NURTURING NEW IDEAS:
LEGAL RIGHTS AND ECONOMIC ROLES

NURTURING NEW IDEAS:
LEGAL RIGHTS AND ECONOMIC ROLES

Edited by
L. JAMES HARRIS

Director
The PTC Research Institute
and Professor of Law, The National Law Center
of
The George Washington University

The Bureau of National Affairs, Inc. • Washington, D.C.

Printed in the United States of America
Standard Book Number: 87179-081-5
Library of Congress Catalog Card Number: 76-83776

This book is dedicated to the memory of

ARTHUR M. SMITH

Associate Judge of the
Court of Customs and Patent Appeals

because of his important contributions
as lawyer, teacher, and judge, his long
association with The PTC Research
Institute, and his great interest in industrial property literature.

LIST OF CONTRIBUTORS

SAMUEL R. BAKER is a partner in the firm of Stitt & Baker, Toronto, Canada.

ROBERT B. BANGS, a Principal Investigator in The PTC Research Institute, is an Economist with the U.S. Department of Commerce.

J. N. BEHRMAN is a Principal Investigator in The PTC Research Institute; Professor of International Business in the Graduate School of Business Administration, University of North Carolina.

JOHN K. CONNOR is a partner in the firm of Baker and McKenzie, Sydney, Australia.

JOHN F. CREED is a Research Associate of The PTC Research Institute; partner in the firm of Baker and McKenzie, New York, N.Y.

WALTER DERENBERG is a partner in the firm of Von Maltitz, Derenberg, Kunin and Janssen, New York, N.Y.; Professor of Law, New York University.

GEORGE E. FROST is Director, Patent Section of General Motors Corporation, Detroit, Mich.; formerly a Principal Investigator in The PTC Research Institute.

LAWRENCE R. HAFSTAD is Vice President in Charge of Research Laboratories, General Motors Corporation, Warren, Mich.

L. JAMES HARRIS is Director of The PTC Research Institute; Professor of Law, The George Washington University.

MARY A. HOLMAN is Associate Professor of Economics, The George Washington University; 1961-1962 Thomas Alva Edison Fellow of The PTC Research Institute.

JOSEPH GRAY JACKSON is a partner in the firm of Jackson, Jackson & Chovanes, Philadelphia, Pa.

STEPHEN P. LADAS is a partner in the firm of Langner, Parry, Card and Langner, New York, N.Y.

EDWIN H. LAND is President and Director of Research of Polaroid Corporation, Cambridge, Mass.

JOSEPH M. LIGHTMAN, a Research Associate of The PTC Research Institute, is with the Foreign Business Practices Division, Office of Commercial and Financial Policy, U.S. Department of Commerce.

DENNIS I. MEYER is a Research Associate of The PTC Research Institute; partner in the firm of Baker and McKenzie, Washington, D.C.

GERALD J. MOSSINGHOFF is Director, Congressional Liaison Division, National Aeronautics and Space Administration.

GERALD D. O'BRIEN is a patent attorney with Bendix Corporation, Arlington, Va.

S. CHESTERFIELD OPPENHEIM is Adviser on Research of The PTC Research Institute; Professor Emeritus of Law, University of Michigan.

MALCOLM J. F. PALMER is a partner in the firm of Baker and McKenzie, London, England.

MALCOLM W. PARRY is a partner in the firm of Langner, Parry, Card and Langner, New York, N.Y.

GILES S. RICH is a Judge on the U.S. Court of Customs and Patent Appeals.

JOSEPH ROSSMAN is a patent attorney in Philadelphia, Pa.; formerly a Principal Investigator in The PTC Research Institute.

SAMUEL RUBEN is President of Ruben Laboratories, New Rochelle, N.Y.

BARKEV S. SANDERS is a Principal Investigator in The PTC Research Institute; Actuarial Consultant to the Graduate School of Public Health, University of Pittsburgh, and to the United Mine Workers Welfare and Retirement Fund.

DAVID SARNOFF is Chairman of the Board, RCA Corporation.

FREDERIC B. SCHRAMM is a patent attorney in Cleveland, Ohio.

JOHN R. SHIPMAN is Director of International Patent Operations, IBM Corporation, Armonk, N.Y.

IRVING H. SIEGEL, a Principal Consultant of The PTC Research Institute, is with The W.E. Upjohn Institute for Employment Research, Washington, D.C.

SCHUYLER M. SIGEL is a partner in the firm of Stitt & Baker, Toronto, Canada.

GORDON K. TEAL is Vice President and Chief Scientist for Corporate Development, Texas Instruments, Inc., Dallas, Texas.

NEIL F. TWOMEY is an attorney in New York, N.Y.; formerly a Research Assistant of The PTC Research Institute.

TABLE OF CONTENTS

ix

INTRODUCTION

Inventive activity occurs in all societies. In the more primitive societies inventions are simple things, serving relatively simple needs. If an invention serves an actual need, it will tend to be used; if not, it will be rejected—or even ignored.

In any type of society, basic invention is not likely to be the result of just one man's efforts. It may be surmised that primitive man did not suddenly come upon the wheel. Small increments of progress, trial and error by many individuals must have been important. Small improvements are made constantly. Innovation also thrives on failures and setbacks. The advance may not be smooth.

Invention is a very important element of a dynamic society's activity. Indeed, innovative behavior is given a legal status in such a society. This status is institutionalized through a patent system based on statutory law and judicial interpretation. By means of the patent system, advantages flow to society and in return society confers a legal right on the creative person. Society shows its favor by recognizing certain types of property and establishes a shelter for the profitable use of such property.

Everyone is interested, directly or indirectly, in inventions and patents, and certain members of society have very specialized roles. Engineers and chemists are constantly exercising innovative talent, whether or not they formalize their contributions as inventions for patent. The Patent Bar mediates between these inventors and society. The importance of invention and patents to the public at large and to technical and other specialists is reflected in the fact that the total funds spent annually on R&D are in the neighborhood of $25 billion in the United States.

The studies included in this book deal with the many-sided relationships involved. Through interdisciplinary, empirical research, they analyze and evaluate the parts played by the patent and related systems in the economic and social performance of the United States and other countries. The studies were planned to investigate these roles, especially because of differences of opinion expressed concerning them.

Many Americans subscribe to the belief that the patent system has been one of the main channels through which the United States has advanced to a position of technological primacy. The common belief is that the system also has fostered inventive resourcefulness,

1

the development of technical know-how, the investment of risk capital, and scientific research—and thus has contributed to a progressively higher standard of living.

These beliefs have been challenged. The doubts have been reflected in the literature and in the hearings, investigations, and reports of various branches of the government. The controversy has involved the related systems of laws such as those of trademarks and copyrights.

Out of these uncertainties and the gaps in existing knowledge, the need for research arises. The major contribution of The PTC Research Institute, which conducted the studies presented in this volume, is diagnosis and the complementary dissemination of findings. The Institute's primary purpose is to ascertain how the systems are functioning, and to make the facts available to citizens of the country in objective reports. These facts could become the basis for sound, remedial action.

The research and educational activity covered in this volume falls into five natural areas, and a chapter is devoted to each:

Individual	(e.g., from the standpoint of creativity, incentives, and the like)
Organization	(e.g., from the standpoint of economic growth, research and development activity, intercompany relations, and executive decision-making)
Government Policy	(e.g., from the standpoint of administrative regulations and procedures, terms of contracts with private firms, judicial actions, antitrust, and taxation)
Legislative Proposals	(e.g., from the standpoint of expert and lay opinion or knowledge)
International	(e.g., from the standpoint of foreign transactions, treaties, and arrangements)

Through publications of the Institute, especially the scholarly journal *IDEA,* the Institute has been monitoring these five broad areas. *IDEA,* published continuously since 1957, and disseminated in more than 30 foreign countries, provides the basis for this volume. The first four chapters spotlight U.S. industrial property issues, and the fifth chapter focuses on U.S. industrial property interests in the world context. This book is intended to make the Institute's research more generally available to students, researchers, and other professional workers in the various disciplines. Since the responsibility for good government rests on an informed citizenry, we are making this special effort to reach a broader public with the research results. In view of world conditions, it is particularly important that more people be informed about the potential of the patent and related systems for technological progress, for world cooperation and trade, and for world peace.

The papers range from a consideration of the motivation of individual inventors to a discussion of the organizational needs of companies, universities, and government agencies, both nationally and internationally. Every successful process or product goes back to the inventor, whether he is the independent or lone inventor, or the equally important "captive inventor" employed by research laboratories or companies. This is true whether the research is conducted by companies, universities, or government. These papers emphasize the practical aspects of applied research, since business and government sponsors are generally interested in use. The papers reflect the patent as a property that belongs to the inventor. The unique function of the patent laws is that they prevent others from making, using, or selling the patented invention without the inventor's consent, or the consent of his assignee, in return for a public disclosure of an inventive concept. The papers exhibit the inventive resourcefulness that has been fostered under the patent systems, and the access the systems have provided to risk capital and to the development of technical know-how.

It is important to recognize the broad mix that is accomplished in this volume. Our purpose is to inform the general reader as well as those with special interests in the patent and related systems. Although the papers are largely based on factual research, some are concerned with planning and others with the interaction of law and the rest of society. Still others have employed the factual information already gathered. In this way we have achieved a broad cultural aggregate, appealing to many publics.

The design of the volume, in a broad sense, is to obtain an intellectual integration. In each of the chapters there is a planned balance of specialization and subject matter. The authors are drawn from different pertinent disciplines and professions, and there is a relationship between the papers in the chapter so as to achieve a reciprocal cross-fertilization that might lead to additional benefits.

In the case of the first chapter, for example, the first three papers are presented by outstanding inventors and the other paper, by a legal specialist. New insights into the incentives and deterrents to technical creativity are gained by several revealing presentations on the aspirations and experience of inventors in context with the paper depicting the actual legal and economic environment in which these inventors work. It is in this opening chapter that we set the tone and provide perspective.

Another example is the second chapter. The first paper concerns the organizational needs and experience of the academic institution. The following two papers direct attention to the needs and experience of industry with respect to industrial property. This juxtaposition leads to a better understanding of the requirements of both types of organization. It reveals the actual operation of the organizational role of industrial property as the relationships are worked out in these presentations.

Similar design appears in the last chapter, which deals with the international role of industrial property. This final chapter provides the reader an opportunity to understand more fully the role of industrial property in the transfer of technical information between countries, including East-West trade and transactions with the lesser-developed nations. It is our belief that such an understanding will lead to more effective action on the part of U.S. private and public interests, as well as those of foreign countries.

Within the confines of this volume we have included papers on some of the major problems that confront the systems. The seasoned judgment and intimate experience of practitioners have been combined in the articles with the technical knowledge and experience of researchers.

This distillation of the essence of particular problems and possible solutions should provide a challenge to strong insularities and to traditional relationships. Thus, in a sense, this volume constitutes an attempt to tap the experience of knowledgeable people and to present their ideas in a broad forum to make the evolution of the systems vital and meaningful to the end that the best traditions, interests, and ideals of America and of other countries will be served by sound industrial property systems in the future.

The papers, reports and other material included in this volume have been edited for the benefit of the whole, and some changes have been made to accommodate them to book publication. An opportunity was also provided for the authors to write a brief postscript to the papers if they wanted to note any current developments or to extend their remarks. Major additions to, or deletions from, .the papers as originally published in *IDEA* are noted in each case. Although the object was to select material that, despite the passage of time, merited reprinting in book form, several of the authors preferred to rewrite their original papers. With Volume 8, Number 1 (Spring 1964), the name of The Patent, Trademark, and Copyright Journal of Research and Education (PTC J. Res. & Ed.) was changed to *IDEA*. To provide style uniformity, all references to that Journal are cited hereinafter as *IDEA*.

PART I

INDIVIDUAL MOTIVATION AND PROTECTION

Doctors Land, Ruben, and Teal view their achievements in three inspiring papers. Though there are dissimilarities, these men have a fascination with new ideas and a deep personal involvement in their work. Dr. Ruben, the independent inventor, Dr. Teal, the research administrator, and Dr. Land, the entrepreneur, vigorously pursue innovative objectives, but each inventor clearly articulates his own dream. For example, Dr. Land (of the Polaroid Corporation) seeks "to induce others to create companies similar" to his own!

The three papers shed light on the creative personality. All the men have considerable training in technology, intensive preparation for original research, and a special ability to analogize from past experience, transferring knowledge from one field to another. Other attributes they show are a strong admiration for the patent system and a recognition of the importance of that system for the support of science-based creative research.

The study by Joseph Rossman illuminates the methods utilized both here and abroad to encourage employee-inventors. His paper presents empirical information on the modern industrial and governmental environment in which R&D activity is being conducted, the policies and procedures introduced to stimulate invention, and the effect of such policies on inventive activity.

Although there are no special provisions in U.S. statutory law concerning compensation, there is support in certain quarters for legislation which would provide for financial participation by the U.S. employee-inventor in profits accruing to the employer from the invention. A number of European countries already have such laws. Account is taken in Dr. Rossman's paper, therefore, of the effect of foreign special laws on company arrangements with inventors. The German law is considered the most comprehensive and complex employee compensation legislation in Europe; conspicuously absent from the list of European nations which have enacted such laws are its next two leading industrialized members, France and England.

From these papers, it is clear that to compile a precise comparative catalogue of the features of the independent and employee inventor would be a very difficult task. Although independents ap-

5

pear to operate under a minimum of constraints and the alternatives open to them seem to be greater, the dynamic forces in our economy require creative people to play different roles in the constantly changing environment—which their own efforts appear to induce. Thus, it is not surprising to find certain key characteristics of the two breeds of innovator that are very much alike. In their papers, both employee and independent demonstrate at least four traits in common, and in abundance: technical ability, perseverance, ingenuity, and vision.

On Some Conditions for Scientific Profundity in Industrial Research

EDWIN H. LAND

For about 20 years I have been interested in the question of how to establish in the United States a large number, perhaps several thousand, of new companies based in science. My dream was that each of these companies would conceive of a new field and would carry on from the basic scientific work in that field through research, development, engineering, production, aesthetic design, lively, honest advertising, and efficient distribution. Our life up until that time in our own technologically creative company had been so satisfying and happy that we wanted not only to continue in the same way ourselves, but also to induce others to create companies similar to ours. Nothing that has happened in the generation that has intervened makes me feel any less faith in the dream I then had, although the fact is that for one reason or another not nearly as many of these companies came into being as I would have hoped. Because I still believe in that dream, I want to describe in some detail the inventive experience in a company based in science.

Before I start on that detail, I must emphasize that the kind of company I believe in cannot come into being and cannot continue its existence except with the full support of the patent system. Since this Conference is dedicated to detailed discussion of understanding the needs of a healthy patent system, I shall make only one comment: namely, that except for the intricacy that has entered into interference procedures, the patent system as I have known it for the last 40 years is satisfactory in principle to support the kind of science-based industrial renaissance that I believe in. For this purpose, all that is required is an expansion of the Patent Office—an expansion of budget, facilities, and equipment, comparable to the expansion of demand being made on the Patent Office.

The specifications I now set for these ideal scientific companies are no different from the ones I set for myself in 1927—pick problems that are important and nearly impossible to solve, pick prob-

EDITOR's NOTE: This paper was presented by Dr. Land upon his acceptance of the 1964 Charles F. Kettering Award from The PTC Research Institute on June 17, 1965. (*IDEA,* Vol. 9 (Conference Number 1965), p. 120.)

lems that are the result of sensing deep and possibly unarticulated human needs, pick problems that will draw on the diversity of human knowledge for their solution, and where that knowledge is inadequate, fill the gaps with basic scientific exploration—involve all the members of the organization in the sense of adventure and accomplishment, so that a large part of life's rewards would come from this involvement. My faith was that in the long run this kind of activity could be self-supporting rather soon, that it would inspire the desire of others, not participating directly, to share indirectly, by contributing sometimes advice, sometimes financial support, and sometimes a market, even though, to begin with, the market may have been created just to encourage us. Over this 40-year period, I have found that Americans bring instinctive optimism, generosity, and enthusiasm to the support of any effort that they believe is fundamentally creative. My only disappointment then is that this instinct has not been tapped in the way I feel it can be to bring into being the thousands of new companies.

I want to review with you case histories from our own experience of the inventive process, in the hope that we may gain insight into how to encourage such companies as I seek.

As I review the nature of the creative drive in the inventive scientists that have been around me, as well as in myself, I find the first event is an urge to make a significant intellectual contribution that can be tangibly embodied in a product or process. The urge, as pure urge, precedes in a perfectly generalized way the specific contribution—so that the individual hunts for a *domain* in which to utilize the urge. The early stage need not be early in life, it can occur intermittently throughout life. The hunting process is fascinating to contemplate because during it there may be many abortive first approaches at the verbal level to fields which are then rejected as being either not significant enough or not feasible enough—and then, quite suddenly, a field will emerge conceptually so full blown in the creator's mind that the words can scarcely come from his mouth fast enough to describe the new field in its full implication and elaborateness.

This domain which neither he nor the world had known until some magic moment, now is for him so vividly real and well populated with ideas and structures that he will lead you around through it like a guide in a European city. Then it appears to him that all that is left to do is to parallel that intricate "reality" which came into being in his mind, with a corresponding reality in the world outside of his mind. Sometimes this process of creating the outside reality may take five years, sometimes five hours. For the creative person this process of establishing the correspondence between the outside reality and the one within his mind is a timeless undertaking, reminiscent of the relativistic trips through space in which people return to earth only a little older while the rest of mankind has aged.

Whether the process is the five-hour process or the five-year process it always turns out to be true that many subsidiary and supporting inventions and insights are required to go from the thing in the mind to the thing in the world. These subsidiary inventions are born of accurate analysis, patient research, broad experience, and total devotion to the perfection of the final outer reality. For this sequence of rather tedious virtues there is available no new series of *grand* excitements. Basic emotional energy must continue to flow from the initial perception of the field and from that first excitement.

Now I take you through these details of the genesis of inventions because it must be clear that this kind of timeless life can be lived only in an appropriate environment, a different kind of environment from what we must establish for some of our important massive engineering undertakings, such as the moon probe, undertakings in which a date must be met at all costs, and in which individual profundity must be largely displaced by rapid-fire interaction between brilliant members of large groups. Since it is somewhat easier for the general public to understand and for the government to manage this latter type of intellectual activity, we must be extremely careful to nurture and protect the former type with which this discussion is chiefly concerned.

Now for examples: As for the generalized urge: Thirty-eight years later, I can still recall the full vividness of my own need at the age of 17 to do something scientifically significant and tangibly demonstrable. At the age in which each week seems like a year, I picked field after field before I decided that the great opportunity was polarized light.

Jumping ahead 17 years, I recall a sunny vacation day in Santa Fe, New Mexico, when my little daughter asked why she could not see at once the picture I had taken of her. As I walked around that charming town I undertook the task of solving the puzzle she had set me. Within the hour, the camera, the film, and the physical chemistry became so clear to me that with a great sense of excitement I hurried over to the place where Donald Brown, our patent attorney (in Santa Fe by coincidence) was staying, to describe to him in great detail a dry camera which would give a picture immediately after exposure.

In my mind it was so nearly complete and so real that I spent several hours describing it, after which it was perhaps more real to him than even the ultimate reality. Only three years later, three years of the timeless intensive work referred to above, we gave to the Optical Society of America the full demonstration of the working system.

What is hard to convey, in anything short of a thick book, is the years of rich experience that were compressed into those three years. It was as if all that we had done in learning to make polarizers, the knowledge of plastics, and the properties of viscous liquids, the preparation of microscopic crystals smaller than the wavelength of light, the laminating of plastic sheets, living in the world of colloids in supersaturated solutions, had been a school and a preparation both for that first day in which I suddenly knew how to make a one-step dry photographic process and for the following three years in which we made the very vivid dream into a solid reality.

Once again we can see the significance of environment, of a corporate life whose managerial center was concerned with scientific ideas, a corporate life in which everyone participated in the mastery, day by day, of the new technological problems that arose in our search for better polarizers and new ways of using them. The transfer from the field of polarized light to the field of photography was for us all a miraculous experience, as if we had entered a new country with a different language and different customs, only to find that we could speak the language at once and master the customs. In short, the kind of training we had given ourselves in the field of polarized light had endowed us with a competence we had not sought and did not know we had; namely, a competence to transfer what must be a common denominator in *all* honestly pursued research, from one field to an entirely different one.

I am inclined to think that only in a corporation, however small or large, in which individuals are expected to make the center of their life the intellectual life of the laboratory can this kind of transferable talent be built. This process must continue for year upon year and decade upon decade. I find men around me in our laboratory who have lived this way and who now seem more alert, creative, and productive than when they were 30 years younger. That creativity is tied to some youthful age is a myth that comes about, I believe, because for one reason or another men stop living this way perhaps because they are encouraged to think there is more dignity associated with tasks implying power over people than with tasks implying power over nature.

Remember that we are searching these case histories not for the purpose of intimate revelation, but to try to find out why more scientific companies do not survive. Whatever the other reasons may be, I think that a primary reason is that at just the time when a man's talent might be maturing, he is drawn off into a variety of so-called managerial activities. It is impossible for the long, long thoughts, the profound thoughts, the unconscious accumulation of insights, to come into being after these serious digressions into management. I am not saying that other good things do not come out of these diversions, but these other good things are not our subject. Actually here is an endless opportunity for use of managerial aptitude of every research man, *within the intimate domain of his own investigation,* and within that domain he may exercise his managerial aptitude without the stress and distractions he will necessarily find outside of the domain of his own scientific investigation.

I think the important and nearly impossible projects such as we set for our goal require prolonged periods of intensive concentration. Frequently, the problems can best be solved, perhaps solved *only* if the work is done in a relatively short time. In most of the worthwhile problems, so many variables are involved that the human mind cannot keep them in order in the presence of interruptions. It is simultaneous mastery of a hundred interacting variables that is the glory of the kind of scientist we are talking about for our scientific companies.

When I started on the actual program of making the black-and-white film for our camera I set down the broad principles that would also apply to color. I invited Howard Rogers who had worked with me for many years in the field of polarized light to sit opposite me in the black-and-white laboratory and think about color. For several years he simply sat, and saying very little, assimilated the techniques we were using in black and white. Then one day he stood up and said, "I'm ready to start now." So we built the color laboratory next to the black-and-white laboratory and from then on until the time many years later when we released our color film, the program of matching the dream of the color process that was in our mind with the reality of the color process in the outside world never stopped. My point is that we created an environment in which a man was *expected* to sit and think for two years. May I suggest that there is a difference between that environment and the one which we tend to create when we think of national projects for massive engineering purposes.

You will note that the qualities that I am concerned about in corporate life are not related to bigness or smallness as such. There are small companies and small businesses that are not oriented towards thoughtfulness and profundity, and there are a few large cor-

porations in which they are encouraged. But our universities do not
train for patient and extended thought, and those few areas in
government which have provided thoughtful environments are in
certain danger of being swamped by the great mass undertakings.
The one *governmental* device for protecting the profound thinker
is the patent system.

    During the period ahead of us, many of us will be working to
invent methods whereby the government can catalyze the formation
and growth of creative companies. We shall also be trying within
the universities to generate men with competence for profound in-
dividuality. It would be most unfortunate if by the time we have
succeeded with these undertakings the patent system is robbed of
the power to perform its part of the new task.

Opportunities Afforded an Independent Inventor by the Patent System

Samuel Ruben

Recognition and encouragement are necessary factors for stimulating imaginative rather than merely memory-oriented thinking. In review of my own efforts, the attempts at imaginative thinking extend back more than 50 years of my life.

I was born in New Jersey in 1900, and shortly thereafter my family moved to New York, where I attended public schools. From an early age I was an avid reader of scientific literature and had an almost compulsive desire to read and to analyze what I read. I owe a great debt to the public libraries. Next was the great pleasure derived from chemical and electrical experimental work, particularly stemming from my interest in radio as a licensed amateur for several years prior to World War I. These interests helped materially to develop experimental methods and persistence for translating imaginative thoughts into practical realities.

Since adverse personal economic conditions required means for support not only for myself but also for family assistance, I could not plan formal college training. This was supplanted by constant home study and later, non-credit evening courses on such basic subjects as mathematics and chemistry.

EDITOR'S NOTE: This paper was presented by Dr. Ruben upon his acceptance of the 1966 Inventor of the Year Award from The PTC Research Institute on April 14, 1966. (*IDEA*, Vol. 10, No. 1 (Spring 1966), p. 116.)

AUTHOR'S NOTE: Most of the work cited in the above related to the study and application of electrochemical systems. This in turn has resulted in the application of those systems to solid state rectifiers, dry electrolytic condensers, and sealed zinc mercuric oxide alkaline cells. My recent electrochemical process development involves producing light-transmitting—or microporous—stainless steel in a continuous manner with control within close limits of the number and size of perforations. The process involves selective electrolytic dissolution of grain boundary precipitates without altering the thickness or surface of the metal, its application being for filters, containers whose walls would pass air or gases but not liquids, and other articles where a long wide sheet with uniform porosity is required. This work further emphasizes the importance to a modern inventor of acquiring a broad mental storage of the facts of technology by continuous study and experience and, more specifically, the understanding of the science of materials in relation to the electronic structure and property of the element.

13

The most important event in the development of creative endeavor came after I had acquired my first job in the winter of 1917 as an assistant in a laboratory of the Electrochemical Products Company. This development company was engaged in perfecting a patented process for the fixation of atmospheric nitrogen by high frequency electrical discharge.

I obtained this job because of my familiarity with high frequency radio transmitters. My amateur radio transmitter experience was directly applicable to the understanding of one phase of the work. The project had been started in a Brooklyn laboratory under the direction of the inventor of the process, but in order to progress they engaged the services of an authority in the field of electrical discharges; namely, Professor Bergen Davis of the Physics Department at Columbia University. Professor Davis was the technical consultant, and he directed the experimental work. To allow him to devote more time to this war effort work, the laboratory was moved, by arrangement with the University in 1918, to the basement (Room 110) of Fayerweather Hall which housed the Physics Department. Professor Davis took a keen interest in me during the time I was associated with this process and for many years thereafter, up to the time of his death in April, 1958. During these 40 years he was always interested in my progress, giving me valuable and appreciated counsel. In the earlier days he spent considerable time in guiding my studies, and in our many hours of discussion I learned a great deal. He arranged for my attending some of his lectures relating to electrical discharges through gases, and the use of the Physics Department library in the same building. Professor Davis' life and career were themselves a great inspiration to me.

The understanding and appreciation of the electronic structure of matter and its relation to chemical and physical properties was an important result of my relation with Professor Davis. Its application to practice can be noted in my early rectifier patents (1925) in which I classify the desirable electrode materials in accordance to their valence position as elements in the Periodic Table. The nature of materials, particularly of the elements, has been a guiding factor in all my work, and so essential to the successful solution of problems involved in my inventions. In my recent book entitled *The Electronics of Materials,* the stress is on the importance of the electron configuration in relation to the valence electron potential arrangement of the Periodic Table of Elements so as to supply a quantitative character to electric parameters. This concept, arranged in chart form, has been useful in our laboratory since 1940.

The honorary degree "Doctor of Science" was conferred on me in 1959 by Butler University for my work in electrochemistry, and on June 9, 1966, the honorary degree "Doctor of Engineering" will be conferred by the Polytechnic Institute of Brooklyn.

Besides encouragement, an inventor needs financial support in carrying out his development to completion. I was fortunate in obtaining such support, for in 1922 Professor Davis suggested to Malcom W. Clephane, (incidentally a former Washingtonian) a patent attorney who had been president of the development company, that he set up an independent laboratory for the investigation of several of my patentable ideas. In 1923 a laboratory was established in New York City, after a temporary set-up in my home. Since 1930, the laboratory has been in New Rochelle, N. Y. Mr. Clephane's support and enthusiastic cooperation contributed greatly to the success of the laboratory.

In order for the inventor to obtain commercial realization of his work, it is desirable to gain the support of a company that has the courage, imagination, and foresight so necessary in carrying an invention to a production stage through the trials and tribulations that most inventions incur before the product has production stability and is commercially sought after. In this matter I was fortunate to contact P. R. Mallory & Co. and particularly its founder, P. R. Mallory, whose interest in research and development is inherent to his make-up. My relationship as licensor and consultant to the company has been maintained over the years with a number of products manufactured on a large scale.

The time and state of the technology are most important, for one can experience the limitations of acceptance if ahead of the art and find that at or after the expiration of a patent, large-scale use is made of one's development. I have experienced both the advantage of having developments at a time when a need existed, and others which went into large volume use after expiration of my patents. My solid-state magnesium rectifier was introduced at a time when charging storage batteries to operate the radio set of the early twenties was a problem. The use of the rectifier as a continuous trickle charger eliminated the necessity of removing the storage battery from the living room for charging. However, my development of the dry electrolytic condenser or capacitor eliminated the need for the storage battery entirely.

The further development of the capacitor for higher voltages later eliminated the need for the B-batteries. In 1928, the use of the A-eliminator was supplanted by the introduction of the indirectly heated A/C tube. This tube was constructed with a ceramic rod which insulated the heater from the electron emitter and had some limitations, such as a rather long time to heat the element, and thermoconductive effects which limited the operating life of the tube. The introduction by the industry of the indirectly heated A/C tube materially reduced the royalties received from A-eliminators. In order to meet this challenge, the integral heater element tube was developed, and rapidly reached large-scale production. I accomplished this by coating and sintering to the heater wire a pure nonconductive oxide which reduced the heating time from several minutes to seven seconds. The elimination of unstable ceramic materials increased the operating life several fold. Development of the refractory insulated copper wire followed. This refractory wire coating was the forerunner of an electrodeposition process which I developed for multilayer wire-wound resistors which were in large production during World War II. These resistors were capable of withstanding military test requirements which could not be met by any of the previous types.

Timing was again important when the sealed alkaline cell was developed at the onset of World War II. This provided the miniature high capacity mercury cell capable of withstanding severe storage and operating conditions that could not be met by the standard dry cell which had been manufactured for about 60 years. It will be noted that there has been a sort of chain reaction between the first commercially successful invention and those that followed.

I believe the independent inventor will always be important because he is in the position of being able to think away from or independently of popular trends with respect to a given project; he does not have the problems of possibly jeopardizing his position if he is wrong. An employee in an organization, unless he is in the top echelon of research and development, may fear to be wrong and thus affect his record or status with his associates and with the company.

The advantage of independent operation is that it forces one to study the problem more thoroughly and allows the freedom to concentrate on a project without interference or the need to utilize time on unrelated matters. It requires a more practical consideration of the problem in order to obtain the necessary data with a minimum amount of equipment; it forces one to depend upon a certain amount of ingenuity to use what he has to the best advantage.

The disadvantages, in respect to technological processes, are that in an organization it is possible to obtain assistance on some phase of the development from sources more competent in some specialty and to have available more complete equipment.

One hurdle an independent inventor sometimes has to overcome, even with demonstrable models or data, is the inherent reluctance of the technical staff of his prospective licensee to accept outside ideas. In industry this is known as the N. I. H. (not invented here) factor. Some managements will override the opinions of their engineering department and depend entirely on trial results.

The recognition and encouragement of the organizational inventor is going to grow in importance for many reasons. The philosophy today seems to be to obtain the safest job with all insurances until death, and many individuals become permanent organization men at an early age. In the years prior to World War I, the opportunities for obtaining employment in research and development projects were very limited. Individuals endowed with that inner sense of direction, with persistence to carry imaginative thinking to practical reality, were willing to take the risks to acquire the rewards of a successful invention.

The American patent system is a basic source of encouragement to the inventor, for it provides him with a means of protecting the practical results of his imaginative thinking by the issuance of a patent which can give him the hope for recognition and reward. This system has enabled me to function as an independent inventor and maintain a development laboratory for the past 43 years with support, except for the first three years, entirely derived from the license or sale of patents. I am most grateful for the opportunities afforded to me by our American system.

Roots of Creative Research

GORDON K. TEAL

My personal inventive career was at Bell Telephone Laboratories, an ideal environment for creative invention and innovation. There, I, like many others, experienced the excitement of learning how to exploit science for the benefit of society. Basic to whatever inventive achievements I may have been able to make was the struggle to acquire a scientific understanding.

Undoubtedly my most important inventions were connected with the development of germanium and silicon single crystals. It is hard to realize now that making single crystals of germanium and silicon could ever have been controversial.

As I look back to see what really influenced me in critical decisions which culminated in the single crystal work and my contributions to the transistor, I note the roots of research leading to my inventions go very deep in time.

The story starts with graduate study at Brown University under Professor Charles A. Kraus, one of the two outstanding experts on germanium chemistry in this country. My Master's and a Doctor's thesis were on the chemistry and electrochemistry of germanium and some of its compounds. Germanium was a useless material, studied only because it was chemically interesting. Had I been "mission" oriented, I may have missed a very exciting career. Concentration on germanium during my graduate study resulted in a continuing personal sentimental attachment for germanium, which to me, at least, was and is an exotic element.

The opportunity to enter a career of creative research and innovation, concerned particularly with electronic materials, I owe to Robert R. Williams and Robert M. Burns, who headed chemical research in Bell Telephone Laboratories. When they invited me to come to work at Bell Telephone Laboratories, I accepted and went there in 1930.

During the 30's, I did research on electron emissive surfaces of photocells for television pick-up, fairly complicated electron multipliers and camera tubes. Preparation, control of the composi-

---

EDITOR'S NOTE: This paper was presented by Dr. Teal upon his acceptance of the 1967 Inventor of the Year Award from The PTC Research Institue on April 20, 1967. (*IDEA*, Vol. 11, No. 1 (Spring 1967), p. 1.)

tion and structure of electronic materials to achieve special electron or photoemissive, conductive or photoconductive properties were the major concern. I made several attempts during this period to start germanium studies.

In 1940 I again proposed research on germanium and when the television activity to which I was assigned was closed down in February 1942, within two weeks I had made some germanium microwave rectifiers, using some digermane gas obtained from one of my Brown University associates of the period 1927 to 1930. While I had thought the germanium rectifier project to be an unusually good idea, I began to doubt my intuition and turned my attention to the development of some new types of resistors, including pyrolytically deposited alloy films of germanium and silicon. At a later date when germanium devices proved to be terrifically important to the war effort, I was very disappointed that I had abandoned my rectifier program. I resolved never again to doubt my own strong intuitions. This crucial, conscious decision is evidenced by my persistence in growing germanium and silicon single crystals.

The transistor invention at Bell Labs in late 1947 convinced me that this was definitely the time to get back on germanium work. In spite of my important challenging assignment handling the chemical development of a silicon carbide varistor for a new telephone handset, my most enthusiastic thoughts were on the potential of germanium and I repeatedly made germanium research program proposals, starting in February 1948, and on through June, July and August of that year, and suggested preparing single crystals. I reasoned that removing the crystal boundaries and other undesirable defects from germanium probably would be as important to the transistor as removing the last traces of gases from the vacuum tube. In spite of this acceptable analogous reasoning, support was difficult to obtain.

One night in the latter part of September 1948, John Little (also at BTL) and I met by pure chance on a bus going into the center of Summit, New Jersey, from the Murray Hills Laboratory. John needed some small germanium wafers for some point contact transistors in a new mechanical design that he had conceived. His needs were an expedient opportunity of getting into an important part of germanium and transistor activity. During the remainder of the bus ride, we busily designed an equipment for pulling germanium rods, and two days later had already set up a crude machine and pulled germanium rods containing large single crystals from a crucible in an atmosphere of hydrogen. During the next few months we made better equipment and large and more perfect crystals.

Soon after growing our first crystals, I proposed a single crystal program on germanium and silicon to J. A. Morton, head of transistor development. He gave financial support and encouragement.

As the work proceeded in 1949, gradually all the scientific studies on transistors began to make use of single crystal material. As Bardeen has pointed out (*Proceedings of the Institute of Radio Engineers* [1958], p. 952) "controlled very perfect single crystals have provided, in a sense, a laboratory for study of such processes" (various electronic and physical solid-state phenomena).

Later, the single crystals were crucial in realizing the first junction transistor. About the time of Shockley's June 1949 paper on the structure and theory of the junction transistor, I suggested to Morgan Sparks, who was working with Shockley, attempting to make a junction transistor, that he and I collaborate. Within less than a year we pulled the first junction transistor.

During 1951 Ernie Buehler and I turned our attention more and more towards silicon. We pulled the first large silicon single crystals, pn, pnp, and npn junction structures.

I collaborated with Howard Christensen during 1951 and 1952 in forming a single crystal pn junction by epitaxial deposition of thin single crystal films on germanium single crystals by decomposition of germanium iodide vapor. The variety of applications of such techniques envisioned has been recorded in U. S. Patent 2,692,839 issued to us in 1954. These early efforts were cut short by my leaving Bell Labs. Much later, June 1960, epitaxial technology became an important and useful part of industrial technology.

One might think oneself lucky to have participated only in the transistor research activity at Bell Telephone Laboratories. I was doubly fortunate, however, in having the satisfaction of also participating in development of the transistor and related industry at Texas Instruments, also a most exciting place.

I went to Texas Instruments January 1, 1953, to set up their Central Research Laboratories. Pat Haggerty's visualization of TI's potentiality and plans impressed me tremendously. The success of TI in the years since has demonstrated clearly that my early confidence in him as an unusually able leader was not misplaced. Let me pay tribute too to the crucially important contributions of my other associates at TI, particularly to Mark Shepherd who is here today and who is well known for his major contributions to the semiconductor industry.

Texas Instruments was unique in industry in emphasizing grown junction transistors. My participation in this critical decision was advice given to Pat Haggerty in 1952 and later in 1953, when I went to TI. While TI captured the market with high quality transistors, competing companies struggled to make "inexpensive" transistors by other methods.

At TI, my job was to establish the environment for and to direct innovation in contrast to performing personal invention. I gradually built up a group of researchers who concentrated on programs that would lead as quickly as possible to important products. The first major goal of our program was a silicon transistor by techniques suited to mass production. We decided to go the grown junction route, by no means a simple or trivial choice. We avoided the problems such as differential expansion between silicon and alloying electrode which are inherent in the alloyed junction. Most companies took the alloy route and some the III-V intermetallics.

W. A. Adcock, M. E. Jones, Jay Thornhill and E. Jackson of our Central Research Laboratories, as history and TI stock have recorded, developed the first commercially feasible silicon transistors. I proudly announced this achievement at a national conference of the Institute of Radio Engineers on May 10, 1954, under rather dramatic circumstances. Earlier speakers had remarked about how hopeless it was to expect the development of a silicon transistor in less than several years and advised people to be satisfied with germanium transistors for the present.

The results are highlighted in an issue of *Fortune* (November 1961), page 226:

> The silicon transistor was a turning point in TI's history, for with this advance it gained a big headstart over the competition in a critical electronic product; there was no effective competition in silicon transistors until 1958. TI's sales rose almost vertically; the company was suddenly in the big leagues.

Another important relevant project undertaken in TI was the development of a chemical reduction method for bulk high purity silicon production that started TI towards becoming the leading supplier of this material to the chemical and electronic industries. Raymond Sangster and Willis Adcock, John Ross, and Jim Fisher spearheaded the effort.

With the broadening and deepening torrent of developments of transistor technology in the 1950's and 60's, it is impossible even to mention, much less trace, the threads of the development. Diffusion, mesa, planar and epitaxial techniques developed and have made use of single crystal materials in a multitude of ways as do integrated circuits, now a major concern of semiconductor industry. TI's Central Research Laboratories contributed to these rapidly developing technologies in a variety of ways. For example, the building of complete subsystems on a silicon wafer was a part of the written plans as early as October of 1957.

My present activity at the National Bureau of Standards may seem unrelated to my efforts to develop useful products at Bell Telephone Laboratories and Texas Instruments, since the National Bureau of Standards does not normally seek to develop products except under national emergency conditions; however, one of our major activities is the characterization of materials that might have important scientific and technological benefits to the nation. Another aspect of our mission is to maintain a data bank of evaluated properties of matter and materials. Industry, government and the scientific community may draw on it to make decisions and progress in areas such as exploratory studies and new product development. Because technology is rapidly becoming science based, accurate numerical data on the properties of matter and materials are increasingly critical in the everyday considerations that affect the rise and fall of corporations and even of nations.

Because science and technology stimulate and aid each other, the inventor even more frequently will be found in science-based environments offered by organizations such as Bell Telephone Laboratories and Texas Instruments. The resulting inventions are essential to creating the era of abundance about which we dream and others demand.

Let me also say in closing that I have been greatly helped in my creative career by the U.S. patent system.

Rewards and Incentives to Employee-Inventors

JOSEPH ROSSMAN

INTRODUCTION

This is a report of the data obtained from questionnaires sent to selected companies and inventors relating to rewards and incentives to employee-inventors.

The importance of bringing about, through industrial research, an uninterrupted flow of new inventions is essential to our economic health and progress and the need to stimulate inventors into activity can scarcely be overemphasized. In Congress and among the federal agencies, as well as in industry, there is some difference of opinion on the effect of the rewards and incentives which are currently offered to employee-inventors. Proposals have been made from time to time that legislative action be taken, similar to that in effect in some foreign countries, to assure that employee-inventors are adequately compensated by their employers.

The importance of research in our economy is now generally recognized not only by industry but by our legislators. For example, the *Twelfth Annual Report of the Select Committee on Small Business of the U. S. Senate,* May 15, 1962 states:

> Just as the industrial revolution, beginning in the 18th century, changed our way of life, the present revolution—the scientific revolution, or the research revolution of the 20th century—will also change our way of life. This revolution consists of the systematic and large-scale application of science to industry. Since World War II it has pervaded almost every phase of our daily lives. The changes going on in the areas of electronics, atomic energy, and automation are in many respects different in kind from any that have occurred before, and will change the world much more. The needs of World War II stimulated organized scientific research. The results were an atomic bomb, synthetic rubber, and great technological achievements in radar and antibiotics.
>
> Many new products, the results of research, helped push the economy upward during 1948-58. Transistors, power steering, power brakes, antibiotics, polyethylene, styrene plastics and resins, vitamins, synthetic detergents, grew more than 40 percent per year during that

EDITOR'S NOTE: Dr. Rossman has added a bibliographical note at the end of his paper. The note covers other work in the field and recent material. This paper appeared in *IDEA*, Vol. 7, No. 4 (Winter 1963-1964), p. 431. The study was begun in 1962 and completed in 1963.

decade. Synthetic fibers, room air conditioners, tape recorders, grew from 30 to 40 percent per year.

This list can be expanded almost indefinitely. The impact of research and development is obvious. Technological progress has been playing a major role in propelling the economy forward, especially since the middle of the 18th century.

The new element in our society is the growing recognition that new products and new processes are the key to a company's growth, an industry's growth, a nation's growth—and these are dependent on the continuous development of innovations to keep the economic system expanding.

Small business, in particular, has a stake in this issue, because, unless the new, dynamic areas of our economy are open to small- and medium-size firms, their role in tomorrow's economy will, undoubtedly, become competitively untenable.

As research has grown, its influence on profitability has also grown to the point where it now either determines or strongly influences profit performance of many segments of industry. One oil company has made as much as $1.45 of annual return per research dollar in some projects, and another estimates that each research dollar yields a total return of $15.40. A paper company estimates a net return of $10 in a typical year from each research dollar. This should be compared with annual return of 20 cents, or less, per dollar of investment in other kinds of projects. It is not surprising that there is a good correlation of percentage of sales devoted to research and development and profits as percentage of net worth. In other words, the higher the percentage of gross receipts spent on research, the higher the rate of return on net worth.

The latest 1960 survey published by the National Science Foundation *Funds for Research and Development in Industry* (NSF 63-7) shows that U. S. industry funds for R&D performance averaged $35,500 per R&D scientist or engineer. There were 307,300 scientists and engineers employed in R&D, the aircraft and missiles employing 85,500, electrical equipment and communication 72,200, chemicals and allied products 34,400, and machinery 31,700. The distribution of the funds was 4 percent for basic research, 20 percent applied research, and 76 percent development. Funds for R&D performed by industrial firms totaled $10.5 billion in 1960 which is three times the total for 1953. Total industrial R&D performance comprised about three-fourths of the $14.0 billion for the economy as a whole.

The patent statistics for the same seven-year period do not reflect a comparable increase in the number of patent applications which totalled 70,343 in the fiscal year 1953 and 79,331 in 1960. The number of patent applications per $1 million R&D expenditures has been steadily declining; in the period 1941-43 it was

53.10 and in 1957-59 it was 9.36.[1] Dr. Brode points out our gross national product increases at 3.5 percent per year while our R&D rate is 15 percent per year and at this rate it will exceed our gross national product before the end of the century.[2]

The question arises are existing company policies in relation to their R&D employees sufficiently effective to stimulate the production of patentable inventions, especially since 96 percent of all current company R&D performance is in the area of applied and development research which is the area in which patentable inventions fall.

In order to obtain current information regarding existing practices in industry, it was decided to send a questionnaire to a random sample of companies to whom U. S. patents were issued during the fiscal year beginning June 7, 1960.

The published abstracts of patents issued from June 7, 1960, to June 27, 1961, starting with patent No. 2,943,327 up to patent No. 2,990,548, and ending with numerals —42, —52, and —61 were cut out and mounted on cards which constituted a systematic 3-percent sample for this period. The patents assigned to U. S. and foreign companies were segregated. The patent numbers were listed in each letter sent to U. S. companies and the last 6 digits of the patents were listed on each inventor questionnaire. The foreign questionnaires were sent on aerogramme letters without any inventor questionnaire cards. This sample contained 837 patents issued to U. S. inventors which were assigned to 495 U. S. companies. A total of 447 questionnaires were mailed to companies with known addresses (48 had no known address) (see Appendix C) with 1,118 inventor cards (see Appendix D). In the 3-percent sample there were 118 patents assigned to 100 foreign companies to whom questionnaires were mailed. An additional 120 foreign companies were selected at random in order to increase the size of the foreign sample (see Appendix B). The sample included 312 unassigned U. S. patents, 46 patents assigned to the government, 6 assigned to partnerships, 29 assigned to foreign individuals, and 40 unassigned patents to foreign inventors. The total U. S. patents assigned to all companies during the fiscal year 1960 was about 70 percent of all issued patents.

A total of 110 (24 percent) replies were received from the U. S. companies. There were 385 (33 percent) filled-in cards re-

---

[1]See Machlup, "Patents and Inventive Effort," *Science,* Vol. 133 (May 12, 1961), p. 1463.
[2]*American Scientist,* Vol. 50 (March 1962), p. 1.

turned by the inventors. Out of a total of 220 foreign questionnaires sent, 84 (38 percent) replies were received (see Appendix A).

Questionnaires were also sent to 74 Research Institute members and 40 (54 percent) replies were received (see Appendix E).

The replies to each of the questions in the questionnaires are summarized in this report.

COMPANY POLICIES IN ENCOURAGING EMPLOYEE-INVENTORS

The following questions were submitted in our questionnaire to obtain information regarding current company practices:

It is often contended that industry could do more to encourage employee-inventors by changing its policy with respect to their conditions of employment (e.g., by way of cash rewards, promotions, salary increases, honors, publicity, retention of title to invention by employee, etc.).

(1) What is your present policy?

(2) How long (years and months) has your present policy with respect to conditions of employment of employee-inventors been in effect?

(3) If a *different policy* was previously in effect, please state:

    (A) What the previous policy was.

    (B) Date it was changed.

    (C) How the change in policy has affected the inventive productivity of your company's R&D employees.

    (D) *Also* please give the following (or equivalent data), if possible:

        (a) Number of ideas submitted for consideration for patenting per capita R&D employee *before* and *after* change in policy.

        (b) Number of patent applications filed per capita R&D employee *before* and *after* change in policy.

        (c) Number of patents issued per capita R&D employee *before* and *after* change in policy.

There were 106 replies from U. S. companies in our 3-percent sample which indicated the following payments are made to sole employee-inventors upon execution of their patent applications and assignment:

ON FILING SOLE PATENT APPLICATION

Number of Companies	Amount
62	0 or nominal $1
5	$5
2	$10
5	$25
16	$50
1	$60
10	$100
1	$125
1	$150
1	$200
1	$250
1	$300

One company makes the following payments for each patent application filed:

Number of Inventors	Amount to Each Inventor
1	$200
2	$175
3	$150
4	$125
5 or more	$500 (prorated)

When joint applications are assigned in general the same amounts are generally paid to each inventor, but payments over $100 are usually prorated. In some cases joint inventors are paid $75 each where $100 is paid to a sole inventor.

When the patent is issued most companies make no further payments. The following payments to sole inventors when a patent issued were reported. Joint inventors were generally paid similar amounts and in a few cases are prorated. In one case maximum total payments to joint inventors was $300.

PAYMENTS WHEN PATENT ISSUED

Number of Companies	Amount
1	$25
1	$35
5	$50
2	$75
9	$100
1	$150
1	$500

The replies thus indicate that it is the general policy of most companies to regard the salaries paid R&D employees as full consideration for the assignment of inventions made during their employment using the time and facilities of the company. Only a few companies pay any substantial amounts or make special awards. Two companies reported that they may pay as much as $5,000 as an annual special company award. Some companies have set up suggestion systems and special awards as high as $25,000 for employees who are not engaged in R & D.

One company pays the inventor in any one calendar year a share of royalties received from licensees or a share of sale of a patent as follows:

40%   of first $1,000
30%   of next $2,000
20%   of next $2,000
15%   of next $15,000
10%   of all further sums collected

One company reported that one of the best ways to encourage R&D employees to produce inventions is to make it possible for them to have some return from their inventions by sharing with the employee any monetary income through the sale or licensing of his assigned patents. By giving the employee, say, 15 percent of such return, important inventions can become lucrative to him and yet the company itself has no "out of pocket" expense in remunerating the employee. This company believes that these ties are strengthened by arranging the agreements so that such income is payable to an individual even under postemployment situations. This not only gives the R&D employee greater encouragement to produce inventions, but creates a sufficient tie should he leave the company to be more than willing to help the company should it become involved in litigation involving a patent.

The 40 replies received from Research Institute members indicated the following payments are made to sole inventors when the patent application is filed:

SOLE INVENTOR WHEN PATENT APPLICATION FILED	
Number of Companies	Amount
27	No payment or nominal $1
2	$ 25
4	$ 50
4	$100
1	$150

In the case of joint inventors, two companies pay $25 to each joint inventor upon filing; four pay $50; two pay $100; and one pays $150.

When the patent is issued four companies pay $50 to the sole inventor; one pays $100. In the case of joint inventors each may be paid the same amount or payments may be allocated.

It is interesting to compare other recent surveys made with our results. The Industrial Research Institute made a study in 1957 of 104 companies regarding awards for inventions made by employees. The results given were:

Number	Amount paid
17	$1
10	$ 2—$25
14	$26—$50
11	$51—$100
5	above $100

Special Bonus Awards If Given	
7	$1,000 or less
6	$1,001—5,000
2	Royalty

The National Industrial Conference Board published a report in *Business Management Record,* August 1952, "Patent Policies for Employees" which gave information obtained from 48 companies. Seventeen of these companies pay a fixed amount per invention: one company pays $150; six companies pay $100; six pay $50; and four pay $1. The latter sum, of course, is more in the nature of a legal consideration than additional compensation. The 13 companies which pay more substantial sums generally split the amount, paying part on application for the patent, and the balance when the patent is issued.

Eleven of these companies also give additional compensation through more liberal salary increases. Three companies recognize meritorious inventions by bonuses: one includes it in the semi-annual discretionary bonus, and two arrive at the amount by bonus plans already in effect for such purposes.

One company gives the employee-inventor 10 percent of income derived by the company from use of the invention by others. Three aircraft companies are the only ones participating in the survey that grant royalties from issuing licenses under the patent. These three royalty plans pay as follows:

Company A
    30%   on first $1,000
    25%   on second $1,000
    20%   thereafter
    (no percentage on company use)

Company B

    30%   of first $10,000 net

    20%   of next $10,000

    10%   of next $50,000

     5%   of all above $70,000

        received by company after cost of exploiting and protecting the invention has been deducted.

Company C

    After all expenses,

    50%   of first $1,000

    30%   of next $1,000

    10%   thereafter

Special award plans are in effect in several companies to stimulate employee-inventors and to give recognition to specially meritorious disclosures.

One company, through a committee, selects the two best inventions made each year and pays the respective inventors $500 each as awards of merit. (The sum is divided equally in the case of joint inventors.) The committee further chooses the most beneficial invention during a five-year period for a grand award of merit of at least $1,000.

Another company's plan provides that from every fifty inventions received each year, a patent disclosures committee will select the "most meritorious," whose inventor will be awarded $200. (Where two or more inventors are involved in the same disclosure, a total of $300 is divided equally among them.) In this company, too, special awards, as high as $5,000, are made for inventions that have proved of outstanding commercial value.

Other companies make special awards for inventions through bonus plans which recognize outstanding service.

A survey made by the National Industrial Conference Board, published in the August 1963 issue of *Business Management Record,* states the following:

Three fourths of the sixty-two respondent companies that pay cash awards for employee inventions grant fixed amounts. These range from $5 to $350. Occasionally the payment is in savings bonds or shares of stock.

Payments are usually made in two installments, part on filing of the application and the balance on issue of the patent. A number of companies have adopted each of the following award schedules:

- $50 on filing, $50 on patent issue
- $50 on filing, $100 on issue
- $100 on filing

Some other award schedules reported by cooperators include:

- $10 on filing, $100 on issue
- $25 on filing
- $50 on filing, $150 on issue

- $10 on disclosure, $100 on filing
- $50 on filing, $300 on issue
- $250 on assignment, $50 on issue
- $50 savings bond on filing, $200 cash on issue

Companies that pay fixed awards for employee patents generally provide for awards to each of two or more co-inventors. A few companies divide fixed awards equally among all the co-inventors, but more often a system like that established by a motor vehicles company is in force:

a. $50 to an applicant who is the sole inventor

b. $40 to each applicant in the case of a joint application where there are only two inventors

c. $35 to each applicant in the case of a joint application where there are three or more inventors

A petroleum company gives each inventor $50 on filing of a patent application, with a proviso that if there are more than four co-inventors they will share a maximum of $200. A further payment of $100 is made to the inventor or each co-inventor upon issuance of the patent. An instruments company, which pays $100 to an individual inventor at the time of filing a patent, divides a total of $200 among all employee co-inventors when a joint patent of theirs is filed.

A fourth of the respondent companies that compensate employee inventors make awards according to an estimate of the invention's worth. Thus a textile company writes that a typical award based on patent value is around $1,000, "although much smaller awards are sometimes made." A manufacturer of electrical industrial equipment, in addition to paying a cash award of $50 on acceptance of a disclosure and $50 on filing of the application, makes a "most meritorious award" to the best disclosure in each block of fifty, the award being $200 for a sole inventor and $300 for a joint invention. This company also provides a special patent award that may be granted on a commercially successful invention. According to the company, these three awards may total as much as $5,000 per inventor.

To emphasize the importance of being first in developing new ideas and to insure a continued high level of inventive activity, an office equipment manufacturer recently devised a three-point patent award system. The first part of the program rewarded employee inventors for work already done at the time the award system started in 1961. Two hundred and twenty-five employees received awards ranging from $1,000 to $3,000 for inventions on which patents had already been filed or issued.

Part two of the company's award program provides awards of from $1,000 to $5,000 or more for outstanding individual inventions. When an invention is judged "outstanding," the inventor receives $1,000 in cash. When a corporate special awards committee determines that any invention is "special" the company pays the inventor $5,000 or more. The third part of the award system pays employee inventors $1,000 and up for a consistent output of significant inventions.

Several companies indicated that in some instances they may release rights to inventions made by their employees when requested.

In such cases the company may at its expense obtain the patent for its employee and retain a royalty-free shop right.

RESULTS OF COMPANY POLICY CHANGES

We sought to obtain data regarding policy changes in rewarding employee-inventors which might offer some clues how effective rewards may be increasing productivity. There were 27 companies in our sample which stated that they made changes in their policies. Also a total of 9 Research Institute member replies indicated policy changes were made. The combined replies indicated that 9 companies increased their payments to inventors which resulted in some increased production of inventions. No significant increase was found by 14 companies. Thirteen made no reply or had no data available for making any judgment. Two companies dropped all cash payments previously made. One company had a policy established for 20 years which provided for cash awards to inventors after issuance of the patent. It recently decided to cancel such policy and require assignments of all inventions without any cash awards for the following reasons. The explanation given to its employees stated:

> Since we entered into an invention award agreement with most employees at the time of their employment, some employees can be expected to ask why a different agreement and related policy are being established now. It will be recalled that the original Agreement provides that the Company will pay employee inventors a cash "award" for each invention that is patented and retained exclusively for use in the Company's business. Our experience shows that this procedure is impractical and is detrimental both to the Company and to employee inventors. Because of the award provision, in each instance in which a possibly meritorious idea has been submitted to the Company it has been necessary to determine if a rather large cash outlay can be justified before decisions can be made to patent and ultimately exploit it. This has presented a virtually insurmountable obstacle since many inventions have little or no obvious practical value and in most cases the dollar value of an invention is speculative unless there has been a considerable period of costly development, experimentation and actual application of the invention. Consequently, the invention award Agreement has caused unfortunate delays and the abandonment of many employee inventions which had at least some potential. As a result, employee inventors have been denied appropriate Company recognition for making useful inventions and the Company has been denied the benefit of these inventions. The depressing effect of our past practice can best be demonstrated by pointing out that during the past twenty years the Company only has pursued invention cases sufficiently to have paid employee invention awards three times.

> Because of the highly complex and technical nature of our industry, our success, and consequently the success of her personnel,

depends to an ever increasing extent on the inventiveness and creativeness of employees, many of whom are highly trained technical professionals who specifically are expected to invent as a normal part of their assignments. Recognition of performance in this area can most appropriately be provided by the personal commendation, formal announcement, salary consideration and other means which may be expected to contribute to employee prestige and satisfaction and which commonly are used to recognize other types of meritorious job performance.

It is hoped sincerely that the changes being effected in the Company's policies and practices covering inventions, discoveries and improvements by employees will result in making available to our company in greater abundance the new and improved products, processes, methods and equipment that are essential to the continued success of the Company and of her personnel.

STANDARDS AND PROCEDURES FOR EVALUATING INVENTIVE PRODUCTIVITY

The rising cost of research in industrial enterprises can be attributed to increased expenditures for research facilities and salaries of research personnel. Assuming all possible action is taken by management to stimulate employees to invent by giving them ample rewards and incentives, by affording them ample research facilities and a favorable creative environment, the question arises, how can the inventive productivity of individual research employees be evaluated so that they may be recognized for their contribution to the company, as well as for comparison with other employees in the same organization? It is generally recognized that not all research activity is necessarily productive because creativity cannot be turned on or off as desired. Furthermore, the production of inventions is often a matter of serendipity or the unlooked for by-product of research. Arthur Bakalar, director of the patent division of Shell Development Company, reported that 5 percent of the research staff of about 1,300 research employees made more than half of the patented inventions during 1937-1954. He quotes the president of Bell Telephone Laboratories as saying: "It has been our experience that invention is not an automatic result of engaging in systematic research and development. . . Actually, only about 4 percent of them [the research workers] make half of all the inventions."[3]

We sought to obtain information from the questionnaire mailed to 447 United States companies selected from the *Official Gazette* of the U. S. Patent Office for the fiscal year beginning

---

[3] 41 *JPOS* 592 (1959).

July 1, 1960, as previously described. The following question was asked:

"What standards and procedures do you employ to evaluate the productivity of R&D employee-inventors?"

We received 92 replies to this question. Several respondents interpreted this question to refer either to judgments whether a submitted idea was patentable or whether it was desirable to file a patent application. Most of these respondents indicated that submitted ideas were referred to their patent department for patentability evaluation. The present study did not explore how company decisions are made when to file or not to file a patent application on ideas submitted by R&D employees.

It appears that many factors must be considered before any judgment can be made regarding the output of any individual R&D employee. The nature of the specific projects he is assigned to work on, the facilities available to him, the technical character of the problems involved, whether the project involves basic or applied research, the time spent on the project, prior successes or failures by others, the value of the project to company business, etc., are just a few of many more factors involved. Thirty-seven replied that no attempt at evaluation of inventive productivity is made. However, in practice some factors are informally considered in assessing the value of R&D employees to their company for salary increases and promotions. The evaluation is generally made by immediate supervisors who are in frequent contact with the R&D employees, consideration being given to their entire performance and overall contribution to the company's growth. Twenty of the responding companies consider the number of applications filed or patents obtained as at least one factor to be considered. In general, R&D people are expected to invent because they are employed to do so, but the number of inventions they make does not necessarily measure the extent of their value to the company.

A questionnaire was also sent to 74 Research Institute members who were not included in the sample selected as previously described containing the same question regarding evaluation of the productivity of their R&D employees. Of the 35 replies received to this question, 17 indicated no direct attempt to evaluate productivity is made, 7 considered the general overall performance of their R&D personnel, 9 took into consideration the number of patents issued and patent applications filed.

The following selected comments made by the respondents

reflect various approaches made in evaluating the productivity of their R&D personnel.

The number of patents obtained is not the sole criterion, since there may be instances of inventions for which patents cannot be obtained, for one reason or another. Moreover, inventive productivity is itself not the sole criterion of desirable scientific accomplishment in the company, since it may happen that a particular scientist is assigned to a task in which a low incidence of inventions would be expected, e.g., some type of fundamental research.

*   *   *

We consider in reference to each R&D employee the number of ideas submitted in relation to opportunity afforded for creativeness by work assignments; the basic nature of inventions; the number of patent applications filed and patents issued; and the extent to which the submitted ideas solve particular problems without necessarily being patentable.

Also, it is obvious that one invention of unusual sophistication and value (in a commercial sense) must outweigh a dozen inventions of a marginal character. An employee who consistently produces inventions of significant value is recognized and advanced in salary and position.

*   *   *

On an annual basis we prepare a detailed statistical summary on each of our professional employees engaged in R&D indicating numbers of conceptions submitted, applications filed, and patents issued. We also prepare a similar statistical summary for each of our research supervisors, the obvious purpose being to attempt to determine whether a given supervisor or type of supervisor is more or less effectual in creating inventive environment than other supervisors. This report is for use by top R&D management to assist in the over-all evaluation of employee performance.

*   *   *

The inventive productivity of R&D employee-inventors is evaluated not only by the number of times they are identified as the inventor or co-inventor of a patentable idea upon which a patent application is filed, but also by the results they obtain in the projects assigned to them, taking into consideration the nature of their activity and various other factors which can be considered to contribute to the expectancy of patentable contributions.

*   *   *

We expect each R&D employee to produce inventions over a period of years at the average rate of one patentable invention every two years. From this base we evaluate an employee's performance by taking into account the field in which he works and the employees with whom he works to determine whether a greater or lesser rate of inventiveness is reasonable.

*   *   *

Not all engineers and scientific personnel are inventors. A rela-

tively small percentage of the engineers make most of the inventions
—so that five engineers might come up with more inventions than
50 other engineers. These five should be given the highest incentives,
and it is these people who are generally advanced in the company
both salary-wise and organization-wise.

*   *   *

As an informal check on the inventive productivity of our R&D
effort, we utilize a standard that for every $75,000 expended by our
engineering development departments, we should produce one patentable invention. I have found it extremely difficult to measure productivity on a per capita basis and prefer to do it on a dollar basis expended or budget basis.

*   *   *

Various factors, including the quality as well as the number of
inventions and innovations, are taken into account. Further, work in
new fields is usually more conducive to making inventions than research activity in well-worked fields; this factor is also considered in
evaluating the performance of employees.

*   *   *

We do not have any standards and procedures for evaluating the
inventive productivity of R&D employees. Because one individual
may be working on a particularly difficult project while another less
skillful individual may be working on a much easier one, any attempt
to compare the inventive productivity of two such people becomes
impossible. We believe that the evaluation of an R&D employee by
his immediate supervisor and other associates is about the best criterion we have found.

*   *   *

Management, at all levels, is made aware, in a number of ways,
of the number and nature of an employee's inventions. For example,
whenever an employee makes an invention resulting in the filing of a
patent application, his supervision, up to the highest level, is ap-
prised thereof by the responsible Patent Attorney. As another example, issuance of patents to employees is noted regularly in one of
the company's journals (which has a wide circulation outside the
company). Further, periodically a report is made to top management
of the applications filed and patents issued which appear to be of
major importance.

*   *   *

Our procedure is to see that the general managers of our various
operations know of the patent applications which are filed on behalf
of his employees, and that he also knows our opinion of the level of
invention involved so that quantity alone is not determinative.

*   *   *

Our standard merit rating and evaluation system, developed for
engineering and technical employees, takes into account the factors
of originality and creativity and constitutes the basis for salary
changes.

*   *   *

The productivity of a chemist or engineer is a primary factor in determining the advancement and annual compensation of the employee. In determining the productivity of a technical man, we give consideration to both his patentable, as well as his unpatentable, technological contributions to the company. As a matter of policy, we have not favored the idea of giving a special award to our technical people because of patentable contributions. It is our belief that this results in a discrimination against many technical contributions which are of substantial value to the company in its day-by-day operations and yet are unpatentable. We have always favored the practice of giving consideration to a man's technical productivity and contribution in determining his annual salary.

*   *   *

Resourcefulness and creativeness in the recognition, analysis and solution of problems are the broad standards employed to evaluate the performance of R&D employees. Performance reviews are made periodically. Inventive productivity is one of the criteria used in applying these standards and such productivity is measured by (a) the volume and character of the material submitted for patent consideration and (b) the number and "quality" of patents for which the employee is responsible.

Conclusions

Any attempt to measure the creative output of a research worker should begin with an examination of the products of his work. After an inventory is made of the products, each product would have to be evaluated from the viewpoint of value to the company. The values may be tangible or intangible. Tangible values may be represented by patents, new products, improvements in going products, reduction of production costs, etc. Intangible values may be represented by significant technical and scientific publications based on company research of general value to the industry, development of test devices and methods, etc. J. H. McPherson,[4] of The Dow Chemical Co., lists the following creative products of a scientist which could be tallied to evaluate his creativity:

1. Patents
2. Patent disclosures
3. Publications
4. Unpublished research reports
5. Unprinted oral presentations
6. Improved processes
7. New instruments
8. New analytical methods

---

[4] "A Proposal for Establishing Ultimate Criteria for Measuring Creative Output," *Scientific Creativity: Its Recognition and Development,* Eds. Calvin W. Taylor and Frank Barron (New York: John Wiley & Sons, 1963), Chapter 2.

9. Ideas
10. New products
11. New compounds

He then points out:[5]

> We could merely add up the number of products in each of these categories, since many of them must go through some screening to obtain their classification, and make a judgment about the "creativity" of the scientist. One of the criteria used at the General Electric Company to prove the worth of its Creative Engineering course is the number of patents produced by graduates of the course.
>
> Most research men would be reluctant to use number of patents alone as a suitable criterion for measuring "creativity." These would be some of their arguments:
>
> 1. There are many valuable creative acts that might meet some standard of creativity but are not patentable.
> 2. There is a wide range of quality in patents. (One researcher may, because he feels that it is a "good thing" to get patents, develop one chemical compound after another and pile up quite an impressive list of patents. Another investigator, less socially motivated to seek patents, may apply for one only after he has done scientific work that meets his own high standards. But, when judges have available the number of patents and patent disclosures that each scientist has, they are inclined, if acting in haste, to make their judgments on this numerical statement, in spite of the realization that the quality of the patents should be considered.)
> 3. An investigator working in a fertile field where little work has been done may accumulate many patents, whereas a worker in a well-plowed field may find a patent hard to come by.
> 4. Some investigators may be so motivated to pursue science for science's sake that they neglect to patent a patentable product.
> 5. Over a long span of time the frequency of patent issue is affected by social conditions and changes in patent laws.
>
> No doubt many other objections could be raised to the use of the number of patents as a criterion of creativity. If the patents were to be used, each patent would have to be subjected to a qualitative analysis. Similarly, each of the other listed products would have to be analyzed before it could be included.
>
> What methods could be used to make the analysis of each of these products more exact? The analyses will always be a matter of human judgment, the only gauge for measuring invention, since objective criteria are lacking.

The replies made by the respondents to our questionnaire indicate that the measurement and evaluation of the productivity of R&D is an unexplored field that deserves intensive investigation. McPherson[6] points out:

> Since we will be struggling with the ultimate criteria problem for some time, I should like to make two suggestions:

[5] *Ibid.*, p. 25.
[6] *Ibid.*, p. 29.

1. The labor involved in determining analytical methods for looking at each of these products and in developing methods for putting these analyses together would be considerable. Some research people feel that their intuitive quick judgment would be valid most of the time and tend to view such labor as a waste of time. Others feel that the mere adding of products would be sufficient. So I propose that to test these judgments a procedure somewhat like the following be tried:

A.   Three sets of criteria should be collected on the same people.

    (1) A group of scientists should be rated in the usual fashion —quick judgments on creative level of the subjects.

    (2) A numerical count of products should be made and a ranking established.

    (3) An analytical scheme for each product should be developed and applied to all the products of each man. Then, all the subjects should be ranked according to these analyses.

B.   The relationship between these rankings should be obtained.

2.   The National Science Foundation might invite the Research Institute, which also is located in Washington, D.C., at The George Washington University, to help with the problem.

EFFECT OF ASSIGNMENT OF INVENTIONS REQUIRED BY COMPANIES

The following question included in our questionnaire brought many interesting comments:

"Since most companies take title to patented inventions of their R&D employees it is often contended that this practice impairs incentives to invent. (1) Do you believe that this is or is not true? (2) If true, can you supply one or more specific examples?"

Practically all U.S. companies replying to this question indicated that incentives of their R&D employees were not impaired because the companies took title to their patented inventions. A number of respondents took strong exception to the statement in our question that "since most companies take title to patented inventions of their R&D employees it is often contended that this practice impairs incentives to invent" as being unfounded in fact. The prevailing company approach is that R&D employees are employed to invent and the resulting rights to such inventions are property rights which they are hired to create. The employee incentives therefore should not be impaired since their salary and advancement are dependent upon, among other things, the inventive ingenuity they bring to bear on their assigned problems. Only four companies indicated impairment of incentive might occur under some situations. However, no specific examples were given because obviously where inventions are not forthcoming many reasons may be responsible. Some companies find that taking title may reduce the incentive of R&D employees to make formal disclosures of new ideas and also the preparation of disclosures to the patent department. Some R&D employees also are reluctant to spend time in assisting the company patent attorneys in prosecution of their patent applications or analyzing cited references.

STIMULATING R&D EMPLOYEES
TO PRODUCE MORE INVENTIONS

Questionnaire cards (4″ x 5″) were sent to 1,118 inventors whose names appeared in the selected sample patents as previously described. We received 385 filled-in cards. All but 2 of the inventors were employees who assigned their inventions. Also all but 4 of the inventors stated that they were employees and had signed agreements to assign their inventions to their company.

One of the six questions asked was:

"In your opinion, can R&D employees be encouraged to produce more inventions? Yes . . . . No . . . . If yes, how?"

There were 28 "no" replies. There were 96 replies indicating cash payments or bonuses would encourage production. There were 20 who indicated a royalty or percentage of sales as desirable; 18 indicated an incentive plan would be desirable. Thus, nearly 35 percent of the inventors thought tangible remuneration would encourage more inventing.

Freedom of research was indicated to be desirable by 18, professional recognition by the company was mentioned by 25, a favorable creative environment by 19, more information regarding patent law and procedure was mentioned by 15, better communication regarding problems to be solved was noted by 14. Various miscellaneous suggestions were made, such as attendance at scientific and technical meetings, permission to publish results of research, better facilities, as factors in stimulating productivity of inventions.

It is interesting to compare the inventor replies with other recent studies. In 1957 a report was published by the Committee on Engineers and Scientists for Federal Government Programs (Government Printing Office 1957) which made a study of the attitudes of scientists and engineers based upon responses made by 17,439 scientific and engineering personnel in federal government service and 3,317 similar individuals engaged in industrial research.

The factors contributing to job satisfaction in order of importance for industry personnel were as follows:

1. Interest potential of work
2. Integrity of management
3. Opportunity to move up in organization
4. Calibre of supervision
5. Living conditions
6. Pay
7. Opportunity to discover and do creative work
8. Chance to feel a part of organization
9. Congeniality of associates
10. Professional recognition
11. Security of employment
12. Physical facilities for research
13. Learning "what makes things go"
14. Chance to contribute to basic scientific knowledge
15. Social value of work

For government employees Item 7 was third in order of importance and Item 14 was eighth. Otherwise, the order was generally close for both.

John Riegel, in *Intangible Rewards for Engineers and Scientists,* Bureau of Industrial Relations, University of Michigan, Report No. 9 (1958), made a study of 276 nonsupervisory engineers and scientists of 10 companies. He also interviewed 44 executives, 91 supervisors, and 276 employees. (Table I below.)

A question put to each executive who was interviewed was, "What does your company do to motivate engineers and scientists to do their best work and to yield them high levels of satisfaction on the job?" In response, many of the executives spoke of salaries and benefits, but there were more references to the treatment of professionals and to the provisions of intangible rewards.

Table I shows a distribution of references to sources of intangible rewards to engineers and scientists. The first column shows the distribution of the 252 references made by 164 nonsupervisory professionals; the second column shows the distribution of 185 references made by 36 executives.

Although the employees and the executives agree to some extent, there are noteworthy differences in the percentages in the two columns. A definitely larger percentage of references was made by the employees to the recognition of their work. Also, the employee spoke more frequently than did the executives about the challenge and variety of their work as a source of satisfaction.

TABLE I

REWARDS OTHER THAN RECOGNITION

Distribution of 252 References by 164 Nonsupervisory Engineers and Scientists to Various Sources of Intangible Rewards, and Distribution of 185 References by 36 of Their Executives to Similar Sources

	Distribution	
Sources	Employees' References %	Executives' References %
Recognition by supervisors and managers of my (our) contributions	28	16
"I know how I'm doing"	4	
The favorable regard of my colleagues because of my work		4
Challenge of projects assigned to me (us)	12	10
Their variety	4	
Having my ideas accepted and	7	
seeing them put to use	10	7
Being treated as a professional	10	1
Being given responsibility for my projects		3
Being allowed to manage my own work	6	5
Being consulted on technical problems		8
Being given business and technical information		10
Having the privilege to publish		5
Being encouraged and permitted to participate in the activities of professional societies		4
Being allowed to select projects on which I can work part-time		2
Miscellaneous references		1
Competent and understanding supervisors and managers	8	1
Who show interest in me as a person and in my welfare		7
Who give me confidence in the management		1
Opportunities to learn in my professional field	6	4
Prospects for promotion and a professional career	2	
Promotions already received		1
Facilities and environment of the work		6
Services provided by the company: testing, calculating, drafting, clerical, etc.		2
Work schedule not strictly enforced	2	1
Miscellaneous references	1	1
	100	100

A study by Dr. Lee E. Danielson, *Characteristics of Engineers and Scientists Significant for Their Motivation,* published by the Bureau of Industrial Relations, University of Michigan Report No. 11 (1960), gives data relating to reasons for job satisfaction given by 277 nonsupervisory engineers and scientists in Table II. Reasons for dissatisfying job activities are given in Table III.

E. V. Murphee, President of Esso Research and Engineering Co., in a recent talk (*The Chemist* [July 1962], p. 241) in referring to Dr. Danielson's study said management must try to understand the needs, goals and behavior of their scientists and engineers.

> Dr. Danielson concluded that technical personnel, as compared with other employees are more responsible, more objective and more deeply involved in their work. They desire greater freedom and more individualized, less routine supervision. They have a greater need for tangible and intangible rewards for their work and ideas. They are more creative, analytical, ambitious, emotional, and introverted. Their goals are broader, higher, and more definite.

> No single pattern of job activity could be singled out as being more or less satisfying by any sizable portion of the group under study. Apparently it is the "whole job" that makes work interesting to the technical man—its variety, the balance achieved between laboratory and other technical work, and the sense of responsibility for a project. Reasons given for technical job satisfaction included: Visible results; completed tasks; new, non-routine and challenging assignments; personal satisfaction; recognition by others; utilization and extension of abilities; relations with others; opportunities for growth and advancement. I conclude that we in industrial research must aim at six major targets in providing an environment best suited to these men:

> 1. A clear definition of their broad responsibilites.
> 2. Simple, direct lines of communication.
> 3. Ample opportunities for expanding their knowledge.
> 4. Sufficient time and opportunity for interchange of ideas and information with colleagues.
> 5. Recognition of technical achievements.
> 6. Adequate rewards for accomplishments.

> The future of U. S. industry, in fact the future of our country, rests on accelerated growth of good research by good research men. We face an urgent need to provide the best kind of environment for the research man of tomorrow. He must be a man who is dedicated to the making of scientific contributions. He must be creative and have drive and initiative. He must be an authority in his field with the ability to communicate his ideas to others.

> We in research management also have an obligation. We must provide him with the environment that will make it possible for him to work to the top of his creative ability.

Dr. Robert E. Wilson (*The Chemist* [May 1962], p. 176) outlined the obligations of management to the research man as follows:

> The first and greatest [company] obligation to the research man

TABLE II

EMPLOYEES' REASONS FOR
SATISFACTION WITH JOB ACTIVITIES

Reasons*	Times Each Reason Was Given
I. Visible Results	
a. I can point to results of *my* effort	42
b. I can see progress toward a goal	9
c. I obtain results that pay off to the company	8
II. Task Completion	
a. I see an idea through from inception to completion	27
b. My predictions or hypotheses work out	10
c. I eliminate problems or "bugs"	7
III. New, Nonroutine, Challenging Work	
a. My work is new, it's pioneering, it requires imagination	38
b. It's nonroutine, there is variety and balance	33
c. It's a challenge, it taxes my ingenuity	35
IV. Personal Satisfaction	
a. My work gives me creative experiences	41
b. I can take personal pride in my job (not related to reward)	20
c. My work satisfies my personal curiosity	10
d. It gives me personal satisfaction and it satisfies the company goals	5
V. Recognition from Others	
a. My supervisor trusts me, lets me work on my own	19
b. As a result of my work, others recognize me as expert	15
c. My supervisor and/or higher management recognizes me for my work	9
d. I perform a service or help others and gain their respect	7
VI. Self-Realization (utilization and extension of abilities)	
a. I am extending my college training (broadening)	29
b. My talents, training and interests are utilized	28
c. I consider my present work training for the future	4
VII. Relations with People	
a. I have contacts with others within and outside the company	31
b. There is teamwork in my work group	9
VIII. Miscellaneous	
a. I have an opportunity to contribute to fundamental knowledge	11
b. I have an opportunity to work on something immediately useful	9
c. I have an opportunity to work on something I consider important	5

*Given by 277 nonsupervisory engineers and scientists.

TABLE III

DISSATISFYING JOB ACTIVITIES AND
EMPLOYEES' REASONS FOR DISSATISFACTION*

Activities and Reasons**	Times Each Activity Was Mentioned
I. Conducting Research or Experiments and Tests_____	34
a. Inability to solve problem	
b. Lack of end result	
c. Old-product research	
d. Stigma attached to unsuccessful research	
e. Type and scheduling of "research"	
II. Designing and Drafting_____	12
III. Constructing Models_____	3
IV. Performing Clerical Tasks (record-keeping, clerical jobs, bookkeeping, etc.)_____	42
V. Performing Routine or Continuous Tasks (calculator, plottery, etc.)_____	70
Reasons for dissatisfaction with Categories II-V:	
a. Poor utilization of abilities and skill	
b. Unable to prove oneself	
c. Lesser trained person could do job	
d. Boredom or monotony	
VI. Supervising and Consulting_____	16
a. Prefer to do things myself	
b. Committee meetings a waste of time	
VII. Preparing and Presenting Reports (written or oral)_____	52
a. Lack of skill in reporting	
b. Inability to meet various standards	
c. Futility of reports	
d. Frequency of reports	
VIII. Establishing and Enforcing Standards_____	7
a. Lack of authority to enforce standards	
b. Conflicts that result from trying to enforce standards	
IX. Performing Other Activities (teaching, expediting and service functions)_____	18
a. Not "engineering" work	
b. Waste of time	
X. Limitations Imposed by Higher Management (procedures, personnel, planning, organization, actions, and relations with other departments)_____	53

*Order of presentation follows the order in which the items appear on check sheet.

**Responses of 277 nonsupervisory engineers and scientists.

is to define the company objectives, which should be specific. "It is not enough to say that the company seeks to make a profit or to improve its products and processes. These are the aims of practically all companies. The research man is entitled to know the specific areas in which he is expected to be creative."

He also stressed 10 other obligations of management:

1. Good research management with scientific and administrative ability;
2. Adequate compensation for the research man;
3. Good working conditions;
4. "Patient" money, or willingness to spend money without being too impatient for returns;
5. Relative freedom for the research man within the objectives set up by the company;
6. Adequate assistance to relieve research men of routine work;
7. The ability of management to listen to worthwhile developments;
8. Nondiversion of too many research men to sales technical service or to manufacturing technical service;
9. A reasonable opportunity for outside technical contacts;
10. An outlook on research as a long-pull proposition not dependent on how the stock market is behaving. "Often there is greater need for research during depression than in times of prosperity."

Effective stimulation by management of R&D employees to create requires an appreciation of the factors involved in the creative process as well as a sympathetic understanding of the creative personality. Creativity cannot be set in motion at will. The psychological basis of creativity has hardly been explored by psychologists, although in recent years this subject has received more attention by them. Most of available data today is crude and inexact. We do have generalized personality impressions of the creative person. He is a nonconformist, shows a high level of initiative and independence of thinking. He also shows curiosity, self-discipline and a drive for accomplishment. He tends to become totally involved in his work.

The truly creative person is not a good organization man, yet as a company employee he is under pressure to adjust to organization life. The conventional restraints required by organization activities tend to impair his creativity because he loses more or less the freedom of action essential to creativity. He cannot always choose his own problem or satisfy his random curiosity without accounting for lost time to his superior or research director. The problem for management is thus to provide a creative atmosphere taking into account the psychological factors of the inventor and at the same time not to impair the productivity of R&D personnel by requiring too rigid compliance with the work discipline imposed on noncreative employees.[7]

Appendix A
FOREIGN QUESTIONNAIRE REPLIES

A total of 220 air letter questionnaires was mailed to foreign companies selected from the *Official Gazette* for the fiscal year beginning June 1960. We received 84 (38 percent) replies as follows:

Australia	1	Holland	4
Belgium	1	Italy	4
Canada	2	Japan	4
Denmark	3	Lichtenstein	1
France	7	Norway	2
West Germany	19	South Africa	1
Great Britain	17	Sweden	10
Hungary	1	Switzerland	7

We received in many instances detailed replies to the question: Does your country have special laws regulating the assignment of patented inventions made by company employees? If yes, how do these laws affect your arrangements with your employee-inventors? Some of the respondents sent copies of their pertinent laws and even included English translations. These replies appear to agree in most instances with a review of various national laws relating to employees' rights in their inventions published by Fredrik Neumeyer, patent attorney in Stockholm, Sweden, *International Labour Review,* January 1961, pp. 1-31, published in Geneva, and also in his recent study *The Law of Employed Inventors,* Study No. 30, published by the U. S. Senate Subcommittee on Patents 1963, and also in an article by William J. Rezac of the patent department of Olin Company concerning "The Validity of Foreign Contracts Assigning Employees' Inventions to Their Employer," published in *JPOS* March 1960, pp. 177-92. A recent book by Christian Englert, *L'Invention Faite par l'Employé dans l'Entreprise Privée,* Verlag für Recht und Gesellschaft AG Basel, Switzerland, 1960, p. 239, is a useful comparative legal study of foreign employer-employee law.

No attempt will be made here to summarize or compare the laws in

---

[7]There is scant literature on this subject. See: Hower, R. H., *Managers and Scientists* (Boston: Harvard Business School, 1963); Rubenstein, A. H., "Setting Criteria for R&D," *Harvard Business Review,* Vol. 35 (1957), pp. 95-104; Drucker, P. E., "Twelve Fables of Research Management," *Harvard Business Review,* Vol. 41 (January-February 1963), pp. 103-108; Quin, J. B. and Mueller, J. A., "Transferring Research Results to Operations," *Harvard Business Review,* Vol. 41 (January-February 1963), pp. 49-66; Phelps, E. D., "Help Your Engineers to Get Ahead," *Harvard Business Review,* Vol. 40 (January-February 1962), pp. 125-132.

the various foreign countries relating to inventions made by company employees in view of the available publications previously referred to.

Judging from the replies received, it appears that the relations between management and employee-inventors and current problems are very similar to those existing in this country. Since we have only a few replies from each country, no definitive generalizations can be made at this time.

As pointed out by Dr. Neumeyer: "There are three main approaches available for setting up national law provisions regarding rights and obligations of employed inventors: (1) creation of a special law (Sweden, Denmark, Germany, and Soviet Union); (2) insertion of provisions into the patent law (Austria, Canada, Finland, Holland, Japan, and Italy); or (3) insertion of provisions into the law of contracts (Switzerland). Other important countries, such as the United States, Great Britain, and France, are still relying upon the precedents given by the courts or statements made by certain official boards." In these countries inventions made by company employees can be conveniently classified as: (1) "Service Inventions," those made by the employee (a) within the scope of his employment; and (b) within the field of business activity of the employer; (2) "Dependent Inventions," those made by the employee (a) outside the scope of his employment; but (b) within the field of business activity of the employer; and (3) "Free Inventions," those made by the employee (a) outside the scope of employment; and (b) outside the field of business activity of the employer.

"Free Inventions" normally belong to the employer but they may be acquired by agreement with the employee. "Service Inventions" belong to the employer without extra compensation. "Dependent Inventions" may or may not belong to the employer depending upon the circumstances and country, and also usually entail special compensation in addition to usual salary paid the employee especially if the invention is of exceptional value.

The West German Employee Invention Law of July 25, 1957 is quite complicated. In addition, regulations for the compensation of employee inventions were established July 20, 1959. A detailed explanation of the German law is given by James W. Brennan, "The Developing Law of German Employee Inventions," *IDEA*, Vol. 6, No. 1 (Spring 1962), pp. 41-86. Also see K. E. Laude, "Compensation for Employee Inventions in Germany," 44 *JPOS* 77 (November 1962).

We received a number of statements from U. S. companies indicating that they did not favor any legislation in the U. S. A. such as exists in West Germany or Japan. One company stated:

> We have wholly-owned subsidiaries in Japan and several European countries where such legislation in various forms now exists. Our experience has been that such legislation complicates employee invention agreement understandings, injects issues between employer and employees which do not exist now in the United States, and in return do not really do anything for the inventor-employee which would not be done anyway.

In regard to the existing employer-employee law in West Germany, the general attorney of a large U. S. company made the following comments:

> The overall impression I received was that management was un-

happy about the fact that the law exercised a disturbing influence on recruiting. The head of the applications laboratory for this company, for example, said he found it difficult to recruit personnel because there is little likelihood that people doing applications work would make patentable inventions. A similar situation exists for the quality control group. Yet, these groups are essential to the successful operation of the company. The recurring thread running through all the comments is that the law made every chemist want to do research—yet research was only one of a large number of fields in which skilled personnel were required.

The actual operation of the law does apparently raise some problems in that at least one member of the patent group finds it necessary to devote a large part of his time to the original and early appellate procedures involved in fixing the remuneration of the inventors. My overall impression is that most remuneration matters are settled at an early stage in the entire established procedure. I did, however, hear of one case in which this had not proved possible. In the resultant appeal, the inventor requested a very much higher remuneration than he had originally requested on the ground that the appeal would jeopardize his standing in the company so that he should, in effect, receive a reward that would compensate him for a loss of position.

One of our U. S. respondents in the Fall of 1960 visited with Dr. Schade, the Head of the Arbitration Court which is authorized to suggest "reasonable compensation" to dissatisfied employee-inventors. At that time, there were 140 cases on the docket of which one-third were finally disposed of on the following basis:

A lump-sum settlement was generally preferred (leaving open the question of reconsideration if conditions change later).

Compensations range between DMs 500 and 1,000. In some special cases, a compensation of DMs 10,000 was paid, generally a half or one monthly salary.

Compensation was based on a 6-year life time of the patent (general average).

The result of the calculation was checked against the sum the company would have been willing to pay an outside inventor for the same invention. Fifteen percent of this sum (1/5 to 1/8) was regarded as reasonable compensation for employee-inventors.

These cases appeared to indicate that inventors tend to over-rate the compensation expected. Dr. Neumeyer outlines in his study a number of reported rulings and opinions under the German employee law.

One German company reported that in a few cases they reassigned the invention to the employee and merely retain a shop right.

Another comment we received states:

Legislation to assure the employee-inventors are adequately compensated by the employers would be difficult to administer and necessarily inequitable. Half of the patents are never used. How can compensation be placed on a purely defensive patent? The basic incentive is the pay check with its size depending on the employee's contribution to the business.

Dr. Neumeyer's study contains a good discussion of the arbitration procedure under the German employer-employee law and he gives summaries of about 20 reported cases. He also gives a summary of 17 published Swedish cases relating to employee-inventor awards. He indicates that many disputes are settled amicably between the parties without resort to arbitration or litigation.

APPENDIX B

AIRLETTER SENT TO FOREIGN COUNTRIES

Gentlemen:

The PTC Research Institute of The George Washington University would very much appreciate your cooperation in the foreign phase of an important research study it has undertaken. The study deals with rewards and incentives to employee-inventors both in American and foreign companies.

As you know, many hundreds of American patents are being currently issued to foreign companies, and because we cannot query all these companies with respect to their inventor-incentive policies and procedures, we have taken a scientific sample of patents issued to them. Since your company originated one of the American patented inventions included in our sample (listed at the end of this letter), we solicit your reply to the following questions. The identity of your company will be held in strict confidence.

A. Does your country have special laws regulating the assignment of patented inventions made by company employees?

                 Yes_____No_____(please check)

     1. If "yes," how do these laws affect your arrangements with your employee-inventors? (Please comment and include, if possible, one or two examples from your own experience.)

     2. If "no," what is your present policy?

B. It is often contended that private industry could do more to encourage employee-inventors by its policy with respect to their conditions of employment (e.g., by the way of cash rewards, promotions, salary increases, honors, publicity, retention of title to invention by employee, etc.) 1. Do you believe this is or is not true? 2. If true, please comment.

C. It is often contended that the practice of companies taking title to patented inventions impairs incentives to invent. 1. Do you believe this is or is not true? 2. If true, can you supply one or more specific examples?

We know that we are asking a great deal of you. We realize that the demands on your time will preclude anything but a brief reply, but we urge you to respond promptly to this letter. Because of the scientific sampling plan employed in this study, the cooperation of every respondent is critically important. Our findings will be published in the Institute's Journal.

Sincerely,

L. James Harris

Patent No.   Date   Inventor   Title

LETTER AND QUESTIONNAIRE SENT TO SAMPLE U.S. COMPANIES

Gentlemen:

The PTC Research Institute of The George Washington University would very much appreciate your cooperation in an important research study it has undertaken. The study deals with rewards and incentives to employee-inventors. Dr. Joseph Rossman, a patent attorney on the research staff of the Institute, is the Principal Investigator.

The importance of bringing about, through industrial research, an uninterrupted flow of new inventions is essential to our economic health and progress and the need to stimulate inventors into activity can scarcely be overemphasized. In Congress and among the Federal agencies, as well as in industry, there is some difference of opinion on the effect of the rewards and incentives which are currently offered to employee-inventors. Proposals have been made from time to time that legislative action be taken, similar to that in effect in some foreign countries, to assure that employee-inventors are adequately compensated by their employers.

We are asking you to help us establish a body of factual knowledge on vital questions concerning rewards and incentive policies of companies on the productivity of employee-inventors. Such factual knowledge does not now exist.

As you know, many thousands of patents are being currently issued to companies, and because we cannot query all these companies with respect to their inventor-incentive policies and procedures, we have taken a scientific sample of the patents issued to them. Since your company originated one or more of the patented inventions included in our sample (listed at the end of this letter), we would like to draw upon your experience, and we also solicit your further cooperation by asking you to have the inventor or inventors complete the card questionnaire(s) and mail in the enclosed envelope. (The last six digits of the patent number appear in the lower right-hand corner of the card.) The identity of your company and the inventor will be held in strict confidence.

A. It is often contended that industry could do more to encourage employee-inventors by changing its policy with respect to their conditions of employment (e.g., by way of cash rewards, promotions, salary increases, honors, publicity, retention of title to invention by employees, etc.)

1. What is your present policy?
2. How long (years and months) has your present policy with respect to conditions of employment of employee-inventors been in effect?
3. If a *different* policy was previously in effect, please state:
   a. What the previous policy was.
   b. Date it was changed.
   c. How the change in policy has affected the inventive productivity of your company's R&D employees.
   d. *Also* please give the following (or equivalent data), if possible.
      a. Number of ideas submitted for consideration for patenting

        per capita R&D employee *before* and *after* change in policy.

    b. Number of patent applications filed per capita R&D employee *before* and *after* change in policy.

    c. Number of patents issued per capita R&D employee *before* and *after* change in policy.

B. What standards and procedures do you employ to evaluate the inventive productivity of R&D employee-inventors?

C. Since most companies take title to patent inventions of their R&D employees it is often contended that this practice impairs incentives to invent. 1. Do you believe that this is or is not true? 2. If true, can you supply one or more specific examples?

D. Another criticism of industry policies with respect to its employee-inventors is that the established policies have become less and less appropriate as government financial support for industry R&D grows. Please comment on this topic.

We know that we are asking a great deal of you. We realize that the demands on your time will preclude anything but a brief reply, but we urge you to respond to this letter and have the inventor(s) complete and mail the enclosed card(s). Because of the scientific sampling plan employed in this study, the cooperation of every respondent is critically important. Our findings will be published in the Institute's Journal and should be very useful to industry.

                   Sincerely,

                   L. James Harris

APPENDIX D

U. S. INVENTOR QUESTIONNAIRE

Date_____

1. Were you an employee of the company to which the invention was assigned at the time you made it? Yes_____ No_____.

2. Did you sign an agreement to assign your invention to the company?

3. a. Have you received any cash compensation for your invention in addition to your salary? Yes_____ No_____.

    b. If yes, state basis of payment:_____

    c. If no, did you receive any other rewards? Please state what:_____

4. Please state your age:_____ Education: grammar_____; high school_____; college_____(no. of years)_____; graduate_____(no. of years)_____.

5. How many U.S. patents have been issued in your name previously?_____.

6. In your opinion, can R&D employees be encouraged to produce more inventions? Yes_____ No_____.

    If yes, how?_____

APPENDIX E
LETTER AND QUESTIONNAIRE SENT TO INSTITUTE MEMBERS

Gentlemen:

The PTC Research Institute of The George Washington University would very much appreciate your cooperation in an important research study it has undertaken. The study deals with rewards and incentives to employee-inventors. Dr. Joseph Rossman, a patent attorney on the research staff of the Institute, is the Principal Investigator.

The importance of bringing about, through industrial research, an uninterrupted flow of new inventions is essential to our economic health and progress and the need to stimulate inventors into activity can scarcely be overemphasized. In Congress and among the federal agencies, as well as in industry, there is some difference of opinion on the effect of the rewards and incentives which are currently offered to employee-inventors. Proposals have been made from time to time that legislative action be taken, similar to that in effect in some foreign countries, to assure that employee-inventors are adequately compensated by their employers.

We are asking you to help us establish a body of factual knowledge on vital questions concerning rewards and incentive policies of companies on the productivity of employee-inventors. Such factual knowledge does not now exist.

As you know, many thousands of patents are being currently issued to companies, and because we cannot query all these companies with respect to their inventor-incentive policies and procedures, we have taken a scientific sample of the patents issued to them. We are also interested in supplementing that study with the experience of the companies which are members of the Institute. We would like to draw upon your experience, by asking you to answer the following questions. The identity of your company will be held in strict confidence.

A. It is often contended that industry could do more to encourage employee-inventors by changing its policy with respect to their conditions of employment (e.g., by way of cash rewards, promotions, salary increases, honors, publicity, retention of title to invention by employees, etc.).
  1. What is your present policy?
  2. How long (years and months) has your present policy with respect to conditions of employment of employee-inventors been in effect?
  3. If a different policy was previously in effect, please state:
     a. What the previous policy was.
     b. Date it was changed, and reason for the change.
     c. How the change in policy has affected the inventive productivity of your company's R&D employees.
     d. *Also* please give the following (or equivalent data) if possible.
        a. Number of ideas submitted for consideration for patenting per capita R&D employees *before* and *after* change in policy.
        b. Number of patent applications filed per capita R&D employees *before* and *after* change in policy.

      c. Number of patents issued per capita R&D employee *before* and *after* change in policy.

B. What standards and procedures do you employ to evaluate the inventive productivity of R&D employee-inventors?

C. Since most companies take title to patented inventions of their R&D employees it is often contended that this practice impairs incentives to invent. 1. Do you believe that this is or is not true? 2. If true, can you supply one or more specific examples?

D. Another criticism of industry policies with respect to its employee-inventors is that the established policies have become less and less appropriate as government financial support for industry R&D grows. Please comment on this topic.

We know that we are asking a great deal of you. We realize that the demands on your time will preclude anything but a brief reply, but we urge you to respond to this letter. Our findings will be published in the Institute's Journal and should be very useful to industry.

                           Sincerely,

                           L. James Harris

BIBLIOGRAPHICAL NOTE

Abel, P., "Employees' Inventions in Austria," *Industrial Property Quarterly* (1960), pp. 31-33.

Beatty, B. P., "Employee-Inventors' Patent Rights and Compensation and Employers' Rights in Foreign Countries," *The Encyclopedia of Patent Practice & Invention Management* (1964), pp. 233-242.

Brennan, J. W., "The Developing Law of German Employee Inventions," *IDEA,* Vol. 6, No. 1 (Spring 1962), pp. 41-86.

Calvert, R., "Patent Policies for Industry," *Journal Patent Office Society,* Vol. 48 (1966), pp. 215-241.

Clesner, H. F., "Innovator's Payment Determination in U. S. S. R.,"*IDEA*, Vol. 6, No. 2 (Summer 1962), pp. 226-240.

Coleman, L., "The Effect of Shifting Employment on Trade Secrets," *Business Lawyer* (January 1959), pp. 319-328.

"Employee Inventor: A Symposium." Moderator: L. J. Harris. An Inventor's View, J. Rabinow; An Executive's View of the Employee Inventor, J. A. Haddad; An Attorney's View, The Employee Inventor, I. L. Wolk; A View From Abroad, F. Neumeyer; The Employee Inventor: An Economist's View, I. H. Siegel; How Many Patentees?, B. S. Sanders; A Psychologist's View, J. N. Mosel. *Journal Patent Office Society,* Vol. 47 (1965), pp. 467-513.

"Employee vs. Company Interests in Trade Secrets and Patents: Panel Discussion," *IDEA*, Vol. 10, Conference No. (1966), pp. 67-90.

"Employer-Employee Stakes in Invention." Moderator: R. E. Gibson; Energizing and Rewarding Inventors. Invited contributors (Tishler, Zworykin). Loss of Trade Secrets Through Changes in Employment. Invited contributors (McPherson, Williams, Wilson). Panel discussion and question period. Research Staff contributors (Bangs, Green, Rossman, Sanders. Siegel). Invited contributors (McPherson, Tishler, Williams, Wilson). *IDEA*, Vol. 8, Conference No. (1964), pp. 24-58.

Englert, C., "L'Invention Faite Par L'Employée Dans L'Enterprise Privée," *Verlag für Recht und Gesellschaft* A. G., Basel (1960), p. 240. A survey of employer-employee rights to inventions in European countries as well as USA.

Hayes, A. J., "Independent Inventor's Interest," *Journal Patent Office Society*, Vol. 47 (May 1965), p. 298.

Hefter, L. R., "Invention—Inventor's or Employer's?" *IDEA*, Vol. 7, No. 3 (Fall 1963), pp. 380-395.

"Independent Inventor and the Small Business Inventor: A Symposium." P. A. Mallinckrodt: Point of view of the individual inventor. C. W. Musser: Acquisition by the federal government of title to patents. D. King: The independent inventor, a community asset. C. E. Branick: Improving the climate for invention. D. V. Simone: The how of invention. C. E. Hastings: The inventor and small business. G. Z. Edwards. *Journal Patent Office Society*, Vol. 47 (1965), pp. 419-459.

Koenig, G. K., "The Shop Right—Time for Limitation," *Journal Patent Office Society*, Vol. 49 (1967), pp. 658-677.

Lassagne, T. H., "The Legal Rights of Employed Inventors," *American Bar Association Journal*, Vol. 51 (1965), pp. 835-839.

Laude, K. E., "The Compensation For Employee Inventions in Germany," *Journal Patent Office Society*, Vol. 44 (1962), pp. 772-781.

Lightman, J. M., "Inventors' Certificates and Industrial Property Rights," *IDEA*, Vol. 11 (1967), pp. 133-150.

Leonard, J. W., "The Protected Rights of the Employee Inventor in His Invention," *Journal Patent Office Society*, Vol. 49 (1967), pp. 357-371.

McTiernan, C. E., "Employees' Responsibilities as to Trade Secrets," *The Encyclopedia of Patent Practice & Invention Management* (1964), pp. 242-248.

McTiernan, C. E., "Employees and Trade Secrets," *Journal Patent Office Society*, Vol. 41 (1959), pp. 820-835.

McTiernan, C. E., "Trade Secrets—The Predicament of the Employer," *Patent Law Developments*, Southwestern Legal Foundation (1964), pp. 75-92.

McTiernan, C. E., "Employee-Inventor Compensation Plans," *Journal Patent Office Society*, Vol. 46 (1964), pp. 475-484.

Maltby, W. R., "Need for a Federal Policy to Foster Invention Disclosures by Contractors and Employees," *Federal Bar Journal*, Vol. 25 (1965). pp. 32-40.

Maltby, W. R., "Division of Rights Between the Sponsor and the Originator of an Invention," *Federal Bar Journal*, Vol. 21 (1961), pp. 258-265.

Neumeyer, F., "The Employed Inventor-Part I, The European Situation," *Lex et Scientia*, Vol. 2 (1965), pp. 233-242; Part II, "The American Situation," *Lex et Scientia*, Vol. 2 (1965), pp. 243-265.

Neumeyer, F., "Employees' Rights in Their Inventions," *Journal Patent Office Society*, Vol. 44 (1962), pp. 674-710.

Neumeyer, F., "The Law of Employed Inventors in Europe," *Study No. 30 of the Senate Subcommittee on Patents*, S. Res. 267, 88th Congress, 1st Session (1963).

Nolte, A. C., Jr., "Shop Rights," *The Encyclopedia of Patent Practice and Invention Management* (1964), pp. 731-736.

"Organization-Individual Confrontation," *IDEA*, Vol. 7, Conference No. (1963), pp. 114-187. A symposium covering various aspects of the inventor in an organization, his incentives and problems.

"Patent Payments to Employees Top $1 Million at Lockheed," *Journal Patent Office Society*, Vol. 47 (1965), p. 346.

Plaisant, R., "Employees' Inventions in Comparative Law," *Industrial Property Quarterly*, Vol. 5 (1960), pp. 31-54.

"Protection of Trade Secrets in the Employer-Employee Relationship," *Notre Dame Lawyer*, Vol. 39 (February 1964), p. 200.

Rezac, W. J., "Assignments of Inventions to Employers Here and in Europe." *New York University Intra. Law Review*, Vol. 15 (1960), p. 219.

"Rights of Employer and Employee in Patentable Inventions," *American Patent Law Assoc. Bulletin* (April-May 1966), pp. 173-207. A panel discussion by six attorneys relating to recent developments and company policies.

Siegel, I. H., "Changing Status of Sole Inventors: A Company Case Study," *IDEA*, Vol. 11, No. 2 (Summer 1967), pp. 151-158.

Siegel, I. H., "Employee Creativity and Organizational Aims," *IDEA*, Vol. 9, No. 3 (Fall 1965), pp. 401-425.

Siegel, I. H., "Independent Inventors: Six Moral Tales," *IDEA*, Vol. 9, No. 4 (Winter 1965-66), pp. 643-655.

"Statutory Requirements of Companies for Protection of Intellectual Creations," *IDEA*, Vol. 8, No. 4 (Winter 1964-65), pp. 483-589. A clinic discussion in depth of forms of statutory protection of intellectual creations American companies need, now and in the future, in the light of recent court decisions and existing company situations.

Takino, B., "The Protection in Japan of Inventions by Employees During Course of Their Employment," *Washington Law Review*, Vol. 39 (1964), p. 564.
Wade, W., "Employee Inventions and Agreements," *Encyclopedia of Patent Practice & Invention Management* (1964), pp. 227-233.

Was, D. A., "The Right of the Inventor to Use His Invention," *Industrial Property Quarterly*, Vol. 6 (1961), pp. 76-82.

PART II

ORGANIZATION NEEDS AND EXPERIENCE— UNIVERSITY AND INDUSTRY

From a consideration, in the previous chapter, of the individual's position and function in the creative process, we turn in this section to the role of the organization in which, or with which, he works. The first paper deals with the academic community. It depicts the academic environment for research and enumerates the opportunities for the utilization of research results. Several programs are elaborated for the productive commercialization of patents to support research, particularly when grants from an outside organization are not available. Stress is placed on the involvement of alumni in this activity.

Another kind of "alumni," those who migrate from one industrial organization to another, are considered in the paper "Trade Secrets in Context of Positive Competition." They are analyzed here as a group that requires special understanding, new responses from companies, and increasing attention by the courts and the legislatures. The character, application, and protection of trade secrets are described as an element of our social system: Trade secrets are a part of the total mechanism for the protection of ideas; the people concerned with trade secrets make their contributions to the economic system mostly in positive and productive ways, providing a unique dynamism to the economy in the process. They do so despite some pathological situations involving actual bad faith (e.g., stealing) and gross carelessness with another's confidential information. Although abuses are abnormal and relatively few, they appear to be increasing; on the other hand, means are being provided through company rules, legislation, and court decision to improve the functionality of trade secrets as an element of our social system.

Among the papers in this section is a pioneer study on the use of modern statistical method to determine the rate of patent utilization. The paper shows the proportion of patents used and the reasons for non-use. The findings—in view of previous estimates by other authors—are quite surprising.

What organizations actually do with the industrial property they seek to protect and use for their profit is the primary concern of all three papers. Although organizations encourage novelty, they must provide for the safety of and maximize the return on, their property: The paper on institute patent programs proposes new plans for patent commercialization; the report on trade secrets deals with attempts to understand the function of trade secrets and with efforts to provide appropriate legal adjustments; and the report on utilization of patents casts light on a primary characteristic of such property that has been grossly underestimated in the past—commercial use.

Protection and Promotion of Products of the Mind Resulting From Research in a Technological Institute

Frederic B. Schramm

INTRODUCTION

The so-called cold war is a grim race for survival, survival of nations, survival of a way of life, survival of human freedom. The race is being run in the arenas of economics and technology. Although the greater emphasis in the popular mind is upon technology, one cannot lose sight of the fact that the race is equally grim in the arena of economics and that economic strength determines the ability to compete in the arena of technology.

Our universities and scientific schools are in the forefront of the technological race. To keep ahead requires ever increasing effectiveness and efficiency in scientific and technological research. Under the grim circumstances, it demands also adequate attention to economics, or financial support.

Arrangements have been employed for tending to the economics and providing financial support for general or unsponsored scientific research conducted at engineering schools and scientific divisions of universities. One of them has been obtaining grants from an outside organization which supplies sufficient funds to get new research projects started and counts on recouping its advances and acquiring funds for future grants by the earnings of the research discoveries and patents resulting from those research projects. Such support can come, of course, only from the projects which have proved to have some commercial or financial value. Such an outside granting organization may be unable to foresee technical or commercial value in the products of research at any particular technological institute and therefore be reluctant or unable to support patenting and industrial promotion.

When grants from an outside organization are not available, some technological institutions may find it to their advantage or may find it desirable to attempt to develop a more direct and closely affiliated mechanism for evaluating, protecting, and promoting the

EDITOR'S NOTE: This paper appeared in *IDEA*, Vol. 6, No. 1 (Spring 1962), p. 150.

products of unsponsored research and development. The term "unsponsored research" is used to apply to research other than applied research sponsored or paid for by an industry or manufacturing company to solve a specific problem or develop a particular product which becomes the property of the sponsor. Where a technological institution utilizes an outside granting organization for obtaining commercial outlets for developments which can advantageously be handled by such an outside organization, there may still be advantages in retaining the right to handle some of its developments individually and being relieved of exclusivity in the arrangement with the outside organization.

The major technological institutes have sufficient human and material assets available to carry the recommended concept of direct and closely affiliated control forward to an optimum degree which will prove mutually advantageous and beneficial to the institute, to the institute's alumni and to the community. This can be accomplished in a variety of ways, some of which have proved highly successful for similar institutions.

It is hoped that this paper will provoke sufficient interest in the problems involved to support additional analysis of existing procedures followed by our technical schools and their advantages and disadvantages and the possibilities in trying new procedures. It would be worthwhile to investigate to what extent possibilities of supporting teaching and research financially from the by-products of research have been lost by lack of suitable procedures, and to find out what percentage of ideas developed by technological university laboratories could become real income producers.

RESEARCH AND PATENT PLAN

In order to obtain full benefits from the research work done at an institute consideration must be given to the matter of processing the results of research work done at the institute's laboratories by members of the institute's faculty and graduate student body and employees, including the extent to which patents should enter into the program.

The matter may be considered under three heads. First, a brief summary of what has been done or considered by various institutions; second, desired objectives of the institute with regard to research and the utilization of the results of the research; and third, the extent to which the manner of operation of an outside research commercializing organization fits these objectives.

What Some Institutions Have Done

It has been said that patentable discoveries and inventions are usually fortuitous by-products of research, particularly with regard to research conducted on the university campus. Moreover, whether seeking a better understanding of the laws of nature or endeavoring to develop new products or improve old products or processes, many scientists working in university laboratories are content to pursue their investigations without giving much, if any, thought to the patentability of the results and often take the attitude that wide dissemination of the results through publication is preferable.

Nonetheless, very often new ideas, discoveries and inventions growing out of experiments and investigations undertaken with quite a different purpose in view may have valuable commercial application and require patent protection and control in the public interest. They may not only be essential to scientific and technological progress and to cultural and social advancement, but also contribute to industrial developments and expansion.

It has also been said that where the protection and control provided under the patent laws may have to be invoked to obtain the maximum public benefit and usefulness from these products of non-profit research, the universities and other non-profit research organizations have the responsibility to the public and to the inventors, to see that the discoveries and inventions are patented and are so administered and controlled that they will produce the greatest benefit to all concerned.

Universities, colleges, and technological institutes are primarily teaching institutions, but research is and always has been an integral part of the overall education program. However, there is much variety in the manner in which research results are handled in different educational institutions. Some eighty-five universities, colleges, technological institutions and professional schools have adopted general research and patent policies as a definite course of action formulated and expressed in systematic statements by the boards of control, state legislatures and other governing bodies of the institution. It is understood that Harvard University and Western Reserve University have formal research and patent policies with respect to inventions and discoveries primarily concerned with therapeutics or public health.

University-Affiliated Research Organizations[1]

There are thirty-five or more special research institutions, foundations, corporations, departments and divisions established as

---

[1]See *Patents and Nonprofit Research,* Study of the Subcommittee on Patents, Trademarks, & Copyrights of the Committee on the Judiciary, U. S. Senate, pursuant to S. Res. 55, Study No. 6, (Washington, D. C.: G. P. O., 1957), p. 27.

units or affiliates of educational institutions to handle for the respective institutions the administration and/or conduct of sponsored research under contract or grant and in some instances the co-ordination of all research activities of the institutions as well as the management of the patentable results of such research. An example is the Ohio State University Research Foundation.

Unincorporated Institutional Units

In some cases sponsored research is conducted and/or administered under contractual arrangements made by unincorporated institutional units such as the Institute for Co-operative Research of Johns Hopkins University.

University-Affiliated Foundations

Where the educational institution has a substantial investment in the discoveries of inventions and in the patents obtained thereon and promotional effort is necessary to exploit the patents, there is the problem of additional investment in money and services being required to place the inventions, or the finished products based upon the inventions, in commercial production, introducing them to the public and gaining their acceptance. Very often these functions are performed on behalf of an educational institution by a separately incorporated non-profit patent management foundation affiliated with the institution. The oldest is the Wisconsin Alumni Research Foundation. This was established in 1925 and acts as the patent-management agent for the University of Wisconsin and for the faculty and staff of the University. The Purdue Research Foundation was created in 1930 and the Cornell Research Foundation in 1932.

At the present time there are more than 50 of these separately incorporated organizations with authority to perform patent management functions.

Although it is primarily a special research organization offering research and experimental engineering services to industry and government, the Armour Research Foundation is authorized to handle the management of patents for the Illinois Institute of Technology, with which it is affiliated, as well as patents on discoveries and inventions growing out of its own research activities and which the Foundation holds in its own name.

There are about 69 colleges and universities which directly or through affiliated patent-management organizations enter into patent development agreements with research corporations.

Litigation and Other Experiences

Educational institutions and other non-profit research organizations have kept relatively free of litigation and other controversial experiences relating to patents and inventions. Prior to 1945 the Wisconsin Alumni Research Foundation was involved in extensive infringement litigation over the Steenbock Vitamin D patents and the copper-iron patent. Although the Vitamin D patents were finally held invalid, a decision in the copper-iron patent favorable to the Foundation was accepted by industry.

The Rutgers Research and Endowment Foundation has been involved in two instances of litigation with respect to its streptomycin patent.

Royalty Income

The Wisconsin Alumni Research Foundation obtained a gross royalty income of $14 million through 1946 from its Vitamin D patents and $1,734,000 from Warfarin through 1955. The expired copper-iron patent yielded $652,000 through 1952 and the stabilized iodine patent $450,000 through 1955. In some instances some other patents in the Foundation's portfolio brought in less than the expenses incurred.

The Rutgers Research and Endowment Foundation has received approximately $7 million in royalties under the streptomycin licenses and $150,000 under those on neomycin, including both the domestic and foreign patents. Other university affiliated research foundations or the universities themselves have also received royalty income but in smaller amounts than the Wisconsin Research Foundation and the Rutgers Research and Endowment Foundation.[2]

Dr. Robert E. Wilson, winner of the Perkin medal, asserted:

> A generation ago most research workers in the medical field and many of those in our universities felt that it was not quite ethical to patent their discoveries, particularly in matters relating to public health. During the past twenty years, however, there has been a growing recognition of three facts: (1) Failure to patent is more likely to delay than to encourage the development and marketing of new products especially if any substantial investment or advertising is required to get them started. (2) Failure to patent leaves new remedies open to widespread abuse by unethical manufacturers and promoters, whereas patenting permits a control of quality and marketing practices which is highly desirable in the case of many new drugs. (3) Failure to patent simply throws away a large potential income from those who benefit from new discoveries, which income might better be collected and used to promote further research in related fields . . . . This is a sound and

---

[2] *Patents and Nonprofit Research, supra,* p. 59.

socially desirable method of financing research work which would be lost if the value of patents were to be greatly reduced.[3]

The Research Objectives of a Technological Institute

Technological institutes and professional schools are primarily teaching institutions. Their principal objective, therefore, is effective teaching of engineering and science.

However, research is an essential adjunct of effective teaching. The research activities of the faculty and staff of the institute enable the institute to fulfill its function of extending the boundaries of human knowledge, of encouraging attitudes of scientific inquiry, of training students for scientific and technical pursuits, and disseminating scientific and technological information. Well organized research may, therefore, be considered another important objective of the institute, second only to its primary teaching function.

Another aspect of university research relates to providing experience in the actual carrying on of research techniques and procedures that can be obtained only through actual participation in experimental research.

However, carrying on research on the requisite scale to supplement the theoretical teaching function and to provide the training obtained in the actual research experience involves substantial expenditures both for equipment and for salaries of personnel. Sponsored research provides income for that portion of the research program, specifically directed in the fields authorized by the sponsors or relating to the solution of specific problems of the sponsors. However, to fulfill its function of extending the boundaries of human knowledge in every area relating to technology and physical sciences, the specific areas of sponsored research are inadequate to cover the field. The teaching budget cannot be depended upon to complete the areas in which research should be carried on.

A third objective of the institute's program should be to find ways and means of adequately supporting the research program. This should encompass making full use of all the assets available to the institute including its teaching faculty, members of its research staff, its superior undergraduate students, its graduate student body, the members of the corporate body, trustees or the like constituting and governing the institute, the entire alumni body in addition to the sponsors of specific research projects and the other organizations which are directly or indirectly supporting the institute in research programs, such as alumni organizations and community groups of manufacturers and local organizations.

---

[3] *Industrial and Engineering Chemistry,* Vol. 35 (1943), p. 177.

Any program is no better than the personnel which carries it out. Adequate support of the program of the technological institute, therefore, involves proper support of the personnel engaged in executing the program.

Wherever possible opportunities should not be neglected for deriving financial income from the research program through royalties and otherwise to provide funds for the requisite salaries and the equipment. With adequate equipment, the results may be accomplished from which personal gratification may come. Recognition to the personnel engaged in research will come in part from the publication of scientific articles and treatises.

Even from the standpoint of the general public the greatest benefit to the general welfare and the maximum improvement of the national economy may come, not alone from making public research findings and rendering them freely available in widely known publications and other media of dissemination, but from patent protection.

Karl T. Compton said in one of his annual reports while President of Massachusetts Institute of Technology:

> Responsibility does not always end with the mere publication of a patentable scientific discovery or invention: the public benefits derivable from patent laws and contemplated by the framers of those laws should not be lost through a failure to solicit patent protection.[4]

Elihu Thompson declared:

> Publish an invention freely, and it will almost surely die from lack of interest in its development. It will not be developed, and the world will not be benefited. Patent it and, if valuable, it will be taken up into a business.[5]

The patent system serves a dual purpose in supporting research activities. First, insofar as research work conducted at the institute may relate to or lead to discoveries of industrial value, the results of research may enable the institute directly, or through a research foundation, to augment the institute's income required for financial support of equipment and personnel and in providing financial incentives to personnel. Secondly, the issuance of a patent may provide a very meaningful stimulus in the form of official recognition following critical examination that the inventor has contributed to advance the sum of human knowledge.

It has been suggested that the academic person should not seek commercial gain from products of original research ostensibly undertaken to enhance knowledge in his academic field. The contradictions which are inherent in this view have been pointed out. Moreover,

---

[4] *Technology Review,* Vol. 35 (Dec. 1932), p. 101.
[5] *Electrical World,* Vol. 75 (1920), p. 1505.

this view is not shared by many persons who have exhibited outstanding success in enhancing knowledge in their academic fields.
While an exhaustive documentation could be prepared, the following tabulation of academic persons who have recognized the desirability of creating valuable rights in the products of their research
is significant.

Professors, Educators, Teachers, Who Have Obtained U. S. Patents

BARNES, John Landes, professor of engineering, UCLA, b. Oct.
16, 1906. Granted U. S. patent on Modulation system.—
WWE, 1959.

CALLAN, John Gurney, university professor, b. Apr. 7, 1875, d.
Dec. 30, 1940. Univ. of Wisconsin 1915-20; Harvard 1920—.
Has taken out about seventy patents, principally in connection
with steam turbines.—*WWWA,* Vol. I.

CARNELL, Paul Herbert, chemistry professor, b. May 7, 1917.
Marietta College 1948-49; Albion College 1948-52; Chair-
man chemistry department, Albion College, 1952 to date.
Nineteen U. S. patents. *Chemical Who's Who,* 1956.

COOKE, Hereward Lester (deceased), professor of physics, Princeton Univ., received patents on toothbrushes.

COPE, Arthur C., Bryn Mawr, Pa., professor of organic chemistry
and head of the Department of Chemistry of Massachusetts
Institute of Technology in 1945, holder of nine patents on
barbiturics.

D'ALELIO, Gaetano F., professor and head, Department of
Chemistry, Univ. of Notre Dame. b. Dec. 26, 1909. 315 patents, synthetic fibers, molding and laminating compositions,
radar insulations, rocket launchers, etc.—*Who's Who in
Engrg.,* 1954; *Chem. Who's Who,* 1956.

EINSTEIN, Albert, physicist and former patent examiner, Institute of Advanced Studies, Princeton Univ., Patent No. 1,781,
541 on refrigeration system.

ERICKSON, J(ulius) L(yman) E(dward), prof. of organic chemistry,
La. State U. b. Lake Charles, La., Oct. 8, 1901. Holds patents
on macrocyclic musk compounds.—*Chemical Who's Who,*
1956.

FERMI, Enrico, b. Italy, Sept. 29, 1901, d. Nov. 28, 1954. Taught
Univ. of Florence 1924-26; Univ. of Rome 1927-38; professor
at Columbia Univ. 1939; Univ. of Chicago 1945. Ten or more
patents in field of atomic energy—2,206,634, July 2, 1940—
Process for production of radioactive substances, etc.

FISHER, Harry Linn, research chemist, b. Jan. 19, 1885. Professor of chemical engineering, Univ. of S. Calif. 1953-56. Holds fifty patents in organic chemistry and rubber technology.— *WWE,* 1959.

FULLER, Richard Buckminster, S. Ill. Univ., research professor Geodesic Dome Patents—structures used in the Air Force's DEW and in commercial structures and factories. Geodesic Domes use only 1% of the material utilized by conventional buildings to shelter the same number of square feet of ground.

GODDARD, rockets. Guggenheim Foundation, paid million to widow.

HAAS, Dr., head of chemistry department, Purdue University. (See McBee).

KARRER, Paul, professor of chemistry, Univ. of Zurich, Zurich, Switzerland, winner of the Nobel Prize in 1937 for sympathetic vitamin structure, granted ten U. S. patents for synthesis of vitamins B_2 and E.

LAWRENCE, Ernest O., professor of physics, Univ. of Calif., 1930—. b. Aug. 8, 1901, d. Aug. 27, 1958. Invented cyclotron. Obtained U. S. patent No. 1,948,384, Feb. 20, 1934 for method and apparatus for acceleration of ions.—*WWE,* 1959.

LOF, George O. G., consulting engineer, b. Dec. 13, 1913, professor, Univ. of Colorado, 1940-47; Univ. of Denver 1948-52. U. S. patents No. 2,680,565, June 8, 1954 for Solar Heating Apparatus and Method; No. 2,909,171, Oct. 10,1959—for Solar Cooker.

MCBEE, Dr., professor of chemistry, Purdue University. Has taken out large number of patents in the field of organic chemistry jointly with Dr. Haas.

PAULING, Linus Carl, professor of chemistry, Calif. Inst. of Tech., b. Feb. 28, 1901. U. S. patent No. 2,416,344, Feb. 25, 1947 for Apparatus for Determining the Partial Pressure of Oxygen in a Mixture of Gases.—*Chemical Who's Who,* 1956.

PEARL, Irwin Albert, research chemist and professor, b. Dec. 25, 1913. Univ. of Wash. teaching fellow in organic chemistry, 1934-37; research assoc. 1938-40. Approx. 150 scientific papers and patents in the fields of synthetic organic chem., wood chem., etc.—*Chemical Who's Who,* 1956.

PINES, Herman, professor of organic chemistry, Northwestern Univ., b. Jan. 17, 1902. Over 125 patents in field of hydrocarbons, hydrogenation, alkylation, etc.—*Chemical Who's Who,* 1956.

RAMBO, William Ralph, professor electrical engineering, Stanford Univ., b. Sept. 3, 1916. Fifteen patents in electronics field.— *WWE*, 1959.

RUGE, Arthur C., Cambridge, Mass., research associate, professor of engineering seismology. Patents included twenty on strain gages and torque, fluid pressure and weight measuring and recording devices.

SALATI, Octavio M., asst. professor electrical engineering, 1948 to date, Univ. of Pennsylvania. Five U. S. patents. Microwave connectors.—*WWE*, 1959.

SZENT-GYORGYI, Albert, 1937 Nobel Laureate in the field of medicine and physiology, Woods Hole, Massachusetts, research biologist—Patent No. 2,834,541.

VAN ALLEN, James A., physicist, educator, b. Sept. 7, 1914. Professor, Iowa State Univ. 1952 to date. U. S. patent No. 2,945,-002, July 12, 1960, for 2.2' -dihydroxy -4.4' -dimethoxybenzil as an ultraviolet stabilizer.—*WWA,* 1960-61.

Moreover, if the research results are patented, knowledge thereof may spread far more rapidly to industry, the engineering profession, and other research scientists because the issued patents are classified with a high degree of subdivision so that information in specific narrow areas may readily be found when sought.[6]

In summary, it is believed that the immediate objectives of a technological institute in support of its research program should be both to cause the research program to help to pay its way through royalties and other income under patent rights utilizing the various facilities and contacts which the institute has for bringing its inventions to industrial use, and to provide the institute's research workers with the maximum possible recognition including that represented by the issuance of patents.

An Individualized Research Promotion Program for a Technological Institute

An individualized research promotion program may prove advantageous because it may well be that some of the discoveries and inventions of the personnel of a technological institute which would have to be rejected by an outside organization might have been made the subject matter of patent applications to the advantage of the in-

---

[6]Simon M. Newman, "Classified Patent Search Files, a Proposed Base for Technical Information Centers," 43 *JPOS* 418 (June 1961); Nathan Reingold, "U. S. Patent Office Records as Sources for the History of Invention and Technological Property," *Technology & Culture,* Vol. 1, No. 2 (Spring 1960), pp. 156-157.

stitute as a possible source of revenue or as an incentive to the personnel involved, enhancing the reputation of the institute in the scientific and industrial world or even among its own alumni.

Since various institutions have employed several different plans, different possibilities may be mentioned for the selection of a suitable plan. Such possibilities include: (1) the establishment of a non-profit patent holding corporation; (2) the holding of patents by the technological institute; (3) an alumni-sponsored foundation to raise funds for research not covered by specific sponsors; (4) the establishment of a separate but affiliated research and development company; (5) the organization of an actual profit-type manufacturing and marketing corporation to acquire developments from the institute and other sources and carry them through the pilot plant and market research stages before resale or spin-off of newly developed industries and; (6) various combinations of these plans.

A Present and Immediate Basic Plan

In order to progress as rapidly as possible to what may ultimately be considered the ideal plan without losing momentum while developing future plans, a technological institute commencing the evaluation of its research results will obviously utilize as much of the mechanism of its present practice as feasible in an immediate plan which will increase the incentive for the research workers of the institute to submit their ideas for legal evaluation and lift the status of the research of the institute and improve the results thereof.

Initially, the institute may hold the patents resulting from the institute's research in which sponsorship contracts do not require assignment to the sponsor. It is desirable to have an individual on the staff of the institute or connected with its faculty who can act as a research correlator and maintain close co-operation with the members of the faculty who have been authorized to direct the channels of the research activity of the institute. If the institute already has some funds available for research not limited to the work of specific sponsors the committee in charge of such funds can co-ordinate the research activities of the institute.

This committee should in effect serve those engaged in research at the institute by relieving the originator of research products from the business aspects of arranging for developments and exploitation of the research products. Thus, the committee should insure prompt and fair distribution of royalties or other monies received from sales of licenses of the products of research. It should also arrange for prompt publication of research results as soon as permissible including a systematic arrangement for publicizing these results, including patents and other forms of recognition in the alumni publication of the institute.

The committee should serve as a channel through which the faculty of the institute would be assured of recognition and enhancement of professional status for research work by the issuance and utilization of patents, by publication of results, by organization of new industries based upon research results, and otherwise, thus acting as a Promotion Committee.

While preserving to faculty and graduate students freedom in the selection of subjects for doctoral dissertations, the Promotion Committee should actively counsel and inform the administration of the institute of open areas where research work could be fruitful, unexplored fields of science, unsolved problems of engineering and industry and industrial fields open for development. In some cases patent state of art searches and scientific literature searches should be made to find these open areas or the areas where problems exist in which research work could profitably be done by those associated with the institute.

In order to start the program, an institute research fund should be established. In the final analysis, the initial operation could take the optimum form illustrated in Chart I, where alumni contributions would be solicited for the institute or university research fund and in return the alumni would have access to the promotion and marketing facilities of the Promotion Committee for their own inventions. Suitable service or commission charges could be levied against the alumni using the facilities or other contractual arrangements made to enable the institute to share the value in any such alumni-originated inventions. If the promotion effort were little more than publicity in the alumni publication of the institute, it would still provide a promotion facility not otherwise available to many alumni.

Future Research Program

The foregoing expedient program is designed to accommodate the situation at an institute where no independent research staff and facilities are available. The research activity at technological institutes is often limited to that which can be accomplished by the faculty and the graduate students. There is often no other research staff or facility at the institute.

However, this interferes unduly with the teaching responsibilities of the faculty and it does not appear that the research objectives of the technological institute are being fulfilled to their optimum degree by this type of practice of limited utilization of

CHART I

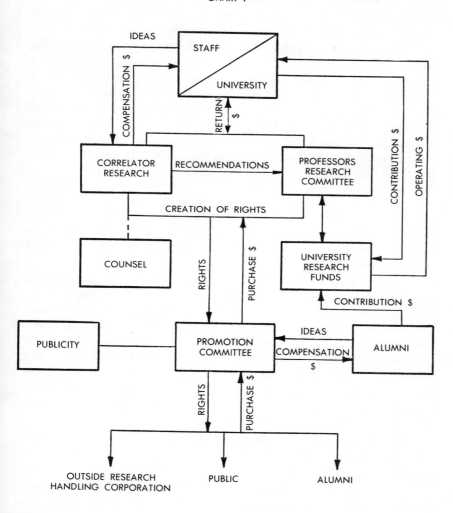

research results, nor are the assets of such an institute being marshalled to their fullest extent in the aid of such fulfillment. Ideally, sufficient, unfettered funds and assets should be made available to support a full-fledged research program, the products of which can be utilized to support the primary educational objectives of a technological institute by providing the requisite funds or facilities to promote the institute and those associated with the institute and its program. Such a program should be an adjunct to the original research objectives for the faculty and graduate students at the institute in that it can carry forward and develop the products of original results in a manner most beneficial to the progress of science and the useful arts. It is within this frame and with this ultimate objective that the following general proposals may be considered.

As soon as practicable it is desirable to establish a non-profit patent-holding corporation with an administrator and a board of directors headed by the president of the institute, including representatives from the board of trustees of the institute or like governing body, the faculty of the institute and the alumni association of the institute. Such a holding corporation should take over the function of the temporary proposed promotion committee and provide management and marketing facilities for the products of research of the institute. Patents and other legal rights acquired and royalties earned should be held for the use and benefit of the institute and net earnings employed for supplementing funds available for research and educational facilities and faculty salaries. Ultimate decentralization of the management and promotion function to the holding corporation is believed desirable for achieving greater efficiency and flexibility of operation.

Supplementing the holding corporation it would be desirable to establish a foundation to raise funds for enabling scope of the institute's research work to be expanded and its quality increased. To this end there may be an alumni-sponsored foundation in which the alumni would assume the responsibility for raising funds for the sponsoring of research generally to cover those areas not included in research supported by specific sponsors. Such a research-supporting foundation would work closely with the holding corporation, with actual administration conducted by a director with the co-operation of the president of the institute.

In consideration of the funds raised, the alumni who sponsored the foundation would receive the right of first refusal to utilize any patents or inventions resulting from such research.

Operation under this first step in an augmented research program is illustrated diagrammatically in Chart II and includes the concept of consideration to the alumni in return for their contributions in the form of a right of first refusal to acquire and utilize the products of the research of the institute. Availability of such rights to the alumni could be publicized by means of the institute's alumni publication, and bidding, if any, would be limited to the alumni contributors to the foundation. The alumni would also retain the privilege of utilizing the management and marketing facilities of the patent holding corporation to promote their own development on a cost or other basis.

The next step in the program could be the formation of a non-

CHART II

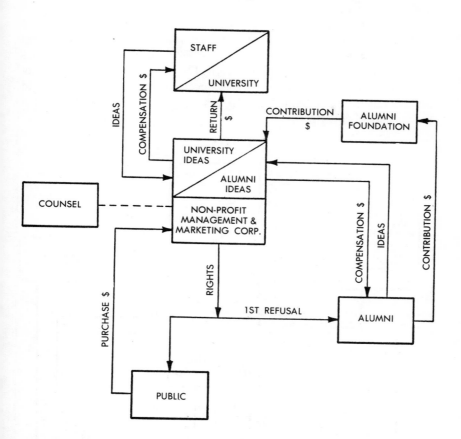

profit research and development, incorporated organization, separate from the institute but affiliated with it, to complement and develop the research done by its faculty and graduate students. Whereas the original research conducted in the laboratories of the institute would be largely for scientific interest and teaching value, the separate but affiliated research company would intentionally look for profitable fields of research and direct its staff into those fields. As impending commercial development of a faculty member's research discovery placed too great demands upon his time and limitations upon his independence, the affiliated research company would take up the faculty member's discovery and carry it through to engineering and commercial completion to enable maximum possible revenues becoming available to the institute. The formation of such a research company would be a major undertaking involving the acquisition of land, laboratories and working capital, but would be a logical forward step.

Operation under this new step in a future research program is diagrammatically illustrated in Chart III where the research and development corporation is shown as an adjunct to the institute's staff in developing original research. The incentives in the form of compensation return for new ideas developed by either staff should be substantially the same in each case and may take the form of a percentage of royalties.

CHART III

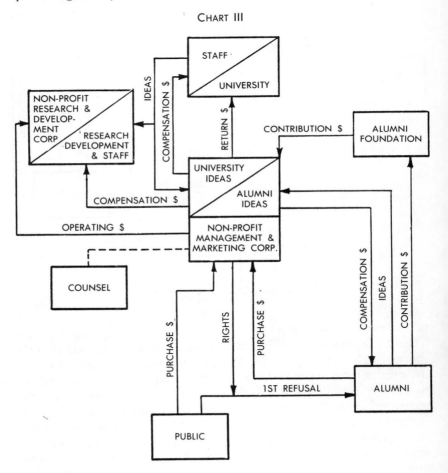

Finally, as an ultimate goal, one may envisage the alumni becoming so interested in the possibilities of the institute's research program and the profits to be derived from it as to form an actual profit-type corporation to acquire the products of research of the institute's staff, its research and development company, other alumni and their companies and employees. In view of the mutually preferential relationship between such a profit corporation on the one hand and the institute and its affiliated organizations on the other hand and the speed and flexibility of operation made possible, it is reasonable to anticipate generous royalty income by the institute and an abundance of profitable developments acquired by the profit corporation. Such a corporation need not be limited in its activities. They would include acquisition of research discoveries, manufacturing, marketing, carrying discoveries through the pilot plant stage or further, market research and even the resale of patents, knowhow, trade secrets, or a subsidiary company to alumni or others, sale of services to alumni and others, and everything relating to science, engineering, and research that could be done in co-operation with the institute and publicized in the institute's alumni periodical.

Operation under this final phase is illustrated in Chart IV which shows that the right of first refusal is transferred to the profit corporation which was capitalized by the alumni, each of whom received warrants to purchase stock in such corporation in proportion to their contributions to the foundation. It is contemplated that the profit corporation would develop manufacturing and marketing divisions or subsidiaries in connection with acquired products of research and development. These divisions and subsidiary companies could ultimately be integrated into an apprentice-educational program which would supplement the educational program at the institute.

Throughout all phases of the research programs there are opportunities for the institute and its alumni to be mutually helpful and to improve the alumni relations. Every research development by the institute, its affiliated organizations and by alumni reported in the alumni periodical represents an opportunity by other alumni to participate in the program, to acquire rights in new developments or to obtain an outlet for their own developments.

Marshalling the Assets of a Technological Institute in Support of Research

A technological institute or university science division has many assets and facilities which might be tapped for the support of an enlarged research program in the geographical area of the institute and employing the physical plant of the institute. Better established technological institutes and scientific schools are for-

CHART IV

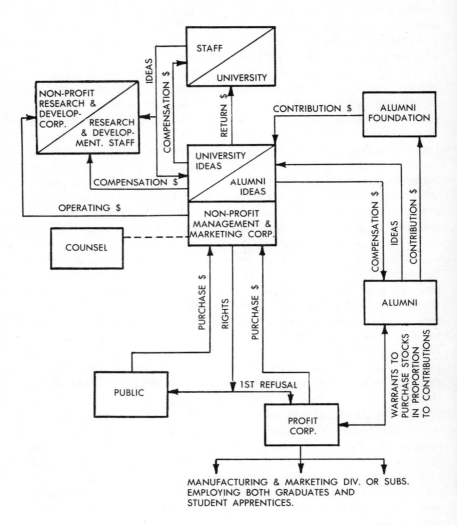

MANUFACTURING & MARKETING DIV. OR SUBS.
EMPLOYING BOTH GRADUATES AND
STUDENT APPRENTICES.

tunate in already having alumni who have distinguished themselves in science and industry and in being the suppliers of
scientific and technical personnel to many of the great and outstanding manufacturing and research laboratories. All these facilities, and in addition the general body of alumni, the entire faculty,
the staff, the graduate students, the subscribers to the institute's
industry-sponsored funds and various other supporting funds, and

the alumni magazine itself should be utilized in supporting and promoting the institute's research program.

Whatever type of organization is employed for administering the program, all of these facilities and assets should be employed in carrying on the research projects, in finding specific sponsors where sponsorship is still required, in disseminating knowledge of the availability of research results, in finding licensees where the research results are patentable, in supplying information as to patent recognition where patents have been issued and in increasing recognition by publication otherwise where the nature of the research is such that patent protection cannot be obtained.

A technological institute's alumni magazine usually reaches many of the outstanding industrialists and engineers of the nation and particularly of the industrial centers of the nation. Such a magazine could well be utilized in supporting the program by carrying a bimonthly or quarterly list of patents issued to the institute's faculty, students and staff, also alumni, and a column listing the outstanding research results or scientific discoveries for the period subsequent to the previous issue of the magazine, whether patented or unpatentable. This recognition in the alumni magazine would be concerned primarily with the unsponsored research, although the results of sponsored research could be included where approved by the sponsors.

Results of some of the institute's research projects such as those in astronomy and mathematics, for example, may not lend themselves to patent protection or to commercial utilization. On the other hand, in other departments such as mechanical engineering, electrical engineering, metallurgy and chemistry, and chemical engineering, a substantial proportion of the projects may have sufficient relation to industrial and commercial end uses to make valuable even those patents applied for originally in large part to provide recognition to the inventor.

Even in the pure science research fields of astronomy, mathematics and physics there may be patentable by-products having valuable use also in industry. Apparatus and methods devised for research purposes may frequently be adaptable for use in industry to accomplish industrial production and control. Similarly, the "know-how" involved in abstract concepts and techniques of pure science may be converted to material value by contractual arrangements even though the usual forms of statutory protection are not readily available.

It is quite possible that only one idea or less for each ten submitted will be patentable. Some may be susceptible of protection by other legal means such as contract, copyright, common law rights against misappropriation of intellectual property, etc.

In the relationship between the alumni and the research and patent development program of the institute, the scientific school or technological institute has the opportunity of pioneering an entirely new concept: using the alumni to promote research and exploitation of patentable results of research—using the research and the patentable results to help the alumni—a unique plan for improving relations between a technology educational institution and its alumni. Many educational institutions have placement programs for employment of young alumni and older ones who need a change of employment, but none is known which has a continuous placement program for ideas of institute staff and alumni and development and manufacturing plant dollars of alumni and their companies.

Can an institute and relations with its alumni fail to benefit if the institute pioneers and brings together on a continuous basis the alumni money which the institute needs and the ideas and inventions and information as to manufacturing outlet which alumni and their companies need?

Initiating a Patenting Program

The professors of the institute and its research staff should be acquainted with the value of the patent system in advancing human progress by bringing knowledge of innovations to possible users, to other interested parties and to those who may be inspired to make improvements and radically different substitutes, establishing new industries and opening up new avenues of research. It should be pointed out, furthermore, that patenting is not only entirely professional but fully in accord with the dignity of a scientist because patented ideas are more likely to become widely disseminated, to be developed and to go into use than those which are merely described in publications. Patents are read widely and by many who seldom see a scientific publication, because patents are well classified. Patented inventions are more likely to be extensively used than those described in publications but with no one having any financial or industrial incentive for undertaking the expensive investment for economical production and adequate commercial acceptance, and with no one having the right to exercise sufficient control to avoid having the idea employed by charlatans or contrary to the good reputation of the inventor.

CONCLUSION

The circumstances under which research work is done at a well-organized technological institute give good prospects of original creative processes and apparatus-developing which will include those that can go into commercial or industrial use and help support the program financially, possibly with good fortune, yielding enough revenue from some developments to build up the endowment for teaching salaries.

Moreover, in any event a consistent program of patenting even the more modest achievements will add to the recognition of faculty and research staff and bring knowledge of the institute's patentable developments before a widened circle of engineers and leaders in science and industry as well as enabling the institute to provide service to alumni which will bring to even higher levels the loyalty and support of the institute's alumni.

One may envision a new approach to the college research problem by welding together effective teaching, research integrated into the teaching program while contributing to advancement of science and the scientific method, and financial support for the research program. A technological institute's special facilities and industrial-connection assets enable the institute to marshal the power of its trustees, faculty, industrial sponsors and alumni in a program which will provide both incentive and recognition to its discoverers in research and insurance of retention of financial values of research to further the objectives of the institute.

Trade Secrets in the Context of Positive Competition

L. James Harris and Irving H. Siegel

INTRODUCTION

Two subjects of continuing research interest to the authors are here brought into conjunction. One of these is positive competition, the nature and implications of which have been explored in three earlier papers on: the patent system, judicial attitudes toward various patent-licensing arrangements, and international transactions in industrial property.[1] The second subject is the protection of trade secrets, a matter that has been, and is still being, investigated under Institute auspices by questionnaire as well as by a review of cases and of other literature.[2]

The basic idea informing this paper and the earlier ones that deal with positive competition may be stated as follows: The pluralistic society of the United States tends to generate, through the interaction of its competing elements, constructive conditions for protecting, using, and limiting the varieties of private property that it creates and that it recognizes as beneficial to the general welfare. Widely shared values and attitudes, established customs and institutions, the extant body of law, and the common circumstances and experiences of economic life and of citizenship seem routinely to support the emergence and profitable social application of many different kinds of private property. While encouraging novelty, however, interaction also brings forth safeguards. Individuals and groups that consider a class of property to be either insufficiently[3]

Editor's Note: This article appeared in *IDEA*, Vol. 10, No. 3 (Fall 1966), p. 297.

[1] The three earlier papers by the same authors and the issues of *IDEA* (or its predecessor) in which they appeared are: "Positive Competition and the Patent System," Vol. 3, No. 1 (Spring 1959), pp. 21-32; "Evolving Court Opinion on Patent Licensing: An Interaction of Positive Competition and the Law," Vol. 5, No. 2 (Summer 1961), pp. 103-113; "Positive Competition and Antitrust in Foreign Transactions Involving Industrial Property," Vol. 7, No. 3 (Fall 1963), pp. 253-276.

[2] For an earlier paper by the authors, see "Protection of Trade Secrets: Initial Report," *IDEA*, Vol. 8, No. 3 (Fall 1964), pp. 360-374.

[3] *Report of the Attorney General's National Committee to Study the Antitrust Laws* (March 31, 1955), p. 226.

"This points to the sound rule that monopoly power individually acquired solely through a basic patent, or aggregation of patent grants should not by itself constitute monopolization in violation of Section 2. It would be a paradox to

appreciated or grossly misused[4] may seek to alter the climate of opinion regarding it and to effect desired adjustments in legal and other pertinent rules. Trade secrets have long been recognized as a valid category of intangible property in our society,[5] and well-publicized efforts are currently being made to improve their functionality and status in the total competitive system in response to new challenges.[6] In this paper, we discuss the character, application, and protection of trade secrets as an element of this system.

NATURE OF POSITIVE COMPETITION

The adaptive system just described is the regime of positive competition. The vigorous pursuit of private interests is a distinctive feature, but also characteristic are an extensive and necessary regard for expressed and latent public wants, a sensitivity to governmental criticism and sanctions, and the existence of an evolving and still permissive framework of custom and law. All of these have contributed to unprecedented levels of material welfare and leisure. Despite the expansion of governmental constraints in recent years, great latitude remains for private decision and action in quest of profit. Furthermore, technical innovation and diffusion remain important modes of profitable self-expression. In this regard, the contrast with other industrial nations, whatever their ideological inclination, is striking.[7]

The American style of positive competition retains its special productiveness and progressiveness even though it has "monopolistic" and other blemishes that claim almost the complete attention of

---

encourage individual invention by grant of a patent and then penalize that temporary monopoly by deeming it 'monopolization.' Hence, violation of the Sherman Act should, as the cases suggest, require abuse of the patent grant or proof of intent to monopolize beyond the lawful patent grants."

[4]For Assistant Attorney General Donald F. Turner's publicly reported negative attitude toward restrictions in licensing agreements, see *Antitrust and Trade Regulation Report* No. 231 (December 14, 1965), The Bureau of National Affairs, Inc., pp. 4-17.

[5]In earlier societies, too. Thus, the guilds of the Middle Ages put great store by trade secrets. See Schiller, Arthur A., "Trade Secrets and the Roman Law," *Columbia Law Review,* Vol. 30 (1930), p. 837.

[6]See also concluding section of Harris and Siegel, "Protection of Trade Secrets: Initial Report," *IDEA,* Vol. 8, No. 3 (Fall 1964), pp. 373-374.

[7]Concerning institutional and attitudinal inhibitions to competition as a source of progress, see, for example, "Can Europe Catch Up with U. S. Technology?," *Business Week* (October 29, 1966), pp. 66ff.; and Stieber, Jack, "Manpower Adjustments to Automation and Technological Change in Western Europe," *Adjusting to Change,* Appendix Volume III to *Technology and the American Economy,* National Commission on Technology, Automation, and Economic Progress (February 1966), pp. 41-125.

various domestic[8] and foreign critics. In principle, at least, these flaws are remediable; and, in practice, considerable and continual effort and experiment are directed toward improvement, with proclaimed doctrine generally subordinated to pragmatics.[9] Although specific avenues of economic and social advance may become clogged, others are kept clear and new ones are opened. The diversity of products, services, and freedoms proliferates as attrition also occurs. We have recently become painfully aware that large numbers of economic and social "dropouts" lose confidence in, or never share, the dominant values of the system, or do not become equipped to garner the advantages offered; yet the size and energy of the competitive majority are awesome.

When we speak of positive competition, we have in mind an order that actually exists, that has demonstrated its merit in ways most people understand, not a theoretical system that ought to be.[10] It is not a textbook model, a matchstick caricature, a simplified abstraction for which claims of perfection and purity may be safely made in a classroom—and for which, alas, practical achievability, acceptability, and viability do not have to be proved. It is a system that is impressively *working*, despite inefficiencies, not merely one claimed to be "workable." It is the competition that almost everyone recognizes to prevail when he uses the noun without a qualifying adjective; or that the antitrust vigilante still acknowledges to be worth protecting even as he daily enlarges his list of observed questionable practices that may "lessen" it or diminish its "potential."[11]

---

[8]See Assistant Attorney General Donald F. Turner's statements in *IDEA*, Vol. 10, Conference Number (1966), pp. 32-38; and in *A. B. A. Journal* Antitrust Section (August 1965), p. 29; 1961 Hearing before the Senate Antitrust Subcommittee on the bill that passed as the Drug Act of 1962; Section 151(a) Atomic Energy Act (42 U. S. C. 218(a)); Brulotte v. Thys Co., 379 U. S. 29 (1964); Walker Process Equipment, Inc. v. Food Machinery and Chemical Corp., 382 U. S. 172; U. S. v. Singer Mfg. Co., 374 U. S. 174.

[9]See the various distinctions with respect to royalty rates made by the courts to the decision of Automatic Radio Mfg. Co. v. Hazeltine Research, Inc., 339 U. S. 827 (1950) in such cases as American Securit Co. v. Shatterproof Glass Corp., 269 F.2d 769 (1954); Brulotte v. Thys Co., 379 U. S. 29 (1964); But see McCullough Tool Co. v. Well Surveys, Inc., 343 F.2d 381 (1965). Also see American Photocopy Equipment Co. v. Rovico, Inc., 148 *USPQ* 631 (1966), for a novel theory advanced by the court which holds that an "exorbitant" rate of patent royalties might be considered a misuse of the patent.

[10]Our choice of the word "positive" was influenced in part by a famous passage in *Scope and Method of Political Economy*, a book by J. N. Keynes (father of the more celebrated economist). Keynes differentiated between a "positive science," comprising a "body of systematized knowledge concerning what is," and a "normative or regulative science," relating to "criteria of what ought to be." See Friedman, Milton, *Essays in Positive Economics* (Chicago: University of Chicago Press, 1953), p. 3.

[11]See session on "Conflicts Between Patent and Antitrust Laws?," *IDEA*, Vol. 10, Conference Number (1966), pp. 29-65.

It is concerned with the totality of economic behavior—most of which is clearly permissible and some of which is still open to challenge and to reclassification as illegal.[12] Antitrust is itself part of the apparatus of positive competition, though only a minor part of it; and the forces that push toward "monopoly," including those fostered by government itself,[13] are likewise to be reckoned as elements of the total system.

The diverse interests that flourish under positive competition and that also produce it naturally opt for contradictory modes and for opposite directions of improvement.[14] Some propose enlargement and sharper definition of the areas of prohibition, interdicted practice, or per se violation,[15] they tend to favor the enumeration and adoption of more explicit proscriptive guidelines and criteria.[16] Others, however, look to a permissive "rule of reason,"[17] call for the weighing of all pertinent circumstances before condemnation of particular practices, point to the multidimensionality and subtleties

[12]The spirit of positive competition in dealing with unsettled issues is interestingly reflected in the Government and company positions disclosed in the press when the Justice Department recently filed its third civil antitrust suit charging General Electric Company with price-fixing and restraint of trade in the sale of light bulbs. Conceding that the challenged practice is half a century old and had been held legal by the Supreme Court as early as 1926, the Department claimed that "those earlier cases were decided erroneously and that more recent court decisions . . . have changed the law." A company official recalled the repeated approvals by the courts and averred that the challenged practice had "served the public well"; but he also pledged full cooperation with the Government "in hope that this new court test will resolve this complicated legal matter once and for all." See *Wall Street Journal*, September 28, 1966, p. 3.

[13]Professor Fritz Machlup told a Senate subcommittee hearing on administered prices that "the antitrust laws are excellent," but "it happens that our Government has done much more to create monopoly than to destroy monopoly," that "we are still going on doing it, day after day." See Kefauver, Estes, *In a Few Hands: Monopoly Power in America* (Baltimore: Penguin Books, 1965), p. 223. Comparable observations were made in the testimony of C. D. Edwards, H. M. Gray, and E. G. Nourse.

[14]On the disagreement among the experts and the differences among the courts concerning the legality of royalty-free compulsory licensing and dedication, see *Report of the Attorney General's Committee to Study the Antitrust Laws* (1955); Hartford-Empire Co. v. U. S., 323 U. S. 386 (1945); U. S. v. National Lead Co., 332 U. S. 319 (1948); U. S. v. General Electric Co. et al., 82 F. Supp. 753 (1949); and U. S. v. Imperial Chemical Industries, Ltd., 105 F. Supp. 215 (1952).

[15]See U. S. v. General Instrument Corp. et al., 87 F. Supp. 157 (1949); U. S. v. Line Material Co., 333 U. S. 287 (1948); U. S. v. General Electric Co. et al., 80 F. Supp. 989 (1948).

[16]See Donald F. Turner's statements in *IDEA*, Vol. 10, Conference Number (1966), pp. 32-38.

[17]See Standard Oil v. U. S., 283 U. S. 163 (1931); Chicago Board of Trade v. U.S., 246 U.S. 231 (1918). Also see the cogent exposition of a "rule of reason" relating to "Patent Right Transferability" in Recommendation No. XXII, pp. 41-43, of the Report of the President's Commission on the Patent System (1966).

of competition, eye with suspicion the efforts to dispose of cases categorically, deplore the apparent concession of guilt in the pleading of *nolo contendere*;[18] they tend to emphasize the "higher-systems" view in the appraisal of the social benefits and injuries incident to any particular behavior.[19]

The publicity attending litigation exaggerates the significance of an occasional pathological situation and obscures the predominant normal situation.[20] Actually, the regime of positive competition, with its automatic signals, rewards, and punishments, achieves a very large degree of self-regulation. The formal policing function, the explicit resort to law enforcement, is minor in view of the volume and variety of business actually transacted. It is not surprising that the dictatorial states of the Soviet bloc have recently come to appreciate the advantages of greater managerial permissiveness for further economic growth and evolution; and it may confidently be assumed that the nations of Western Europe will also seek to loosen the manifold constraints on competition that have seemed in the postwar years to offer economic security but have more surely limited the productivity advance on which this security ultimately depends.

In concluding these brief remarks on positive competition, we refer to two of many recent writings that might be cited to illustrate the esteem in which such competition is really held, by whatever name it happens to be called. In his final book (1961), J. M. Clark, who had pioneered the concept of "workable competition" in 1940, had this to say in the preface:

---

[18]Harris and Siegel, "Positive Competition and the Patent System," *IDEA*, Vol. 3, No. 1 (Spring 1959), pp. 21-31.

[19]See discussion of patent interchange in *Report of Attorney General's National Committee to Study the Antitrust Laws* (1955).

[20]Relatively few patent antitrust court cases decided in the Sixties have received much public notice. The following appear to have had more than passing attention in legal circles: Binks Mfg. Co. v. Ransburg Electro-Coating Corp., 281 F.2d 252 (1960); U. S. v. Columbia Pictures Corp., 189 F. Supp. 153 (1960); U. S. v. Jerrold Electronics Corp., 187 F. Supp. 545 (1960); Dehydrating Process Co. v. A. O. Smith Corp., 292 F. 2d 653 (1961); U. S. v. Lever Bros. Co., 216 F. Supp. 887 (1963); U. S. v. Singer Mfg. Co., 374 U. S. 174 (1963); Berlenbach v. Anderson and Thompson Ski Co. Inc., 329 F.2d 782 (1964); Brulotte v. Thys Co., 379 U. S. 29 (1964); International Mfg. Co., Inc., v. Landon, Inc., 336 F.2d 723 (1964); Preformed Line Products Co. v. Fanner Mfg. Co., 328 F.2d 265 (1964); Atlantic Refining Co. v. FTC, 381 U. S. 357 (1965); Hazeltine Research, Inc. v. Zenith Radio Corp., 239 F. Supp. 51 (1965); Laitram Corp. v. King Crab, Inc., 146 *USPQ* 640 (1965); McCullough Tool Co. v. Well Surveys, Inc., 343 F.2d 381 (1965); U. S. v. Huck Mfg. Co., 147 *USPQ* 464 (1965); Walker Process Equipment, Inc. v. Food Machinery and Chemical Corp., 382 U. S. 172 (1965); American Photocopy Equipment Co. v. Rovico, Inc., 148 *USPQ* 631 (1966).

... I am shifting the emphasis from "workable" to "effective competition" . . . because "workable" stresses mere feasibility and is consistent with the verdict that feasible forms of competition, while tolerable, are still inferior substitutes for that "pure and perfect" competition which has been so widely accepted as a normative ideal. And I have become increasingly impressed that the kind of competition we have, with all its defects—and these are serious—is better than the "pure and perfect" norm because it makes for progress. Some departures from "pure and perfect" competition are not only inseparable from progress, but necessary to it. The theory of effective competition is dynamic theory.[21]

The second item is a published 1966 interview with the current head of the Antitrust Division, who disclosed more than just a preference for guidelines (as an aid to voluntary compliance), a tolerance for no-contest pleas, and a desire to preserve "potential competition" through the discouragement of certain mergers. He expressed himself in favor of the somewhat general and vague wording of the antitrust laws, which makes them "capable of refinement and development as we go along," as economic thought itself evolves. While asserting that certain industries have "essentially noncompetitive" pricing policies, he also recognized the growth of inter-industry competition and the proliferation of competitive products—so "it's not a bad guess that things are at least not getting worse."[22]

CHARACTER OF TRADE SECRETS

A fuzzy penumbra around the concept of "trade secrets" is to be expected. The meaning is not self-evident. The concept, in fact, is like many, many others that are encountered in the world of positive competition and that constantly have to be interpreted and reexamined.[23] Indeed, our concept of positive competition itself

---

[21]Clark, J. M., *Competition as a Dynamic Process* (Washington, D. C.: Brookings Institution, 1961), p. ix. Curiously, Clark's new term, "effective competition," was the title of a report made to the Secretary of Commerce by the Business Advisory Council in December, 1952. The term there described "a business community which is characterized by ceaseless striving among competitors, all endeavoring to expand their share of the market—and the total size of the market as well—by producing relatively more and better goods and services at relatively lower prices; provided that there must, of course, continue to be safeguards against unfair or predatory competition" (p.2). This concept approaches what we call positive competition, but it is less inclusive and seems to have a normative intention.

[22]Interview of Turner, D. F., "Guidelines for Fair Competition," *U. S. News and World Report* (February 21, 1966), pp. 76 ff.

[23]Some authorities argue that the Supreme Court has, by implication, questioned the validity of trade secrets in Sears Roebuck and Company v. Stiffel Company, 376 U. S. 225 (1964); and Compco Corporation v. Day-Brite Lighting, Inc., 376 U. S. 234 (1964). See Handler, Milton, "Product Simulation: A Right or Wrong?," *Columbia Law Review*, Vol. 64 (1964), p. 1183.

has had to be defined here, and this competition is open-ended and still evolving.

"Trade secrets" encompass every kind of information that a firm would like to keep confidential. The term is not legally transformable, however, into a blanket limitation on the subsequent use of the knowledge that a professional worker acquires, on the future applicability of the technical competence and maturity that he attains while in a company's employ.[24] While most of the published court decisions involve trade secrets of a scientific or technical nature, the term also covers the large bulk of business information that is deemed valuable enough to keep private.[25] The

---

However, in Schulenburg v. Signatrol, Inc., 212 N.E. 2d 865 (Sup. Ct. Ill. 1965) the court observed:

"The defendants cite [Sears and Compco] for the proposition 'that no state may, by laws dealing with unfair competition, impose damages or enjoin the copying, manufacturing and sale of an article which is protected by neither a Federal patent nor a copyright.' In a proper case, we would concur with this statement. However, a reading of Sears and Compco clearly indicates that they are inapposite here. There, the defendants had copied the plaintiffs' unpatentable products by legal means. No problem concerning trade secrets was present. Plaintiffs here readily concede that their finished products may be copied by legal means (such as acquiring one of the finished products and measuring and analysing it, until a copy can be produced), but maintain that employees in positions of confidence may not surreptitiously copy plaintiff's blueprints while in their employ and subsequently use them to establish a competing business."

Derenberg, Walter, J., in "The Nineteenth Year of Administration of the Lanham Trademark Act of 1946," Part II, 150 *USPQ* 42 (1966), states:

"The gradual whittling away at the pillars of the private law of unfair competition, particularly since the Supreme Court's decisions in Sears and Compco, has already been referred to in previous reports and in Section IV of the present survey . . . .

"As now proposed, the Unfair Competition Act of 1966 [S. 3681 introduced by Senator McClellan on August 2, 1966, in the 2nd Session of the 89th Congress] would take the form of an amendment to Section 43(a) of the Lanham Act, but would in its most basic provisions follow the predecessor bill. More specifically, S. 3681 includes a 'general clause' in proposed Section 43(a) (6), providing a civil action for unfair competition against any act or conduct 'contrary to commercial good faith or to normal and honest practices of the business or vocational activity.' This general proviso is preceded by a catalogue of specific practices which will be deemed to constitute unfair competition."

Section 43(a) (4) of the proposed Act reads as follows:

"[Any person who shall engage in any act, trade practice, or course of conduct, in commerce, which] results or is likely to result in the wrongful disclosure or misappropriation of a trade secret or other research or development or commercial information maintained in confidence by another, or . . . ."

Also see section on "Interplay of Patentability and Trade Secrets," *supra,* note 2, at pp. 366-369.

[24]See Fairchild Engine and Airplane Corp. v. Cox, 50 N.Y.S.2d 643 (1944).

[25]At the annual meeting of stockholders on July 26, 1966, the president of Sperry Rand Corporation reported that detailed operating information was issued only for Divisions experiencing a loss: "For each Division of our business that has a profit, the amount of that profit and the exact shipping volume would be of great interest to competition to such a degree that the information could be detrimental to the Corporation's interests. Consequently, it is our policy not to

putative financial importance of data to a company's current or future status is a criterion for legal protection of controlled information as a "trade secret."[26]

According to Section 757 of the *Restatement of the Law of Torts,* "a trade secret may consist of any formula, pattern, device or compilation of information which is used in one's business, and which gives him an opportunity to obtain an advantage over competitors who do not know or use it." This definition goes on to state that "generally it relates to the production of goods" and to set forth six criteria "to be considered in determining whether given information is one's trade secret." The six criteria affecting an employer's secret are:

(1) the extent to which the information is known outside of his business;
(2) the extent to which it is known by employees and others involved in his business;
(3) the extent of measures taken by him to guard the secrecy of the information;
(4) the value of the information to him and to his competitors;
(5) the amount of effort or money expended by him in developing the information;
(6) the ease or difficulty with which the information could be properly acquired or duplicated by others.[27]

Evidently, from the foregoing, a trade secret has certain tangible attributes, but it also has intangible, relational, subjective qualities. The more definite characteristics include "formula," "pattern," "device," "compilation of information which is used in one's business"; the less objective notions include "an advantage over competitors," "extent to which the information is known," "extent of measures taken," "the value of the information," "the amount of effort," "the ease or difficulty with which the information could be properly acquired."

The courts have asserted different grounds for the exercise of their jurisdiction. "In some cases it has been referred to as property, in others to contract, and in others, again, it has been treated as founded upon trust and/or confidence."[28] For example, *Pea-*

---

reveal such figures." These figures, of course, refer to "trade," are "secret," and may be quite valuable to Sperry. They, therefore, come under the rubric of "trade secrets," but they do not automatically become legally protected.

[26]The expenditure by the employer is an important criterion in determining whether a trade secret is established. Sperry Rand Corp. v. Rothlein, 241 F. Supp. 549 (1964).

[27]*Restatement of the Law of Torts,* Vol. IV (St. Paul: American Law Institute Publishers, 1939), §757, Comment b., p. 6.

[28]Morison v. Moat, 9 Hare 241 (1851); Robinson, William C., *The Law of Patents for Useful Inventions* (Boston: Little, Brown, and Co., 1890), p. 4: "By the performance of an inventive act the inventor acquires a property in the

body v. *Norfolk* (1868)[29] considered a trade secret to be a property right, protectable as a contract or confidence against violation or breach. In recent years, the courts have been following the theory advanced in 1917 by Justice Holmes in *E. I. du Pont de Nemours Powder Company* v. *Masland:*

> The word "property" as applied to trademarks and trade secrets is an unanalyzed expression of certain secondary consequences of the primary fact that the law makes some rudimentary requirements of good faith. Whether the plaintiffs have any valuable secret or not, the defendant knows the facts, whatever they are, through a special confidence that he accepted. The property may be denied but the confidence cannot be. Therefore the starting point of the present matter is not property or due process of law, but that the defendant stood in confidential relations with the plaintiffs, or one of them. These have given place to liability, and the first thing to be made sure of is that the defendant shall not fraudulently abuse the trust reposed in him. It is the usual incident of confidential relations.[30]

The significance of the theory of a breach of confidence can be better appreciated when an examination is made of the holdings of the courts with respect to protection of the trade secrets after the general public has had access to them. The general rule is that any member of the public may practice the secret without being obligated if the secret falls into the public domain. There are numerous ways in which a trade secret can be dedicated to the public.[31] Dedication may occur, for example, when the subject matter of the trade secret is invalidly claimed in an issued patent. It may also occur when the subject matter is described in a publication or in a patent but is not claimed therein.

---

invention which he thus creates, irrespective of its future protection by a patent. This property vests in him by the law of nature, and by the same law may be divested in any manner which places it in the possession of the public. . . .The property which thus vests in him by the law of nature, enlarged in its enjoyment by the provision of our Patent Law, is recognized as entitled to the same protection as any other form of property . . . ."

[29]98 Mass. 452. Amedeé E. Turner, in his treatise on *The Law of Trade Secrets* (London: Sweet and Maxwell, Ltd., 1962), shows that only in the last hundred years has much law on trade secrets developed in the United States and in England.

[30]244 U.S. 100 (1917). The Headnote to §871 of Robinson's excellent treatise *op. cit. supra* note 28 states: "The Disclosure or Misuse of an Inventor's Secret by those to whom it was Confidentially Communicated is a Breach of Trust and Actionable."

[31]Robinson, *op. cit. supra* note 28, p. 31. "In the absence of any provision of positive law relating to the subject, the unrestricted disclosure of his secret by the inventor is destructive to his property therein. His idea of means then passes into the possession of mankind, becomes a portion of the common stock of knowledge, is open to the enjoyment of all who choose to use it, and thus escapes entirely from the ownership and control of the inventor . . . . Nor is the method by which the disclosure is accomplished of any consequence provided that it be complete and voluntary. . . ."

To what extent do the courts consider a person who had confidential knowledge of a trade secret prior to its publication a member of the general public with respect to the secret after publication? When the subject matter no longer has unique economic value to the original firm, can it continue to be the basis for a breach of the confidential relationship? This is a test that bears directly on the ethics of the problem.[32]

Generally, the pattern of decisions of the Sixth and Seventh Circuit Courts has been distinguishable from that of the Second. The Sixth and Seventh Circuits seem to have been strictly enforcing confidential information concerning trade secrets received before publication. The different position of the Second Circuit has been succinctly stated by Judge Hand:

> The Seventh Circuit, and apparently the Sixth as well, have however, held that if before issue one has unlawfully obtained and used information which the specifications later disclose, he will not be free to do so after issue; his wrong deprives him of the right which he would otherwise have had as a member of the public. We have twice refused to follow this doctrine, and we adhere to our decisions.[33]

Curiously, when the parties enter into an agreement with no termination date expressed therein, the Second Circuit holds that subsequent public disclosure does not relieve the recipient from payment for secret information. The case of *Warner-Lambert Pharmaceutical Company* v. *John Reynolds*,[34] involving Listerine, is an example. The court here decided in favor of the plaintiff. The public disclosure of the Listerine formula was the fault of neither the plaintiff nor the defendant; but Warner-Lambert, which had already paid almost $25 million, had to continue paying almost $2

---

[32]Some take the position that the law of trade secrets should only protect a secret and should not be concerned with the ethical question or the punishment of the wrongdoer. In the Conmar Products case, Judge Hand agrees with this theory, but also explains that the doctrine of the 6th and 7th Circuits, which appears to hold a contrary view, "must rest upon the theory that it is a proper penalty for the original wrong to deny the wrongdoer resort to the patents; and for that we can find no support in principle." However, see Monsanto Chemical Company v. Miller, 118 *USPQ* 74 (1958) on the position that it is the defendant's wrong which should determine the nature of the relief.

[33]Conmar Products Corp. v. Universal Slide Fastener Co., Inc., 172 F.2d 150 (2d Cir. 1949).

[34]178 F. Supp. 655 (S.D.N.Y. 1959), aff'd, 280 F.2d Cir. 1960). A sizable body of law has developed concerning agreements, express or implied, relating to the disclosure of secrets to another for the latter's use. The courts are fully aware that inventors must often sell inventions that are unpatented or unpatentable. This situation may arise, for example, with respect to outside inventors who submit ideas to corporations with the intention that use be made in the corporate business, but confidentially, and with compensation. See Ellis, Ridsdale, *Trade Secrets* (New York: Baker, Voorhis and Company, Inc., 1953). pp. 170-190; *IDEA*, Vol. 3, Conference Number (1959), pp. 82-91.

million a year, although its competitors were now free to copy the formula. Thus, after public disclosure of a trade secret, the Second Circuit is more likely to enforce a contract relating thereto than to continue the obligation based on confidentiality of one who had prior knowledge of the secret.

The cases decided in the Sixth and Seventh Circuits against the recipient of confidential information after publication have usually involved improprieties on the part of the recipient.[35] Where breach of confidence or an inequity was not involved, the Seventh Circuit appears to have acted more like the Second.[36]

Moreover, the cases in the Second Circuit that have favored the recipient of confidential information have generally not involved improper conduct on his part.[37] Where the conduct is improper, the Second Circuit will act against the wrongdoer by assessing damages.[38] The standards for improper conduct may vary among the Circuits. The language in the cases of the Sixth and Seventh Circuits encompasses the innocent in its sweep, although the cases actually deal with commercial improprieties.[39] For the Second Circuit, the language refers to the grossly improper, while the cases are actually limited to instances of proper conduct.[40]

NEW CIRCUMSTANCES AND CHALLENGES

Surely, both the volume of proprietary information classifiable as trade secrets and the traffic in such information have increased prodigiously in the past generation; and the expansion of both has provided new opportunities and new problems for disposition by the forces of positive competition. These interacting forces, which include the government and the courts, are ever determining, ever

---

[35]Shellmar Products Co. v. Allen-Qualley Co., 87 F.2d 104 (7th Cir. 1936); A. O. Smith v. Petroleum Iron Works Co., 74 F.2d 934 (6th Cir. 1935).

[36]Northrup v. Reish, 200 F.2d 924 (7th Cir. 1953); see also Powers, George R., "Relief in Trade Secret Cases after Publication," *PTC J. Res & Ed. (IDEA)*, Vol. 5, No. 1 (Spring 1961), pp. 70-80.

[37]Conmar Products Corp. v. Universal Slide Fastener Co., Inc., 172 F.2d 150 (2d Cir. 1949); Pennington Engineering Co. v. Houde Engineering Corp., 136 F.2d 210 (2d Cir. 1943); Picard v. United Aircraft Corp., 128 F.2d 632 (2d Cir. 1942); also see Koehring Co. v. National Automatic Tool Co., Inc., 150 *USPQ* 777 (S. D. Ind. 1966).

[38]Schreyer v. Casco Products Corp., 190 F.2d 921 (2d Cir. 1951). But see the strong negative reaction by Justice Brink of the New York Supreme Court (Broome County) to the defendant's contention that at some time after the breach of confidence he could have obtained the information elsewhere (General Aniline and Film Corp. v. Frantz et al., 151 *USPQ* 136 [1966]).

[39]*Supra* note 35.

[40]*Supra* note 37.

reappraising, the equities and benefits incident to the creation, ownership, and productive use of the large supply of trade secrets. Thus, trade secrets constitute one of the innumerable fields in which positive competition operates in our kind of society.

The order-of-magnitude increase in the inventory of trade secrets and in transactions involving them is traceable, in large part, to the impressive gains made in research and development activity, under both private and public auspices, since World War II. These gains have been accompanied by significant growth in the number of scientists, engineers, and technical support personnel engaged in industry. Billions of private dollars, in addition to larger sums of public money, have come to be spent annually in the design, realization, and improvement of processes and products destined for business, government, and households.

The increase in the supply of, and in the dependence upon, trade secrets is not restricted to manufacturing. For example, services—consulting and other—also merit notice. They are often based on, or otherwise involve, sophisticated novel technologies— especially in the data-processing and communication fields, where patent protection for know-how and for "software" may be difficult or impossible to obtain.

Another point should be made here: The proliferation of trade secrets and the increase in the number of people having legitimate access to them are phenomena ascribable to economic expansion as well as to the enlargement of the scale and scope of research activity. High levels of business investment over a number of consecutive years, the diffusion of processes and products that have already been proved, the establishment and growth of firms and industries, the increase in employment of skilled workers, the mobility of managerial and technical employees—these too have a relation to the amount of confidential business information available, the degree of sharing required, and the problems of protection, control, and remuneration.

In the adjustments being worked out by the processes of positive competition, due account is being taken of custom, traditional values, and the services provided through social and other institutions. Private arrangements seem much more important—in the determination of company, employee, and social roles and benefits —than the active intervention of government agencies, legislatures, and the courts. This statement does not mean, however, that new legislation or that administrative and judicial clarification will not be sought, forthcoming, or welcome. External correctives are obviously needed in those instances in which unethical behavior by employees or employers is manifested. In the next section, some directions of desirable improvement in public as well as private provisions for trade secrets are indicated.

Happily, the court cases involving disputes over trade secrets seem few, when consideration is given to the huge supply and the heavy traffic. Advance company-employee agreements and the alertness of firms in setting compensation scales have doubtless contributed significantly to the inhibition of litigation. Crowded court calendars, however, may also discourage quests for legal rectification where other modes of settlement have failed. On the whole, positive competition may be expected to achieve a fairly good record with respect to trade secrets; the system, as already noted, is sensitive to opposing demands,[41] is flexible, and contains mechanisms for self-improvement.

The judgment just expressed about the future record cannot be reached lightly. At every stage of United States history, an acute awareness of the active and latent threats to dominant values, customs, and institutions has encouraged dire appraisals of the plight and prospects of competitiveness. Nowadays, there are many grounds for dismay concerning even more profound relationships than those between employer and employee in the realm of trade secrets. A partial catalogue of these well-advertised grounds would include conformity, consensus, attenuation of the two-party system, shifting balance of enterprise toward government initiative, federal welfarism, declining parental discipline, the waning influence of religion on ethics, civil-rights disorders, crime, urban blight, technological disruption, economic insecurity, undeclared wars, and so forth. Perhaps our plight is worse than England's when Lord Bacon replied to charges of corruption with a plea that the general *vitia temporis* (the sins of the times) should be differentiated from his own *vitia hominis* (the sins of man).[42] On the other hand, the situation today may only be noisier and seem worse to us because it is the situation with which *we* have to deal.

---

[41] The principle of shop rights is an example of the equity involved in the creation of trade secrets and patent rights. The conception of the effort of the employee and of the time and the facilities of the employer are both utilized and therefore the rights are divided. "A shop right, with reference to the employer-employee relationship, is an implied, irrevocable, non-assignable, non-exclusive license of an employer to use in his business, without paying for its use, a trade secret created, discovered, or invented by his employee. The mere fact that the trade secret is discovered, perfected or invented during the employee's hours of employment does not give rise to a shop right; there must be conduct on the part of the employee which will estop him from denying such license." Toner v. Sobelman, 86 F. Supp. 369 (1949).

[42] Bowen, C. D., *Francis Bacon: The Temper of a Man* (Boston: Little, Brown and Co., 1963), p. 196.

DIRECTIONS FOR IMPROVEMENT

In our democratic society of positive competition, the law reflects social mores, and the courts tend to evolve a law of trade secrets in directions they believe to be in the public interest, proceeding as far as the public is deemed ready to go. In civil cases at least, the courts seem to have achieved a generally acceptable balance between technical competition (as expressed in personnel transfer) and property rights in trade secrets.[43]

Increased reliance on trade secrets in recent years is sometimes attributed to the time lag in processing patent applications;[44] but this argument is not persuasive.[45] A much more important factor, it would seem, is the vast increase in industrial research activity. Inventions, whatever their quality, are probably being generated at an unprecedented rate in today's setting, and the companies sponsoring them are naturally interested in profitable use. Positive competition encourages early utilization. A company that makes use of an invention more than a year prior to patent application, however, may be able to depend only on secrecy for protection. The temptation to test the market before patenting has always existed, but nowadays it may be stronger as the number of potential patent applications increase due to the extraordinary increase

[43]See Space Aero Products Co., Inc. et al., v. R. E. Darling Co., Inc., 145 *USPQ* 356 (Md. Ct. App. 1965), where the court seeks to balance the promotion of scientific progress, by protecting the originator, with free competition, by permitting the employee to use skill learned during employment.

[44]See "Clinic on Statutory Requirements of Companies for Protection of Intellectual Creations," *IDEA*, Vol. 8, No. 4 (Winter 1964-1965), pp. 561-573; in an earlier paper *supra* note 2, at p. 366, Harris and Siegel mention factors favorable to company reliance upon trade secrets: ". . . As industrial arts expand and become more complex, the chances of obtaining patents diminish and the danger of invalidity of issued patents increases. Furthermore, the increasing difficulty of reconstruction of products such as chemicals places a premium on secrecy. To be patentable, as is well known, an invention must come within one of the statutory classes of invention: process, machine, manufacture, or composition of matter. Other hurdles have to be negotiated; questions of public use, novelty, utility, and unobviousness must be determined. A company has to decide whether the use of matter disclosed can be policed, whether adequate claims can be obtained, whether the litigation costs incident to enforcement are worth the gain. . . ."

[45]See Commissioner Brenner's reference to the testimony relating to the backlog presented on behalf of the Patent Office to the House Appropriations' Committee in a dinner address before the American Patent Law Association, *APLA Bulletin* (October-November 1966), p. 550. The Commissioner states that ". . . our long-range plans are to add 150 examiners plus the necessary supporting personnel in order to assist us in reaching our goal of 18 months pendency within the next few years.

"Our program calls for adding 75 examiners in fiscal '67 and 75 more examiners in fiscal '68. This additional manpower, according to our studies, combined with our capability of operating with present staff in the range of about 100,000 disposals a year, should enable us to meet this goal of 18 months pendency within the next three or four years."

in research. In any case, studies of the Institute indicate that 48.8 percent of the patents used by very large companies are put to use before application for patent is made. The proportion is 31.1 percent for the companies of intermediate size.[46]

Any lag in patent processing should not, of course, affect the degree of reliance upon unpatentable "know-how," which generally has come under the heading of trade secrets. Of prime importance is the fact that the technology represented by this type of know-how could, with proper precautions, remain undisclosed very much longer than the technology included in patent applications.[47] The Patent Office will, in most cases, eventually disclose application information in the form of issued patents.

We should recall that the patent system replaced the system of trade secrets flourishing in the guilds of the Middle Ages. Under the guild codes an innovation remained secret indefinitely; and, in certain instances, the technology died with the last members of the guild. The patent system discloses the trade secret to the public upon the issuance of the patent in return for a "monopoly" right over a limited period of time.[48] The patent idea gradually supplanted trade secrets until every industrial country in the world boasted a patent system. Many writers have attributed the technical progress of their country to the type of incentives and protection offered by the system. In our own country, the system from the very beginning became a part of the apparatus for positive competition. It has always had its critics, who presumably would not be prepared, however, to propose return to a world dominated by technical trade secrets.[49]

It does not appear that much needs to be done legislatively to develop better protection for trade secrets subject to loss as a result of the indiscretion of migrant technical personnel.[50] To increase the protection accorded to trade secrets beyond what the

[46]Sanders, Barkev S., "Speedy Entry of Patented Inventions into Commercial Use," *IDEA*, Vol. 6, No. 1 (Spring 1962), pp. 87-116.
[47]"Clinic on Statutory Requirements of Companies for Protection of Intellectual Creations," *IDEA*, Vol. 8, No. 4 (Winter 1964-1965), pp. 561-573.
[48]*Ibid.*
[49]Machlup, Fritz, *An Economic Review of the Patent System*, Study No. 15 of The Subcommittee on Patents, Trademarks, and Copyrights of The Committee on the Judiciary, United States Senate, 85th Cong., 2nd Sess. ". . . If we did not have a patent system, it would be irresponsible, on the basis of our present knowledge of its economic consequences, to recommend instituting one. But since we have had a patent system for a long time, it would be irresponsible, on the basis of our present knowledge, to recommend abolishing it. This last statement refers to a country such as the United States of America—not to a small country and not a predominantly nonindustrial country, where a different weight of argument might well suggest another conclusion."
[50]See *supra* note 47, "Clinic on Statutory Requirements of Companies for Protection of Intellectual Creations."

adjudicated cases already provide would involve serious economic, social, and legal issues. Clearly, the antitrust implications alone should discourage action along this line. We should note here that even the patent exception to the antitrust laws, based on a Constitutional mandate, has come under increasing pressure from the courts.

The courts have not been reluctant to provide appropriate means for maintaining a balance between personnel transfer and company investment in trade-secrets cases.[51] Proper precautions in the light of judicial interpretations, however, have not always been taken by employees,[52] employers, and third parties.[53] Moreover, alleged malfeasances are often of an ambiguous nature. In short, there is adequate legal theory[54] for justice to be done

---

[51]The courts have made an effort to suit the remedy to the actual need for secrecy. See Sperry Rand Corp. v. Rothlein, 241 F. Supp. 549 (1964); Franke v. Wiltschek, 209 F.2d 493 (1953); B. F. Goodrich Co. v. Wohlgemuth, 137 *USPQ* 389 (1963); E. I. du Pont de Nemours and Co. v. American Potash and Chemical Corp., 200 A. 2d 428 (1964). Judge Kaess, in Allis-Chalmers Co. v. Continental Aviation and Engineering Corp., 151 *USPQ* 33 (Dist. Ct., E. D. Mich. S. Div. 1966), states that ". . . the injunction granted is as restricted as possible to protect the secrets involved without undue restraint on Mr. Wolff's right to pursue his chosen vocation, only prohibiting work in the design and developing of distributor type pumps. Mr. Wolff is able to work at Continental in application engineering without limitation as to the field of activity, and to engage in design and development in all kinds of fuel injection systems and pumps except a distributor type pump. Furthermore, the injunction granted is limited in time. Being a preliminary injunction it will last in any event only until final hearing in the action, and it may terminate earlier by its own terms, if the confidential information comes into the possession of Continental by legitimate means." Also see Larx Co., Inc. v. Nicol, 71 *USPQ* 115 (1946) where the court's test was the "reasonableness of the restraint imposed;" Harris and Siegel, *supra* note 2, pp. 362-363.

[52]Injunctive relief prior to disclosure would generally be denied unless disclosure was imminent or a valid provision relating to trade secrets was included in the employment agreement. See H. B. Wiggins Sons' Co. v. Cott-A-Lap Co., 169 Fed. 150 (1909); S. S. White Dental Mfg. Co. v. Mitchell, 188 Fed. 1017 (1911).

[53]For examples of the high standards established by the courts for second employers, see Colgate-Palmolive Co. v. Carter Products, Inc., 230 F.2d 855 (1955); Monsanto Chemical Co. v. Miller, 118 *USPQ* 74 (1958); Although a bona fide purchaser of the secret for value is protected (Chadwick v. Covell, 151 Mass. 190 [1890]) unless he has changed his position on the faith of his ignorance, the innocent user may not continue to use the secret after notice (Vulcan Detinning Co. v. American Can Co., 75 N. J. Eq. 542). See also Ellis, *op. cit. supra* note 34, at pp. 101-105.

[54] Robinson, *op. cit., supra* note 28, at p. 29: "The remedy for wrongs already committed against an inventor by persons entrusted with his secret is an action at law for damages in the State courts, or, where citizenship confers the necessary jurisdiction, in the Federal courts. This action has been variously regarded as one of tort based on the fraud involved in the breach of trust or as one of contract on the express or implied agreement to respect the reserved rights of the inventor, but in one form or the other adequate compensation is awarded for the injury sustained. Against a future and expected invasion of the inventor's rights equity will interpose an injunction, forbidding the unauthorized use of the knowledge of the defendant or his disclosure to others of the secret of the invention. The latter remedy is open to the personal representatives of a deceased inventor, and to those whose fiduciary relations toward the defendant are derived from and identical with his."

in these cases, and the courts have provided sufficient remedy and imposed satisfactory sanctions,[55] but evidence is often equivocal or difficult to obtain.

The outright theft of trade secrets has been a subject of recent Congressional attention. The McDowell Bill[56] was introduced in the 88th Congress to amend the National Stolen Property Act.[57] Unlike the statutes in foreign countries, our federal statute does not cover the theft of technical information. The McDowell Bill did not receive general industry support since it included non-technical business information and did not clearly distinguish inadvertent disclosure by migrant personnel from actual theft. Thus, although business firms are keenly interested in disclosure of trade secrets by the migrant employee, they seem to want additional legislation mostly to prevent and to penalize outright theft. The responses by companies to the Institute's early questionnaire indicate a similar attitude.[58]

How can companies assist the courts, in our regime of positive competition, to fulfill their proper role with respect to trade secrets? Employers would be well advised to institute security measures that assure sufficient evidence of the factors set forth in the previously mentioned Section 757 of the *Restatement of the Law of Torts*.[59] A company security system ought also to protect the employer against subjecting himself to liability through hiring personnel acquainted with trade secrets of competing companies.[60]

[55]See Minnesota Mining and Mfg. Co. v. Technical Tape Corp., 192 N.Y. S.2d 102 (1959), aff'd 226 N.Y.S.2d 1021 (1962); Smith v. Dravo Corp., F.2d 369 (1953) for a limited use of the injunction to a specific process or product. In Head Ski Co. v. Kain Ski Co., 158 F. Supp. 919 (1958), the court practically enjoined former employees from engaging in the same business. In Schulenburg v. Signatrol, Inc., 50 Ill. App. 2d 402, 412, the court stated that the injunction may be a drastic remedy, but imposed it nevertheless in order to "give to plaintiffs their just due."

[56]H. R. 5217.

[57]18 U.S.C. § 2311-2317.

[58]See section on "Legislative Gaps," *supra* note 2, at pp. 371-373.

[59]*Supra* note 2, at p. 362; see Messrs. McPherson, Williams and Wilson, "Loss of Trade Secrets Through Changes in Employment," *IDEA*, Vol. 8, Conference Number (1964), pp. 36-49. In General Aniline and Film Corp. v. Frantz et al., 151 *USPQ* 136 (1966), Justice Brink of the New York Supreme Court states that "the degree of secrecy . . . required for a trade secret need not be absolutely 100% perfect," that the plaintiff need not "meet the stringent requirements necessary in the case of a patent application." Justice Brink explains: "The reason for this is that the gravamen of this action is breach of confidence and the fact that at some later time after he violated his agreement and trust he could have obtained information elsewhere does not excuse his conduct. Protection is given against the reprehensible means, such as a breach of confidence, employed in gaining the secret."

[60] See "Safeguarding Confidential Information," *Management Record*, Vol. 22, No. 12 (December 1960), p. 26, a study by the Committee on Employment Conditions of the Engineers Joint Council. Information is here set forth on the attitude of, and attention by, employers to their employees' problems with respect to confidential information.

Furthermore, the security system should, by advice, help employees and others to avoid inadvertent involvement in trade-secret misunderstandings with employers.[61] Procedures should also be designed for avoidance of misunderstandings between the current employer and a previous[62] or subsequent employer.[63] An employer who institutes adequate security precautions permits the courts without strained interpretation to recognize the confidential relationship, to assert the importance of good faith, and to point up its presence in a very practical and ethical way. Such precautions provide an effective learning opportunity and reaffirm high social standards under different combinations of meaningful circumstances.[64]

A carefully worded non-disclosure provision should be included by companies in all employment contracts.[65] It should be simply and clearly worded and explicitly brought to the attention of the employee so that he understands the implications of confidential relationships and is impressed with their importance. Extraneous matter and unusual or unfair requirements, however, should be avoided. A non-disclosure provision is not essential legally in an employee agreement,[66] since courts generally deter-

---

See in "Injunctions to Protect Trade Secrets—The Goodrich and Dupont Cases," *Virginia Law Review*, Vol. 51 (1965), p. 937:

"The real threat came from the nature of the position Wohlgemuth was to occupy for his new employer, and where this, rather than intent, is the source of the threat, substantial probability and inevitability become very difficult to distinguish."

[61]Wohlgemuth was alleged to have said that "loyalty and ethics had their price." 192 N.E.2d 99, p. 104.

[62]*Virginia Law Review, supra,* note 60, at pp. 940-941:

"That Latex intended to induce Wolgmuth to disclose Goodrich's secrets was suggested by the fact that Wolgemuth had been sought out by Latex, had been offered an increase in salary to manage its space suit department, and was the only one of more than ten applicants who was actually interviewed for the new position. Potash likewise acted suspiciously when it advertised in a newpaper in Wilmington, Delaware, the site of du Pont's home office, for a manager of plant technical services who 'must hav TiO_2 experience.' Moreover, Potash had as recently as 1961 been refused a license from du Pont to use the chloride process and had subsequently begun to recruit key technical personnel to develop the process on its own."

[63]See Solo Cup Co. v. Paper Machine Corp., 144 *USPQ* 729 (1965), for action by court where third party competes unfairly with respect to trade secrets possessed by a new employee. Also see Herold v. Herold China and Pottery Co., 257 Fed. 911 (1919), concerning the invocation of the law against those having actual or implied knowledge of a confidential relation of others.

[64]Improvement in employer-employee relations, establishment of courses in professional ethics in universities for scientists and engineers, and avoidance of positions for new employees that may involve the utilization of secret information belonging to a former employer are among the suggestions offered at the 1964 Annual Public Conference of The PTC Research Institute, *supra* note 2, at p. 360.

[65]See McTiernan, Charles E., "Employees and Trade Secrets," 41 *JPOS* 820 (1959).

[66]Obligation not to disclose may rest on implied contract based on employer's

mine a case on the basis of trust, but they may well balk at upholding an unreasonable provision.[67] A written agreement provides
a good legal way of putting an employee on notice and also provides
an opportunity to deal with him fairly and equitably. In the event
of litigation, it provides a sufficiently high standard to which the
courts can repair.

Another type of provision that should be included in an employment agreement relates to competition with the employer
after separation.[68] It should be drawn with even more care than
the non-disclosure type, since an unreasonable restraint of trade
and a more serious threat to the employee's future livelihood may
be involved.[69] This type of provision may subsequently be considered anti-competitive in nature, and it has features that directly
involve the public interest. Since the courts in these cases will generally ground their relief on the actual agreement made between
the parties,[70] explicit language should be used and steps taken to
do justice to the two parties and provide adequately for the public
interest.[71] The courts, in effectuating a fair and reasonable[72]

---

great efforts to maintain secrecy and employee's participation in such efforts. See
Winston Research Corp. v. Minnestoa Mining and Mfg. Co., 146 *USPQ* 422 (Ct.
App. 9 1965); Furr's Inc., et al. v. United Speciality Advertising Co., et al., 144
USPQ 153 (Tex. Ct. Civ. App. 1965).

[67]Hudson Foam Latex Products, Inc. v. Acken, 82 N.J.Super. Ct. 508 (1964).

[68]Blake, Harlan M., "Employee Agreements Not to Compete," *Harvard
Law Review*, Vol. 73 (1960), pp. 625-691; Irving Varnish and Insulator Co., v.
Van Norde, 138 N.J.Eq. 99, 46 A.2d 201 (1946).

Ellis, *op. cit., supra* note 34, at p. 128: "For the former employer to have to
wait until his former employee has disclosed the secret to his new employer is like
telling a man: you cannot lock the stable door until the horse has been stolen.

"There is another difficulty in connection with a requirement that unauthorized disclosure must precede court action and that is the fact that in many cases the
trade secrets are of such a nature that the former employer may have great trouble
in proving the disclosure of the secret to end its use by the competitor."

[69]Ellis, *op. cit., supra* note 34, at pp. 96-117; McClain, Joseph A., Jr.,
"Injunctive Relief Against Employees Using Confidential Information," *Kentucky
Law Journal*, Vol. 23 (1935), p. 248; *Virginia Law Review*, Vol. 47 (1961), p. 583.

[70]For information on the prospects for obtaining an injunction where there
is no actual disclosure or a valid restrictive convenant, see *Virginia Law Review,
supra* note 60 at pp. 932-935. In B. F. Goodrich Co. v. Wohlgemuth, 137 *USPQ*
389 (1963) the court pointed out that "without exception . . . where injunctive
relief has been granted it has been in a situation where there is a restrictive noncompetitive covenant. . . ."

[71]McClain, *supra* note 69, at pp. 246-248:
"Cases involving right of employees to leave and compete are examples of
'balancing interests or equities.' See Cook. *Cases on Equity*, 2 ed. C.3, Sec.4 (1932).
. . . . On the one hand, we have the desire to encourage competition and to facilitate
the exercise by an individual of all his skill and knowledge, and, on the other hand,
there is the wish to give reasonable protection against unfair competition to established businesses."

[72]Carpenter, Charles E., "Validity of Contracts Not to Compete," *University of Pennsylvania Law Review*, Vol. 76 (1928), p. 254:
"If the restraint is no more than is reasonably necessary to protect the employer

provision of this kind, could significantly contribute to enforcement of ethical standards.

Some suggestions may also be offered for making license agreements relating to trade secrets more effective instruments of positive competition. These agreements allow the licensee to use know-how without restraint by the licensor. There is always the danger that the secrecy of the information might be lost through inadvertent disclosure by one of the parties; and if the trade secret becomes involved in litigation, this danger becomes even greater. Accordingly, it seems prudent, where the hazard warrants, to make an assignment instead of to license, and to provide for sale of the information for a lump sum (or for payment in some other relatively quick manner).[73]

Another precaution is for the licensor to spell out the metes and bounds of the secret information very precisely. The relative lack of statutory protection for trade secrets makes the licensor and licensee dependent on the trade-secret contract to a much greater extent than the parties to other types of industrial-property contracts (e.g., those relating to patents, designs, and trademarks). Also important is the careful preparation of provisions of an agreement when more than one type of industrial property is included to assure separate consideration of these types by the parties and by the courts. Furthermore, attention should be given to the kinds of restrictions included in trade-secret licenses. The restrictions

---

against the deflection of customers or misuse of trade secrets by the employee through the opportunity which his employment has given him, the courts uniformly uphold the covenant and give relief either at law or in equity. But the promise by the employee not to compete will be bad if the restraint is more extensive territorially than is reasonably necessary to protect the employer's business . . . or if the restraint is for a length of time not needed to protect the employer's business . . . [or] where the purpose is to prevent the employee from quitting the employer's service and not to prevent use of detrimental information gained through employment."

[73]See Ladas, Stephen P., "Problems of Licensing Abroad," *The Trademark Reporter*, Vol. 56, No. 7 (July 1966), p. 526. However, Ellis, *op. cit., supra* note 34, at p. 495, states: "Most trade secrets are exploited by their discoverers or their successors in business. Secret processes and formulas are almost always developed by manufacturers for their own use. If they have manufacturing facilities, they have no incentive for licensing competitors. Also, where a process or formula is capable of producing a product which, by examination or analysis, does not reveal the nature of the process or formula by which it is made, it is difficult to check on the operations of a licensee.

"Lists of customers, credit data and commercial material of various kinds are never voluntarily transferred to actual or potential competitors."

A colleague expresses some doubt as to the feasibility of lump sum payments:

"It is always wise in business transactions to bet cash on the barrelhead, where this is possible, but there's the rub. In my experience, for what it's worth, trade secret deals typically demand great ingenuity on the part of the lawyers in working out an acceptable payment scheme, and lump sum payment only rarely meets the needs of the parties. . . ."

permitted in a trade-secret license may be somewhat different from those in other industrial-property licenses (due to the secret nature of the information and its non-statutory character); yet the courts generally apply tests with respect to the restraint of competition similar to the tests applied to patents.

Know-how licensing to the lesser industrialized nations, which has flourished since the end of World War II, is impeded in some degree by the difficulty of maintaining the secret character of information in agreements. Such licenses afford striking opportunities for these nations to share in the progress offered by modern technology.[74] A pioneer study of foreign licensing conducted by the Institute[75] found that the principal asset often wanted by a foreign company was know-how, sometimes by itself, sometimes to supplement a patent license, and sometimes to support a trademark. A majority of the 180 United States companies replying to a questionnaire, furthermore, reported that know-how was much more important to them as a licensable asset than were patents or trademarks; that know-how was indeed more sought after by potential licensees. In determining its license policy, a company may wish to: (1) confine the agreement to non-secret know-how; (2) entrust the secrets to personnel provided by the licensor to the licensee for the duration of the agreement; or (3) press for sale of the secret information at a price taking into account the recipient's (or his government's) ability to pay and the seller's own economic situation (including tax aspects). Care in drawing the contract is at least as important as in domestic licensing agreements. Another comment is made on international licensing arrangements below.

---

[74]See U.N. General Assembly Res. No. 1713 (XVI), "The Role of Patents in the Transfer of Technology to Under-Developed Countries," U.N. General Assembly Plenary 1084 (December 1961).

[75]Behrman, J. N., "Foreign Licensing" (Project 5a, "Relation of American Patents, Trademarks, and Techniques and American-Owned Foreign Patents to Foreign Licensing"), *IDEA*, Vol. 1, No. 2 (December 1957), pp. 220-243; Behrman, J.N., "Advantages and Disadvantages of Foreign Licensing," *IDEA*, Vol. 2, No. 1 (March 1958), pp. 137-158; Behrman, J.N., "Licensing Abroad Under Patents, Trademarks, and Know-How by U.S. Companies," Report on a Survey of Problems and Practices and Their Relation to the American Patent and Trademark Systems, *IDEA*, Vol. 2, No. 2 (June 1958), pp. 181-277; Behrman, J.N., and Schmidt, W.E., "Royalty Provisions in Foreign Licensing Contracts," *IDEA*, Vol. 3, No. 3 (Fall 1959), pp. 272-302; Behrman, J.N., and Schmidt, W. E., "New Data on Foreign Licensing," *IDEA*, Vol. 3, No. 4 (Winter 1959), pp. 357-388; Behrman, J.N., "Foreign Licensing Investment, and U.S. Economic Policy," *IDEA*, Vol. 4, No. 2 (Summer 1960), pp. 150-172; Behrman, J.N., "Foreign Licensing," *IDEA*, Vol. 4, Conference Number (1960), pp. 19-21.

POSTSCRIPT

The foregoing remarks on trade secrets are hardly definitive. The subject, furthermore, is open-ended and evolving, like positive competition itself. The nonlegal literature, including trade and professional journals, is also giving more attention to trade secrets, so that public consciousness of the subject is expanding. This growing public awareness itself may tend to increase the volume of litigation and legislation. This developing interest was anticipated in our "initial report" in *IDEA*. The present paper emphasizes that the realm of positive competition includes the domain of trade secrets.

In any consideration of the role of trade secrets in the real world of positive competition, it is obviously necessary to include: (1) the relationship between employee and employer; (2) their treatment in national and state legislation and by the courts; and (3) their status in international arrangements and agreements. Some additional remarks pertaining to these three levels are offered in the remainder of this section.

A constructive relationship between the employer and employee with respect to trade secrets is essential to progress in invention and innovation under modern circumstances. Such a relationship must derive from a mutuality of interest recognized by the parties. Employer and employee are clearly interdependent in their pursuit of creativity and enterprise. They are well served in dealing with one another by fair and reasonable provisions in agreements voluntarily entered.

Our "initial report" in *IDEA* contemplated that "pressures will be exerted by interested parties to extend, to strengthen, and to render more uniform the state laws covering trade secrets."[76] The business and professional communities are indeed becoming more concerned with problems of loss and protection. Increasing demands for coordination and clarification of state laws, and for systematic testing of the legality of those laws, may accordingly be expected.

The state-federal legal frontier is fluid, and no equilibrium is yet in sight. Recent state legislation has been mostly of a criminal nature.[77] The satisfactory protection of property and of individual rights will require some reduction of the wide variations

---

[76]*Supra* note 2, at p. 374.

[77]Georgia, Illinois, Minnesota, Nebraska, New York, New Jersey, Pennsylvania, and Wisconsin have in the past few years either introduced bills or enacted important statutes concerned with trade secrets. See Sutton, John P., "Trade Secrets Legislation," *IDEA*, Vol. 9, No. 4 (Winter 1965), pp. 587-607.

in state laws. Greater uniformity is required since competition in research and development is national, even international. The interstate and international needs may encourage a quest for federal legislation to cover criminal acts relating to trade secrets. As already noted, it is unlikely that civil federal legislation specifically directed to trade secrets will find sufficient support. On the other hand, the difficulty of determining just what trade secrets are will continue to exert pressure against enactment of criminal legislation. It may also imply likelihood of narrow interpretation.

The proposed federal legislation on unfair competition[78] reflects the expanding interest in protection of confidential information. The original broadly phrased legislation has been sharpened specifically to include trade secrets—partly in response, no doubt, to the *Sears* and *Compco* decisions of the Supreme Court. If enacted, federal civil legislation would for the first time be taking account of a species of proprietary information historically left to the common law for protection. Thus, despite the apparent lack of demand for a trade-secret civil law, such legislation may yet be enacted on the national level as part of a more general effort to provide for unfair competition in the federal statutes. A statute relating to unfair competition would indeed seem to be an appropriate place to assert that trade secrets are recognized by federal law. The law of unfair competition is based on the general principles of fairness and equity, principles especially pertinent to the governance of trade-secret relations.

Although increasing account is being taken of trade secrets in international arrangements (generally on a theory of unfair competition), trade secrets have still been less subject to regulation by specific international agreements than patents and trademarks. Moreover, trade secrets have been less subject to national codification than the latter two, so it is not surprising that American companies appear to depend on foreign specialists for expertise on the law concerning confidential information in the different countries. Furthermore, the practical difficulties involved in maintaining the secrecy of technical information licensed abroad place severe limitations upon contracts involving such transfers.

Despite these obstacles, modern conditions require that increasing attention be given to the international role of confidential information. Among these conditions are the advance in communications and transportation, the importance of research for the aspirations of smaller countries, the technological character of national defense, the global effort to industrialize, and intensifying

[78]See note 23, *infra*.

competition for foreign markets. Feasibility, fairness, and public accountability must be considered in drawing trade-secret agreements; but these considerations must be supplemented by an understanding of the foregoing conditions.

In conclusion, in the challenging circumstances of the future and within the context of positive competition, new arrangements for safeguarding trade secrets will be fostered and instruments already available will be used more extensively. The vigor of positive competition ensures variety and ingenuity in the mechanisms devised or used to meet employer-employee, third-party, national and international needs. The directions of improvement are more readily discernible, of course, than any distant or final pattern of actual arrangements.

The Patent Utilization Study

Joseph Rossman and Barkev S. Sanders

SUMMARY AND CONCLUSION

The Patent Utilization Study is a trial attempt to apply present-day statistical methods to patents in force to determine empirically the number of patents that are actually used in production and the extent of such use.

The present report sets the stage for the pilot study, describes the general procedures followed, indicates the returns that might be expected from the mail questionnaires, and gives findings with respect to the proportion of patents used commercially and reasons for current non-use of patents.

Present indications, from a prepilot subsample, are that some information through mail questionnaires can be expected from 70, and at most 80 percent of the assigned patents in terms of completed assignee and/or inventor questionnaires.* Of the unassigned patents, returns might be expected from 35 to possibly 45 percent.** With such incomplete returns, it will not be possible to arrive at any firm conclusions on patent utilization and other characteristics of patents studied because of the possibility of bias in the returns. It is planned, therefore, to remedy this situation at least partially by interviewing a subsample of nonresponding inventors and assignees to ascertain to what extent the characteristics studied of the patents of such inventors and assignees are different from the patents of those assignees and inventors who have returned completed questionnaires. Other methods might also be found useful to supplement personal interviews, so as to be able to test the extent, if any, that the patents of inventors and assignees who could not be reached by mail or personal interviews are different with respect to utilization and other significant characteristics from those for which questionnaires have been returned or interviews have been made.[1]

Editor's Note: This paper, a pioneer in the use of modern statistical methods to determine the rate of patent utilization, appeared in *IDEA*, Vol.1, No. 1 (June 1957), p. 74.

*The final response was 75 percent.

**The final return was 33 percent.

[1]Because greater effort was required to complete questionnaires for a patented invention which was put to commercial use as compared with one that was not used, it is believed that the bias in returning a completed questionnaire favored

The analyses of completed questionnaires received so far indicate a somewhat higher utilization rate of patents reported by inventors of assigned patents in comparison with unassigned patents.[2] Comparison of inventor replies with respect to utilization of assigned patents with assignee replies shows a tendency for inventors to over-report the current use of patents. In terms of assignee replies, it would seem that of the sampled patents about 50 percent were in current use or had been used in the past. These are divided roughly as follows: about 30 percent in current use and 20 percent used in the past. An additional 10 to 15 percent are patents with prospects for use in the near future. This would suggest that, by the time assigned patents expire, 55 to 65 percent have been used in production to some extent and at some time. For sampled unassigned patents, the proportion used is closer to 40 percent, including current and past use. If patents with prospects for future use are also included, it will approach 50 percent. It would appear, therefore, that between 40 and 50 percent of unassigned patents are used to some extent at some time before expiration.

In the findings the most frequent reasons given for current non-use of the patent by inventors of assigned patents are, in the order of relative frequency: (1) lack of market demand; (2) development of the art has taken a different course; (3) competitively at a disadvantage. The most frequent reasons for non-use reported by assignees are: (1) lack of market demand; (2) competitively at a disadvantage; and (3) other, reasons different from those listed specifically in the questionnaire. The most frequent reasons for non-use given by the inventors of unassigned patents are: (1) shortage or lack of venture capital; (2) patent does not provide sufficient protection; and (3) lack of market demand.

When the pilot study is completed and the findings are mechanically tabulated, it will be possible to establish many more tests of internal consistency and reliability of the returns. To generalize the findings, however, and to determine their range of variability in time

---

patented inventions which had not been put to commercial use. Other evidence, such as proportionately fewer completed questionnaires from the smallest companies, which had the highest utilization rate, bolstered the conclusion that the utilization rate was probably lower for patented inventions for those with completed questionnaires than for those from which no questionnaires were received. (See B. S. Sanders, J. Rossman, L. J. Harris, "Patent Acquisition by Corporation," *IDEA*, Vol. 3, No. 3 (Fall 1959), pp. 217-261.

[2] The higher utilization rate of assigned patented inventions vis-à-vis the unassigned was sustained by subsequent returns. The conclusion based on all returns indicates a utilization rate of 40 to 50 percent for nonassigned patent inventions and 50 to 60 percent for assigned (including the subsequently assigned patented inventions). (See B. S. Sanders, "Patent Utilization," *IDEA*, Vol. 2 (Conference No. 1958), pp. 179-198, 217-229).

and in response to various economic and social forces, it is essential to extend studies of this type over the entire life of the patent to isolate and measure the impact of various forces on utilization and related characteristics of patents.[3]

THE PROBLEM

Considerable speculative literature has been published by social scientists, engineers, industrialists, and others regarding the role of inventions in our economy. However, few of the conclusions are based on objective, factual data derived from a first-hand appraisal of the effects of inventions on our economy. We believe that such a factual appraisal is feasible with respect to the use of patented inventions provided the term *use* is given a functionally narrow definition.[4]

Such a study would attempt to determine the proportion of patents issued in a particular year, which are used in actual production before the expiration of the patent. It would determine how soon patents used in production were put to use after the filing of the patent application, how many of these were put to use prior to the issuance of the patent, for what periods, the length of time patents are generally used, and the extent of such use. One measure of the extent of use would be the monetary income inventors derive from patented inventions and the monetary returns of assignees from assigned patents. The study would yield information on the economic or competitive value of patents which are not used in actual production. Information would be obtained on specific social, economic, or technological factors which stimulate or inhibit the

---

[3]As mentioned, these internal analyses plus a follow-up postal-card questionnaire mailed in 1962 to those assignees who had returned a completed questionnaire led us to believe that patented inventions for which questionnaires were returned had a lower utilization rate than those for which no questionnaire was returned. (See B. S. Sanders, "The Upgrading of Patented Inventions and Their Use Here and Abroad," *IDEA*, Vol. 7, No. 1 (Spring 1963), pp. 45-83, especially pp. 52-60.

[4]The term "patent" is used in place of the more formal term "Letters Patent." The patent statute defines a patent as the legal right to exclude others from making, using, or selling the patented invention. In this sense a patent is an intangible property right which gives the owner the right to bring suit against an infringer in order to restrain the unauthorized use of the patented invention. The invention itself exists separate and distinct from the patent. The term "invention" thus refers to the subject matter covered by the patent and is often used interchangeably with the term "patent." However, in this article, the term "patent" will be used generally as referring to the invention covered by the patent since the study is restricted to the universe of patented inventions. Occasionally it will be used to refer to the exclusive legal rights inherent in Letters Patent, and such usage will be apparent from the context.

industrial utilization of different patents and the extent to which these effects are uniform or different for the various classes of patents. Many other relationships between utilization and other attributes such as the classification of the patent, the year of issue, the characteristics of inventors, etc., could be studied.

It would be necessary to interview a sufficiently large number of inventors and assignees conforming to the statistical requirements of a probability sample to obtain the kind of information referred to above. The results derived from such a sample could then be applied, with a relatively narrow margin of error, to all patents to determine the extent of patent utilization. If the results thus obtained over a period of years yield consistent patterns of patent utilization, it should then be possible to evolve a patent utilization index which could be projected into the future.[5] We hope it will be possible to predict the number of patents that will come into commercial use in a given year and thereby evaluate to some extent the impact that the use of these patents will have on our economy.

To do this, sampling is necessary in view of the nearly 600,000 patents in force in the United States. It would be impractical to attempt a study of all of these patents. Before such a study could be completed an appreciable number of these patents would have expired, and others would have taken their place. Moreover, in any study of patent utilization, the necessary emphasis is not on the patents that have been issued, but on the dynamic phenomena that may occur in the future. Unless it can be demonstrated that characteristics of utilization observed in one period are useful in forecasting similar utilization in another period, any empirical approach to the study of this problem would be futile for practical purposes. In this respect, therefore, this pilot study of patent utilization is an experiment to determine the extent to which patent characteristics remain constant from year to year, so that future events may be forecast. Ideally this would require interviewing thousands of inventors and assignees in different parts of the country to obtain a representative sample of all the patents in force over a representative period of time. However, it would be foolhardy to embark on such a costly project before we have explored its potentialities and practicalities beyond reasonable doubt. It was therefore proposed to conduct this pilot study of patent utilization, and the present article is a presentation of the approach and findings that have resulted from this effort.

---

[5]Such a projection would have to take into consideration changes in economic and social environment, to the extent that these can be anticipated and would affect patent utilization.

SCOPE OF PILOT STUDY

In this pilot study the term *use* means that prior to the expiration of the sampled patent the patent is being produced for sale or is being used in the manufacture of articles for sale. It is believed that with this limitation it should be possible to arrive at an operationally useful differentiation of patents which have proved of immediate and direct economic significance from those that have not as yet done so.

The patent utilization study does not merely differentiate patents utilized from those not utilized; it goes beyond this basic distinction. It differentiates used patents *inter se* in terms of the extent and nature of such use. It further seeks information on the effect that the use of the patent has had on sales and production costs of assignees or inventors. Furthermore, an effort is made to obtain the net monetary results from the use of the sampled patent as of the time of the preparation of the questionnaire.[6]

The study also seeks information as to interrelationships between the above characteristics of use and other attributes of the patent, such as the year of application, the year of issue, the lapsed time in the Patent Office between the date of application and the date of issue, the classification of the patent, the number of claims made by the patentee, the assignment status, etc. It will provide information regarding certain personal characteristics of the inventors and the extent that these are associated with use.

In the case of assigned patents, certain correlations will be sought among various characteristics of patents, the extent and nature of their utilization, and assignee characteristics. Assignee characteristics may include the type of industry, amount of capitalization, annual expenditures for research, etc.

THE METHOD

A 2-percent sample from all the patents issued in 1938, 1948, and 1952 was selected for this pilot study. Ideally the sample would have included some patents from each of the 17 years covering the term of a patent.[7] The three years were selected because it was felt more could be learned from a study where the sample represents the two extremes and roughly the midpoint of the 17-year period. The sample is what in statistics is regarded as a probability

---

[6]For the scope and content of the inventor and assignee questionnaires, see Appendix B.

[7]The statutory period of a patent is 17 years, after which the invention becomes public property.

sample; that is, initially every patent in these three years had a known probability (in this case the same probability) of being included in the sample. The method used in selecting the sample was systematic sampling, using the patent numbers as the basis for sampling.[8]

Instead of interviewing the inventors and assignees, it was felt that many of these could be reached by mail questionnaires. However, initial interviews were conducted with a limited number of inventors and assignees in order to develop and pre-test mail questionnaires. It is assumed that the bulk of the study can be carried out by means of mail questionnaires. To determine whether refusal to respond to the questionnaire introduces a bias in the returns, and if so, the extent of such bias, it is necessary to solicit personally and interview a subsample of inventors and assignees who fail to respond to the mail questionnaire. It is possible that in addition a number of substitute means might be found, some of them reflected in this report, to test the representative nature of the working sample.

PURPOSE AND SCOPE OF THIS REPORT

The present report, aside from describing briefly in the preceding pages the purpose and method of the pilot patent utilization study, aims to deal with the following:

----

[8]To select the sample, from a table of random numbers, two sets of two-digit numbers were drawn. These turned out to be 10 and 59. Thus all patents issued in 1938, 1948, and 1952 with numbers having terminal digits of 10 or 59 were selected as the sample. This gave a 2-percent sample for each of the years selected. This assumes two things: (1) In assigning numbers to patents all numbers are used; there is no pattern or design in assigning numbers to patents by the Patent Office. (2) One type of patent has the same probability of being assigned a particular number as any other type. The second assumption is fully met; with respect to the first prerequisite the requirements are closely approximated. Thus in *Distribution of Patents Issued to Corporations (1939-55)*, Study of the Subcommittee on Patents, Trademarks, and Copyrights of the Committee on the Judiciary, U.S. Senate, 84th Congress, 2nd session, Pursuant to S. Res. 167, Study No. 3, p. 3, note 2, it is stated: "If the number of the first patent issued in 1939 (2,142,080) is subtracted from the number of the first patent issued in 1956 (2,728,913) the result would be slightly higher than the total given here. This is due to the fact that some patent numbers were not used: an application might be in process of issue with the patent number assigned and then be withdrawn for some reason and the patent not issued (or issued later with another number), in such event the assigned patent number could not be used for some other case. These withdrawals averaged 26 per year during the period involved here."

Accordingly, the use of a table of random numbers was not a necessary condition to the selection of a random sample from the patent population. For an explanation of the use of a table of random numbers to prevent possible bias in sampling, see G. W. Snedecor, *Statistical Methods* (Ames: The Iowa State College Press, 5th ed., 1956), p. 9 *et seq.*

1. Present the gross characteristics of the 2-percent sample, showing the number from each of the years sampled and their distribution according to the residence of the inventor and the assignment status of the patents, and the homogeneity of the patents in terms of these characteristics for the individual years sampled.

2. Compare a few patent characteristics derived from the present sample with the characteristics of the population sampled in terms of a complete count or other samples.

3. Present the phases or stages in which questionnaires were mailed to inventors. The division of the 2-percent sample into sub-samples[9] provides a basis to test the reliability of the findings in terms of the internal consistency of these subsamples.

4. Present an analysis of the returns from the prepilot phase of the sample. This was the first phase in which mail question-naires were used. Therefore, the percentage of returns will give an indication of the returns of completed questionnaires that might be expected from the completed pilot-study mailings.

5. Present some findings with respect to the percentage of patents utilized and the reasons given by inventors and assignees for current non-use of patents.

Much of the work in preparing this report has involved exten-sive statistical testing of the early returns from the different phases of the 2-percent sample to check their consistency and to ferret out any evidence of possible selectivity in the early returns in com-parison to later returns—some of these in response to repeated requests to inventors and assignees. In this report only the general conclusions will be considered. Because this is the first systematic study of patent characteristics by modern statistical methods, the detailed analysis and the detailed methodological implications will be presented in a subsequent report.[10]

Table 1 presents certain characteristics of the 2-percent sample selected for the pilot patent utilization study.

Table 1 shows the distribution of the 2-percent sample of patents according to the year in which issued, and the residence of the inventor (whether residing in the United States or else-

---

[9]See Appendix A.

[10]See B. S. Sanders, J. Rossman, and L. J. Harris, "The Non-Use of Pat-ented Inventions," *IDEA*, Vol. 2, No. 1 (1958); "Attitudes of Assignees Toward Patented Inventions," *IDEA*, Vol. 2, No. 4 (Dec. 1958); "Sources and Uses of Patented Inventions," *IDEA*, Vol. 5 (Conference No. 1961); "Patterns of Com-mercial Exploitation of Patented Inventions by Large and Small Corporations," *IDEA*, Vol. 8, No. 1 (Spring 1964).

TABLE 1

NUMBER OF PATENTS ACCORDING TO YEAR IN WHICH
ISSUED AND PERCENTAGE DISTRIBUTION ACCORDING
TO RESIDENCE OF INVENTOR AND ASSIGNMENT
STATUS OF SAMPLED PATENT

Assignment Status of Patents and Residence of Inventors	Year of Issue of Sampled Patents						All Three Years	
	1938		1948		1952			
	Number	Percent	Number	Percent	Number	Percent	Number	Percent
(1)	(2)	(3)	(4)	(5)	(6)	(7)	(8)	(9)
Total	762	100.0	479	100.0	873	100.0	2,114	100.0
Total assigned:	502	65.9	317	66.2	552	63.2	1,371	64.9
Initially	462	60.0	307	64.1	539	61.7	1,308	61.9
Subsequently*	40	5.2	10	2.1	13	1.5	63	3.0
Unassigned	260	34.1	162	33.8	321	36.8	743	35.1
U.S. residents	645	84.6	436	91.0	768	88.0	1,849	87.5
Foreign residents	117	15.4	43	9.0	105	12.0	265	12.5
U.S. residents:								
Total assigned	437	57.3	288	60.1	485	55.6	1,210	57.2
Initially	397	52.1	278	58.0	472	54.1	1,147	54.3
Subsequently	40	5.2	10	2.1	13	1.5	63	3.0
Unassigned	208	27.3	148	30.9	283	32.4	639	30.2
Foreign residents:								
Assigned initially†	65	8.5	29	6.1	67	7.7	161	7.6
Unassigned	52	6.8	14	2.9	38	4.4	104	4.9

*Based on assignment records of the U.S. Patent Office checked in the spring of 1955 to ascertain the number of patents assigned subsequent to the time the patent was issued.
†Subsequent assignments by foreign inventors were not determined.

where) and according to the assignment status. Column 9, for instance, indicates that of the total number of patents included in this sample, nearly 65 percent were assigned. About 62 percent were initially assigned, 3 percent were subsequently assigned, and 35 percent were unassigned. For the three years, nearly 88 percent of the patents were issued to residents of the United States. It further shows the percentage of patents issued to residents of the United States according to assignment status, and the corresponding percentages with respect to patents of nonresidents. It will be noted that the proportion of the initially assigned patents does not vary widely from year to year in the three years studied. The proportion of subsequently assigned patents does vary as one would expect. The number as well as the proportion of such patents is highest in 1938;[11] this number and percentage is considerably lower in 1948, and lowest of all in 1952.

---

[11]When this study began 1938 patents were still in force. When the search was made for assignment of patents subsequent to issue some of the 1938 patents

In 1938 about 5 percent of the patents not assigned initially were assigned subsequently. This figure, however, is in terms of subsequent assignments of patents issued to residents divided by all the patents issued. For inventors residing in the United States these percentages of subsequent assignments are 6 (6.2) for all the patents and 16 (16.1) for patents unassigned at the time of issue. Of course, the constancy of this percentage of patents assigned subsequently would have to be tested by further parallel studies, using different terminal years.

The percentage of 1948 patents not assigned initially, but assigned subsequently, is only 2, and for 1952 patents it is less than 2 (1.5).[12] It is apparent that, during the life term of the patent, the number of patents that become subsequently assigned increases. If 1938 patents are typical in this respect, for inventors residing in the United States, of all the patents issued about 6 percent, and of the initially unassigned patents about 16 percent, became assigned subsequent to issue.[13]

The proportion of patents issued to residents of foreign countries was highest in 1938 and lowest in 1948. This is understandable in the light of circumstances during World War II which prevented many foreign residents from taking out patents in the United States, and economic and other differentials since the war that would affect the decision of foreign inventors to apply for United States patents.

Regarding the percentage of patents initially assigned, statistical tests applied to the proportion of patents assigned in the three years indicate that there are no significant differences between these years. If these three years are typical of other years, it would seem that the proportion of patents initially assigned does not change markedly from year to year. In this connection, a study (U.S. Senate Study No. 3) prepared by the Patent Office for the Senate Subcommittee on Patents, Trademarks, and Copyrights[14]

---

had expired. This was by design, so that the prospects for future assignments would be nil (as it probably was for patents of 1938).

[12]In terms of patents issued to resident inventors, these percentages are 2.3 and 1.7, respectively.

[13]Subsequent studies indicated that the Patent Office assignment files were apparently incomplete. In many cases where an inventor indicated to us that subsequent to issuance his patent had been assigned to some specific company, there was no record of this in the assignment files. Our best estimate on the basis of these returns is that a minimum of 15 percent of the patents issued as unassigned become assigned subsequently, but only about a third of these assignments are recorded in the Patent Office assignment files. There is some indication that the proportion recorded in the official file has been declining.

[14]*Distribution of Patents Issued to Corporations (1939-55)*, Study of Subcommittee on Patents, Trademarks, and Copyrights of the Committee on the

shows that the percentage of patents issued in these three years to corporations does not differ markedly from the average percentage of all patents in force as of December 31, 1955. The percentage of patents assigned to corporations (domestic or foreign) for the three years, derived from the Patent Office study, is 56.6, which does not differ materially from the average for the 17-year period, given as 58.5. It may be inferred, therefore, that it is probable that many of these percentages remain reasonably constant over a protracted number of years, or fluctuate within relatively narrow ranges. This inference is borne out by Figure 4, page 15, and Table 7 on page 12 of the U.S. Senate Study No. 3. The percentage range over the entire period is 54.5 to 64.5 and much of the deviation from the norm was concentrated in the war years when the proportion of patents issued to corporations was the highest. The figure indicates that, in the 20-year period, 1936-1955 inclusive, the percentage of patents issued to corporations has not changed materially.[15] On the other hand, the proportion of patents issued to foreign residents, like subsequently assigned patents, shows statistically significant variation from year to year, in the war and postwar period.

TESTING OF THE SAMPLE

The nature of the sample readily provides two equivalent subsamples, patented inventions ending with the number 10 and those ending with the number 59.

A test may be made by multiplying the sample for the individual years shown in Table 1 by 50, to estimate the total number of patents issued in each of these years.[16] These yield the numbers of 38,100, 23,950, and 43,650 for 1938, 1948, and 1952, respectively. The United States Senate Study No. 3 gives the total number of patents issued in these three years as 38,060, 23,963, and 43,616, respectively. It is apparent that the estimates very closely approximate the actual number of patents issued in these years. The total number of patents issued in these three years

---

Judiciary, U.S. Senate, 84th Congress, 2nd Session, Pursuant to Res. 167, Study No. 3. See Committee print 1957, p. 3, Table I, and see also note 7, *supra*.

[15]This proportion has changed in recent years. At present 75 to 80 percent of U.S. patents are issued to corporations, including the U.S. Government.

[16]Of course to derive any other estimate of patents of a certain type for any one year or all three years, the number of such patents found in the sample would be multiplied by 50—for instance, if we wished to estimate the number of patents issued to a particular corporation in these three years, or the number of chemical patents, etc., we would have to multiply the number of such patents in our sample by 50.

was 105,639, and the estimate for this from the 2-percent sample is 105,700.[17]

Another type of comparison may be made with respect to estimates of the proportion of patents initially assigned, derived from this study with percentages obtained by the Patent Office from a much larger sample. The Patent Office sample, however, is not a *probability* sample. This comparison is shown by Table 2.

TABLE 2

COMPARISON OF ESTIMATES OF PERCENTAGE OF PATENTS INITIALLY ASSIGNED BASED ON PATENT UTILIZATION STUDY, WITH ESTIMATES PREPARED BY PATENT OFFICE, FOR EACH YEAR SAMPLED AND FOR THREE YEARS COMBINED.

Year	Percent of Patents Initially Assigned		
	From Patent Utilization Study	From Patent Office*	Percentage Difference
(1)	(2)	(3)	(4)
1938	60.6	63.1	—2.5
1948	64.1	63.4	+ 0.7
1952	61.7	61.6	+ 0.1
Three Years	61.9	62.5	—0.6

*Supplied by the Patent Office.

The comparison indicates very close agreement. If the sampling variation of the percentages derived from the patent utilization study are taken into consideration, in no case are the differences between the percentages derived from this study and those obtained by the Patent Office statistically significant. The largest difference found is in 1938 when the Patent Office estimate was 2.5 percent higher. The smallest difference is for 1952 when the percentage obtained from the patent utilization study was 0.1 percent higher. For the three-year period the difference between the two sets of estimates is approximately 0.6 percent, well within the margin of sampling variation.

Table 3 presents another comparison between the estimates derived from the patent utilization study and estimates obtained by the Patent Office.

This table compares the estimates derived from the patent utilization study showing the percentage of patents issued to residents of foreign countries with similar estimates obtained by the Patent Office.

---

[17]We have ignored adjusting for the fact that certain numbers have no assigned patents—see note 8, *supra*. Nevertheless, the estimates check very closely with the actual count of the total patent population.

TABLE 3

COMPARISON OF ESTIMATES OF PERCENTAGE OF PATENTS
ISSUED TO FOREIGN RESIDENTS, FROM PATENT UTILIZATION
STUDY, WITH ESTIMATES PREPARED BY PATENT OFFICE, FOR
EACH YEAR AND FOR THREE YEARS COMBINED

Year	Percent of Patents Issued to Foreign Residents		
	From Patent Utilization Study	From Patent Office*	Percentage Difference
(1)	(2)	(3)	(4)
1938	15.4	15.2	+ 0.2
1948	9.0	8.3	+ 0.7
1952	12.0	12.9	—0.9
Three Years	12.5	12.7	—0.4

*Supplied by the Patent Office.

It should again be noted that the differences are small. When the sampling variations are taken into consideration, none of the differences is statistically significant.

A fourth comparison is available in terms of the duration of time elapsed between the date when the patent was applied for and the date when it was granted. This comparison is presented in Table 4.

TABLE 4

COMPARISON OF ESTIMATED MEAN DURATION OF TIME IN
MONTHS ELAPSED BETWEEN APPLICATION FOR PATENT AND
GRANTING OF PATENT, FOR PATENTS ISSUED IN SPECIFIED
YEARS, BASED ON PATENT UTILIZATION STUDY AND
PATENT OFFICE DATA

Year	Mean Duration of Time Elapsed in Months		
	From Patent Utilization Study	From Patent Office*	Difference in Months
(1)	(2)	(3)	(4)
1938	29.9	29.41	+ 0.49
1948	39.5	40.51	—1.01
1952	44.2	43.65	+ 0.55
Three Years	38.0	37.81	+ 0.19

*Supplied by the Patent Office.

It is to be noted again that the differences between the estimates derived from the 2-percent sample of this study and those obtained by the Patent Office are small and statistically not significant.

These various comparisons indicate the essential statistical soundness of the 2-percent sample. It is not possible to determine from these comparisons of parallel estimates whether the Patent Office estimates or those derived from this study are closer to the true values of the population from which the samples were taken. As already indicated, the distinction between the two estimates is that the Patent Office samples were commonly larger, but they were not *probability* samples. Therefore, it is not possible to derive any measure of sampling error for the Patent Office estimates. Measures of sampling errors for this study will be presented in the forthcoming second report.

In the prepilot subsample extensive effort was made to follow all possible leads to obtain a current address for the inventor.[18] Once an address was found, efforts were made to persuade the inventor to return a completed questionnaire. While telephone contact has been used occasionally, there is no indication that this will increase completed questionnaires substantially where efforts through the mails have failed, although telephone calls may materially reduce the number of inventors classed as nonrespondents.[19] The percentage of completed questionnaires, with respect to the patents in the prepilot subsample, might be used as an indication of the proportion of completed mail questionnaires that we are likely to get from the more recent mailings.

Table 5 shows the distribution of inventors in the prepilot subsample by response status, as of January 10, 1957, separately for inventors of assigned and those of unassigned patents, and for the two groups combined.

Of the 211 inventors in the subsample, questionnaires were received from 112, or 53 percent of the total. Three of these were questionnaires completed for deceased inventors.[20] Of the 99 inventors from whom no questionnaires had been received as of January 10, 1957, 25 were deceased and two others were seriously incapacitated. Eighteen inventors have not been reached because of the lack of a current address. Perhaps many of these are deceased. Forty-nine inventors have presumably received the questionnaires but for one reason or another have failed to respond; and finally, five indicated that they did not care to complete the questionnaire. There is reason to believe that a number of these 49 cases are not in any real sense nonresponse, but at this

---

[18]See Appendix A.

[19]See Appendix A, note 39.

[20]Relatives of deceased inventors were not solicited to complete the questionnaires. However, these three completed questionnaires were returned without solicitation.

TABLE 5

NUMBER AND PERCENTAGE DISTRIBUTION OF INVENTORS IN PREPILOT SUBSAMPLE BY RESPONSE STATUS SEPARATELY AND COMBINED FOR ASSIGNED AND UNASSIGNED PATENTS

Response Status	Assigned		Unassigned		Assigned and Unassigned	
	Number	Percent	Number	Percent	Number	Percent
(1)	(2)	(3)	(4)	(5)	(6)	(7)
Inventors in the sample	152	100.0	59	100.0	211	100.0
Completed questionnaires:	91	59.9	21	35.6	112	53.1
Inventor living	89	58.6	20	33.9	109	51.6
Inventor deceased	2	1.3	1	1.7	3	1.4
No questionnaire:	61	40.1	38	64.4	99	46.9
Inventor deceased	19	12.5	6	10.2	25	11.8
Inventor incapacitated	2	1.3	--	- -	2	.9
No current address	10	6.6	8	13.6	18	8.5
No response	26	17.1	23	39.0	49	23.2
Refusal to answer	4	2.6	1	1.7	5	2.4

stage we could not estimate what proportion of these cases classified as nonrespondent in Table 5 should be reclassified.[21]

It should be noted that an appreciably smaller proportion of inventors of unassigned patents in the sample have returned completed questionnaires in comparison with inventors of assigned patents, 36 percent and 60 percent, respectively—a difference which is statistically significant. A larger proportion of inventors with unassigned patents are among those whose current address is unknown to us, nearly 14 percent as compared with less than 7 percent for inventors with assigned patents.[22] Similarly, in the group who apparently have received questionnaires, nonrespondents are proportionately greater among inventors of unassigned patents, 39 percent as compared with 17 percent. It

[21]From our attempts to telephone non-respondents, we have learned that some of these inventors are deceased, though the mail was not returned to us by the Post Office. In other instances the letter was mailed to a person bearing the same name, who was not the inventor. In the latter cases the true inventor might be deceased, or, if living, his current address is not available to us.

[22]According to a prelimianry analysis of the age, as of January 1, 1957, of inventors of assigned and unassigned patents, the age distribution of inventors of unassigned patents indicates this group has many more inventors of advanced age, yet the proportion of deceased and incapacitated inventors known in this group is actually smaller in comparison to inventors with assigned sampled patents. This would tend to strengthen the belief that an appreciable number of inventors with unassigned sampled patents, who have not been heard from, are deceased. This is probably true also for inventors of assigned sampled patents, but to a much lesser extent proportionately.

is probable that a substantially higher proportion of inventors with unassigned patents, about whom we have no specific information, are deceased, compared with inventors of assigned patents.

Table 5 has dealt with the number of inventors who have returned completed questionnaires and the further classification of others who have not returned questionnaires. Table 6 shows the number and percentage of patents with respect to which inventor questionnaires were received.

TABLE 6

NUMBER AND PERCENTAGE DISTRIBUTION OF PATENTED INVENTIONS IN PREPILOT SUBSAMPLE, BY WHETHER OR NOT AT LEAST ONE COMPLETED QUESTIONNAIRE WAS RECEIVED FROM THE INVENTOR, SEPARATELY AND COMBINED FOR ASSIGNED AND UNASSIGNED PATENTS

Receipt of Questionnaire	Assigned		Unassigned		Assigned and Unassigned	
	Number	Percent	Number	Percent	Number	Percent
(1)	(2)	(3)	(4)	(5)	(6)	(7)
Patents in the sample	124	100.0	54	100.0	178	100.0
One or more questionnaires received	76	61.3	21	38.9	97	54.5
No questionnaire*	48	38.7	33	61.1	81	45.5

*Since joint inventors could have had different reasons for failure to return a questionnaire, no attempt was made at this stage to indicate the apparent reason for failure to have received a completed questionnaire.

Table 6 indicates that completed questionnaires received from inventors in the prepilot sample by January 10, 1957, constitute less than 55 percent of the patented inventions in that subsample. It is problematic whether with further effort this percentage for the prepilot group could be raised to 60. Table 6 confirms what was observed in Table 5, that is, a higher response rate from inventors with assigned sampled patents. Thus, for assigned patents in the subsample, inventors have supplied information with respect to 61 percent of the patents, while the corresponding percentage for the unassigned group is 39. This percentage difference is statistically significant.

Questionnaires were mailed to most of the assignees of patents in the prepilot subsample. These mailings were made initially in the spring of 1956.[23] The 124 assigned patents have 116 different assignees. One hundred four of these assignees are companies

---

[23] Assignees who fail to return a completed questionnaire are sent a first follow-up letter; if this proves ineffective after an interim, a second follow-up letter is sent requesting the return of completed questionnaires.

and 12 are individuals.[24] The latter, very often, is either the wife or some other close relative of the inventor. The number and percentage of patented inventions with respect to which questionnaires have been received from assignees are shown in Table 7.

TABLE 7

NUMBER AND PERCENTAGE DISTRIBUTION OF ASSIGNED PATENTS IN PREPILOT SUBSAMPLE BY RESPONSE STATUS OF ASSIGNEES

Response Status	Number	Percent
Assigned inventions in the sample	124	100.0
Assignee questionnaire received*	60	48.4
No questionnaire	64	51.6
No current address†	13	10.5
No response‡	51	41.1

*These are all corporate assignees.
†Of these, six are individual assignees.
‡Of these, six are individual assignees.

Although the assignee questionnaires for the prepilot subsample had been mailed initially early the previous spring, less than 50 percent of the assignees had responded by January 10, 1957. While some increase in this percentage is still expected, again it is improbable that the percentage of assignees returning completed questionnaires will exceed 60.[25] The probability of receiving a completed questionnaire from an individual assignee appears to be very small. Of the 12 such assignees in the prepilot subsample, no current address could be found for six, and with respect to the remaining six, for whom presumably there were current addresses when the questionnaires were mailed, none has responded.

Of course, as expected, many of the questionnaires completed by assignees are for the same patents for which questionnaires were also received from one or more inventors. This is reflected in Table 8.

The overall results are given by the percentages in the last line of Table 8. It will be seen that inventors and assignees have not returned completed questionnaires for nearly 26 percent of the assigned patents in the prepilot subsample; no questionnaires

[24]In subsequent analyses it was deemed more appropriate to treat patents assigned to wives or other relatives as nonassigned. Actually assignee returns, including assignees who acquired the patent subsequent to its issuance averaged about 55 percent. This is exclusive of any individual assignee, of course.

[25]For assigned patents, returns were received from inventor(s), assignees, or both. The number of assigned patents with at least one questionnaire from either of these represented 75 percent of assigned patents in the sample.

Table 8

NUMBER AND PERCENTAGE DISTRIBUTION OF PATENTS IN
PREPILOT SUBSAMPLE BY RESPONSE STATUS FROM INVENTORS
AND/OR ASSIGNEES FOR ASSIGNED PATENTS, AND INVENTOR
RESPONSE FOR UNASSIGNED PATENTS

Response Status	Assigned		Unassigned		Assigned and Unassigned	
	Number	Per-cent	Number	Per-cent	Number	Per-cent
(1)	(2)	(3)	(4)	(5)	(6)	(7)
Number of inventions	124	100.0	54	100.0	178	100.0
One or more questionnaires:	92	74.2	21	38.9	113	63.5
Inventor questionnaire only	32	25.8	21	38.9	53	29.8
Inventor and assignee questionnaires (all inventors)	41	33.1	---	- -	41	23.0
Inventor and assignee questionnaires (some inventors)	3	2.4	---	- -	3	1.7
Assignee questionnaire only	16	12.9	---	- -	16	9.0
No questionnaire	32	25.8	33	61.1	65	36.5

have been returned with respect to 61 percent of the unassigned
patents; these give a combined group of between 36 and 37 percent
of the patents for which there are no completed questionnaires.
Without knowing something about the characteristics of this 36 to
37 percent of inventions in the subsample, no firm prediction can
be made with respect to the characteristics of all the patents from
which the subsample was derived. Before such a partial sample can
be used as a probability sample, it must be demonstrated that the
characteristics of patents under study, for which no questionnaires
have been returned, are no different from those for which questionnaires have been returned.

It is evident that information in the subsample is particularly
deficient with respect to unassigned patents. Questionnaires have
been received in the prepilot subsample for less than 40 percent
of the unassigned patents included. For assigned patents, this
percentage is 74. It is improbable that the response rate for unassigned patents could be raised to as high as 50 percent or that
the overall response rate for the combined group, assigned and
unassigned, could be raised to 70 percent from the less than 64 percent shown in Table 8.[26]

---

[26]The final returns indicated 33 percent for those patents which were
issued unassigned and were not reported to have been assigned subsequently; while
for about 75 percent of assigned patents, including those assigned subsequent to
issuance, we had at least one questionnaire from an inventor or the assignee.

The conclusion, therefore, which may be derived on the basis of the prepilot phase of the study is that when the work on the mailings for the study is concluded, the percentage of patents with one or more completed questionnaires will range between 35 and 45 for the unassigned, and between 70 and 80 for the assigned patents.

The implication of incomplete returns is the possibility that patents for which no questionnaires are returned may be different in certain respects, particularly with respect to utilization, from those for which questionnaires have been returned. The most effective way to test this possibility would be, as planned, to interview a subsample of inventors and assignees who failed to respond. If this nonresponse group is not significantly different from the group responding, it would indicate, in effect, that the mail questionnaire approach is sufficient, by itself, to produce a reasonably representative sample, at least for those characteristics used in this study. Information for all the patents in the entire sample cannot be obtained, even through the use of personal interviews as a follow-up method. A significant proportion of inventors, especially those of unassigned patents, are deceased; other inventors and some assignees cannot be located; and some inventors and assignees will not cooperate. For these groups, other methods should be devised to assure that the characteristics of the patents of interest to us in this study are not different from those for which information has been obtained or will be obtained through personal interviews.[27]

One possible approach for testing the adequacy of the working sample (the sample for which information has been obtained) is in terms of internal analyses. These include comparison of the different subsamples with one another. This has been done intensively in terms of the intercomparison against one another of different phases of the interviews and mailings. We have compared the characteristics of assigned patents from questionnaires completed only by assignees with those of patents for which both the inventor and assignee have completed questionnaires. We also have compared the converse, the characteristics of patents with inventor replies only with those patents with both inventor and

[27]It should be stressed, of course, that if through conventional means it is not possible to reach 100 percent, but information is available for, let us say, 90 or 95 percent of the patents in the sample—and that either specifically, or as a group, they do not differ from the ones for which specific information is unavailable—the study would still be an overwhelming success as a fact-finding study in utilization. It will give for the first time firm figures of the proportion of patents used with a margin of uncertainty far below anything that has been available to date.

assignee replies. We have also compared replies of assignees with replies of inventors for identical patents. Characteristics of assigned and unassigned patents with two or more inventors have also been compared; contrasting the utilization patterns of patents in which all the inventors have replied against those in which only some of the inventors have replied. We have compared characteristics of patents for which replies were received as a result of the initial mailing with those for which completed questionnaires were received after one or more follow-up requests. The internal checks and comparisons available at this stage have been used in appraising the findings presented in this article. Their detailed presentation and discussion, however, will be given in the forthcoming methodological report.[28]

When the pilot study is ready for mechanical processing, there will be many more internal checks and correlations which, although not conclusive in themselves, will give an inferential basis for determining whether the working sample is appreciably different from a truly random sample with which the study began. These tests should also aid in appraising the level of reliability of information supplied. These internal tests will also include comparisons of the patents for which questionnaires have been completed with those patents for which no questionnaires have been completed with respect to known characteristics, such as the year of patenting. This information may indicate the extent that nonresponse reflects old age, death of the inventor, or other differential characteristics which might influence the prospect of response but which may have little, if any, association with patent utilization. Similarly, comparisons will be made to determine whether there are differences in these two groups of patents (those with questionnaires and those without) in terms of class of patent, length of time pending in the Patent Office, geographic location of the inventor, number of claims, and other factors for which information is available for the entire 2-percent sample.

THE FINDINGS

It has already been indicated that at this time the pilot study is incomplete. Errors and inconsistencies in reported information are another limitation characteristic of studies of this type. Only

---

[28]This analysis snowballed into a typescript monograph of more than 200 pages. It was decided not to publish it, though it gave strong assurance of internal consistency of the data obtained from interviews, those received early, those received late, and those received after numerous follow-ups, and many other consistency checks.

repeated studies and intensive analysis of the returns supplemented by special inquiries can reveal the presence and the magnitude of such errors.

Percentage of Patents Utilized

Since the determination of the proportion of patents utilized by industry is the capstone of the current study, it is natural that this ratio has been a key item of information looked for as soon as the completed questionnaires began to come in. Information with respect to patent utilization was obtained independently from inventors, and for assigned patents, from assignees. Table 9 summarizes these returns from inventors separately for assigned and unassigned patents and for the combined group.

Table 9 summarizes all the information obtained so far from inventor questionnaires with respect to utilization of the sampled patent. The questions were designed to obtain information as to whether or not the patent has been used at any time and, except in the personal interview questionnaire, separate information was obtained as to whether the patent was still in use or had been used only in the past. If the patent was not in either of these classes, information was sought as to whether there was a prospect for use in the near future. Other replies provided for were: "Never used and no prospect of use" and "Don't know whether used or not." So far seven inventors of assigned patents and four inventors of unassigned patents have failed to answer this question. Column 2 shows the frequency distribution of the assigned patents according to these replies. The sub-items "In current use" and "Used in the past" do not add up to the total of patents used at any time, because the latter are based, as indicated in Table 9, on all the questionnaires, while the two sub-items are based on questionnaires exclusive of those completed by personal interviews. The percentage distribution of these is shown in Column 3. The tentative findings indicate, according to the replies received from inventors, approximately 58 percent of the patents were used, about 41 percent being in current use and about 18 percent used in the past. Between 2 percent and 3 percent of the inventor replies for assigned patents indicate that there is a prospect for use of the sampled patent in the near future. Twenty-one percent indicate that the patent was not used, and there is no prospect for its use; about 17 percent said that they did not know whether the patent was used. The majority of these, as indicated from the assignee replies for these same patents, were never used.

With respect to unassigned patents, Column 4 shows the

Table 9

NUMBER AND PERCENTAGE DISTRIBUTION OF PATENTS IN 2
PERCENT SAMPLE ACCORDING TO UTILIZATION STATUS,
BASED ON ALL RESPONSES RECEIVED FROM INVENTORS FOR
ASSIGNED AND UNASSIGNED PATENTS, SEPARATELY AND
COMBINED AFTER WEIGHTING

Utilization Status	Assigned		Unassigned		Assigned and Unassigned (weighted)*	
	Number	Per-cent	Number	Per-cent	Number	Per-cent
(1)	(2)	(3)	(4)	(5)	(6)	
Total number of patents represented by one or more completed questionnaires	457	100.0	152	100.0	100.0	
Patents used at any time:	267	58.4	64	42.1	53.9	
In current use†	178	41.1	46	33.3	39.1	
Used in the past†	76	17.6	12	8.7	14.8	
Expected use in the near future	11	2.4	9	5.9	3.7	
Don't know whether in use	76	16.6	12	7.9	13.8	
Never used and no prospect of use	96	21.0	63	41.4	28.6	
Unanswered	7	1.5	4	2.6	– –	

*This column is derived by weighting the percentages in Columns 3 and 5 by the relative proportion of assigned and unassigned patents granted to residents of the United States in the three years under consideration (1,218 assigned and 631 unassigned—see Table 15 in Appendix A). The questionnaires in which the inventor failed to indicate utilization were not taken into consideration.

†Since for the personal interview cases the information regarding current or past use was not differentiated, the figures, for "current use" and "used in the past," as separate categories, are based on mail questionnaire responses only, which constitute 433 assigned, and 138 unassigned patents.

distribution according to utilization status based on inventor questionnaires. In all, 152 inventors of unassigned patents have replied. The percentage distribution for these patents indicates that some 43 percent are used currently or were used in the past. About one-third of the unassigned patents are used currently and about 9 percent were used in the past. Nearly 6 percent of the inventors of unassigned sampled patents indicated that the patent is to be used in the near future. Forty-one percent indicated that the patent had never been used and there is no prospect for use, and about 8 percent said that they did not know whether the patent was used or not. Since the proportion of completed questionnaires is quite different for assigned and unassigned patents, it would be misleading to combine Columns 2 and 4 to obtain combined utilization rates. Therefore, Column 6 percentages have been derived by weighting each group according to its proportionate representation in the original 2-percent sample shown in Table 1 in Appendix A. In doing this, we have assumed that these assigned patents with replies on utilization are representative of all the assigned patents in the 2-percent sample, and the unassigned patents likewise are representative of the unassigned patents in the sample.

Comparisons of Columns 2 and 3 with Columns 4 and 5 indicate marked differences between assigned and unassigned patents as to utilization based on inventor replies. These differences have been tested and found to be statistically significant. There is no basis to assume that these differences in the utilization patterns for assigned patents will vanish with more complete returns. There is a possibility, however, that the reliability of the information with respect to utilization reported by inventors of assigned patents is of a different quality from those reported by inventors of unassigned patents. Therefore, the replies on utilization received from the inventors of assigned patents are checked against the corresponding replies of assignees on identical patents. This is shown in Table 10.

TABLE 10

COMPARATIVE UTILIZATION REPORTED BY INVENTORS AND ASSIGNEES WITH RESPECT TO SAME PATENTS OBTAINED TO DATE THROUGH MAIL QUESTIONNAIRES

Inventor Replies	Assignee Replies				
	Total	Current Use	Past Use	Expected Use	Never Used
(1)	(2)	(3)	(4)	(5)	(6)
Total	136	46	21	20	49
Current use	62	43	9	5	5
Past use	12	1	9	1	1
Expected use	3	--	--	2	1
Don't know	30	2	1	3	24
Never used	28	--	2	8	18
Unanswered	1	--	--	1	--

The marginal total of Table 10 based on 136 patents in which concurrent replies with respect to utilization were available through mail questionnaires received from the inventors and assignees indicates that, while inventors reported 62 patents to have been in current use, the corresponding number reported by the assignee is 46. In only 43 patents did both the assignees and the inventors agree that the patent had been used in the past. Of the inventors, 12 reported that the patent had been used in the past. The corresponding total reported by assignees is 21. On nine patents inventors and assignees agree that the patent had been used in the past. Only three inventors indicate that there is a prospect for future use of the patent. The corresponding number reported by assignees is 20. There is agreement between inventors and assignees for two patents that will be used in the near future. For 30 patents inventors reported they did not know whether the patent is in use; for 24 of these patents the assignees report the patent was never used. None of the assignees reports that it is not known whether the patent was used. Inventors report 28 patents as never used; the total number of never used patents reported by assignees is 49. With respect to 18 patents, both the inventor and the assignee agree on the identical patents that were never used. Further details of cross-distribution of these patents, according to utilization reported by inventors and assignees, may be observed in Table 10.

We may conclude from Table 10 that there is a tendency for the inventors to overreport the number of patents in current use, assuming that the assignee reply in this respect is a reliable criterion. This exaggeration, however, may not be due to intentional falsification, but rather a lack of correct information. On the other hand, with respect to overall percent of patents utilized, if one takes into consideration future use as well, assignee replies do not give results materially different from those of inventor replies—this may be true particularly near the end of the 17-year term.

The unreliability of replies with respect to utilization from inventors of assigned patents, however, cannot be the basis for judging the reliability of replies of inventors of unassigned patents, since inventors of unassigned patents are in a better position to know the utilization status of their patents. However, a glance back to Table 9 indicates that nearly 8 percent of the inventors of unassigned patents stated that they did not know whether the patent was used or not. This may suggest that there is a degree of uncertainty in the replies of inventors of unassigned patents as well—though not to the same extent as is true with respect to inventors of assigned patents.

Since the assignee is in a better position to know the utilization status of the sampled patent, subject to further exploration and inquiry, we believe that greater reliance should be placed on returns based on assignees' replies. In Table 11 are shown the assignee replies as to whether or not the patent was being used or had been used, etc., in terms paralleling those employed in the inventor questionnaires.

Table 11 shows the assignee replies, and compares replies

in terms of two subsamples, summarizing all the assignee questionnaires received as of February 18, 1957. Columns 2 and 3 are based on assignee replies with respect to patents in the prepilot subsample and those included in the initial personal interviews. The figures showing patents in current use, and those patents used in the past, however, are based on the prepilot subsample only. In the initial interviews current use was not distinguished from past use only. In Columns 4 and 5 are shown assignee returns from the December 1956 mailings. The frequency distribution of these patents according to utilization agrees closely with the frequency distribution of patents in the prepilot subsample and in the personal interview cases. The use of various statistical tests for possible significance of the differences indicates none of these percentages is statistically significantly different from one another; therefore, the two sets of returns can be regarded as different samples from the same universe and can be combined to give a larger sample, with a higher degree of reliability and stability. This has been done in Columns 6 and 7.

TABLE 11

NUMBER AND PERCENTAGE DISTRIBUTION OF ASSIGNED PATENTS BY UTILIZATION STATUS, BASED ON ASSIGNEE RESPONSES, SEPARATELY AND COMBINED FOR THE PREPILOT SUBSAMPLE RETURNS AND INITIAL INTERVIEWS, COMPARED WITH RETURNS FROM DECEMBER MAILINGS*

Utilization Status	Prepilot and Personal Interviews		December Mailing		Combined	
	Number	Per-cent	Number	Per-cent	Number	Per-cent
(1)	(2)	(3)	(4)	(5)	(6)	(7)
Patents represented by completed assignee questionnaires	78	100.0	183	100.0	261	100.0
Patents used at any time:	38	48.7	92	50.3	130	49.8
In current use	17†	28.8†	61	33.3	78†	32.2†
Used in the past	11†	18.6†	31	16.9	42†	17.4†
Expected use in the near future	8	10.3	16	8.7	24	9.2
Don't know whether in use	1	1.3	--	--	1	.4
Never used and no prospect of use	31	39.7	74	40.4	105	40.2
Unanswered	--	--	1	.5	1	.4

*See Appendix A.

†Since for the personal interview cases the information regarding "current use" and "past use" was not differentiated, the figures showing current use and those showing past use are based on the responses from the mail questionnaires only. This represents 59 patents in Column 2 and 242 in Column 6.

On the basis of Table 11, if it can be assumed that the assign-ees from whom questionnaires have been received are not signif-icantly different from those who have not responded, it may be concluded that about half of the assigned patents in the sample are being used or were used in the past.[29] Almost another 10 per-cent of patents are expected to be used in the near future. The overall conclusion, therefore, seems to be that if these statistics are not biased, by the time assigned patents expire, about 60 percent of them will have been used in production at one time or another. Stated in these terms the conclusions derived from the assignee replies would not be materially different from the conclusions that could be derived from the inventor replies. In other words, much of the difference apparent between inventors and assignees is with respect to the time axes; as far as overall percentages of used pat-ents are concerned, inventors tend to report all patents used in the past or to be used, as being in current use.

Table 11 shows that there is no significant difference between two subsamples of assignee replies, in one of which every effort has been made to maximize the returns, while in the other there has not been time for a similar effort as yet.[30]

In Table 12 all the direct and indirect evidence available at present regarding the utilization patterns of assigned patents in terms of assignee replies has been summarized.

Columns 2 and 3 of Table 12 are derived from the relation-ship shown in Table 10 between inventor and assignee replies on patent utilization. Using that relationship, we have estimated for the 304 patents, for which there were inventor replies but no assignee replies, what the probable assignee replies would have been. These estimates have been compared with Columns 4 and 5 where the distribution of patent utilization is shown in terms of

---

[29]This is far greater than the percentage of patents believed to be used in commercial production in terms of estimates which have been found in the litera-ture. For example, L. J. Carr, in an article, "The Patenting Performance of 1,000 Inventors During Ten Years," *American Journal of Sociology*, Vol. 37 (1932), pp. 569-580, refers to estimates of 1 percent of the patents issued as having any practical utility. Edward Thomas, "Are Patents Worthwhile?" *Journal Patent Office Society*, Vol. 13 (1931), pp. 232-235, refers to estimates of 5 percent of patents being used. His own estimate is that 10.8 percent to 18 percent of patents are actually put to use. A number of our correspondents have written that it is commonly believed that about 5 percent of the patents are used—some have in-dicated more specifically that one fourth or one third of their company patents are in current use.

[30]In the prepilot subsample and initial interviews, questionnaires were available for 78 out of 150 assigned patents, 52 percent of the total; in the remain-ing segment of the 2-percent sample there are 1,048 assigned patents with only 183 replies to date or about 17 percent of the total.

TABLE 12

PROBABLE REPLIES OF ASSIGNEES AS TO UTILIZATION OF
PATENTS BASED ON INVENTOR REPLIES—PATENTS WITH
RESPECT TO WHICH ONLY INVENTOR QUESTIONNAIRES HAVE
BEEN RECEIVED, COMPARED WITH ASSIGNEE RESPONSES
ON UTILIZATION

Utilization Status	Inferred Assignee Replies		Assignee Responses					
			Assignee Questionnaire Only		Assignee and Inventor Questionnaires		Combined	
	Number	Per-cent	Number	Per-cent	Number	Per-cent	Number	Per-cent
(1)	(2)	(3)	(4)	(5)	(6)	(7)	(8)	(9)
Patents represented by completed question-naires by inventor or assignee	304	100.0	120	100.0	136	100.0	560	100.0
Patents used at any time:	162	53.3	60	50.0	67	49.3	289	51.6
In current use	90	29.6	36	30.0	47	34.6	173	30.9
In past use	72	23.7	24	20.0	20	14.7	116	20.7
Expected use in the near future	45	14.8	5	4.2	20	14.7	70	12.5
Don't know whether in use	--	- -	1	.8	--	- -	1	.2
Never used and no prospect of use	97	31.9	53	44.2	49	36.0	199	35.5
Unanswered	--	- -	1	.8	--	- -	1	.2

120 patents with respect to which no inventor has replied, and
Columns 6 and 7, showing the distribution of 136 patents with
respect to which there were both assignee and inventor replies—
the distribution as to utilization being based on assignee replies.
Examination of these columns indicates that with respect to overall patent utilization the percentages are quite close across the
board, the maximum being 53 and the minimum 49, a variation
that one may well expect in samples of this size. The same may be
said of the percentage of patents in current use. The range among
these percentages across the board is from almost 30 to less than
35. There is considerable difference regarding past use between the
group of 120 assignees of patents the inventors of which had not
replied and the 136 assignees of patents with respect to which both
inventors and assignees had replied (see Columns 5 and 7 as well
as 3 and 7). The test of significance shows that in random samples
drawn from the same population, differences as large as this could

occur with less than 5-percent frequency. It is to be noted that this difference is between two groups of assignee replies—differences between Columns 3 and 5 are not significant. The 120 assignees who replied without the inventor having replied reported a much lower expectancy of use in comparison to parallel percentages in Columns 2 and 7 respectively. Again this difference is statistically significant. This might suggest that for this group of patents with respect to which the assignees only replied, the inventors may have been of more advanced age so that more of them were deceased or were incapacitated and therefore unable to reply to the inventor questionnaire. For such a group of patents—heavily weighted with patents issued in 1938—there will be a concentration of those used in the past and a corresponding deficit of patents used in the future. But this, of course, is purely conjectural at this time, though subject to checking. In any event, even though some of these differences are large enough to be statistically significant, the overall pattern shown in the three columns is nevertheless reasonably consistent and therefore Columns 8 and 9 may be said to give us, as of this stage of our study, the best approximation of the proportion of patents utilized, from the patents granted in these three years.

The percentage of assigned patents utilized, based on assignee replies, is not significantly higher than the percentage of unassigned patents utilized. This may be seen by comparing the percentages given in Column 5 of Table 9, with Column 7 of Table 11 and Column 9 of Table 12. We believe, nevertheless, that the percentage of unassigned patents used is probably somewhat lower, and there is also some reason to believe that the period over which the unassigned patents come into use is much more restricted.

Tentative Conclusions on Utilization

Because utilization is the central theme of this study, despite its preliminary and incomplete state, the returns to date have been subjected to intensive analysis, subject to the limitation that the information has not been mechanically processed as yet. It would not have been economical to attempt many cross classifications, even by the year in which the patent was granted which, it appears, exerts marked influence on the selective factors which differentiate patents for which information has been received from those for which no information is as yet at hand. Subject to these limitations, the analysis seems to suggest that at a given time, from one fourth to one third of the assigned patents in force are likely to be in current use. For unassigned patents it is probable that this proportion would be somewhat lower. Between one sixth and one fourth of the assigned patents are likely to have been used, but are no longer in current use. Therefore, at any given time, of all the assigned patents in force, approximately one half would be in current use or would have been used at some time. The corresponding percentage for unassigned patents may range between one fourth and two fifths, that is, one fourth and two fifths of such patents would be in current use or have been used in the past. The percentage for patents expected to be used in the near future may range from one out of 12 to one out of six for assigned patents. In this respect, the reported information for unassigned patents is likely to be less reliable and shows a somewhat higher percentage than that for assigned patents.

The above indicated ranges will depend, in part, on the composition of what is sometimes called the "mix" of patents, that is, the relative proportion of patents that are in their first, second . . . to 17th year; partly on the times in relation to the economic cycle; partly on the time lapse in the Patent Office, between the filing and the granting of the patent; and probably many other factors.

The tentative findings of this study suggest that at the time of expiration of the patents from 45 percent to 65 percent of the assigned patents have had some commercial use, however limited. The probable comparable percentage for unassigned patents may range from 30 to 45.

There are indications that by the time patents are granted some 20 to 30 percent of those assigned have been used. Some of these would be already obsolete. In this respect the pattern of use for unassigned patents is likely to be quite different—a far smaller proportion of unassigned patents are probably in use at the time the patent is granted. The majority of patents will probably be used close to the time of granting. In other words, the period for "usability" as defined in this study is probably much more restricted, comparatively speaking, for unassigned than for assigned patents. Even with respect to assigned patents the chances for utilization probably decline rather rapidly after the patent is granted. In all probability for both groups of patents a very small percentage would come into commercial use toward the end of the 17-year period.

We assume that as the study progresses it will be possible to narrow the ranges of some of these guestimated percentages.[31]

---

[31]For the entire sample of 245 assigned patented inventions reported in current use or used in the past, in 39.2 percent such commercial use preceded the

We also hope to be able to trace more sharply the utilization curve in relation to the 17-year term for assigned and unassigned patents, since there is every indication that the patterns of utilization for the two groups will be markedly different. Another related matter that has hardly been touched upon, though present inferentially in these statistics, is the time span over which patents are used. The completed study should shed considerable light on this area in which it is also probable that the patterns will differ markedly for assigned and unassigned patents.

While our findings are tentative, the internal consistency of the data leads us to believe that the overall results regarding the high proportion of patents used are reasonably firm.

Reasons for the Non-Use of Patents

An important aspect of the utilization project is to ascertain the reasons for the current non-use of the patent. Question 32 in the inventor questionnaire and question 12 in the assignee questionnaire, which is similar, provide the bases for such analyses.[33] Table 13 shows the distribution of replies to Question 32 from inventors, for inventors of assigned patents and those of unassigned patents with respect to reasons for current non-use of the patent.

Columns 2 and 3 indicate that of the 289 replies, 25 percent indicated lack of market demand as the reason for current non-use of the patent. Nearly 19 percent gave as the reason the fact that the development of the art had taken a different course. About 14 percent indicated that competitively the patent was at a disadvantage. Over 12 percent gave rapid obsolescence as the reason for current non-use. Eleven percent replied they did not know the reasons for current non-use. Nearly 10 percent wrote in different reasons for current non-use instead of checking one of the choices given in the questionnaire. Finally, 4 percent indicated neglect to exploit the patent. These written-in replies have not been studied or analyzed as yet. A few inventors gave reasons such as "patent

---

patent application, in 49.0 percent the use began while the patent was still pending, and in only 11.8 percent did the commercial use begin subsequent to the granting of the patent. (See B. S. Sanders, "Speedy Entry of Patented Inventions into Commercial Use," *IDEA*, Vol. 6, No. 1 (Spring 1962), pp. 87-116.)

[32]A large proportion of the patented inventions put to commercial use remain in such use for many years. On the basis of our sample of 1938 patents, about 52 percent of the inventions put to commercial use were still in commercial use even though the patent had expired. (See B. S. Sanders, "Longevity of Patented Inventions Put to Commercial Use," *IDEA*, Vol. 8, No. 3 (Fall 1964), pp. 337-359.)

[33]See questionnaire in Appendix B.

TABLE 13

NUMBER AND PERCENTAGE DISTRIBUTION OF PATENTED
INVENTIONS ACCORDING TO REASON FOR CURRENT NON-USE
OF PATENT, BASED ON INVENTOR REPLIES SEPARATELY
FOR ASSIGNED AND UNASSIGNED PATENTS

Reasons for Current Non-use or Very Little Use	Assigned		Unassigned	
(1)	(2)	(3)	(4)	(5)
Replies to question 32	289	100.0	85	100.0
a. Lack of market demand	72	24.9	16	18.8
b. Rapid obsolescence	36	12.5	2	2.4
c. Competitively at a disadvantage	41	14.2	3	3.5
d. Shortage or lack of venture capital	7	2.4	27	31.7
e. Development of the art has taken a different course	54	18.7	5	5.9
f. Foreign competition	--	--	--	--
g. Supporting arts have not developed sufficiently	7	2.4	2	2.4
h. Patent does not provide sufficient protection	3	1.0	--	--
i. Neglect to exploit it	10	3.5	20	23.5
j. Do not know the reason	31	10.7	4	4.7
k. Other	28	9.7	6	7.1

does not provide sufficient protection," "supporting arts have
not developed sufficiently," and "shortage or lack of venture capital."[34]

In order of their importance, as determined by the relative
frequencies of the replies, the reasons for current non-use are:
(1) lack of market demand; (2) development of the art has taken a
different course; (3) the patent is competitively at a disadvantage;
(4) rapid obsolescence; (5) reason for current non-use unknown;
and (6) other.[35]

The distribution of replies from inventors of unassigned patents regarding the reasons for current non-use of the sampled
patent is distinctly different. For these, the highest frequency,
almost one third, gave shortage or lack of venture capital as the
reason for current non-use. The next largest category, nearly 24
percent, gave neglect to exploit the patent as the reason. Nineteen

---

[34]For a detailed study of causes of current non-use of patented inventions,
see B. S. Sanders, J. Rossman, and L. J. Harris, "The Non-Use of Patented Inventions," *IDEA*, Vol. 2, No. 1 (March 1958), pp. 1-60.

[35]In Question 32 it was deemed possible that there might be more than
one reason why the patent was not in current use. Therefore, respondents were
not instructed to check only one specific reason, but more than one if applicable.
A number have given multiple reasons for current non-use of the sampled patent.
For the sake of simplicity, in this preliminary analysis only one reply has been
used, the first reason listed in the questionnaire. There is no information about
the relative importance if an inventor indicated two or more reasons.

percent gave lack of market demand as the reason. Seven percent stated they did not know the reason. Smaller percentages gave other reasons. It is reasonable to assume that the reasons for non-use would be quite different for assigned and unassigned patents, so there is no justification to combine these two groups.

The assignee replies to the reasons for current non-use of the sampled patent are given in Table 14. Column 3 shows the percentage distribution of all the replies, including those in current use and those who failed to reply to Question 12. Column 4 shows the percentage distribution of those who specifically replied to the question requesting reasons for current non-use of the

TABLE 14

NUMBER AND PERCENTAGE DISTRIBUTION OF PATENTED INVENTIONS ACCORDING TO REASON FOR CURRENT NON-USE OF PATENT, BASED ON ASSIGNEE REPLIES RETURNED

Reasons for Current Non-use or Very Little Use of Sampled Patent	Number	Percent	
		All Replies	Specific Replies
(1)	(2)	(3)	(4)
Total replies	320	100.0	– –
Replies to question 12, assignee questionnaire	202	63.2	100.0
a. Lack of market demand	81	25.3	40.1
b. Rapid obsolescence	18	5.6	8.9
c. Competitively at a disadvantage	51	15.9	25.3
d. Shortage or lack of venture capital	1	.3	.5
e. Foreign competition	––	– –	– –
f. Patent does not provide sufficient protection	1	.3	.5
g. Neglect to exploit it	––	– –	– –
h. Other	50	15.6	24.8
Question does not apply	106	33.1	– –
Unanswered	12	3.8	– –

patent.[36] Two fifths of the assignees gave as the reason for current non-use of the sampled patent, lack of market demand. One fourth gave as the reason that the patent was competitively at a disadvantage; another 25 percent listed reasons other than those specifically given in the questionnaire, using the category "other." These reasons have not been specifically analyzed at this time though they will be eventually.[37] Nearly 9 percent gave "rapid

---

[36]Some assignees also checked more than one reason for non-use, but at this time only the first reason checked has been used.

[37]Two items listed in the inventor questionnaires specifically, "Development of the art has taken a different course" and "Supporting arts have not devel-

obsolescence" as a reason. "Shortage of capital" and "patent does not provide sufficient protection" each had only one assignee respondent.

To determine what insights and meaning these replies might have on questions such as non-use or suppression of patents, more intensive and detailed analysis is needed of these returns in relation to other information regarding the patent, as well as possibly the cross-analysis of inventor and assignee replies with respect to the same patent.

APPENDIX A

PHASES OF THE PILOT STUDY

This study has been conducted in certain phases. The number of patents included in each of these phases and the number of the inventors to whom these patents were issued are shown in Table 15 of this Appendix. The patents studied as to utilization were confined to those inventors who, at the time when the patent was granted, were residents of the United States.

TABLE 15

NUMBER OF PATENTS AND INVENTORS ACCORDING TO ASSIGNMENT STATUS OF SAMPLED PATENTS, BY SUBGROUPS DEVELOPED IN COURSE OF STUDY—LIMITED TO INVENTORS RESIDING IN THE UNITED STATES* WHEN PATENT WAS ISSUED

Category†	Sampled Patents			Inventors of Sampled Patents		
	Combined Number	Assigned Number	Un-assigned Number	Combined Number	Assigned Number	Un-assigned Number
(1)	(2)	(3)	(4)	(5)	(6)	(7)
Total	1,849	1,218	631	2,150	1,460	690
Initial interviews	40	26	14	45	28	17
Prepilot Subsample	178	124	54	211	152	59
October mailing	1,428	936	492	1,663	1,126	537
January mailing	168	112	56	195	133	62
All others‡	35	20	15	36	21	15

*The study of utilization was restricted to inventors residing in the United States.

†The inventor questionnaires were mailed in three groups; the assignee questionnaires were mailed in two groups, one in the spring of 1956 for the prepilot subsample and the balance in December 1956.

‡This category represents deceased inventors and those for whom no address could be found, as well as assignees for whom no address could be found.

---

oped sufficiently," were excluded from the list of specific reasons in the assignee questionnaire. Although this makes the comparison of reasons for current non-use by inventors and assignees a little more difficult, it may provide evidence on how specific the reasons given are if these missing reasons are reflected in the "written-in" answers under "Other." It might be noted that in Table 13 fewer than 10

The first phase of the study consisted of initial interviews conducted with inventors and assignees in greater Washington, D. C.; Maryland; Delaware; and greater Philadelphia. All the inventors who could be contacted cooperated in the study. However, these interviews with inventors and assignees are, at best, suggestive since there were only 40 patents involved in this phase, of which 26 were assigned. Forty-five inventors were involved.

The second phase, the prepilot subsample, consisted of a subsample of 10 percent, taken randomly from the 2-percent sample; limited, of course, to inventors who had not already been interviewed. The purpose of the prepilot phase was to test the mail questionnaires and the mailing procedures before launching the larger study involving some 1,850 patents and more than 2,000 inventors. This 10-percent subsample represented 178 patented inventions and 211 individual inventors. In this phase, one of the aspects explored was the effectiveness of the use of certified mail in comparison to regular mail.[38] Furthermore, this subsample was used to ascertain which avenues are useful in finding current addresses for inventors, and ways of inducing inventors and assignees to respond. The prepilot mailing to inventors was made in the fall of 1955. We are still attempting to maximize the number of returns by using all avenues available to us. Assignees of patents in the prepilot subsample were sent questionnaires in the spring of 1956. Efforts are being continued to maximize these returns.

The addresses used for mailing questionnaires to inventors were the latest available in the Patent Office files of patents granted. In the prepilot phase of this study about 41 percent of the initial mailings were returned by the Post Office because the address obtained was not current. For many of these inventors current addresses were obtained eventually by writing to assignees, if the patent was assigned, and/or to attorneys. Where these means proved unproductive, we resorted to others, such as writing to co-inventors and searching various directories. The same procedures are being followed in subsequent phases of mailing of questionnaires to inventors. Various standard manufacturers' indexes and registers have been used in securing current addresses of assignees. Few difficulties have been encountered, except in cases where the assignee is an individual.

In this report the prepilot subsample is used to indicate the proportion of returns that may be expected from the subsequent mailings to inventors and assignees.

The largest group of questionnaires was sent by certified mail to inventors in October 1956. These questionnaires included over 1,400 patents and nearly 1,700 inventors. Enclosed with the questionnaires was an explanatory covering letter and instructions.[39]

---

percent of the inventors of assigned patents gave reasons under "Other." In Table 14, for assignees, 25 percent wrote in reasons other than those listed in the questionnaire.

[38] In the prepilot mailing questionnaires to inventors of odd numbered patents were sent certified. Questionnaires covering even numbered patents were sent by regular mail. In subsequent phases where questionnaires were sent to inventors for the first time certified mail was used exclusively. In all phases, the first follow-up letter was sent by regular mail. With respect to assignee questionnaires, regular mail was used exclusively.

[39] Two months after the initial mailing, a follow-up letter was sent to those who presumably received the initial mailing but had returned no completed ques-

The last phase of the study consisted of mailing the remaining questionnaires to inventors in January 1957. This mailing included some 168 patents representing 195 different inventors. There was a residue of 35 patents for which the inventor, and in some instances the assignees, could not be identified, or from other sources it was known that the inventor was deceased.

All assignee questionnaires not included in the initial or the prepilot subsample were mailed in December 1956. The number of assigned patents shown in Table 5 is slightly larger than the number shown in Table 15. This results from the fact that communication with the inventors has indicated that the patent had been assigned even though the Patent Office files failed to reveal an assignment as of the spring of 1955. However, it should be noted that the differences between the two are relatively slight.

APPENDIX B

INSTRUCTIONS FOR FILLING OUT THE QUESTIONNAIRE ON THE PATENT UTILIZATION STUDY

(For the Inventor)

All the information supplied by the inventor in this questionnaire will be treated as confidential.

To save the respondent's time, the questionnaire is so designed that the replies can be made by a check mark in most instances. In questions calling for numbers and amounts, where the number or amount is zero enter "0."

Part I. The information in Part I was abstracted from the official records of the U.S. Patent Office. Please check this information for accuracy and completeness and enter necessary corrections or additions.

Part II. Most questions in Part II are self-explanatory.

3. This question is to obtain information on the number of years of full-time or equivalent part-time school attendance. As a rule, a person who has only completed grade school will circle "8"; one who has attended high school for two years should encircle "10" or "11" depending on the highest grade completed. A high school graduate should encircle "12," a college graduate with no further graduate work should encircle "16," and so on for graduate work, depending on the number of full years (or equivalent) of graduate work.

---

tionnaire. This is now being followed by a second follow-up letter urging the return of a completed questionnaire. If this brings no result, then the individual will be considered as a nonrespondent. Recently, attempts have been made, where convenient, to telephone nonresponding inventors. This experience has indicated that in some instances the inventor is deceased even though the letters, including certified letters, were delivered to the address by the Post Office. In other instances the inventors, presumably identified through a telephone directory, turn out to be someone other than the inventor but with the same name. Therefore, some of the nonresponses should have been listed as deceased or without current address rather than nonresponse.

6. Major occupation refers to the occupation in which you have the greatest skill; as a rule it is the occupation which you have pursued the longest. "Sampled invention" or "sampled patent" is your patent indicated on page 1.

10. The position to be recorded here should be the current position with the company. If you are no longer with that company, please record the last position you held with the company.

11. What was the impetus, "trigger," as it were, that gave you the idea for the sampled patent?

13. The answer desired is, as accurately as possible, the lapse of time (in months) between the time when you had the initial idea and the development of this idea to a stage at which a patent application could be filed. For instance, if you conceived the idea in May, 1951, and did enough work on it so that you could have filed for a patent in September, 1951, but you actually did nothing about it until January, 1952, when you filed for a patent—the time interval desired is that between May and September, 1951.

14. This includes laboratory tests, construction of a model and any other concrete means of testing the workability of the machine, process or product. If certain phases were tested but others not, indicate the extent of testing in the space provided for "Other."

16. Include in your replies patents issued to you jointly with other inventors. Patents in force are those for which the 17 years has not elapsed since the date of their issuance. A patent is considered "used commercially" if it is produced for sale. Production, merely to test the workability, or the cost, or the method of production is not to be regarded as "used commercially."

18. The purpose of this question is to see whether most inventors work in a limited field of technology and what these fields are. Therefore, please describe the field as specifically as possible.

19. Include only inventions which you believe could have been patented.

20. "Out-of-pocket" expenses means payments from your own personal funds. (a) Refers to any expenditures in developing the idea; (b) any expenditures to have a search made, prepare the patent application, file for a patent, etc., and pay all the necessary fees to obtain the patent; (c) refers to trying to sell the patented invention (there may have been costs of attempts to sell the idea even before the patent was applied for or granted—if so, these should be included in c, also the initial costs incidental to producing the patent invention for the market).

22. "Assigned to your employer by special agreement" means that there was no standing contract to assign it to your employer at the time the invention was made. "A company" in c, d, or e refers to a firm other than the one in which you are employed or were employed at the time of the invention.

23. Difficulties would include obstacles in seeing the responsible officials of various companies you felt would be interested in your sampled invention, or difficulties encountered in securing needed capital to produce the patented article, process or product yourself, etc.

25. Do not count as income from your sampled patent any promotion which you received from your employer or increase in salary, though the invention was the direct or contributory cause. Income in reply to the question means payment for your sampled patent—such as a monetary award. Sometimes an award is made to the employee at the time of disclosure and a subsequent payment is made if the disclosure is patented; both of these are to be included. Where the employer pays you *pro forma* $1 in consideration of your assigning the patent to him, count it as income, and any other direct income from any sources whatsoever paid to you for the use of the patent or its product. Of course, if you have produced the patented item yourself, then the income which you have had from the sale of it, less the production cost, should be included. If the patent rights were sold outright report the amount received from such sale.

26. This refers to costs incurred in developing special machinery or other preparation necessary to produce and market your invention—not, however, the routine cost of production for the market.

29. Interference means there was at least one other application filed in the Patent Office which duplicated one or more of the claims made by you, so that you were required to submit evidence to show that your invention preceded in time this other invention(s) on file in the Patent Office.

30. Have you or your assignee(s) sued or threatened to sue any individual or corporation for infringing your sampled patent or has anyone sued or threatened to sue you or your assignee(s) or licensee(s) in connection with the use of your sampled patent?

34. Means one or more foreign patents were taken out on the same invention as the sampled patent. The reply to this question should be affirmative whether the foreign patent has expired or lapsed—the question is: was there a foreign patent granted at any time on this invention? If the answers for (b) are different, that is, the invention was patented, let us say, in England by you; in Sweden by an assignee; and in France by a licensee—indicate these by adding sub-numbers after each country (1) to indicate you, (2) the assignee, and (3) a licensee. If the relationships are more involved, explain under "Remarks" at the end of Part II.

Note: If the space provided for any question proves insufficient, use the space provided for "Remarks" at the end of Part II. In all such instances, however, be sure you give the number of the question. If the space allowed for "Remarks" proves insufficient, use additional sheets and attach these to your questionnaire. The space under "Remarks" is otherwise left for you to make any observations explanatory or otherwise that you may wish.

THE PATENT UTILIZATION STUDY

Mailed_____

Order number_____ Sample number_____ Date

Received_____

PART I—Basic information on sampled patent (Derived primarily from the *Official Gazette*)

1. Patent number_____ 2. Number of claims_____

3. Class_____

4. Title_____

5. Name(s) of inventor(s)_____

6. Address_____

7. Application date (earlier priority date if any)_____

8. Date patent granted_____ 9. Date of assignment_____

10. Date of subsequent assignment (from file or other source)_____

11. Name(s) and address(es) of assignee(s). Give names and addresses of *all* assignees and indicate whether all or a part of the interest was assigned

12. Never assigned (check)

QUESTIONNAIRE FOR INVENTOR

Strictly CONFIDENTIAL

PART II—All references to invention or patent in this section are with respect to the sampled patented invention, unless indicated otherwise.

1. When were you born?_____
   (day)   (month)   (year)

2. Give the state or country of your birth_____

3. Encircle the highest grade of schooling completed

   1 2 3 4 5 6 7 8   9 10 11 12_____
       Grade School   High School

13 14 15 16
College

17 18 19 20+
Graduate and
post-graduate
work

4. Did you show early interest in inventions—before age 20? (check)
Yes_____ No_____ Do not recall_____

5. How old were you when you received your first patent?_____

6. What do you consider your major occupation?_____
What was your occupation at the time of your sampled invention?_____
_____

7. What industry have you been in primarily?_____
What industry were you in at the time of your sampled invention?
_____

8. Are you: (check) (a) Self-employed_____ (b) Employee_____
(c) Other (specify)_____

9. At the time when you made your sampled invention were you:
(check) (a) Self-employed_____ (b) Employee_____
(c) Other (specify)_____

10. If you are, or were an employee of a company to which the sampled
patent was assigned, please indicate your official position with such
company
_____
(President, Vice-President, Research Director, etc.)

11. What stimulated or gave rise to your sampled invention? (check one
or more) (a) The demands of your job_____ (b) Financial prob-
lems_____ (c) Studies you were engaged in_____ (d) No known
stimulus_____ (e) Accidental_____ (f) Other (specify)_____
_____

12. Was your sampled invention associated with your: (check one or
more) (a) Business_____ (b) Training_____
(c) Hobbies_____ (d) Other (specify)_____

13. How many months elapsed between the initial conception of the idea
of your sampled invention and your development of it to a stage ready
to apply for a patent?_____

14. Was your sampled invention actually produced (in the laboratory or
otherwise) to test its feasibility? (check) Yes_____ No_____
Other (specify)_____

15. What led you to seek patent protection for your sampled invention?

　　　_____

16. What is the total number of your patented inventions?　(a) All the patents issued to you to date_____　(b) All the patents issued to you that are still in force_____　(c) All the patents issued to you which are assigned_____　(d) All the patents issued to you that were or are being used commercially_____　(e) All the patents issued to you before the sampled patent_____

17. What is the number of your patent applications which are pending? _____ Number of these pending applications that are assigned_____ Number that are not assigned but will be assigned before issue_____

18. Are your patented inventions in a specified field of technology? (check)　(a) One patent only_____　(b) All of them_____ (c) Most of them_____　(d) They are in different fields_____ (e) Other (specify)_____ If your answer is other than (a) please indicate the specific field or fields:

　　　_____

19. Have you made patentable inventions which were not patented? (check)　Yes_____　No_____　If "yes," why were these not patented?_____

20. In developing your sampled invention did you have any out-of-pocket expenses for the following?　(If yes, give the amounts; if no, enter zero)　(a) In developing your idea so as to be able to apply for a patent $_____　(b) In applying and obtaining the patent $_____ (c) In trying to interest others to purchase or use your patent or to develop means for producing and marketing it yourself $_____

21. Are the amounts shown in 20 based on:　(a) Expense accounts_____ (b) Recollection_____　(c) Estimates_____　(d) Other (specify)

　　　_____

22. Is your sampled patent assigned?　(check)　Yes_____　No_____ If "yes"　(a) Was it assigned to your employer by prior agreement to assign_____　(b) Was it assigned to your employer by special agreement_____　(c) Was it assigned to a company through the assistance of an agent_____　(d) Was it assigned to a company through your own negotiation_____　(e) Was it assigned to a company which approached you for purchasing_____　or licensing it_____ (f) Other (specify)_____

23. What, if any, difficulties did you experience in trying to market your sampled invention?

　　　_____

24. Is your sampled patent licensed?: (check) Yes_____ No_____
Do not know_____ If "yes," how many licensees does it have____
____? If "no," were efforts made to license it? Yes_____
No_____ Do not know_____

25. What is the net income from your sampled patent to you (enter the amounts; if none, enter zero)? (a) Realized to date $_____

26.* Do you know the amount that the assignee(s) or licensee(s) had to spend to put your sampled invention or its product on the market? (check) Yes_____ No_____ If "yes," give the amount (including zero) $_____

27.* Do you know the total net amount that the assignee(s) or licensee(s) have realized from the use of your sampled invention? Yes_____ No_____ If "yes," give the amount (including zero) $_____

28.* Are the amounts given in Questions 26 and 27 based on: (check) (a) Belief_____ (b) Records (royalties, etc.)_____ (c) Other (specify)_____

29. Was your sampled patent involved in interference? (check) Yes_____ No_____ If "yes," (a) What out-of-pocket costs did you incur as a result $_____ (b) What costs did the assignee(s) or licensee(s) incur $_____ (c) What was the outcome (describe)_____

30. Has there been any litigation or threat of litigation with respect to your sampled patent? (check) Yes_____ No_____ Do not know_____ If "yes," what was the outcome (describe)_____

31. What, if any, use has been made of your sampled invention? (check) (a) Is the sampled invention presently being used? Yes_____ No_____ Do not know_____ If "yes," check whether slightly _____ moderately_____ extensively_____ (b) If it is not presently being used, was it ever used? Yes_____ No_____ Do not know_____ If "yes," check whether slightly_____ moderately _____ extensively_____ (c) If it has not been used to date, is it expected that it will be used in the near future? Yes_____ No_____ Do not know_____

32. If your sampled invention is not being used in production at this time, or it is being used only slightly, is it because of: (check) (a) Lack of market demand_____ (b) Rapid obsolescence_____ (c) Competitively at a disadvantage_____ (d) Shortage or lack of venture capital_____ (e) Development of the art has taken a different course_____ (f) Foreign competition_____ (g) Supporting arts have not developed sufficiently_____ (h) Patent does not

provide sufficient protection_____ (i) Neglect to exploit it_____
(j) Do not know the reason_____ (k) Other (specify)_____

33 * Do you feel that the assignee(s) or licensee(s) of your sampled patent
have done all that could be done to make the maximum use of your
patent? (check) Yes_____ No_____ Do not know_____
If "no," what do you believe is the reason for their failure to do so?
(describe)_____

34. Is your sampled invention patented in other countries? (check)
Yes_____ No_____ Do not know_____ If "yes," (a) List
all the foreign countries in which it was patented_____

35. In your opinion: (a) Does the present patent system in the United
States encourage invention? (comment)_____
_____ (b) Does it encourage utilization of
patents by industry? (comment)_____
(c) Are inventors sufficiently protected? (comment)_____

36. On the basis of your experience, would you say that large corporations
are receptive to outside inventions, such as inventions by free-lance
inventors? (comment)_____

37. In terms of your own experience have you found the 17-year period:
(check) (a) Too long_____ (b) Just about right_____ (c) Too
short_____ (d) Other (specify)_____ If your an-
swer is other than (b), please indicate what period you consider most
appropriate and why?_____

38. Do you believe that on the average the large corporations have a
stimulating or a retarding influence on: (a) Number of patented
inventions (comment)_____ (b) On the use of
patents in industry (comment)_____

39. What questions would you add to a questionnaire on the utilization of
patented inventions which you deem appropriate, but have been overlooked in this questionnaire? (use additional sheets if necessary)

40. Which questions in this questionnaire do you deem inappropriate or
worthless for one reason or another? (indicate the questions by numbers)_____

Remarks: (use additional sheets if necessary)

Note: For underscored question numbers read the Instructions.
*To be answered only in cases in which the sampled patent is assigned.

INSTRUCTIONS FOR FILLING OUT THE ASSIGNEE QUESTIONNAIRE ON
THE PATENT UTILIZATION STUDY

(For the Assignee)

The first page of the questionnaire provides basic information with respect to the sampled patent, abstracted from the *Official Gazette.* Please check this information and enter any corrections or additions in the space for remarks on this page. If the space is insufficient, please attach extra sheets.

There are 31 questions. A number of these questions will be inapplicable to you. For instance, Question 2, dealing with a purchased patent, will not concern an assignee who did not acquire the patent by purchase. Conversely, the assignee who acquired the sampled patent by purchase will not be concerned with Question 3. There are a number of other questions that are used alternatively so that *any particular assignee has considerably fewer than 31 questions to answer.*

Most questions can be answered by a check mark or a number.

In most questions there is a sub-item "other" in the event your reply does not fit in the specific category provided. If you find it necessary to use "other," please do not check but write out the appropriate answer.

Please base your replies on records where possible. Where records are not available please give your best estimate. Please answer *all* applicable questions.

Question 3. This question seeks to determine the expenditures in connection with the sampled invention from its conception to the time at which a patent application was or could have been filed. It should *exclude* expenditures looking toward the sale, the manufacture, or in general, the commercial use of the invention. Where separate cost records have not been kept, please give your best estimate. Include the actual cost, fees, etc., incidental to obtaining the patent (and foreign patents, if any).

Question 5. This is the period in which the costs reported in Question 3 were incurred.

Question 6. The costs sought in Question 6 are those incurred in addition to the costs reported in Question 3. Such costs should be included whether or not the patent was actually commercially exploited. These are costs looking toward commercial exploitation of the patent whether they were incurred before applying for the patent or afterwards. Please note that all costs incidental to patenting are included in Question 3 and should not be duplicated in Question 6.

Question 7. Please answer regardless of the extent of use.

Questions 10 and 11. Please give actual dates.

Question 26. Net loss means all expenses incurred in inventing, patenting, and/or developing the sampled invention for commercial exploitation, plus actual production costs, less the total income realized to-date from sales, royalties, inventory, etc., derived from the sampled patent. Net gain represents the excess of income from sales, royalties, inventories, etc., above all the expenses incurred in inventing, patenting, and/or developing the sampled invention for commercial exploitation plus actual production costs.

The "expenses incurred in inventing and patenting" is the amount you reported in Question 3. The expenses for "developing the sampled invention for commercial exploitation" is the amount you reported in Question 6.

If accounting figures are not available please give your best estimate.

Question 27. This question is primarily intended to ascertain the current practice in patent cost accounting.

Questions 28 and 29 relate to a phase of the study contemplating an intensive examination of sampled patents involved in litigation or interference.

Questions 30 and 31. If you are an assignee with two or more questionnaires, please record your responses with respect to Questions 30 and 31 on only one of these questionnaires.

Definitions of Words and Phrases Used:

Commercial exploitation, (used commercially): Making or selling the patented invention, or using the patented invention in the production of goods or services, or making financial arrangement(s) with a third party(s) for the production, use, or sale of the patented invention.

Use (used) in production: Making or selling the patented invention, or using the patented invention in the production of goods or services.

Unexpired: This was underlined for emphasis.

Know-how: Factual knowledge not suitable for precise, separate description but which, when used in an accumulated form, after being acquired as the result of trial and error, gives to the one acquiring it an ability to produce something which otherwise he would not have known how to produce with the same accuracy or precision found necessary for commercial success.

THE PATENT UTILIZATION STUDY

Order number_____   Sample number_____   Date_____

PART I—Basic information on the sampled patent (Derived primarily from the *Official Gazette*)

1. Patent number_____   2. Number of claims_____   3. Class____

4. Title_____

5. Name(s) of inventor(s)_____

6. Application date (earlier priority date if any)_____

7. Date patent granted_____   8. Date of assignment_____

9. Name(s) and address(es) of assignee(s). (If more than one assignee, give names and addresses of all, and indicate whether all or a part of the interest was assigned to each)

_____

10. Legal status of the assignee_____
     (Corporation, Partnership, or Individual)

Remarks:

QUESTIONNAIRE FOR ASSIGNEE

All replies will be kept strictly CONFIDENTIAL

PART II—Information concerning the sampled patent

All references to invention or patent are with respect to the sampled patent under consideration unless indicated otherwise.

1. How did you acquire your right(s) in the sampled patent?   (check)
    (a) Purchased_____   (b) Developed by own employe(s) :
    (1) Under contract to assign_____   (2) Not under contract to assign
    _____   (c) Other (specify)_____

2. If purchased, what was the amount paid?   (Give the amount if lump sum payment; otherwise, indicate both the method of payment and the amounts involved)_____

3.* If the invention was produced by your employe(s), give the actual or estimated costs incidental to the conception, research and all other expenditures incurred including the cost of patenting (exclusive of any separate costs for commercial exploitation) $_____

4. If purchased, when was it purchased?   (month and year)_____

5.* How many months elapsed between the initial conception of the idea of the sampled invention and the development of it to a stage ready to apply for a patent?_____

6.* What expense (in addition to those given in Question 2 or 3) did you incur to develop the sampled invention to the stage where it was ready for commercial exploitation (production for sale or use in production)? $_____

7.* Is the sampled patent used in production now?   (check)   Yes_____
    No_____   Other (specify)_____

8. If not used in production now, has it ever been used in production?
    (check) Yes_____   No_____   Other   (specify)_____

9. If it has never been <u>used in production</u>, are there indications that it will be used in the foreseeable future? (check) (a) Definite indication it will be used_____ (b) Some indication it might be used_____ (c) No indication that it will be used_____ (d) Other (specify)

10.* If the sampled invention is or was ever <u>used in production</u>, what is the date when it was first used? (month and year)_____

11.* If the sampled invention was in use but is no longer in use, what is the date when it was last used? (month and year)_____

12. If the sampled invention is not being <u>used now in production</u>, check the reason why it is not being used: (a) Lack of market demand_____ (b) Rapid obsolescence_____ (c) Competitively at a disadvantage_____ (d) Shortage of venture capital_____ (e) Foreign competition_____ (f) Patent does not provide sufficient protection_____ (g) Outright neglect to develop _____ (h) Other (specify)_____

13. If the sampled patent is or was <u>used in production</u>, indicate if it is or was used: (check) (a) Extensively_____ (b) Moderately_____ (c) To a limited extent_____ (d) Other (specify)_____

14. Can the sampled invention be <u>used commercially</u> by itself (with or without expired patents) or must it be used in conjunction with other <u>unexpired</u> patented inventions? (check) (a) Can be used by itself, but that is not the way it is being used_____ (b) Is being used by itself_____ (c) Cannot be used to advantage by itself_____ (d) Would have to be used in conjunction with others_____ (e) Other (specify)_____

15. If the sampled invention is or was <u>used in production</u> in conjunction with one or more other patented inventions, is or was the sampled invention a major or minor item? (check) (a) Major_____ (b) Equally important_____ (c) Minor_____ (d) Other (specify)_____

16. If the sampled patent is or was <u>used in production</u>, is or was the "know-how" an essential element in that production? (check) (a) Yes_____ (b) No_____ (c) Other (specify)_____

17. Did you devote your attention to the development and perfection of the "know-how" because of the patent protection on the sampled invention? (comment)_____

18. Has the sampled invention increased your sales? (check) (a) Markedly_____ (b) Moderately_____ (c) Slightly_____ (d) Not at all_____ (e) Other (specify)_____

19. Has the sampled invention resulted in the reduction of your production costs? (check) (a) Markedly_____ (b) Moderately_____ (c) Slightly_____ (d) Not at all_____ (e) Other (specify)____
_____

20. Describe any other benefits which you have derived or expect to derive from your right(s) in the sampled invention_____
_____

21. Have licenses been issued by you to others for the sampled patent? (a) Yes_____ (b) No_____ If "no," would you be willing to license it? (1) Yes_____ (2) No_____ (3) Other (specify) _____ If "yes," did the license contain provisions relating to: (check) (a) Quantity_____ (b) Territory _____ (c) Price_____ (d) Other (specify)_____
_____

22. If it has been licensed, what were the reasons for licensing it? (comment)_____

23. Would you have manufactured, used, or sold the sampled invention if you did not have the patent protection? (check) (a) Yes_____ (b) No_____ (c) Other (specify)_____

24. What relationship or dealings did you have with the inventor prior to the assignment of the sampled patent? (describe)_____
_____

25. Do you own or are you licensed to use other patents issued to the inventor of the sampled patent? (a) Total number of such patents owned_____ (b) Total number of such patents licensed to you____ (c) Total number of such patents which have not expired_____

26.* What would you estimate as the net loss or gain that you have had to date from the sampled invention? (give the estimated amount) (a) Net loss $_____ (b) Net gain $_____ (c) Other (specify)
_____

27.* Is the amount in 26: (a) a recorded figure_____ (b) an informed guess_____ (c) Other (specify)_____

28.* Was the sampled patent involved in interference? (check) No_____ Yes_____ If "yes," what was the outcome? (indicate)_____

29.* Has the sampled patent been involved in litigation? (check) No_____ Yes_____ If "yes," what was the outcome? (indicate)_____

30.* What questions would you add to a questionnaire on the utilization of patented inventions which you deem appropriate, but which have been overlooked in this questionnaire? (use additional sheets if necessary)_____

31.* Which questions in this questionnaire do you deem inappropriate or worthless for one reason or other? (indicate the questions by numbers)_____

Remarks:

_____

Note: For definition of words or phrases underlined see instructions.
*Asterisked question numbers are explained in the instructions.

PART III

GOVERNMENT POLICY

Now we come to the government's role in industrial-property policy. The extraordinary rate of growth of government-financed R&D since World War II (outlays, including R&D facilities, are about $18 billion for 1969) suggests a need for a broader view of the patent implications stemming from such financial support. A great deal of attention has been directed in the literature to government patent policy, particularly the relative merits of the license and title policies—and rightly so, since so many people are directly concerned with these policies. Much consideration has also been given to the effect of government-subsidized R&D on higher education and to the dangers of the concentrated nature of awards to industry. Negligible attention, however, has been devoted to the implications for our expanding economy of an increasing governmental focus on control, as demonstrated, for example, in the decisions relating to trade practice. Unfair-competition policy, which is designed to establish the rules of competition, and antitrust and tax policy are ways—though sometimes very subtle—in which the government influences transactions in industrial property. Indeed, legislation and its court interpretation relating to patent misuse and antitrust violation dominate the nature of restrictive provisions included in industrial-property licensing agreements.

The paper "An Economic Analysis of Government Ownership of Patented Inventions" directs attention to the R&D activities of government, providing empirical information on the number of government-owned patents and the commercial use of the inventions they cover. The second paper presents the history of unfair competition law and shows how the freedom of the individual is protected by the authority exercised by government over competition, keeping it fair. This paper traces unfair competition from 1410 in the *Schoolmaster's* case through *Keeble* v. *Hickeringill* (1706) and the *prima facie* tort cases, the passing-off doctrine of the common law, broadened to include misappropriation in the *INS* and associated cases, and concludes with a plea for "judicial mapping of the metes and bounds of the unwritten law of unfair competition." The third paper examines certain patent arrangements that have been attacked as patent misuse or antitrust violation. It offers constructive views with respect to advancement of both the public and private long-term interest.

153

The parking meter industry report, a pioneering study, covers the effects of the compulsory licensing decree rendered against Vehicular Parking, Ltd., a patent holding corporation, and substantially all of the prewar members of the parking meter industry. Although the decree apparently eliminated price-fixing agreements in the industry, the report indicates that its effects "have been very mild"; the decree helped very little in opening the industry to new companies. The research method utilized by the author was developed by him in a study of the concrete-block-making-machine industry, and further elaborated in his study of professional color motion picture antitrust decrees. This method could be employed in other cases to measure the technological and economic effects of antitrust decrees in which patents are a major factor.

The three papers on taxation place in perspective the effects of tax law on industrial property rights. The dearth of analytical and empirical material on taxation and industrial property in the literature makes these three papers especially important for patent practitioners.

An Economic Analysis of Government Ownership of Patented Inventions

MARY A. HOLMAN

INTRODUCTION

The federal government currently (June 30, 1961) owns about 12,000 patented inventions, acquired mainly from its vast R&D program. The nature and extent of the utilization of these government-owned patented inventions are points at issue in public debates about government patent policy. The controversy is over the disposition of patent rights originating from government-financed R&D work.

Objective of the Study

The primary goal of this study is to determine the nature and extent of the commercial utilization of government-owned patented inventions and the causes for nonutilization. The study is undertaken to test empirically the validity of the hypotheses developed by advocates of the title policy—that government ownership of patents promotes the greatest possible commercial use of inventions arising from federally financed R&D, and that government ownership of patents prevents dangers created by patent monopolies. For comparative purposes, and also because the matter has been neglected almost completely, attention is given to the utilization of government-owned patented inventions by the government itself.

Exaggerated Views

In an effort to effectuate a change in government patent policy, combatants in the struggle to achieve a government-wide title policy or a government-wide license policy have tended to distort, by overemphasis, the importance of the utilization of patented inventions originating from government-financed R&D. In addition, the matter is entangled in legal, political, and economic issues on the role that properly should be assumed by the government in this country.

EDITOR'S NOTE: At the end of this paper (which appeared in *IDEA*, Vol. 7, Nos. 2 and 3, Summer and Fall 1963), the author has added a section on research which corroborates the findings of this study.

Although the government is now the largest single owner of patented inventions, government-owned patents constitute only 2 percent of all unexpired U.S. patents. These government-owned patents are a single aspect of the entire patent system, which, in turn, is but one of many factors contributing to economic growth. Similarly, the patent system is only one element that can cause monopolization and economic concentration. Neither should the utilization of government-owned patented inventions be expected to play a significant role in the process of economic growth, nor should any exclusive use of these inventions be expected to contribute greatly to difficulties associated with monopoly and increased economic concentration. This does not mean that widespread use of government-owned patented inventions is unimportant. On the contrary, all the results of public R&D should be used as extensively as is feasible and economic. It does mean that any favorable effects of innovation on economic growth, or unfavorable effects on competition, will be far less than is claimed by the defenders of the license policy and of the title policy.

THE ECONOMICS OF GOVERNMENT-OWNED PATENTED INVENTIONS

To put it as briefly as possible, the economics of the patent system rests on the advance of technology by means of granting exclusive or monopoly rights. Advances in science and technology can stimulate economic growth. On the other hand, the exclusive use of patented inventions can preclude widespread diffusion of the technology and can hinder the maintenance of competition. The economy derives social benefits from economic growth, whereas social costs can be incurred when monopoly power increases. The philosophy underlying the patent system, of course, is that social benefits gained from advances in science and technology outweigh the social costs of exclusive rights.

Government ownership of patented inventions strikes the heart of the patent system. With relatively insignificant exceptions, it is and has been the policy of the government not to permit exclusive use of the patented inventions it owns. The government usually grants revocable, nonexclusive, royalty-free licenses upon request. Does government ownership of patents promote the most widespread commercial use because the inventions are freely available to all? Or instead, does government ownership of patents mean that some inventions holding commercial potential will not be developed because patent protection is absent?

Economists' Views of the Patent System

For centuries economists have been debating the relative merits of the patent system. The issues have been disentangled, but they have not been settled. In general treatises, the classical economists of the late 18th and 19th centuries expressed incidental opinions accepting patent protection as a stimulant or reward for the inventor-producer. The one well-known dissenter was the French economist, Simonde de Sismondi.[1] Spurred by a controversy in the third quarter of the 19th century as to whether European patent systems should be abolished, economists gave more direct attention to exclusive rights to patents as an incentive. The more important arguments evolving during that period are basically the same as those used today—patents are a stimulus for disclosure of new technology, for invention, and for innovation.[2]

Disclosure of New Technology

The patent is granted to the inventor in exchange for complete disclosure of the new technology embodied in his invention. In the absence of a patent system, the information disclosed would be a free good, which producers could use at will. To the extent that information is disclosed, social benefits exceed private profits. If information were not forthcoming, potential social benefit would be foregone. When patents are granted in exchange for incomplete or faulty disclosures, private profits exceed social benefits. It is alleged that such is a common occurrence today. It has been said that writing patent applications so as to obtain the maximum protection and the minimum disclosure is one of the arts in the patent profession.[3] Statistics on the rising number of patents that have been declared invalid by the courts are cited to give partial empirical support to this contention. In addition, it is argued that society actually secures no benefit because only those inventions that cannot be kept secret are patented.

Patents as an Incentive for Invention

As a result of the change in the organization of research, an

---

[1]Fritz Machlup, *An Economic Review of the Patent System*, Study No. 15 of the Subcommittee on Patents, Trademarks, and Copyrights of the Senate Committee on the Judiciary (Washington, D. C.: G.P.O., 1958). pp. 19-20.

[2]Fritz Machlup and Edith Penrose, "The Patent Controversy in the Nineteenth Century," *Journal of Economic History*, 10 (May 1950), pp. 11-20.

[3]Seymour Melman, *The Impact of the Patent System on Research*, Study No. 11 of the Subcommittee on Patents, Trademarks, and Copyrights of the Senate Committee on the Judiciary (Washington, D. C.: G.P.O., 1958), pp. 46-47.

appraisal of the effect of the patent system on incentives requires a distinction between kinds of inventors. The major division is between individual inventors and the captive or hired ones. The latter group can be further divided into inventors employed by private business, nonprofit organizations, and the government. Ideally, economic and statistical tools should provide a means of measuring the elasticity of the supply of inventive efforts for each of these groups to changes in the amount of patent protection.

Using historical patent statistics, several authorities on the patent system indicate that the elasticity of supply of inventive activity appears to be low. The soaring increase in R&D expenditures and the number of scientists hired are not reflected by corresponding increases in the number of patents issued. Other researchers contend that patent statistics are a poor means of measuring inventive activity for several reasons: (1) the average input per patentable invention has increased; (2) standards of patentability change over time; (3) the reliance on secrecy as opposed to patents changes; and (4) a substantial amount of the research has been basic in nature and undertaken by the government.

Development and Utilization of Inventions

The introduction of new products and the use of new processes have at least three stages—development of new scientific knowledge, application of basic research, and commercial exploitation. Exploitation or innovation proceed from invention and the development of new knowledge. Defenders of the patent system contend that even if exclusive rights do not operate as an incentive to encourage the disclosure of new technology or to stimulate invention, temporary monopoly rights are necessary to promote the utilization of inventions. The exclusive rights compensate for future uncertainties or uninsurable risks.

The patent grant puts into operation forces that have social benefits and social costs. In the short-run, exclusive rights give producers an incentive to innovate, but the monopolistic position retards competitive imitation and diffusion of the new technology embodied in the invention. Society benefits from the introduction of new products and processes. If the innovation would have materialized in new products effectively marketed in the absence of the patent system, society incurs a social cost because immediate adoption by other producers is precluded by the monopoly rights given to the owner of the patent.

However, with dynamic competition in the long-run, society can gain from a proliferation of new innovations because of the monopoly rights. In Schumpeterian terminology, this is the "process of creative destruction." Anticipation of short-run monopoly profits tends to promote competition in the long-run because of the compulsion among competitors to keep ahead of rivals by developing superior substitute products or cost-reducing processes. The patent system can facilitate dynamic competition by disclosing advances in new technology to the public. The system operates to widen the production frontier. The resulting enlarged stock of new and useful technical knowledge creates greater opportunities for competitive ventures.

The social costs of exclusivity depend upon whether or not the research and competitive innovation result in superior processes and products, and whether such research and innovation would have been undertaken in the absence of the patent system. A net social loss is thought to be suffered when exclusive rights are carried beyond that contemplated by the patent grant. Such alleged abuses of the patent system include: prolonged monopoly, unwarranted suppression of patents, and cartel arrangements. These actions, however, are illegal and subject to antitrust laws. The patent system can operate to increase economic concentration by strengthening monopolistic positions and by creating opportunities for illegal collusive action. It can function, however, in the opposite direction and increase competition. The patent grant can shelter the market position of a firm entering a concentrated industry.

The tools of economic analysis have not yet been developed to the required degree of precision or level of sophistication to permit a quantitative measurement of these social costs and benefits.[4] Only recently have economists and statisticians undertaken case studies of individual industries to determine the role played by patents as an incentive for investment in innovation.[5] Except for spotty data from antitrust cases, virtually no empirical infor-

---

[4]Possibilities for determining the net economic value of the patent system recently have been considered by well-known economists in the fields of public policy and economic growth. Agreement exists that economics can provide only the most shadowy answers to questions about the net social benefit of the patent system. Economics, however, is helpful in understanding the direction of relative changes in social benefits and social costs which might result from changes in the patent system. See Jesse W. Markham, James S. Worley, Dwight S. Brothers, "The Value of the American Patent System: An Inquiry into Possible Approaches to its Measurement," *IDEA*, Vol. 1, No. 1 (June 1957), pp. 20-56; Fritz Machlup, *An Economic Review of the Patent System, op. cit.*, pp. 56-80; and Alfred E. Kahn, *op. cit.*, pp. 318-336.

[5]The studies reveal that patents have made a contribution to the incentive to innovate. However, the findings are not universally applicable to all investment decisions or all patented inventions. No theory of patent-induced innovation can

mation is available on the nature and extent to which patented inventions are used for purposes other than actual commercialization, i.e., used for blocking competitors or control of markets.

Government-Owned Patents and Disclosure, Invention, and Innovation

The patent system as an incentive for the disclosure of new technology and invention affects the number and cost of inventions arising from government-sponsored research and development. Exclusivity to stimulate innovation affects the utilization of government-owned patented inventions.

Assuming that the patent grant operates as an incentive for the disclosure of new technology, secrecy can be detrimental to the effectiveness of public research in enlarging the base of technical knowledge. For example, if contractors were not permitted to retain titles to inventions, they might be reluctant to disclose technical findings not specifically defined by the terms of contracts. The tendency would be strongest for new technology that appeared to hold commercial potential.

Another crucial matter for government-sponsored research is whether or not patent rights function as an incentive to increase the inventive efforts of government employees; to induce contractors to employ their most productive scientists on government research projects; and to encourage the most efficient business concerns to accept government contracts. The cost of government research, and the cost of maintaining a given level of national security, would increase if these incentive effects were adverse. Advocates of a license policy contend that such is the case.

The current administrative policy of the government to make the patents in its portfolio available on a nonexclusive basis, in effect, assumes either that patent-induced innovation is not important for the commercialization of these inventions, or that social costs that arise from exclusive use exceed the social benefits that would accompany an increase in the rate of commercial use. These assumptions are not justifiable on a priori grounds. If anything, the reverse is more probable. Without examination, it is likely that inventions arising from military research will require more development effort before commercial utilization is possible than those growing out of industrial research. In addition, since ownership of the inventions rests with the government, control can be

be derived from these studies. For a summary of the case studies, see Alfred E. Kahn, *op. cit.*, pp. 319-321; and Jesse W. Markham, James S. Worley, and Dwight S. Brothers, *op. cit.*, pp. 44-46.

exercised to avoid monopolistic abuse. The current administrative policy also assumes that the administrative problems of providing for exclusive rights on some politically acceptable basis are too great.

Economic Growth

Rapid and widespread utilization of inventions is one of the significant forces in the process of economic development. A substantial part of our economic growth has been achieved through the general results of the research and development process: new products and new processes. Simply conceived, economic growth is a per capita increase in real goods, services, and leisure. Economic growth depends upon: (1) a quantitative increase in the factors of production, generated mainly by capital formation; and (2) a qualitative improvement in the utilization of a given amount of resources, propelled principally by technological change.

Capital Formation

Although more attention has been focused on the role of innovation on capital improvement, it also vitally affects capital formation. The introduction of new consumer products and new and more efficient capital goods has a strong impact on aggregate investment spending.

Product innovation can be viewed either as having a catalytic action on consumption expenditures or as having been induced by the desire of consumers to have a greater flow of goods. In the first instance, the annual proliferation of new and improved consumer goods stimulates the desires of consumers and brings about an increase in spending. In the second, consumer spending plays an active role, rather than the traditionally conceived passive one, in the process of economic growth. The insatiable desires of consumers spur businesses to introduce new or improved products and to increase output. In either case, the usual net result is an expansion in plant and equipment, greater output, capital formation, and a higher level of real income.

New Technology

The second prime mover for economic growth is a change in the quality of inputs used in the production process. Increases in per capita income have resulted from major shifts in the production function, or a more efficient arrangement of inputs because of technological change. These changes in the production function have materialized in part from a continuous flow of process innovations. Increased productivity from a given amount of factors of production arises from changes in the quality of one or more inputs, as well as from economies of scale. Technological change relates only to productivity gains derived from improvements in the quality of capital.

Innovation

Economic growth, which originates from inventions, is not realized unless producing units actually commercialize inventions. Although innovational investment shades into replacement investment, it can be distinguished from it. Replacement investment is investment in new capital equipment for proved processes and products. It can be considered as the routine aspect of investment; the reproduction of capital equipment that already exists. Innovational investment pertains to the use of new and unproved processes and products. Some innovational investment takes place in the replacement process because new models of standard equipment usually embody some technological improvements. Also, some product innovations are minor and require little or no modification of equipment.

Innovation can be induced or autonomous. Producers can be forced, by competitive market pressures and falling profits, to employ cost-reducing processes and to introduce product improvements to stay in business; or they can assiduously seek new techniques and new markets to reap the profits of innovation. When survival of the firm depends on innovation, patent protection probably plays a less significant part in the decision to invest than when entrepreneurs actively pursue possibilities for innovation.

As an integral part of the process for competitive survival, much product-oriented research, invention, and innovation are believed not to be directly affected by patent protection. Since the 18th and 19th centuries, there has been a change in the direction of applied industrial research. In an earlier era, invention and innovation were concentrated on developing more efficient means of producing relatively well-known products, whereas today the most substantial portion of industrial research is devoted to product improvement or to the development of new products. The introduction of new products, or at least quality variation, now is thought to be a variable in the competitive process as important as changes in prices and quantities offered for sale. Because of the contest to keep abreast or ahead of rivals for survival, it is possible that product innovation would continue at a rapid rate in the absence of a patent system.

If the innovation is required for survival, the primary executive decision probably is whether or not to continue to reinvest capital in the firm. The gamut of alternative investment opportunities is wide for firms actively seeking innovational investment opportunities. Noninnovational investment possibilities probably are even larger. Innovational projects can include: development of trade secrets, unpatented inventions, patented inventions owned by the firm, patented inventions developed by independent inventors or competitors and available by purchase or by license, and government-owned patented inventions.

Executive decision-makers probably make at least rough calculations on the expected yield of the contemplated innovational investment compared with the productivity of other investment outlets. Allowances, even if little more than guesses, are made for uncertainty concealed by the future. Patent protection can reduce the risks associated with immediate imitation by competitors. Other human and physical risks, however, exist. A few of these risks include: reaction of competitors, or creative destruction in the Schumpeterian sense, which can bring about premature obsolescence; products might not be accepted by consumers or manufacturers; innovations might be launched too close to business recessions; or essential raw materials might be excessively scarce and costly.

To some extent, the value of the patent system as an incentive for innovational investment depends on personal and subjective judgments. Executive decisions are not made in a vacuum. They reflect personal opinions concerning institutional surroundings. They also mirror innate tendencies toward pessimism, optimism, or conservatism possessed by the decision maker. The benefits that can be derived from patent protection, in any given situation, probably would vary from firm to firm.

Government-Owned Patents and Economic Growth

Some unknown proportion of the new products and new processes contributing to the economic growth of this country are covered by patents. A small number of these are patented inventions owned by the government. Although the great majority of all government-owned patents are military-oriented, about 10 percent were developed by civilian departments to satisfy commercial needs. Of the civilian departments, only the Tennessee Valley Authority avowedly attempts to develop inventions to the point where they can be used commercially without further development effort. With the exception of inventions administered by that agency, there is no self-evident reason to believe that government-owned patented inventions originating from research designed to improve civilian technology require less engineering or financial development before commercialization is possible than those developed by private industry for similar purposes. In addition, it is doubtful that many products and processes covered under government-owned patents and originating from defense research activities are important for the induced innovation process and competitive survival. As an incentive for the commercial utilization of all but a few government-owned patented inventions, patent protection is probably at least as necessary for government-owned patented inventions as it is for privately owned and developed patented inventions.

The utilization of inventions by the government also contributes to increases in real income through capital formation and the use of new technology. The government produces social goods to satisfy social wants—primarily national defense. Between 1946 and 1961, government procurement of goods and services for national defense rose from 5 percent to 10 percent of the gross national product. Because the profit motive is absent in government, patent protection is not necessary for government investment in innovation. Patent rights are necessary, however, to protect the government against costly infringement suits. The government can be protected in its procurement activities by actual ownership of patented inventions or by licenses to use inventions.

Government-Owned Patents and Monopoly

Advocates of a title policy contend that government ownership of patents is necessary to maintain free access to technology developed at government expense and to prevent further economic concentration. Inseparably interrelated with the prevention of monopoly is avoidance of any adverse effect that might occur when the public is left at the mercy of a single firm owning a revolutionary new invention originating from government-financed research. Although patented inventions usually are small components of complete products and processes, it is conceivable that a revolutionary new invention might embody all the necessary technology for something as important as weather control or a cure for cancer.

The problem of monopoly and economic concentration arising from market imperfections is compounded, so advocates of the title policy argue, when titles to patented inventions are retained by contractors. Most of the dollar volume of R&D contracts is awarded to the largest firms and it is possible that a license policy would increase industrial concentration. The monopoly aspect of the patent grant also is a potential tool for abuse of the competitive system. Extension of monopolistic practices beyond those intended by the patent system, however, collides with the antitrust laws, the principal means for maintaining competition. Patent law does not specifically exempt patent matters from antitrust legislation, nor does antitrust law release patents from its authority. Consequently, patent monopolies are subject to antitrust regulation.

There are four major abuses of the patent system in attempts to monopolize. First, patent owners have limited the ways in which licensees can utilize patented inventions. The courts have upheld price and quantity restrictions imposed by an individual licensor upon an individual licensee, but they have invalidated industry-wide price-fixing, for example. Tying clauses controlling supplementary products by means of license agreements are also unreasonable under the law. Secondly, competitors have used patent pools as a basis for collusion. Thirdly, patentees have attempted to monopolize by blocking competitors from manufacturing or from selling in a market by holding exclusive rights to almost all complementary and competing patents in a particular field of technology. Finally, patent owners have suppressed patents. They do not use some inventions which hold commercial potential, nor do they license other business firms to use them.

With a few minor exceptions, there is no monopoly element in the utilization of government-owned patented inventions originating from the patent grant. These inventions are freely available to all. A change in administrative policy, providing for exclusive use, however, would put the utilization of these patented inventions in a position similar to that of privately owned patents in relation to the antitrust laws.

ACQUISITION OF PATENTS BY GOVERNMENT

Nearly all of the patented inventions owned by the government arise from work of government employees and contractors. The government does, however, acquire a few patented inventions by means of purchase, donation, and international treaty.

Argument Against the Acquisition of Employees' Inventions

Defenders of the license policy argue that if the government permits its employees to retain titles to patented inventions originating from their work, better qualified scientific and technical personnel would be induced to enter into government service. This is important, they contend, because of the inability of the government to match salaries offered by industry. This argument is valid only if patent rights act as an incentive and if other compensations offered by the federal government are insufficient to attract qualified scientific personnel into federal service.

Arguments Against a Title Policy for Contractor Inventions

In addition to the contention that government ownership of patented inventions retards commercial utilization, advocates of a license policy hold that retention of patent rights by contractors promotes efficiency in procurement. If the value of patent rights is a significant factor for contractors, then acquisition of title can provide an incentive for superior research and development work. It can also act as an inducement to the more efficient private enterprises to accept government research and development contracts. Greater efficiency can result in either: (1) more, and presumably better, research and development with the same utilization of resources; or (2) the same amount of research activity using fewer factors of production.

Arguments for a Title Policy for Contractor Inventions

Advocates of title policy also have arguments to supplement those on economic growth and prevention of monopoly against retention of patent rights by contractors. They hold that economic injustice occurs when the public is forced to make a double payment for a patented invention. This can happen when titles to the patented inventions remain in private hands. The public initially pays for the research and development from which the inventions originate. Then there is a second payment in the form of monopolistic prices when the public buys the finished product. This, to be certain, assumes that the patented inventions are developed and commercialized.

There are three counter arguments to this: First, that contractors pay for a substantial part of the costs of developing inventions in the form of existing experience, knowledge, and skill. Secondly, that the public pays for and receives the full benefit of research and development work specified in contracts. Public payment is not for the inventions but for the research and development work. Finally, if there is a double payment, such a payment is analogous to subsidies to farmers, the merchant marine, and other interest groups.

Proponents of the title policy also contend that if the government retains patent rights, it can recover all or part of its research and development expenditures through royalty-bearing licenses. The recovery of these expenditures is deemed to be equitable because it shifts the burden of paying for research and development from the general taxpayer to the purchasers of the final products who benefit from the inventions.

METHOD

To estimate the nature and extent of commercial and government use it is necessary to conduct an analytical and empirical study. An investigation based on a complete census, or the entire universe of all government-owned patents, is impractical. In addition, a scientific study of government-owned patents does not require a complete census. Sampled observations can be employed to infer facts about the entire population of government-owned patents.

To obtain factual information about the utilization of government-owned patented inventions, three distinct groups of individuals and business firms were sent questionnaires or letters: (1) inventors of government-owned patented inventions; (2) individuals and firms licensed to use government-owned patents; and (3) individuals and firms requesting information about government-owned patents from the Small Business Administration.

Count of Patents and Licenses

Before it was possible to take a random sample from the universe of all government-owned patents and one from the number of licensed patents, it was necessary to have an accurate count of the patent portfolio of the government, as well as the number of patents on which licenses have been issued. When this study began in the fall of 1961, no precise figure on the number of government-owned patents was available from government sources. In the spring of 1962, the Office of Technical Services in the Department of Commerce began to maintain a current index of all unexpired government-owned patents.[6] Table 1 shows the number of government-owned patents recorded in the Assignment Branch. The total number, 11,674, is the universe from which the random sample of patents was taken for the purposes of requesting information from inventors.

---

[6]Since the mid-1960's the Federal Council for Science and Technology has maintained current information about government-owned patents.

Table 1
U.S. GOVERNMENT-OWNED PATENTS
(Assignment Branch of the U.S. Patent Office)
By Agency, 1944-1961

Year	Department of Agriculture	Atomic Energy Commission	Department of Commerce	Department of Interior	Tennessee Valley Authority	Department of Army	Department of Air Force	Department of Navy	Other Agencies	Total
1944 [a]	33	—	10	3	4	10	—	5	2	67
1945	47	1	2	6	5	21	—	3	2	87
1946	52	6	3	7	1	51	—	30	—	150
1947	41	18	3	9	1	60	—	25	—	157
1948	100	35	6	11	1	161	1	57	2	374
1949	80	65	7	16	6	223	1	96	4	498
1950	94	151	15	20	6	217	10	121	3	637
1951	90	167	5	26	7	188	14	167	11	675
1952	87	149	7	42	7	217	14	182	7	712
1953	61	124	8	18	6	258	28	166	9	678
1954	44	142	5	13	1	166	40	212	1	624
1955	59	150	13	16	2	174	34	250	3	701
1956	76	267	24	12	6	185	60	309	—	939
1957	71	257	15	7	2	231	61	332	4	980
1958	53	307	23	4	3	305	94	401	3	1,193
1959	98	511	24	11	2	253	153	373	9	1,434
1960	64	197	21	7	6	287	137	447	4	1,170
1961 [a]	42	143	3	3	3	133	50	215	6	598
Total	1,192	2,690	194	231	69	3,140	697	3,391	70 [b]	11,674
Percent	10.2	23.0	1.7	2.0	0.6	26.9	6.0	29.0	0.6	100.0

[a] 1944 includes only July through December. 1961 includes only January through June.
[b] Includes the patent holdings of the following agencies: Department of Health, Education, and Welfare, 31; Department of Justice, 10; National Aeronautics and Space Administration, 7; Office of Civil Defense, 1; Federal Aviation Agency, 1; Civil Production Administration, 1; Federal Communications Commission, 1; Federal Power Commission, 1; Federal Works Agency, 3; Department of Treasury and Internal Revenue Service, 4; Veterans Administration, 1; General Services Administration, 1; and Reconstruction Finance Corporation, 2.
Source: Card Index of Patents Maintained by the Assignment Branch of the U.S. Patent Office. Compiled in October, 1961.

Table 2 shows the number of government-assigned patents on which licenses have been issued. It should be noted that the number of licenses issued is considerably larger than the number of patents on which licenses have been issued. More than one license has been granted on some patents.

TABLE 2
GOVERNMENT-OWNED PATENTS ON WHICH LICENSES
HAVE BEEN ISSUED[a]
By Agency
July 1, 1944—June 30, 1961

	Number	Percent of Total
Department of Agriculture	263	17.7
Atomic Energy Commission[b]	949	63.8
Department of Defense	193	13.0
All Other Agencies[c]	82	5.5
Total	1,487	100.0

[a] Includes only those patents issued between July 1, 1944, and June 30, 1961, on which licenses had been granted between July 1, 1944, and June 30, 1961.
[b] This does not include over 100 patents administered by the Atomic Energy Commission on which the sole license issued was to a foreign government.
[c] Includes the following: Department of Commerce, 30; Department of Interior, 24; Tennessee Valley Authority, 24; and Department of Health, Education, and Welfare, 4.
Source: Information supplied by the various government agencies and departments administering government-owned patents.

THE SURVEYS

The 271 patented inventions, randomly sampled from all government-owned patents, were developed by 387 individuals. In February 1962, questionnaires were sent to those inventors for whom a current address was available. A follow-up letter was sent to inventors who had not responded by April 1962. By September 15, 1962, the cutoff date, completed returns had been received for 180 different sampled patents—or 66 percent of the 271 patents in the random sample. The rate of response was considerably higher in terms of the number of sampled patents for which at least one inventor was located—75 percent.

A letter requesting information on the commercial use of government-owned patented inventions was sent to firms licensed to use the patents in February 1962. The follow-up letter sent to nonresponding firms was mailed in June 1962. An informal letter, rather than a questionnaire, was sent in the belief that firms are more willing to reply to a letter than to a questionnaire. At least one reply was received for 55 percent of the sampled patents.

THE COMMERCIAL USE OF GOVERNMENT-OWNED PATENTED INVENTIONS

The commercial use of government-owned patented inventions has much to do with the kinds of inventions in the patent portfolio of the government. What proportion of government-owned patents holds little commercial potential because of the nature of the products or processes covered under the patents? A second question is this: What amount of further engineering or financial development is necessary before commercialization is possible?

The Patent Portfolio of the Government

There can be a close relationship between the kinds of inventions owned by the government and the amount of further development required for use. This relationship can be visualized as a spectrum. At one extreme are inventions holding no potential commercial use; further development is not relevant for these inventions. They have military application only. Such inventions might include bomb ejector mechanisms or radio jamming systems. A short quotation from a reply received by an inventor in the Department of Defense when queried about the commercial potential of his invention illustrates the point: ". . . is not applicable to commercial use until mercenary armies become popular again." At the other extreme are inventions that are ready for commercialization without development. These inventions might include devices for the modification of fibers or the production of foods. Between these extremes are those inventions requiring various degrees of further development—extensive, moderate, or slight. To be sure, the kind of invention can affect the amount of development required for commercial use. Some military-oriented devices have commercial application after extensive engineering and financial development. Other inventions developed for military purposes, however, have immediate commercial application. Some inventions developed for industrial use need extensive development to bridge the gap between success in a laboratory and actual commercial exploitation.

Kinds of Inventions Owned by Government

Table 3 shows a classification of government-owned patents issued between January 1, 1955, and December 31, 1961. Except for minor adaptations, the title of the classes are the official titles. The format of the *Index of Patents*, published by the U. S. Patent Office, does not readily permit a classification of patents issued

TABLE 3

CLASSIFICATION OF PATENTS ISSUED BETWEEN 1955 AND 1960,
GOVERNMENT-OWNED AND ALL PATENTS

Title of Classification	Class Number	Government-Owned Patents		All Patents [a]		Government-Owned as a Percentage of all Patents
		No.	Percent	No.	Percent	
Radiant Energy	250	695	10.8	5,072	1.9	13.7
Inorganic Chemical Procedures	23	525	8.2	3,263	1.2	16.1
Chemistry, Electrical and Wave Energy	204	318	5.0	2,087	0.8	15.2
Ammunition and Explosive Devices	102	285	4.4	947	0.4	30.1
Ordnance	89	270	4.2	708	0.3	38.1
Communications, Radiant Energy	343	264	4.1	1,703	0.6	15.5
Chemistry, Carbon Compounds	260	255	4.0	1,252	0.5	20.4
Measuring and Testing Devices	73	177	2.8	2,942	1.1	6.0
Electricity, Measuring and Testing	324	167	2.6	1,976	0.7	8.5
Communications, Electrical	340	143	2.2	2,939	1.1	4.9
Repair and Manufacture of Electrical Lamp and Discharge Devices	315	143	2.2	2,699	1.0	5.3
Wave Transmission Lines and Networks	333	139	2.1	1,248	0.5	11.1
Metallurgy, Production of a Metal or an Alloy	75	122	1.9	1,887	0.7	6.5
Power Plants and Motors	60	113	1.8	2,438	0.9	4.6
Electric Lamp and Discharge Devices	313	105	1.6	1,995	0.7	5.3
Foods and Beverages	99	99	1.5	2,627	1.0	3.8
Electrical Circuit Makers and Breakers	200	89	1.4	4,952	1.8	1.8
Aeronautics	244	88	1.4	1,453	0.5	6.1
Machine Elements and Mechanisms	74	84	1.3	4,888	1.8	1.7
Optical Instruments	88	84	1.3	2,222	0.8	3.8
Telephony	179	83	1.3	3,331	1.2	2.5
Registers	235	81	1.3	1,884	0.7	4.3
Coating, Processes and Miscellaneous Products	117	78	1.2	2,589	1.0	3.0
Manufacture of Articles from Metal	29	66	1.0	2,755	1.0	2.4
Electricity, Motive Power Systems	318	64	1.0	1,533	0.6	4.2
Total Above		4,537	70.7	61,390	22.9	7.4
Total Issued		6,417	100.0	268,428	100.0	2.4
Percent Classified		70.7		22.9		

[a] Includes government-owned patents.
Source: U.S. Patent Office, Assignment Branch, and U.S., Patent Office. *Index of Patents* (Washington, D.C.: G.P.O., 1955 through 1960).

before 1955. Over 55 percent of the patents included in this study, however, can be classified by kind of invention. The 25 classes shown in the table are ranked in order of the number of patents issued. The table gives a comparison of the number and percent of government-owned patents in a particular class and the number and percent of all U.S. patents in the same class. Government-owned patents are also shown as a percentage of all patents issued.

The defense orientation of government-sponsored research and development is reflected in the kinds of inventions assigned to the government. The first five ·classes include about one-third of all government-owned patents, but only 5 percent of all U. S. patents issued. These five classes include patents covering technology on radiant energy, inorganic chemical procedures, electrical and wave energy chemistry, ammunition and explosive devices, and ordnance. Government-owned patents constitute a significantly greater proportion of all U.S. patents in these and the next two highest ranking classes than the proportion in other classes. Government-owned patents comprise between 14 percent and 39 percent of all patents in these classes. In contrast, government-owned patents are about 2 percent of all unexpired patents.

Amount of Development Work

Patent protection to induce innovational investment is less important when inventions are completely developed. This does not mean that all risks are eliminated and that patent protection has no incentive effect. Risks, such as those associated with advertising and marketing of the product, still exist. Inventors were asked to state whether their inventions required further development for commercialization. As Table 4 shows, inventors supplied information on 154 sampled patents.

About half of all government-owned patented inventions require further development for commercial use. With the excep-

TABLE 4
SAMPLED PATENTED INVENTIONS REQUIRING FURTHER
DEVELOPMENT FOR COMMERCIALIZATION

Agency or Department	Total No.	Yes No.	Percent	No No.	Percent
Department of Agriculture	19	9	47.4	10	52.6
Atomic Energy Commission	38	16	42.1	22	57.9
Department of Defense	87	41	47.1	46	52.9
Other Agencies	10	8	80.0	2	20.0
TOTAL	154	74	48.1	80	51.9

tion of the combined group, "other agencies," very little difference exists in the amount of development required on inventions administered by the military departments and the civilian. It is not unexpected that the "other agency" category has proportionately more completely developed inventions. The avowed R&D policy of the Tennessee Valley Authority is to develop inventions to the point where industry can profitably employ them. The proportion of patented inventions administered by the Department of Agriculture that requires no development for use is only slightly lower than that for inventions held by the Atomic Energy Commission and the Department of Defense. The R&D mission of the Department of Agriculture is to improve technology in the agricultural sector of the economy. Generally, commercialization of the results of the research is the primary end. This evidence gives some support to the contention that an exclusive licensing policy for some Department of Agriculture patents is necessary to encourage private firms to invest in the development of inventions. As previously indicated, officials in that Department advocate an exclusive licensing policy.

Commercial Use Reported by Inventors

Information supplied by inventors shows that the rate of commercial use of government-owned patented inventions is between 10 percent and 15 percent.

Commercial Use of Sampled Patented Inventions

Table 5 presents data on the commercialization of 158 sampled patented inventions owned by the government. Of these, inventors report that 23, or 15 percent, have been commercialized. The level of use does not differ significantly among the agencies

TABLE 5
COMMERCIAL USE OF SAMPLED PATENTED INVENTIONS
REPORTED BY INVENTORS

Agency or Department	Total No.	Used		Not Used	
		No.	Percent	No.	Percent
Department of Agriculture	20	3	15.0	17	85.0
Atomic Energy Commission	38	6	15.8	32	84.2
Department of Defense	90	12	13.3	78	86.7
Other Agencies	10	2	20.0	8	80.0
TOTAL	158	23	14.6	135	85.4

administering the inventions. The estimated rate of use reported for inventions administered by the Department of Agriculture is

15 percent, for the Atomic Energy Commission the rate is 16 percent, and 13 percent for the Department of Defense. There is a
somewhat higher rate of commercialization on inventions administered by all of the other agencies—20 percent.

No attempt was made to elicit information from inventors
about the commercial value of utilized patented inventions. There
is little reason to believe that inventors are able to provide information on the effect of use of the sampled patented inventions on
the sales or costs of firms using the inventions. However, information was obtained on the extent of commercial use. Of the 23
commercialized patented inventions, 8 have been used extensively,
7 moderately, and 6 only slightly. No information was supplied
for two inventions.

There are two checks to test the accuracy of the reported
incidence of commercial use. The first comes from multiple responses on the same sampled patented invention. The other is an
estimate of the level of commercial use of all government-owned
patented inventions developed by the inventors. Almost without
exception, when more than one inventor supplied information on
the same sampled patent, the inventors agreed that the invention
was or was not used. When one inventor could not supply information about the commercial use of the invention, his partner did
have such information. Inventors were asked to indicate the number of *all* of their U. S. patents assigned to the government and
also to give the number of those inventions that have been commercialized. The 206 responding inventors have assigned title to
1,216 patents to the government. Of these, 116, or slightly less
than 10 percent, have been commercialized. Even though the check
provides but a rough estimate of the commercial use of government-owned patented inventions, the discrepancy between the
estimates is slight—10 percent of *all* of the inventors' government-
assigned patents as compared with 15 percent of the *sampled* patents. By agency the rates of commercial use for the 1,216 patents
are: the Department of Agriculture (11 percent), the Atomic
Energy Commission (17 percent), and the Department of Defense
(10 percent).

Extent of Further Development

Of the 23 sampled patented inventions reported commercialized, only one required extensive development before commercialization was feasible. Another needed moderate development.
Eleven of the inventions required slight additional development,
and 10 were completely developed by the government before use.

None of the commercialized inventions administered by the Department of Defense or the Department of Agriculture required more than a slight amount of development for commercial use. Caution should be exercised in accepting the precision of these estimates because they are qualitative in nature based only on the considered judgment of the inventor.

One question asked inventors was designed to elicit additional information about the relationship between commercial use of government-owned patented inventions and the amount of further development work required for that use. Inventors employed by industry were asked whether they or their employers had ever undertaken any further engineering or development efforts for the commercialization of any government-owned patented invention. They were also asked to indicate whether these development efforts resulted in the commercialization of the invention, and whether a patent was issued on the improvements.

Among the 147 inventors who had industrial employment experience, 22 knew of instances when commercialization materialized because of further development work. Five inventors cited instances when development work was undertaken, but commercial use did not result. Patents were issued on 12 of the 27 improved inventions. From the hundreds of government-assigned patents about which inventors must have first-hand knowledge, it is surprising that only 12 actual examples of improvement patents were cited.

Inventions Held Under Secrecy Orders

For reasons of military security, some government-owned patents are held under secrecy orders for years. When any patent application is held under a secrecy order, information about the invention cannot be made public. Although the U.S. Patent Office keeps all patent applications secret until the application is allowed, officials in government agencies can disseminate information about these inventions before patents are issued. Also, inventions that are to be assigned to the government can be, and are, licensed and used before patents are issued. Such procedures are not permitted for applications held under secrecy orders. Some government patent attorneys believe that inventions held under secrecy orders lose commercial potential because they become obsolete.

From the data, it is difficult to discern any strong effect of secrecy orders on the rate of commercial use. In fact, the average time lag is slightly higher for commercialized patents than for all sampled patents—58 months compared with 56 months. This information, coupled with the fact that rapid obsolescence is not one of the more important reasons cited for nonuse of inventions, indicates that obsolescence arising from reasons of national security probably is not great.

Reasons for Non-Use of Government-Owned Patents

An appraisal of the effect of government ownership of patented inventions on economic growth must consider reasons for non-use of inventions as carefully as the extent of actual commercialization. Some patented inventions originating from government-sponsored R&D hold little commercial potential. It does not matter whether the government or private individuals hold titles to them.

Overwhelmingly, inventors cited the same two reasons for nondevelopment of these inventions for commercial use as those given by contractors when they retained title to inventions arising from government-sponsored research—the invention is for government use only (27 percent) and there is insufficient market demand (27 percent). See Table 6. Insufficient market demand is also an important reason given by private firms for not commercializing patented inventions that are developed from private funds.

No invention administered by the Department of Agriculture was reported to have government application only. This reason, however, is the most important cause for nondevelopment of Atomic Energy Commission and Department of Defense patents. To check on the precision of replies, as well as to gain additional insight on the kinds of government-owned patents that hold little commercial potential, inventions that inventors stated are for government use only were classified. About one-fourth of the patents cover technology on ordnance, ammunition, and explosive devices. Over half of these inventions can be put into the five most important classification groups for all government-owned patents.

Seventeen inventors believed that their patented inventions would have been commercialized if the government had not held title to the patent. About three-fourths of these inventions required a moderate or a slight amount of development work for commercialization. Only one needed extensive development.

Commercial Use Reported By Licensees

Licensees were questioned about their use of government-owned patented inventions primarily to determine the extent to which the number of outstanding licenses reflects the rate of com-

TABLE 6

REASONS FOR NON-USE OF GOVERNMENT-OWNED PATENTED INVENTIONS REPORTED BY INVENTORS

Reasons for Nonuse	Total		Department of Agriculture		Atomic Energy Commission		Department of Defense		Other Agencies	
	No.	Percent	No.	Percent	No.	Percent	No.	Percent	No.	Percent
Rapid obsolescence	21	10.3	1	3.8	9	17.6	10	8.4	1	14.3
Insufficient time	5	2.5	1	3.8	2	3.9	2	1.7	0	--
For government use only	54	26.6	0	--	14	27.5	39	32.8	1	14.3
Insufficient market demand	54	26.6	10	38.5	11	21.6	31	26.1	2	28.6
Government holds title to patent	17	8.4	2	7.7	7	13.7	6	5.0	2	28.6
Insufficient venture capital	1	.5	0	--	1	2.0	0	--	0	--
Outside product line	15	7.4	1	3.8	1	2.0	12	10.1	1	14.3
Insufficient competitive advantage	21	10.3	8	30.8	5	9.8	8	6.7	0	--
Neglect to develop invention	11	5.4	2	7.7	1	2.0	8	6.7	0	--
Other	4	2.0	1	3.8	0	--	3	2.5	0	--
TOTAL	203	100.0	26	100.0	51	100.0	119	100.0	7	100.0

mercial use. The rate of licensing sometimes is considered synonymous with actual commercialization. Firms licensed to use government-owned patents reported that 19 percent of the inventions have been used commercially—25 out of 129 sampled patents. See Table 7.

Information supplied by licensed firms supports the belief that the rate of commercialization of patented inventions originating from R&D conducted by the Department of Agriculture is not substantially different from the rate of use for patented inventions administered by the Department of Defense. As a matter of fact the rate of use reported on Department of Agriculture patents is slightly lower than that on Department of Defense patents—27 percent compared with 32 percent.

TABLE 7

COMMERCIAL USE OF SAMPLED PATENTED
INVENTIONS REPORTED BY LICENSEES

Agency or Department	Total No.	Used		Not Used	
		No.	Percent	No.	Percent
Department of Agriculture	22	6	27.3	16	72.7
Atomic Energy Commission	80	11	13.7	69	86.3
Department of Defense	19	6	31.6	13	68.4
Other Agencies	8	2	25.0	6	75.0
TOTAL	129	25	19.4	104	80.6

The rate of commercial use for all government-owned patented inventions cannot be determined from the rate of use for licensed government-owned patented inventions. Considering only the proportion of firms actually commercializing licensed government-owned patented inventions, and neglecting for the moment the possibility of use without a license, the rate of use for all government-owned patents is slightly less than 3 percent. About 20 percent of the licensed sampled patented inventions were reported to have been used commercially. Twenty percent of all the 1,487 government-owned patents on which licenses have been issued amounts to 297 patents. These 297 commercialized licensed patents are slightly less than 3 percent of the 11,674 patented inventions in the portfolio of the government. By agency, the extent of commercialization derived by this method is 6 percent for the Department of Agriculture, 5 percent for the Atomic Energy Commission, 1 percent for the Department of Defense, and 4 percent for all other agencies.

Extent of Further Development

By chance, in no instance did both a licensee and an inventor report commercial use on the same invention. Licensees as a group, however, indicated a slightly larger amount of development work was required for the commercial use of sampled patented inventions than that estimated by inventors. Fourteen licensees undertook further development work to commercialize the sampled inventions. Of these, five inventions required an extensive amount of development, five moderate, and four slight. Six inventions needed no further development for commercialization. Many licensees wrote that the know-how of the firm was the most important element in the commercialization of the invention. Only two licensees stated that know-how was not essential.

Commercial Value of Utilized Inventions

Licensees revealed very little information about the commercial value of inventions. This probably resulted from difficulty of allocating benefits of increased sales or reduced costs to that portion of the final product contributed directly by the patented invention. Approximately one-third of the responding firms did not make reference to the commercial value of the inventions. Use of the patented inventions, however, results in an increase in sales more frequently than a reduction in costs. Licensees did not quantitatively estimate the value of greater sales or lower costs. Other studies on the utilization of inventions also indicate that inventions result in increased sales more frequently than reduced costs.

Reasons for Non-Use of Government-Owned Patents

One of the most curious findings of this study is the large number of firms that denied being a licensee, or were not able to find evidence of a license agreement in their records. Table 8 shows that 10 percent of the responding firms stated they are not licensed to use the sampled invention. Lack of knowledge or information about being a licensee might have resulted from one or a combination of factors. The employee making the arrangement for the license might no longer be with the firm. Files and records of the organizations, or perhaps those of the government agencies, might be in error or incomplete. Or, it might have been the result of indifference toward government-owned patents because they are available on a royalty-free basis and available to all. Licensees frequently expressed such indifference.

Licensees most frequently cited the five following reasons

TABLE 8

REASONS FOR NON-USE OF GOVERNMENT-OWNED PATENTED
INVENTIONS REPORTED BY LICENSEES

Reasons for Nonuse	Total		Department of Agriculture		Atomic Energy Commission		Department of Defense		Other Agencies	
	No.	Percent	No.	Percent	No.	Percent	No.	Percent	No.	Percent
Not a licensee	14	9.5	2	6.9	10	10.4	1	6.7	1	12.5
Rapid obsolescence	2	1.4	–	–	2	2.0	–	–	–	–
For government use only	17	11.5	6	20.7	17	17.7	–	–	–	–
Insufficient market demand	14	9.5	3	10.3	5	5.2	2	13.3	1	12.5
Government holds title to patent	16	10.8	2	6.9	11	11.5	1	6.7	1	12.5
Insufficient venture capital	3	2.0	1	3.4	1	1.0	–	–	–	–
Outside product line	20	13.5	3	10.3	18	18.8	1	6.7	–	–
Insufficient competitive advantage	9	6.1	–	–	6	6.3	–	–	–	–
Neglect to develop invention	1	.7	–	–	1	1.0	–	–	3	37.5
Too much sales or development effort	21	14.2	5	17.2	10	10.4	3	20.0	2	25.0
Substitutes available	20	13.5	5	17.2	10	10.4	3	20.0	–	–
Did not meet specifications	8	5.4	2	6.9	4	4.2	2	13.3	–	–
Academic interest only	2	1.4	–	–	1	1.0	1	6.7	–	–
Other	1	.7	–	–	–	–	1	6.7	–	–
TOTAL	148	100.0	29	100.0	96	100.0	15	100.0	8	100.0

for nonuse of the sampled patented inventions: (1) too much sales or development effort is required; (2) the product is outside the usual market line of the firm; (3) comparable or better substitutes are readily available; (4) the product is for government use only; and (5) the market position of the final product is in doubt because the government holds title to the patent.

Use Without Licenses by Small Businesses

To obtain information on the use of government-owned patented inventions without licenses by small businesses, a very short questionnaire was sent to individuals and firms requesting information about these patents from the Small Business Administration. The method used for selecting these firms was arbitrary because there is no clearly defined universe from which to take a random sample. Files of the Small Business Administration contained letters dating from December 1960. The first 100 letters, written between December 1960 and March 1961, were selected and the individuals and firms writing these letters were sent questionnaires. Letters with the earliest dates were chosen because it was necessary that a sufficient amount of time had elapsed to permit commercialization or a decision against use. The 100 individuals and firms had requested information about 88 different patented inventions. Questionnaires were sent in June 1962.

Respondents supplied information about the commercial utilization of 51 of the 88 different patents. Only two firms reported commercialization of an invention, and the same invention is used by both firms. The patented invention is in the patent portfolio of the Department of Agriculture. The patent covers the production of food. Neither concern is licensed by the Department of Agriculture to use the patented invention. Both firms indicated that the end product covered by the patent has an established market. The end product is also within the usual product line of the firm. An official of one firm said that the invention required only a slight amount of financial and engineering development for commercialization. A representative of the other said the required development work was extensive.

GOVERNMENT USE OF ITS OWN PATENTED INVENTIONS

In 1961, the federal government spent approximately $50 billion on goods and services for the national defense—about 10 percent of the $520 billion gross national product. Some of the final goods purchased by the government embodied patented inventions owned by the government. The use of government-owned patented inventions by the government itself is one facet of utilization that has received virtually no attention.

Definition of Government Use of Patented Inventions

For every patented invention it owns, the federal government holds licenses to about two more. The government uses many of the inventions it owns, as well as those it is licensed to use. This analysis is limited to government-owned patented inventions.

For this discussion, government utilization of patented inventions is defined to mean the use of patented items and processes in the production of goods and services for the satisfaction of defense and civilian requirements. Government use includes the utilization of government-owned patented inventions in: (1) production in government installations; (2) research and development in government laboratories; (3) production of final products for the government by private contractors; and (4) research and development activity for the government by private contractors. This definition excludes uses of patented inventions for purposes of control. The government exercises control when it uses patented inventions for such purposes as earning income from royalties and issuing licenses which contain terms and conditions appropriate for the particular desired end.

Government Production of Goods and Services

In the private sector of the economy, R&D activities and the utilization of inventions that arise therefrom are spurred by the profit motive. Such, of course, is not the case for the federal government. Two forces propel the government to undertake research and development work: (1) military and defense requirements; and (2) meritorious or vital civilian needs. If left alone, the price and resource allocating mechanism of the private market system would not supply, or would supply in insufficient amounts, the goods and services that satisfy these needs.

National Defense Requirements

Goods and services for the national defense must be provided by the government because they must be consumed collectively or not at all. It is neither possible to divide national defense into units that directly benefit individuals, nor is it possible to sell units of national defense on the market. Because most of the R&D undertaken by the government is designed solely to increase the effectiveness of our national defense, about 85 percent of all government-owned patented inventions are for purposes of national security. If these inventions also hold commercial potential, the economy derives additional benefits.

Civilian Requirements

About 15 percent of the patents in the portfolio of the government originate from R&D work undertaken to advance specific technologies—agriculture, mineral resources, saline water, and chemical fertilizers. Also, the Atomic Energy Commission holds some inventions that were developed to foster civilian uses of atomic energy. The nondefense needs are technological advances with civilian applications. The government develops more efficient processes and technologically superior goods for civilian use, because private producers do not find it sufficiently profitable to engage in the necessary amount of R&D work. If only the private sector of the economy provided new technology, the advances would not be sufficient because the financial gains to producers are less than the benefits to society as a whole.

The government can use some of its civil-oriented patented inventions. For example, new devices and techniques might be developed by the government for use in its flood control projects; its programs for conservation and improvement of soil and mineral resources; its activities for peaceful uses of atomic energy; or its postal operations. However, the main objective of most civil-oriented research and development work financed by the government is commercial utilization of the results by private firms. Unlike commercial use of military inventions, commercialization of civilian inventions owned by the government does not yield additional benefits to the economy. For example, government-owned patents covering inventions on new food products are designed to be used by private firms and sold on commercial markets. An ultimate objective of the research is to increase the demand for farm products and to raise incomes in the agricultural sector of the economy. Commercial use of other inventions developed by civilian agencies is designed to increase productivity.

The Reported Rate of Use

To obtain specific and factual data about the use of government-owned patented inventions by the government, inventors were asked whether the sampled inventions have been used by the government. In addition, they were requested to provide information on how, when, and where the inventions were used by the government. Before the questionnaires were sent, it was fully

recognized that inventors might encounter difficulties in responding to the questions because of security restraints.

Of the 271 sampled patents, information on government use
was supplied for 148, or 55 percent of the total. Similar information on commercial use was provided for a slightly larger proportion of the sampled patents. The author believes that the lower
rate of response about government use results from a reluctance on
the part of inventors to disclose possibly security-classified material.
The percentage of employee-inventors answering this question is
somewhat lower than that for contractor-inventors.

As Table 9 shows, inventors reported government use on 94
of the 148 sampled patented inventions, or about 63 percent. A
rate of government use of government-owned patented inventions
as high as 60 percent is not out of line with estimates of commercial
utilization of about 55 percent to 65 percent on privately developed
and owned patented inventions.

TABLE 9

GOVERNMENT USE OF GOVERNMENT-OWNED
PATENTED INVENTIONS

Agency or Department	Total Reply No.	Used		Not Used	
		No.	Percent	No.	Percent
Department of Agriculture	20	0	0	20	100.0
Atomic Energy Commission	40	30	75.0	10	25.0
Department of Defense	78	58	74.4	20	25.6
Other Agencies	10	6	60.0	4	40.0
TOTAL	148	94	63.1	54	36.9

The rate of government use of inventions administered by the
Atomic Energy Commission is about the same as that of the Department of Defense—75 percent and 74 percent, respectively.
The R&D mission of the Department of Defense is to provide new
and more effective equipment and techniques for the national
defense. Use of these new technological advances for national
security is a governmental function. Although the Atomic Energy
Commission has an R&D mission encompassing both civilian and
military needs, the latter certainly is the more important.

The government did not use any sampled patented inventions administered by the Department of Agriculture. It is not surprising that there was no government use of these patented inventions. The research work of the Department of Agriculture is
undertaken mainly to increase agricultural productivity and the
demand for farm products through commercial utilization of the

results by private firms. With the exception of one invention, government use of patented inventions administered by "Other Agencies" also was for national security or civil defense. No government use was reported for Tennessee Valley Authority patented inventions. These inventions also arise from research designed to increase productivity through commercial use of the results by private businesses. One invention, developed by the Bureau of Mines, Department of the Interior, was used by the government to satisfy a nondefense need. Although the inventor did not provide adequate information about that use, the government probably used the invention for soil and mineral conservation purposes.

The majority of patented inventions used by the government, about 65 percent, are components of final or end products. Approximately 35 percent of the inventions cover processes. Unfortunately, more precise information on how the government uses its patented inventions cannot be ascertained from the replies received from inventors. The responding inventors were scrupulous not to disclose information that might have a bearing on national defense. The following are typical examples of the replies: "in moderate use," "in certain instrumentation," "for atomic energy," "sorry," "AEC plant," and "in military equipment."

CONCLUSIONS

Government ownership of patents is new and is becoming increasingly important. The patent portfolio of the government is now large and it is growing. The government is the largest single owner of patents in the United States. It is probable that the patent portfolio of the government will continue to expand, and that the policy issues surrounding government ownership of patents will become more important. The number of patents owned by the government can easily double during the next decade. Federal expenditures and obligations for R&D continue to increase substantially. The National Aeronautics and Space Administration, a title policy agency, is growing in importance.

Most patented inventions are privately developed and owned, and most inventions must be exploited by private enterprise. In the United States, there is a political and economic predisposition against the government's conducting commercial activities. With the exceptions of electric power and lending programs, the commercial activities undertaken by the government can usually be explained by national defense requirements. Furthermore, the patent system is an institution, under the patent law, designed to encourage invention and innovation by private individuals and organizations. The patent system was established and is maintained under the auspices of the federal government. Despite assertions to the contrary, it is not self-evident that the government will undertake risks associated with the development and commercialization of the patented inventions it owns.

If government-owned patented inventions are to be exploited commercially, this must be done by private industry. Under the title policy, these inventions are freely available to all. This policy implicitly assumes either: (1) that patent protection is not necessary to stimulate innovation; or (2) that the social costs that can be incurred from the monopoly exceed the social benefits that can be derived from innovation. Except for a few patented inventions administered by the Tennessee Valley Authority which are completely developed, there is no factual evidence indicating that patent protection is less important as an incentive for the development and exploitation of government-owned patented inventions than it is for those developed and owned by private firms and individuals.

The patent portfolio of the government, however, differs from any other collection of patents. Most government-owned patented inventions originate from research undertaken by the Department of Defense and the Atomic Energy Commission. The research and the resulting inventions are designed to increase the effectiveness of the national defense. Many of the patents owned by the government cover technology on radiant energy, ordnance, ammunition, and explosive devices. There is, however, a substantial block of patented inventions, administered by the Department of Agriculture, that are intended for commercial use. These patents cover technology on carbon compounds, foods and beverages, bleaching and dyeing processes, and fermentation.

The government itself does use a large proportion of the patented inventions it develops for military requirements. The rate of government use of its own patented inventions is at least as high as 60 percent. Because of national security restrictions, some government use of its own inventions is enshrouded in mystery. Government use of new technology contributes to economic growth in a manner similar to that of commercial use—formation of new capital and more efficient use of a given amount of resources from technological change. However, the impact of government use of new technology on economic growth should not be exaggerated. Government purchases of goods for the national defense comprise about one-tenth of the gross national product.

In contrast with government use, the rate of commercial use of government-owned patented inventions is low—between 10 percent and 15 percent. Nonexclusive rights, arising from government ownership and a policy on the part of the government to grant only revocable, nonexclusive, royalty-free licenses are not the main reason for noncommercialization. The low rate of commercial use results from more advantageous alternative investment opportunites. Many of these inventions have only government applications. For others, there is either an insufficient commercial market demand for the final product, or substitutes for the inventions are readily available. Because of the kinds of inventions owned by the government, they hold little commercial potential. Other studies show that privately owned patented inventions originating from government-sponsored research also have slight possibilities for commercial use.

The specific R&D projects from which most government-owned patented inventions originate do not have the dual goal of providing for military and commercial requirements. Any commercial benefits the economy derives from military-oriented patented inventions can be considered as additional social benefits to the economy.

Proposed methods for widening the commercial use of government-owned patented inventions frequently include the establishment of a central administrative agency. Because the possibilities of increasing the commercial use of government-owned patented inventions are slight, the desirability of establishing a central agency is not great. The principal responsibilities of a central agency would be to transmit information about patents to the private sector of the economy and to make arrangements for licensing these patented inventions. Government agencies sponsoring the R&D from which the inventions arise would be unwilling and unable to relinquish complete responsibility for all administrative chores. Undoubtedly, there would be some unavoidable and unnecessary duplication of facilities and activities. Duplication would be particularly prevalent for agencies such as the Department of Agriculture, the Atomic Energy Commission, and the Tennessee Valley Authority. These agencies have had close working arrangements with industry for years.

Conceivably, a central administrative agency could also sponsor development work on government-owned patented inventions to compensate for risks associated with the lack of patent protection. As indicated, in the United States, the government does not usually undertake commercial activity. In addition, it is doubtful whether a development program would be self-supporting. Even without an invention development program, the possibility of recovering substantial R&D expenditures made by the government through a system of royalty payments is remote. In fact, it is possible that income from royalties might not be sufficient to cover administrative expenses. The Tennessee Valley Authority discontinued its policy of charging royalties because the receipts were small and the administrative burdens great. The British National Research Development Corporation incurs a loss on 84 percent of the patents it acquires.

Provision for exclusive use of government-owned patented inventions would probably increase the rate of utilization. Some advocates of the title policy, particularly officials of the Department of Agriculture, contend that exclusivity should be granted for inventions that require extensive further development work. On the average, the amount of further development required for commercialization of utilized inventions is less than that for all inventions in the patent portfolio of the government. Of the inventions reported to have been commercialized, well over half needed no or only a slight amount of additional development. Many licensees said that they did not commercialize government-owned patented inventions because too much development or sales effort is required.

The possibility of raising the rate of commercial use by providing for exclusive use, however, is not great. It is estimated that no more than an additional 10 percent of the patented inventions owned by the government would be used commercially. Although a detailed outline of the administrative arrangements providing for exclusive use is beyond the scope of this paper, it is suggested by the author that sale of licenses by a system of competitive bids conforms to the competitive principles of our economy. In addition, competitive bidding schemes are widely used by the government in procurement and surplus disposal activities.

Because government-owned patented inventions hold slight commercial potential, and because the commercial value of these inventions is small, the possibilities for monopolistic abuse are also slight. If, however, the sale of an exclusive license on a patented invention would create a clear and present danger of monopoly, the government could grant nonexclusive licenses or none at all. In addition, the government has the legal authority to control the use of revolutionary inventions, such as a means to modify weather or a cure for cancer. Governmental authority to control inventions that vitally affect public health, safety, and welfare also extends to privately developed and owned patented inventions.

The title policy may adversely affect incentives. The attitudes and opinions of inventors and licensees reflect a strong sentiment against the ownership of patents by the government. These negative attitudes toward government ownership of patents might adversely affect the incentives of government employees to invent, the incentives of government contractors to disclose new technology that holds commercial potential, and the incentives of government contractors to employ their most productive scientists and engineers on government research contracts.

The policy of the government's taking title to patented inventions arising from federally financed research, and making these inventions freely available to all, does have a slightly adverse effect on commercialization. Some patented inventions probably would be developed more rapidly and additional inventions commercialized, if business firms were given exclusive rights to the inventions. The title policy, however, can be modified to permit greater commercialization of government-owned patented inventions. Provision for exclusivity can be made by the sale of licenses.

The contribution of government-owned patented inventions to economic growth is slight. The rate of commercial use is low, and the inventions that are used do not have much commercial value. The rate of government use is high, but government purchases of goods for the national defense constitutes only 10 percent of our gross national product. If most of the R&D sponsored by the government continues to be directed toward defense requirements, there is little reason to believe that patented inventions arising from government research will have a greater impact on economic growth than those currently owned by the government.

Recent Research—

Since the initial publication of this study, additional research has been conducted by the author and others. The results of these studies confirm and strengthen the principal findings about the use of patented inventions resulting from government-financed R&D.

One source of additional information about the use of government R&D inventions comes from a study of the patent policies of the National Aeronautics and Space Administration undertaken by Donald S. Watson and me during 1966.[7] The other source comes from a two-year (1966-1968) study on various facets of gov-

---

[7]Donald S. Watson and Mary A. Holman, *An Evaluation of the Patent Policies of the National Aeronautics and Space Administration*, Report of the Committee on Science and Astronautics, U. S. House of Representatives, 89th Cong., 2nd Sess. (Washington, D. C.: G. P. O., 1966).

ernment patent policy conducted by Harbridge House, Inc., Boston, Mass.[8]

In 1961, the research and development sponsored by the National Aeronautics and Space Administration was too recent in origin to have had an impact on the patent portfolio of the federal government. This, of course, resulted from the existence of time lags between the inception of R&D and any ensuing patented inventions. Recent investigations show that the utilization of inventions resulting from research sponsored by the Space Agency follows the same pattern as that for other federal departments—the rate of commercial use is low and the measurable commercial value of the inventions is small.[9]

The Space Act of 1958 provides (Section 305[a]) that titles to inventions made under NASA contracts shall go to the United States. However, the Act permits the Administrator to waive part of the rights of the government if he determines that such action will serve the interests of the United States. At the end of 1965, NASA owned 268 issued patents and 512 inventions on which patent applications had been filed. On the same date, NASA had granted waivers to 181 individual inventions. Of those inventions owned by NASA, the agency had granted 107 nonexclusive licenses on 46 different inventions and one exclusive license.

Information about the commercial use of NASA-owned inventions comes from responses to a questionnaire sent out to each firm granted a license and to each inventor of a NASA-owned patented invention. The questionnaires were sent out in February 1966. At least one reply was received for 91 percent of all licensed inventions and for 73 percent of all patented inventions. By mid-1966, five inventions licensed by NASA were in actual commercial use; four of them were used by the companies where they originated. Firms anticipated the commercial use of five additional licensed inventions. No inventor reported that commercial use of his NASA-owned patented invention had materialized by mid-1966. As in the case of inventions administered by other government agencies,

---

[8]The results of the research undertaken by Harbridge House have not yet been published. A mimeographed report was submitted to the Federal Council for Science and Technology in May 1968.

[9]Here brief comment is made on only one of several aspects of the public interest served by NASA's patent policies. In line with my earlier study, it is the utilization of NASA's inventions. The report prepared for NASA analyzed the matters of the disclosure of inventions, the transfer of technology, the best contractors, the protection in procurement, the protection of health and welfare, and the avoidance of economic concentration and monopoly, as well as that of the invention utilization.

the main reasons for the lack of commercial use were: insufficient market demand, government applications only, and the availabilities of superior substitutes.

Replies to another questionnaire sent to companies holding waivers to NASA inventions found that of the 181 waived inventions about 11 percent were in actual commercial use. The value of these inventions was low. At the end of December 1965, the combined expenditure on development of inventions by the companies holding waivers exceeded income from sales attributed to the waived inventions. The major obstacles to commercialization of waived inventions were: availabilities of superior substitutes, expected market failed to materialize, and excessively high development costs.

Again, like inventions ensuing from research sponsored by other federal agencies, the rate of government use of NASA's inventions is high. The combined replies of inventors show that two-thirds of NASA-owned patented inventions are used by the government. Companies holding waivers to inventions reported approximately the same rate of government use. A high rate of government use is to be expected because one of the main reasons that the government seeks patent rights is for protection in the procurement process.

The results of the research conducted by Harbridge House show the rate of commercial use for all government R&D inventions is 12.5 percent. The survey of that research group included patented inventions that issued in 1957 and in 1962. For these government-financed patented inventions, the rates of use did not vary much by funding agency. Not only was the financial return from commercialization small, but most of that return was derived from a few inventions. The main reasons for lack of commercial use were, again, insufficient market demand and sole applicablility of the inventions to government requirements.

The Judicial Process in Unfair Competition Law

S. CHESTERFIELD OPPENHEIM

The PTC Research Institute was established to explore through research and the empirical method the ramifications of legal systems for the protection of industrial and cultural creations. It is interesting to recall that among the names suggested for this undertaking was The Intellectual Property Foundation—a designation which would embrace all products of the mind the law might secure against unfair appropriation. This breadth of potential coverage is in fact recognized by the Institute's Declaration of Trust which covers systems cognate to those pertaining to patents, trademarks, and copyright.

It therefore seems fitting on this occasion to place in perspective, and thereby perhaps bring into focus, some fundamental aspects of the private law of unfair competition as it evolved at common law and in courts of equity. Unfair competition is one area of law that is either pendent to the three systems mentioned or independently presents doctrinal aspects of great significance. In the accommodation of the judicial to the legislative process, what legal doctrines have marked out the boundaries of protection of the fruits of private enterprise in commercial and intellectual pursuits?

The premise of American private enterprise is that the discipline of competition is the generating force of a free society in keeping with our political, economic, and social traditions. We reject extensive authoritarian controls in order to preserve for individuals and business firms freedom to fashion their own destinies with the greatest scope the public interest allows. Two interrelated bodies of law limit this liberty. One is our antitrust policy designed to maintain competition by prohibiting its suppression or substantial lessening. The other is a policy against unfair competition designed to regulate the level of competition by insuring its fairness and honesty with resulting benefits to the consuming public.

COMMON LAW ORIGIN OF PRIVILEGE TO COMPETE

Unfair competition law developed from the judicial process of

EDITOR'S NOTE: This paper was presented by Professor Oppenheim upon his acceptance of the first Charles F. Kettering Award from The PTC Research Institute on June 19, 1958. (*IDEA*, Vol. 2, Conference No. 1958.) The author has added a postscript to this paper.

the law of torts or civil wrongs. "Unfair" and "competition" are terms that defy precise definition or exact formulation. It is no over-simplification, however, to say that common law and equity sought to moderate the excesses of competition by redressing business wrongs arising from unprivileged interferences with existing and prospective business relations. Later, this was extended to safe-guarding literary, artistic and similar types of intellectual creations. In a broad sense, fair competition is recognized as privileged conduct. Unfair competition is condemned as out-of-bounds tortious conduct. Some economists have constructed a game theory of competition from which analogies can be drawn. In popular parlance of sports, we use the terms "fair play" and "rules of the game" to characterize fair competition and expressions like "foul play," "hitting below the belt," or "dirty tricks" to condemn unfair competition.

We first turn to the common law to see in broad outline the theories of liability that evolved to distinguish between fair and foul competitive play in commercial relations. The story starts with the fascinating *Schoolmaster's Case* in 1410 in the English Court of Common Pleas. (Hilary Term. Y. B. Hen. J. V., f. 47, pl. 21.)

Two masters of a grammar school in Gloucester brought an action on the case against the defendant who had the temerity to open a competitive school there. The plaintiffs sparred with all kinds of legal technicalities, including a claim of an exclusive franchise from the church. They were aggrieved because they lost pupils and fees and apparently the defendant was a fee cutter. The court held there was no cause of action.

Here is a foundation stone of the privilege to engage in a private business in good faith and to compete for customers. This privilege still prevails as a cardinal principle of the American common law of torts. We sometimes lose sight of the reasoning that a competitor must have freedom to inflict harm on his rivals so long as that injury results from constructive rather than destructive competition.

TWO THEORIES OF TORT LIABILITY—
ENGLISH LAW

When the competitive market economy emerged in England, two theories of tort liability evolved which later found their way into the fabric of American unfair competition law. This dichotomy must be explained, for, in my view, it provides a key to an understanding of the present posture of judicial doctrine pertaining to protection of both commercial relations and intellectual productions. This is done only in broad outline and sweeping retrospect.

One common law theory of the cause of action for illegal competition stems from the concept that all actionable wrongs must fall within one of the so-called nominate torts. This simply means that the plaintiff must show he has been harmed by such traditional wrongful conduct as fraud or misrepresentation, negligence, libel and slander, including disparagement of business conduct, conspiracy and inducing breach of contract. This exemplifies the rigidity of the common law systems in denying a remedy where there was no specific writ. It has nevertheless not precluded the courts from liberalizing the requirements for redress. As we shall see, unfair competition also became a nominate tort but it has been expanded as a classification covering various kinds of unfair conduct.

A second common law theory relevant to unfair competition is that there is a general principle of tort liability. This might encompass conduct within the previously mentioned categories of wrongs, including unfair competition, but it is broader than, and independent of, such rigid classifications. It provides an element of flexibility. It vests in the courts wide judicial discretion in case-by-case adjudication of new private claims that press for recognition and legal security as the economic, technological, and cultural life of society progresses. It supplies to a considerable extent a unifying principle not hemmed in by predetermined types of legal and equitable remedies or a rigid property right concept.

While differing in basic concept, these two theories are not wholly antithetical. Both of them have been applied in the United States in federal and state courts in causes denominated unfair competition and in other actions designed to resolve similar issues under the more plastic general principle of tort liability. In helping to bring into focus contemporary doctrines in this field, a few pages of legal history remind us of fundamentals which are sometimes blurred by failure to re-examine them.

Among the early English cases *Keeble* v. *Hickeringill*, 11 East 574, 103 Eng. Rep. 1127 (Queens Bench, 1706), decided in 1706 is epochal. There the plaintiff owned a pond to which wild fowl were accustomed to come. The plaintiff invested capital in decoys and nets for enticing the game. The defendant, it was alleged, wilfully and maliciously fired guns which frightened the fowl and caused them to forsake the plaintiff's pond. Lord Holt sustained the plaintiff's action on the case for damages.

The great teaching of this case for the modern law is its doctrine that there is a common law right to conduct a lawful business for profit without unjustified interferences of others, whether they be competitors or noncompetitors. In 1706 private enterprise in Merrie

England was on the march. The plaintiff may have been partly motivated by the love of the sport, but Lord Holt said he was seeking to supply the markets of England with wild game. This was in the public interest and so "He that hinders another in his trade or livelihood is liable to an action for so hindering him" by unprivileged behavior.

IMPACT ON AMERICAN LAW

Is the general principle of tort liability formulated in the *Keeble* case living law today in unfair competition litigation? There are indications that the bar is not sufficiently aware of the impact *Keeble* has made upon the development of a similar doctrine in America under the strange designation of the prima facie tort. Its genesis is in the writings of Justice Holmes, Dean Wigmore, and Sir Frederick Pollock, who sought a rationale for unifying the law of torts by breaking away from the orthodox notion that all wrongful conduct must fall within one of the particular torts. The classic formulation of the prima facie tort concept first appeared in Justice Holmes' Supreme Court opinion in *Aikens* v. *Wisconsin,* 195 U.S. 194 (1904), in these words:

"It has been considered that, prima facie, the intentional infliction of temporal damages is a cause of action, which, as a matter of substantive law, whatever may be the form of pleading, requires a justification if the defendant is to escape."

Suggestive of this same breadth is Justice Brandeis' statement in another Supreme Court opinion that "The right to carry on business—be it called liberty or property—has value. To interfere with this right without just cause is unlawful." It is not so well known that this broad doctrine has been accepted in some of the federal and state courts and applied to unfair competition cases involving wrongful interference with business relations. We turn to some illustrative cases.

In *Original Ballet Russe, Ltd.* v. *Ballet Theatre,* 133 F.2d 187, in the federal Court of Appeals for the Second Circuit in 1943, the parties were competitors in producing ballet performances. The plaintiff sought damages alleging that defendant had deliberately set out to destroy the plaintiff's business by inducing dancers to break their contracts with plaintiff and by maliciously circulating false statements to injure plaintiff's reputation. The court held that the complaint stated a single cause of action for intentional destruction of the plaintiff's business without justifiable excuse. It expressly stated that this cause of action goes back at least to the early English case of *Keeble* v. *Hickeringill* and to the philosophy brilliantly expounded by Justice Holmes. The particular wrongful acts might independently have been deemed separate wrongs but here they were only parts of the over-all plan to ruin the plaintiff's enterprise.

In 1946 in *Advance Music Corporation* v. *American Tobacco Company*, 296 N. Y. 79, the New York Court of Appeals re-affirmed its adoption of this approach. In this case the defendant sponsored the "Hit Parade" radio program which purported to list and perform the leading song hits of the country reported by an independent survey. Plaintiff alleged that as a publisher of sheet music sold through distributors it was dependent upon the rating of its songs in promoting sales. The complaint further alleged that defendant intentionally omitted plaintiff's songs or devalued their ratings and this diminished plaintiff's revenues and impaired its business reputation and property rights. This was held to state a good cause of action for relief either at law or in equity with the caveat that defendant's justification must be one the law will recognize.

One more example is *Mackey* v. *Sears, Roebuck & Company*, 238 F.2d 86, decided in 1956 in the Seventh Circuit Court of Appeals. There Sears was charged by plaintiff with predatory price cutting, threats of boycott and other practices alleged to be inten-tionally aimed at driving the plaintiff out of business. The value of this case is underscored by the action of the Court in dismissing plaintiff's counts for violation of the federal Sherman and Clayton Acts, while sustaining a count based upon the prima facie tort of predatory price cutting beyond the bounds of justified competition.

These and other cases that could be cited are illustrative of the prima facie tort as the modern version of the historic tort remedy known as an action on the case which was used in the *School-master* and *Keeble* litigation, an alternative remedy which permits the courts to keep pace with changing economic and social values in case-by-case adjudication. The New Jersey Court of Equity as far back as 1902 in *Jersey Printing Company* v. *Cassidy*, 63 N. J. Eq. 759, summed up this approach in these prophetic words:

> ... A large part of what is most valuable in modern life seems to depend more or less directly upon "probable expectancies." When they fail, civilization as at present organized may go down. As social and industrial life develops and grows more complex, these "pro-bable expectancies" are bound to increase. It would seem that courts of law, as our system of jurisprudence is evolved to meet the growing wants of an increasingly complex social order, will discover, define, and protect from undue interference more of these "probable expectancies."

EXPANSION OF UNFAIR-COMPETITION CONCEPT— FROM MISREPRESENTATION TO MISAPPROPRIATION

At this point we sketch one more common law development as a means of redressing conduct deemed offensive to a fair and equitable rivalry for personal gain. Coexistent with the tort remedy of action on the case and the prima facie tort concept is the category that carries the specific label of unfair competition. There are thus three main common law headwaters from which relief for essentially the same generic type of wrong can flow.

In its narrow common law meaning, the nominate tort of "unfair competition" was confined to what is called the "passing off" practice. This was a species of misrepresentation first emerging in trademark infringement cases. A trademark is a symbol of identification to distinguish the particular source of one's goods from those of another. "Passing off" means that a person uses an identical or confusingly similar mark to palm off his goods as those coming from the owner of the goodwill of the mark. This deceit occurs whenever there is likelihood of confusion of prospective purchasers which tends to divert customers from the owner of the trade symbol. Similar passing off can be accomplished by imitation of the appearance of a product, its labeling or packaging, and other multifarious features. There are numerous doctrinal refinements not here relevant, since my purpose is simply to characterize the essence of this type of misrepresentation the law seeks to curb.

In 1918 in the classic *International News Service v. The Associated Press* case, 248 U.S. 215, the Supreme Court of the United States expanded the unfair competition concept to include situations where one misappropriates what equitably belongs to another. Instead of misrepresenting by selling his goods as coming from the plaintiff, the defendant tells the world that he is the creator of what he has appropriated from the plaintiff. This has been called inverse passing off.

The facts of the *Associated Press* case were these. International News Service was copying news items from the AP bulletin boards and early editions of AP member papers. As a result the newspapers on the West Coast subscribing to INS service were frequently able to scoop papers using AP service. The Supreme Court condemned this practice as a misappropriation species of unfair competition. The Court did not decide whether there was a general property right in the news or whether the form of expression in the write-up of the news was protected by the Copyright's Law. It cut to the core of the wrong by characterizing the defendant's conduct as reaping where it had not sown. AP and INS were competitors in gathering and disseminating news. INS, without cost to itself, was appropriating for its profit the fruits of AP's labor, expenditures, skills, and money while the news still had commercial value as "fresh" or "hot" news. As one writer has aptly said, this introduced into the law of unfair competiti⟨ . a remedy against unjust enrichment of the defendant to the detriment of the plaintiff. This is deemed contrary to good conscience. It is not cricket.

The generality of this misappropriation doctrine is comparable to the prima facie tort and the plastic action on the case. The Supreme Court indicated as much in articulating a general proposition applicable to both competitive and non-competitive relationships.

> . . . when the rights or privileges of the one are liable to conflict with those of the other,

Justice Pitney said,

> each party is under a duty so to conduct its own business as not unnecessarily or unfairly to injure that of the other.

I shall return later to a summation of the extent of application of the misappropriation doctrine.

We have looked back at the development of three theories of liability and remedial processes. From this perspective I now venture suggestions which may be helpful in evaluating the contribution the judicial process, apart from the legislative process, is capable of making to unfair competition law.

This is a mixture of diagnosis and prognosis one can tremble to make. It brings into view the interactions of the judicial and legislative processes. It calls for recognition that in conceptual structure and operation the private law of unfair competition cannot be reduced to a unified rationalization. In this branch judicial and legislative law-making have manifested both progression and retrogression. There have been inconsistencies and contradictions. Another shortcoming has been lack of uniformity of doctrines which has been accentuated since the Supreme Court's decision in *Erie Railroad* v. *Tompkins,* 304 U.S. 64 (1938), required federal courts, in the absence of a relevant federal or state statute, to apply the decisions of the courts of the particular state as the applicable law in adjudication. This has tended to produce a checkerboard of conflicting decisions.

I do not overlook these deficiencies in setting forth some beliefs which may bring into sharper focus the considerations relevant to the means of giving greater coherence to the law of unfair competition.

JUDICIAL v. LEGISLATIVE PROTECTION AGAINST UNFAIR COMPETITION

The basic choice is between the judicial and legislative processes for resolving conflicting interests of claimants for legal protection of business and cultural values on the one hand, and for freedom of sharing those values on the other hand. The common law and equity general principles we have sketched place in the courts broad discretion in projecting the growth of private unfair competition law. In my view this capacity of the unwritten law should not be underestimated when weighing the alternative of relying upon extension of the legislative and administrative processes as others have advocated.

This is not an all or none choice, since obviously legislation is necessary in certain situations to supplement the unwritten law. The patent and copyright laws illustrate legislation indispensable to fulfillment of the constitutionally sanctioned purposes of these systems. Implementation of common law and equity in the Trade-Mark Act of 1946 to broaden protection is another example of salutary legislation. In federal public law proceedings, not directly relevant here, Section 5 of the Federal Trade Commission Act delegates to the Commission initial administrative and quasi-judicial authority to determine what constitutes unfair methods of competition and unfair or deceptive acts or practices. Other instances of needed regulation can be found in the confused mass of state legislation.

Without denying the need for legislation as a check and balance to fulfill purposes to which the judicial process is ill-adapted or which it has failed to achieve, I believe that doubts should be resolved in favor of primary reliance upon traditional Anglo-American lawmaking by judicial decision as against legislation in adjudicating unfair competition issues in adversary proceedings between private parties. I stress this as a preference. This does not mean that further study should not be given to proposals, for example, for a federal law of unfair competition applicable to private suits or for a uniform state unfair competition statute. I believe, however, that there has been a tendency to undervalue the potential progress that can still be made toward achieving a greater degree of coherence and uniformity of doctrine in this field by application of the general principles of common law and equity which we have previously described. The time lag in judicial response through unwritten law may be no greater or no more costly than the time lag in fulfilling declared legislative purposes. There is also risk that by either method desired objectives will be frustrated.

Two chief contentions favoring legislation are disclosed either in court opinions or in legal literature. One contention is that the legislature is better equipped than the courts to define and limit in uniform, comprehensive, and orderly fashion the interests worthy of protection and the scope of remedies in unfair competition law. The other contention is that, absent such legislative guides, the courts may create judge-made monopolies incompatible with the goals of a free society. In particular situations, this concern is expressed when relief for unfair competition is sought for subject matter not covered by the patent and copyright laws or, if covered, where such protection has not been obtained. Here the fear is expressed that perpetual monopoly might be given judicial sanction instead of the limited time monopoly of the statutory patent or copyright. We shall briefly deal with each of these contentions.

It should be noted that in any given case the court of equity must find that the claimant has some interest of substance and value the law will protect. This may be a contract right, a trust or confidence, or other relational interest. In most unfair competition cases, however, the courts have applied the property concept and initially determined whether the interest sought to be secured has attributes of either an absolute or a qualified property. This property concept, however, can be expanded, and some courts have so stretched it to cover a conglomerate of intangible values. There is truth in the assertion that any value a court decides to protect can be labeled a property right. This makes property more a legal conclusion than a formulary description. It takes in all manifestation of business good will and literary, artistic or other intellectual productions.

EVOLUTION OF MISAPPROPRIATION DOCTRINE

Let us return to the misappropriation doctrine as a vehicle for demonstrating the conflicting judicial attitudes toward this problem. Some courts have applied the misappropriation doctrine with the conviction that they are capable of utilizing the method of a Rule of Reason in determining what constitutes unprivileged or unjustified conduct of competitors and parties that are not in a competitive relationship. They have sought to do this by resort to economic, ethical and social criteria of unfairness with due regard for the overall public policy of maintaining effective competition. Here is a typical expression of this attitude in these words of a

New York state court judge in *Dior* v. *Milton,* 155 N.Y.S. 2d 443 at 451 (S. Ct. N. Y. 1956):

> In passing upon the question of the sufficiency of this complaint alleging unfair competition, it is helpful to bear in mind the origin and evolution of this branch of the law. It originated in the conscience, justice and equity of common-law judges. It developed within the framework of a society dedicated to the freest competition, to deal with business malpractices offensive to the ethics of that society. The theoretic basis is obscure, but the birth and growth of this branch of the law is clear. It is a persuasive example of the law's capacity for growth in response to the ethical, as well as the economic needs of society. As a result of this broad background, the legal concept of unfair competition has evolved as a broad and flexible doctrine with a capacity for further growth to meet changing conditions. There is no complete list of the activities which constitute unfair competition.

Courts that are hospitable to these postulates have not hesitated to apply the misappropriation doctrine of the *Associated Press* case to novel situations. Leaving to one side other issues frequently raised in the same case and problems of patent or copyright protection, let us cite a few examples of extensions of unfair competition.

In *Waring* v. *WDAS Broadcasting Station,* 327 Pa. 433 (1937), Waring's Pennsylvanians orchestra made licensed recordings of musical compositions it broadcast over the air. The records were sold at retail at 75 cents. The defendant broadcasting station purchased these records and broadcast them as part of its sustaining program. This conduct was enjoined. Recognizing that Waring had a common law property right in the particular artistic style of rendering the composition, the Supreme Court of Pennsylvania reasoned that the defendant had unfairly appropriated for its profit the product of the labor and talents of the musical artistry of Waring's orchestra. In the competition of furnishing entertainment to the public, defendant was diluting the value of the exclusivity of Waring's live broadcast for which the sponsor was paying substantial sums.

In the world of sports, *Pittsburgh Athletic Club* v. *KQV Broadcasting Company,* 24 F. Supp. 490 (W. D. Pa. 1938), furnishes another illustration. There the Pittsburgh Pirates contracted for the exclusive right to broadcast play-by-play descriptions of its ball games. Defendant stationed paid observers at vantage points outside the ball park and broadcast the game as it progressed. This was enjoined by a federal court as a misappropriation of the fruits of the plaintiff's enterprise and expense in maintaining an organization and originating a sporting contest where the essence of the commercial value was exclusivity in reporting the play-by-play descriptions. Defendant was privileged to report the news of the results of the game inning by inning. It was not legally justified in taking a "free ride" on the expenditures and the other composite of values attributable to the ball club, the advertising sponsor, and the broadcasting company. Under similar circumstances, unauthorized broadcast of blow-by-blow descriptions of a boxing match or the taking of motion pictures of the bout have been enjoined even though the appropriator was located outside the plaintiff's premises.

New York is a jurisdiction where the state courts have not faltered in balancing the interests of the parties by applying the general equitable principles of the misappropriation doctrine. One of the most recent is *Metropolitan Opera Association* v. *Wagner-Nichols Recording Company,* 101 N.Y. S.2d 483 (S. Ct. N. Y. 1950), *affirmed* 107 N. Y. S.2d 795 (App. Div. 1951). It was alleged that Metropolitan Opera had granted Columbia Records the exclusive right to make records of its operatic performances broadcast under exclusive rights sold by the Met to the American Broadcasting System. Defendant made an "off the air" master recording of certain Met performances and from this made and sold records in competition with those sold by Columbia. These allegations were held to state a cause of action for unfair competition. Applying the *Associated Press* doctrine, the court mentioned as factors relevant to misappropriation the income the Met derived from its contracts, its substantial investment in its organization, the employment of famous opera singers, an orchestra, chorus and other creative intangible goodwill values involved in the Met performances and in maintaining their high quality and favorable reputation.

Some commentators have concluded that the misappropriation doctrine has been sparingly applied by the courts and does not offer the promise the *Associated Press* case portended. My review of the cases has led me to agree with writers who believe the doctrine has had considerable influence in the growth of this segment of the law.

CONFLICTING VIEWS ON
MISAPPROPRIATION DOCTRINE

We now turn to an examination of a judicial attitude which repudiates the breadth of the misappropriation doctrine of the cases just described. It can be traced in significant part to the prestige and impact of the opposing rationale articulated in the dissent of

Justice Brandeis in the *Associated Press* case and in the opinions of Judge Learned Hand.

In his dissent Justice Brandeis recognized that the unwritten law possesses capacity for growth. He shied away, however, from enlarging the scope of unfair competition beyond conduct condemned by the traditional torts. He reasoned that to grant additional relief would require the making of a new rule of law rather than satisfying new demands for justice by invoking analogies or by applying an existing rule to new facts. In his view the legislature, and not the courts, is equipped to recognize a new private right and to define its boundaries when the complexities of conflicting claims need resolution in harmony with the overriding public interest. Justice Brandeis felt that the obvious injustice of giving a competitor a "free ride" could not be corrected by judicial action alone without opening the door to greater evils.

In similar vein Judge Hand declined to grant injunctive relief in a suit against a defendant who had copied a published popular design for silk fabrics created by the plaintiff. He rejected the contention that this inequitable conduct came within the reach of the majority opinion in the *Associated Press* case. He glossed the broad language of that opinion by interpreting its rationale as limited to substantially similar factual situations. Though he felt the plaintiff had suffered an injury for which there should be a remedy, he said there are larger issues at stake in correcting what he called "an hiatus in completed justice." This, he continued, judges cannot do when the subject has been entrusted to Congress for determination under the patent and copyright laws. Plaintiff might have secured a design patent, Judge Hand pointed out, and an amendment of the copyright law might be sought if it does not already cover the case. To create by judicial fiat a common law patent or copyright would give plaintiff a monopoly contrary to the limited time exclusiveness the Constitution allows only Congress to grant. Judge Hand further observed that since the court must judge on the limited record prepared by litigants, its vision is inevitably more contracted than that of the legislature which can view the whole horizon. In this he concurred with Justice Brandeis' conservative approach.

In *RCA* v. *Whitman*, 114 F.2d 86 (2d Cir. 1940), Judge Hand reiterated that the *Associated Press* case must be confined to its facts and denied there was misappropriation in a situation virtually identical to that in the *Waring* orchestra case we have previously described.

SUGGESTED JUDICIAL RULE-
OF-REASON APPROACH

We can now evaluate these conflicting approaches. In my view the Brandeis-Hand conclusion that the courts are not equipped to define and limit novel private rights seems unwarranted in theory and practice. The courts which have undertaken this judicial task have not set sail on entirely uncharted seas. It has not proved impossible to identify the tangible and intangible embodiments of such values as the talents and skills of performing artists, the investments and expenditures in organizations like the Associated Press, Metropolitan Opera, Waring's orchestra and the Pittsburgh Pirates, and other manifestations of subject matter that have the attributes of substance and value associated with property rights. Nor have the courts lacked perception in distinguishing and rejecting spurious claims of property in mere abstract ideas for which there is no legal protection once they are voluntarily disclosed without the safeguard of contract or confidential relationship.

I do not underrate the judicial burden of determining whether or not the defendant's conduct is privileged or justified, once the court has found the requisite protectible interest and that defendant has invaded that interest. There is ample precedent at law and equity for exercise of this broad discretion. There is a tendency to overlook the striking parallel in application of the Rule of Reason in public law areas such as our antitrust and trade regulation laws. The generality of the three fundamental concepts we have traced through the common law—the action on the case, the prima facie tort and unfair competition as one of the nominate torts—are comparable to the general standards in which enacted public laws are couched. A prime example is the Sherman Act's prohibition of unreasonable restraints of trade and monopolization. Chief Justice Hughes distilled the essence when he characterized the Sherman Act as "a charter of freedom" which "has a generality and adaptability comparable to that found to be desirable in constitutional provisions."

Resort to this legislation did not, and, in my view, could not provide a substitute for ultimate judicial resolution of licit and illicit conduct. It is well known that antitrust doctrines are judge-made. The Supreme Court in 1911 adopted the Rule of Reason as the master yardstick of judicial interpretation and in 1956 the Court categorically stated that it "has not receded from its position on the Rule." This standard has generated controversy and will continue to do so because of divergent views regarding its role and applications in varying factual situations. There is consensus, however, that the

Rule of Reason vests discretion in the courts "to decide whether conduct is significantly and unreasonably anticompetitive in character and effect."

The general principles in unfair competition law we have sketched likewise rely upon the courts to decide whether the defendant's conduct is by nature and effect significantly and unreasonably unfair in the context of a free economic and cultural society. Certain types of conduct can be quickly and positively adjudged unreasonable per se with greater assurance than in the more complicated antitrust field. Fraud, misrepresentation, the gross forms of physical interference, boycotts, disparagement and the like do not require extravaganza of judicial inquiry and analysis beyond the competence of judges and the efficacy of fact-finding processes in private adversary litigation. To be sure, there are differences in the degree of difficulty when the novelty of the plaintiff's claims reach into areas theretofore unmapped in common law and equity suits. It is not apparent, however, why the Anglo-American tradition of growth of law through the judicial process cannot be equal to this exploratory task. If we are persuaded that the American industrial and cultural order is too diverse and changeable to make realistic and workable a comprehensive code of specific fair or unfair practices, then it follows that general legislative standards will in any event throw into the lap of the courts the ultimate function of giving content to such standards in case-by-case adjudication.

DANGER OF JUDGE-MADE MONOPOLIES EXAGGERATED

As previously stated, advocates of primary resort to legislation, in addition to stressing the inadequacy of the judicial process in the twilight zones of unfair competition, have also emphasized the danger of creating or expanding judge-made monopolies contrary to the overriding public interest in maintaining effective competition. This is an exaggerated fear. It may at times stem from ideological resistance to exclusiveness of rights in industrial and intellectual values beyond the traditional concept of private property in land and chattels. In part it may be attributable to an undiscriminating and emotional use of the word "monopoly," as though it uniformly meant the power to control the market by fixing prices and excluding competition. We cannot deal here with the various refinements of economic and legal analysis of the monopoly concept. Suffice it to say, our society is suffused with differential advantages accruing to particular persons. These are illustrated by product differentiation in brand names, quality, design, or packaging that distinguish one's source from other sources of goods. The Supreme Court in the recent *Cellophane* case, *United States* v. *E. I. du Pont de Nemours and Company,* 351 U.S. 377 (1956), judicially recognized the economists' characterization of these advantages as forms of imperfect competition in the sense that the owner of good will of the differentiated products has a monopolistic element in consumer preferences for what he produces and sells. Yet the Supreme Court did not equate this with illegality. The majority opinion of the Court warned against this fallacy by saying:

> . . . one can theorize that we have monopolistic competition in every non-standardized commodity with each manufacturer having power over the price and production of his own product. However, this power that, let us say, automobile or soft-drink manufacturers have over their trademarked products, is not the power that makes an illegal monopoly. Illegal power must be appraised in terms of the competitive market for the product.

JUDGE LEARNED HAND'S CAVEATS

In the unfair competition field, some of the opinions of Justice Brandeis and Judge Learned Hand warned against judicial sanction or extension of monopoly rights for which there is no constitutional or statutory basis or common law precedent. In part this solicitude is expressed in situations where the claimant is put to an election between the limited-time exclusiveness of a statutory patent or copyright and the perpetual exclusiveness of common law property rights not lost by reason of the owner's conduct. This reasoning is conditioned by the legal concept of publication which we can treat here only in summary form.

As a word of legal art, a general publication results when the owner of subject matter having the attributes of property makes it available for common use. A classic example is literary or artistic property. The rubric is that common law rights in such works continue indefinitely until a first publication is made. There are many acts which may bring this about. A common example is making copies of a book or musical composition and placing them on public sale. Since these are also copyrightable works under our law, publication with notice of copyright paves the way for 28 years' protection with one renewal for a like term. If the subject matter is not copyrightable, the owner may lose all of his rights of exclusion.

Judge Hand has consistently said that the owner cannot have it both ways. If he embodies his literary or artistic property in a tangible chattel for public sale or distribution, his common law exclusive rights are terminated. If this subject matter is within the copyright law and he fails to comply with the statutory formalities. such as notice of copyright, he dedicates his work to the public.

There are various oddities in the publication concept. For example, contrary to the layman's idea of a general publication in the dictionary sense, a public performance of a play, a broadcast or telecast of a musical composition or script, an oral delivery of a teacher's lecture or a minister's sermon is not a general publication if, in all the examples cited, no tangible copies are made accessible to the public. One may hear or see but is not privileged to reduce the subject matter to possession.

In Judge Learned Hand's view, public sale of copies of a work divests the owner of his common law property and if he does not or cannot secure the limited-time monopoly of statutory copyright, the court should not give him the bonanza of a perpetual monopoly by ignoring the general publication. There are conflicting decisions, however, on whether the owner can impose restrictions which manifest a subjective intention to make only a limited publication. For example, in the *Fred Waring* case we previously mentioned, each phonograph record placed on public sale contained a notice restricting the purchaser to non-commercial uses of the record, thus prohibiting broadcast for profit. This restriction was upheld as a so-called equitable servitude on chattels. In the *Whiteman* case Judge Hand refused to give effect to a similar restriction deemed to be an unreasonable restraint upon use by the purchaser.

This suffices to indicate the resistance of some courts to common law or equity recognition of exclusive rights in the types of subject matter we have illustrated. Judge Hand's view, it should be noted, is in conflict with the extension of the misappropriation doctrine in the *Metropolitan Opera* case where the New York Court held that it could enjoin as unfair competition the copying of phonograph records of the Met operas even though these records had been placed on public sale. In the 1955 *Capitol Records* v. *Mercury Records* case, 221 F.2d 657, the Second Circuit Court of Appeals applied this New York doctrine to enjoin the defendant's copying of the records of musical compositions which are in the public domain. The records as such were held not copyrightable under our Copyright Law. Judge Hand's dissent recognized that this was in conflict with his views, but agreed that the *Metropolitan Opera* decision is conclusive if the issue is to be decided by the law of New York where the records were sold.

JUDICIAL EXTENSION IS COMPATIBLE
WITH COMPETITIVE SYSTEM

To what extent is the fear of judge-made monopolies justified? In some of my writings on this subject I have stressed the need for the Rule of Reason in unwritten unfair competition law comparable to the Rule of Reason in the Sherman Antitrust Act. In applying the standard of reason to unfair competition doctrines, there is relevance in Judge Jerome Frank's warning against succumbing to the "monopoly-phobia" which he described as "both a symptom and cause of a neurotic tendency which, in refusing bravely to face facts, cannot yield intelligent advice." We also should give heed to Judge Hand's equally relevant caveat that "In the guise of protecting against unfair competition, we must be zealous not to create perpetual monopolies." My study of the case law has nevertheless inclined me to believe that generally the extension of the unwritten law in unfair competition through judicial decisions has not been out of harmony with American aversion to monopoly rights. The judicial conscience has been sensitive to spurious and inflated claims of exclusive rights. It seems fair to say that judicial expansion of unfair competition doctrines has been conservative rather than daring. The open market for industrial and intellectual productions outside the patent and copyright systems does not appear to be in danger of foreclosure. Unprivileged poaching on the good will of trademarks and trade names, to mention one area of unfair competition, has been weighed against the freedom to make use of undeceptive common words of the language, geographic terms, personal names, and functional features essential to the making and sale of goods. In fact, members of the trademark bar at times complain that some courts have allowed the catch-word of monopoly to restrict unduly the scope of protection of these trade symbols. In the borderland areas where Judge Hand has placed judicial barriers to expansion of unfair competition doctrine, some might wonder why there should be such fear of exclusive rights in designs and styles recognized by Judge Hand himself to be as ephemeral as the changing moods of the dictators of women's fashion. Hemlines rise and fall. Today it is the chemise, the sack, and the trapeze. Women's hats are first off the face and later on the face. The repertoire of currently popular musical compositions, apart from the imperishable classics available to free use of all, cannot long withstand the whimsies of the public. Today's public insatiability for the words and lyrics of "Hound Dog" becomes surfeited tomorrow.

The thesis that primary reliance should be placed upon judi-

cial mapping of the metes and bounds of the unwritten law of unfair competition has been presented with due acknowledgment of
its imperfections and with recognition of the necessity for legislation to meet purposes unfulfilled by the judicial process. It is understandable, for example, that the failure of the courts to bring piracy of industrial designs within the reach of unfair competition
doctrine has resulted in long-time efforts to obtain legislative
protection beyond the present prospects of securing copyright
registration as a "work of art" or a design patent. We must also
note that lack of effective private remedies against false advertising, other than the "passing off" practice, has accounted for
Section 43 (a) of the Trade-Mark Act of 1946 designed to redress
in broader scope false descriptions or representations. This provision has been both strictly and liberally construed and its effectiveness is not yet fully assured. We again remind you that when
these types of legislation are formulated in general standards, the
judges will tend to have the final word anyway with respect to
legislative intent and interpretations that give content to the
meaning of the general language.

In conclusion, I suggest that while judicial evaluation of
conduct as fair or unfair competition inescapably involves subjective elements, such as the sensibilities or intuitive judgment of
the tribunal, case-by-case adjudication is not and need not be
divorced from objective processes. Here, as in other fields of the
law, the courts need procedural improvements in fact-finding.
They also need the aid of the empirical method for introducing
into the record of a particular case factual information relevant
to the interests of the parties seeking protection of industrial and
intellectual productions and the parties contending for freedom
to share in these creations. From these sources, always subject to
the right of cross-examination in the trial of cases, can come more
realistic and sure-footed judicial consideration of objective data
for equitable adjustment of the private claims in accommodation
to aims of the American economic and social order.

Author's Postscript—

Apart from the stream of judicial decisions within the historic
framework of unfair competition law since this paper was written
in 1957, two notable Supreme Court decisions set precedents the
limits of which are still unclarified.

In both *Sears, Roebuck & Co.* v. *Stiffel Co.*, 376 U.S. 225
(1964) and *Compco Corp.* v. *Day-Brite Lighting Co.*, 376 U.S.

234 (1964), the plaintiff sought to enjoin a competitor's copying of the plaintiff's product as patent infringement and unfair competition. The patents were declared invalid but relief was granted on the ground of unfair competition. The Seventh Circuit Court of Appeals affirmed, ruling that proof of "palming off" need not be made under Illinois law. In reversing both decisions, the Supreme Court held that "when an article is unprotected by a patent or a copyright, state law may not forbid others to copy that article."

Whether these decisions will be limited to cases of product simulation or will further restrict unfair competition relief on the misappropriation or unjust enrichment theory of *International News Service* v. *Associated Press,* 248 U.S. 215 (1918), is still unclear. But see *Columbia Broadcasting System* v. *De Costa,* 377 F.2d 315 (1st Cir. 1967). Consider also congressional proposals to accord protection against unfair competition as a matter of federal law, e.g., Senator McClellan's latest bill (S. 1154, 90th Cong., 1st Sess. 1967) and Professor Walter Derenberg's comments and citation of cases on page—of this book.

Whether or not such legislation is enacted, the thesis of my paper that primary reliance upon the judicial process is to be preferred as the ultimate means of marking out the scope of protection against unfair competition appears to me to be still valid.

The Parking Meter Industry

George E. Frost, S. Chesterfield Oppenheim, and Neil F. Twomey

SUMMARY

On March 28, 1944, Judge Leahy rendered decision in favor
of the Government and against Vehicular Parking, Ltd., a patent
holding corporation, and substantially all of the prewar members
of the parking meter industry. The government complaint had
alleged, and Judge Leahy found, that the patent licenses entered
into by Vehicular Parking and the associated business activities
of the defendants, gave rise to illegal price fixing and other violations of the Sherman Act. The decision indicated that the patents
of Vehicular would be made subject to compulsory licenses.
Later decrees so ordered.

There have been two major entries into the parking meter
business since the decision and decrees. One was Magee-Hale
Park-O-Meter Company. The other was International Meters,
Incorporated, whose product did not involve features covered by
any of the Vehicular patents and did not give rise to any patent
infringement controversies. In 1952 the International meter business was sold to Mi-Co—a prewar meter concern which has since
marketed the meter.

Vehicular charged that the Magee-Hale Meter construction
infringed four Vehicular patents. After some initial legal proceedings. Magee-Hale (organized by Carl Magee and others who
had been instrumental in building up Dual Parking Meter Company, the principal prewar concern) elected to take a license under
the compulsory licensing decree provisions. The principal stock-
holder of Magee-Hale finally purchased the Vehicular patents for
$95,000, bringing the controversy to an end.

There are six significant parking meter manufacturers at the
present time, the same number as in the prewar period. Data indicate that Duncan Parking Meter Corporation, the chief competitor
to the Dual Parking Meter Company during the prewar period, is
the leading concern in terms of sales, with substantially more than
a third of the sales volume, followed by Magee-Hale with about

EDITOR'S NOTE: This paper, a pioneer study on the effects of compulsory
licensing decrees in which patents are a major factor, appeared in *IDEA*, Vol. 2,
No. 3 (Fall 1958).

a third of the total sales volume. The other four concerns share the remaining portion of well under one-third of the meter sales.

The effects of the compulsory licensing decree provisions have been very mild. Activity on both the Magee-Hale meter and the International meter commenced well before the antitrust opinion and decrees and for this and other reasons cannot be credited to the compulsory licensing provisions. In addition, the patents in the industry during the postwar period have been of the detailed engineering improvement variety for which alternative fully competitive structures are available. While the members of the industry do have a lively interest in product improvement, attention is directed to improving existing meter designs and not to basically new forms of meters. The only recent meter design that can be classed as wholly new terms of principle is the Duncan Automaton, which has not been stressed by Duncan in its sales effort and has not enjoyed any large sales volume.

INTRODUCTION

This report relates to the second of two case studies selected as pilot projects on the effects of compulsory licensing decrees in antitrust cases. The first study was of the so-called *Besser* case, relating to the concrete block making machine industry. This study is reported in Volume 2, Number 1 (March 1958) of *IDEA* at pages 61 to 134. The second and present study is directed to the so-called *Vehicular Parking* case, involving the parking meter industry. The conclusions of the present report, beginning at page 401, include a comparison of the results of the two studies and a discussion of their significance in relation to the conditions in other industries.

The parking meter industry can be traced to the first commercial installation of such meters in Oklahoma City in 1935. When the war interrupted meter production, the importance of parking meters to municipalities was evident. By that time, some 150,000 meters had been sold by six major concerns. At the conclusion of the war there was a tremendous accumulated demand for meters, with the consequent sellers' market that prevailed until about 1950. The peak year for the industry as a whole was probably 1948, when about 195,000 meters were sold at a dollar volume of about $12 million.

Meters are sold to municipalities for installation on street curbs and in parking lots to control parking. In most instances the price of the meter is paid to the manufacturer out of the revenues produced by the meter, a fixed percentage of such revenue—

such as 50 or 75 percent—being paid over to the manufacturer. Once paid for, the meters constitute a substantial source of revenue to the municipality. For example, Rochester, New York, in 1944 collected $90,017 from 1,855 meters, or about $50 per meter. The City of Chicago in 1956 collected $2,412,835 from 28,909 parking meters, or about $85 per meter.* This substantial revenue, coupled with the effectiveness of the meters as a policing device, accounts for the present wide popularity of the meters.

PREWAR HISTORY OF THE
PARKING METER INDUSTRY

The rudiments of the parking meter idea find expression in proposals made in the 1920s.[1] However, the first commercial parking meter installation was not made until 1935, when Dual Parking Meter Company installed 2,000 meters in Oklahoma City.[2] This installation was largely the result of the efforts of Carl C. Magee, who was the first effective proponent of parking meters and remained an outstanding figure in the industry until his death in 1946. Magee's efforts began at least by 1932 and progressed in successive steps to the 1935 construction.[3]

The Oklahoma City installation was a well-publicized im-

*Chicago Daily Tribune, Part 4, p. 8 (Jan. 17, 1957).

[1] The early proposals are recorded in a series of patents issued on applications filed around 1930. They include Homan patent 1,620,098, filed in 1925 and directed to a "Parking Meter" in the form of a clock to be affixed to the automobile; Hutches patent 1,749,977, filed in 1923 and directed to a similar device; Doyle patent 1,752,071, filed in 1926 and directed to a device carried by the automobile which was to be run (with an indicator showing that fact) while the auto was parked and was to be periodically recharged by the police upon payment of a prescribed charge; Ogilvie patent 1,879,438 filed in 1930 to a "Parking Device" consisting of a curb-mounted coin-operated timer in which a green disk showed during a passage of the time paid for and a red disk appeared upon expiration of that time; and Babson patents 1,731,839 and 1,973,275, filed in 1929 and 1930, respectively, and similarly directed to a curb-mounted coin-operated timing device.

In addition to the antecedent parking meter patents, the parking meter industry may also be traced to coin-operated timers generally. Prior to 1930 these had been used to control coin-operated hotel radios, appliances, gas and electric supply, and other things. An example of such a patent that became important in later parking meter patent litigation is found in Miller patent 1,799,056, filed in 1930 and ultimately assigned to Duncan Parking Meter Corporation.

[2] The history of the parking meter industry—and this initial installation by Dual—is discussed in Business Week, April 21, 1945, p. 44. See also Business Week, May 17, 1947, p. 31.

[3] The Magee 1932 construction is shown in Magee patent 2,039,544, issued in 1936 to a "Parking Meter." This unit consisted of a box similar in shape to a farm mail box, mounted on a post. The user inserted a coin and pulled a lever to actuate the timing mechanism and lower the signal flag. Upon expiration of the paid-for time, the timer in the device elevated the signal flag to "violation" position. No time indication was otherwise provided. In 1933 Magee filed patent 2,088,300 to a "Parking Device." This patent related to the internal mechanism

mediate success. Dual promptly engaged in the substantial manufacture of parking meters. As then manufactured, the Dual meter
included all of the essential elements of the modern "manual"
type meter. In this type meter, the user inserts a coin and turns
a handle. Turning the handle winds the clock mechanism and
sets the clock pointer to the paid-for number of minutes. The
clock mechanism thereafter drives the pointer toward the zero
time position as time passes, thus causing the pointer to indicate
zero time and a parking violation upon expiration of the paid-for
time. The essential elements of this mechanism—curb mounting,
coin operation to set the paid-for time, manual setting, and indication of elapsed time—are shown in patents issued well prior to the
1935 Oklahoma City installation.[4]

The earlier patents prevented Dual from obtaining any broad
patent protection to the meter developed by 1935. This meter did,
however, become the subject matter of Magee patent 2,118,318
which attained later importance as a major patent owned by Vehicular Parking, Ltd. Claim 10 of this patent is of rather broad
scope to a meter in which a flag is moved to a retracted position
when the meter is in operation and—at the conclusion of the paid-
for time—is swung to signalling position to indicate a parking
violation.[5]

Following the success of the Dual installation in Oklahoma
City, a number of other business concerns began the manufacture
and sale of parking meters. The principal competitor was Duncan
Parking Meter Company of Chicago, Illinois, which began manufacture about 1935. Its entry into the industry was due to the similarity between parking meters and the coin-operated timers made
for other purposes by Miller Meters, a related company. Similar
considerations dictated the entry of M. H. Rhodes of Hartford,

---

of the meter. In 1935 Magee filed patent 2,118,318 to a "Coin Controlled Parking Meter." This patent is discussed in the text.
    [4]The Ogilvie patent, see note 1 *supra*, showed a parking meter with all of
these features, except an indication of the time as it passes. All of these features,
including the indication of time are in the timer for radio sets and similar applications shown in Miller patent 1,799,056.
    While these earlier patents thus showed the essential features of the parking
meter as later developed, they did not—with the exception of the Doyle patent
1,752,071—pose any significant patent infringement threat to the manufacture
of parking meters. The Doyle patent contained claims that could be construed
broadly to cover the later-developed commercial parking meter. This patent was
ultimately acquired by Vehicular and was emphasized by Vehicular to induce
manufacturers to take licenses.
    [5]Claim 10 of patent 2,118,318 is directed to the combination of the viola-
tion-indicating flag with the time-indicating mechanism. The prior art Ogilvie
patent, see note 1 *supra*, showed such a violation indicator without the time-
indicating mechanism.

Connecticut, which began manufacture at least by 1940. Rhodes was then, and still is, in the business of manufacturing timer mechanisms for other purposes. Parkrite Corporation began the manufacture of meters by 1936 and by 1938 was absorbed by the Karpark Corporation. The parties in interest in these companies were financiers, together with Walter J. Herschede who was in the business of manufacturing clocks. The remaining major pre-war parking meter manufacturer was Mi-Co Meter Company, which began manufacture in 1936. Mi-Co was initially operated as a subsidiary of Michaels Art Bronze Company of Erlanger, Kentucky, a manufacturer of nonferrous architectural and ornamental products for use on public buildings. Michaels entered the parking meter field because of the similarity of market between the new product and products then being sold by the company. The other substantial pre-war concern in the industry, Standard Meter Corporation, did not survive the war period.

Dual was the leader in the prewar parking meter industry, and had sold about 43 percent of the meters installed at the end of 1941. Duncan had sold about 17 percent of the meters at this time. Rhodes was third, with about 15 percent of the meters, Karpark was fourth with 13 percent and Mi-Co was fifth with about 11 percent of the aggregate sales. About 150,000 meters had been sold by all companies by the end of 1941.

The "automatic" type meter was the major pre-war technical development. In the automatic meter the user merely inserts a coin. The meter is thereupon automatically set for operation and proceeds to time. The user is not required to operate a handle to wind the clockwork mechanism or otherwise condition the meter for operation. Operating power in the automatic meter is provided by an electrical or a spring drive mechanism which is activated upon insertion of the coin. The spring type automatic meter must be periodically wound by meter maintenance personnel. Electrically driven coin-operated timers not using an actuating lever had previously been designed to control appliances.[6] The principal patent to the "automatic" meter is patent 2,168,302 which issued to Magee and his co-workers on an application filed in 1936.[7] The claims of this patent are important but not essential to the manufacture of a practical automatic type meter.[8]

[6] *E.g.*, Seeburg patent 2,038,963, filed in 1931, to a coin-operated electrically driven timer mechanism for radios, refrigerators, etc.

[7] In the mechanism of this patent one end of the spring is connected to drive the clock mechanism continuously. At the other end the spring is connected to the violation flag and time pointer and serves to set the time pointer and lower the flag when the coin is inserted.

[8] The broadest claim is claim 12, which calls for spring means driving both

In short, by the time World War II interrupted parking meter production, parking meters were recognized as an effective solution to the parking problem, a number of manufacturers were well established, and both the manual and automatic type meter had been commercially developed. Patents had issued to both types of meters, but were directed to specific constructions because of the prior art patents to parking meters and coin-operated timers generally.

THE PARKING METER ANTITRUST LITIGATION

In July 1942 the Department of Justice filed a civil complaint under Section 4 of the Sherman Act charging violation of that act by the principal concerns then in the parking meter industry, the patent holding company (Vehicular Parking, Ltd.), and the principal officers of these companies.[9] The alleged violation centered about the formation and activities of Vehicular Parking, Ltd. which—by that date—had acquired ownership of the principal patents to the parking meter and had licensed the participating manufacturers to make meters.

Vehicular Parking, Ltd. had been formed in 1937 by the management of Parkrite. The first agreement was made in that year with Karpark and Parkrite. It provided for the assignment of the patents owned by these concerns to Vehicular Parking and a license back from Vehicular to each of these concerns. The patents so assigned included Doyle 1,752,021, which could be literally construed to cover essentially all parking meters.[10] Mi-Co agreed to take license in September 1939, conditioned on the taking of similar licenses by at least five of the seven meter manufacturers. In January 1940—after its prospective customers had been given

the resetting mechanism and the timer. An example of an automatic meter not involving such mechanism is found in Fink patent 2,359,754. In this meter the setting mechanism is gravity operated. The Fink unit was initially made by International Meters and is now manufactured and sold by Mi-Co.

[9]The defendants were Vehicular Parking Ltd., The Karpark Corp., Dual Parking Meter Corp., M. H. Rhodes, Inc., The Standard Meter Corp., Peerless Oil and Gas Co., Duncan Meter Co., Frank L. Michaels and Alfred R. Miller, doing business as Mico-Meter Co., Vernon L. Taylor, John Howard Joynt, Walter J. Herschede, Guy Kelsey, H. D. Timberlake, George E. Tribble, Carl C. Magee, M. H. Rhodes, Donald F. Duncan, and T. W. L. Newson.

[10]The Doyle patent is described in note 1 *supra*. It should be emphasized that the Doyle structure was intended for use inside the vehicle, was not coin operated, and in appearance and actual operation was quite unlike the parking meter as it subsequently commercially developed. The broad construction of this patent was based on the sweeping language of some of its claims. Under the doctrine expressed in Westinghouse v. Boyden, 170 U.S. 537 (1898) and more recent cases such as The Texas Company v. Globe Oil & Refining Co., 225 F.2d 725, 735 (7th Cir. 1955), the commercial parking meter would not be considered to infringe the Doyle patent, irrespective of the language of the claim.

patent infringement notices by Vehicular Parking—Rhodes took a license conditioned on Dual taking a similar license. Duncan agreed to take a license when Dual did so.

The management of Dual resisted the licensing efforts of Vehicular Parking. In March of 1940, Vehicular brought a patent infringement suit against Dual on the Doyle patent and on Toce patent 2,190,553.[11] Dual retaliated in May of the same year by bringing a patent infringement action against Karpark in the same court on Magee patent 2,118,318[12] and McGay patent 2,168,302.[13] Both Vehicular and Dual notified cities and municipalities of the litigation. In consequence, the sale of meters by both Dual and Karpark was—in the words of a Vehicular attorney—"virtually at a standstill."[14] In June of 1940, one Tribble acquired a controlling stock interest in Dual and became a director. Dual then took a license from Vehicular and sold its existing patent rights to Vehicular for the sum of $55,000. At that time, or shortly thereafter, the licenses to Mi-Co, Rhodes, and Duncan became effective. Standard took a license in October 1940, after its customers had been given patent infringement notices.

Thus by fall 1940, Vehicular had acquired the patents of Karpark, Parkrite, and Dual, and had licensed all the substantial companies in the business, namely Karpark, Parkrite, Dual, Duncan, Standard, Mi-Co, and Rhodes.

The licenses issued by Vehicular were essentially uniform and embodied a number of provisions charged by the Government and held by the district court to violate the Sherman Act. The significant provisions in this respect were summarized by Judge Leahy as follows:[15]

(1) "Manual" meters would not be sold below $35 and "automatic" meters not below $45.
(2) "Reasonable" prices would be charged for standards, collars, other parts and services.
(3) A 2 1/2 percent discount would be maximum. 5 percent interest per annum would be charged on deferred payments.
(4) No trade discounts in the form of free meters.

---

[11]The Toce patent, entitled "Parking Meter Expansion Clamp," originated with Karpark Corporation. The patent is directed to an expansion clamp to which a parking meter may be mounted on the open top of a support post or pipe. The scope of the patent is confined to the specific clamp structure, for which numerous perfectly practical substitutes are available and are in use.
[12]See note 5 *supra* and accompanying text.
[13]See notes 7 and 8 *supra* and accompanying text.
[14]Letter of June 4, 1940, written by Mr. John Howard Joynt, Plf. Ex. 57 in the Government suit.
[15]United States v. Vehicular Parking Ltd., 54 F. Supp. 828, 833, 61 *USPQ* 102, 109 (D. C. Del. 1944).

(5) 40 percent of the sales price would be the maximum commission payable to salesmen and distributors. No commissions in advance and not more than $75 per week would be paid as selling expense to salesmen.

(6) No free service or maintenance. Guarantees against defective workmanship to be limited to one year.

(7) Installation of meters for trial periods of less than six months prohibited.

(8) No rental of meters.

(9) Giving of a patent infringement bond in excess of $10,000 to cities prohibited.

(10) No deliveries in anticipation of price advances.

(11) Used and reconditioned manual meters not to be sold below $25, such automatic meters not below $35.

(12) Maximum of $15 for trade-in allowance on second-hand meters.

(13) Sales to cities on credit only if 75 percent of meter income to go to seller until purchase price is paid and payment to be completed within 15 months.

(14) Minimum prices fixed for manual type of meter not to exceed those established for the automatic type.

(15) Each manufacturer to have an agreement no more favorable than the other.

(16) Violations of agreement subject to fines.

(17) Vehicular to enforce patents held by it against other manufacturers of parking meters.

(18) Corporate defendants to pay Vehicular 4 percent of the sales price of each meter in order to police the industry.

(19) Agreements to terminate on the expiration date of the last patent listed in the agreements.

(20) Each manufacturer admitted its own meters were within the scope of the patents held by Vehicular and agreed to mark its meters with the numbers of the patents held by Vehicular.

(21) If any of the pooled patents were held invalid royalty payments to abate.

On March 28, 1944, Judge Leahy rendered his decision in favor of the Government.[16] With respect to the terms of the license agreements, he stated that "Assuming Vehicular's patents are valid, the agreements in suit attempt to extend the lawful patent monopoly in an illegal manner." With respect to the overall patent pooling relationship of the defendants, he stated:[17]

> Where the defendant corporations control from 95 percent to 98 percent of an industry, with threat of competition removed, upon agreement that others will be refused "to join the fold," a tight mo-

---

[16]See note 7 *supra*. The decision of Judge Leahy was preceded by the decision of the Kenton Circuit Court of Kentucky in Vehicular v. Mi-Co., No. 44,455, decided July 22, 1942. In that case the Kentucky court dismissed an action by Vehicular against Mi-Co to recover royalties due under the license agreement, holding that the agreement was invalid under the Sherman Act. See n. 12, 54 F. Supp. 834, 61 *USPQ* 110.

[17]110 F. Supp. 838, 61 *USPQ* 113.

nopoly exists, especially where the parties to the agreement before they became parties to it were in free and open competition and sold the devices at prices to the public much below those established by the agreement.

In his conclusions of law, Judge Leahy declared that covenants in the various license agreements were unenforceable because of the violation of the antitrust laws. Conclusions 19 and 20 were directed to patent enforcement and read: [18]

19. The defendants have effectuated a conspiracy to obtain and use patents and patent rights in violation of the Sherman Act and therefore should be enjoined from enforcing those patent rights, whether by suits for infringement or suits to collect royalties.

20. The defendants have effectuated a conspiracy to obtain and use patents and patent rights in violation of the Sherman Act, and therefore should be required to grant licenses under such patents and patent rights to any applicant therefor.

In his opinion, Judge Leahy indicated doubt that the patents should "be virtually cancelled by the inclusion in the proposed decree of the provisions commanding royalty-free licensing." In an opinion rendered a few months later, he postponed consideration of this matter in view of the pending decision of the Supreme Court in the *Hartford-Empire* case. [19] He did, however, enjoin the defendants from instituting or threatening to institute suits for past infringement or to collect royalties.

On May 6, 1946, a final decree was entered. [20] This decree provided for the compulsory grant of patent licenses on reasonable royalties in the following language:

Each of the individual defendants, each of the company defendants, and each of their directors, officers, agents, employees, successors and assigns be and they are hereby ordered to grant to any applicant therefor, to the extent to which the defendants or any of them possess the power to do so, an absolutely unrestricted, whether

---

[18]61 *USPQ* 118. The Government had concluded its brief with the following paragraph:

"In the present case the only means of restoring competition to the industry is to remove the source of the monopoly power of the defendant. In accordance with prayer 7 of the complaint, this can be accomplished by enjoining the defendants from instituting patent infringement litigation and compelling the defendants to give all applicants royalty-free and unrestricted licenses under their respective patents and patent applications for the lives of such patents and applications.

"The patent pool and the licensing system created by Vehicular in collaboration with the other defendants are the nucleus of the monopoly. Simply to decree a dissolution of the monopoly without neutralizing the patents would be totally ineffective. Such a decree would leave the defendants free to use the source of their monopoly power." (Govt. Main Brief. p. 67).

[19]United States v. Vehicular Parking. 56 F. Supp. 297. 63 *USPQ* 54 (1944).
[20]United States v. Vehicular Parking. 61 F. Supp. 656. 67 *USPQ* 115 (1945).

as to the duration or otherwise, license or sublicense to use, manufacture and sell under any or all United States letters patent and patent applications including all renewals, extensions or reissues of such patents or patent applications, listed in Schedule A which is annexed hereto, provided, after the date of the entry of this order amending the judgment entered July 18, 1944, a reasonable royalty may be charged for such licensing of the United States letters patent and patent applications, including all renewals, extensions, or reissues of such patents or patent applications, listed in Schedule A annexed hereto, provided, further, the provisions of this paragraph 9 shall not be deemed to adjudicate any defense which any person might raise or claim in any suit or proceeding by any defendant, its successors or assigns for infringement, damages, injunction or compensation on account of the patents and patent applications, including all renewals, extensions or reissues of such patents or patent applications, listed in Schedule A annexed hereto.

This provision applied to a list of patents owned by Vehicular Parking.[21]

In a press release at the time of the 1944 opinion, the Department of Justice stated:[22]

As a result of the Court's decision upholding the Government's charges against eight companies and ten individuals engaged in the manufacture and sale of parking meters, cities throughout the country will be free to purchase such equipment from any manufacturer at competitive prices, terms and conditions of sale.

Heretofore parking meters could be purchased only from the defendants in this case at fixed, high and arbitrary prices. Furthermore, purchasers were required to review their bid specifications to conform with the restrictions imposed upon them by the defendants.

The Court's decision, therefore, is of particular interest to all municipalities of the country as well as an important step in the Department's program to clarify the relationship between the antitrust laws and the patent laws. The Court by limiting the patent to the precise terms of its claims, re-affirmed the position of the Department that the patent grant contains no implied license to violate the antitrust laws.

DEVELOPMENTS IN THE PARKING METER
INDUSTRY SINCE 1944

The decrees in the government antitrust proceedings approximately coincided with the end of the wartime moratorium on parking meter production and the resumption of parking meter manufacture. The demand for parking meters evident during the early war years fully materialized, with the consequence that the

---

[21]The list was modified on July 16, 1953, in respects not here pertinent.
[22]See CCH Trade Reporter 54,019 (1944).

meter manufacturers enjoyed a sellers' market for a considerable period, followed by strong meter demand running beyond 1950. Meter production promptly rose to many times the pre-war rate. As compared with the pre-war peak of 48,000 meters in 1941, 1946 production was about 190,000 meters and orders taken in the latter year have been estimated at about 300,000 meters. In 1948—probably the peak production year—the Federal Trade Commission estimated that some 195,000 meters were sold for a total price of about $12 million.

The accumulated wartime meter demand has now tapered off. Current sales are for new installations incident to continued urban growth, additional meter locations in existing urban areas, and replacement meter sales. These, however, add up to a considerable total meter production which at present writing probably exceeds 120,000 meters per year.

Substantial changes have taken place in the business concerns in parking meter business. Magee left Dual soon after Tribble gained control in 1940. In August of 1945 Magee formed Magee-Hale Park-O-Meter Company with Gerald Hale and two other individuals who had a part in the pre-war activity of Dual. A second post-war entry into the industry took place when International Meters began operations. This company was a subsidiary of American LaFrance Foamite Corporation. Its meter design can be traced back at least to 1942. With these two additions, the major meter concerns at the start of the post-war period were Dual, Duncan, Mi-Co, Rhodes, Karpark, International, and Magee-Hale. In 1952 International sold its assets to Mi-Co, thereby leaving Dual, Duncan, Mi-Co, Rhodes, Karpark, and Magee-Hale as the principal concerns in the industry. As a result, the number of major manufacturers of parking meters at the present writing is the same as the number immediately before the war.

No data are available with respect to the year-by-year production of the individual parking meter manufacturers. However, the last Vehicular Parking survey of 1948,[23] the American City survey of 1954,[24] and the list compiled by Magee-Hale of its own

---

[23] Vehicular Parking Ltd., Parking Meters in the United States, year ending Dec. 31, 1948.

[24] The American City List of Parking Meter Installations, American City Magazine. This list was compiled in 1954 upon the basis of an extensive survey and compilation of data from the cities and from the manufacturers. Some question arises as to the date that can be assigned to this survey, since it includes data from different sources at different times. The date of Dec. 31, 1953, appears to be a reasonable approximation of the time for which the survey data applies.

installations as of August 15, 1957,[25] and data supplied by the management of Duncan, provide the following figures:

	ACCUMULATED TOTAL METER PRODUCTION			
	Dec. 31, 1948	Dec. 31, 1953	Aug. 15, 1957	Sept. 1958
Dual	134,000	231,000		750,000
Duncan	174,000	401,000		
Karpark	76,000	128,000	561,000	
Magee-Hale	140,000	385,000		
Mi-Co	58,000	136,000		
Rhodes	92,000	117,000		
International	4,000			
Others	4,000	13,000		

From the above figures, the following average annual production figures can be derived:

	AVERAGE ANNUAL METER PRODUCTION		
	1949-1953	1954-Aug. 15, 1957	Calendar 1954-1957 Annual Average
Dual	19,000		65,000
Duncan	45,000		
Karpark	10,000	51,000	
Magee-Hale	49,000		
Mi-Co	16,000		
Rhodes	5,000		

The above figures must be taken with some caution because the respective surveys were not necessarily made on the same basis, it has been necessary to assign a specific effective date of the American City survey, and other factors are believed to render the figures not exact. The data nevertheless do show the general relationship of the respective meter manufacturers, and support a conclusion that Duncan and Magee-Hale are each doing over one-third of the business, Dual and Mi-Co are each selling about 10 percent of the meters sold, and that the remaining sales are primarily by Karpark and Rhodes, with each selling well under 10 percent of the total number of meters.

Parking meter prices in the postwar period reflect a number of factors, including particularly the accumulated wartime demand and seller's market (which tended to increase prices) and the maturity of the industry (which tended to decrease prices). In

---

[25] Magee-Hale Park-O-Meter Company, Park-O-Meter Installations as of Aug. 15, 1957.

this setting it is not possible to isolate the effect of the compulsory licensing decree provisions on prices. The prices do, however, generally reflect a somewhat smaller increase over the prewar figures than would be expected on the basis of declining dollar values.[26]

From the standpoint of product improvement, the parking meter industry now has the characteristics of a mature industry. In the post-war period only three wholly new meter designs have been introduced. These are the "Alfco Twin," made by International, the "Park-O-Meter" of Magee-Hale, and the Duncan "Automaton." Improved operating mechanisms, improved coin collection arrangements, and other refinements have been incorporated in many of the other meters, but the operating principles have remained unchanged. There is considerable product rivalry between Magee-Hale—which sells only the traditional type "automatic" meter—and Duncan—which sells only the traditional type "manual" meter and the "Automaton" which is wound by the act of inserting the coin. Other manufacturers also stress their own product improvements, but generally make available both the "manual" and "automatic" meter types. At the present time, however, this product competition is largely confined to the incorporation of specific advantages in existing mechanisms and not to radically new meter designs.

Patent rights are of limited importance in the parking meter industry today. Indeed, the chief importance of such rights at the present writing appears to be that of preventing the copying of specific meter features by competitors. In a number of instances patent rights have been the occasion for royalty payments. Patent rights in no way foreclose the manufacture of the basic manual and automatic meter types, or the inclusion of refinements as necessary to make fully competitive meter designs.

---

[26] As noted above, the prices set by the Vehicular licenses were $35 for manual meters and $45 for automatic meters. These prices were in effect for the 1940-1941 period. The ratio of the 1950 consumer price index to that for 1940 is 1.72, the ratio of the 1950 price index for metals and metal products to that for 1940 is 1.76, and the ratio of the 1950 price index for motor vehicles to that for 1940 is 1.86 (see, Department of Commerce, Office of Business Economics, 1957 Biennial Edition, pp. 26, 31, and 30, respectively). Based on these ratios, the prices set in the licenses, in 1950 dollars, were in the $60-$65 range for manual meters and the $77-$84 range for automatic meters.

The Federal Trade Commission figure of 195,000 meters sold for $12 million in 1948 leads to an average price of $61.50 per meter. In 1949 the average Magee-Hale price was $60. In April 1950 the City of Chicago invited bids on parking meters and initially received bids averaging $70 per meter (the highest figure being about $84 and the lowest about $65). The city thereupon called for new and lower bids. The average price on the second set of bids was $53 (the highest figure being about $70 and the lowest about $40).

There are no indications of agreements in the parking meter industry today similar to those that accompanied the activity of Vehicular Parking prior to the war.

With these introductory remarks we shall now turn to a discussion of the activities and history of the individual companies.

Duncan Parking Meter Corporation

There is a consensus in the industry—borne out by the tabulation above—that Duncan and Magee-Hale are the leading concerns in the parking meter industry today. As the tabulation also indicates, Duncan currently is selling a somewhat greater number of meters than Magee-Hale.

During the pre-war period Duncan was the chief competitor to Dual, then the industry leader. In the post-war period, Duncan became a leader in sales and by the close of 1948 the aggregate Duncan sales had exceeded those of Dual.

As is discussed above in connection with the pre-war history of the industry.[27] Duncan started in the parking meter business in the middle 1930's in cooperation with the Miller Meter Company, a related company. Miller was engaged in the manufacture of timing devices, including coin-operated devices for washing machines. hotel radios. and the like. from which entry into the parking meter business was a natural change. Miller Meters makes all of the parts for the Duncan meter (except for die castings) and assembles the meters. Die castings are made by another concern owned by the same parties. Total employment of Miller and Duncan is about 250 persons.

Duncan maintains a plant in Montreal to supply the Canadian market.

Duncan has sold all the meters used by the City of Chicago.

Prior to 1950, Duncan manufactured only manual meters. In that year it brought out the "Automaton." This meter was designed by Robert Broussard who testified in the Magee-Hale tax proceedings[28] that he was paid a license royalty of 50 cents per meter. Broussard also testified that 30,000 "Automaton" meters had been sold prior to 1955, an average of about 6,000 per year. The "Automaton" employs a distinctive semispherical glass upper case design.

Duncan currently sells three meter models. One of these—

---

[27]See p. 214, *supra*.
[28]Magee-Hale Park-O-Meter Co. v. Commissioner. No. 43,058 (Tax Court of the United States). R. 355.

the Duncan-Miller Model 50—was designed prior to the war.[29] It is a manual meter. The second current Duncan meter—the Duncan-Miller Model 60—is a modernized version of the Model 50 featuring among other improvements a more refined coin collection mechanism, improved case design, and improved visibility of the time scale and pointer.[30] It is likewise a manual meter. The third meter—the "Automaton"—is discussed above.[31] It is an automatic meter in the sense that the user does not have to rotate a handle to initiate meter operation. It differs from other automatic meters (and is like a manual meter) in that the spring winding required for meter operation is supplied by the operator, in this case by the force exerted on the coin as it is forced into the meter.

Current Duncan advertisements stress the absence of winding operations with the Duncan meters (including the "Automaton"). In this respect Duncan offers an advantage over Magee-Hale and the automatic meters made by other competitors, for all of these involve either the cost of electrical apparatus or require periodic winding by city officials. By way of disadvantages, the Duncan manual meters (like all manual meters) require the hand operation to set the meter when the coin is inserted, and the "Automaton" requires finger pressure in inserting the coin.

Duncan follows a policy of obtaining patents to its meter improvements where possible, including patents in Canada.[32] In

---

[29] The structure of this meter is shown in patent 2,070,445, filed July 30, 1936.

[30] The appearance of this meter is approximately that shown in patent 2,768,783.

[31] This meter is shown in its general appearance in patent 2,483,805.

[32] The following patents are assigned to Duncan: Broussard, 2,465,146, filed Dec. 23, 1946, entitled "Coin Gate Mechanism"; Broussard and Sollenberger, 2,483,805, filed March 5, 1948, entitled "Coin Mechanism Housing" (Canadian 470,354); Broussard, 2,594,388, filed Sept. 23, 1946, entitled "Automatic Pay Station" (Canadian 470,492); Broussard, 2,596,123, filed March 27, 1945, entitled "Parking Meter and Coin Slot Therefor"; Broussard, 2,596,124, filed March 27, 1945, entitled "Parking Meter"; Broussard, 2,596,122, filed March 27, 1945, entitled "Parking Meter and Coin Slot Therefor"; Broussard and Sollenberger, 2,613,792, filed July 12, 1948, entitled "Coin Handling Apparatus"; Broussard and Miller 2,613,871, filed April 12, 1949, entitled "Coin Handling Apparatus," (Canadian 470,694); Broussard, 2,618,371, filed Dec. 23, 1946, entitled "Parking Meter"; Broussard, 2,633,960, filed Jan. 14, 1948, entitled "Coin Handling Apparatus" (Canadian 476,061).
The following patents are assigned to Miller Meters: Anderson, 2,604,259, filed Feb. 2, 1949, entitled "Coin Box for Coin Operated Machines"; Broussard, Miller, and Christensen, 2,660,283, filed Feb. 2, 1950, entitled "Parking Meter"; Broussard 2,685,953, filed Sept. 22, 1951, entitled "Parking Meter"; Broussard, Miller, and Sollenberger, 2,695,090, filed Feb. 2, 1950, entitled "Parking Meter"; Broussard, 2,752,924, filed Jan. 14, 1948, entitled "Coin Handling Apparatus"; Arzig, 2,768,783, filed July 29, 1954, entitled "Coin Receptacle" (Canadian 497,420); Canadian 497,053, filed April 16, 1953, entitled "Coin Handling Apparatus."

the case of the Model 50 manual meter, the patents marked on the meter have now expired.[33] Detail patents to specific aspects of the Model 60 construction, especially the coin collecting arrangement, remain alive.[34]

With respect to the "Automaton," a series of patents have issued, of which some cover the spring winding mechanism based on coin pressure in fairly broad terms.[35]

Duncan brought a patent infringement suit against Rhodes in 1946.[36] Claim 15 of Miller patent 1,799,056 was asserted to be infringed. This patent, as discussed above,[37] was directed to a coin controlled timer and includes no description of a parking meter as such. Duncan took the position that claim 15 was of sufficient scope to cover the accused Rhodes parking meter, which was a manual type meter. The district court held the claim invalid, but infringed if valid.[38] The Court of Appeals for the Third Circuit affirmed per curiam.[39] The patent expired almost concurrently with the Court of Appeals decision.

Following the antitrust decree, Duncan refused to take a patent license from Vehicular. In 1948, Vehicular filed the so-called "Chicago" suit alleging patent infringement by Duncan.[40] The charges were initially directed to the Model 50 manual meter. A total of five patents and 12 claims were listed in the complaint.[41] It is believed that the most troublesome of the infringement charges was claim 10 of Magee patent 2,118,318, relating to the flag mechanism on the meter.[42] In May 1950 the complaint was amended to add charges of infringement by the "Automaton." Vehicular named four patents and six claims in this infringement

---

[33] The patents so marked are Miller 1,799,056 (expired in 1947); Miller 2,070,445 (expired in 1954); and Design 101,237 (expired in 1950).

[34] *E.g.*, Arzig 2,768,783, filed July 29, 1954, entitled "Coin Receptacle."

[35] *E.g.*, Broussard 2,580,400, filed March 27, 1945, entitled "Parking Meter and Coin Slot Therefor."

[36] Duncan Meter Corp. and S. L. Miller v. M. H. Rhodes, Inc., No. 740 D. Del.

[37] See note 1, *supra*.

[38] Duncan Meter Corp. *et al.* v. M. H. Rhodes, Inc., 68 F. Supp. 89 (1946).

[39] Duncan Meter Corp. *et al.* v. M. H. Rhodes, Inc., 161 F.2d 1022 (1947).

[40] Vehicular Parking Ltd. v. Duncan Meter Corp., 48 C 1899. On the same day, Duncan sued Vehicular in the Northern District of Ohio, seeking declaratory judgment of patent invalidity and non-infringement. This case was dismissed on Dec. 31, 1948, apparently by agreement of the parties to litigate the issues in Chicago.

[41] Patent 2,088,300 (claims 2, 3, 4, 5, and 6); patent 2,118,318 (claims 10 and 11); patent 2,137,111 (claim 8); patent 2,262,783 (claims 2 and 3); patent 2,328,043 (claims 6 and 8).

[42] See p. 214, *supra*.

charge.[43] The principals in Magee-Hale purchased the Vehicular patents soon after this amendment to the Complaint. The "Chicago" litigation was then settled for a $25,000 payment by Duncan and, on April 16, 1951, an order was entered on stipulation dismissing the complaint, declaring four patents non-infringed, and ordering their dedication to the public.[44]

The activities of Duncan are of particular interest to the present study for a number of reasons. First, Duncan is one of the two largest manufacturers of parking meters today, with a sales volume of the order of a third of the industry sales and in excess of the sales volume of Magee-Hale. Second, the Duncan manufacturing and product improvement efforts do not appear to have been influenced one way or another by the compulsory license provisions of the antitrust decree. As the Chicago suit shows, Duncan was ready to face the Vehicular patents rather than pay the royalties sought by Vehicular. Third, in introducing the "Automaton" Duncan made the most recent substantial innovation in the parking meter industry. Finally, Duncan is of interest in that it does not make a conventional automatic meter and in this respect is in product competition with the manufacturers of automatic meters, including Magee-Hale which makes only an automatic meter.

Magee-Hale Park-O-Meter Company

Magee-Hale requires detailed discussion because of its important role in postwar parking meter industry developments.

It will be recalled that Dual Parking Meter Company was organized mainly through the efforts of Carl C. Magee. Magee initially owned 50 percent of the stock and Gerald A. Hale, J. B. McGay and George Nicholson, with others, had minority stock holdings. Magee was president of Dual when Tribble acquired a majority interest in its stock in 1940 and remained president for a time thereafter. Hale also continued as an employee of the new majority owner for a time. McGay and Nicholson owned and operated Macnick Company which fabricated meters for Dual.

Magee, Hale, McGay and Nicholson organized Magee-Hale Park-O-Meter Company on August 9, 1945.

In 1943, prior to the formation of Magee-Hale, Hale undertook the design of a new parking meter to be made and sold after

---

[43]Patent 2,162,191 (claims 9 and 10), patent 2,262,783 (claim 2), patent 2,328,043 (claims 6, 7 and 8). patent 2,190,555 (claim 1).
[44]The patents dedicated were 2,162,191, 2,190,555, 2,262,783, and 2,328,043.

the war. Magee, McGay and Nicholson also worked on the project. The meter is shown in patent 2,625,250 issued on January 13, 1953, on an application filed on October 1, 1945. All meters sold by Magee-Hale to date closely conform to the design of this patent. The patent claims are confined to specific improvements, including (a) actuation of the tripping mechanism by the force exerted by the operator on inserting a coin into the meter, (b) operation of the meter by various combinations of coins or multiples of coins, (c) resetting the time indicator according to the value of the coin inserted and (d) a coin display window to discourage the use of slugs.

In recognition of the work of Magee, McGay, and Nicholson, Hale assigned to each an undivided one-fourth interest in the meter design and patent rights. On September 5, 1945, an exclusive license was entered into between these parties and Magee-Hale, providing for a royalty of $4 per meter. These same four parties (Magee, McGay, Nicholson and Hale) each also owned a one-fourth interest in each class of Magee-Hale stock.

Operations by Magee-Hale were a success from the start. By 1947 its sales volume was in excess of that of the entire industry for 1941, the best pre-war year. The record for the first four years of operation is as follows:

	*1946	*1947	*1948	*1949
Net meters sold	9,480	49,164	59,191	49,251
Earned revenue on meter sales	$45,777.24	$707,540.03	$1,337,612.87	$1,460,262.93
Net parts sales and other income	3,697.75	8,875.29	20,213.81	37,783.57
Gross income	49,474.99	716,415.32	1,357,826.68	1,498,046.50
Expenses other than taxes and royalties	52,083.93	479,127.89	959,115.79	1,040,767.27
Net income before taxes and royalties	**(2,608.94)	237,287.43	398,710.89	457,279.23
Royalty paid	3,868.00	66,272.00	112,256.00	190,076.00
Net income before taxes	**(6,476.94)	171,015.43	286,454.89	267,203.23
Federal and state taxes	--	65,693.55	113,150.80	103,179.85
Net income after taxes	**(6,476.94)	105,321.88	173,304.09	164,023.38

*Fiscal years ending on July 31 of each year indicated.
**Deficit.

The extent of the business success of Magee-Hale through

fiscal 1949 is best brought out by the relationship of the earnings before taxes and royalties to investment. The aggregate par value of the issued stock was only $70,500. Earnings for the period totaled $1,090,668.61 before taxes and royalties, or about 15.5 times the investment. This is equivalent to about 12 percent return compounded annually over the four-year period. Over and above this return "officers commissions" paid during the period totaled $246,277.02. These figures become even more impressive when it is recalled that Carl Magee died prior to the close of the first year of business of Magee-Hale, leaving management essentially in the hands of Hale, whose major interest lies in the engineering aspects of the business.

Initially, the Macnick Company fabricated the Magee-Hale meters on order from Magee-Hale. Magee-Hale, however, owned essentially all of the tools and dies. In March 1957 Magee-Hale began to manufacture meters in its own plant in Oklahoma City. It is interesting that in April 1947, Rockwell Manufacturing Company—which later bought Dual—bought the capital stock of Macnick. Precision Products Company of Delaware makes the timers used in the Magee-Hale meters.

On May 23, 1946, Vehicular wrote Magee-Hale that it was ready and willing to grant a patent license to Magee-Hale. Considerable correspondence followed, culminating in a letter dated November 28, 1946, from Vehicular to Magee-Hale stating specifically that the Magee-Hale meter infringed claim 10 of Magee patent 2,118,318, claims 4, 5, 6, 8, 9, 10, 11, 12, 13, and 14 of McGay patent 2,168,302, claims 1-3, 5, and 9 of Woodruff patent 2,198,422 and claims 4 and 5 of McGay patent 2,284,221. The Vehicular standard blanket license offered to Magee-Hale called for a 4 percent royalty, but not less than $1.40 per manual meter and $1.80 per automatic meter. Early in December 1946 Magee-Hale asked for a royalty rate as to the specific four patents alleged to be infringed, to which Vehicular replied that it could not make any exceptions to the standard license terms. On December 18, 1946, Magee-Hale filed petition for leave to intervene in the antitrust proceeding, seeking an injunction against interference by Vehicular with its business and an order fixing the rate for a compulsory license.

An initial question arose as to whether Magee-Hale was entitled to apply for a determination of reasonable royalties under the judgment.[45] Paragraph 13 stated that jurisdiction was retained to enable "any of the parties to this judgment" to apply to

---

[45] United States v. Vehicular Parking, Ltd., 74 *USPQ* 289 (1947).

the court for such determination. It was argued that Magee-Hale was not a "party" to the judgment.

Judge Leahy granted leave to intervene. reasoning that the compulsory license provision of the decree would be rendered ineffective unless such intervention was permitted.

Five months later Judge Leahy also decided that Magee-Hale need only take licenses under the four patents for which license was sought and not under all the patents of Vehicular. He also held that the court should fix a reasonable royalty if Magee-Hale so desired. The only other important issue was whether Magee-Hale would be required to take a license after the court had fixed a reasonable royalty. Judge Leahy did not consider his court as a "place for litigious business men to stress and strain as they try to make a deal."[46] and therefore held that a license was mandatory if a royalty was fixed pursuant to the decree procedure.

On November 26. 1947. Magee-Hale filed a written election to take license under the four Vehicular patents. Judge Leahy appointed Arthur G. Connelly. Esq.. as special master to determine a reasonable royalty. The order of reference. dated October 19. 1948.. provided that the master should consider the prior art in fixing the scope of the patents. but not to the extent of concluding that any patent was without meaning. Eight days later Magee-Hale filed suit in the same court for a judgment declaring the four patents invalid. Judge Leahy dismissed this complaint on the ground that so long as Magee-Hale was a potential licensee it could not question the validity of the patents for which it sought license. This order was affirmed on appeal. The Court of Appeals noted. however. that the Magee-Hale motion to test validity in the license proceeding was not finally disposed of.[47]

In the reasonable royalty proceedings before the special master. Vehicular placed its main emphasis upon an agreement under which Magee-Hale paid $4 per meter royalty to Hale. Magee McGay. and Nicholson. It contended that this payment for an exclusive license on a single narrow improvement patent showed conclusively the reasonableness of the 4 percent offer to Vehicular (which would amount to about two dollars per meter at the October 1946 Magee-Hale sales price). Magee-Hale took the rather extreme position that only nominal royalties should be ordered. It argued that Vehicular paid only a small purchase price for the patents to be licensed. that Vehicular only charged 4 per

---

[46] This opinion is not published.

[47] Magee-Hale Park-O-Meter Co. v. Vehicular Parking. Ltd.. 180 F.2 897. 899; 84 *USPQ* 395. 398 (3rd Cir. 1950).

cent royalty for a license under its entire group of 31 patents and did not increase this rate when the patents involved in the royalty proceedings were included, that the patents were of limited scope in view of the prior art, that the parking meter industry was one of low profits, and that Vehicular had failed to restrict its proofs on the value of the patents to the portion of the parking meters covered by them.

The special master filed a preliminary report on April 20, 1950. He concluded that Magee-Hale was entitled to a nonexclusive license at the rate of 1 percent royalty for each of the patents in question, with a maximum royalty rate of 3 percent for any three or all four of the patents.

The preliminary report of the master is reproduced as Appendix A. In summary, the master—after noting that there was no evidence relating to the Patent Office histories of the respective patents—concluded that the prior art patents relied upon by Magee-Hale did not compel a narrow patent construction. He considered that the structures of these patents required substantial modification to make a parking meter. The special master also concluded that the prices paid by Vehicular for the patents did not represent arm's length transaction but rather involved an element of duress. He accordingly considered that the purchase prices did not indicate the value of the patents or a license to them. The royalty previously charged by Vehicular for licenses was not considered controlling because the licenses were taken to police the industry rather than to repay the patent owner. The argument that the industry would not support substantial royalties was dismissed as contrary to the record. Finally, the master concluded that Vehicular was justified in not segregating the patented structure from the parking meter as a whole. On this point he noted the doctrine of earlier patent accounting decisions to the effect that where a complete product is made possible by the patented invention the complete product and not just the patented combination is the measure of the damages for patent infringement.

As above noted, the Magee-Hale stockholders purchased the stock of Vehicular for $95,000. This took place before further proceedings on the master's report and brought the litigation to an end.

The Magee-Hale Tax Proceedings[48]

It will be recalled that on September 5, 1945, Hale executed an exclusive license to Magee-Hale to make, use, and vend the

[48]Magee-Hale Park-O-Meter Co. *et al.* v. Commissioner, 15 T.C.M. 254 (1956).

subject matter of what became patent 2,625,250. The exclusive license required a royalty of $4 per meter manufactured. On September 17, 1945, Hale assigned an undivided one-fourth interest in the patent rights to Magee, McGay, and Nicholson, so that each of the four principals in Magee-Hale received a royalty of $1 per meter.

Royalties were thereafter paid out pursuant to the agreement. Magee-Hale deducted the royalties paid as a reasonable allowance for depreciation of a capital asset, namely its exclusive license interest in the patent. The Hales (and evidently the other parties as well) paid tax at capital gains rates on the theory that the exclusive license constituted a sale of a capital asset held for over six months. The government contended that the payments made by Magee-Hale to the Hales were dividends and assessed a deficiency against the Hales based on the difference between the tax paid and the tax based on ordinary income rates and a deficiency against the company in the amount of the tax due on the amount deducted from the corporate income to make the payments.

The Tax Court held for the Hales and Magee-Hale. Judge Tietjens concluded that the agreement between Magee-Hale and its majority shareholders was genuine. The court noted that Magee-Hale not only received an exclusive license to the prospective patent but also received rights to an accumulative indexing mechanism, the parking meter design and the trade name "Park-O-Meter." The value of the patent rights was proved, in the court's opinion, by the later commercial success of the Park-O-Meter. The court considered the $4 per meter royalty paid by Magee-Hale's Canadian licensee and the sum of over $4 per meter paid by the British licensee as a measure of the value of the patent rights to the Park-O-Meter.

The court also held that the exclusive license granted by the Hales to Magee-Hale was the sale of a capital asset entitling them to treat the royalties as capital gains.

The Present Status of Magee-Hale

Magee-Hale is currently in a strong position in the parking meter field. As above noted, it and Duncan each sell about one-third of the current meters, with the additional third of the meters being divided among Dual, Mi-Co, Rhodes and Karpark.

Magee-Hale meters are manufactured in Canada by the Park-O-Meter Company of Canada, Ltd., operated by David A.McGowan, 81 Main Street, Toronto. License was entered into with Magee-Hale on July 1, 1950. Just prior to this date the Canadian patent to the Park-O-Meter (No. 459,961) was assigned to Magee-Hale for $40,000. According to the Tax Court testimony the Park-O-Meter sells for $86 in Canada and 9,000 were sold between 1950 and 1955. Park-O-Meter of Canada was sued for patent infringement by Dual's Canadian licensee. The same infringement charges were made as in the U. S. compulsory license proceedings. The proceedings lasted one and one-half years and ended in a settlement under which McGowan (the Magee-Hale licensee) agreed to pay a royalty of $1.75 per Park-O-Meter manufactured.

Magee-Hale meters are sold in Europe[49] by the British licensee, Venner Time Switches, Ltd. of London. This license was entered into on January 1, 1953. The royalty amounts to 8 percent of the sales price of the meters, which ranges from $70 to $84.

While Magee-Hale emphasized the value of the Hale patent, 2,625,250 in the tax proceedings, other considerations indicate that its value is limited. No domestic competitor is known to have sought a license, nor has any infringement notice been sent. There is considerable evidence, including some of the Tax Court testimony, indicating that the principal reason Canadian and British licenses were taken was the desire to make the successful Magee-Hale meter without change or other expense and not because an equally effective design could not be made without access to the patent. Moreover, there were no claims in the tax proceeding that the patent covered more than the specific mechanisms.[50]

Gerald Hale has been issued a total of six patents since 1945.[51] The original patent (2,625,250), however, is the only one marked on the meter. The management of Magee-Hale considers that the basic structure of patent 2,625,250 is so complete that no important

---

[49] See *Business Week*, April 6, 1957, p. 81.

[50] The Tax Court stated that the 13 claims of the '250 patent ". . . related to improvements in the operation of the parking meter, such as (a) actuation of the tripping mechanism by the force of the operator's insertion of a coin in the meter, (b) operation by various combinations of coins or multiples of coins, (c) resetting the time indicator according to the value of the coin inserted, and (d) a coin display window to decrease the use of slugs . . ." 15 TCM 254, 256-57 (1956). In the 1949 meter survey for the City of Chicago these features received no emphasis, and the report is critical of the coin window which could easily be pushed out. See City of Chicago Parking Meter Survey 1949. Results of Investigation of Commercial Parking Meters.

[51] Patent 2,532,906, filed May 7, 1949 entitled "Cumulative Indexing Mechanism"; patent 2,599,912, filed January 12, 1951 entitled "Coin Tube and Opener Therefor"; patent 2,620,971, filed June 10, 1950 entitled "Coin Collector"; patent 2,625,250, filed August 1, 1945 entitled "Automatic Parking Meter"; patent 2,631,710, filed August 3, 1950 entitled "Automatic Parking Meter"; patent 2,655,797, filed March 21, 1949 entitled "Timer Apparatus for Parking Meters."

changes are necessary. The company undertakes research and engineering directed to improvements in materials and construction and other engineering refinements.

The success of Magee-Hale prompts inquiry as to the reasons the company went into the business and the reasons for this success. In the first place, it seems clear that formation of Magee-Hale was motivated by a desire on the part of Magee and Hale to reenter the parking meter business, and to do so outside the Vehicular group. Magee and Hale were cognizant of the Vehicular patents at the time. They considered, however, that the key need was that of developing a meter fulfilling existing operating requirements and adjustable to meet future needs. They were ready to take their chances on the patents when and if the problem became acute. They felt that the Vehicular patents were not entitled to a broad interpretation, and that the patents were unenforceable because acquired under duress, with little investment, and in violation of the antitrust laws.

There can be no doubt that the principals in Magee-Hale found comfort in the antitrust proceedings. By March 28, 1944, when Judge Leahy entered his first decision, it was evident that in all probability at least reasonable royalty licenses would be available under the Vehicular patents. This decision was regarded by Magee-Hale as giving "back stop" protection with respect to charges of infringement of the Vehicular patents. This decision came before full scale manufacturing activity had commenced and before the major production investments in the Park-O-Meter had been made. In addition, the Vehicular decrees were of value to Magee-Hale in minimizing patent infringement threats against prospective Magee-Hale customers.

While the antitrust proceedings thus eased the entry of Magee-Hale into the parking meter business, the present writers believe that Magee-Hale would have entered the business and would have had essentially the same success whether or not the decree was entered. The past resistance of Magee to the Vehicular group and his past success with Dual made it almost certain that he would re-enter the business with a new company just as soon as the wartime moratorium on meter production was lifted. The major design efforts of Hale and Magee took place while the war was still in progress and during a time when the outcome of the antitrust proceedings was not certain. While a different termination of the antitrust proceedings could have prompted a change in plans by Magee-Hale, every present indication is that it would not have done so, and it is considered almost certain that Magee-Hale could and would have entered the industry regardless of the decree.

Duncan and Magee-Hale are the present leaders in the parking meter industry. Magee-Hale's success, like Duncan's, appears to be the consequence of the combination of a high quality product, a favorable price, and aggressive sales technique, all based on prior experience in the business. Although Carl Magee died before the middle of 1946, he did have an opportunity to carry the business over its initial efforts. As to the meter design, Hale's earlier experience with Dual doubtless enabled him to avoid pitfalls such as those that plagued International. In the postwar seller's market, Magee-Hale was able to take full advantage of its resources and establish itself in a manner that assured its present position in the industry. The Vehicular antitrust proceedings were of some aid to Magee-Hale, but were not responsible for the entry of Magee-Hale into the industry or for the success of the company.

Dual Parking Meter Company

Dual is the oldest parking meter manufacturer, having been founded in 1935 by Carl C. Magee. The company was operated by Mr. Magee in Oklahoma City until shortly before World War II when Tribble purchased a majority stock interest and brought the company into the Vehicular patent licensing arrangement.[52]

In July 1944, Union Metal Manufacturing Company of Canton, Ohio, purchased the assets of Dual and made Dual a subsidiary. Union was then, and now is, a manufacturer of street lighting and other equipment for sale to municipalities. It made the purchase to expand the line of products it sold to municipalities. The meters were manufactured by Superior Switchboard and Devices Company, another subsidiary of Union. Soon after purchasing Dual, Union also purchased Vehicular. Vehicular was operated as a statistical agency for a period of time, publishing statistics of parking meter installations for the benefit of municipalities. This operation was discontinued by 1947. After this date, Vehicular was only a patent holding company.

During the prewar period Dual was the clear leader in the parking meter industry, with about 41 percent of the sales. Postwar sales, however, have been at a much smaller volume. Currently, as above discussed, Dual is probably selling less than half the volume of either Duncan or Magee-Hale.

As is discussed above with reference to Magee-Hale, Union Metal sold the Vehicular patents to the Magee-Hale management in 1950. A paid-up license was retained by Union to assure to Dual a continued freedom to manufacture under the Vehicular patents.

---

[52] See p. 217, *supra*.

In late 1956 Rockwell Manufacturing Company of Pittsburgh announced that it had acquired Dual Parking Meter Company and certain other Union Metal assets relating to the parking meter business. Rockwell is in the business of manufacturing valves and other products for sale to municipalities. Its own manufacturing experience in connection with taxi meters provided it with a fund of knowledge as to the manufacture of timing mechanisms generally. Rockwell had prior contact with the parking meter industry when it purchased Macnick Company, which was manufacturing parking meters for Magee-Hale.

Rockwell has since moved Dual from Canton, Ohio, to Pittsburgh and has transferred manufacturing operations to its own plants. Following the acquisition, Dual advertised that it would have the benefits of the Rockwell research laboratories.

The principal meter construction manufactured by Dual since the war is an automatic meter. This meter uses a housing shape similar to that of the pre-war Dual meters.[53] Improvements have been made in the operating mechanism, as represented by a number of patents that have issued to Superior Switchboard.[54] The changes involved, however, are of the detail variety and represent no fundamental changes in the meter design.

Dual also manufactures a manual meter, to which minor sales emphasis is given. While the housing of this meter was restyled after the war, and detailed improvements have been made over the years, the construction of this meter is fundamentally the same as prior to the war.

Dual parking meters are made and sold in Canada by Dual Parking Meter, Ltd., which is an independent operating company.

It is too early to evaluate the effect of the Rockwell purchase on Dual and on the parking meter industry. Rockwell employs almost 7,000 persons and its sales volume is in excess of $100 million

---

[53] See, e.g., Clough patent 2,570,920.

[54] Patent 2,551,914, filed September 10, 1949, entitled "Coin Register Parking Meter"; patent 2,556,123, filed September 21, 1949, entitled "Flywheel Governor for Parking Meters" (Canadian 473,164); patent 2,570,920, filed June 4, 1949, entitled "Parking Meter Coin Discharge Guiding Construction" (Canadian 482,883); patent 2,588,271, filed March 12, 1951, entitled "Hinge Construction for Parking Meter Doors"; patent 2,696,899, filed August 22, 1949, entitled "Time Selecting and Coin Handling Mechanism" (Canadian 501,700); patent 2,718,954, filed July 3, 1951, entitled "Parking Meter" (Canadian 532,861); patent 2,755,904, filed June 6, 1951, entitled "Manually Operated Parking Meter."

Dual has been issued Canadian patent 390,658, filed January 16, 1936, issued 1940; (U. S. 2,118,318); patent 390,659, filed March 17, 1936, issued 1940 (U. S. 2,137,111); patent 390,660, filed May 26, 1936, issued 1940 (U. S. 2,168,302) and patent 395,164 filed June 17, 1937, issued 1941 (U. S. 2,162,191).

.nnually, making it far larger in size than any other parking meter manufacturer. Its experience as the manufacturer of about 70 per-ent of all domestic taxi meters,[55] as well as other products, in-licates an impressive production know-how. Its water meters and ▸ther products sold to municipalities give it experience with the ales side of the parking meter business. With all of these assets it eems clear that Rockwell could alter greatly the status of Dual, both n terms of meter design and production and in terms of sales effort. To date, however, there are no indications of activity in this direc-ion, and Dual continues its advertising and sales at essentially the ame level as prior to purchase by Rockwell. Indeed, with the ex-eption of advertisements made at the time of the purchase by Rock-vell, Dual continues to place major advertising stress on the success ▸f past Dual installations.

International Meters, Inc.

International Meters, Inc., was formed in 1945 as a subsidiary ▸f American LaFrance Foamite Company. The latter company is he leading producer of fire engines and similar equipment sold to nunicipalities. The parking meter business was thought to be a natural avenue for expansion in the postwar era.

The meter manufactured by International was the twin type neter of Louis F. Fink patent 2,359,754, filed in 1942. An inspec-:ion of the patent and the operation of the meter indicates that in :erms of overall complexity and effectiveness of operation the struc-:ure could form a competitive parking meter. The twin meter ̄eature had a positive advantage at the time of its introduction in 1946 in that it reduced meter stands, housings, and the like by nearly ɔne-half and simplified collection and winding operations. The meter was introduced with a vigorous advertising program in 1946 and the company followed an optimistic policy as to the prospective sales. The company is reported to have contracted for 100,000 clockworks per year in 1946, to supply the equivalent of 200,000 single meters.

International had difficulties from the start. The Vehicular survey for 1946 indicates that no International meters were installed as of the end of that year. As meters were installed, difficulties of a mechanical nature plagued International. Meters were returned in considerable quantities and considerable delay was encountered in diagnosing the trouble and correcting it. By 1949 International had made less than 1 percent of the meter installations in the

---

[55] See *New York Times*, Sept. 2, 1957, and *Christian Science Monitor*, June 4, 1957.

United States. Moreover, the unfavorable experience of municipalities with the parking meter imposed a risk that the American LaFrance sales of other products would be adversely affected International discontinued advertising in 1951.

An indication of the difficulties encountered by International is found in a report made for the City of Chicago. With respect to the Alfco-Twin meter, this report states:[56]

> These meters gave considerable trouble throughout our tests. I is possible to "operate" these meters continuously (until the spring runs down) by placing of a penny in the slot and following with a single nickel partially inserted into the coin slot.

American LaFrance sold the International Meter assets to Mi-Co in 1952. The International twin meter became the Mi-Co automatic meter. The experience of Mi-Co in making and selling the International type meter since the purchase has been satisfactory.

International appears to have had no difficulty with Vehicular Parking. An examination of the Fink patent structure and the various patents owned by Vehicular indicates that Vehicular could not justifiably charge International with patent infringement. Indeed, the indications are that International studied the Vehicular patents and took them into account in the design of its meter. The experience of International thus shows that it was possible to design a competitive meter in 1946 that would not infringe the Vehicular patents.

There are no indications that the antitrust proceedings had any influence on the activity of International. The meter design must have commenced well before the 1942 filing date of the Fink patent and hence well before the antitrust decision. Also, since infringement of the Vehicular patents was not a problem, International had little to gain or to lose by the antitrust proceedings.

Moreover, the difficulties experienced by International appear to have no relation to the patent aspects of the meter. Rather, they appear to have been wholly related to production problems. The subsequent experience of Mi-Co with the International meter confirms this conclusion and shows that there was no fundamental difficulty in the International meter design as such. The experience of International thus stands as a practical demonstration of the conclusion derived from a study of the Vehicular patents that a competitive non-infringing meter could be made.

---

[56] Results of Investigations of Commercial Parking Meters, Jan. 7, 1949 included in City of Chicago, Parking Meter Survey, 1949.

Mi-Co Meter Company

Mi-Co, now a division of Michaels Art Bronze Company, is a manufacturer of non-ferrous and stainless steel architectural metalwork sold primarily to general contractors. Mi-Co entered the parking meter business in 1936 and has been in the business ever since.[57]

Mi-Co is located in Erlanger, Kentucky. The basic meter parts, with the exception of the clock mechanism, are made on the premises and stocked for use in meter manufacture. Parking meters constitute about a quarter of the total business of Michaels Art Bronze Company.

Prior to 1952 Mi-Co confined its manufacture and sale to a manual type meter. In that year it purchased the assets of International Meters and began the manufacture and sale of the "Alfco" automatic twin meter as a Mi-Co meter. Like the other pre-war meter manufacturers, Mi-Co enjoyed a considerable sales volume in the immediate post-war years, but due to reduced market demand its sales volume has decreased in more recent years. Current sales volume has been estimated by Mi-Co management to be in the neighborhood of 10 percent of the domestic total of original and replacement meters.

Mi-Co currently employs one experimental engineer who devotes his time exclusively to improving the meters and their accessories. The company management does not feel that either the commercial or patent opportunities in an over-all meter redesign are as favorable as those associated with improvements in accessories and portions of the meters, such as the coin collection equipment and related devices. For this reason product improvement emphasis is placed on accessories and specific portions of the meters. The current Mi-Co manual meter incorporates the same over-all meter construction as the pre-war models. The automatic meter utilizes the same over-all construction as was embodied in the meter at the time Mi-Co purchased the business from American LaFrance.

The numbers of six patents are currently placed on the Mi-Co manual meter.[58] All but two of these patents were filed prior

---

[57]See p. 214, *supra*.

[58]Patent 2,268,716 filed May 12, 1936, entitled "Parking Meter"; patent 2,311,242, filed July 3, 1939, entitled "Parking Meter"; patent 2,397,878, filed October 30, 1941, entitled "Parking Meter Mechanism"; patent 2,429,478, filed October 30, 1941, entitled "Counting Attachment for Parking Meters" (Canadian 422,427); patent 2,563,182, filed Jan. 21, 1949, entitled "Parking Meter Mechanism" (Canadian 498,656) design patent 100,975.

to the war. The automatic meter is marked with three patents.[5] All of these patents relate to details of construction and no assertion have been made by Mi-Co that competitors are infringing eithe these or any other of the patents it owns. Mi-Co has followed ; rather active policy of filing patent applications, and currentl owns about 29 patents.[60] The company is not currently intereste in foreign patents, but management indicates that a different polic will be followed in the event foreign sales become more significant.

Mi-Co meters are sold in Canada by Mi-Co Meter Sales an Service, Ltd. The Canadian company was sued under th Canadian Vehicular patents by Dual Parking Meter Company o Canada, which case has been settled.

The Mi-Co postwar experience is of particular interest witl respect to the Mi-Co twin meter. The Mi-Co activity since pur chasing this business from American LaFrance indicates that Mi Co regards the meter as a fully effective competitive meter. Indeed this meter is stressed in Mi-Co advertising on an equal basis wit the manual meter. Available trade information indicates that th Mi-Co experience with the twin meter is entirely satisfactory an that the twin meter has been accompanied by no more than th usual servicing and other problems. This experience strongl indicates that the difficulties with the twin meter initially put ou by International were not inherent in the meter design as such bu rather were due to other matters.

M. H. Rhodes, Inc.

M. H. Rhodes is located in Hartford, Connecticut, and begar the manufacture of parking meters in 1935. The company was then and still is, engaged in the manufacture of other timing devices, o which expansion into the parking meter business was a natura extension.[61] About a quarter of the Rhodes business is in parking meters.

Rhodes makes the "Mark-Time" meter. This meter is manu- factured in the manual type only. It is distinctive in the use of only a single window permitting the dial to be viewed only from one side.

---

[59] Patent 2,213,240; patent 2,359,754, filed June 26, 1942, entitled "Plura Parking Space Meter"; and design patent 154,716.

[60] The most recently issued patents are 2,563,182, filed Jan. 21, 1949, en titled "Parking Meter Mechanism"; patent 2,628,699, filed May 28, 1948, entitle "Parking Meter Mechanism"; patent 2,642,170, filed Sept. 29, 1949, entitle "Coin Loss Preventer"; (Canadian 493,224) patent 2,721,641 filed June 30, 1949 entitled "Parking Meter Mechanism"; and patent 2,749,978, filed Sept. 1, 1953 entitled "Twin Parking Meter."

[61] See p. 214, *supra*.

The meter uses a rotating shield rather than the pointer and violation indicator used on the Magee-Hale, Dual, and Duncan meters. All parts for the meter, including the timing mechanism, are made on the premises.

Rhodes shared in the large meter sales volume of the immediate postwar years. The Vehicular survey for 1948 showed that as of the end of that year Rhodes had made about 14 percent of the parking meter installations. Since that time the Rhodes volume has decreased in both relative and absolute terms. The management feels that the sales volume is about 10 percent of the total domestic volume, although the computations made above suggest that the figure is under 5 percent.[62]

Rhodes does not apply any patent numbers to its meters. Since the war it has been issued two patents to such meters.[63]

Rhodes meters are manufactured and sold in Canada by Sperry Gyroscope of Ottawa, Ltd.

As above discussed in connection with Duncan,[64] Rhodes was sued by Duncan for patent infringement in 1946. This litigation terminated in favor of Rhodes in 1947. Aside from this suit, Rhodes has not been engaged in any patent litigation since the war and has neither received nor sent any patent infringement notices. Rhodes' freedom from action on the Vehicular patents appears to be due to the use of the shield construction mentioned above.

CONCLUSIONS

Insofar as the court found a violation of the Sherman Act, the *Vehicular Parking* decision rests on traditional principles of antitrust and patent law. The effort to monopolize the industry by collecting the available patents in a single entity, the understandings respecting the number of licensees, the price fixing license provisions, the restrictive license terms directed to unpatented subject matter, the agreements not to contest the patents, and similar practices had all been held illicit in closely analogous prior cases.[65] In enjoining these practices, and in declaring the various agreements illegal and unenforceable, the court applied the traditional remedies for like cases under Section 4 of the Sherman Act.[66] No

[62]See p. 222, *supra.*

[63]Patent 2,437,556, filed October 25, 1943, entitled "Timing Device"; patent 2,553,332, filed October 25, 1943, entitled "Timing Device."

[64]See p. 226, *supra.*

[65]*E.g.,* Standard Sanitary Mfg. Co. v. United States, 226 U.S. 20 (1912).

[66]For a general discussion of antitrust relief measures in patent cases, see Frost, Oppenheim, and Twomey, "Compulsory Licensing and Patent Dedication

facts coming to the attention of the authors of the present study cast any doubt on the success of these decree provisions in bringing the Sherman Act violations to an end.

The decree provisions requiring compulsory licensing of the patents rest on a somewhat different footing.[67] They were necessarily based on the premise that restoration of normal competition in the industry required something more than cessation of the prior illegal conduct. These decree provisions were implicitly based on the conclusion that access to the patents on at least a reasonable royalty basis would make some measurable contribution towards undoing the anticompetitive effects of the prior agreements. To what extent does the subsequent experience of the industry bear out the effectiveness of these decree provisions?

The compulsory licensing provisions of the *Vehicular Parking* decree have had little effect in initiating the entry of substantial new firms into the parking meter industry. This was probably inherent in the limited nature of the patent rights of Vehicular. The only patent that could possibly be accorded broad scope covering all practical parking meters was the Doyle patent. Its application to the commercial parking meter was at best dubious, as the principals in the Vehicular program repeatedly observed. In any event the Doyle patent expired in 1947. Meter manufacture in 1946— the first complete postwar year—and after was practically free from any risk of injunction under this patent (even if it were accorded an unexpected validity and scope) because of the time required for trial and possible appeal. As to the other Vehicular patents alternative constructions not involving significant infringement problems were available.

Only two firms of significance entered the parking meter industry in the postwar period. These were Magee-Hale and International. Their histories indicate that at best the compulsory licensing decree provisions gave their managements some comfort with respect to patent infringement claims by Vehicular. Neither firm was moved to begin manufacture by the compulsory license decree provisions.

Magee-Hale was founded by persons previously associated with the highly successful operations of Dual Parking Meter Company. It was the activity of these persons—especially Carl Magee— that had established the commercial importance of the parking

---

Provisions of Antitrust Decrees— A Foundation for Detailed Factual Case Studies,' *IDEA*, Vol. 1, No. 1 (June 1957), p. 127. And see *Report of the Attorney General's National Committee to Study the Antitrust Laws*, 225.

[67] See Frost, Oppenheim, and Twomey, note 66 *supra*, pp. 136-8.

meter. Once Magee lost control of Dual and had left that firm, it was probably inevitable that he would re-enter the industry as soon as the wartime parking meter moratorium was lifted. There is ample evidence that he and his associates had this thought in mind from the start. Initial design activities on the Magee-Hale meter began in 1942, when the content of the ultimate antitrust decree was at best conjectural. To be sure, the Magee-Hale meter was later charged to infringe a number of Vehicular patents, and the special master on the limited record before him refused to give the patents a narrow construction. It seems clear, however, that a designer with the capabilities of Gerald Hale could have devised an entirely successful meter without running afoul of the patents, as did International and others.

The Magee-Hale history is revealing in another respect. From the outset the company was a success. Gross income was over $700,000 in 1947 and by 1949 was essentially $1,500,000. In relation to either gross sales or invested capital the company income was most impressive. At the same time Vehicular, then without any license income, had limited resources and at best faced highly speculative patent infringement proceedings if it was to prevail against Magee-Hale, even if the patents were not subject to compulsory licenses. One could go far to resolve doubts favorably to Vehicular and against Magee-Hale in such patent infringement proceedings and still not have a situation where Vehicular was likely to deter Magee-Hale in its activities. As it turned out, the master's preliminary report in the compulsory licensing proceeding was quite favorable to Vehicular—largely because the issue of patent validity was foreclosed and the record did not include the Patent Office histories of the patents involved. The strong likelihood is that Vehicular was in a stronger position vis-a-vis Magee-Hale by reason of this decision than it ever would have been in any conventional patent infringement proceeding. Yet the Vehicular patents were promptly sold outright to the Magee-Hale principals for the comparatively modest sum of $95,000 which imposed little hardship on Magee-Hale.

The judgment of Magee-Hale and Duncan as to the worth of the Vehicular patents is indicated by the prompt settlement of the Chicago suit after the Magee-Hale principals purchased the patents, the $25,000 consideration paid by Duncan in the settlement, and the dedication of the patents required by the consent decree in that suit. This sum was less than one year's royalties on Duncan's sales at the rate set by the master.

Unlike Magee-Hale, International commenced operations

with a meter that was apparently designed to avoid the use of the violation flag and other structures involved in the principal Vehicular patents. The meter design had been started well prior to 1942, when the nature of the antitrust decree provisions was conjectural. Had the International management thought the violation flag and other features of the Vehicular patents to be worth a reasonable royalty, the meter construction could have been modified after the March 1944 antitrust decision to include these features. No such modification took place. For these reasons it seems clear that the compulsory licensing provisions had no significant influence on the entry of International into the parking meter business or on its subsequent activity.

To be sure, International was not successful and the reliability of the meter construction was one of its problems. This difficulty, however, appears to have had little if any relation to the presence or absence of structure to which the Vehicular patents related. The subsequent experience of Mi-Co with the International meter indicates that the International meter construction was not inherently impractical.

The Government unsuccessfully sought royalty-free compulsory licensing in the *Vehicular Parking* case. The present study indicates that such relief, if granted, would not have substantially altered subsequent competition in the industry. To be sure, such decree provisions would have made the Magee-Hale compulsory licensing proceedings unnecessary, and would have prevented the Chicago litigation involving Duncan. None of these proceedings, however, involved expenses of substantial amount in relation to the other sums involved in the activity of Duncan and Magee-Hale, and it seems perfectly clear that no activity these concerns might have undertaken was prejudiced by the litigation.

The further question arises of whether the compulsory licensing decree provisions in the *Vehicular Parking* case altered product improvement activity in the industry. Analytically, it would seem that the decree provisions would not be likely to have significant effect, since they affected only certain existing patents owned by Vehicular, leaving all the other concerns in the industry (including those named as defendants in the antitrust proceedings) free to use their patent rights in the normal fashion. The actual experience has been that the concerns in the field proceed with product improvement activities uninfluenced by the antitrust decree.

This does not mean, however, that patents are a strong factor in the parking meter industry today. In terms of product design the industry is quite mature. Indeed, many of the meters on sale today are covered only by expired patents. To be sure, many of the concerns point with pride to their product improvement efforts, but the resultant meter changes in the last decade (with the exception of the Duncan "Automaton") relate only to specific features of a character not leading to broad patent rights. Indeed, the principal role of patents in the industry in recent years is that of preventing the copying of specific features and requiring royalty payments. Such payments have been made in the case of the Duncan "Automaton" and the $4 per meter payments from Magee-Hale to the principals in that concern. Significant royalty payments have also been made by foreign licensees of domestic manufacturers. In no instance, however, do patent rights limit the ability of competitors to devise practical noninfringing constructions.

There is, of course, the possibility of some radically new meter design. The most recent change that might fall in this classification is the Duncan "Automaton," with its departure from both the manual and the automatic meters of the past. Duncan prefers, however, to place its major sales emphasis on the manual meter. At the present writing there are no signs of specific acitivity by any of the companies directed towards a radically new meter. This observation, however, is hardly very significant in view of the probability that such activity would be highly secret. A number of the companies interviewed indicated an alertness to the possibility of a radically new meter and indicated that they would actively pursue any such development with the expectation of obtaining significant patent rights.

The conclusions here reached invite a comparison with the results of the study of the antitrust decree in the concrete block making machine industry.[68]

There are substantial similarities between the industries studied. Each involves a rather small number of manufacturers. Each involves what is now a well-developed product with limited present prospects for radical change and the incident broad patent rights. The important technology in each instance is freely available to all the concerns. In each of the industries the principal competitive effort is directed to product reliability, cost, service, and sales, and the compulsory licensing provisions of the antitrust decrees have had very mild effects.

In each of the industries studied, moreover, a clear antitrust law violation was found before the decrees were entered. In the parking meter case, the key activities were the effort to obtain

---

[68]*IDEA*, Vol. 1, No. 1 (March 1958), p. 61.

patent rights to form a pool monopolizing the industry, the restrictive patent license policy, and similar activities directed towards elimination of price and other competition between the six concerns then in the industry. In the concrete block case the acts were in the nature of individual monopolization by Besser, the major concern in the field, and to a smaller degree were related to the patent licensing agreements involving Stearns.

In the concrete block case two concerns credited the compulsory license decree provisions with bringing about their entry into the business. Neither of these concerns is now a major concern in the field, although there is the possibility that one might develop to such position in the future. In the parking meter case the compulsory licensing provisions of the judgment cannot be credited with the entry of any substantial concern into the business. However, the time since the judgment has seen the growth of Magee-Hale, which is now one of the two major concerns in terms of current meter sales volume.

Caution must be observed, however, in drawing general conclusions from these results. Each of the industries studied is characterized by application engineering rather than organized research activities. Neither industry has had any radical product changes during the periods the judgments have been in effect, and there are no indications that the situation would have been any different absent the decrees. For these reasons the results of the present two studies form no basis for assuming that similar conclusions would be drawn in industries where product improvement is carried on at a more rapid rate, especially where the decree provisions impinge upon the activities of research laboratories with substantial budgets. The conclusions to be drawn in these other situations must await a substantial number of additional case studies.

APPENDIX

In The
United States District Court
District of Delaware

United States,
         Plaintiff
  vs.

Vehicular Parking, Ltd. *et al.*,   *Civil Action No. 259*
        Defendants

Magee-Hale Park-O-Meter Company,
        Intervenor

MASTER'S PRELIMINARY REPORT

This is a proceeding to determine a reasonable royalty for a license under certain patents pertaining to parking meters. The patents in issue are McGee 2,118,318. McGay et al. 2,168,302. Woodruff et al. 2,198,422. and McGay 2,286,221.

There are numerous other patents and patent applications concerned with parking meters owned by Vehicular Parking, Ltd. They had been licensed previously to selected parking meter manufacturers under substantially similar agreements which provided, inter alia, for royalties of 4% of the sales price of each meter. price fixed without regard to the scope of the licensed patents, and many restrictive practices designed to eliminate competition. These practices were held to be in violation of the antitrust laws, the license system was held to be void, and the parties were enjoined from future performance thereunder. U. S. v. Vehicular Parking et al., 54 F. Supp. 828. 841 (D. C. Del. 1944).

To carry into effect the purpose of the antitrust laws, and restore a broad base of competition in the parking meter industry, Vehicular was ordered to license its patents for a reasonable royalty. Magee-Hale thereupon was permitted to intervene and seek a license under the four patents here in issue. The present reference was made for the purpose of ascertaining a reasonable royalty for the Magee-Hale license.

Under the order of reference Vehicular was charged with the burden of proof. Its prima facie case was in large part confined to the examination of Magee-Hale officers and books. As noted in the memorandum filed herein on September 16, 1949. this evidence was sufficient to meet the minimum requirements of a prima facie case. but left many pertinent inquiries undeveloped. Magee-Hale then had the opportunity to complete the record, but rested without introducing any evidence. Hence this determination of reasonable royalty must necessarily be based on a record which leaves many questions unanswered.

Vehicular based its position largely on the undisputed fact that Magee-Hale pays to its officers four dollars per meter pursuant to the terms of an agreement whereby it acquired an exclusive license under a pending patent application of its president for an improved parking meter. Vehicular asserts that the sole consideration for this payment is the license under the Hale application. which is of much less value to this industry than any of the four patents in issue. Hence, urges Vehicular, it should receive at least this amount for a license under its patents of established merit. In answer Magee-Hale asserts that the patent license is but a small part of the consideration for the four dollar payment. so inferentially the transaction should be ignored.

Magee-Hale was not dealing at arms length with its officers when it entered into this agreement. and in any event, the payments which it made involved more than the mere purchase of a license under the Hale application. This license. however. constituted an important part of the consideration of the agreement. Thus. it is entitled to substantial weight in this proceeding.

Magee-Hale in addition to attacking the materiality of the agreement discussed above. asserts several additional grounds for reducing the rate to an insignificant basis. These grounds are (a) the small purchase price

Vehicular paid for the patents in issue; (b) the fact that Vehicular charged but 4% royalty for the licenses held to be illegal in the antitrust suit, covering 31 patents, and did not increase this royalty when the patents now under consideration were included therein; (c) the very limited scope to which the patents are entitled in view of the prior art; (d) the small profits in the parking meter industry; and (e) Vehicular's failure to restrict its proofs to the portion of the parking meters covered by the patents at bar.

Considering the foregoing contentions seriatim, I find that neither individually nor collectively do they justify the conclusion that a reasonable royalty hereunder should approximate a nominal amount. As to point (a), the purchase price of the patents is not persuasive inasmuch as the record shows they were acquired under duress, first by suing their former owners for patent infringement and, secondly, by a change of stock control of the owner. *United States* v. *Vehicular Parking Ltd., supra,* at page 832.

The royalty previously charged by Vehicular under its illegal licensing program (point *b supra*) is not persuasive inasmuch as the main consideration for these licenses was the restrictive provisions designed to eliminate competition, which the Court condemned in the antitrust suit. It appears that the sole purpose of this royalty was to defray the expense of policing the industry, rather than repay the patent owner for the license. *United States* v. *Vehicular Parking Ltd.* at page 833.

The patents need not be narrowly construed in view of the prior art (point *c supra*). The prior art patents for the most part are not concerned with parking meters, and the most pertinent structures which they disclose would have to be modified substantially to adapt them for use in this industry. Whether the required modifications would be within the knowledge of the man skilled in the art is doubtful from the present record, but in any event it bears on the question of validity and is forbidden territory under the Order of Reference. File wrappers of the patents at bar were not introduced in evidence, so there can be no finding that a restricted interpretation of the patent claims is required by the proceedings in the Patent Office. There is a serious question that at least two of these patents made a profound impression on the parking meter industry, and have been widely followed by Magee-Hale and others. Hence these patents claim commercially important devices, and, on the present record, are entitled to a liberal construction.

The contention that the profits in this industry are so small that they could only support an inconsequential royalty (point *d supra*) is at variance with the record. The exhibits and testimony establish that Magee-Hale's operations resulted in a most attractive return on the investment. Mr. Hale, its president, testified that while he had no way of knowing the profits of competitors they should be greater than those of Magee-Hale (Transcript 109). Thus the industry profits are substantial, and can defray a sizeable royalty.

The last contention which appeared to be seriously urged by Magee-Hale concerned the failure of Vehicular to segregate the patented structure from the parking meter as a whole (point *e supra*). Inasmuch as the patents in issue do not include in their claims such elements as the coin box, counter, meter, support, and sidewalk flanges, the failure of Vehicular to eliminate such unclaimed elements from its proofs is asserted to be fatal. The very heart of the parking meters under discussion is the combination covered by the patents at bar. Without them the meters could not be sold as marketable articles. Hence, under the controlling doctrine of *Garretson v. Clark*, 111 U. S. 120 (1884), the entire value of the parking meter may be considered.

From the foregoing discussion it is evident that, in my opinion, Vehicular should not be reduced to an insignificant royalty for its patents. They have a broad scope and describe and claim devices of great commercial importance, which are being sold in large quantities at a substantial profit. At the same time, I believe that the $4 per meter payments made by Magee-Hale to its officers (in part for an exclusive license under the Hale application) is too high, even though a non-exclusive license under the four patents in suit should be considerably more valuable to the recipient than an exclusive license under the Hale application and any patent which may ultimately issue thereon.

It is self-evident that a non-exclusive license under all Vehicular patents which are infringed by Magee-Hale's parking meter is essential to the latter. The antitrust litigation established that a competitor who infringed a patent was practically at the mercy of the patent owner. When sued his only alternatives were to capitulate or face bankruptcy. Mr. Hale testified herein, without contradiction, that "cities would not buy meters from a company involved in patent litigation" (Transcript 41). Inasmuch as the main market for these meters is closed to an infringer involved in litigation, it is apparent that virile competition will prevail only if patent litigation is minimized by suitable patent licenses.

To restore competition a simple and workable royalty schedule should be adopted. Unquestionably, each of the patents at bar is not of equal importance to the industry or each licensee. Yet, the uncertainty and delay which would accompany any attempt to meticulously appraise each patent as applied to each device would defeat entirely the fundamental objective of the proceeding—"to restore a broad base of competition in the parking meter industry." See *United States* v. *Vehicular Parking et al, supra,* at page 841.

It might also be noted in passing that a meticulous calculation of a fair patent royalty is for all practical purposes a physical impossibility. The field of economics is not subject to the uncanny precision of mathematical sciences such as astronomy and electronics, since, unfortunately, business men do not behave like heavenly bodies or charged particles. To strive for such precision would only serve to defeat the purpose of this reference.

To accomplish the objectives of this proceeding I find that each patent should be subject to the same royalty rate. The total royalty for a license under all four patents in issue, however, should not be the arithmetic sum of all the patents licensed, but rather three times the royalty for a license under any one patent. The same rule would apply if all of Vehicular's patents were licensed instead of four.

This is a rough rule of thumb, but I find it much more workable, and fairer to all parties concerned, than any of the numerous formulas which I originally attempted to evolve from the record in this case.

For the royalty rate per patent, I find that 1% based on the sale or rental price of each licensed meter is fair. This is preferable to basing royalties on a flat sum per meter, as fluctuations in the prices of different meters due to changes in design or competition might make such an arrangement onerous to the licensee.

Under this formula, Magee-Hale would pay a royalty of 3% of its sale or rental price for each licensed meter which infringed three or more licensed patents in return for an unrestricted non-exclusive license under the four patents in issue. If it wished a license under additional patents of Vehicular its maximum royalty would still be 3%, regardless of the number of licensed patents. On the other hand, if it redesigned its meters so that they infringed but one or two Vehicular patents it would have to pay but 1% or 2% royalty respectively on the redesigned meters.

An order may be submitted providing for the filing of exceptions to the above report, with supporting memoranda, within a reasonable time. The order may also provide for the filing of proposed findings of fact and conclusions of law, with supporting memoranda, if the parties so desire.

                                                        Arthur G. Connolly
                                                        Special Master

April 20, 1950

Evolving Court Opinion on Patent Licensing

L. James Harris and Irving H. Siegel

This exploratory paper has two related objectives. One is to examine the trend and flux of court opinion respecting certain patent licensing arrangements that have been regarded as inconsistent, in varying measure, with the public interest—viz., "tie-ins,"[1] package licensing, and grant backs. All three have been directly or indirectly attacked as forms of patent misuse or antitrust violation. They may be said to have the common characteristics of permitting benefits to the patent owner which do not necessarily derive from the use of the patented invention. This paper takes the view that, since these arrangements have developed through the exercise of opportunities afforded in free societies for pursuing private gain while meeting felt social needs, they merit evaluation on the basis of existing legal standards generally applied to economic affairs as well as legal standards concerning the exclusivity of patent rights.

The second objective is to point up an important consequence of the frequent avoidance of court tests of the legal validity of business arrangements, particularly those affecting patent licensing. In our kind of society, it is desirable to make an energetic legal defense of challenged business practices that have been pursued in good faith—that is, on the assumption of compliance with the law. Indiscriminate quests for settlement by consent decree, like other failures to defend assumed economic rights, impede the fullest development of positive competition, hamper the functional and self-correcting evolution of law through proper court test, and even threaten the vitality of a free society.

POSITIVE COMPETITION

At this point, we should recall the meaning of "positive competition," a term introduced by the authors in an earlier article to

EDITOR's NOTE: This paper represents the second of a series on the concept of "positive competition." It appeared in *IDEA*, Vol. 5, No. 2 (Summer 1961).

[1] The term "tie-in" is used in this paper in a limited sense. It comprises arrangements (1) requiring the licensee to purchase from the patentee unpatented articles outside the scope of the licensed patent when such articles are not suitable for substantial non-infringing use; or (2) in which the tying product is patented and the patent does not create illegal market power in the entire factual setting.

emphasize the pervasiveness and variety of constructive "normal" behavior in transacting the nation's business. The term refers to the very large, unspectacular "core" of economic behavior, in contrast with the pathological or deviant fringe which, regrettably, attracts much greater popular and professional attention. It refers to accepted modes of action in the world in which we live—permissive and inventive, as well as repetitive and routine. These modes are dynamic and varied, unlike the rigid, mechanical behavior encountered in textbook models which abstract, simplify, and idealize. Related terms are "economic freedom" and "competition in free markets," as these are understood in the literature of antitrust. All connote a "style" which we as a nation are historically committed to preserve and foster: maximum scope for profitable private economic decision-making and organization, subject to custom and law and to such paramount common needs as national defense.

In the patent field as in other parts of the economic domain, many avenues of positive competition are well marked and well traveled. Indeed, despite the existence of uncertain paths, some useful guidelines already fairly well delineated lead to the very frontiers of the specialized area of licensing.

COMPLEX PATTERN OF INTERPLAY

Another preliminary matter that requires explicit notice is the reciprocal dynamic influence of positive competition and the larger cultural environment, including the law. Modes of private behavior interact continually through time, with each other and also with the elements of this environment. Indeed, conduct and institutions always are reshaping each other in varying respects and in varying degrees.

Since the citizens of a free society have considerable control over, and also have a stake in, the outcome of this interaction, they should participate with deliberateness and foresight. Specifically, they should seek to avoid the erosion of their economic and political freedoms, especially through failure to exercise adequately the range of options currently available to them. Vigilance must include the active use of available instruments, legal as well as other, for enlightened pursuit of self-interest. Through the exercise and defense of existing rights, atrophy of these rights is avoided and their positive significance is retained. Recourse to adjudication when the law is unclear helps to make law responsive and to keep law vital. Only through the appropriate test of cases, especially widely representative ones, can the law meaningfully evolve to serve the broad needs of changing times and circumstances. This evolution may, of course, entail reconsideration of presumably settled issues and reversal of earlier dominant opinion.

SOME ESTABLISHED GUIDELINES

Certain propositions command wide judicial acceptance and already provide guides to persons and firms seeking economic reward in patent licensing activities.

In *United States* v. *General Electric Company*,[2] the Supreme Court formulated the classic yardstick that a patentee may license "for any royalty, or upon any condition the performance of which is reasonably within the reward which the patentee by the grant of the patent is entitled to secure." This comprehensive principle sanctions various patent license arrangements as reasonably ancillary to the exclusive rights conferred by the patent.

The *General Electric* principle is consistent with guidelines marked out in a number of other cases. For example, it has been held in 1938 that any conveyance of a right under a patent constitutes a license if it does not amount to an assignment of a part, whole, or fractional interest in a patent.[3] It has also been held that a license gives permission to do what the licensor could otherwise legally seek to prevent. Further, a license is granted on conditions reasonably necessary to give the patentee a reward to which he is legally entitled.[4] In addition, it has been determined that a patent owner may limit the price at which the licensee sells,[5] the persons to whom the licensee sells, as well as the location of licensee operations,[6] and the volume of licensee production.[7] Another point well settled is that, when the patentee imposes restrictions beyond the scope of the claims of his patented invention, he may be denied relief in infringement suits because of patent misuse or may be held in violation of the antitrust laws for conduct amounting to unreasonable restraint of trade, an attempt to monopolize, or actual monopolization.[8]

[2]272 U.S. 476 (1926); See also the *Report of the Attorney General's National Committee to Study the Antitrust Laws* (March 31, 1955), pp. 231-233.
[3]L. L. Brown Paper Co. v. Hydroiloid, 32 F. Supp. 857 (1939); General Talking Picture Corp. v. Western Electric Co., 304 U.S. 175 (1938).
[4]Extracted Process Limited v. Hiram Walker & Sons, 153 F.2d 264 (1946).
[5]U.S. v. General Electric Co., 272 U.S. 476 (1926). See *Attorney General's Report, supra*, pp. 233-236 for differing views on price limitations.
[6]Westinghouse Electric & Manufacturing Co. v. Tri City Radio Electric & Supply Co., 23 F.2d 628 (1927). See *Attorney General's Report, supra*, pp. 236-237.
[7]American Equipment v. Tuthill Building Material Co., 69 F.2d 406 (1934). See *Attorney General's Report, supra*, pp. 236-237.
[8]Ethyl Gasoline Corp. v. U.S., 309 U.S. 436 (1940). A patent monopoly

We should also note at this juncture three general changes that have occurred over the years in the circumstances of patent licensing. First, the patentee can no longer include any condition he pleases in a license on the grounds that he can license or not as he chooses (*Motion Picture Patents Company* v. *Universal Film Mfg. Co. et al.*)[9]—although this choice is still permitted in many foreign countries. Second, in contrast with the experience in early years of our country, inventions are now generally part of a large group embodied in a machine or they are combined with many others in a process or product. Third, certain patent antitrust issues are no longer the subjects of vigorous controversy that they were prior to World War II.

MISUSE—EQUIVALENT TO ANTITRUST VIOLATION?

Some courts have held antitrust violations involving patents to constitute misuse and have also held misuse to amount to an antitrust violation. The latter position was asserted in a dictum in the *Mercoid* case. This decision tends to reflect a public distrust of all "monopolies"[10] even though the patent monopoly has an explicitly lawful status[11] and does not limit any preexisting public right: "An inventor deprives the public of nothing which it enjoyed before his discovery."[12]

The history of patent tie-in cases reached a turning point in 1917, when the doctrine of misuse was explicitly stated in *Motion Picture Patents*.[13] In this case the court held that no need existed to test an alleged patent tie-in violation against the standards set up in the Clayton Antitrust Act since this type of misuse could be tested against the criteria of patent law. In contrast, Justice Douglas's *Mercoid* decision in 1944[14] stated that patent misuse was *also* an antitrust violation.

---

is lawful and not a monopoly in the familiar economic sense. See *Attorney General's Report, supra,* pp. 247-259.

[9]243 U.S. 502 (1918).

[10]Monopoly is in bad odor, not only because of its connotation in economic literature, but also because of the public impression of it, which may have been reinforced by the widely publicized recent electrical equipment criminal conspiracy convictions under the Sherman Act. The popular view seems to be reflected in the Supreme Court's *per curiam* opinion in Radiant Burners, Inc. v. Peoples Gas Light and Coke Co., *et al.,* 81 S. Ct. 365 (1961) in which the court held that it was not necessary for the plaintiff to allege and prove "public injury" in a private treble damage action. Many Sherman Act cases had been dismissed by the courts on this ground in the past.

[11]Title 35 U.S.C. Sec. 101.

[12]U.S. v. Dubilier Condenser Corporation, 289 U.S. 178 (1933).

[13]See note 9 *supra.*

[14]320 U.S. 661 (1944).

Since an antitrust violation involving patents may unreasonably restrain commerce and exceeds the lawful patent monopoly, it could indeed be considered. as some courts have, a form of misuse. However, to consider misuse always as an antitrust violation, even when the misuse does *not* violate the standards of the antitrust statutes. is to say that anything done outside the lawful patent monopoly expands that monopoly into a violation of these statutes. Even though the courts have not generally gone as far as Justice Douglas, a confusion of the two concepts is frequent and some authorities even perceive a trend toward his position.[15]

Since, in a certain sense, patent law and antitrust law are concurrent or supplemental to each other, the conclusion that violation of one also automatically represents violation of the other seems illogical. However, developing case experience provides a constructive basis for confrontation of both types of law and should eventually harmonize their interpretation and impact.

TIE-INS

Though tie-ins are generally regarded as incompatible with positive competition, experience with such arrangements has actually served to clarify acceptable modes of behavior. This statement is not intended to justify tie-ins, but to point up their contribution to the trial-and-error process of mutual adaptation of business practice and the law. Indeed, certain arrangements that have been forbidden at one time as tie-ins have later been recognized as legal. thus becoming additional guidelines for positive competition.

Most authorities agree that the courts have primarily objected, from *Motion Picture* to *Mercoid*, to the fact that benefits were derived by the patentee from sources other than the patented invention. Unless a case is excepted under Section 271 of the 1952 Patent Act, courts still consider this objection valid. (The 1952 Act in Section 271 (d) excepted the derivation of revenue from licensing to perform acts which, if performed by another without consent, would constitute contributory infringement. It also permitted the patent owner to enforce patent rights against contributory infringement.)

Pursuant to Section 271 (b) and (c), an action may be brought against a contributory infringer who knowingly sells a staple article not suitable for substantial non-infringing use or against anyone who actively induces infringement. Explicit recognition is thus given in the statute to the doctrine of contributory infringement

---

[15]See *Attorney General's Report, supra*, p. 238.

which was questioned in the *Mercoid* case.[16] An inventor is now enabled to sue a single contributory-infringer company instead of pursuing many small direct infringers, as in the manufacture of household articles.

Here is an example of the law returning to a former interpretation as it seeks to facilitate what is generally recognized as economically constructive. In the *Mercoid* case there was some question as to whether there was anything left of the contributory infringement doctrine. The 1952 revision undertook to remove that question and to reestablish the doctrine firmly, thus also demonstrating that the law regarding patents is eminently practical and that, when misused, it can cope with the misuse. The same practical orientation is further demonstrated by the decisions in cases requiring the licensee to purchase from the licensor all of the patented item that he uses.[17] The requirement is held to be an agreement that properly provides against infringement.

Concerning the other type of "tie-in" arrangement considered in this paper,[18] some authorities maintain that the courts have perhaps gone too far in the condemnation of tie-in clauses in patent licenses from an antitrust standpoint. The following statement, appearing on page 238 of the *Report of the Attorney General's National Committee to Study Antitrust Laws*, expresses succinctly the majority and minority positions of the Committee members:

> From an antitrust standpoint, a tying clause in a patent license is like a tying clause in any other contract. The Committee feels, however, contrary to the apparent trend of Supreme Court opinions,[57] that in determining whether a tying clause may substantially lessen competition under the Clayton Act, or is unreasonable under the Sherman Act, the fact that the tying product is patented need not be decisive of illegality. The patent may be broad and basic, in which event the economic power incident to the patent makes the tying clause illegal. On the other hand, the patent may be narrow and unimportant, in which event it may confer virtually no real market power.

---

[16]"When the patentee ties something else to his invention, he acts only by virtue of his right as the owner of property to make contracts concerning it and not otherwise. He then is subject to all the limitations upon that right which the general law imposes upon such contracts. The contract is not saved by anything in the patent laws because it relates to the invention. . . .

"That result may not be obviated in the present case by calling the combustion stoker switch the 'heart of the invention' or the 'advance in the art.' The patent is for a combination only. Since none of the separate elements of the combination is claimed as the invention, none of them when dealt with separately is protected by the patent monopoly." (From the majority opinion delivered by Mr. Justice Douglas. See also Mr. Justice Frankfurter's dissenting opinion.) Mercoid Corp. v. Mid-Continental Investment Co., 320 U.S. 661 (1944).

[17]Steiner Sales Co. v. Schwartz Sales Co., 98 F.2d 999 (1938).

[18]See note 1 *supra*.

Accordingly, where the tying product is patented, the patentee should be permitted to show that in the entire factual setting, including the scope of the patent in relation to other patented or unpatented products, the patent does not create the market power requisite to illegality of the tying clause.

A few Committee members, however, approve the recent trend of Supreme Court opinions in this area. A monopolistic position in the market for the tying product is a prime criteria [sic] of illegality and, in his [sic] opinion, a patent which has any validity at all necessarily gives the owner market control over that product. Thus, he [sic] does not agree that a tying clause in a patent license is like a tying clause in any other contract. With this dissent, Louis B. Schwartz agrees.

---

[57] "On a number of occasions the Court has regarded the patent itself as involving sufficient market power to make any tying clause a violation of the antitrust law. See United States v. Columbia Steel Co., 334 U.S. 495, 522 (1948); Times-Picayune Pub. Co. v. United States, 345 U.S. 594, 601 (1953); International Salt Co., Inc. v. United States, 322 U.S. 392, 396 (1947). Cf. Mr. Justice Frankfurter's statement in Standard Oil of California v. United States, 337 U.S. 293, 307 (1949) that '* * * A patent, moreover, although in fact there may be many competing substitutes for the patented article, is at least prima facie evidence of * * * [market] * * * control.' "

PACKAGE LICENSING

In package licensing, the patentee may seek to tie in subject matter from articles outside the scope of the patents he owns. In *United States* v. *Paramount Pictures, Inc.*,[19] the licensing of one block of pictures was made contingent on the licensing of another block from the distributor. However, the court stated: "We do not suggest that films may not be sold in blocks or groups, when there is no requirement, express or implied, for the purchase of more than one film." *American Securit Company* v. *Shatterproof*[20] clearly held that refusal to license a patent except with others is misuse, and it appears from the opinion on appeal that the royalty should be reduced as patents in the package expire.

The Supreme Court has held that, where royalties were computed on the basis of a licensee's total sales,[21] a package license is valid and the sale could even include unpatented items. The question of coercion was practically eliminated since royalties were based on total sales and the licensor had no difficulty convincing the licensee to take the package. The court recognized the reasonableness of using package licensing to avoid questions of infringement and bookkeeping and other practical problems arising from the increasing complexity of the arts.

---

[19]334 U.S. 131 (1948).

[20]154 F. Supp. 890 (1957); 268 F.2d 769 (1959).

[21]*Automatic Radio Manufacturing Inc.* v. *Hazeltine Research Inc.*, 339 U. S. 827 (1950).

Almost ten years later, the *Securit* case left unclarified points: Is it a misuse to continue to collect royalties for all patents in the package without any reduction for those that expire? How do you determine whether coercion is present? Do simple request and refusal suffice? Is there any consideration of reasonableness of conditions?

We can see from these questions that there still is room for interpretation of law in subsequent cases to define, clarify, and establish additional guidelines for positive competition. The subsequent interpretation of law will mark out new channels of opportunity in our enterprise system. Although some decisions criticize normal practice, most adhere to the view that the normal is also functional.

The few critical cases, like *Securit*, have been the basis for considerable professional writing. The volume and tenor of this writing may give a distorted impression of the situation which actually prevails. Specifically, they exaggerate the prevalence and consequences of the abnormal and dysfunctional behavior manifested in a relatively few cases. Witness the amount of literature on such atypical and comparatively rare cases as *Hartford-Empire*,[22] and consider also the enduring impact of such literature.

It is sometimes thought that there is a distinction between package licensing and tie-in arrangements, because the former involves only patented items that are generally related while the latter involves only unpatented items. This distinction certainly is not valid with respect to Section 3 tie-in cases of the Clayton Act,[23] for the Act there expressly states "whether patented or unpatented." Some limitation of this aspect of the tie-in rule was expressed in *Libbey-Owens-Ford Glass* v. *Sylvania Industrial Corporation*.[24] However, in this case, the licensed process and the tied patented item were in the same patent. Whether tie-in limitation or package licensing is involved, it appears that the convenience of the parties will not be considered (compare *U. S.* v. *Paramount Pictures, Inc.,* in which copyrighted films were not licensed unless other copyrighted films were accepted).

GRANT BACKS

Despite economic and other differences among block booking,

---

[22]Hartford-Empire v. United States, 322 U.S. 386 (1945).

[23]International Business Machines Corp. v. U. S., 298 U.S. 131 (1936).

[24]Libbey-Owens-Ford Glass v. Sylvania Industrial Corp., 154 F.2d 814 (1946).

"tie-in"[25] arrangements, and package licensing, the fact that the patentee seeks to derive revenue from sources other than the specific patented invention might cause the courts to treat such arrangements as in restraint of trade or outside the lawful patent monopoly. In *Transparent-Wrap Machine Corp.* v. *Stokes & Smith Co.*,[26] the classic grant back case, the Supreme Court reversed Judge Hand, who had attempted to extend by analogy a ruling to what he considered a similar situation. In this case the Supreme Court felt "that the monopoly which the licensor obtains when he acquires the improvement patents extends beyond the term of his basic patent, but . . . that is not creating by agreement a monopoly which the law otherwise would not sanction." This opinion does seem to contradict the theory of Judge Biggs in *Securit*, who stated "that that agreement shall continue 'in full force and effect to the expiration of the last to expire of any' of *Securit's* patents set out in 'Schedule A' constitutes a patent misuse for it extends the payment of royalties of patents under patents which may expire to the expiration date of that patent most recently granted to *Securit*."

It is of interest that the same Supreme Court Judge, Justice Douglas, wrote the *Mercoid* and *Transparent-Wrap* decisions, both of which involved benefits to the patentee from sources other than the patent, and that he came to opposite conclusions. The grant back restriction (*Transparent-Wrap* decision) required the licensee to assign or license all improvements on the licensed invention to the licensor. The District Court in the *Transparent-Wrap* case found for the licensor on the ground that he was trying to protect himself so that he could manufacture and sell a marketable product on expiration of the license or on default by the licensee. The opinion of Judge Hand[27] reversed the District Court largely on the basis of the *Motion Picture Patents* and *Mercoid* line of cases. Justice Douglas, writing for the Supreme Court, reversed the Court of Appeals and stated that the consideration might be "services, or cash, or the right to use another patent." Thus grant backs are not in the category of illegal per se violations.[28]

An important private benefit derived from the grant back is the incentive it offers to patentees who might otherwise fear the potential competition of licensees and refuse to license. In this

---

[25]See note 1 *supra*.

[26]329 U.S. 637 (1947).

[27]Transparent-Wrap Machine Corp. v. Stokes & Smith Co., 156 F.2d 198 (1946).

[28]Some have distinguished between the scrutiny to be given to exclusive, as opposed to nonexclusive, license grant backs (*Attorney General's Report, supra,* pp. 228-229).

respect the grant back may differ from tie-in arrangements, block booking, and package licensing, which do not promise such protection. Other than the royalties collected, there is no inducement to the patentee to license his competitor. The grant back is in effect an instrument that widens industry utilization, for it opens an avenue that might otherwise remain closed because of a reluctance of the patentee to give a competitor an "in."

The key question for these misuse violations still remains whether the patentee seeks to benefit from sources other than the patented invention as marked out by its claims. With respect to antitrust violation, Justice Douglas's dictum in *Mercoid* considered misuse an antitrust violation per se; but, in his subsequent *Transparent-Wrap* opinion, he cautioned that only grant back limitations that unreasonably restrain trade or monopolize are illegal for violation of the antitrust laws.

The preceding discussion prompts two observations that bear on positive competition. First, grant backs and package licensing are *not* per se illegal and still may provide possibilities for action that industry might wish to explore. Second, the variety of decisions described above and the differences expressed by Justice Douglas suggest that new cases may disclose new opportunities for distinction and reversal as further judicial clarification is sought in the changing economic environment.

LICENSING AS AN AVENUE OF COMPETITION

The mere fact that licensing exists may reduce the tendency to monopolize, although this probability is rarely mentioned in the literature. Licensing assures that companies which may be better equipped than the patentee to serve a market will have an opportunity to do so. It also readies a number of additional sources of supply for the period after the patent expires or in event of emergency. Thus, licensing may serve to encourage maximum volume and to dilute monopoly control.

Although multiple licenses may differ from a single license in its potential to restrain trade unreasonably,[29] there is law on the subject to deal with this contingency too, as there is with respect to "tie-in"[30] clauses, block booking, package licensing, and grant backs. Thus, existing law lights the way to acceptable practice and constructive economic behavior, and fulfills an essential mission in our enterprise system.

---

[29]Newburgh Moire v. Superior Moire Co., 237 F.2d 283 (1956); *Tinnerman Products, Inc.* v. *George K. Garrett Co.*, 185 F. Supp. 151 (1960).

[30]See note 1 *supra*.

Positive competition affects the character and alignment of the law with respect to licensing, and the law in turn affects economic functioning. As already indicated, a reciprocal dynamic relationship exists between positive competition—between what is, what works, what actually occurs—and the law, which is the guide, a perfectible chart that helps us over the complex course of history.[31] Specifically, patent law has developed in the endeavor to foster and encourage technical advance. It serves as a guide for positive competition to the extent that it actually promotes "the progress of science and useful arts" and contributes to both the public welfare and private benefit.

POSITIVE COMPETITION AND CHALLENGED BUSINESS PRACTICE

At this point we must call attention to the failure to utilize to full advantage the possibilities for constructive interaction of positive competition and the law in the area of patent licensing and in other areas in which business practices have been challenged. A conspicuous type of failure is the resort to negotiation or consent procedures that may prejudice or compromise the future exercise of rights now clearly possessed, or now widely believed to exist. Such procedures seem particularly attractive when there is doubt or fear concerning the outcome of litigation. Although it is desirable not to burden the courts with excessive or trivial litigation and to burden the law with every small difference of opinion, it is also possible to go too far in the direction of abstinence. It is a duty of citizenship to defend challenged rights to the extent that we believe in them lest they be attenuated by default. It is the give-and-take of controversy in particular cases that helps positive competition and the law to evolve in a complementary, compatible, and functional manner—in a manner that enriches, rather than hobbles, enterprise.

A distinguished authority on the antitrust law has effectively expressed this view in a recent address:

". . . [I]t is extremely important that a corporation charged with antitrust violation it believes is not within the settled per se violation areas, should have the fortitude to litigate the case whenever it believes that the issues involved are fairly justiciable and are significant to itself and to the industry in which it operates. . . . Complacency in avoiding litigation under the circumstances stated,

---

[31]In *Navy JAG Journal*, October, 1959, Representative Carl Vinson, of Georgia, Chairman of the House Armed Services Committee stated that: "Laws are nothing more, and nothing less, than the needs and concerns of the people, expressed in words and requirements."

or docile acceptance of hard bargains in antitrust consent settle-
ments, will tend to create the very peril of undue interference with
freedom of lawful private enterprise managerial decision-making
business should at all costs strive to preserve. Remember that the
ultimate safeguards against unwarranted antitrust charges are the
independent courts to which the issues are submitted."[32]

Let it not be thought that this position is rooted in narrow
political considerations. According to a Staff Report of the Senate
Judiciary Subcommittee published on February 19, 1960, from
August 1941 to January 9, 1959, patent relief was obtained in 107
judgments filed in civil antitrust cases brought by the United States
government. Ninety-four of these judgments were entered by consent. This report concludes, in part: "In short, compulsory patent
licensing relief, when negotiated by consent, without prior specific
judicial finding that it is appropriate relief in a particular case, may
have created competitive disadvantages as well as benefits."

Implicit in the United States two-party system and the general
theory of American government is a continuing contention of fairly
balanced forces. Victories are regarded as reversible, and it is also
recognized that majorities may be transient. The achievement of
power is not to be used for the aggrandizement and crystallization
of power to resist future challenge. Accordingly, it is important for
our citizens and organizations to exercise rights with vigilance
and diligence, to prevent a setting of unequal relationships. In particular, rights should be exercised in traditional and established
forums, such as the courts, lest these prerogatives be forfeited to
administrative expediency.

What has just been said applies with equal force to other
processes vital to positive competition and its healthy interaction
with the law. For all kinds of legislative deliberations or hearings,
full debate by representative, informed, articulate spokesmen is
desirable. Maximum participation, direct or indirect, in national
decision-making processes provides a basis for maximum acceptance
of outcomes, even though change or reversal of these outcomes may
still be sought by legal means. Great damage is done to positive
competition when vigorous argument is eschewed, or when it is
hampered by the misuse of political power to discredit opposition.

Perhaps, we have entered a period of American history in
which we shall have to rely increasingly on the courts to uphold
traditional rights. Protracted international tensions create a habit

[32]Address by S. Chesterfield Oppenheim, Advisor on Research to The
Patent, Trademark and Copyright Foundation, before the Michigan Patent Law
Association (February 1961) and the Patent Law Club of Washington (April 1961).
See also *IDEA*, Vol. 3, No. 1 (Spring 1959), p. 31.

of coalition between the executive and legislative branches and also encourage the rise and spread of "bipartisanship." Both developments may proceed too far and persist too long in the face of public indifference or indulgence. In such circumstances, the courts alone may be able to show the independence and objectivity required for uncompromising support of traditional rights. Ironically, it may be the "conservative" courts that protect the "liberal" fountainhead when the system of checks and balances partially breaks down, when the doctrine of the separation of powers loses sharp definition with popular acquiescence or support. Ironically, it may be the protest of "big business" in the courts that helps to maintain or salvage the rights which its antagonists hazard by trustful concurrence in the aggrandizement and fusion of executive and legislative power.

Salvation by the courts cannot be guaranteed, however, nor is it automatic. The important thing for our citizenry is that court opinion evolves, that there is an interaction between positive competition and the law, that proper resort to court test contributes to the general health and tone of a democratic society. It should be recalled that, in our country as in England, the concept of "reasonableness" was developed by the judiciary. In the *Dyer* case,[33] in early fifteenth century England, restraint of trade was held illegal without reference to any subsidiary criterion. Not until the eighteenth century was the criterion of "reasonableness" explicitly introduced. Our own Sherman Act was at first interpreted by the courts as meaning exactly what it said, so that all agreements in restraint of trade were considered illegal. However, in *Standard Oil of New Jersey v. U. S.,*[34] Justice White proposed as a criterion "the rule of reason guided by the established law." This case also developed the per se invalidity doctrine, which has over the years appeared pertinent to many kinds of business arrangements challenged by the government. Clearly, the judicial branch is a factor that should not be overlooked by those who believe that both private and public long-term interests can be concurrently advanced.

---

[33] *Dyer Case* (variant spelling *Dier*), *Yearbook* 2 Henry V, fol. 5, pl. 26; Maynard's edition, part 6, 2 Henry V. p. 5, pl. 26.
[34] 221 U.S. 1 (1911).

"Know-How" Licensing and Capital Gains

John F. Creed and Robert B. Bangs

The licensing of "know-how" either separately or perhaps more usually in conjunction with patents and trademarks[1] is a business practice of extensive and growing importance in both domestic and foreign licensing. Our inquiry is into the federal tax aspects of know-how licensing, with the principal focus on the eligibility of proceeds therefrom for capital gains treatment under the income tax law.

DEFINITION OF KNOW-HOW

The term "know-how" is not susceptible to exact definition. In the broadest sense, it may consist of inventions, processes, formulae, or designs which are either unpatented or unpatentable; it may be evidenced by some form of physical matter, such as blueprints, specifications, or drawings; it almost invariably includes trade secrets; and it may involve accumulated technical experience and skills which can best, or perhaps only, be communicated through the medium of personal services.[2]

It can be seen that know-how as a general descriptive term comprehends a variety of forms and natures. This fact necessarily complicates a tax analysis of know-how licensing and renders

---

EDITOR'S NOTE: This paper illuminates an important area of tax law about which considerable uncertainty has existed. (*IDEA*, Vol. 4, No. 2, Summer 1960.) The law remains essentially unchanged from that set forth herein.

[1]See Berhrman and Schmidt, "New Data on Foreign Licensing." *IDEA*, Vol. 3, No. 4 (Winter 1959), p. 370, in which the authors' analysis of more than 1,200 foreign license agreements of 55 large U. S. corporations resulted in the following breakdown of the subject matter covered by the agreements:

	Number of Agreements
Patents only	585
Patents, Trademarks and Know-How in combination	246
Patents and Know-How	172
Trademarks only	111
Trademarks and Know-How	57
Know-How only	40
Patents and Trademarks	4
	1215

[2]For a full discussion of the subject matter of know-how, see Eckstrom, *Licensing in Foreign Operations*, Chapter VI (Foreign Operations Service, 1958).

unfeasible any broad statement regarding the availability of capital gains treatment on resulting proceeds.

CAPITAL GAINS—THE LEGAL PROBLEM

To result in long-term capital gains under the Internal Revenue Code, the transfer of know-how must generally constitute: (1) the "sale or exchange" (2) of a "capital asset" (3) held for more than six months by the transferor.[3] There exists scant judicial precedent for the application of these requirements to know-how transfers. Accordingly, the analysis which follows must in great part rest on the analogous cases involving the taxation of patents and on the judicial precedents interpreting know-how for purposes other than taxation.

KNOW-HOW AS A CAPITAL ASSET

Section 1221 of the Internal Revenue Code defines a "capital asset" as "property held by the taxpayer (whether or not connected with his trade or business)" other than certain specified or excluded categories of property. The first essential then is that know-how qualify as "property" if it is to be accorded status as a capital asset.

"Property" as a general term is frequently used but not precisely defined in the Internal Revenue Code.[4] The only specific references in the Code to the property aspect of a species of know-how are found in Sections 861 and 862 (dealing with determination of income from sources within and without the United States), which construe rents and royalties to include payments for the use of "patents, copyrights, *secret processes and formulae*, goodwill, trade-marks, trade brands, franchises *and other like property.*"[5] The implication is clear that not only secret processes and formulae, but probably also other forms of licensable material falling within the scope of know-how, have the character of property.

INVENTIONS, SECRET PROCESSES, AND FORMULAE AS PROPERTY

It is indisputably clear that patented inventions constitute

---

[3]Int. Rev. Code of 1954, Sec. 1222(3).

[4]Specialized definitions of property are contained in the following sections of the Code: §317, (corporate distributions); §614, (depletion allowance); §1231, (property used in a trade or business); and §1235, (patents as property). These sections, however, contribute little to the generic definition of the term.

[5]Emphasis added.

property for purposes of taxation.[6] The case of *Samuel E. Diescher*[7] demonstrates that the property in an invention does not derive from issuance of a patent. The following language is pertinent:

> Under the common law, the property right of the inventor, to make, use and vend, was recognized. The patents issued under statute are merely the grant of the right to exclude others from that use for a period of 17 years. The inventor's property right in his invention does not come into being upon his obtaining of a patent but exists prior to that time upon his reduction of an original invention to actual practice. *Crown Die & Tool Co.* v. *Nye Tool & Machine Works,* 261 U.S. 24; *Six Wheel Corporation* v. *Sterling Motor Truck Co.,* 50 F.2d 568. As the court said in the last cited case:
>
>> "From the foregoing, it will be seen that the irreducible quantum of the inventor's right in the res [the invention], even under the common law, is that of making, using and vending. The Federal Constitution and the statutes passed thereunder simply make that right exclusive. The statutes certainly do not curtail the natural right; they enlarge it."
>
> We think, therefore, that petitioners had a property right in each of the inventions which they had reduced to practice. These rights represented something of exchangeable value which the partnership possessed since it was able to exchange them for a valuable consideration. See *Gayler* v. *Wilder,* 10 How. 477; *Individual Drinking Cup Co.* v. *Osmun-Cook Co.,* 220 Fed. 335; *Hershey Manufacturing Co.,* 14 B.T.A. 867; affd., 43 F.2d 298; *George Washington, Sr.,* 36 B.T.A. 74. That answers the only question presented here. So, we conclude that these particular patents and inventions perfected and demonstrated more than two years prior to September 28, 1932, constituted property owned by the partnership for more than two years.[8]

It is apparent from the above passage that property inheres in an invention upon its reduction to practice, and that the patent grant merely creates the additional monopoly right to exclude others from the use of the invention for 17 years.[9]

Several tax cases have dealt with the status of secret processes as property. In *George S. Mepham*[10] the taxpayer, engaged in

---

[6]The United States Code, Title 35, §261, provides that "patents shall have the attributes of personal property." The Internal Revenue Code of 1954, Sec. 1235, explicitly describes patent rights as property. In the cases dealing with capital gains on patent transfers, the Treasury has usually grounded its case on the theory that the patents were held primarily for sale to customers and therefore were not capital assets [e.g., Harvey v. Comm., 171 F.2d 952 (9th Cir. 1949)], or that the patent was not sold or exchanged [e.g., Edward C. Myers, 6 T.C. 258 (1946)]. The Treasury did not contest the property nature of patents in these cases.

[7]36 B.T.A. 732 (1937), aff'd, 110 F.2d 90 (3rd Cir. 1940), *cert. denied,* 310 U. S. 650 (1940).

[8]*Id.* at 743-44.

[9]*Accord,* Franklin S. Speicher, 28 T.C. 938 (1957), Edward C. Myers, 6 T.C. 258 (1946).

[10]3 B.T.A. 549 (1926).

the manufacture of dry color and pigments, acquired the rights to certain inventions (formerly covered by British patents) which at considerable expense he adapted to his business. He was thereby able to eliminate the emission of sulphuric fumes from his manufacturing operation while his competitors continued to encounter constant trouble from this source. The process as adapted was never patented and at the time the taxpayer sold his business it was unknown both to the trade and to the public. The Board of Tax Appeals[11] acknowledged the property nature of the secret process when it stated that ". . . the taxpayer, in disposing of his business, sold not only the tangible property used in the business, but also the good will and other intangible assets, including the secret process. . . ."[12]

In *Wall Products, Inc.,*[13] the question involved was the deductibility of royalty payments to two stockholders for use of a secret formula employed in curing concrete. The formula was never patented. The government contended that the licensors had no property interest in the formula, which admittedly was simple and could be broken down into its constituent parts by a competent chemist. In sustaining the deductions the court found that the formula was secret and was therefore *property* which formed a proper basis for the payments made under the license agreement. The property rights of the licensors were held to be unaffected by the fact they had not applied for a patent on the formula.

The case of *Nelson* v. *Commissioner*[14] involved similar facts. The taxpayer in that proceeding was the president and majority shareholder of a corporation which had contracted to pay royalties to his mother in consideration of the assignment of a secret process involved in spinning metals. The Commissioner argued that the royalties were in fact disguised dividends to the son. The process incorporated the "know-how" acquired by long experimentation and experience in spinning heavy metals. It did not consist alone of mechanical skill but involved ingenuity and was evidenced by notes, sketchings, and drawings. In finding against the Commissioner the court stated:

> It is well settled that secret processes may constitute property and be dealt with contractually as such. Moreover, the courts will prevent the unlawful use of processes without the permission of the owner of the process. *Durand v. Brown*, 6 Cir. 236 F. 609; *Allen-Qualley Co. v. Shellmar Products Co.*, D. C. Ill. 31 F.2d 293 affirmed

---

[11]Predecessor of the Tax Court.
[12]3 B.T.A. at 553.
[13]11 T.C. 51 (1948).
[14]203 F.2d 1 (6th Cir. 1953).

7 Cir., 36 F.2d 623; *O. & W. Thum Co.* v. *Tloczynski,* 114 Mich. 149, 72 N.W. 140, 38 L.R.A. 200; *Glucol Manufacturing Co.* v. *Schulist,* 239 Mich. 70, 214 N.W. 152; *Hoeltke* v. *C. M. Kemp Mfg. Co.,* 4 Cir. 80 F.2d 912, certiorari denied 298 U. S. 673, 56 S.Ct. 938, 80 L. Ed. 1395; *A. O. Smith Corp.* v. *Petroleum Iron Co.,* 6 Cir., 73 F.2d 531, 538, 539.[15]

TRADE SECRETS AS PROPERTY

It can be seen from the foregoing tax cases that the courts recognize the property aspects of invention and secret processes and formulae. A broader inquiry is into the status of trade secrets as property. "A trade secret may consist of any formula, pattern, device, plan, or compilation of information which is used in one's business and which gives him an opportunity to obtain an advantage over competitors who do not know it or do not use it."[16] As so defined, trade secrets comprehend all or nearly all of the varied elements and forms which comprise know-how.

Litigation involving trade secrets has occurred principally in the area of "unfair competition." It is well settled that the possessor of a trade secret may enlist the aid of equity to enjoin its use or disposition by another to whom it has been disclosed in confidence.[17] The cases have typically involved the right of an employer to preclude disclosure or exploitation by an employee or former employee of confidential information or data gained in the course of his employment.[18] The relief accorded the employer in·these circumstances extends to prohibiting the use of such trade secret by one acquiring it from another with knowledge of its secret character.[19]

The unfair competition cases have referred variously to an owner's "property" or "right of property" or "kind of property" in trade secrets.[20] But without necessarily contradicting these prem-

---

[15]203 F.2d at 6.

[16]4 Restatement of Torts, §757, cited in the following cases: Sandlin v. Johnson, 141 F.2d 660 (8th Cir. 1944); Schreyer v. Casco Products Corp., 97 F. Supp. 159 (D. Conn. 1951). International Industries, Inc. v. Warren Petroleum Corp., 99 F. Supp. 907 (D. Del. 1951).

[17]E. I. du Pont de Nemours Powder Co. v. Masland, 244 U.S. 100 (1917); John D. Park & Sons Co. v. Hartman, 153 Fed. 24 (6th Cir. 1907). See also cases listed at 170 A.L.R. 449, 451 at n. 11.

[18]See, *e.g.,* Pomeroy Ink Co. v. Pomeroy, 77 N.J. Eq. 293, 78 Atl. 698 (1910). See also 43 C.J.S. Injunctions, Section 148 (1945).

[19]Lamont, C., & Co. v. Bonnie Blend Chocolate Corp., 135 Misc. 537, 238 N.Y. Supp. 78 (Sup. Ct. 1929).

[20]Wilson v. Rousseau, 4 How. (45 U.S.) 646 (1846); Sandlin v. Johnson, 141 F.2d 660 (8th Cir. 1944); Herald v. Herald China & Pottery Co., 257 Fed. 911 (6th Cir. 1919); Allen-Qualley Co. v. Shellmar Products Co., 31 F.2d 293 (N.D. Ill. 1929).

ises, it should be apparent that the rights inhering in trade secrets are something different from and lesser than the absolute and exclusive property rights—as to use, dominion, and disposition—accruing to the owner of physical things, or the monopoly rights granted by a patent; in other words, if a trade secret is property, it is not such in the full sense. The owner of a trade secret, provided he takes the necessary cautions to safeguard its secrecy, is merely protected in the unfair competition cases against its use and disclosure without his consent.

The following language of Mr. Justice Holmes in *E. I. du Pont de Nemours Powder Co.* v. *Masland* might suggest that the relief accorded owners of trade secrets in such cases is not grounded on a concept of property:

> The word "property" as applied to . . . trade secrets is an unanalyzed expression of certain secondary consequences of the primary fact that the law makes some rudimentary requirements of good faith. Whether the plaintiffs have any valuable secret or not the defendant knows the facts, whatever they are, through a special confidence that he accepted. The property may be denied but the confidence cannot be. Therefore the starting point of the present matter is not property . . ., but that the defendant stood in confidential relations with the plaintiffs, or one of them. These have given place to hostility, and the first thing to be made sure of is that the defendant shall not fraudulently abuse the trust reposed in him. It is the usual incident of confidential relations. If there is any advantage in the fact that he knew the plaintiffs' secrets he must take the burden with the good.[21]

This case should not be interpreted as contradicting the existence of property rights in trade secrets. While the injunctive relief granted by the Court in that case may have been premised on the confidential relationship of the parties, the existence of intangible property in the trade secrets may nonetheless—as the opinion perhaps implies—be the consequence of such relief. Such a conclusion is consonant with the definition of intangible property as a relationship between persons which the law recognizes by attaching to it certain sanctions enforceable by the courts.[22] In other words, it would seem that intangible property rights by their nature *normally* derive from or are an expression of some primary relationships between persons which entail legal responsibility.

The unfair competition cases are perhaps not conclusive of the status of trade secrets as property. More appropriate for the purposes of this inquiry are the precedents involving the sale of trade secrets. It is firmly established that trade secrets may form the subject matter

---

[21] 244 U.S. at 102.
[22] Curry v. McCanless, 307 U.S. 357 (1939).

of a sale (or assignment).[23] A "sale" is legally defined as the transfer of *property* for a valuable consideration.[24] Accordingly, it is necessary to conclude, at least for the special purpose of sale, that trade secrets are property.

Our concern, of course, is whether trade secrets constitute property within the tax meaning of that term. The courts have consistently given a broad interpretation to the term "property" as applied in the field of taxation. As stated by the 10th Circuit in *Citizens State Bank of Barstow, Texas* v. *Vidal:*

> "Property" is a word of very broad meaning and when used without qualification may reasonably be construed to include obligations, rights and other intangibles, as well as physical things. "Property" within the tax laws should not be given a narrow or technical meaning.[25]

That property in the tax sense includes intangibles is confirmed by other cases. A franchise or good will can be the subject of property.[26] So also can be a partnership interest,[27] a lease,[28] or an exclusive agency.[29] Most of the tax cases dealing with the property status of intangibles have involved their sale or exchange. And the fact that these various incorporeal subjects could be sold has been cited as proof of their nature as property. As stated by the 7th Circuit in *Commissioner* v. *Stephens-Adamson Mfg. Co.:* "We think it a fair definition to say that what may be sold or assigned is property."[30]

On the basis of the foregoing discussion, it can be reasonably concluded that trade secrets, and hence know-how, constitute property for purposes of taxation. This conclusion is supported by a number of private rulings issued by the Commissioner under Sections 367 and 351 of the Internal Revenue Code in transactions involving the transfer of know-how by United States corporations to foreign subsidiaries.[31]

Section 351 provides for the nonrecognition of gain (or loss)

---

[23]Fowle v. Park, 131 U.S. 88 (1889); Coca-Cola Bottling Co. v. Coca-Cola Co., 269 Fed. 796 (D. Del. 1920); Anderson v. Distler, 173 Misc. 261, 17 N.Y.S.2d 674 (Sup. Ct. 1940).

[24]Jones v. Corbyn, 186 F.2d 450 (10th Cir. 1950).

[25]114 F.2d 380, 382-83 (1940).

[26]Grace Bros., Inc. v. Comm., 173 F.2d 170 (9th Cir. 1949); Cleveland Allerton Hotel, Inc. v. Comm., 166 F.2d 805 (6th Cir. 1948).

[27]Comm. v. Shapiro, 125 F.2d 532 (6th Cir. 1942).

[28]Louis W. Ray, 18 T.C. 438 (1952).

[29]Elliott B. Smoak, 43 B.T.A. 907 (1941).

[30]51 F.2d 681, 682 (1931).

[31]Such rulings include one dated January 20, 1960, and another dated September 28, 1959.

arising from the exchange of property for stock in a controlled corporation. Where the transferee of such property is a foreign corporation, taxation of such gain cannot be averted unless, prior to the transaction, a ruling or clearance is obtained from the Internal Revenue Service under Section 367 to the effect that tax avoidance is not a principal purpose of the exchange. In the private rulings referred to above, the Commissioner in granting the Section 367 clearance has thereupon ruled that under Section 351 no gain will be recognized on the transfer of know-how in exchange for stock of the foreign subsidiary. Since the very essence of a Section 351 transaction is the transfer of property in exchange for stock, it necessarily follows that the Commissioner has construed know-how as property in these rulings.

KNOW-HOW AS A CAPITAL ASSET

Having determined the property character of know-how, we turn next to the question of its qualification as a capital asset. The latter term is defined in the Internal Revenue Code to comprise all "property" other than specified categories which are excluded from this status. The relevant portions of the definition statute are set forth below:

> [T]he term "capital asset" means property held by the taxpayer (whether or not connected with his trade or business), but does not include—
>
> (1) stock in trade of the taxpayer or other property of a kind which would properly be included in the inventory of the taxpayer if on hand at the close of the taxable year, or property held by the taxpayer primarily for sale to customers in the ordinary course of his trade or business;
>
> (2) property, used in his trade or business, of a character which is subject to the allowance for depreciation provided in section 167, or real property used in his trade or business. . . .[32]

Regarding the second exception to the classification of property as a capital asset, it should be recognized that know-how normally cannot be depreciated since it has no fixed or ascertainable life, but rather has an indefinite duration.[33] In this sense know-how differs from a patent which, because of its certain statutory life of 17 years, can be depreciated if used in the taxpayer's trade or business, in which circumstance it is not a capital asset.[34] Thus, the classifica-

---

[32]Int. Rev. Code of 1954, Sec. 1221.

[33]Inecto, Inc., 20 B.T.A. 566 (1930), aff'd per curiam, 50 F.2d 1078 (2d Cir. 1931). See also A. R. R. 339, 3 Cum. Bull. 169.

[34]It should be noted, however, that a patent not qualifying as a capital asset because it is depreciable will normally be a Section 1231 asset (a depreciable asset

tion of know-how as a capital asset will generally hinge on whether or not it falls within the first excluded category described above.

It should be readily apparent that know-how is not "property included in the inventory of the taxpayer." Hence the salient question is whether and in what circumstances know-how is "property held by the taxpayer primarily for sale in the ordinary course of his trade or business." (Our reference is basically to corporate taxpayers, as they are principally responsible for the development and hence licensing of know-how.) The question has never been judicially decided. However, it would seem that the nature and origin of know-how normally tend to refute any contention that it is held primarily for sale. Know-how is essentially an accumulation of the methods, techniques, and processes derived from experience and experimentation in manufacturing a product. Thus, know-how is normally an incident—and indeed a derivative—of manufacture, rather than property held primarily for sale.

It is significant that in analogous cases involving capital gains from corporate transfers of patents the Commissioner has not usually urged that the patents were held primarily for sale.[35] And while in these cases the patents, as depreciable property, were Section 1231 assets rather than capital assets, the point is the same since a finding that the patents were held primarily for sale would have defeated any attempt to classify them as Section 1231 property and accordingly would have resulted in ordinary income rather than capital gain on their sale or exchange. The inference to be taken from these precedents is that, when it is evident that patents have been developed and used for manufacturing purposes, the Commissioner does not attempt the difficult argument that they are held primarily for sale. It would appear that this analysis applies *a fortiori* to the corporate sale of know-how, which, unlike a patent or invention owned by a corporation, is inevitably involved in and a product of manufacturing operations. The reasonable conclusion must then be that know-how is normally held by a corporation for manufacturing purposes and not for sale. There may, of course, be exceptions to this statement.

It may be that fragmented sales of know-how, for example, on a country-by-country or item-by-item basis, will incur risk of classification as property held primarily for sale.[36] Even in these

_____

used in a trade or business) with the result that its sale or exchange will result in capital gain under that section.

[35]See, *e.g.*, Merck & Co., Inc. v. Smith, 155 F. Supp. 843 (E.D. Pa. 1957); National Bread Wrapping Machine Co., 30 T.C. 550 (1958).

[36]In cases involving individual inventors, a past history of selling patents has sometimes led to the finding that the patent in controversy was held by the inven-

circumstances, however, it would seem that an attempt at such classification should fail if it can be shown (as it normally can) that the corporation develops and uses its body of know-how principally in connection with its own manufacturing operations and that the sale of know-how is merely incidental to this much broader purpose.[37] This would seem especially true where the corporate taxpayer can point to a long history of utilizing the transferred know-how in its business.[38]

We have concluded that know-how will generally satisfy the statutory definition of a capital asset. It should be recognized that this definition has in some instances been narrowed by judicial determination. The Supreme Court decision in *Corn Products Refining Co.* v. *Commissioner*[39] represents perhaps the leading example of this practice and must be considered for purposes of the present analysis. In that case the taxpayer, a manufacturer of corn products, engaged in the purchase of corn futures in order to assure itself of adequate supplies of corn. The sale of these futures gave rise to income which the taxpayer reported as capital gain on the theory that the futures were capital assets. In rejecting this argument the Court stated:

> We find nothing in this record to support the contention that Corn Products' futures activity was separate and apart from its manufacturing operation. On the contrary, it appears that the transactions were vitally important to the company's business as a form of insurance against increases in the price of raw corn. Not only were the purchases initiated for just this reason, but the petitioner's sales policy, selling in the future at a fixed price or less, continued to leave it exceedingly vulnerable to rises in the price of corn. Further, the purchase of corn futures assured the company a source of supply which was admittedly cheaper than constructing additional storage facilities for raw corn. Under these facts it is difficult to imagine a program more closely geared to a company's manufacturing enterprise or more important to its successful operation.

*　　*　　*

Admittedly, petitioner's corn futures do not come within the

---

tor primarily for sale. See, *e.g.*, Harold T. Avery, 47 B.T.A. 538 (1942). It should be appreciated, however, that these cases have involved inventors who have not utilized their patents in any manufacturing trade or business and accordingly could not argue that the inventions were held primarily for manufacturing purposes.

[37]Cf. Carl G. Dreymann, 11 T.C. 153 (1948).

[38]This standard is somewhat analogous to the "age test" employed by the courts (prior to the Revenue Act of 1950) in determining whether livestock was held for purposes of breeding or dairy as opposed to sale. The presumption created by this test was that if animals were sold at an immature age, they were held for sale, and that otherwise they were held for breeding or dairy uses, with the result that proceeds from their sale were capital gains. See Fox v. Comm., 198 F.2d 719 (4th Cir. 1952).

[39]350 U. S. 46 (1955), *rehearing denied*, 350 U.S. 943 (1956).

literal language of the exclusions set out in that section [now Section 1221]. They were not stock in trade, actual inventory, property held for sale to customers or depreciable property used in a trade or business.

*   *   *

Since this section is an exception from the normal tax requirements of the Internal Revenue Code, the definition of a capital asset must be narrowly applied and its exclusions interpreted broadly.[40]

It is perhaps no answer to the holding in *Corn Products Refining Co.* to characterize the Court's redefinition of the term "capital asset" as yet another illustration of judicial legislation. But that point aside, it appears from a close examination of the decision that it has questionable application to the problem before us. That case involved hedging transactions which, on the basis of prior cases and rulings, were found to be a form of insurance rather than a dealing in capital assets.[41] It is unlikely that the decision can reasonably be applied to situations not concerned with commodity futures. It is perhaps significant that the Commissioner has not attempted to apply the holding to patent assignment or to the sale of good will. Its application to know-how transfers would appear to be equally without warrant.

SALE OR EXCHANGE REQUIREMENT

It is reasonable to assume that the sale or exchange requirement as interpreted in the patent cases applies generally to know-how transfers. It is well settled that the transfer of the exclusive right to make, use, and sell a patented article for the full term of the patent results in an assignment, that is, a sale, rather than a mere licensing of the patent.[42] Certain later cases have employed a less rigid standard in allowing capital gains upon a showing that the transferor had retained no right of "provable substantial value."[43]

The application of either of these standards to the transfer of know-how presents this very difficult problem: the transferor cor-

---

[40]*Id.* at 50-52.

[41]Moreover, the Internal Revenue Code of 1954, Sec. 1233, explicitly excepts hedging transactions from classification as the sale or exchange of capital assets.

[42]This was the test employed in the classic infringement case of Waterman v. MacKenzie, 138 U.S. 252 (1891), and adopted by subsequent tax cases in determining whether the transfer of rights had effected an assignment of the patent. See Edward C. Myers, 6 T.C. 258 (1946); Ernest Gustave Hoffman, 8 B.T.A. 1272 (1927).

[43]United States v. Carruthers, 219 F.2d 21 (9th Cir. 1955). Cf. Rollman v. Comm., 244 F.2d 634 (4th Cir. 1957).

poration's continued use or reserved right to use the know-how in licensing its use to others would apparently mean that it had granted something less than the *exclusive* right to make, use, and sell under the know-how; or in the alternative, that it had retained a right of provable substantial value. And, of course, in normal circumstances the transferor will wish to reserve the right to make continued use of the subject know-how.

On the other hand, there is ample authority that the exclusive licensing of a patent within a given industry or limited geographically results in the sale of the patent. In *Vincent A. Marco*[44] the Tax Court ruled that the transfer of the exclusive right to make, use, and sell a patented article in that portion of the United States west of the Mississippi River amounted to a sale of the patent.[45] In *First National Bank of Princeton* v. *United States*[46] the taxpayer invented and patented a method of rounding ends of brush bristles. He exclusively licensed the right to make, use, and sell the invention with respect to toothbrushes, but reserved to himself the right to use and license the invention for other types of brushes. The court held that there had been a sale of the patent.[47]

These precedents as applied to our inquiry would appear to provide sound support for construing the exclusive licensing of know-how with territorial or industry limitations as a sale of the property. The geographical limitation would seem to have special practical application in the foreign licensing of know-how, which could be on a country-by-country basis.

The grant of exclusive rights to a patent must extend for its full term if a sale is to result.[48] The elements of know-how, unlike patents, do not have a fixed or ascertainable life, but are of indefinite duration and capable of perpetual existence. Accordingly, to accomplish a sale of this property, it is probably necessary to grant the licensee not only exclusive but perpetual rights. This conclusion is confirmed by the cases involving the licensing of trademarks, which can also be said to be capable of perpetual existence.[49]

---

[44]25 T.C. 544 (1955).

[45]*Accord,* Thornton G. Graham, 26 T.C. 730 (1956); Lamar v. Granger, 99 F. Supp. 17 (W.D. Pa. 1951).

[46]136 F. Supp. 818 (D. N.J. 1955).

[47]See also Carruthers v. United States, 219 F.2d 21 (9th Cir. 1955), involving the exclusive licensing of a patent for use in the tuna industry.

[48]Waterman v. MacKenzie, 138 U.S. 252 (1891); Arthur M. Young, 29 T.C. 850 (1958).

[49]See Thomas D. Armour, 22 T.C. 181 (1954), where it was held that the transfer of rights to a trademark must be perpetual in duration to constitute a sale. See also Seattle Brewing & Malting Co., 6 T.C. 856 (1946).

METHOD OF PAYMENT

The courts have traditionally held that the method of payment is not a factor in determining the eligibility of a patent transfer for capital gains.[50] Notwithstanding this fact, the Commissioner, in Mimeograph 6490,[51] issued in 1950, took the official position that the assignment of a patent in consideration of payments measured by the assignee's production, sale, or use of the patented article was *not* to be regarded as a "sale" of the patent. The arrangement was said rather to provide for the payment of royalties taxable as ordinary income. While this position continued to meet consistent defeat in the courts, it nonetheless resulted in considerable uncertainty in the tax law. Recently, however, the Service, because of its repeated failure to obtain judicial support on the question, has revoked Mimeograph 6490.[52] Thus, the existence of a royalty arrangement no longer poses a threat to the realization of capital gains on patent assignments. This conclusion would seem logically to apply also to transfers of know-how.

SERVICE ELEMENT OF KNOW-HOW TRANSFERS

In the usual case, the grant of know-how involves some element of personal services which are to be rendered by the grantor. These services may take the form of teaching and instructing, or may involve consultation or technical assistance in adapting the know-how to the particular manufacturing operations of the grantee. In certain situations such technical services may be the principal or only medium of communicating the know-how to the transferee.

It is, of course, clear that the performance of personal service in the normal course results in ordinary income rather than capital gains. Where it has been determined that proceeds arising from the transfer of know-how are basically eligible for capital gains, the question arises as to what portion, if any, of such payments must be allocated to the personal services and reported as ordinary income. In cases involving the sale or assignment of a patented device which is technical and intricate, services of an advisory nature have generally been construed as ancillary and subsidiary to the sale of the patent and the complete proceeds of the transaction held taxable as capital gains.[53] The duration and extent of the services are important

[50]Comm. v. Hopkinson, 126 F.2d 406 (2d Cir. 1942); Edward C. Myers, 6 T.C. 258 (1946).

[51]1950-1 Cum. Bull. 9; Rev. Rul. 55-58, 1955-1 Cum. Bull. 97.

[52]Rev. Rul. 58-353, 1958-2 Cum. Bull. 408.

[53]Arthur C. Ruge, 26 T.C. 138 (1956); Raymond M. Hessert, 6 T.C. Memo. 1190 (1957); William M. Kelly, 6 T.C. Memo. 646 (1947).

factors in determining whether such services are ancillary and subsidiary to the patent grant. In *Arthur C. Ruge*[54] the taxpayers, in transferring all right, title, and interest to certain inventions, agreed to give the assignee a certain number of man-days consulting service per year if requested, but not to exceed 60 days per year. Certain percentage payments called for by the agreement were in consideration of the inventions and of the consulting services. The Tax Court found that the services were merely ancillary to the assignment of the patents and of a type and kind usually called for to implement the sale of highly technical and intricate inventions. Accordingly, the percentage payments in their entirety were held to constitute consideration for the sale of the inventions and were thus taxable as capital gains.

The application of the "ancillary and subsidiary doctrine" to technical services rendered in connection with know-how transfers would appear wholly reasonable. This conclusion finds support in Revenue Ruling 55-17,[55] which involved these facts: A foreign corporation not engaged in business in this country licensed a domestic corporation to use certain techniques and methods ("commonly referred to as 'know-how' ") for recovery and purification of chemicals, which know-how the domestic corporation wished to apply to commercial production in the United States. The foreign corporation was to provide instruction in certain techniques to the employees of the domestic corporation, and these services were to be performed abroad. The question at issue was the allocation of payments made by the U. S. company between royalties attributable to the use of know-how, on which portion tax was to be withheld, and amounts attributable to personal services on which no withholding was required. The following extract from the Ruling is significant for our purposes:

> The essence of the contract is the making available to the domestic corporation the technical knowledge, methods, experience, that is, the "know-how" of the foreign corporation. While manufacturing "know-how" is of a nonpatentable nature, it is something that its possessor can grant to another for a consideration. The right to use such "know-how" is not materially different from the right to use trademarks, secret processes and formulae, and, if the right thereto is granted as part of a licensing agreement, it becomes, in effect, an integral part of the bundle of rights acquired under such an agreement.
>
> The payments made under the contract are applicable both to the specific rights therein granted, that is, the right to use the "know-how," and to services performed abroad in instructing and training the employees or technicians of the domestic corporation. Such payments

---

[54] Arthur C. Ruge, 26 T.C. 138 (1956).
[55] 1955-1 Cum. Bull. 388.

should therefore be allocated between the license to use the "know-how" and the personal services. Since the personal services have only nominal value apart from the license to use such "know-how," all but a nominal sum should be allocated to the license.[56]

The Ruling in its provision for an allocation of only a nominal sum to the personal services is basically consonant with the "ancillary and subsidiary doctrine" enunciated in the cases involving the sale or assignment of a patent. Hence, it can be reasonably concluded that if technical services are merely incidental to the grant of know-how, all, or nearly all, of the payments made under the transfer agreement will be eligible for capital gains, provided, of course, the transfer effects the sale or exchange of a capital asset as discussed earlier in detail.

The Ruling is not directly concerned with the problem before us, that is, the allocation of payments between capital gains (representing the price of the property [know-how] which was sold or exchanged) and ordinary income (representing compensation for personal services). But the essential thrust of the Ruling is the same, in that it segregates payments into amounts attributable respectively to the know-how and the personal services. The Ruling reflects a realistic appreciation of the fact that technical services have little intrinsic value apart from their connection with the know-how, and accordingly, it limits the sum allocated to such services.

It would appear that the Revenue Ruling has a broader application than the "ancillary and subsidiary doctrine" developed in the patent transfer cases. It would appear appropriate to those situations in which technical services are not merely incidental to the know-how grant, but in fact constitute the principal or only method of transferring the know-how. Even in these circumstances, it would seem, as stated in the language of the Ruling, that "[t]he essence of the contract is the making available to the domestic corporation of the technical knowledge, methods, experience, that is, the 'know-how' of the . . . [transferor] corporation" and that "the personal services have only nominal value apart from the . . . [grant of] such 'know-how'. . . ."

The point would seem to be this: Even where the technical services are extensive and the primary means of communicating the know-how, they have little independent value. Accordingly, in these cases it would appear reasonable to fix this value at the cost, including salaries, of the employees of the transferor company who perform these services. In this manner, the predominantly greater part of the payments made by the transferee would be attributed to

---

[56]*Id.* at 389.

the transfer of the property in the know-how, and hence eligible for capital gains if the requisite conditions for this treatment are satisfied. As a practical matter, it is probably advisable in these circumstances to make specific provision in the know-how agreement for the grantor to be compensated for the services of its technical personnel (if extensive) on such a cost basis. This would tend to assure that all other payments would relate to and be in consideration of the know-how grant.

THE SIX-MONTH HOLDING PERIOD

We have concluded that know-how will generally qualify as a capital asset which is capable of sale or exchange. It is, of course, necessary that the know-how—as any capital asset—be held by the transferor for more than six months if long-term capital gains, to which preferential tax rates attach, are to result from such sale or exchange.[57] In the usual situation, the holding period would appear to pose no problem with respect to the grant of present know-how. This is because such know-how will normally consist of proven techniques, processes, and accumulated experience which by their very nature and development have existed for a time substantially greater than six months. And even in the exceptional circumstances where some such element of know-how may have existed for a shorter duration, it is a relatively simple matter to defer its assignment until the holding period requirement is satisfied.

A more difficult problem is presented in the case of the grant of continuing know-how. Frequently, a corporation acquiring the existing know-how of another corporation will also wish for obvious reasons to have the use of future improvements and developments of the know-how of the transferor corporation. In view of the holding period requirement, it is highly questionable whether payments made for or allocated to the grant of rights to such future know-how will be eligible for treatment as long-term capital gains.

The question is similar to that involved in assignments of future patents and inventions. It is clear that such assignments are valid and may be specifically enforced.[58] There is, however, a conflict as to whether such transactions can result in capital gain. Denial of this treatment has been predicated on either of these two grounds: (1) The inventor, because of the future assignment, never owned the invention and hence could not sell it;[59] or (2) assuming own-

---

[57]Int. Rev. Code of 1954, Sec. 1222.

[58]Littlefield v. Perry, 88 U.S. (21 Wall.) 205, 226 (1875); Conway v. White, 9 F.2d 863, 866 (2d Cir. 1925).

[59]Blum v. Comm., 183 F.2d 281 (3d Cir. 1950).

ership, the inventor had not satisfied the six-month holding period required for long-term capital gains, the complete rights to the invention being deemed automatically to vest in the assignee upon its reduction to practice.[60]

Other decisions adopted the theory that the future assignment could not affect a present sale of an asset not yet in being, and that ownership of the invention could vest in the transferee only upon formal assignment by the inventor after the invention had come into existence. Thus, if the inventor held the invention for six months prior to formal assignment, he was entitled to long-term capital gains.[61]

These precedents would appear to have logical application to transfers of future or continuing know-how, with the result that the capital gains eligibility of payments therefor is most uncertain, if not unlikely, and probably would be opposed by the Treasury. If a corporation contemplates the grant of rights to continuing know-how in conjunction with the transfer of existing know-how in a capital gains situation, it is clearly advisable to provide for a specific and reasonable allocation of total payments between such existing and future know-how. (It may even be desirable to employ separate agreements for this purpose.) Failure to make a fixed and definite allocation may result in an allocation being made by the Commissioner in a manner which will minimize the amounts attributed to existing know-how and hence available as capital gains.

It has been suggested that the holding period problems arising in connection with assignment of future inventions and improvement patents can be averted if the inventor or assignor merely gives the prospective assignee an option to acquire such future inventions or patents.[62] It has also been suggested that these problems can be eliminated, and the transferee's interest at the same time protected, by requiring in a formal agreement that all future inventions or improvement patents must be offered to such party by the inventor or assignor once they come into existence.[63] Either of these methods can be utilized to guarantee that there will be no completed sale of the future property until the six months holding period has elapsed. There appears to be no reason why these solutions cannot be adapted to the future know-how situation in order to produce a capital gains result.

---

[60]Paul L. Kuzmick, 11 T.C. 288 (1948).

[61]Carl G. Dreymann, 11 T.C. 153 (1948). Cf. Richard W. Te Linde, 18 T.C. 91 (1952).

[62]Bailey, *The Inventor*, 15 N.Y.U. Inst. on Fed. Tax. 285, 308 (1957).

[63]*Patent Licensing*, Practising Law Institute, 95, 96 (1958).

CONCLUSION

We conclude that know-how is property and that it usually constitutes a capital asset. To accomplish its sale or exchange, it is necessary that there be a grant of the exclusive right to make, use, and sell under the know-how. The continued use or retention of the right to use such know-how by the transferor—which is the normal practice—will generally prevent the transfer of *exclusive rights*. There is, however, authority to support the proposition that the transfer of exclusive rights to know-how for utilization within a given industry or limited geographically will be construed as a sale, with capital gains as a consequence. The exclusive grant in these circumstances would permit the continued use of the know-how by the transferor. The transfer with territorial limitations would appear to have special practical application to foreign licensing, which could be on a country-by-country basis.

It should be recognized that the path to capital gains on know-how transactions is both tortuous and uncharted. There is presently lacking the body of direct precedents necessary to achieve a definite clarity and predictability in resolving the many issues we have raised. Nonetheless, our exploratory analysis, which relies principally on the analogous tax cases involving patent transfers, leads us to conclude that, within the limitations outlined here and with proper attention to drafting of license agreements, the grant of know-how can yield capital gains results.

Tax Experience of American Corporations Owning Numerous Patents

ROBERT B. BANGS AND JOHN F. CREED

What tax problems do American corporations that own extensive patent assets most frequently encounter? How do tax considerations shape their administration of these assets. if at all? Is there uniformity of tax experience among American corporations with regard to earnings from their intangible industrial property. or diversity? Are transactions in patents and related industrial property frequently or only rarely tax-motivated? Does experience indicate any need for change in our income-tax rules as they apply to patents and knowhow? These and similar questions are typical of those asked by people who have thought deeply about our tax and patent systems and their interrelationship.

Such questions as these touch important issues about which much has been written and spoken and about which. as with all complex issues. there may be differences of opinion among reasonable men. The questions themselves emerge from the circumstances that we have. on the one hand. formal income-tax rules that are intended to apply uniformly to all comparable situations. These rules derive from statutory language. from regulations amplifying this language. and from litigated cases. We have. on the other hand. individual taxpayer experiences with tax rules that may appear harsh or inequitable in special situations. or that do not appear to follow either the letter or the logic of the statute.

In the welter of controversy about taxation. the special area selected for study in this Research Institute—within the general field of interaction between the tax and patent systems—is actual. representative tax experience. This area needs to be distinguished from the subject matter of the usual legal or accounting studies of taxation; these latter are concerned primarily with the precise boundaries of existing law. Witness the typical article in any of the better known tax law journals.[1] These articles review the leading

EDITOR'S NOTE: This paper represents a first comprehensive survey of representative tax experience among corporations owning substantial patent portfolios. (*IDEA*. Vol. 5. No. 3. Fall 1961.)

[1]Cf. the bibliography appended to J. A. McFadden and C. D. Tuska, *Accounting and Tax Aspects of Patents and Research* (New York: Van Nostrand. 1960).

cases, which establish the marginal applications of particular tax rules stated in general language. The characteristic question is whether a given type of transaction falls under rule A or rule B. Is it capital gain or ordinary income? Business expense or capital investment? Taxable or not?

Our concern in the tax studies of the Institute is less with the marginal than with the modal or typical tax situation. We seek answers to such questions as: how do corporations ordinarily handle their patents for tax purposes? Do tax considerations influence business policies with regard to patent licensing, and if so to a great or merely a minor extent?

To answer these and related questions requires more than the usual study of tax law. It requires the accumulation of a body of empirically based knowledge that may be treated statistically. To begin building such a store of knowledge the Institute, in 1960, addressed a detailed questionnaire to all American corporations that, in 1955, had owned 150 or more patents. We reasoned that by dealing first with substantial blocs of patents, we might accumulate useful and broadly based experience more quickly than by querying corporations generally. Many corporations own few if any patents, and consequently have only limited experience with the tax problems that accompany patent ownership.

Our questionnaire focused primarily on experience under the U.S. federal income tax; but it also called for details about foreign patenting, and for problems encountered under foreign income taxes because of patent ownership or use.

Since 1954, patents owned by corporations have, for U.S. income tax purposes, been classified as depreciable property used in trade or business. This is a special sort of property. Patents are by definition not capital assets, although treated as such for certain purposes. Patents share this classification as depreciable property with business structures and machinery.

The tax treatment of depreciable property is as follows: If the property is sold for a loss, that loss is a business loss; it may be offset against business income of any kind and, if unrequited, carried over to other years. If sold for a profit after book depreciation, this profit is treated as though it were a long-term capital gain, and taxed at lower effective rates than ordinary income. Whether the depreciable property can be sold for a profit or a loss depends on whether tax depreciation corresponds well or ill with actual depreciation, and on such other factors as the general trend of prices over the life cycle of the depreciable property.

In contrast to the gain or loss from outright sale of a patent, or other depreciable property, income from use of such property, earned either in direct commercial operations or by licensing the patent, is typically ordinary income; however, in special cases, when an exclusive licensing arrangement transfers all substantial rights in the patent, the transaction may be viewed by the tax authorities as the equivalent of a sale—so that capital gain or ordinary loss may result.

THE UNIVERSE OF THE STUDY AND OF THE RESPONSES RECEIVED

Questionnaires were mailed to the 252 American corporations that owned 150 or more patents according to a 1955 list.[2] Completed questionnaires were received from 62 of these, forming the main body of information available for analysis. Letter replies were received from 27 corporations that were unable, for various reasons, to supply all the details requested but who wished nevertheless to supply some information. These letter responses vary in completeness and in the nature of the information they supply; but a considerable number contain statements of company policy with regard to licensing, foreign patenting, or other transactions in industrial property that have tax implications. The letter replies thus add useful detail to that supplied by the completed questionnaires.

Because the questionnaires were directed only to corporations that were known to have title to substantial numbers of patents, the coverage represented in our responding group is quite broad. Slightly more than 50,000 U. S. patents and nearly 44,000 foreign patents were owned on December 31, 1959 by corporations who returned questionnaires. Of all the U.S. patents estimated to have been owned by American corporations at the end of 1959, we can account for about 16 percent among our respondents.

Since the number of U.S. corporations that file income-tax returns is about 180,000, and since a substantial fraction of these corporations may own at least one patent, a large sample would have been required to obtain 16 percent coverage of corporate patent ownership, had the sample been selected in some other manner.

Because we surveyed only corporations known to have large numbers of patents, our results are not necessarily typical for all

---

[2]*Distribution of Patents Issued to Corporations* (1939-55). Study #3 for the Subcommittee on Patents, Trademarks, and Copyrights, Senate Judiciary Committee Print, 84th Cong. 2nd Sess., Dec. 29, 1956.

corporations, nor representative of those that own only a few patents; but, by and large, the tax problems of such corporations arising from administration of their patent assets will be minor in comparison with those of corporations that have large patent portfolios. Our interest, after all, is primarily in tax problems and tax experience. We sought to locate it in the most accessible place.

The number of patents owned by companies filing completed questionnaires is shown in Table 1. Tables 2 and 3 give frequency distributions of reporting companies by number of U.S. and foreign patents owned, respectively. The average number of U.S. patents

TABLE 1
NUMBER OF PATENTS OWNED BY REPORTING CORPORATIONS
(Dec. 31, 1959)

Company Number	U.S. Patents	Foreign Patents	Company Number	U.S. Patents	Foreign Patents
1	227	248	33	190	58
2	[1]	[1]	34	220	91
3	75	75	35	298	197
4	1250	450	36	265	147
5	397	300	37	406	246
6	196	208	38	292	488
7	626	491	39	[1]	[1]
8	1451	738	40	564	200
9	542	526	41	[1]	[1]
10	2339	2993	42	480	108
11	1100[2]	400[2]	43	269	127
12	520	800	44	151	0
13	750[2]	400[2]	45	[1]	[1]
14	183	176	46	200[2]	250[2]
15	1950	3280	47	355	176
16	385	262	48	600	228
17	634	[1]	49	403	95
18	83	30	50	400[2]	100[2]
19	1853	286	51	3000[2]	4750[2]
20	5000[2]	3000[2]	52	437	0
21	1188	784	53	142	27
22	513	46	54	936	558
23	250	600	55	114	200[2]
24	1132	895	56	7600[2]	8500[2]
25	1082	120	57	481	1500[2]
26	450	179	58	297	448
27	578	450	59	184	376
28	380	750	60	3527	1151
29	292	488	61	775	2425
30	1150	2010	62	250[2]	50[2]
31	250	200			
32	524	136	TOTALS	50,186	43,817

[1]Not reported.
[2]Estimated by respondent.
Source: Replies to Institute Questionnaire.

Table 2

NUMBER OF U.S. PATENTS OWNED

(Dec. 31, 1959)

Number of U.S. Patents Owned	Number of Companies
Less than 100	2
100-399	23
400-699	16
700-999	3
1000-1499	7
1500-1999	2
2000 and over	5
No report	4
Total	62

owned by each reporting company was 865, but the median was only 443. This latter average is less affected by the very large patent collections in the sample.

In four cases the number of U.S. patents owned was not reported, while in five cases the number of foreign patents owned was not reported. Generally, the number of foreign patents ran below the number of U.S. patents, although in 16 cases it was higher. The number of foreign patents does not correspond with the number of inventions, as a single invention may be patented in ten foreign countries, and thus count as ten foreign patents.

A number of companies reported that it was their practice to take out foreign patents only in those countries and for those products or processes which they believed would be productive of some income. In a few cases it was apparently the policy to patent a basic invention in the principal foreign industrial countries for defensive or protective reasons.

The reporting companies covered a broad range but by no means a complete classification of industrial groups. Chemical and electrical manufacturing companies are well represented, as are petroleum refiners and distributors and also machinery manufacturers. Transportation equipment manufacturing, apart from aircraft, is poorly represented. Several manufacturing companies in this field reported by letter that patents are relatively unimportant to their operations although they owned substantial patent portfolios.

The preponderant sources of these large collections of patents represented in Table 1 were the company's own research programs or their own employees. In nearly every case it was reported that well in excess of 90 percent of all patents owned had been assigned to the company by employees. For at least half of the reporting

TABLE 3
NUMBER OF FOREIGN PATENTS OWNED
(Dec. 31, 1959)

Number of Foreign Patents Owned	Number of Companies
Less than 100	10
100-399	22
400-699	11
700-999	5
1000-1499	1
1500-1999	1
2000 and over	7
No report	5
Total	62

companies, employees are the sole source of patented inventions. The remaining companies acquire a few patents from outside individuals or by purchase from another corporation, usually when they take over the assets of that other corporation in a merger.

It appears, however, that large corporations do not ordinarily treat patents as articles of commerce, to be bought and sold, but as operating business assets, primarily for their own use. This corresponds with our findings from responses of individual inventors, who in an earlier survey reported that they had few opportunities to sell their patents outright to corporations, and thus obtain capital gains treatment for themselves.

The number of patents not owned but licensed for their own use by the reporting corporations typically ran well below the number of patents owned. In the relatively few cases where the licensed patents were more numerous than the owned patents, they were often far more numerous. Three companies, for example, reported that they licensed more than ten times as many patents for their use as they themselves owned. These three companies were in three different industries, so this sort of relationship is not specific to one branch of technology. Evidently the explanation in these cases was that access to certain methods the companies wished to use required the licensing of large blocs of patents owned by others. The others were typically other corporations, although six corporations reported that one-third or more of the patents they licensed came from individuals.

The basic data on number of patents licensed for the use of our reporting corporations are given in Table 4. Tables 5 and 6 give distributions of reporting corporations by number of patents licensed from others.

Extensive use of licensing is customary in certain industries.

but not in others. Likewise, custom varies as between licensing individual patents and blocs of them covering an entire field of technology. In the petroleum industry, for example, field licensing is usual. One letter received, in lieu of a completed questionnaire, puts it this way:

> It has been customary in our business, for a great many years, to both issue and accept patent licenses on a basis of defined fields rather than individual patents. This practice is so prevalent that it makes it a virtual impossibility for us to enumerate the patents we have licensed to others or the patents under which we have accepted licenses from others.

In other industries, field licensing is also common and cross-licensing arrangements more prevalent. One manufacturer of optical equipment reported as follows:

> Most of the patent licensing arrangements into which we have entered are cross-licensing agreements which involve the exchange of nonexclusive licenses in certain fields, usually a field or fields which are of little interest to the licensor and considerable interest to the licensee. These licenses are generally fully paid, the consideration being the grant of a corresponding license from the other party.

Such a barter system of exchanging patent licenses may be appropriate when there are several firms in an industry all with intangible industrial property in about equal amounts. Barter systems break down or are not suitable when the exchanging corporations are not similar in assets or complementary in technology. For this reason such arrangements are probably not widespread.

On the general subject of the sources from which licenses used by American corporations are derived, the distribution of licenses obtained from foreign corporations is quite interesting. Among the 60 companies reporting, 20 said they obtained no licenses whatever from foreign corporations, but only from U.S. corporations and individuals. Those corporations which did obtain licenses from abroad frequently obtained a relatively high proportion of their licenses from this source. Thus seven companies stated that 50 percent or more of their licensed patents were from foreign corporations, and three additional companies put the proportion at from 30 to 50 percent. The explanation is, of course, to be found in the relative state of the industrial arts as between the U.S. and other countries in specialized fields of manufacture. In chemicals and drugs foreign technology is quite advanced; American corporations license many product and process patents for use in this country. In automobiles and heavy machinery, on the other hand, few if any licenses are obtained from foreign companies.

Additional summary information on the sources from which

TABLE 4

NUMBER OF PATENTS LICENSED FOR OWN USE BY
REPORTING CORPORATIONS

(Dec. 31, 1959)

Company Number	U.S. Patents	Foreign Patents	Company Number	U.S. Patents	Foreign Patents
1	0	0	33	54	12
2	[1]	[1]	34	91	7
3	5	[1]	35	30	50
4	13,500	1500	36	20	0
5	2	2	37	7	0
6	2	1	38	31	0
7	20	2	39	[1]	[1]
8	211	[1]	40	100	20
9	7500[2]	7500[2]	41	[1]	[1]
10	500[2]	100[2]	42	[1]	[1]
11	30	6	43	10	0
12	8	100[2]	44	[1]	[1]
13	25	[1]	45	[1]	[1]
14	75	5	46	40	35
15	50	[1]	47	75	0
16	0	0	48	49	2
17	[1]	[1]	49	89	0
18	1	0	50	10	5
19	57	[1]	51	15,500	50
20	[1]	0	52	4	[1]
21	[1]	[1]	53	2	0
22	5	2	54	[1]	0
23	30	60	55	72	11
24	149	62	56	800[2]	350[2]
25	271	155	57	60	0
26	655	96	58	25	10
27	400[2]	300[2]	59	2	0
28	30	8	60	[1]	[1]
29	31	0	61	[1]	[1]
30	150[2]	100[2]	62	10	0
31	3	[1]			
32	[1]	[1]	TOTALS	40,791	10,551

[1]Not reported.
[2]Estimated by respondent.

licenses granted to American corporations are derived is given in Table 7.

The international patent-licensing pattern has been explored in other studies of the Research Institute;[3] it is not the intention here to supplement those studies. The point to be made is simply

[3]Cf. *IDEA*, Vol. 2, No. 2 (June 1958); Vol. 3, No. 3 (Fall 1959); Vol. 3, No. 4 (Winter 1959); Vol. 5, No. 1 (Spring 1961).

TABLE 5
NUMBER OF U.S. PATENTS LICENSED FOR OWN USE
(Dec. 31, 1959)

Number of Licenses	Number of Reporting Corporations
None	2
1-9	11
10-49	15
50-99	9
100-249	4
250-999	5
1000 and over	3
No report	13
Total	62

TABLE 6
NUMBER OF FOREIGN PATENTS LICENSED FOR OWN USE
(Dec. 31, 1959)

Number of Licenses	Number of Reporting Corporations
None	16
1-9	10
10-49	5
50-99	5
100-249	4
250-999	2
1000 and over	2
No report	18
Total	62

TABLE 7
SOURCES FROM WHICH U.S. PATENTS LICENSED FOR OWN USE WERE DERIVED

Source of Licenses	Number of Reporting Corporations
Solely from other U.S. corporations	10
90-99% from other U.S. corporations	15
50-89% from other U.S. corporations	22
10-49% from foreign corporations	8
10-49% from individuals	23
Over 50% from individuals	2
No report	7
Total	87[1]

[1]As the source categories are not mutually exclusive. the total is greater than the number of reporting corporations.

that a diversity of practice does exist; a range of practice is represented in our reporting sample, and this variety of practice does produce some special tax problems, which will be explored in detail later.

TYPICAL TAX SITUATIONS—SALE OF PATENTS

Present law allows a U.S. corporation to sell patents outright, or to grant exclusive licenses conveying all substantial rights to the patents and to treat the proceeds from such sales, in large part, as capital gain—subject to a maximum tax rate of 25 percent. The gain is, of course, the excess of the proceeds over the cost or other basis of the patent. If the patent has been developed in the selling company's own laboratory, the research and development cost will have been expensed—as the tax law allows. The patent itself will be capitalized only for the filing fees and legal expenses that sometimes cannot be taken as tax deductions; alternatively it may be carried at only a nominal value—such as $1. Virtually all the proceeds will therefore be capital gain. If the patent has been purchased rather than developed, it may have a substantial unamortized cost basis, and the gain may be only a fraction of the proceeds realized.

In our sample, 27 corporations reported that they had, on some occasion, sold patents outright. About half of this group said they did so rarely. The typical sale situation was either one in which some portion of the business assets was sold (including the patents) or one in which the company by chance developed a patent that had no foreseeable application in the company's own business. Therefore they sold the patent to some other operator more likely to use it. The other operator was typically another corporation.

Twenty-nine corporations reported they had never, on any occasion, either sold patents outright or licensed them exclusively. Six companies failed to reply to this question.

In every case where patents had been reported sold, the reporting companies indicated they had experienced no difficulty in qualifying these transactions for capital-gains treatment. It is impossible from this evidence to conclude otherwise than that the law in this area is well understood and uniformly administered. The reporting companies are, of course, relatively large corporations, served in nearly all cases by competent tax counsel. Smaller corporations may have less consistent experience. In marked contrast to this experience of large corporations we found in an earlier survey[4]

[4]"Tax Problems of the Individual Inventor," *IDEA*, Vol. 3, Conference Number 1959, pp. 35-47.

that a substantial fraction of individual inventors who sold patents were unaware they could claim capital-gains treatment for the proceeds.

Among the companies that had sold patents, the majority had made sales of both U.S. and foreign patents. In only four cases had foreign patents been sold but no U.S. patents. In another four cases, U.S. patents had been sold but no foreign patents. The remaining 19 companies had sold both U.S. and foreign patents. What this distribution suggests is that company policy in most cases tends to be fairly uniform with regard both to U.S. and foreign patents; broadly similar practice is usually followed with regard to all patent assets, in whatever country based. However, the present evidence is too slender to be conclusive.

The mere fact that nearly as many corporations reported they had sold patents as reported they had not does not mean that such selling is common or usual corporate practice. The question as worded asked whether patents had *ever* been sold; in other words, a single sale out of possibly 1,000 patents under administration called for a "yes" answer. The information given by our respondents regarding the circumstances surrounding sale, however, clearly indicates that patent sales by corporations are atypical or unusual. By and large, major corporations treat patents as business assets for their own primary (often exclusive) use; they only sell them when they do not fit into their regular operations or as part of a package made up largely of other assets. The typical sale results when a division or some other administrative segment of a business is sold. In such sales the proceeds are often not allocated as between the patents and the other business assets. The capital gain, if a gain results, is simply the difference between the sales price and the adjusted basis of all the assets in the package.

When patents are sold, it is not necessary that the proceeds be received either in a lump sum or in a single taxable year in order to qualify for capital-gains treatment. An exclusive license, calling for a running royalty based on production or use, can also be a sale for tax purposes, provided all substantial rights in the patent are transferred. In an exclusive license with a running royalty we have a rarity in tax law—one of the few situations where a stream of receipts, extending over a number of years and varying from year to year, becomes capital gain instead of ordinary income. The transaction is not analogous to an installment sale, but rather is a sale for an unknown amount—to be finally determined only after the invention has ceased to be of any use to the licensee.

Selling a patent by giving an exclusive license for a periodic royalty can be a highly advantageous arrangement for an individual inventor. In such a sale he spreads his income over several years, thus deferring part of his tax liability and perhaps lessening its total amount. Buyers may also prefer such terms since their initial investment in an invention of uncertain commercial success may be minimized.

For a corporation, the tax advantages in a patent sale by the exclusive license, running royalty route are less obvious than for an individual inventor. The corporation income-tax rate is basically flat rather than progressive, as is the rate on individuals. Nevertheless exclusive licenses may still be advantageous to a corporation—if only in postponing tax liability and permitting the use of and income on the funds equal to the tax postponed. By giving exclusive licenses the seller also retains basic legal title and can provide for termination of the exclusive license in case royalty payments are defaulted. This gives some measure of protection which is an advantage over an outright assignment.

To determine corporate practice concerning the form in which proceeds are taken in the relatively rare cases when patents are sold, we included a question on this point. The three possibilities are sale for a fixed sum (ordinary sale), a sale for fixed installments (installment sale) and a sale for a running royalty (exclusive license). The replies are summarized in Table 8.

It is plain from this distribution that the running royalty is by far the most popular form of taking proceeds, outweighing both other forms by a substantial margin.

Table 8 should not be interpreted as indicating that tax considerations dictate the method of taking payment for patent sales. While there is a temporary tax advantage in the running royalty, its use is probably determined more by prudent business practice than by tax saving. When a patent is sold there is often considerable uncertainty about its commercial value in the minds of both buyer and seller. The fairest arrangement to both parties may well be the running royalty. It is also in a sense the least speculative form of payment, since it is directly related to the value of the patent in actual use.

LICENSING PRACTICE AND TAX CONSIDERATIONS INVOLVED

Although corporations do not sell patents frequently, they do a much more extensive business in nonexclusive licensing, both in this country and abroad. To gain some insight into the licensing pattern and the tax problems involved therein, several questions were asked in the present survey. The first was calculated merely to establish the extent of licensing and whether the pattern differed as between licensing in this country and abroad. A classification of patents as between chemical, mechanical, and electrical was also called for to check the representativeness of the sample and whether practice varied significantly among the three classes of patents.

TABLE 8

FORM IN WHICH PAYMENT WAS TAKEN WHEN PATENTS
WERE SOLD OR LICENSED EXCLUSIVELY

Form of Payment	Percent of Companies Reporting	
	U.S. Patents	Foreign Patents
Running royalty exclusively	35	59
Running royalty in 51-99% of cases	31	22
Lump sum payment exclusively	10	4
Lump sum payment in 51-99% of cases	7	0
Fixed installments exclusively	7	4
Fixed installments in 51-99% of cases	10	11
Totals	100	100

In our reporting group of 62 corporations, all but three gave information about licensing within the U.S. Sixteen gave no information about foreign licensing, either because they did none, or because details concerning this activity were not available. Some American companies assign their foreign patents to foreign subsidiaries and consequently have no direct information on the licensing activity of those subsidiaries.

Appendix Table A gives the basic data on patents, distributed percentagewise by chemical, mechanical, and electrical, that are owned by our group of reporting corporations. This table may be read in conjunction with Table 1, which gives the number of patents owned.

The distribution of patents owned, by classes, is summarized in Table 9.

All the reporting companies had the majority of their U.S. patents in one class, although 28 companies owned some patents in all three classes. Company by company, the classes of foreign patents owned followed those of U.S. patents owned fairly closely. This reflects the fact that the underlying inventions are the same in both cases.

To determine the part played by tax considerations in company decisions whether to license its own patents to others on an exclusive or non-exclusive basis, a question was included on this point.

We simply asked whether tax considerations *sometimes* influenced these decisions, not whether taxation was the sole or the determining consideration. As already noted, only the proceeds from exclusive licensing arrangements are eligible for capital-gains treatment.

The replies to this question were distributed as follows: With regard to U. S. patents

12 companies reported tax considerations did influence their decisions concerning the form of licensing for patents they owned;

44 companies reported tax considerations did *not* influence their decisions.

With regard to foreign patents, the results were broadly similar—

12 companies were influenced by tax considerations, while 24 were not.

The decision about how to license a patent to others is inevitably a complex business decision, dependent on many factors; these vary from case to case. There is always present, for example, the

TABLE 9
CLASSES OF PATENTS OWNED

Class of Patent	Number of Companies Reporting	
	U.S. Patents	Foreign Patents
Chemical patents only	0	2
Mechanical patents only	5	6
Electrical patents only	0	1
51-99% chemical patents	19	13
51-99% mechanical patents	27	16
51-99% electrical patents	8	8
No reports	3	16
Totals	62	62

Source: Appendix Table A.

question whether it is better to have several licensees contributing incremental royalties than a single licensee making sole use of the invention. There may also be questions of trade custom, and of business policy concerning the maintenance or strengthening of competition.

Our evidence indicates that exclusive licensing is somewhat more common with regard to foreign than U.S. patents; but this may be a result primarily of the fact that potential markets are smaller in some other countries than in the U.S.; consequently, to have a minimum economic operation it may be necessary to license only one supplier in the foreign country. Additionally, a U. S. company may be willing to give an exclusive license on a foreign patent when it has determined not to operate directly in the foreign country, whereas the grant of an exclusive license to the corresponding domestic patent would foreclose the U.S. company from its use in this country. These and other factors of economic advantage generally outweigh the tax factors in determining license policy; nevertheless corporations do unquestionably bear taxation in mind when calculating their market strategy in patent licensing.

When a license is given to other producers it very often carries with it considerably more than the unadorned right to use the patent rights in production. Frequently the patent disclosure must be supplemented with "know-how" to enable advantageous use to be made of it. Trademarks may also be included as part of the license package. Among our reporting companies, 44 (or 71 percent) stated that they customarily licensed some combination of patents, know-how, and trademarks—the most usual combination being patents and know-how. Only 12 companies (or 19 percent) said they regularly licensed patents only, not in combination with either know-how or trademarks. Four companies said they had no customary policy but made decisions on a case-by-case basis. Only two companies failed to reply to this question.

In foreign licensing it is apparently more usual to include know-how in the package than to license only the patent, as is sometimes done with U.S. patents. However, the practice varies less within a company, as between U.S. and foreign patents, than it does from company to company. Particular companies tend to follow the same general policy with regard both to U.S. and foreign licenses, if they have an established general policy—as many of those in our reporting group do.

The use of package licenses raises an interesting tax question. Proceeds from exclusive patent licenses can normally be reported as capital gains. It is less well established that proceeds from exclusive licenses to know-how can safely be so reported. In an earlier article[5] we have examined this question at length, and cited precedents indicating that certain kinds of know-how are industrial property and may be licensed exclusively for capital gains. Other forms of know-how, particularly if capable of transmission only through personal services, are less palpably depreciable property within the meaning of the Internal Revenue Code. At the time this article appeared, it was plain that not all corporations were fully aware that know-how-licensing proceeds might, on occasion, be taken as capital gains.

---

[5] "'Know-How' Licensing and Capital Gains," *IDEA*, Vol. 4, No. 2 (Summer 1960), pp. 93-108.

For further information on practice within this area, we inquired of our group of reporting corporations whether, when package licenses including know-how were employed, it was usual to allocate some portion of the proceeds to the know-how. Eight corporations said they did allocate the proceeds; 36 did not. Seventeen corporations had no experience with exclusive licensing arrangements of the sort where a division of the licensing proceeds might be important. Among the eight companies who did allocate the licensing proceeds, only four had claimed capital gains treatment for the proceeds attributable to the know-how. In no case had these claims been denied by the Internal Revenue Service, although two corporations reported that audits for certain taxable years in which sales of know-how were reported as capital gains had not been completed. This evidence, while too slender to be conclusive, does in a general way confirm our earlier impression that not all corporations are getting maximum tax advantage on their licensing proceeds.

Apart from tax saving, there may be other advantages in allocating the proceeds from package licensing. License fees may be set more accurately if account is kept of precisely what is being licensed; moreover, costs of furnishing the know-how may be compared directly with the income earned. A number of companies that do not now do so might well consider separating the proceeds from know-how licensing, if only for purposes of better internal management control.

As already noted, licensing practice within a single corporation tends to be fairly uniform with regard to both U.S. and foreign patents, with perhaps a slightly greater tendency to grant exclusive licenses in the case of foreign patents. Further support for this general conclusion is available from the answers to a question reading, "Is your licensing practice and/or tax reporting substantially different in foreign than in domestic licensing?" Thirty-five companies (69 percent of those reporting) stated it was not; they followed the same policies with respect to both kinds of patents. Ten companies said their practice was different. Seventeen companies either had no experience with foreign licensing, and hence could make no valid comparison, or for some other reason failed to respond to this question.

In the case of the ten companies reporting differences between domestic and foreign licensing practice, the reasons for the difference, which each was asked to give, are significant. One company included know-how in its foreign licenses but not in those granted to other U.S. corporations. Four companies had assigned all their foreign patents to foreign-based subsidiaries; these subsidiary companies, located in low or non-income-tax countries, received the license income without any liability for U.S. tax being incurred. The device of foreign-based companies is a well known technique of tax postponement that is useful whenever there are foreign earnings that it is desired to shelter from U. S. tax. Patent proceeds, as well as earnings of any other type originating abroad, are amenable to this treatment. Four companies reported they granted exclusive licenses abroad, although none in this country. One company reported that, although its licensing practice was different as between foreign and U. S. patents, the tax treatment of the proceeds was the same.

These results, while not conclusive, indicate no sharp difference in licensing practice within corporations, and no special tax considerations that would make for such a difference. There are, of course, differences in tax-base definition and in rates between the U.S. corporation income tax and foreign income taxes. These differences are too numerous to be examined in detail here. Use of foreign-based companies to shelter foreign earnings from the U. S. tax is a general technique, available to any U. S. company that has earnings abroad from any source, whether sales, manufacturing, or licensing. It is not a specific technique for treating earnings from patent licenses. It is recognized, of course, that valid business reasons, rather than merely tax incentives, often underlie the use of such foreign companies.

When patents are licensed out to others for their use, the proceeds may be taken in a lump sum, in installments, or as running royalties (perhaps with special limits). We have already seen in the case of patents licensed for intra-reporting-company use, that the running royalty is by all odds the most usual form of payment. The same might be expected for patents licensed to others.

That this is indeed the case is apparent from the data in Table 10, which classify the type of royalty (or other payment) received by type of patent and by number of corporations reporting income in this form. It is plain from this table that the running royalty is more common than any other form of payment.

It would appear that there is no significant variation among the different types of patents and that either straight or slightly modified running royalties are the rule.

The overwhelming proportion of these royalty receipts are reported as ordinary income for tax purposes. Only a small fraction, probably not more than 1 or 2 percent and certainly not more than 5 percent at the most, is reported as capital gain—in spite of the fact that running royalties, if from exclusive licenses, are eligible for capital-gains treatment.

That the general arrangements for payment on licenses received and on licenses granted are broadly similar is further confirmed by responses to another question included (largely to test consistency) in our questionnaire. Twenty-seven corporations reported that, in case of U. S. patents, the type of royalty paid and received was generally similar between licenses received and licenses granted. Nine companies reported differences. Concerning foreign patents, the results were consistent, namely 23 companies reporting similarity and six reporting difference.

TABLE 10
FORM IN WHICH PAYMENT IS RECEIVED FOR
PATENTS LICENSED TO OTHERS

Type of Payment	Number of Companies Reporting		
	Chemical Patents	Mechanical Patents	Electrical Patents
Lump-sum payment	9	8	4
Flat rate royalty	25	36	19
Flat rate royalty with minimum	14	16	10
Sliding scale royalty	12	11	7
Totals	60	71	40

No customary practice, varies with each license 2
Take all types of royalty and non-royalty payments 4
Cross-licenses only—no royalties paid or received 4

INCOME FROM PATENT LICENSING

To get some picture of the income earned from patent licensing activities, questions were included that called both for the number of patents licensed to others and for the income resulting therefrom. In all, 42 corporations with more than 19,000 patents (both U. S. and foreign) responded to these questions. From these responses it is possible to contruct some rough estimates for all corporations. The aggregate income from licensing reported by the 42 corporations was $38.5 million or just over $2,000 per license. There was considerable dispersion about this average in the earnings per license reported by the different companies.

The basic data on number of patents licensed to others and earnings from these licenses are given in Table 11.

The income figures in Table 11 represent company averages for the five-year period ending with 1959. The number of patents licensed is for the single year 1959. This may differ considerably from the average number of patents licensed during the five-year period and thus may help to explain some of the variation in average income per patent licensed from company to company.

TABLE 11
NUMBER OF PATENTS LICENSED TO OTHERS
AND INCOME FROM LICENSING

Company Number	Number of Patents Licensed	Income from Licensing ($ thousands)	Company Number	Number of Patents Licensed	Income from Licensing ($ thousands)
3	112	10	34	56	21
4	193	800	36	11	17
7	45	500	37	123	50
8	131	42	38	140	4000
9	21	85	40	38	5
10	799	1660	42	57	390
11	15	110	43	11	60
12	442	125	44	11	1
13	575	2500	46	245	495
14	46	50	47	18	200
16	326	2400	48	30	24
18	25	2	51	1688	2250
19	1056	0	52	218	2
20	1000	1752	54	511	350
22	102	378	55	6	12
23	133	500	56	9080	9500
25	248	183	57	58	1502
26	219	227	58	432	50
27	15	15	60	740	4200
28	15	2	62	8	12
29	140	4000			
33	58	42	TOTALS	19,197	38,524

This variation in income per license is readily apparent from Table 11 and may be summarized as follows:

    2,450 patents produced only $909,000 or less than $400 per patent licensed;

  14,141 patents produced $20.2 million or nearly $1500 per patent licensed;

   1,149 patents produced $7.1 million or nearly $6200 per patent licensed;

     261 patents produced $6.2 million or nearly $24,000 per patent licensed.

By company, license income ranged from zero to $9.5 million.

Additional parts of the variation in income per patent licensed are attributable to variation in the intrinsic worth of different patents, and to inclusion of more than the simple right to use the patent in many of the license arrangements. It is likely that many of the more valuable licensing contracts included in the summary above conveyed substantial amounts of know-how in addition to the patent rights. Our available information does not permit a breakdown between simple licenses and package licenses so far as the income information is concerned.

On the basis of our reported information, it is possible to extrapolate rough estimates of the aggregate amount of patent license income earned by U. S. corporations. The calculation is as follows. In our reporting group we have 8,713 U. S. patents licensed, out of a total of 44,495 owned by those corporations that reported on their licensing arrangements, a licensing rate of just over 18 percent.[6] For foreign patents the rate of licensing is considerably higher, namely 13,420 out of 32,207 patents owned, or nearly 42 percent. This higher rate probably is attributable, in part at least, to the fact that foreign patenting is more selective; only those inventions which have a likely valuable use are protected by patents abroad.

If the corporations in our reporting group that did not report licensing activity had roughly the same rates of licensing as the corporations who did report, we can raise our figures of number of patents licensed to a full group coverage of about 9,200 U. S. and 18,200 foreign—or a total of 27,400 for all the corporations in our universe.

It will be recalled that our reporting group included about 16 percent of all patents owned by U. S. corporations; on this basis the estimated total number of patents licensed by corporations may be projected at in excess of 171,000. It is probable that this figure is too high, since it is doubtful whether the licensing rate runs as high for small corporations owning only a few patents as for larger corporations owning numerous patents. Discounting for this lower rate of licensing among unsurveyed corporations, it is still probable that the number of patents licensed by all U. S. corporations falls somewhere in the range of 100,000-150,000.

We also know from our reporting group that licenses to 19,197 patents produced $38.5 million of income on the average during the five-year period 1955-1959. Applying the same method used to extrapolate number of patents licensed, if the ratio of income per licensed patent in our group is applied to the estimated total of all patents licensed by corporations, the projected average annual income of all U.S. corporations from licensing works out to $200-$300 million. It is probable that the lower figure is somewhat nearer the truth since the patents owned by smaller corporations may be somewhat less valuable on the average than those owned by larger corporations. It should be emphasized again that the $200-$300

---

[6]This compares with a licensing rate of 23 percent obtained in the patent utilization studies of the Institute. These studies cover all corporations on a sample basis and the reporting period is different.

million is a five-year average, not an estimate for any single year.
A current estimate would in all probability be considerably higher.

The extrapolations made above should, of course, be treated
with every caution. They may well be fairly wide of the mark. Nevertheless, for what they are worth, they do indicate that patent
licensing is a large and important activity and that substantial sums
are paid each year for the industrial property represented by patents
and related know-how.

RESEARCH AND DEVELOPMENT COSTS

Since 1954, it has been well established that corporations may
charge off as business expenses for tax purposes all annual costs of
research and development work. This does not mean that outlay on
permanent facilities for research and development work, *i.e.,* costs
of constructing laboratories, may be expensed; but it does mean
that all costs for specialized equipment, having no use apart from
R&D, may be treated as expense. Prior to 1954, the law was somewhat unsettled on this point. The statute was silent as to whether
R&D was an "ordinary and necessary" business expense, and also as
to what costs could properly be allocated to R&D. In practice, expensing of R&D was generally allowed, but individual corporations
were often required to capitalize certain R&D expenses. Enactment
of Section 174 in the 1954 Revenue Code removed most of this
prior uncertainty by establishing the principle of expensing as the
general rule.

For information on actual tax practice concerning R&D costs,
a number of questions were asked of our reporting corporations.
The answers contained few surprises and tended to confirm our
earlier impression that there are few problems in this area of income-
tax law. To the question, "Do you expense all possible R&D outlays?" 58 corporations reported that they did; none reported they
did not, although four companies failed to answer this question.

Section 174 of the Code contains an option allowing R&D
costs to be capitalized over a period of not less than five years in
lieu of expensing. This option is of value chiefly to corporations
(and other taxpayers) having no net income; such taxpayers would
waste the tax value of the deduction if they expensed R&D currently. By capitalizing they can carry the deduction forward to subsequent years instead of wasting it. None of our reporting corporations
was sufficiently unprofitable so that they stood to benefit from this
option.

Few significant problems in qualifying research and development costs as tax deductions were found. In our reporting sample, 51 corporations stated they had encountered no problems with the Internal Revenue Service in expensing R&D. Five corporations had met with some difficulty, but in four of these cases the problems had arisen prior to 1954, when the law was still not specific. Only one company had had a tax problem with R&D since 1954. The nature of this problem was not stated. Six companies did not reply to this question.

Although no tax question is directly involved, some interest may attach to company practice with regard to patentable subject matter discovered in the course of research. Among our questions about R&D, we asked whether it was usual to patent all results not in the prior art that was uncovered in the course of R&D. Twenty companies said this was their practice; two additional companies patented practically all eligible new discoveries from R&D. Thirty-five companies did not patent all eligible results from R&D, for reasons that are quite interesting. These are summarized below:

Reason for Not Patenting	Number of Companies Reporting
Probable market for invention too small	24
Cost of patenting greater than probable benefit	4
Unwilling to make disclosures necessary to secure patent	4
Doubted that patent would be enforceable against infringers	3
Total	35

On the question whether any unpatented inventions had been purchased from outsiders, 54 companies said they had never done so. Six companies had made such purchases. In five of the cases the purchase costs had been deducted as a current business expense. In only one case had the purchase been capitalized.

The primary reason for purchasing an unpatented invention, as far as the buyer is concerned, is probably the desire to maintain the invention as a trade secret. There is a minor tax advantage in that in practical terms expensing is probably easier than if the invention were patented. In that case strict adherence to tax rules would require capitalization. For the seller, disposing of an unpatented invention avoids the formalities involved in securing a patent. In any case, it was plain from our replies that transactions in unpatented inventions were rare occurrences.

EXPERIENCE WITH TAX ADMINISTRATION

In our survey of corporation tax experience, with special

reference to patents and related industrial property, relatively few sources of friction in relations with the Internal Revenue Service were found. On the whole, it would appear that the law is well understood and quite uniformly administered. This is apparent both from our questionnaire replies and from letter replies received in lieu of completed questionnaires.

For example, one letter from a large manufacturer of transportation equipment states:

> We do not have any substantial activities with regard to our patents which create tax problems. By and large our patents are developed and used by us; we have had no problems in qualifying research costs as current income deductions.

In reply to a specific question about whether problems had been encountered in dealing with the Internal Revenue Service on matters relating to patents and know-how, 52 companies said they had encountered no problems. Only four had experienced problems. One of these problems related to the World War II excess-profits tax; two involved the question of offsetting expenses incurred in U.S. against income earned abroad from foreign licenses. One problem related to proper valuation in the case of a purchased patent. In none of these cases was sufficient detail either asked for or received to determine the merits of these particular controversies. It is significant, nevertheless, that their number was so small.

In reply to another question as to whether any unusual tax problems had been met in licensing foreign patents, 45 companies replied they had had none. Nine companies had had no experience with foreign licensing, and three failed to report. Only five companies mentioned having any problems. Two of these problems concerned the allocation of royalty receipts among different foreign countries; two others concerned accounting relationships between the parent company and foreign subsidiaries; one involved a technical problem under the British income tax. It is evident from this summary that, although foreign licensing can give rise to some unusual tax situations, the number of problems arising in this area is actually small—less than we had anticipated would be the case.

While our study of tax experience has been oriented primarily toward problems and practice under U. S. federal income taxes, we sought also, when questioning corporations, to determine whether any significant difficulties had arisen under state income or property taxes—particularly in regard to patent valuation. In our reporting group, 55 companies stated they had experienced no difficulty with state or local taxation so far as their patents were concerned; in all cases where a reply on this point was given, the company's book value for patent assets had been accepted—even where these assets were carried at a purely nominal valuation. Seven companies gave no reply to this question; none reported specific tax difficulties with state or local governments.

In our earlier interviews with corporation executives, the question of inadequate depreciation of purchased patents had arisen on several occasions. Generally, the Internal Revenue Service takes the position that the useful life of a patent, for purposes of the annual depreciation rate, is its remaining legal life. Enough is known from Institute surveys of patent utilization and from other sources to make clear that the economically useful life of patents is often shorter than the legal life. Subsequent inventions and other changes in technology or in market demands often make patents obsolete before they expire. In such cases the patent, while not actually abandoned, ceases to have any value.

The only recourse a company has, when faced with this problem, is to use one of the methods for accelerating depreciation that are permitted under the 1954 Revenue Code. These methods allow a greater write-off during the earlier years of ownership of depreciable property than does the straight line method. The methods, however, are generally available only for assets acquired in 1954 or thereafter.

In our reporting group we found (unexpectedly) that practically all corporations used the straight line method of depreciating patent assets. Forty-five companies so reported. Only one reported use of the sum of the years' digits method—one of the permitted techniques of acceleration. Eight companies reported they had no accounting for patent depreciation—presumably because purchased patents were negligible. It will be recalled from a summary given earlier in this paper that the overwhelming majority of patents owned by corporations are either developed in their own laboratories or by their own employees rather than purchased. Eight companies failed to reply to the question concerning depreciation; but a number of letter replies contained statements on this point. For example, a manufacturer of electrical equipment wrote:

> We do use the straight line method of depreciating patents, and our research and development outlays are expensed without any problems with the income-tax people.

CONCLUSION

It may be useful, by way of summary, to contrast the tax experience of large corporations having numerous patents with that of individual inventors, as revealed in one of our earlier surveys.

Both corporations and inventors have the privilege of selling patents outright, usually by giving an exclusive license, and of receiving capital-gains treatment on the proceeds. Inventors do this fairly frequently and would do it even more if they could more easily arrange exclusive licensing contracts that were advantageous to themselves. Many inventors, however, are poorly informed about income-tax law; large corporations almost never are.

Many individual inventors have great difficulty in obtaining tax deductions for their research and development costs. This is because many inventions are a product of spare time or hobby activities; no income can be shown against which R&D is a proper offset. Large corporations, on the other hand, have no difficulty in taking R&D costs as current tax deductions; they do this as a general practice.

The overwhelming proportion of patents owned by corporations are either developed in their own laboratories or assigned by their employees. Purchases of patent rights from individual inventors are a minor, but still important, source of new technology. Sales of patents by corporations are rare except when some part of a business is sold, or a patent accidentally developed that has no foreseeable application in the company's regular business.

Licensing of patents by corporations is extensive, both in this country and abroad. The bulk of these licenses is nonexclusive and produces ordinary royalty income; some, however, are exclusive and yield capital gains which corporations claim without undue difficulty. Royalty income is estimated to have totalled $200-$300 million annually for all U. S. corporations on the average during the period 1955-59.

Research is undertaken by most corporations in hope of improving their products and bettering their competitive position. As one letter from an oil company puts it:

> Differences between the small after-tax-return from royalties, on the one hand, and the after-tax profit from manufacturing and sales operations, on the other hand, are especially great in technical fields where we are already established, and the manufacturing and sales costs are incremental. For this reason our basic research, development, and patent activities are most frequently directed to new products and processes in support of manufacturing and sales efforts rather than to create inventions for royalty income.

The great majority of corporate-owned patents, having been created by internal R&D which can be expensed, have a negligible cost basis. Often they are carried at a purely nominal valuation in corporate balance sheets. Purchased patents are depreciable property that must be written off over the remaining legal life, which often extends beyond the useful life. Few corporations use other than straight line depreciation for patent assets, although inadequate depreciation of purchased patents is sometimes a problem.

In general, corporate tax experience with intellectual industrial property is more uniform than is the experience of individual inventors with their patent assets.

Tax considerations play a role in corporate decisions about the manner in which they license patents they own, but rarely are these considerations a major or determining factor; they are merely a datum in the complex leading to the final decision.

In presenting the results of this survey of corporate tax experience, we believe the information is the first of its kind devoted to average or representative experience as opposed to individual cases that establish the marginal application of income-tax law. Our results are naturally tentative and limited; they await confirmation or disproof from other studies.

APPENDIX TABLE A
PATENTS OWNED BY REPORTING CORPORATIONS,
PERCENTAGE DISTRIBUTION BY CLASS

Company No.	U.S. Patents			Foreign Patents		
	Chemical	Mechanical	Electrical	Chemical	Mechanical	Electrical
1	0	90	10	0	95	5
2	98	2	0	98	2	0
3	0	95	5	0	95	5
4	5	10	85	2	6	92
5	5	85	10	—	—	—
6	1	77	22	0	97	3
7	70	30	0	70	30	0
8	2	98	0	—	—	—
9	0	20	80	0	20	80
10	85	10	5	85	10	5
11	0	100	0	0	100	0
12	30	65	5	40	58	2
13	—	—	—	—	—	—
14	0	99	1	0	99	1
15	—	—	—	—	—	—
16	80	—	—	70	—	—
17	20	60	20	—	—	—
18	0	100	0	0	100	0
19	3	95	2	—	—	—
20	9	11	80	—	—	—
21	10	20	70	10	20	70
22	80	15	5	90	10	0
23	95	5	0	98	2	0
24	90	9	1	95	5	0
25	2	93	5	1	99	0
26	5	62	33	32	38	30

APPENDIX TABLE A *(Continued)*

PATENTS OWNED BY REPORTING CORPORATIONS, PERCENTAGE DISTRIBUTION BY CLASS

Company No.	U.S. Patents			Foreign Patents		
	Chemical	Mechanical	Electrical	Chemical	Mechanical	Electrical
27	1	19	80	0	20	80
28	91	7	2	—	—	—
29	54	44	2	65	35	0
30	60	40	0	60	40	0
31	1	99	0	—	—	—
32	61	23	6	100	0	0
33	1	97	2	0	100	0
34	0	100	0	0	100	0
35	0	95	5	0	97	3
36	0	98	2	—	—	—
37	0	5	95	0	5	95
38	54	44	2	65	35	0
39	90	10	0	90	10	0
40	99	1	0	100	0	0
41	5	95	0	—	—	—
42	90	5	5	94	3	3
43	0	50	50	0	50	50
44	92	6	2	—	—	—
45	—	—	—	—	—	—
46	20	80	0	20	80	0
47	98	2	0	—	—	—
48	5	90	5	—	—	—
49	0	90	10	0	90	10
50	0	80	20	0	0	100
51	0	100	0	—	—	—
52	1	99	0	0	100	0
53	25	75	0	25	75	0
54	0	99	1	0	99	1
55	7	5	88	7	5	88
56	35	60	5	35	60	5
57	11	89	0	29	71	0
58	0	100	0	—	—	—
59	75	15	10	95	3	2
60	67	33	0	40	60	0
61	0	10	90	0	10	90
62	10	80	10	10	80	10

Trademarks and Taxes

DENNIS I. MEYER AND JOHN F. CREED

"What's in a name?" was the now famous query posed by Juliet. If presented to the corporate community today, the reply of many would undoubtedly be, "Millions in sales"—evidencing the economic status trademarks and trade names have attained in the market places of the world.

This article will examine the federal tax aspects of trademarks and trade names, with emphasis on the tax treatment of costs incurred in acquiring and maintaining such property rights, and the tax consequences to both the seller and the buyer upon disposition.

SECTION 177

The costs of acquiring a trademark, including attorney's fees, design and registration costs, generally constitute capital expenditures.[1] Subsequent amounts expended to enjoin an infringer or defend the validity of a trademark, as well as payments to a competitor in settlement of a controversy relating to the right to use a trademark, are also ordinarily treated as nondeductible capital items.[2] Furthermore, the unlimited useful life of a trademark or trade name precludes an allowance for amortization or depreciation of such capital expenditures.[3]

The foregoing tax implications are applicable to years governed by the 1954 Code, as well as years subject to prior revenue laws. Section 177, added to the 1954 Code in 1956, does, however, afford the taxpayer an opportunity to treat many trademark or trade name expenditures of a capital nature as deferred expenses.

A trademark or trade name expenditure is defined by Section 177 as any expenditure which is directly connected with the acquisi-

---

EDITOR'S NOTE: This paper was published in *IDEA*, Vol. 8, No. 3 (Fall 1964). The authors have added a postscript to the paper.

[1]See, *e.g.*, Duesenberg, Inc. of Delaware, 31 B.T.A. 922 (1934), *aff'd*, 34 F.2d 921 (7th Cir. 1936); Stuart Co., 9 CCH Tax Ct. Mem. 585 (1950), *aff'd per curiam*, 195 F.2d 176 (9th Cir. 1952); Rev. Rul. 55-158, 1955-1 Cum. Bull. 319.

[2]See, *e.g.*, Clark Thread Co. v. Commissioner, 100 F.2d 257 (3d Cir. 1938); Danskin, Inc., 40 T.C. 318 (1963), *aff'd*, 331 F.2d 360 (2d Cir. 1964).

[3]Treas. Reg. § 1.167(a)-3; Seattle Brewing & Malting Co., 6 T. C. 856 (1946), *aff'd*, 167 F.2d 216 (9th Cir. 1948); Norwich Pharmacal Co., 30 B.T.A. 326 (1934).

tion, protection, expansion, registration or defense of a trademark or a trade name; is chargeable to the capital account and does not constitute the consideration paid for a trademark or trade name.[4] If an expenditure comes within the purview of the above definition and an election is made, the taxpayer is allowed to amortize the expenditure rateably over a period of not less than 60 months, beginning with the first month in the taxable year in which the expenditure was paid or incurred, depending upon the method of accounting employed by the taxpayer in computing taxable income.[5]

The Senate Finance Committee, in reporting on the addition of this ameliorating provision to the 1954 Code, stated that:

> Under present law, expenditures paid or incurred by small companies in connection with trademarks and trade names, such as legal fees, are not deductible but must be capitalized. Moreover, such expenditures ordinarily are not amortizable over any period of time since the useful life of most trademarks and trade names is indefinite and not ascertainable. However, certain larger corporations are in a position to hire their own legal staffs to handle such matters. Because of difficulties of identification, these large corporations deduct, in some instances, compensation paid to their legal staffs for performing the same functions. Smaller companies, however, cannot afford to maintain their own legal staffs but must acquire outside counsel to perform their legal work.[6]

The stated purpose of Section 177, therefore, is to provide equality of tax treatment among similarly situated taxpayers, which is always a laudatory objective in a self-assessment system.

Acquisition

The regulations provide that:

> Generally, Section 177 will apply to expenditures such as legal fees and other costs in connection with the acquisition of a certificate of registration of a trademark from the United States or other government, artists' fees and similar expenses connected with the design of a distinctive mark for a product or service . . . .[7]

In addition, other costs incurred in the development of a trademark or trade name will clearly qualify for Section 177 treatment. Recently, for example, a company with a substantial proliferation of products used a computer in its search for new and unique trade names. Obviously, many companies will be able to deduct such initial acquisition costs because they can be easily merged into other operating expenses. When such services are performed by a public relations firm or an advertising agency, the expenditures

---

[4]Int. Rev. Code of 1954, § 177(b).
[5]Int. Rev. Code of 1954, § 177(a).
[6]S. Rep. No. 1941, 84th Cong., 2d Sess. 8 (1956).
[7]Treas. Reg. § 1.177-1(b)(1).

involved may be more readily identified, necessitating resort to Section 177.

The construction of an effective trademark, generally, entails substantial expenditures for advertising and other promotional activities. Television, although costly, provides in many cases an attractive medium for the projection of the product personality embodied in the trademark. Newspapers, magazines and billboards are other media commonly utilized to incite a demand for the advertiser's products. Although such advertising expenditures may produce a benefit extending beyond the taxable year, the courts have held that such advertising costs are deductible in the year paid or incurred, depending upon the taxpayer's accounting method, because the indefinite period over which such benefits extend does not permit deferral of the expenses to future years.[8] Where, however, the expenditure is extraordinary and obviously designed to reap benefits over several years in the future, a portion of the cost has been allocated to the capital account.[9]

Many marks, not susceptible to exclusive appropriation as a technical trademark or trade name originally, have obtained protection under the trademark laws by acquiring a secondary meaning, principally through extensive advertising. Although such expenses may have been incurred with the dual objective of selling the product bearing the mark and establishing a public awareness of the personal identity of the manufacturer or seller, the expenditures are generally considered an item of current expense. In the event the mark does acquire a secondary meaning, the costs of effecting a registration would be capital in nature and could be amortized under Section 177.[10]

Expansion, Protection, or Purchase

Although the regulations are devoid of any examples of expansion expenditures, it is assumed that amounts paid or incurred in the extension of a trademark to a different line of products or to a new geographic area would come within the ambit of a trademark expenditure. The recent trend to mergers and diversification acquisitions will undoubtedly spawn many such expenditures.

Because such an expansion of an existing trademark is, in essence, an acquisition of a trademark for the new area or line, the

---

[8]Treas. Reg. § 1.162-15(c)(1); See, *e.g.,* Sheldon & Co. v. Commissioner, 214 F.2d 655 (6th Cir. 1954); Three-in-One Oil Co. v. United States, 35 F.2d 987 (Ct. Cl. 1929).

[9]Best Lock Corp., 29 T.C. 389 (1957), superseded, 31 T.C. 1217 (1959), *appeal dismissed* 7th Cir; X-Pando Corp., 7 T.C. 48 (1946).

[10]Int. Rev. Code of 1954, § 177(b); Treas. Reg. § 1.177-1(b).

expenditures involved will parallel closely the amounts initially expended in acquiring the trademark. For example, the expansion into a new state or region may entail registration under state law with accompanying legal fees, or the adaptation of the mark to a new product line may require additional design costs.

Such an expansion may also involve advertising and other promotional costs. As discussed above, unless the advertising expenditure incident to the expansion is extraordinary in nature, no part will be allocated to the trademark as a capital expenditure; but the cost can be deducted currently as an ordinary and necessary business expense.

Certain payments, however, which are concededly connected with the expansion of a trademark may not qualify for Section 177 treatment. This is so because the statute, as noted earlier, specifically excludes from the definition of a trademark expenditure, "the consideration paid for a trademark, trade name or business."[11] The regulations, in implementation of this exclusion, state:

> Amounts paid in connection with the acquisition of an existing trademark or trade name may not be amortized under Section 177 even though such amounts may be paid to protect or expand a previously owned trademark or trade name through purchase of a competitive trademark. Similarly, the provisions of Section 177 and this section are not applicable to expenditures paid or incurred for an agreement to discontinue the use of a trademark or trade name (if the effect of the agreement is the purchase of a trademark or trade name) nor to expenditures paid or incurred in acquiring franchises or rights to the use of a trademark or trade name.[12]

Accordingly, a taxpayer which has attached its trademark to a new product, only to find that a similar mark is being used by the manufacturer of a related product, may encounter difficulty in amortizing under Section 177 any payment or payments made pursuant to an arrangement whereby the other user agrees to desist from further use of the conflicting mark.[13]

Payments of a similar nature to protect an existing trademark may, likewise, not qualify for the benefits of Section 177. Illustrative of such a protection expenditure which may not satisfy the statutory definition of a trademark expenditure was the payment in *Aluminum Products Co.*[14] In that case, a controversy arose between the taxpayer and a competitor regarding the use of the word "Lifetime" in connection with aluminum ware. An agreement was reached as a

---

[11]Int. Rev. Code of 1954, § 177(b)(3).

[12]Treas. Reg. § 1.177-1(b)(1).

[13]See, J. I. Case Co. v. United States, 32 F. Supp. 754 (Ct. Cl. 1940), a case involving a payment of $700,000 to a competitor to discontinue use of a confusing and conflicting trademark.

[14]24 B.T.A. 420 (1931).

consequence of negotiations between the parties under the terms of which the competitor agreed to discontinue immediately the use of the word "Lifetime" in consideration of the payment of $15,000 by the taxpayer. The Tax Court, with little pause, held that "by obtaining the promise to discontinue the use of the word 'Lifetime' the [taxpayer] acquired the right to the unmolested use of the trademark."[15]

Suffice to say, when the payment is substantial and founded upon the earnings of the purported infringer, the taxpayer is clearly vulnerable to a contention that "the agreement has the effect of a purchase." This was the situation in *Clark Thread Co. v. Commissioner.*[16] The taxpayer there initiated equity proceedings to enjoin perpetually the use of a competing mark. Prior to trial, the taxpayer, in accordance with a settlement agreement, paid the user of the competing mark $500,000, which was based on the earnings of the recipient over a ten-year period.

A taxpayer in a situation similar to *Clark Thread* may attempt to extricate himself from the Commissioner's deficiency determination by asserting that he did not actually acquire anything but that the payment was to protect and preserve the value of his existing mark. Judicial acceptance of such an argument is doubtful where, as in *Clark Thread,* the facts establish that the prime purpose of the payment was to acquire rights in a competitive mark and, thereby, eliminate competition.

A taxpayer may, however, be able to prevail against an allegation by the Commissioner that the agreement was tantamount to a purchase if he is able to demonstrate factually that the payment in compromise was computed by reference to the cost of infringement litigation; and, therefore, the payment should be treated as legal expenses for purposes of Section 177.

A gratuitous statement by the court in *The Sanymetal Products Co., Inc. v. Carey*[17] adds substantial support to such a position. The taxpayer, there, paid $15,000 to the alleged infringer which consented to a perpetual injunction and stipulated in the Patent Office that the trademark was cancelled. In characterizing the payment, the court stated:

> In order to be fair, it must be conceded that [taxpayer] paid the $15,000 not as a purchase of a substantial right but only as a compromise. If the case had come to trial, [taxpayer] undoubtedly would have prevailed, but the legal expenses would have been greater than

---

[15]*Id.* at 424.
[16]100 F.2d 257 (3d Cir. 1938); *accord,* J. I. Case Co. v. United States. note 13 *supra.*
[17]57-2 U.S. Tax Cas. ¶9865 (N.D. Ohio 1957).

they were. Therefore, in order to properly analyze this matter, we should treat the $15,000 payment as if it were an additional legal expense connected with the lawsuit rather than as a payment of the kind involved in the *Clark* case.[18]

An admission by the user of the competitive mark in the settlement agreement that he possessed no rights in the trademark would further buttress such a contention and not require the court to draw an inference from the facts as in *Sanymetal*. Such an admission may not be readily obtainable, however, because of its effect on the tax incidence of the payment to the recipient. This is discussed in detail in a subsequent section dealing with the sale of a trademark.

The above-quoted regulations appear responsive to the statute and seem to reflect the intendment of the legislature in enacting Section 177 inasmuch as the payment generally involved in such settlement, for example, a *Clark Thread* type situation, cannot be easily hidden by even a large corporate taxpayer.

Attorney's Fees

Amounts expended for legal assistance in connection with the acquisition of a trademark or trade name will ordinarily be treated as capital expenditures and added to the payer's basis in the trademark or trade name. Similarly, when the primary purpose of a suit is to perfect or defend title in the trademark, the legal fees arising therefrom are not deductible but must be capitalized.[19]

Exemplar of the latter situation is *Food Fair of Virginia*[20] where the taxpayer brought suit to enjoin another from using its trade name, alleging that it had established the trade name in Virginia and held the exclusive right to use it there. The suit was dismissed in accordance with an agreement between the parties in which the competitor agreed to discontinue the use of the trade name in Virginia.

Although the taxpayer argued that the expenditure was primarily for the purpose of protecting and maintaining its income by estopping a competitor from employing a trade name which was resulting in a loss of income, the Tax Court thought it obvious that:

. . . basically and primarily the suit was one to defend or perfect the petitioners' title to, or property right in, the trade name. . . .[21]

Continuing, the court stated:

That the suit was disposed of by a settlement agreement between th

---

[18]*Ibid.*

[19]See, *e.g.*, Safety Tube Corp. v. Commissioner, 168 F.2d 787 (6th Cir 1948); William A. Falls, 7 T.C. 66 (1946).

[20]14 T.C. 1089 (1950).

[21]*Id.* at 1093.

parties in no way detracts from the fact that the primary purpose of the litigation was to obtain a judicial determination as to ownership and that the attorney's fee was incurred in defense of the ownership of and property rights in the name. Since in substance the attorney's fee was a cost of defending or perfecting title to property, it was not an allowable deduction.[22]

Where, as in the *Food Fair* case, the purpose of the suit is to determine which party has the right to use a particular trademark or trade name, the legal costs of the unsuccessful party are, of course, deductible.[23] Such litigation, however, often extends beyond one taxable year. Legal fees paid or incurred in those years prior to the final resolution of the issue are capital in nature and, accordingly, should be entitled to Section 177 treatment.[24] In the event that the outcome is unfavorable to the taxpayer, the fees paid or incurred in the year the final decision is rendered, as well as the unamortized portion of fees paid in prior years, would be deductible in full.[25]

An interesting question arises when title is involved, but its defense or protection is only incidental to the primary object of taxpayer's retention of counsel or, where the validity or title of the taxpayer in the trademark is not challenged, by the alleged infringer.

The Tax Court recently had occasion to consider a case, *Danskin, Inc.*,[26] involving the latter situation. In *Danskin,* the sole question was whether the trademark of a competitor was so similar to the taxpayer's mark that, when used in association with the respective goods, it would likely cause confusion and deceive purchasers.

In determining that the legal expenses were not ordinary and necessary business expenses, the Commissioner did not contend that the expenditures were incurred to defend or perfect title, but rather, that the payment removed impending future loss of income by eliminating a competitor's mark. Thus, the Commissioner concluded that the benefit derived from the competitor's agreement to desist from using the competing trademark would be enjoyed over an extended period of business operations and, accordingly, should be capitalized.

The Commissioner's theory of the case is surprising in light of

---

[22]*Ibid.*

[23]Int. Rev. Code of 1954, § 162(a); See, Kornhauser v. United States, 276 U.S. 145 (1928); Ruoff v. Commissioner, 277 F.2d 222 (3d Cir. 1960).

[24]See, Treas. Reg. § 1.177-1(b)(1).

[25]Int. Rev. Code of 1954, § 1016(a)(16) requires an adjustment to basis for amounts allowed as deductions for expenditures treated as deferred expenses under § 177.

[26]40 T.C. 318 (1963).

Revenue Ruling 60-261.[27] There, the Commissioner was requested to rule on the question of whether legal expenditures, incurred to establish the fact that a municipal ordinance prohibiting the operation of a certain business within municipal limits did not apply to taxpayer's business, may be deducted as an ordinary and necessary business expense.

In holding that the legal expenses were deductible under Section 162, the ruling stated that:

> . . . where the expenditure is for a business purpose, such as the use and enjoyment or operation of a business asset already owned, the amount thereof would be deductible as a business expense.
>
> The question as to whether an expenditure is classifiable as a business expense or as a capital expenditure is one of fact. Generally, amounts paid for assets having a more or less permanent value are capital expenditures; however, capital expenditures are not limited to the purchase of physical assets. Thus, legal expenses incurred in defending or perfecting title to property also are capital expenditures.
>
> The instant taxpayer's expenditure clearly was proximate to its business and more specifically related to an asset thereof, the use and enjoyment of which had been hindered by the municipality. The expense of removing the hindrance is directly connected with the use of the business asset, rather than its acquisition, replacement or improvement, or for perfecting or recovering title thereto.[28]

In conclusion, the ruling declared that an earlier ruling[29] was modified

> . . . to remove the implication that legal expenses incurred to protect the continued use of property for income producing purposes are capital expenditures.[30]

In contrast to Revenue Ruling 60-261, the Tax Court in *Danskin* found the Commissioner's deficiency determination correct and held the payments were capital outlays because the "disbursements were made for the purpose of securing a right to increased income for an indefinite period."[31] Needless to point out, there is a definite cleavage between the reasoning in *Danskin* and the rationale of Revenue Ruling 60-261.

In affirming the holding of the Tax Court,[32] the Second Circuit stated:

> The financial gain which petitioner realized from these legal proceedings, through the enhancement of the value of its registered trademark, is an increment of a sort which will endure for many years to come; and therefore the pattern of the revenue laws of accurately matching

---

[27]1960-2 Cum. Bull. 42; *accord,* A.R.R. 98, 2 Cum. Bull. 105 (1920).
[28]1960-2 Cum. Bull. at 43.
[29]I.T. 1382, I-2 Cum. Bull. 146 (1922).
[30]1960-2 Cum. Bull. at 43.
[31]40 T.C. at 324.
[32]331 F.2d 360 (2d Cir. 1964).

income and expenses within annual accounting periods requires that these legal expenses be classified as capital outlays. Financing the removal of a threat to a trademark posed by an infringing mark resembles the cost of perfecting or preserving title to property, a cost well established as a capital expenditure, . . . much more than it resembles a current business expense.[33]

It is interesting to note that the appellate court, in its resolution of the question, retreated to the settled concept that the "cost of perfecting or preserving title to property" is a capital expenditure, although its applicability in *Danskin* is, at best, doubtful.[34]

The determination of the Third Circuit in *Urguhart* v. *Commissioner*,[35] which was not cited by either the Tax Court or the Second Circuit in *Danskin*, appears to be in conflict with the *Danskin* decision. In *Urguhart*, the taxpayers were engaged in the business of inventing, experimenting, developing and exploiting new patents and processes primarily as a licensor. Litigation expenses were incurred in a patent suit which the taxpayers deducted currently as business expenses. The Tax Court held the expenses were capital in nature. On appeal, however, the Third Circuit reversed the decision stating:

> . . . we are the more clear that the litigation expenses were incurred to prevent (and recover) damage to their business, that is, to protect, conserve and maintain their business profits. There is no conflict apparent to us, as urged by the Commissioner, with the principle that expenditures which yield benefits over a period of years are not current operating expenses. . . .[36]

The Tax Court's subsequent citation of the *Urguhart* case appears to indicate that it believes that the Third Circuit's result was predicated upon the fact that the taxpayers were engaged in the business of exploiting and licensing patents.[37] From the language of the court, it is apparent that it would have arrived at the same result in *Danskin*.

Taxpayers who have, through advertising and other promotional activities, created a demand for goods bearing their trademark,

---

[33]*Id.* at 361.

[34]In the course of its opinion the court also noted that:

the language and legislative history of a related section of the Code [§ 177] support the determination that the funds taxpayer expended in conducting its infringement litigation should be classified as a capital expenditure. 331 F.2d at 361.

Neither §177 nor the legislative history thereunder mentions litigation expenses connected with an infringement action. The only references to such costs are in the regulations. Treas. Regs. §1.177-1(b)(1) and §1.177-1(b)(3) Example (3). Thus, there is no clear indication by Congress that it intended to cover the expenses of trademark infringement litigation under §177.

[35]215 F.2d 17 (3d Cir. 1954).

[36]*Id.* at 20.

[37]See, George F. Arata, 31 T.C. 346 (1958).

must be continually vigilant for other marks designed to confuse or deceive the public and, thereby, dilute the drawing power of their mark. In such policing activities, the owner of a valuable trademark may find it necessary to institute a number of suits each year to enjoin the infringement of his mark.

After ownership has been acquired, it would seem aberrational to treat as an additional cost of the trademark, attorney's fees expended to enable the owner to use the mark free from infringement. In light of the decision in *Danskin,* prudence, however, would seem to dictate handling such costs as capital expenditures and electing Section 177 treatment.

Method of Amortization

A trademark or trade name expenditure may be amortized over a period of not less than 60 continuous months.[38] The amortization period commences with the first month of the taxable year in which the expenditure is paid or incurred regardless of the period selected by the taxpayer.[39]

By way of illustration, assume that X corporation, an accrual basis calendar year taxpayer, incurs design costs of $3,000 in April of 1965 in developing a unique trademark for a new product and elects under Section 177 to amortize the charge over 60 months. January, 1965, the first month of the taxable year in which the expense was incurred, will begin the amortization period, and X corporation will be able to deduct $600 or 12/60 of $3,000 in 1965.

The election under Section 177 is irrevocable.[40] As a consequence, the period designated by an electing taxpayer for a particular trademark expenditure cannot subsequently be changed.[41] Section 177, however, permits a taxpayer to elect for each separate trademark expenditure.[42] It follows that, where several trademark expenditures are paid or incurred in a taxable year, a taxpayer, by separate elections, may choose a different amortization period for each trademark expenditure.[43] An obvious further corollary is that the taxpayer need not elect Section 177 treatment for certain separate trademark expenditures arising during the taxable year.[44]

Although the regulations are not definitive on the point, it appears, especially in the absence of any indication to the contrary,

---

[38]Int. Rev. Code of 1954. § 177(a); Treas. Reg. § 1.177-1(a)(1).
[39]Treas. Reg. § 1.177-1(a)(2).
[40]Treas. Reg. § 1.177-1(a)(1).
[41]Treas. Reg. § 1.177-1(a)(2).
[42]Treas. Reg. § 1.177-1(a)(3).
[43]*Ibid.*
[44]*Ibid.*

that separate elections can be made for separate trademark expenditures relating to the same trademark. Thus, under the above example, if X corporation incurred legal fees of $6,000 in December, 1965, defending the same trademark in an infringement action, a separate election could be made and a different amortization period selected for such expenditure.

A separate election may not be permissible, however, where various expenditures are an integral part of a specific transaction. If X corporation, in the above example, incurred attorney's fees, filing fees, and other related costs in the Federal registration of the trademark in June, 1965, X corporation may not be allowed to segregate these costs and elect separately for each. It is manifest, however, that the aggregate costs would constitute a separate trademark expenditure.

Time of Election

Section 177 (c) requires that the election be made within the time prescribed by law, including extensions thereof, for filing the return for the taxable year in which the expenditure is paid or incurred.

The Commissioner will undoubtedly refuse to grant an extension of time within which to make an election for Section 177 treatment. Although Section 6081 provides that, "the secretary or his delegate may grant a reasonable extension of time for filing any return, declaration, statement or other document required . . ." by the 1954 Code, the Commissioner has taken the position that he does not have authority under Section 6081 to grant an extension of time for filing an election in such a situation because the election is an option provided by the Code and does not constitute a return, declaration, statement or document required by the Internal Revenue Code or the regulations thereunder.[45]

In *Danskin*, the Tax Court became the first forum to consider the right of a taxpayer to elect under Section 177 as the taxpayer in that case alleged alternatively that, if the court should find that the litigation expenses were capital expenditures, then it could elect to amortize such expenditures under the provisions of Section 177. A holding by the court that the trademark litigation costs were "capital outlays" necessitated a consideration of this alternative argument.

After reviewing the language of the statute, the court, in holding against the taxpayer, observed that "it is apparent that Congress

---

[45]Cf. Rev. Rul. 60-183, 1960-1 Cum. Bull. 625; William Pestcoe, 40 T.C. 95 (1963).

has set forth the specific terms by which an election to amortize trademark expenditures may be made."[46]

The Second Circuit, on appeal, affirmed this holding stating that "having failed to make an election during the period fixed by statute [taxpayer] cannot now decide to take advantage of the provisions of Section 177."[47]

Thus, administratively, an extension of time to make the election is not available; and judicially, the clear and unambiguous language of the statute leaves no leeway insofar as the time for filing the election is concerned. An incorrect determination by the taxpayer that an expenditure is a deductible expense would, therefore, foreclose amortization under Section 177 unless a protective election is filed with the return. It is implicit from both courts' discussion of this point in *Danskin* that the taxpayer would have prevailed under its alternative argument had such a protective election been filed.

Although there is no printed form for purposes of making the election, the regulations describe in precise terms the statement which the taxpayer must attach to his return "signifying his election under Section 177."[48] The statement must contain the name and address of the taxpayer, and the taxable year involved; an identification of the character and amount of each expenditure and the amortization period. Moreover, the taxpayer must agree to make an accounting segregation on his books and records of the expenditure sufficient to permit easy identification on audit.

ABANDONMENT

In the event of an abandonment, an ordinary loss deduction is permitted under Section 165 (a) to the extent of the taxpayer's adjusted basis in the trademark at the time of the abandonment. The taxpayer, however, is only entitled to such an abandonment loss deduction in the taxable year in which the loss is actually sustained.[49]

While abandonment, of necessity, must involve nonuse, evidence of nonuse alone is not sufficient.[50] An actual intent to abandon, coupled with an act or acts of abandonment, must be present.[51]

---

[46]40 T.C. at 324.

[47]331 F.2d at 362.

[48]Treas. Reg. § 1.177-1(c)(1).

[49]Treas. Reg. § 1.165-2(a); Hazeltine Corp. v. United States. 170 F.Supp. 615 (Ct. Cl. 1959).

[50]I. Lewis Corp., 22 CCH Tax Ct. Mem. 35 (1963) (Trademarks); *In re* Rae's Estate. 147 F.2d 204 (3d Cir. 1945) (Patents).

[51]Hazeltine Corp. v. United States. note 49 *supra;* W. B. Davis & Son, Inc.. 5 T.C. 1195 (1945).

As is evident, the existence of these subjective and objective elements in a particular tax year can only be determined by an analysis of the surrounding facts and circumstances.

The act of abandonment may be the cessation of business either involuntarily because of the enactment of legislation prohibiting the future conduct of such a business[52] or voluntarily, due to continual losses from operations.[53]

An apparent identifiable event will be disregarded, however, if the facts reveal the absence of an intent to abandon. Thus, litigation culminating in a finding that a trademark is invalid is not an event upon which an abandonment loss can be predicted if the taxpayer seeks reversal of the decision by resort to an appellate court.[54] Continuing to carry the trademark as an asset on the balance sheet[55] or an action to recover royalties under a license agreement[56] are other acts inconsistent with an intent to abandon.

Since the ownership of a trademark is not based upon registration, but rather the right to use the trademark exists independently from the registration statutes, passiveness by the taxpayer resulting in expiration of such registration is not an overt act constituting an abandonment.[57] Similarly, the expiration of a patent which is associated with a trademark is not an identifiable event unless the trademark has been the generic designation of the patented article, in which event the generic designation passes into the public domain upon the expiration of the patent.[58]

Since mere nonuse does not establish an abandonment and consistently showing the trademark as an asset on the balance sheet discredits an intent to abandon, the question arises whether the taxpayer can delay the deduction to a more advantageous tax year by the device of retaining as an asset a trademark which otherwise has been permanently discarded from use.[59] The Internal Revenue Service has attempted to avert such a postponement of the deduction by providing in the regulations that:

> The taxable year in which the loss is actually sustained is not necessarily the taxable year in which the overt act of abandonment, or loss of title to the property, occurs.[60]

---

[52]Sheffield Dentifrice Co., 13 B.T.A. 877 (1928).
[53]Rev. Rul. 57-503, 1957-2 Cum. Bull. 139.
[54]George Gordon Urguhart, 20 T.C. 944 (1953), rev'd on other grounds, 215 F.2d 17 (3d Cir. 1954).
[55]In re Rae's Estate, note 50 supra; W. B. Davis & Son, Inc., 5 T.C. 1195 (1945).
[56]George Gordon Urguhart, note 54 supra.
[57]Hazeltine Corp. v. United States, note 49 supra.
[58]Ibid.
[59]Compare, Rev. Rul. 54-581, 1954-2 Cum. Bull. 112.
[60]Treas. Reg. § 1.165-2(a).

In contrast to the above-quoted regulations, the cases to date disclose a definite judicial willingness, in fixing the year of abandonment, to rely upon the unilateral acts of the taxpayer. This is best illustrated by the leading case of *Hazeltine Corp.* v. *United States.*[61] In that case, the taxpayer discontinued the use of certain trademarks in 1930 because the patented inventions with which they were associated became obsolete. The taxpayer, however, continued to carry the trademarks on its books as an asset. In 1943, the Board of Directors considered the approaching expiration of the federal registration and adopted a resolution not to re-register the trademarks, but instead to abandon them.

The registration expired in August, 1943, but no affirmative action was taken by the taxpayer until December, 1944, when a second resolution was adopted to abandon the trademarks accompanied by a resolution instructing the officers to make the appropriate adjustments on the books. Subsequently, in March, 1945, the abandonment of the trademarks "as of and from December 1, 1944" was announced by the taxpayer in a trade publication.

In concluding that the abandonment occurred in 1944, the court cited the action of the Board abandoning the trademarks implemented by a directive to the officers to write them off on the corporate books.[62] Also persuasive was the public notice of abandonment in the trade journal.

The case development in the abandonment area has placed the Commissioner in a somewhat precarious position. When the taxpayer, in reply to the Commissioner's contention that the abandonment occurred in a year other than the year in which the deduction was claimed, introduces evidence, self-serving as it may be, the Commissioner is confronted with the task of going forward with affirmative evidence substantiating his contention. Needless to say, this is a difficult burden to discharge because, generally, there is a paucity of evidence if the taxpayer has done nothing other than terminate the use of the mark in an earlier year.

This is not to suggest, however, that the taxpayer can delay indefinitely the deduction, although it is obvious that the taxpayer does have control, to a limited extent, in determining the year of

---

[61]170 F.Supp. 615 (Ct. Cl. 1959).

[62]See I. Lewis Corp., 22 CCH Tax Ct. Mem. 35 (1963), where the taxpayer's board of directors adopted a resolution discontinuing and abandoning a substantial number of trademarks some of which were acquired by the taxpayer from its predecessor in 1910. Although many of the marks had not been used for many years the Tax Court found an abandonment in 1954, pointing out that mere nonuse is not equivalent to abandonment, especially where the asset may be used again in the future.

deduction. It would be imprudent to delay claiming the allowance for an unduly long period because of the risk of loss of an otherwise clearly deductible item. Moreover, the taxpayer would be well advised, when it decides to formalize the abandonment of the mark, to document carefully the intent to abandon and perform promptly those acts necessary to consummate this intention so that, should an audit occur and litigation ensue, the record will be replete with evidence supporting the deduction in that year.

DAMAGES

Receipt of Damages

In addition to enjoining any further trademark or trade name infringement, a taxpayer may receive damages either in accordance with a judgment or in settlement of the suit.

The tax treatment of such damages is generally determined by reference to the nature of the item the damages are intended to replace.[63] It is settled law that, since business profits are taxable, damages recovered for lost profits likewise constitute ordinary income.[64] On the other hand, where the damages are a substitute for assets, whether tangible or intangible, destroyed by the acts of the defendant, they represent a return of capital and are only taxable to the extent that they exceed the taxpayer's adjusted basis for such property.[65] With respect to punitive damages, the Supreme Court in *Glenshaw Glass Co. v. Commissioner*[66] removed all doubt that they constitute ordinary income to the recipient.

In a trademark infringement suit where damages are also sought, the *gravamen* of the action is generally that the goodwill of the taxpayer has been injured inasmuch as the trademark is the embodiment of such goodwill. Merely alleging an injury to goodwill in the complaint is, however, not alone sufficient to verify that the amount subsequently received represents a recovery for the alleged injury.[67] The allegation must be supported by substantial evidence from which damage to goodwill can reasonably be inferred.[68]

[63]Farmers' & Merchants' Bank v. Commissioner, 59 F.2d 912 (6th Cir. 1932); Raytheon Production Corp. v. Commissioner, 144 F.2d 110 (1st Cir. 1944).

[64]See, e.g., Mathey v. Commissioner, 177 F.2d 259 (1st Cir. 1949), cert. denied, 339 U.S. 943 (1950); Phoenix Coal Co. v. Commissioner, 231 F.2d 420 (2d Cir. 1956).

[65]Highland Farms Corp., 42 B.T.A. 1314 (1940); Strother v. Commissioner, 55 F.2d 626 (4th Cir. 1932), aff'd on other grounds, 287 U.S. 308 (1932).

[66]348 U.S. 426 (1955).

[67]Phoenix Coal Co. v. Commissioner, note 64 supra; Ralph Freeman, 33 T.C. 323 (1959).

[68]Raytheon Production Corp. v. Commissioner, note 63 supra.

If the facts do substantiate that the basic claim was to recover damages for the destruction of goodwill, evidence of profits to establish the value of the taxpayer's goodwill will not change the nature of the recovery.[69]

The fact that the suit is concluded by a compromise between the parties will also not alter the tax consequences of the recovery if the action was brought to compensate for an injury to goodwill.[70] In the latter situation, substantial documentation is important where a lump sum settlement is comprised of several different components such as punitive damages, damages for injury to goodwill and damages for lost profits. If there is no conclusive proof that the recovery was, in part, intended to compensate for injury to goodwill, the entire amount will be allocated to lost profits.[71] Where, however, the pleadings, issues presented and the release agreement disclose that a portion of the payment was a substitute for destroyed goodwill, the settlement will be allocated accordingly.[72]

As mentioned earlier, in the event the taxpayer's goodwill has no basis, the entire amount allocated to it will be taxable.[73] This raises the intriguing question of whether the payment constitutes ordinary income or is entitled to capital gains treatment.

In an early case, *Farmers' & Merchants' Bank* v. *Commissioner,*[74] the Sixth Circuit held that an amount received in settlement of an action for injury to the goodwill of a bank was not taxable at all because it was impossible to determine the extent of the injury to the business; and, therefore, there was "no logical basis upon which [taxpayer] could be charged with gain."[75]

Thereafter, the First Circuit in *Raytheon Production Corp.* v. *Commissioner,*[76] involving the settlement of a suit where the entire goodwill of the taxpayer was destroyed, held that "compensation for the loss of goodwill in excess of its cost is gross income."[77] The *Farmers' and Merchants' Bank* case was distinguished on the basis that:

---

[69] *Ibid.*

[70] *Ibid.*

[71] Chalmers Cullins, 24 T.C. 322 (1955); Ralph Freeman, note 67 *supra.*

[72] Telefilm, Inc., 21 T.C. 688 (1954); Durkee v. Commissioner, 162 F.2d 184 (6th Cir. 1947).

[73] Raytheon Production Corp. v. Commissioner, note 63 *supra;* Telefilm, Inc., note 72 *supra.*

[74] 59 F.2d 912 (6th Cir. 1932).

[75] *Id.* at 914.

[76] 144 F.2d 110 (1st Cir. 1944).

[77] *Id.* at 114.

. . . the bank's business was not destroyed but only injured and since it continued in business, it would have been difficult to require the taxpayer to prove what part of the basis of its goodwill should be attributed to the recovery.[78]

Raytheon was followed by another Sixth Circuit case, *Durkee* v. *Commissioner.*[79] In that case, the court, without discussion, appeared to withdraw from its earlier position in *Farmers' and Merchants' Bank* and, after finding an injury to goodwill, remanded the case to the Tax Court to determine the taxpayer's basis in the goodwill. On remand,[80] the Tax Court considered the opinion of the appellate court as deciding that the recovery was for goodwill and, therefore, capital gains to the extent that it exceeded the taxpayer's basis. The court then found that the taxpayer's basis in the goodwill was zero and concluded that the entire recovery was a capital gain. This result was affirmed *per curiam* on appeal.[81]

Subsequent cases, all in the Tax Court, have also held that a recovery to the extent that it exceeds the taxpayer's basis constitutes capital gain.[82] Unfortunately, they assume that the overage is entitled to capital gains treatment and, therefore, do not provide any reasoning in support of the conclusion.

Since taxpayers will have a zero basis for goodwill unless the goodwill has been acquired by purchase, they can apparently expect capital gains consequences for a recovery for injury to the goodwill, at least, in the Tax Court and Sixth Circuit.

Payment of Damages

The payment of damages pursuant to a judgment or in settlement of a suit is generally deductible either as an ordinary and necessary business expense under Section 162[83] or as a loss under Section 165.[84] The payment may, however, be capital in nature in

---

[78]*Ibid.*

[79]162 F.2d 184 (6th Cir. 1947).

[80]8 CCH Tax Ct. Mem. 701 (1949).

[81]181 F.2d 189 (6th Cir. 1950).

[82]Anna Levens, 10 CCH Tax Ct. Mem. 1083 (1951); *accord,* Levy Collins, 18 CCH Tax Ct. Mem. 756 (1959), a case in which the Tax Court held the excess to be entitled to capital gains treatment even though it found that there was no sale or exchange of a capital asset, involuntary conversion or other disposition of property. But see, Jack Rosenzweig, 1 T.C. 24 (1942), where the Tax Court found that the amount recovered for infringement of a copyright was ordinary income because the taxpayer "did not sell or exchange anything."

[83]See, *e.g.,* Helvering v. Hampton, 79 F.2d 358 (9th Cir. 1935); Camloc Fastner Co., Inc., 10 T.C. 1024 (1948).

[84]See, *e.g.,* International Shoe Co., 38 B.T.A. 81 (1938); North American Investment Co., 24 B.T.A. 419 (1931).

the event the taxpayer by such expenditure acquires a capital asset[85] or clears title to property.[86]

Caution should be exercised where part of the payment is to compensate the recipient for lost profits and the remainder for the acquisition of assets because the entire amount may be a nondeductible capital expenditure if the taxpayer is unable to establish a basis for allocating the payment between the two items.[87]

Fines and penalties are ordinarily not deductible since the allowance of such payments would frustrate public policy.[88] The rationale is that to allow a deduction would lessen substantially the impact of the fine or penalty and, correspondingly, the effectiveness of the law violated. It should be noted, however, that where the law makes a distinction between innocent violators and those who have violated the law deliberately or intentionally, a deduction has been allowed for unintentional violations because it would not frustrate the effectiveness of the statute in question.[89] It would appear that treble damages paid under Section 35 of the Lanham Trademark Act would be deductible since they are compensatory and not punitive in nature.[90]

SALE

Seller

The criteria which must be satisfied to obtain capital gains treatment on the transfer of a trademark are (1) a "sale or exchange," (2) of a "capital asset" (3) held for more than six months by the transferor.[91]

---

[85]Cf. Battle Creek Food Co., 8 CCH Tax Ct. Mem. 207 (1949), aff'd, 181 F.2d 537 (6th Cir. 1950); Automatic Shifters, Inc., 19 CCH Tax Ct. Mem. 694 (1960); but see, Industrial Aggregate Co. v. United States. 284 F.2d 639 (8th Cir. 1960).

[86]Blackwell Oil & Gas Co. v. Commissioner, 60 F.2d 257 (10th Cir. 1932); Wilma M. Imm. 11 CCH Tax Ct. Mem. 258 (1952).

[87]Battle Creek Food Co., note 88 supra; Blackwell Oil & Gas Co. v. Commissioner, note 86 supra.

[88]Cf. Commissioner v. Longhorn Portland Cement Co.. 148 F.2d 276 (5th Cir. 1945), (involving a compromise settlement for violation of a state antitrust law which was held not deductible because the payment was in full satisfaction of the statutory penalties) and William F. Davis, 17 T.C. 549 (1951), (where a payment to a corporation under the Securities Exchange Act of 1934 was found to be in the nature of a penalty and nondeductible, with Lilly v. Commissioner, 343 U.S. 90 (1952), (a case in which the Supreme Court held that payments by the taxpayers who were engaged in the retail optical business, to physicians of one-third of the sales price of glasses sold to their patients were deductible because the public feeling against such practices was not so sharply defined to require disallowance of the payments).

[89]Jerry Rossman Corp. v. Commissioner. 175 F.2d 711 (2d Cir. 1949); I.T. 3530, 1942-1 Cum. Bull. 43.

[90]But see, Tank Truck Rentals, Inc. v. Commissioner. 356 U.S. 30 (1958).

[91]Int. Rev. Code of 1954, § 1222(3).

A capital asset is defined as property held by the taxpayer whether or not connected with his trade or business, but does not include property held primarily for sale in the ordinary course of business or property which is depreciable under Section 167.[92]

The status of a trademark as property for tax purposes is conceded by the Commissioner.[93] As discussed earlier, trademark expenditures may be amortized under Section 177, but trademarks are generally not depreciable under Section 167.[94] Thus, a trademark comes within the definition of a capital asset unless the facts of the particular situation indicate that it was held primarily for sale.[95]

In view of the fact that the property right in a trademark does not come into existence upon registration of the mark but exists prior to registration when the trademark has been reduced to actual use, the holding period for a trademark may, correspondingly, commence prior to registration for purposes of determining whether the mark has been held for the period prescribed by the statute.[96]

An assignment of a trademark clearly satisfies the sale or exchange requirement.[97] Likewise, the grant of an exclusive and perpetual license is ordinarily sufficient to transfer the property interest of the licensor in the mark.[98]

The fact that the transferee in consideration of the transfer agrees to make a periodic payment measured by a fixed percentage of the selling price of products bearing the trademark or based on the units manufactured or sold, or any other similar method predicated upon production, sale or use, will in no way affect the capital gains aspects of the transaction.[99] The relevant inquiry is whether

[92]Int. Rev. Code of 1954. § 1221.

[93]Rev. Rul. 55-694, 1955-2 Cum. Bull. 299.

[94]Treas. Reg. § 1.167(a)-3. In view of the fact that a trademark is not subject to the allowance for depreciation provided in section 167. it would appear that section 1239, which denies capital gains treatment to a sale or exchange of depreciable property between an individual and a corporation more than 80 percent in value of the outstanding stock of which is owned by such individual. his spouse. and his minor children and grandchildren, would not be applicable to a sale or exchange of a trademark.

[95]See, e.g., Harold T. Avery, 47 B.T.A. 538 (1942); cf. Joseph A. Fields. 14 T.C. 1202 (1950), aff'd, 189 F.2d 950 (2d Cir. 1951). But see Pike v. United States, 101 F.Supp. 100 (D. Conn. 1951).

[96]See, e.g., Edward C. Myers, 6 T.C. 258 (1946); Carl G. Dreymann, 11 T.C. 153 (1948).

[97]United States v. Adamson, 161 F.2d 942 (9th Cir. 1947).

[98]Seattle Brewing and Malting Co., 6 T.C. 856 (1946); see also Thomas D. Armour, 22 T.C. 181 (1954); National Bread Wrapping Machine Co., 30 T.C. 550 (1958).

[99]Rose Marie Reid, 26 T.C. 622 (1956); Commissioner v. Hopkinson, 126 F.2d 406 (2d Cir. 1942); Rev. Rul. 58-353, 1958-2 Cum. Bull. 408.

the transferor has retained, under the agreement, any rights of substantial provable value.[100]

For example, the retention of bare legal title under an exclusive and perpetual license agreement will not in any manner restrict the transferee's enjoyment of the trademark. Accordingly, such title retention is inconsequential in determining whether the requisite property transfer has occurred.[101]

The courts, in their consideration of agreements in which the transferor has retained certain rights, have made a clear distinction between the situation where the transferor retains the right to terminate the agreement upon the occurrence of an event which is entirely within its control and an arrangement where there is a termination of the agreement and a recapture of the property rights only upon the happening of a subsequent event which is entirely beyond the control of the transferor, such as expropriation, nationalization or bankruptcy. The preponderance of legal precedent is precisely expressed by the court in *First National Bank of Princeton v. United States:*

> The government is in no better position when it argues that the various cancellation clauses of the 1940 agreement show the party's intent to create a license and not a sale. It is uniformly held that such provisions may be construed as calling for the reversion of title upon the occurrence of a condition subsequent and as such do not impair passage of title at the time the contract is executed.[102]

In addition to the common protective provisions normally embodied in a transfer agreement, a trademark agreement usually includes a provision under which the transferor retains some degree of control over the quality of the product bearing the mark to avoid a possible constructive abandonment.[103]

---

[100]Seattle Brewing and Malting Co., note 98 *supra.*

[101]*Ibid.*

[102]136 F.Supp. 818, 822 (D. N.J. 1955) (vendee could cancel after six months and had no right of resale; vendor could cancel if Federal Trade Commission issued a cease and desist order or if vendor defaulted). Accord, Allen v. Werner, 190 F.2d 840 (5th Cir. 1951) (vendor could cancel if vendee violated the agreement "in any way"); Commissioner v. Celanese Corp., 140 F.2d 339 (D.C. Cir. 1944) (vendor could cancel if vendee went into bankruptcy or receivership); Kronner v. United States, 110 F.Supp. 730 (Ct. Cl. 1953) (vendor could cancel if vendee failed to "use its best efforts in marketing the invention"); Pike v. United States, 101 F.Supp. 100 (D. Conn. 1951); Lamar v. Granger, 99 F.Supp. 17 (W.D. Pa. 1951) (vendor could cancel if royalties were not paid or in event of vendee's bankruptcy); Carroll Pressure Roller Corp., 28 T.C. 1288 (1957) (vendor retained right to exploit patent in foreign markets, limited vendee's right to sublicense, prohibited vendee from assigning and could terminate upon vendee's breach); Vincent A. Marco, 25 T. C. 544 (1955); Edward C. Myers, 6 T.C. 258 (1946).

[103]Cf. Dairy Queen of Oklahoma v. Commissioner, 250 F.2d 503 (10th Cir. 1957). It would seem advisable to establish definite quality standards so that

In *Seattle Brewing & Malting Co.,*[104] two trade brands, "Rainier" and "Tacoma" were transferred in an exclusive license agreement. The agreement provided that the beverages manufactured by the transferee and marketed under the trade names covered by the license would at all times equal "the quality of similar products then manufactured and marketed under the said trade names and brands by the transferor. . . ."[105] Moreover, the agreement provided that a

failure should be considered an event of default and [the transferor] might cancel the agreement . . . in which event all the rights of [the transferee] should terminate. . . .[106]

Thus, the transferor could definitely control the quality of the product produced by the transferee and marked with the trade names. A failure by the transferee to comply with such quality standards would result in a default and bestow upon the transferor the right to terminate the agreement. It is significant to note that the standard of quality required of the transferee was based on the quality of products then manufactured by the transferor.

The Tax Court held the transfer to be a sale stating:

Other provisions in the contract giving [the transferor] the right to require [the transferee] to do certain things, such as keeping the quality of the malt and beer manufactured equal to [the transferor's] quality, were but conditions subsequent. . . .[107]

A restriction against sublicensing without the consent of the transferor will also not preclude capital gains treatment.[108] It should be noted, however, that, in certain situations, the quantitative effect of retaining numerous rights may constitute the retention of a substantial right.[109]

Insofar as exclusivity is concerned, the agreement may be exclusive even though limited to a designated geographical territory.[110] The restriction on use of a trademark to a specific class of items will also not defeat the exclusive nature of the transfer.[111] In *United*

the transferor does not, in essence, have the unrestricted right to cancel the agreement for breach because the transferee has not maintained acceptable standards of quality.

[104]6 T.C. 856 (1946).
[105]*Id.* at 859.
[106]*Id.* at 861.
[107]*Id.* at 870.
[108]See, *e.g.,* Watson v. United States, 222 F.2d 689 (10th Cir. 1955); Parke, Davis & Co., 31 B.T.A. 427 (1934).
[109]See Arthur M. Young, 29 T.C., 850 (1958) *aff'd* 269 F.2d 89 (2nd Cir. 1959); Joe Schmitt, Jr., 30 T.C. 322 (1958), *aff'd,* 271 F.2d 301 (9th Cir. 1959); Treas. Reg. § 1.1235-2(b)(4).
[110]Seattle Brewing and Malting Co., note 98 *supra; accord,* Vincent A. Marco, 25 T.C. 544 (1955).
[111]See First National Bank of Princeton v. United States, 136 F.Supp 818 (D. N.J. 1955); United States v. Carruthers, 219 F.2d 21 (9th Cir. 1955).

States v. *Carruthers,*[112] involving a patent license for use only in the tuna industry, the Commissioner attempted to distinguish a transfer restricted to a geographical area from a transfer limited to a particular industry. The Ninth Circuit was unreceptive to the contention and held that there was not basis for such a distinction.

The reservation of certain rights in the transfer agreement has obvious merit as a control mechanism, especially when the purchase price is in the form of royalty payments. Fortunately, it is a satisfactory device from a tax standpoint, resulting in capital gains to the seller. It would not appear advisable, however, to include unnecessary restrictions which have not received administrative or judicial approval.

Buyer

As discussed earlier, the consideration paid for a trademark or trade name may not be amortized under Section 177.[113] Although Section 167 contains no specific prohibition against a depreciation deduction for a trademark, the regulations under Section 167 provide that:

> If an intangible asset is known from experience or other factors to be of use in the business or in the production of income for only a limited period, the length of which can be estimated with reasonable accuracy, such an intangible asset may be the subject of a depreciation allowance. Examples are patents and copyrights. An intangible asset, the useful life of which is not limited, is not subject to the allowance for depreciation. No allowance will be permitted merely because, in the unsupported opinion of the taxpayer, the intangible asset has a limited useful life.[114]

Obviously, it would be impossible in the ordinary situation for the taxpayer to demonstrate to the satisfaction of the Commissioner that the trademark had a limited useful life. This arbitrary position of the Commissioner has been vigorously challenged by at least one commentator.[115] An amendment to the Code was the proposed solution of another group.[116] The Commissioner, however, stands

---

[112]*Ibid.*

[113]Int. Rev. Code of 1954, § 177 (b)(3).

[114]Treas. Reg. § 1.167(a)-3.

[115]Kragen & Pearce, "Tax Problems in the Trademark and Trade Name Field," 44 *Calif. L. Rev.* 511 (1956).

[116]On February 28, 1961, the American Institute of Certified Public Accountants, Committee on Federal Taxation, submitted the following recommendation to Congress:

> The cost of purchasing trademarks should be amortizable over their useful life as determined by the taxpayer, or over a stated period to be fixed by statute, whichever is longer, to the extent such items are not otherwise treated under other sections of the Code.

unwavering in his attitude toward the depreciation of intangibles with an unlimited useful life such as trademarks.

The rationale of the Tax Court in *Associated Patentees, Inc.,*[117] does, however, provide some basis for a contention that a current deduction should be allowed when the purchase price is a royalty payment measured by the production or sale of products bearing the trademark. In *Associated Patentees,* the taxpayer acquired patents of varying lives. The sellers, controlling shareholders of the taxpayer, were to receive as consideration, 80 percent of taxpayer's annual income from any license agreements it negotiated. The deduction claim by the taxpayer for such royalty payments was disallowed by the Commissioner who contended that only a proportionate part of the royalty payment should be allowed currently with the balance prorated over the remaining lives of the patents. In each succeeding year, the taxpayer would be allowed a deduction for a proportionate part of the payment in that year plus the amount allocated to such year from prior payments.

This method of computation was summarily discarded by the court which recognized that it would result in "inadequate" deductions in the early years and "excessive" allowances in the concluding years of the agreement. Well aware of the unique nature of the issue presented, the court held that the royalty payments made each year were deductible in full and provided a reasonable allowance.

Similarly, in the *Seattle Brewing* case, the court, in discussing certain royalty payments made by the taxpayer, noted that

> It makes no difference whether we designate [the agreement] a license or as tantamount to a perpetual assignment of a right of use with a condition subsequent which might defeat it upon the happening of the event specified. In any event, there was a definite term measured from year to year when the expenditure applicable to income for the period could be definitely determined and exhausted.[118]

Such a royalty arrangement may, however, not be desirable from the buyer's standpoint because it would involve a perpetual commitment to make annual royalty payments or lose the right to use the mark.

If the agreement specifies a fixed period for such payments, the reasoning of *Associated Patentees* would, apparently, not be applicable; and the purchaser would be required to capitalize the annual amounts paid. An attempt to obtain a benefit by the use of a declining royalty schedule would also, undoubtedly, meet with stiff

---

[117]4 T.C. 979 (1945).
[118]6 T.C. at 867.

opposition from the Commissioner since the purchaser could, by agreement, establish an "excessive" allowance in the early years.

A possible arrangement of effecting the sale acceptable to both parties is suggested by the *Seattle Brewing* case. There, the rights were granted in consideration of a royalty payment with an option in the transferee to terminate all royalties after a specified period by the payment of a lump sum. Such a preconceived arrangement would enable the purchaser to deduct a substantial portion of the consideration with only the lump sum payment being a nondeductible item.

From the buyer's standpoint, a more advantageous approach would be an ordinary license agreement with an option to purchase because it would apparently insure deductibility of the royalty payments.[119] Conversely, the latter scheme would be clearly less desirable to the seller since the royalty payments would be taxable at ordinary income rates.

In either of the foregoing situations the Commissioner would closely scrutinize the transaction to determine whether the parties, by such an arrangement, intended to disguise a sale predicted upon a predetermined price.[120] Harmful in this regard would be a provision in the agreement whereby the option price would be reduced by the aggregate royalties paid prior to the exercise of the option.[121]

Sale to a Controlled Foreign Corporation (Section 1249)

Section 16 of the Revenue Act of 1962 (H.R. 10650), inserted a new provision, Section 1249, in the Internal Revenue Code of 1954. Under this new provision, gain from the sale or exchange of a "patent, an invention, model or design, a copyright, a secret formula or process, or any other similar property right" by a U.S. person[122] to a controlled foreign corporation attracts a tax at ordinary income rates. Control for purposes of Section 1249 means the ownership by the transferor, directly or indirectly, of more than 50 percent of the total combined voting power of all classes of stock entitled to vote.[123]

The inclusion of the catchall phrase "any other similar prop-

---

[119]See Seattle Brewing and Malting Co., note 98 *supra*.

[120]See Rev. Rul. 55-540, 1955-2 Cum. Bull. 39 which sets forth the guides which will be employed by the Internal Revenue Service to determine whether an agreement for the use of industrial equipment is a lease or a sales contract.

[121]See East Coast Equipment Co., 21 T.C. 112 (1953), *aff'd*, 222 F.2d 676 (3d Cir. 1955).

[122]Int. Rev. Code of 1954, § 1249(a).

[123]Int. Rev. Code of 1954, § 1249(b).

erty" presents the interpretive problem of whether trademarks and trade names come within the purview of Section 1249. Indispensable in the resolution of this question is a careful analysis of the legislative history to ascertain the Congressional purpose in denying capital gains treatment to the aforedescribed property transfers.

The House version of H. R. 10650 took a somewhat different tack from the bill eventually enacted by including in the gross income of the U.S. person the rentals, royalties or other income derived by the controlled foreign corporation from the license, sublicense, sale, exchange, use, or other exploitation of patents, copyrights and exclusive formulas and processes substantially developed, created or produced in the United States.[124] Thus, the House Bill specifically enumerated the property rights covered and clearly omitted trademarks and trade names.

The House Committee Report, in explanation of this provision, stated that:

> For the income from these patents, copyrights, etc., to be included they must have been substantially developed, created, or produced in the United States, or, alternatively, acquired directly or indirectly from related U. S. persons. Your committee concluded that it was desirable to tax this income to the U.S. shareholders on the grounds that where a patent, copyright, etc. was developed or created in the United States, it is likely that, if it were not for lower taxes abroad, the rights to it would still be held by the domestic company with this company merely licensing its use by the foreign corporation. This, of course, would result in rental or royalty income taxable to the U. S. company.[125]

Extensive hearings were held by the Senate Finance Committee on the bill as passed by the House. Thereafter, Secretary Dillon made a second appearance before the Finance Committee to recommend various changes in the House bill.[126] These suggested revisions included the proposal of Section 1249, which Mr. Dillon explained as follows:

> This change obviates the need under the House bill to determine the amount of income generated by the use of U. S. patents, etc. It eliminates abuse by insuring that patents will be transferred abroad in arm's length transaction producing a full U. S. tax at the time of transfer or on an annual basis.[127]

It is readily apparent from a review of the legislative history

---

[124]Section 13, H.R. 10650 as passed by the House, March 29, 1962.

[125]H.R. Rep. No. 1447, 87th Cong., 2d Sess. 61 (1962).

[126]Hearing on H.R. 10650 Before the Senate Committee on Finance, 87th Cong., 2d Sess., pt. 10 at 4250 (1962).

[127]Hearing on H.R. 10650 Before the Senate Committee on Finance, 87th Cong., 2d Sess., pt. 11 at 4419 (1962).

that Section 1249 and its House counterpart were directed to the transfer of property rights which were "substantially developed, created or produced in the United States." There exists, then, a precise criterion for determining whether a property right is a "similar property right" for purposes of Section 1249.

In applying the foregoing template to trademarks, it becomes immediately evident that there is an essential distinction between trademarks and the property rights set out in Section 1249. Trademarks are essentially territorial in nature. As a consequence, a trademark has little, if any, value in a particular territory until it has been used there. While a patent is also territorial in scope, in that it bestows upon the holder a monopoly right in a specific territory, the rights are obviously dissimilar since a patent derives its value from the underlying invention and could be of substantial worth even though the patented product has never been sold in the particular country or territory.

It is submitted, then, that, since Congress was dealing in Section 1249 with property rights "substantially developed, created or produced in the United States," the rule of *ejusdem genesis* would require the restriction of "any other similar property right" to property rights that are similar in character to a patent, an invention, model or design, a copyright, a secret formula or process which clearly excludes trademarks.[128]

The final regulations under Section 1249 were recently promulgated and consistent with the foregoing view provided that Section 1249 does not include "property such as . . . a trademark or a trade brand."[129]

TRANSFER UNDER SECTION 351

A taxpayer conducting his business as a sole proprietorship may, after a period of sustained growth, decide to change the form of his business organization to that of a corporation. Such a transition, of course, involves a transfer of the assets of the sole proprietorship to the new separate entity. This transaction can, in most cases, be accomplished without the recognition of gain to the transferor under Section 351.

To come within the ambit of Section 351, property must be transferred to a corporation in exchange for stocks or securities of the transferee by a person or persons who, immediately after the exchange, hold at least an 80 percent interest in the transferee cor-

[128]See Lyman v. Commissioner, 83 F.2d 811 (1st Cir. 1936).
[129]Treas. Reg. § 1.1249-1(a).

poration.[130] A trademark often has a fair market value far in excess of its adjusted basis. Thus, the utilization of Section 351 to postpone the recognition of gain is an important consideration to the transferor.

Although the transfer can be accomplished by an assignment, an exclusive and perpetual license agreement is the usual vehicle. The Commission has taken the position, in numerous private ruling letters, that the quantum of rights which must pass to the transferee under such a license arrangement must be the same as those which must be transferred under an exclusive and perpetual license agreement to constitute a sale for tax purposes.

Since the Internal Revenue Service makes no distinction between a sale and a Section 351 transfer, the foregoing discussion of the rights which may be retained by the transferor is equally applicable to a Section 351 exchange. There would appear to be economic justification for the retention of certain rights since the trademark transferred to the new enterprise generally represents part payment for the transferor's equity interest. Thus the transferor's financial remuneration from the transaction will depend upon the ultimate profitability of the transferee and, correspondingly, the transferor will have a continuing interest in how effectively the new company uses the trademark.

Transfer to a Foreign Corporation

It is not an unusual situation when a United States company, selling in foreign markets, finds it impossible to compete on a parity with its local counterparts because of transportation costs, importation duties or the wage differential. To offset these advantages of local manufacture, the United States company often establishes a manufacturing facility within the market area.

When a subsidiary corporation is employed to conduct the manufacturing operations, the United States company is generally faced with the problem of transferring productive assets to the foreign entity.

Such a transfer to a domestic corporation can, as discussed above, be effected tax free under Section 351. Because of the involvement of a foreign corporate transferee, the United States transferor can only invoke Section 351 to avoid the current recognition of gain if a favorable ruling from the Internal Revenue Service under Section 367 has been obtained. Such a ruling represents approval and recognition by the Internal Revenue Service that the proposed

---

[130]Int. Rev. Code of 1954, § 351 (a).

transaction does not have as one of its principal purposes the avoidance of federal income tax. In this regard, the general policy of the Internal Revenue Service is to rule favorably only when the property rights will be used in conjunction with a manufacturing operation.[131]

Because of foreign legal considerations, it may be necessary in certain situations to effect the transmission of the trademark to the foreign company in two parts. Initially, the United States company acquires stock in the foreign entity for cash. Thereafter, the proceeds of the foregoing stock purchase are used by the foreign company to acquire the property rights from the United States transferor. For ruling purposes the Commissioner, consistent with judicial precedent,[132] considers the two transactions related steps of a single transaction, namely, the transfer of property to the foreign corporation in exchange for an equity interest in such enterprise.

Similarly, the Commissioner has approved as a step transaction an arrangement where the transferor, to avoid foreign legal complications, has cancelled its foreign trademark and the new foreign entity has simultaneously made application for the same mark.

Authors' Postscript—

When the preceding article was prepared, there were no decisions dealing with the question of whether a purchaser of a trademark for a consideration based on production, use or sales of the product bearing the mark could deduct such periodic payments as an allowance for depreciation under Section 167.

The authors, citing as authority the *Associated Patentees* case (4 T. C. 975), speculated that such payments were deductible in full in the year made since they constituted a "reasonable allowance" as required by Section 167.

In *Dunn v. United States* (259 F. Supp. 828), a district court in Oklahoma held that payments for the right to use the trade name "Dairy Queen" (based upon the gallonage of mix used) were not deductible as depreciation of a capital asset. The government argued that such payments must be capitalized because they constituted a part of the cost of an asset with an unascertainable useful life. In sustaining the position of the government, the court held that the

---

[131]See H.R. Rep. No. 2508, 87th Cong., 2d Sess. 40 (1962).

[132]See, *e.g.*, Aqualane Shores, Inc. v. Commissioner, 269 F.2d 116 (5th Cir. 1959). See also May Broadcasting Co. v. United States, 200 F.2d 852 (8th Cir. 1953).

indeterminate life of a trademark precludes any depreciation allowance.

It is the view of the authors that the decision in the *Dunn* case is incorrect and could produce harsh and unjustifiable consequences. This position is predicated upon the fact that although a trademark may be of an indefinite duration, the "sale" agreement generally provides for termination and recapture of the trademark in the event that the annual royalty-type consideration is not paid. As a consequence, there is a definite term measured from year to year when the payment clearly based on income for the period can be definitely determined and exhausted. The district court decision in *Dunn* has been appealed, and the disposition of the case at the appellate level should be examined where the purchase price will take the form of a periodic payment geared to production, use or sales of the articles bearing the trademark or trade name.

PART IV

LEGISLATIVE OBJECTIVES AND PROPOSALS

The papers in this section were selected primarily for their expository value respecting legislative proposals and legislative objectives in the industrial property field. The first paper, by Walter J. Derenberg, deals with proposed legislation on unfair competition. In a sense, it might be considered a companion paper to that on the judicial process in unfair competition law by S. Chesterfield Oppenheim, the second one in the previous section. Professor Derenberg refers to S. 3681 of the 89th Congress (the McClellan Bill) and S. 1154 of the 90th Congress, amending Section 43 (a) of the Lanham Trademark Act, as worthy of support. He distinguishes previous attempts to establish a separate statute by means of the Lindsay Bill, explaining that some government critics considered that bill an anticompetitive instrument. Proposals for federal legislation were inaugurated in 1920, and the need was crystallized by the *Erie* v. *Tompkins* case in 1938 and accentuated by the *Sears* and *Compco* cases in 1964. The 1967 *"Paladin"* decision, *Columbia Broadcasting* v. *DeCosta*, grounded in *Sears* and *Compco*, evidences the possible inequities inherent in the latter opinion. Professor Derenberg points out that the catch-all clause of the unfair competition bill is patterned on the laws of Germany, Switzerland, and other countries; on the Paris Convention; the 1929 Inter-American Trademark Convention; and Section 5 of the Federal Trade Commission Act.

The second paper is based on the Kettering Award Address by Judge Giles Rich. He examines the test of unobviousness which replaced the concept of invention. The standard discussed here, like those proposed on unfair competition, was difficult for the courts to apply because of its broad, general nature. The concept of invention, in the subjective sense, first arose in *Hotchkiss* v. *Greenwood*. Later, a sizable number of negative tests were proposed to determine whether invention was present. Although courts have held, as in the 1966 *Graham* v. *Deere Co.* decision, that a standard of invention was set forth in the Constitution, namely: "to Promote the progress of . . . useful Arts," only two words in the constitutional clause relating to patents, the words "inventors" and "discoveries," could be interpreted as applying a relevant standard to particular inventions.

Section 103 (one of the two major changes of the Patent Act of 1952), deriving from the latter standard, is entitled "Condition for Patentability: Non-Obvious Subject Matter." Judge Rich suggests that the unobviousness concept be considered a third requirement for patentability (novelty and utility being the other two). After the passage of the 1952 Act, courts were slow to replace the old standard-of-invention concept with the test of unobviousness. Judge Learned Hand, however, in *Lyon* v. *Bausch & Lomb* (1955) and *Reiner* v. *I. Leon* (1960), based his decisions on the newly proposed test of unobviousness; and these decisions had significant impact on bench and bar.

The third paper, the Kettering Award Address of Dr. Lawrence Hafstad, reviews three subjects on industrial property with which he has had personal experience. He sees an overwhelming taxpayer equity in the R&D component of government contracts for the AEC and an industry equity in such components for the Department of Defense; accordingly, he is inclined to accept the government patent policies practiced by these agencies. Although he recognizes the shift of many companies since World War II from civilian business to government contracting, and the growing importance of this type of government transaction, he believes that patent give-aways resulting from government contracts are grossly exaggerated.

In the second part of his paper, Dr. Hafstad discusses inventors' incentives and inventors' rights. He believes engineers like to consider themselves professional problem-solvers and, whether they are on a salary or otherwise, recognition by their peers is of prime importance. The team approach represents the assumption of large risks for large rewards; and the patent system provides the incentive for management to encourage its inventors.

The President's Commission Report is the third topic discussed by Dr. Hafstad. He proposes that the objective of patent reform be the combination of the best features of different systems to achieve the most effective system, rather than the convenience of the Patent Office. In considering the first-to-file proposal, he asks: First to file what? A flood of half-baked ideas? To provide for the current heavy Patent Office workload, Dr. Hafstad suggests that some procedural change be inaugurated that calls for less effort on important claims; however, he admits that this type of solution requires further study.

The last four papers are concerned primarily with the Patent Reform Bill. The first of these, by Mr. Jackson, is in large part opposed to the recommendations of the Commission, as set forth in S. 1042; Mr. Mossinghoff's presentation is primarily in support of the bill; and the paper by Mr. Parry discusses foreign experience with provisions similar to the President's Commission Report, and is generally critical. Mr. Shipman's paper deals with the international implications of the bill and supports it. The positions taken by the authors indicate very strong differences of opinion on the merits of the proposed legislation.

Mr. Jackson directs his attention particularly to the repeal of the grace period, the introduction of the first-to-file provisions, and the discontinuance of interferences. He charges that the urge to file quickly will lower the quality of patents; pendency in the Office will be lengthened due to the allowance of a year for completion of pre-liminary applications; disclosure will be delayed because use and sale will be retarded; and technological-journal publication will be postponed until after filing. He thinks the enactment of the Reform Bill will breed more widespread secrecy. Pointing out that the laws of foreign countries differ (some provide for operation of a registra-tion system, some for examination of applications), Mr. Jackson maintains that it would be quite difficult to harmonize with them; specifically, he faults the Commission because the absolute novelty they recommend is present only in a limited number of countries.

Among the provisions of the bill he supports are filing by as-signee and the publication of applications; he also suggests a limited experiment with deferred examination. On the other hand, Mr. Jackson presents a considerable list of omissions and inclusions he considers unwise: He regards as imprudent the proposals dealing with terminal disclaimer, broadened reissues, cutting off continua-tion-in-part, appeal to court of appeals from CCPA, and unpatent-ability of computer programs. Omission from the bill of provisions dealing with the problem of claims, disclosure, and petty patents is also noted.

Mr. Mossinghoff discusses the major premises of the Johnson Administration's proposed Patent Reform Act: (1) industrial prop-erty protection is fundamental to a free enterprise system; and (2) if industrial property is strengthened internationally, it in turn will (a) strengthen the free enterprise system and (b) have a beneficial impact on U.S. foreign trade. Early disclosure and early use, fostered by the bill, would promote progress of the useful arts as required by the Constitution. Mr. Mossinghoff stresses that the purpose of the bill is not, principally, to serve the inventor's natural and moral rights in the invention, but rather to promote the progress of the useful arts. He thinks the first-to-file procedure will result in the award of the patent to the inventor who took the first steps to make the invention available to the public; and it will increase the quality and reliability of patents by removing the need of proof of events and dates before filing, and eliminate the defense of prior inventorship.

Mr. Parry points out that one of the main motivations of the Commission's Report was harmonization—despite the fact that practitioners previously had held foreign law in rather low esteem. He agrees with Mr. Jackson that it is difficult to compare foreign experience because of the different national environmental conditions and the variety of provisions in the foreign laws. He stresses the need for the patent law to reflect the legal, social, and political philosophies of a country. From his experience there is a race to the Patent Office in first-to-file countries, and the inventor is in the nature of a speculator.

Mr. Parry presents a weighty catalog of the different requirements in, and the consequences of, the patent laws of foreign countries. For example, absolute novelty—and with no grace period—is provided in France, Holland, and Italy; but in these countries the invention, to constitute prior art, must be known to the public sufficiently to be carried out, and proof of that knowledge must be established by documents. Yet the requirement of no divulgence before filing hinders tests on drugs in France—because they are tested by code numbers to avoid premature publicity. Publication is a bar in Switzerland, Sweden, Norway, Denmark, and Austria only if it is in printed form; and patents of importation are peculiar to Belgium, Spain, and most Latin American countries.

Mr. Shipman emphasizes that the proposed act seeks harmonization where consistent with U.S. objectives, and that the changes proposed are for our benefit. He offers statistics on the substantial U.S. filing abroad, and asserts that the rate of increase of U.S. filing abroad is greater than the increase of U.S. filing at home. A number of his other points emphasize the international implications: We are moving toward a universal patent system and higher living standards will result; the first-to-invent system is really a first-to-file system, with exceptions; and inventors do not work with the necessity of proof of recording in mind. Mr. Shipman notes that only 1 percent of patents are in interference, but *all* inventors must keep the required records—and foreign inventors are discriminated against. He supports preliminary applications because papers could then be published in journals without the loss of foreign rights, and no more proof would be necessary than the recordings and descriptions now required to provide against future interferences.

Mr. Shipman sees it as a choice between two imperfect systems, with the more practicable being the first-to-file.

Proposed Federal Legislation
On Unfair Competition

WALTER DERENBERG

A revised draft of S. 3681, the McClellan Bill, on the subject of a federal law of unfair competition, was introduced by the Senator in the Second Session of the 89th Congress, and differs only in minor respects from the previously introduced S. 3681. It is, however, different in some important respects from H.R. 4651, the Lindsay Bill, which had been introduced in the 88th Congress, 1st Session, as an entirely separate statute on this subject and had met with some opposition on the part of a few practitioners and the government based on certain alleged anticompetitive effects thereof. The bill as now introduced (S. 1154, 90th Cong., 1st Sess.) has been revamped in the form of an amendment to Section 43(a) of the Lanham Trademark Act of 1946 and consists of 12 sections.[1] This bill has already been endorsed in its present form by several organizations, including the American Patent Law Association, the United States Trademark Association, and the American Bar Association.

Efforts to pass a federal unfair competition act started in the 1920s, but became more pressing after the Supreme Court's decision in 1938 in *Erie R. R. Co.* v. *Tompkins*, 304 U.S. 64. As a result of that decision, unfair competition issues were relegated to state law even in cases where they were appended to trademark infringement actions and even though they may have been based upon substantially the same facts. (See *National Fruit Products Co.* v. *Dwinell-Wright Co.*, 47 F. Supp. 499 (D. Mass. 1942), *aff'd*, 140 F.2d 618 (1st Cir. 1944).)

Moreover, it soon became apparent that our courts would be burdened in multistate unfair competition cases with applying the various state laws of all those states in which the unfair practices may have occurred. "Unfair competition is a tort governed by the law of the State where it occurs. If it occurs in a number of States it must be dealt with in accordance with their laws . . . ." (*Purcell* v. *Summers*, 145 F.2d 979 (4th Cir. 1944)). Some of our most eminent federal judges have, therefore, long argued for the enactment of a uniform

---

EDITOR'S NOTE: This paper was delivered at a Conference of The PTC Research Institute on June 22-23, 1967. (*IDEA*, Vol. 11, Conference No. 1967.)

[1] For the text of the bill, see *Trademark Reporter*, Vol. 57 (February 1967), p. 109.

federal act along the lines now included in the McClellan Bill. The late Judge Clark, in 1956, spoke of the need for a "complete and uniform law." (*Maternally Yours, Inc.* v. *Your Maternity Shop, Inc.*, 234 F.2d 538 (2nd Cir. 1956)) And Judge Medina observed in 1959 that "Since most cases involve interstate transactions, perhaps some day the much-needed Federal statute on unfair competition will be passed." (*American Safety Table Co.* v. *Schreiber*, 269 F.2d 255 (2d Cir. 1959))

However, since that time the need for passage of this type of legislation has been even more accentuated as a result of the two recent decisions of the United States Supreme Court in *Sears, Roebuck & Co.* v. *Stiffel Company*, 376 U.S. 255, and *Compco Corp.* v. *Day-Brite Lighting, Inc.*, 376 U.S. 234 (1964), in which the Court held in two sweeping opinions that, at least in the area of misappropriation, there had been complete federal preemption by the patent and copyright laws and that the state courts lack jurisdiction even in cases of slavish imitation of nonfunctional features of products and even upon proof of secondary meaning, as long as the products sought to be protected did not come within the scope of existing patent or copyright legislation.

As a result of these decisions, our law of unfair competition has been almost completely emasculated, and defendants in this type of action today enjoy something of a heyday since it has become almost impossible to prevail in actions of this type in the absence of patent or copyright protection.[2] It is, of course, true that some fair-minded and courageous courts have already attempted to limit the scope of the *Sears* and *Compco* decisions, at least to cases of product simulation, so that relief may still be available in situations in which the defendant's unfair practices are not of this type.

Thus, in *Flexitized, Inc.* v. *National Flexitized Corp.*, 335 F.2d 774 (1964), the Second Circuit remarked: "We do not read the recent U.S. Supreme Court decision in *Sears, Roebuck & Co.* v. *Stiffel Co.* as establishing any Constitutional bar to the application of state law in the instant case." Similarly, an Illinois court had held in a trade secret case, *Schulenburg* v. *Signatrol, Inc.*, 212 N.E.2d 865 (1965), that *Sears* and *Compco* did not cover trade secret situations.

The Pennsylvania District Court has said, in the case of *Pottstown Daily News Publishing Company* v. *Pottstown Broadcasting Company*, 247 F. Supp. 578 (E.D. Pa. 1965), that it did not consider the famous earlier decision of the Supreme Court in the *International News* case (*International News Service* v. *Associated Press*, 248 U.S.

---

[2]See Derenberg, "Product Simulation: A Right or a Wrong?" *Columbia Law Review*, Vol. 64 (1964), p. 1192.

215 (1918)), overruled by *Sears* and *Compco*. Similarly, the New York Appellate Division observed in the *World's Fair* case: "This court does not read either of those cases [*Sears* and *Compco*] as striking down or intending to strike down all state laws of unfair competition in all cases and for all purposes. A leading case on the law of unfair competition, *International News Service* v. *The Associated Press*, was not even mentioned in either opinion. . . . No attempt is being made in this case to give 'patent protection' to an article in trade 'too lacking in novelty to merit any patent at all' but to give protection for a brief two-year period to the valuable property rights of the spectacular and economic educational effort of a nonprofit organization." (*New York World's Fair 1964-1965 Corp.* v. *Colourpicture Publishers,* 141 USPQ 939 [Sup. Ct. 1964], *aff'd*, 21 A. D.2d 896 (2d. Dept. 1964))

However, another deadly blow was dealt the law of unfair competition when the First Circuit in the *"Paladin"* case held, for the first time, that in its opinion the *International News* decision must be considered overruled by *Sears* and *Compco*, although the court in the two latter opinions did not as much as mention that case. (*Columbia Broadcasting System, Inc.* v. *DeCosta*, 153 USPQ 649 (1st Cir. 1967)) Although the court agreed with the jury that the defendant broadcasting system in the *"Paladin"* case had been a "pirate," it went on to say: "Our Paladin is not the first creator to see the fruits of his creation harvested by another, without effective remedy; and although his case is undeniably hard, to affirm the judgments below would, we think, allow a hard case to make some intolerably bad law."

While, in my opinion, the adverse result reached by the appellate court in the *"Paladin"* case might have been justified on other grounds, it is always distressing—not only for the party involved—to read decisions which deny individual justice on grounds of overall policy considerations. We are reminded of a statement by a district court judge in one of the lamp cases before the Supreme Court's decision in *Mazer* v. *Stein*, 347 U.S. 201 (1954), where Judge Picard of Detroit had said, in denying relief: "While plagiarism in any form is to be deplored and certainly not condoned or encouraged, we are concerned here not with one's sense of fairness, but with the law." (*Stein* v. *Benederet*, 96 USPQ 13 (E.D. Mich. 1952))

Moreover, it would seem difficult to take seriously the First Circuit's suggestion that the plaintiff in the *"Paladin"* case may perhaps have been entitled to relief if he had placed a copyright notice on the visiting card, which, among other things, displayed the picture of a chess knight. This sort of reasoning would seem to encourage members of our profession to advise clients to place copyright notices on products or materials obviously not within the scope of existing legislation, with the thought that they might conceivably persuade a judge that statutory protection may be had where the law of unfair competition will now be entirely unavailable.

But let us briefly revert to the pending McClellan Bill.[3] Most interesting and important for our present purposes is Section 7 thereof, which amends existing Section 43(a) of the Lanham Trademark Act of 1946 by including a catalog of unfair practices which will be deemed to be actionable provided they occur in interstate or foreign commerce. The first five enumerated specific practices include such activities as disparagement of a competitor, misrepresentation of goods, services or vocational activities, wrongful disclosure or misappropriation of trade secrets, and misappropriation of quasi-property of another not otherwise protected by federal statute.

This catalog of practices is then, however, followed by a most important catchall or general clause, under which any practice which is "otherwise contrary to commercial good faith or to normal and honest practices in the business or vocational activity" may give rise to a civil action for unfair competition. This provision is patterned not only after corresponding general clauses in the laws of many foreign countries, such as Germany, Switzerland, and others, but also reflects the policy embodied in two international conventions to which the United States is a party, the Convention of Paris for the Protection of Industrial Property of 20th March, 1883, as revised, and the General Inter-American Convention for Trademark and Commercial Protection of Washington, 1929. Article 10[bis], paragraph 2, of the former Convention, expressly provides that: "Any act of competition contrary to honest practices in industrial or commercial matters constitutes an act of unfair competition"; and Article 20 of the Inter-American Convention reads: "Every act or deed contrary to commercial good faith or to the normal and honorable development of industrial or business activities shall be considered as unfair competition and, therefore, unjust and prohibited." Moreover, the proposed general clause is but a restatement of the broad language of Section 5 of the Federal Trade Commission Act, under which any "unfair methods of competition" in commerce and unfair or deceptive acts or practices are declared unlawful.

I have never been able to understand why we should hesitate to confer such broad general equitable powers on our courts when we have not been hesitant to vest an administrative agency with similarly

[3]A complete analysis of the bill may be found in the "Brief in Support of Congressional Passage of Proposed Unfair Competition Amendment to the Lanham Trademark Act of 1946," prepared by The National Coordinating Committee, and published in *Trademark Reporter*, Vol. 57 (Feb. 1967), p. 87.

sweeping powers. Furthermore, all of us who have been practicing in this field, both here and abroad, realize that no specific enumeration of unfair trade practices will ever give adequate protection in the absence of a general catchall clause of the type now embodied in subsection 6 of Section 43(a).

The late Justice Brandeis stated, as far back as 1920 in his dissenting opinion in the famous case of *Federal Trade Commission* v. *Gratz*, 253 U.S. 421, at 437, that "an enumeration, however comprehensive, of existing methods of unfair competition must necessarily soon prove incomplete, as with new conditions constantly arising novel unfair methods would be devised and developed." And the late Edward S. Rogers, who was the first to recognize the need for a federal unfair competition act even during the 1920s, had said: "Experience shows that by the time the judical machinery arrives at a place where the pirate was yesterday, ready to deal with him, that elusive person has moved forward and is still a little ahead—at a place where the courts will not reach until tomorrow—and is there engaged in doing something which will enable him to advantage himself at someone else's expense in some manner hitherto unthought of."[4]

It is my belief and hope that during the next Congress this legislation finally will be enacted since in its present form it does not present any problems of preemption or any constitutional issue. I consider it unfortunate that in the admirable Report on Copyright Law Revision, H. R. Rep. No. 83, 90th Congress, to accompany H.R. 2512, it is stated in connection with proposed Section 301(b)(3), under which state law remedies with regard to certain specified types of unfair competition such as passing-off and false representation would not be deemed preempted, this would not be true with regard to misappropriation and similar unfair activities. On page 100, the report says in this regard:

> Use of the term unfair competition itself has been avoided because of its inherent ambiguity. In accordance with the Supreme Court's decision in *Sears, Roebuck & Co.* v. *Stiffel Co.*, Section 301 is not intended to preempt common law protection in cases involving activities such as false labeling, fraudulent representation and passing-off, even where the subject matter involved comes within the scope of the copyright statute. However, where the cause of action involves the form of "unfair competition" commonly referred to as "misappropriation," which is nothing more than copyright protection under another name, Section 301 is intended to have preemptive effect.

I suggest, however, that actual enactment of the pending McClellan Act before the passage of the new copyright legislation would take the sting out of this comment and, since it would be based on the

---

[4]Rogers, "New Concepts of Unfair Competition Under the Lanham Act," *Trademark Reporter*, Vol. 38 (1948), p. 259.

Commerce clause, would not give rise to any further preemption problem.

Finally, I will briefly mention one other collateral feature of the McClellan Bill. The Supreme Court has recently decided, contrary to overwhelming prior judicial authority, that a victorious party in a trademark infringement case cannot be awarded reasonable attorney's fees even in a case of willful and deliberate infringement. (The *Fleischmann Distilling Corp.* v. *Maier Brewing Co.*, 153 USPQ 432 (1967)) In other words, the Court adopted the *en banc* decision of the Ninth Circuit to this effect (*Maier Brewing Co.* v. *Fleischmann Distilling Corp.* 149 USPQ 89 (9th Cir. 1966)), on the ground that, contrary to the copyright and patent law, the present trademark statute does not specifically provide for such remedy. The McClellan Bill is attempting to change this recent Supreme Court ruling by statute, in expressly providing for recovery of reasonable attorney's fees in the discretion of the Court. In my opinion, this would seem to be particularly necessary in the United States since we are one of the very few countries in the world that have not provided any federal criminal sanction whatever for deliberate or willful trademark infringement.

Test of "Unobviousness" v.
Concept of "Invention"

GILES S. RICH

I believe in incentive systems. Over 20 years ago a prize competition lured me into some intense study and writing.[1] I did not win the prize. Neither did the other contestants, save one.[2] But they all contributed something. That is the way incentive systems work. They bring out out all kinds of efforts, excellent, good, mediocre, indifferent, and bad. But the *system* brings forth the effort. Society benefits from the good and mediocre, as well as the excellent, efforts. The bad efforts don't hurt it any. They may even prevent others from making mistakes if they are made known.

The patent and copyright laws create such incentive systems. The copyright laws provide an incentive which brings out the greatest works of literature and art as well as a lot of trash. The patent system works in a similar way. But you can't get cream without producing milk, and, anyway, it is the milk that society lives on.

Herein I consider an aspect of the patent system which I think causes the most trouble: the most evasive of the criteria for determining what constitutes a patentable discovery or invention.

CONSTRUCTIVE PATENT MONOPOLY

As groundwork, I will first state an axiomatic but too-little-recognized principle. A monopoly, presupposing a demand for the thing monopolized, merely gives rise to *power* which can be put to either good or bad uses. Hence, in the case of monopolies created by government grant, which is all patents are so far as the rights they create are concerned, we have to distinguish between good and bad monopolies.

I will take two well-known examples from history. First, the

EDITOR'S NOTE: Judge Rich presented this paper upon his acceptance of The PTC Research Institute's Charles F. Kettering Award on June 18, 1964. (*IDEA,* Vol. 8, Conference No. 1964). He edited the paper for publication in this volume.

[1]The Linthicum Foundation Competition, 1941, Dean John H. Wigmore, Northwestern University Law School, Chairman. The writer's contribution was published in five installments in JPOS, Vol. 24, pp. 85, 159, 241, 328, and 422, commencing February 1942.

[2]The winner was Laurence I. Wood, whose paper was published in book form, 1942, by Commerce Clearing House, Inc., under the title *Patents and Antitrust Law.*

bad monopoly. Queen Elizabeth granted to one Darcy, a member of her court, a monopoly of playing cards for 21 years so that he could make some money. But playing cards were old and well known, and others were making a living from making and selling them in England. This monopoly, which was by Royal Letters Patent, therefore took from the public a freedom in business which it had long enjoyed before the patent; and it was bad.[3]

In Venice in 1594 the Doge, on behalf of the government, granted to the great Galileo a "privilege," which was the Venetian name for a patent, on a machine which he had *invented* "for raising water and irrigating land with small expense and great convenience," on the condition that it had never before been thought of or made by others.

Galileo made a couple of significant remarks in his petition for the privilege. He said, "it not being fit that this invention, which is my own, discovered by me with great labor and expense, be made the common property of everyone"; and also, that if he were granted the privilege, "I shall the more attentively apply myself to new inventions for universal benefit." In short, he was not inclined to divulge his invention only to have it copied; but if the government would give him some reasonable protection he would not only divulge it and build it but might even apply himself to making some more inventions. Deeming this to be a *good* use to which to put a limited monopoly, the Council voted to grant him a "privilege" or patent of monopoly for 21 years.[4]

The Venetians were accustomed to doing this, having granted about 1,600 "privileges" in the 15th and 16th centuries.[5]

The English in 1624 enacted a statute[6] abolishing and prohibiting future monopolies of the bad Darcy sort and authorizing the continuing grant of Letters Patent for new inventions within the realm, which has continued to this day.

The Founding Fathers came to America from the mother country, bringing with them knowledge of this practice of granting monopolies. In the nearly 150 years of the Colonial period preceding the Federal Constitution, the colonies and then the states grant-

---

[3]Darcy v. Allin, 11 Co. Rep. 846; 1 W.P.C. 1. See Fox, *Monopolies and Patents,* p. 318 (1947). The case also has the popular title "The Case of Monopolies."

[4]*History of the Patent Office,* JPOS, Vol. 18, p. 23 (separate pagination) (1936).

[5]*Ibid.* Most of the privileges were for copyrights, but a small percentage were for inventions.

[6]Statute of Monopolies, May 25, 1624, 21 Jac. I, c. 3. For its history see Fox, note 3, *supra,* at pp. 113-126.

ed numerous patents for new inventions as well as monopolies to encourage the founding of new industries, including, as the English did, encouragement of setting up in America industries already practiced abroad.[7]

It is not surprising that, when it came to the writing of the Constitution, provision should be incorporated, with no controversy at all, for Congress to make laws for the granting of patents to inventors, or that George Washington should urge its speedy enactment, or that the very first Congress should enact our first Patent Act of 1790.[8]

Then began our patent system. One might describe it as a great experiment which goes on continuously, getting more complex all the time. Serious systematic efforts have but recently been undertaken to find out how the system actually works, as an aid to preserving its basic principles and saving the obvious good that is in it.

In this experiment, which involves a mixture of economics, law, technology, and psychology, we still have the centuries-old problem of monopoly power being utilized for socially good and socially bad ends and of deciding which is which.

The greedy nature of some men is such that there are always pressures toward the creation of bad monopolies. Undue preoccupation with countering this pressure, however, has blurred the vision of many well-intentioned but not too well-informed people to the good uses monopoly can be put to and to the good that monopoly power can do, properly channeled and not so proscribed as to lose its effective power.

Paradoxically, in the working of the patent system, monopoly often promotes competition. Numerous instances are all around us, wherever two products serving the same general purpose have achieved, with the aid of patent protection, commercial production. And only after such production is there any possibility of market competition.

The nature of the patent right as a constructive monopoly was pointed out by Dean John H. Wigmore of Northwestern University Law School, who wrote:

> . . . neither Courts nor treatise-writers have been radical enough in defending the legitimacy of the "monopoly" in a patent, as distinguished from the ordinary trade-monopoly. Is it not a fact that every property-right we have is a "monopoly"? The right to our house or our automobile is simply a right to keep anyone else from entering or using it without our consent; and is that not a monopoly?

*   *   *

---

[7]See *History of the Patent Office*, note 4, *supra*, at pp. 35-58.
[8]*Id.* at pp. 55-62.

Of course patent-rights can be so *used* as to merit the distrust attaching to a monopoly,—by contracts fixing prices, by tying agreements, by pools and the like. But so can gold-mines and all the necessities of life by bargains be used monopolistically; yet no one blames the mine-owning right itself or the food-ownership right itself; the blame is directed to the use of it.

And so I for one regard it as unfortunate that courts and treatise-writers have not stood up more boldly for the fundamental right-ness of the patent right itself. I say "for one," because I do not recall reading anywhere an adequate defense of the theory of the patent-right.[9]

CONDITIONS FOR PATENTABILITY

To this point, I have taken note that the *primary* distinction between good and bad patent monopolies is that the good patent does not monopolize something the public *already has,* so as to take something away from the public. The invention covered by the good patent must be *new*; and so our statutes have always provided, though the provision was not always enforced.[10]

But beyond bare novelty one must go one further and troublesome step to have a sound system and keep the monopoly on the good side.

As we refrain from granting patents on inventions that are not new, we must also refrain from granting patents on those inventions which would arise *spontaneously,* given the need or the desire for them, as the yelp of the dog surely follows from stepping on his tail, or with *only a nominal expenditure of time, effort, money, or wit*—especially if the invention is one of real utility likely to meet with popular demand.

Hotchkiss v. *Greenwood*—"Ordinary Skilled Mechanic" Test of Patentability

It was not long after the Patent Act of 1836—in 1850, in fact—that the U.S. Supreme Court made this clear in the "doorknob case," *Hotchkiss* v. *Greenwood*.[11] What was involved was the trial judge's charge to a jury that if *no more ingenuity or skill was required* to construct the patented doorknob *than was possessed by an ordinary mechanic acquainted with the business,* then the patent was invalid.

The Supreme Court approved the charge. The opinion said:

[9]Wigmore, *Forward to Wood,* note 2, *supra.*

[10]*Id.* at pp. 77-82, 230. Under the 1793 Act, for example, there was no examination for novelty over a period of 43 years. About 10,000 patents issued under that act for terms of 14 years, less than the number issued today in three months.

[11]52 U.S. 248 (1850).

"In other words, the improvement is *the work of the skilled mechan-ic, not that of the inventor.*" (Emphasis added.) The decision made clear that patents are not to be granted on inventions which are no more than what the ordinary mechanic acquainted with the business would produce as a matter of course in the pursuit of his calling. Such mechanics are *expected* to produce new things, such as were involved in that case, which involved the attaching of an old clay doorknob to an old metal shank in precisely the same manner as metal doorknobs had been attached to such shanks before. Technically the assembly was *new*, but the Court found that novelty was not enough.

In referring to "mechanics" in this matter we can take them to be representative of a class—all those with ordinary skill in the various callings, ordinary shoemakers, ordinary chemists, electronic technicians of ordinary skill, etc.

What came out of the case after 1850 and is still with us, as a result of the reasoning that the new doorknob "was the work of the skillful mechanic, not that of the inventor," was an injection into the law of what has ever since been called the "requirement for invention."

As is usual with a "doctrine" derived from a court opinion, the doctrine persists although the facts out of which it arose are forgotten. The opinion in the first case is quoted to the judge in a second and he does an opinion embroidering on it, his words being quoted in turn and reembroidered and so on. Judicial rhetoric led to the requirement for "invention" or the "standard of invention," which, however, could not be defined, according to the courts.

The Requirement For "Invention"—The "Undefinable Something"

The resulting situation with respect to the law on the "requirement for invention" was well summed up by Judge Learned Hand, who knew as much patent law as any judge ever has, at a Senate hearing in which I participated in 1955, as follows:

> You could find nearly anything you liked if you went to the opinions. It was a subject on which judges loved to be rhetorical. . . . patent lawyers . . . like to quote all those things. There are lots of them.[12]

This proliferation of views on what did and did not amount to "invention" went on for 100 years. We were enlightened with the view that "invention" resulted from the exercise of the "inventive fac-

---

[12]*Hearings on the American Patent System before the Subcommittee on Patents, Trademarks, and Copyrights of the Senate Committee on the Judiciary,* 84th Cong., 1st Sess., p. 113 (1956).

ulties" and other circular reasoning. Our present standard text, Walker, now in its seventh edition, says that "An invention is the result of an inventive act."[13] Whole books on the patent law were written around such concepts. People collected the statements pro and con in volumes equally divided about in the middle—"invention" on one side, lack of it on the other. Negative and positive tests for detecting its presence evolved. So did exceptions to each test. And patent lawyers selectively quoted all this mass of material as though it proved something. Judges like Learned Hand found, in his words, that "they never seemed to tend toward enlightenment."[14]

This requirement finally evolved into a *"standard* of invention" which the courts pretended was being raised and lowered like an elevator as though it were something tangible. Thus, the Supreme Court, in reversing a decision sustaining a patent, proclaimed that the lower court had applied too low a standard of invention.[15] The courts also proclaimed in all seriousness that this "standard" was to be found in the Constitution, where there are only two words on which it could possibly be predicated, the word "inventors" and the word "discoveries."[16]

"Discovery" and "Invention" Distinguished from "Patentability"

Some judges got it fixed in their minds that if a thing is an "invention" then it is patentable and if it is not patentable then it is not an "invention." They did not realize that the same things are invented over and over—by the use of the inventive faculties or by inventive acts or what have you—and, although clearly "inventions," their originators being as firmly convinced of it as was Galileo, they are not patentable for want of novelty. So it is customary for judges to approach all inventions gingerly in their opinions by referring to them as "alleged" or "supposed" inventions.

All an invention is, however, is something which has been

---

[13]1 Walker, Patents 110 (Deller ed. 1937).

[14]*Hearings on the American Patent System,* note 12, *supra,* at p. 113.

[15]See Great Atlantic & Pacific Tea Co. v. Supermarket Equipment Corp., 340 U.S. 147, 87 USPQ 303 (1950), where the two concurring opinions below were held to have applied a "standard of invention . . . that is less exacting than that . . . required . . . ."

[16]I am not unaware of the statement of the *objective* in Art. I, sec. 8, clause 8, "To promote the progress of . . . useful arts." See "Principles of Patentability" by the writer, 28 GEORGE WASHINGTON LAW REVIEW 393; JPOS, Vol. 42 (February 1960), p. 75. When Congress exercised its power under that clause and set up a patent system, so long as the *system as a whole* functions to further the constitutional objective, it would not seem that the statement of the objective could set any "standard" for patentability of any single invention.

found out, or devised, or discovered. The question today is not what to call it but whether under the statute it is patentable. Hundreds of "real" or "true" inventions, all resulting from "inventive faculties," are held unpatentable every day for lack of novelty.

The Patent Office, of course, proceeded on the same basis, rejecting applications for want of "invention" and granting them when it could be persuaded that "invention" was present. It still does so to a dwindling extent. And through it all the patent lawyers and the judges persisted in telling all concerned that "invention" was something which could not be defined, like God! Patent validity came as a matter of grace, from on high. This was a messy state of affairs. The surprising thing is it worked so well. But not well enough.

In 1941 a Commission appointed by President Roosevelt and headed by Charles F. Kettering[17] came out with a report which said:

> One of the greatest technical weaknesses of the patent system is the lack of a definitive yardstick as to *what is invention*. To provide such a yardstick and to assure that the various courts of law and the Patent Office *shall use the same standards*, several changes are suggested. It is proposed that Congress shall declare a national standard whereby [mark these words] *patentability* of an invention shall be determined by the objective test as to its advancement of the arts and sciences. [Emphasis added][18]

One apparent thought there was—to stop talking about whether a thing is or is not an "invention," to take anything presented as an invention, and then to determine its *patentability* according to a standard which Congress was to declare, Congress never having said anything about it up to that time.

For some years nothing came of the Kettering Commission proposal, but in the 79th, 80th, and 81st Congresses, from 1945 through 1949, identical bills were introduced entitled, unfortunately but almost inevitably, "A bill to declare a national policy for determining invention." Now I have just said that the problem was not really to determine "invention" but to determine the *patentability* of inventions, and this matter of language is one of major concern. Kettering got a hold on the distinction, but it keeps fading away like Alice's cat.

People don't think so much as they talk; and when they do

---

[17]For a note on who Kettering was and his prolific accomplishments in the fields of business, research and inventing, see Jackson, "The Kettering Archives." JPOS, Vol. 46 (1964), p. 331.

[18]Report of National Patent Planning Comm., H.R. Doc. No. 239, 78th Cong., 1st Sess., pp. 6, 10 (1943).

think, they tend 'to think in words, at least about legal abstractions. Words are used to describe things, concepts, and experiences we have in common so that we can communicate. This thing, this concept, this experience every patent examiner, lawyer, and judge had come up against in practice was called the "requirement of invention," or just "invention"—the undefinable something or other that has to be there. This proves to be a cliché, meaningless though it is, that is hard to break away from. I taught for many years, and presumably my students learned, that the prerequisites to patentability were novelty, utility, and invention. There was nothing else to teach.

Thinking and its concomitant words had not progressed beyond that point in the 1930s and 1940s. But today they have. Any current textbook and most cases, you will find, use the old terminology. But it isn't true any more and hasn't been since the Patent Act of 1952 became effective. However, my not believing in ghosts or angels doesn't mean, *in law,* that there are no ghosts or angels, because if you think there are, and are frightened or informed by them, then they exist. As long as judges say there is a requirement for "invention," and many still do, then there is one. If you take a patent into court and the judge invalidates it for want of "invention," you *know* there is one.

But why am I saying there is none? There is none because Section 103 of the Patent Act of 1952 replaced "invention" or "standard of invention" with "non-obvious subject matter" as a condition for patentability. This was recognized by the Supreme Court in three 1966 decisions applying to Section 103.[19]

Section 103 "Non-obvious" Condition of Patentability Replaces "Standard of Invention"

In the late 1940s, Congress became interested in revising and codifying the patent law and did so.[20] Section 103 of the resulting law (Title 35 U.S.C.) was described at the time[21] as providing a *"condition* which exists in our law and has existed for more than 100 years . . . by reason of decisions of the courts." (Emphasis added) And that "condition" is described in the title of Section 103 as one for the existence of "non-obvious subject matter." The

[19]Graham v. John Deere Co., 383 U.S. 1, 148 USPQ 459 (1966); Calmar, Inc. v. Cook Chem. Co. 383 U.S. 1, 148 USPQ 459 (1966); United States v. Adams, 383 U.S. 39, 148 USPQ 479 (1966).
[20]See "Congressional Intent—Or, Who Wrote the Patent Act of 1952?" by the writer, in *Patent Procurement and Exploitation,* (Washington: BNA Books, 1963), p. 61.
[21]H.R. Rep. No. 1923, 82nd Cong., 2d Sess., p. 7 (1952).

addition of Section 103 was stated in the House report on the bill[22] to be *one of the two major changes or innovations in the statute.*

What Section 103 itself says is that what is patented must *not* have been *obvious* to one of *ordinary* skill *in the art involved,* at the *time* the invention was made. The parallel with what would be expected of the "ordinary mechanic acquainted with the business" in the "doorknob case" should be clear.

This is not a "standard of invention"; and it is not called a "requirement of invention." The presence or absence of "invention" is not mentioned. The use of the term "invention" was, in fact, carefully avoided with a view to making a fresh start, free of all the divergent court opinions and rhetorical pronouncements about "invention."[23] And in doing that it was contemplated, as the House report states,[24] that "This section should have a stabilizing effect and minimize great departures which have appeared in some cases."

As has been pointed out by one of the drafters of that section, Mr. P. J. Federico, in his Commentary,[25] what Section 103 sought was

> . . . some modification . . . in the direction of moderating the extreme degrees of strictness exhibited in a number of judicial opinions over the past dozen or so years; that is, that some change of attitude more favorable to patents is hoped for. This is indicated by the language used in Section 103 as well as by the general tenor of remarks of the Committees in the reports and particular comments.

The real vice or inadequacy of the judicial requirement for "invention" was in the truism Mr. Federico also restated, "the so-called standard of invention . . . is an unmeasurable quantity having different meanings for different persons." It left every judge practically free to decide this often-controlling factor according to his personal philosophy of what inventions should be patented, whether or not he had any competence to do so or any knowledge of the patent system as an operative socio-economic force. This was too great a freedom because it involved national policy, which should be declared by Congress and not by individual judges or even groups of judges on multiple-judge courts. In Section 103 Congress made such a policy declaration. It did not there declare what should constitute "invention." It was a statement of something to take the place of this vague concept. And it

---

[22]*Id.* at p. 5.

[23]The writer states this from personal knowledge as one of the drafters. See note 20, *supra.*

[24]Note 21, *supra.*

[25]Federico, *Commentary on the New Patent Act,* 35 U.S.C.A. 1 (1954).

was made in the face of judicial declarations, made in the *absence* of a statute, which Congress expressly desired to modify.

I would like to inject a new term into the patent law so we can discuss the matter rationally. I would like to call it the THIRD REQUIREMENT of patentability. In the Patent Act of 1952, the statute sets out all the requirements in the clearest possible form. Section 101 says inventions must be *new* and *useful*, requirements one and two; Section 102 defines novelty; and Section 103 lays down the *third requirement*. I repeat its clear-cut title: *"Conditions for patentability; non-obvious subject matter."*

Upon examination in the Patent Office or upon adjudication in court, under the statute, when novelty, utility, and unobviousness as defined in Section 103 are found to exist, and there is no statutory time bar under Section 102, there is *patentability* and *that is the end of the matter.* An examination for the presence or absence of "invention," or of precedents on that muddy issue, is not called for and is not proper. It is a work of supererogation. It illustrates, furthermore, a failure to grasp the meaning of the statutory provisions. There is no such prerequisite in the statutory law.

When, as is the case with the "requirement for invention," the century's accumulation of judicial precedents ranges from A to Z, and Congress, looking at the situation under the guiding light of Kettering's statement that *this is no yardstick and the greatest technical weakness of the patent system*, determines to make a yardstick and says the measure shall be "M," right in the middle of the alphabet, it behooves everyone concerned with administering that law to follow the measure "M" and to stop flitting about arbitrarily from A to Z, lighting upon that letter which seems most appealing.

But, even today, lawyers, examiners, and judges are not uniformly following the law as Congress wrote it in the Patent Act of 1952, for a number of reasons. What we have today is a mishmash. Why do we have a mish-mash?

First: A century of thinking and writing about a phenomenon in one set of nomenclature is a hard thing to overcome. Also, a lot of people go on administering the patent laws and practicing under them without bothering to read the revision of them, so they are not aware that there has been a change.

Second: By hindsight it is apparent that those most intimately concerned with the writing and expounding of the Patent Act of 1952, themselves brought up in the "requirement for invention" tradition (and I speak as one of them), did a very poor job of

informing the public what it was they had done. One reason for
that was that, on the average, their own comprehension of what
they had done was not too clear. Remember, they were all of the
persuasion that "invention" *could not* be defined, yet there they
were, trying to put a provision on that very subject into the statute. In going as far as seemed to be possible in that direction, they
knew they were not making a *definition* but rather a *statement of
policy*, a *specific required approach* to a difficult problem, which
approach they thought would stop some of the nonsense deroga-
tory of the patent system that had been going on.

In pursuit of the objective of a statement of policy to counter-
act a judicial trend, the drafters and Congress did one thing which
has had a clear-cut effect. Following a phrase casually dropped
by the Supreme Court in *Cuno* v. *Automatic*,[26] in 1941, that
"the new device, however useful it may be, must reveal the flash of
creative genius," some courts took off on a quest for such a flash
and, not finding it, invalidated patents. The last sentence of Section 103 stopped this abruptly with the legislative command:
"Patentability shall not be negatived by the manner in which the
invention was made." But the judicial reaction to the first sentence,[27] in contrast, was all fouled up.

Third: The members of the bar have a lot to answer for in
creating and perpetuating the problem because it is they who,
desiring to make use of some of the extreme cases antedating the
1952 Patent Act to invalidate patents in litigation, played down
Section 103 and early in its life persuaded a number of courts that
it made no change whatever but was "mere codification."[28] It
would be hard to find a trial lawyer for an infringer who would
not urge on the court, as the existing test for "invention," the
views expressed by the Justices of the Supreme Court in *A & P* v.
Supermarket, in 1950,[29] two years before the effective date of

[26]Cuno Engineering Corp. v. Automatic Devices Corp., 314 U.S. 84, 51
USPQ 272 (1941).
[27]§ 103. *Conditions for patentability; non-obvious subject matter*
      A patent may not be obtained though the invention is not identically dis-
closed or described as set forth in section 102 of this title, if the differences
between the subject matter sought to be patented and the prior art are such
that the subject matter as a whole would have been obvious at the time the
invention was made to a person having ordinary skill in the art to which said
subject matter pertains. Patentability shall not be negatived by the manner in
which the invention was made.
[28]A little reflection should show that when judicial precedents constituting
the "law" range from the very liberal to the most strict, it is a patent absurdity to
speak of a statute taking a middle ground as a "codification" of existing law. See
note 20, *supra*.
[29]340 U.S. 147, 87 USPQ 303 (1950). This was a case preeminently in the

Section 103. Herein lies a grave defect in the development of sound law through adversary proceedings. Lawyers are now paying more attention to Section 103 as they learn that it can help them when they are on the other side, but they are learning slowly. And my generation of lawyers, at least, is still talking, out of habit, in terms of "invention."

Fourth: The nonuniformity and confusion have been described in detail, up to 1957 (the first five years of the 1952 Patent Act), in Senate Committee Study No. 7. What is its title? "Efforts to Establish a Statutory Standard of Invention."[30] The Senate Patent Subcommittee is still striving to bring about a higher degree of uniformity in the courts, in the various groups of the Patent Office, and between the two organizations, but in what terms does it do its own thinking? (See the Subcommittee's *Annual Report No. 107*, April 3, 1963; and *Annual Report No. 1018*, May 1, 1964.) Meanwhile, the U. S. Patent Office Academy has been teaching patent examiners that, under the 1952 Patent Act, there is no "standard of invention," that "invention" is meaningless, and that the prerequisite is as stated in Section 103 of the 1952 Act.

Amid the confusion, there are now encouraging signs in the courts. During the first few years after the 1952 Act, many courts took the position that Congress really had done *nothing* in enacting Section 103 and went about their old business of looking for "invention." Then in 1955 came Judge Learned Hand's *Lyon* v. *Bausch & Lomb*[31] opinion and in 1960 his *Reiner* v. *I. Leon*[32] opinion, both of which realistically appraised and appreciated what Section 103 had done, namely, to restore the law to what it had been 20 or 30 years earlier and, as he said, "to change the slow but steady drift of judicial decision that had been hostile to patents . . . ." In the former opinion he remarked that " 'invention' became perhaps the most baffling concept in the whole catalogue of judicial efforts to provide postulates for indefinitely varying occasions." In the latter he said "It is not for us [the judiciary] to decide what 'discoveries' shall 'promote the progress of science and the useful arts' sufficiently to grant any 'exclusive right' of [to?] inventors. Nor may we approach the interpretation of Section 103 . . . with a predetermined bias." While saying "The

---

minds of the drafters of the 1952 Patent Act, having been decided during the writing of the first drafts. See note 20.

[30]Senate Comm. on Judiciary, 85th Cong., 1st. Sess., *Efforts to Establish a Statutory Standard of Invention* (Comm. Print 1958).

[31]Lyon v. Bausch & Lomb Optical Co., 224 F.2d 530, 106 USPQ 1 (2d Cir. 1955).

[32]Reiner v. I. Leon Co., 285 F.2d 501, 128 USPQ 25 (2d Cir. 1960).

test laid down [in Section 103] is indeed misty enough," he was able, with the evidence provided, to follow it. Certiorari was denied in both of these cases. In both cases the patents were sustained. The Supreme Court could easily have upset him had it wanted to. Judge Hand testified at that Senate hearing in 1955[33] that "whether we were right in construing it [Section 103] as meaning that the old rules were to apply, remains to be seen. I hope the case will go up." From the viewpoint of the writers of the law, he was right!

In 1964, the Fourth Circuit Court of Appeals, which in 1954 had said that Section 103 merely codified the law, came to the conclusion, in *Marvel* v. *Bell*,[34] after reading a number of cases which "have undertaken to comprehensively set forth the standard of invention to be used as a test," that: "When the mass of verbiage has been distilled, however, we have little more to guide us than the test which is incorporated in Section 103 . . ."; and that the court should search for and apply the "objective criteria of [un]obviousness." Hopefully, the court will, in the future, uniformly *start* with the statute, ignoring the "mass of verbiage" it replaces. It seems a logical place to start, especially since it was intended to displace some of those cases in which the verbiage appears.

In 1964, the Sixth Circuit Court of Appeals, in *Monroe Auto Equipment Co.* v. *Heckethorn Mfg. Co.*,[35] said, "It is virtually a practical impossibility to define adequately that abstraction which we call invention,"[36] and then, in spite of that difficulty, said "we must have objective references and a place from which to start. For this we turn to the statute . . . Section 103." A very good place to start! But then the court came to a very unnecessary conclusion "that invention is synonymous with unobviousness. Thus to say that a device lacks invention and that it is obvious is to state the same legal proposition in two ways."[37] It concluded that

_____

[33]*Hearings on the American Patent System*, note 12, *supra*, at 120.
[34]330 F.2d 164, 141 USPQ 269 (1964).
[35]332 F.2d 406, 141 USPQ 549 (1964).
[36]The full quotation is:

It is virtually a practical impossibility to define adequately that abstraction which we call invention. Long ago the Supreme Court said: "The truth is the word cannot be defined in such a manner as to afford any substantial aid in determining whether a particular device involves an exercise of the inventive faculty or not. In a given case we may be able to say that there is invention of a very high order. In another we can see that there is lacking that impalpable something which distinguishes invention from simple mechanical skill." McClain v. Ortmayer, 141 U.S. 419, 427 [Nov. 2, 1891]. This court consistently has echoed this view. [Cases cited] *Id.* at p. 410, 141 USPQ at 553.
[37]A case was cited for this proposition, *In re* Jacoby, 50 C.C.P.A. 734, 309

while obviousness "does not begin to solve the problem," it "gives us a touchstone for the contextual meaning of invention." It also concluded that, in a patent case, decision is arrived at by three steps: a determination of what the prior art was, what the patentee has made, and whether it would have been obvious, viewing the prior art from the time just prior to when the patented device was made. That is just what Section 103 says! When the unobviousness question has been determined according to Section 103, there is nothing more to do and the question of "invention" can be forgotten.

Along with it can be forgotten the "complexities" of another issue wrestled with by the court in deciding whether "unobviousness" is a question of law or fact. Compare *Armour & Co. v. Wilson & Co.*, 274 F2d 143, 124 USPQ 115 (7th Cir. 1960). The presence or absence of "invention" before 1953 was always, in my judgement, the determination of an issue of public policy—what inventions *should* be patented. As such it is a "question of law." This policy has now been legislatively expressed in Section 103.

In Section 103 (see note 27 for text), the following potential *issues of fact* appear: (1) What are the *differences* between "the invention" and "the prior art"? (2) What is disclosed by the prior art presumed to have been available to the inventor? (3) What was the level of ordinary skill in the art at the time the invention was made? (4) Other fact issues relating to *circumstances* indicative of the presence or absence of obviousness, such as long-felt need, immediate copying, sudden displacement of existing practices or devices, difficulty of achievement, failure of others, etc.[38]

Once these *facts* have been assembled, there remains the *ultimate statutory requirement of unobviousness*, the third requirement for patentability, which becomes a matter of statutory *application* and as such must be a *question of law*. As the court

---

F.2d 513, 135 USPQ 317 (1962), in which the opinion was by the writer. The Patent Office Board of Appeals had said the claimed invention "must be unobvious and involve invention." In a footnote to a reluctant but needed quotation of that statement, the writer said:

> To add to the statement that it must be unobvious, as required by 35 U.S.C. 103, the further statement that it must "involve invention" is merely to state the same legal proposition in two different ways. It would seem to suffice to state it once, and that, preferably, in the words of the statute.

> It should be clear that this was intended to put the proposition, developed more forcefully in the present paper, as gently as possible and that it was *not* intended to suggest that "invention" and "unobviousness" as provided in Section 103 are alternative *equivalents* for determining patentability, which they are not.

[38]Such factors were frequently taken into account as objective criteria in determining "Invention."

concluded in the *Armour* case, *supra*, "The development of the factual content necessary to statutory construction is a question of fact." It may be *several* such questions, however. After the fact issues are settled, the determination of unobviousness is necessarily a legal conclusion arising out of the facts, pursuant to the statute—a question of law.[39]

The U. S. Court of Customs and Patent Appeals has been turning out a consistent stream of opinions, during the years since 1956 of which I have personal knowledge, strictly applying the obviousness formula of Section 103 to determine *patentability*, not the presence of "invention." Our court finds Section 103 very workable as a standard of patentability.

The decisions of the Court of Customs and Patent Appeals are slowly but surely causing the Patent Office to base its actions on the statutory provisions of Section 103. The results are beginning to show in the actions and board opinions we review. The Patent Office Academy trains patent examiners to apply Section 103. The Solicitor's Office writes its briefs in the language of the statute.

In discussing this subject, and urging that we should all stop talking about the "standard of invention," in view of Section 103, I have been asked, "What difference does it make?" That is a fair question which has to be answered.

The differences it will make—the reasons why we *must* learn to make this change—are these, among others:

—Until we stop talking about a "requirement for invention," it will never be clear that THE THIRD REQUIREMENT is that stated in Section 103 *and no other*; that when 103 has been complied with, there is no further and different requirement called "invention"; that compliance with 103 is the policy judgment of Congress on how to bring the invention within the constitutional purpose.

—Because looking for the presence of "invention" in addition to compliance with Section 103 defeats the legislative purpose.

---

[39]The Armour case concluded (1960), in the separate opinion devoted to the fact or. law question, that after the facts were settled, "We examine the *standard of invention* applied to these facts as a question of law." (My emphasis.) But under Section 103 there is no "standard of invention." The directive of the statute is to determine whether the invention as a whole "would have been obvious" on the basis of the *differences*, the *ordinary* skill, and as of the *time* of invention. *These* are the factors, and these alone, by which courts are to determine the existence of the third requirement. Note that it is not the obviousness of the differences which must be decided but the obviousness of the *invention*. Leastwise, that is what the statute provides. See 1966 Supreme Court decisions cited in note 19, *supra*.

—Because talking about unobviousness and "invention" as different things leads to weird and confused thinking.

—Because testing patentability by the presence of "invention" gives judges and the Patent Office too much freedom to decide patentability of new and useful inventions on the basis of a personal view as to what *should* be patentable, instead of accepting the view of the legislature on that question of national policy.

—Because it will get all those concerned with the administration of the patent system—Patent Office, courts, and the bar—speaking the same language, a *sine qua non* to the communication of intelligence.

—Because you cannot use "invention" as both an abstract noun and a concrete noun in the same statute or opinion without confusion. The invention is the *thing* that has been produced by the "inventor." There will be muddy thought as long as one has to say: this invention (in the concrete sense) is unpatentable because it is not an invention (in the abstract sense).

—Because it will do more than anything else I can think of to bring about that long-sought-for greater uniformity of opinion on patentability.

—Because it makes the prerequisites to patentability intelligible.

Lay Comments on the
Proposed Patent Law

LAWRENCE R. HAFSTAD

We have all long been interested in the U.S. patent system and no little concerned that it should seem to be under attack. Its purpose, as well as its effectiveness, is being questioned, and claims are made that conditions are now so changed that the patent law as we know it is obsolete. I read that the law has not been changed for 130 years, and this is given as a need for a basic overhaul. While need for changes may be indicated, this specific argument leaves me cold. Our Constitution is considerably older than our patent system, and I am tempted to add that the Ten Commandments are a lot older than either. What endures must contain some element of good, and in my mind this should be a symptom of strength, not of weakness.

As this group is well aware, one can find roots of the patent system in reports on ancient Greece, in the patents to Galileo and others during the Italian renaissance, and in the Tudor monopolies in Great Britain. But it is too often overlooked that in the Colonial period, the Colonies granted a relatively large number of patents, and, in fact, by the time of the Revolution the patent activity in the Colonies was very substantial. We cannot perhaps claim to have originated the patent system, but there is much to support an argument that the Colonies created a new and independent center for the growth of the patent concept.

Our first patent act, adopted in 1790, was much more of an innovation than is sometimes recognized. It led the first British patent act by many years. It is the first specific statute to start an enduring patent system. It said that anyone complying with the statutory terms had a right to a patent—a vital and basic change from the concept of the royal grant made by the British Crown as a matter of favor.

While there is much to view in the U.S. patent system as representing the results of an economy and of political thinking that was independent and leading in its day, we must not belittle what other countries have done. Indeed, depending on how one wants

EDITOR'S NOTE: Dr. Hafstad presented this paper upon his acceptance of The PTC Research Institute's Charles F. Kettering Award on June 22, 1967. (*IDEA*, Vol. 11, Conference No. 1967.) The author's postscript is printed herewith.

to argue the history, some of them may lay claim to earlier ante-
cedents than our own. At the very least, I suggest that those who
so lightly assume that the world should adopt our particular system should bear in mind that—while we have a case to be proud
of—we did not originate patents, and others may have some good
ideas, too.

If we ignore the extremists, there is agreement that some system of incentives is desirable. Even the Russians have found that
out. The argument really is about the details of the system which
will be most effective at least cost. Here I wish to emphasize that I
speak not as a professional expert in this field, but as a concerned
and interested amateur. My grown life has been spent not in wor-
rying about patents, but in learning how to bring to bear on real
social problems the reservoir of knowledge created by, or which
can be created by, science. For this reason, as I talk about patents
and patent law, I can only give my impressions, based on my frequent but only incidental contact with this field.

In recent months we have all been exposed to the pros and
cons of the proposed new patent law. The objectives are unassailable—namely, (1) to raise the quality and reliability of U.S. patents, (2) to reduce the time and expense of obtaining and protecting a patent, and (3) to speed public disclosure of scientific and
technological information.

In the fine print, however, and in the discussions, one encounters confusing questions of both procedure and policy. There is lip
service to the underlying need to provide incentive for the actual
inventor, but the real worry is all about the excessive work load
for the Patent Office; whether title to inventions from government
R&D should go to the government or a contractor; and the inherent iniquity of any monopoly, even one created by the government
itself. Finally, there is much concern about the patent rights of
the professionally employed inventor as against that of his employer, whether in private industry or in government. I will comment on these matters later.

I have been interested in patents all my life, for as a child I
had older brothers who were enthusiastic but unsuccessful basement inventors. Encouraged by patent lawyers, they got patents
all right, but made no sales! I can say from first hand observation
where much of the overload of the patent system comes from.

Since those days I have been interested in reading all I could
about patents. I have found it instructive but confusing to peruse
the literature, for while the same words—such as the word "invention"—are used repeatedly, the game is to guess from the context

in which the word is used what that particular author really meant by his use of the word. When sociologists and economists write about inventions and how they are made and laboratories and how they operate, I find it hard to recognize their description of a field in which I have spent most of my life.

I am reminded of an anecdote related by my favorite math professor at Johns Hopkins in my student days. He was warning us that mathematicians were usually socially unpopular, and he had a very plausible explanation. Social conversation, he reminded us, was like a game of tossing a small balloon from one person to another. Each makes some polite remark and passes the conversational lead to a neighbor. When the conversation reaches the mathematician, he is apt to ask rudely, "Will you please define your terms?" This is equivalent to poking a pin in the balloon and completely ruins the game.

In the patent law discussions I've been reading, a little more mathematical precision in definitions would be most useful. I could give you many examples, but one will make the point. In a recent article the proponents of government ownership of title to inventions are said to "view the alternative as analogous to building a bridge with government funds and then turning it and the toll rights over to the contractor." Here the word "invention" is clearly taken to mean the completed, commercially-proven entity, quite contrary to the usual meaning of the word as referring to conception alone—but then perhaps the misinterpretation is deliberate!

In reading on this subject it is especially necessary to consider the source and to allow for the motivations of the authors. The patent lawyers and other professionals in the field certainly know the meanings of their use of the words, but authors distort meanings in accord with their emotional bent. There is also some vested interest in the confusion in terms, even for the "pros." From the rich collection of quotes in Gilfillan, for example, we can find a statement that patent litigation has become a game . . . and "the better the player, the more complicated and uncertain he likes the game to be, and the more likely the result is to be a triumph of the skill of counsel rather than a determination of the real merit of the patent or of the defenses."[1] In contrast to engineers, many lawyers are not problem solvers—they are paid to be argument winners! I cite the current United Nations debates as evidence.

The above comments are made to emphasize the distinction

---

[1] S. C. Gillfillan, *Invention and the Patent System*, Report for Joint Economic Committee, 88th Cong., 2d Sess. (Washington: G.P.O., December 1964).

and the wide gap between an invention and a successful commercial product. This distinction is basic to much of the current controversy. In recent professional R&D literature, invention is recognized to be a first step in the process of innovation. Further, it is recognized to be a small step in most cases. In the recent Charpie report, "invention" is estimated to represent not more than 5 percent to 15 percent of the cost of innovation.[2] There is really a long row to hoe between "invention"—which for this use may be taken as meaning proven technical feasibility of a novel potentially useful device or process—and commercial application, let alone commercial financial success. Even within a single company, and for people with great prestige and influence, innovation is recognized as being an even tougher job than invention. To quote C. F. Kettering, "[The] greatest durability contest in the world is trying to get a new idea into a factory."

In my personal opinion much of the current controversy about our patent system arises because this recognition of the distinction between invention and innovation is at odds with our popular American folklore and mythology, and the hopes and dreams of individual inventors. Many patent lawyers may disagree with this statement, but patent lawyers talk mainly to each other and draw their conclusions from a highly unrepresentative sample. As the American dream has it, based on conditions a century ago, the lone basement or backyard inventor gets a simple, novel, but revolutionary idea, like putting a wiggle in the hairpin wire, gets a patent, and his fortune is made. In such simple cases invention and innovation are synonymous. In this day and age, however, especially for industrial applications based on modern science, most inventions involve much more sophisticated ideas. It is not so much that the inventive process itself has changed, as that the innovation component of the overall process is assuming a continually increasing role. Invention is still absolutely essential, for this triggers the rest of the process, but we now need at least equal incentive for innovation in addition. This is an unpleasant fact of life which our liberals find it convenient to ignore. To quote H. L. Nieburg,[3] himself certainly no reactionary: "The small band of Liberals that opposes 'give-aways' fails to grasp the inefficacy of the solution proposed (strict public title) to solve the problems which it vividly describes."

Before giving my comments on the proposed law itself, I

---

[2]*Technological Innovation: Its Environment and Management*, Panel on Invention and Innovation, Technical Advisory Board, Department of Commerce. (Washington: G.P.O.).

[3]H.L. Nieburg, *In the Name of Science* (Quadrangle Books, 1966).

would like to discuss a bit more some of the problem areas with which the law seems to concern itself.

The basic question of "monopoly"—which is, after all, what is created by a patent—I will pass quickly, for it is outside my area of competence. As a layman I assume it is the government's business to devise equitable rules for the game to be played by our competing free enterprise activities, and that the government will, further, police the activities to prevent cheating.

The question of government title to government-financed inventions is one with which I have had considerable experience, and this may make my impressions in this area of some value.

I would like first to talk about the situation with respect to the Atomic Energy Law, where the government holds all titles, and then the practice at the Department of Defense where there is more flexibility.

Having been an "atom smasher" by trade since 1928, I am personally aware of the step-wise development of the technology in this field, both prior to and during the secrecy period of World War II. I was indirectly involved during the formulation of the McMahon Act, and after the war served with the AEC in administering many contracts under the patent provisions of the 1946 Act.

To be candid, though my basic bias is that of a free enterpriser, I had no difficulty in either accepting or defending the policy of government title to patents, even those emerging from embryonic privately financed research. Here, in addition to the overwhelming taxpayer equity in the technology, where an entire new industry was created at government expense, there were the urgent national security arguments.

My experience with the Department of Defense patent policy has led to quite different conclusions. I served in the Pentagon for several years under James Forrestal and Vannevar Bush as Executive Secretary of the Research and Development Board. At about that time I was also Chairman of the then Interdepartmental Committee on Science, wherein we made one of the early determined efforts to get a uniform patent policy throughout the government. This experience gave me an appreciation of the number and diversity of the problems to be met in an activity as large and ramified as that of the United States government.

In military procurement it has long been traditional to give title for patents to the contractor, retaining royalty-free use for the government. This policy has always worked well through the years, for with the extra carrot of patent rights, the contractor could and would assign his best and most experienced men, as well as his backlog of technology, to the solution of any urgent military problem. No real conflict of interest from either direction arose as long as the military business for any company was small compared to the civilian business which was carried on by that company.

It is this picture that has changed since World War II, with the enormous expansion in government procurement and expenditures, especially in the R&D area. Now with many companies concerning themselves primarily with sales to the government and only incidentally to the civilian segment of the economy, it is understandable that the question of who should get title should be raised, since in many cases the government is already paying for the development as well as the product.

The series of recent bills relating to patent law in Congress address themselves to this problem. The wording of these bills is technical, but the intent (for example of McClellan S. 1809) can be adequately indicated for our purpose here by a paraphrase from a recent magazine article:[4]

For activities financed by the government this bill "provides that the government usually shall acquire the principal rights in inventions: (1) made during contracts whose purpose directly concerns public health, welfare or safety; (2) intended to develop an item intended for commercial use by the general public; or (3) in a field of science or technology where there has been little experience outside of work funded by the government."

These principles and conditions seem eminently sound as far as the equities in the inventions themselves are concerned. As stated above, it is part of American folklore that a patent represents a path to riches since it provides a monopoly on manufacture and sale of the product. In fact, this is still true for simple items such as hula-hoops, plastic toys, household gadgetry, et cetera. But these are not the kinds of inventions that come out of defense technology. In my opinion the key question is, "What happens next *after* the patent is turned over to the public?" If, when an invention financed by the government is turned over to the public, several manufacturers immediately start production and begin to compete for lower price—then the public is served and public-title approach is a success. If, on the other hand, the manufacturers shun the patent since they no longer have any hope of protecting their chance of recovering high development or tooling costs—then

---

[4]*Scientific Research*, Vol. 2, No. 4 (April 1967), p. 43.

the high sounding operation of "giving the patent to the public" becomes a completely useless gesture, regardless of its political appeal. In fact, it is worse than useless; it is negative. By "giving the patent to the public" in such instances, it ensures that no manufacturer can pick it up, and the public will not receive its benefit in the marketplace.

Based on my experience in the government, the wide variety of cases makes for exceptions to any fixed rule.

In the Pentagon situation the R&D program is so large and diverse that, by selection of examples, a case can be made for either government or contractor ownership of title. There can be cases where new technology is developed entirely at government expense, with automatic fall-out in the civilian economy. At the other extreme there can be cases where technology developed completely at private expense is brought to bear on urgent military problems.

The most recent review of this problem area led to the Kennedy Memorandum and Statement of Policy of 1963. This has proven to be realistic in that it provides flexibility for the responsible administrators to protect the government's interest but yet be sensitive to the just deserts of contractors in specific situations. Any residual problems that have been experienced have been more in the carrying out than with the intent or authority involved in this policy.

The possibilities of give-aways are in any case probably greatly exaggerated. Government developments usually come in the military or space "cost-is-no-object" category, and much further development is needed before products can compete in the extremely cost-conscious civilian market. On balance, the public is more likely to profit in the long run from a policy encouraging the further development for the civilian market, rather than one which tends to freeze a development at the governmental cost level. Here, as in many cases, the time-proven adage applies that "everybody's business is nobody's business."

For this reason I feel that the burden of proof should be on the government to show that the public would really profit in some manner by a patent not given to the contractor.

Another of the areas of major controversy, according to current literature, is that involving the individual inventor and his incentives and rights. As one extreme we can read that under modern conditions all inventions are team inventions, so that the individual inventor and the patent system are no longer needed. This is indeed patent nonsense! The individual inventor is still as important as ever. Xerography by Carlson and the electrolytic capacitor by Ruben are examples of such contributions made well after the era of large-scale laboratory R&D was begun. Creativity is a very personal thing, and no matter how large the laboratory, the "invention" or contribution to the invention is always made by some individual. The team does not make the invention; it is made by a member of the team. For those of us in the business of research and development I think this is axiomatic.

I have always had the uncomfortable feeling that lawyers know all about patents except how they are made, or as I would prefer to express it—how they come about. According to my observations, the key idea emerges or crystallizes out of a slow process of trial and error with respect to many ideas. There may be the "flash of genius" experience frequently cited in patent literature, and the feeling of elation when the key idea is finally recognized as a path to success. The invention, however, is rarely born full blown—so that by noting the day and time, calling a witness and writing furiously in a note book, the exact nature and time of the invention can be recorded for all of posterity. The key idea emerges from among a host of other ideas; it does not descend suddenly out of a clear sky like a bolt from the blue.

For an invention to be made there is invariably a need, or a problem to be solved. Such a need will normally be attacked by many people using great skill and competence and state-of-the-art techniques. Many technical problems yield to this approach, without ever reaching the invention stage. Quoting Judge Hand: Nothing is an invention which is the product of "the slow but inevitable progress . . . through trial and error" and of "the exercise of persistent and intelligent search for improvement." It is when this conventional approach reaches an impasse or at least obviously diminishing returns that the stage is set for an invention.

At this point each individual concerned begins to tell himself that there must be a better way, and begins to generate ideas for new approaches to the problem. These ideas are then filtered for practicality, first by the individual and then further by the group if the individual is a member of a team. Most of the ideas go by the board, but in rare cases a germ of an idea emerges with which no obvious fault can be found. With further careful nurturing, this idea begins to take form as promising a qualitatively different approach to the solution of the original problem. It can only then begin to be recognized as an invention—or as a quantum jump or breakthrough, in more recent vernacular. No matter how large the organization, some certain individual had the key idea and can at this point be established as the inventor with at most a few other individuals as contributors.

As a corollary to the above continuous and sequential process of invention (as contrasted with the isolated step-function concept which would be more conveniently administered by the Patent Office), it is worth emphasizing here that it follows that a claim for an early date for an invention can always be made if the criteria for proven feasibility are correspondingly reduced. I will mention this again later.

In addition to the controversy as to whether inventions are made by individuals or by a team, there is the question of how to reward inventors who choose to work as part of a team. It is true that this was not visualized in the early days when the patent system was devised, and the patent system is certainly supposed to give incentive to the potentially creative individual to go ahead and create.

Does our present patent system provide adequate incentive for an inventor to invent when he is part of a large team?

I cannot presume to answer this very fundamental question, but can only give my impressions. First, let me say that I have been signing papers giving patent rights to some employer or other since 1940 when I left work in pure science. I have never felt "forced" to sign these papers, as current liberal writings never miss an opportunity to imply. Neither threats nor torture were used that I can remember, and to the best of my knowledge I wasn't drugged. Then why did I sign?

I believe the answer is that, for me as for most engineers, I like to consider myself a professional problem solver. The problems may or may not involve the need for inventions, but if they should, I feel as competent to invent as the next man. So many technical problems exist which do not involve inventions that as a "pro" I personally have preferred to work as a problem solver on a salary, with invention being incidental, rather than as a free lancer seeking riches from a single invention.

Some people just seem to want to work on something difficult, challenging, and socially significant—problems too large for attack by a single individual. The hope is to make a contribution toward the overall solution which will result in the recognition and approval of one's peers. In these large affairs many kinds of problems arise and many different kinds of people are needed—and we are all problem solvers. The people making the inventions are making contributions with their particular expertise, as professionals, just as is each other member of the overall group. If the overall group is successful, each member is or should be rewarded—by money, if the operation is commercial, by personal satisfaction in addition if it is in the national interest.

A comparison might be instructive. Let us compare a laboratory to a baseball team, with the inventor analogous to a home run hitter. The latter could conceivably be paid a fixed amount for each home run, with even a bonus for a game-winning home run. No one seems to feel that home run hitters are abused, however, for working on a salary and getting salary increases and bonuses as rewards for good performance. The professional inventor whether in industry or in government is similarly rewarded, and is even more free than the baseball player to seek a new employer if he has reason to feel inadequately appreciated.

The team approach to invention is an effective method for spreading very large risks for very large rewards. In this sense it is no different from other forms of insurance. The inventor who chooses to "go-it-alone" is the reciprocal of the home owner who chooses not to insure his house. The inventor accepts a long period of low returns in the expectation of high rewards later; the home owner saves a small premium over a long period of time and hopes to avoid the possible conflagration at some future time.

This is the way it is—but this is not the way American folklore has it. From what I read, the employed inventor "alienates his stake in possible patents, et cetera, et cetera. . . ." The implication is that his rights are usurped by management and that the incentive to invent intended by the patent system for the individual is no longer effective. However, so long as the patent system provides the incentive for management to encourage its employees to invent, what has been lost?

It is the business of management to function in such a manner that the productivity of "n" people working together is greater than the productivity of "n" people working as individuals. I like to call it introducing drift or direction into what would otherwise be Brownian motion. Profit is the index or measure of the effectiveness with which management does its job. Management has, therefore, every incentive for so arranging the working conditions of its technical employees as to encourage invention. In fact, the competition between industrial laboratories is specifically that of maximizing the output of useful technology and therefore of profitable inventions per dollar expended for research.

The myths, however, persist. One of the first things I was able to do when joining General Motors a few years ago was to satisfy myself directly regarding the persistent myths that steam-powered cars were known to be better than gas-engine powered cars but were held back for commercial reasons—that 40-mile-per-gallon carburetors had been patented and were suppressed to prevent reduction in sales of gasoline—and so forth. I can add my observation to that of others that the suppressed invention is most certainly a myth.[5] In fact, my experience with big industry has found it to lean quite in the opposite direction. On numerous occasions when inventions are made which the corporation chooses not to exploit, the patent rights are transferred or licensed to the inventor, who then (often with associates) resigns from the corporation as a "spin-off" and starts a small business of his own. In the GM laboratories this has occurred mainly in connection with instruments which were developed for specific uses in the business, but which for commercial reasons the corporation did not wish to manufacture.

Based on the above impressions, I would like to give my reaction to some of the more critical aspects of the proposed new patent law. Most important to me is the attempt to seek compatibility with other Free World patent systems. Modern communications have made the world shrink dramatically. This was brought home to me some time ago when I read the following comparison: The horse and buggy of a generation or two ago permitted travel at say six miles per hour. The 707 jet plane goes 600 miles per hour. When we apply this factor of one hundred to distance, the world is no longer 25,000 miles in circumference, but only 250! It is no longer 8,000 miles in diameter, but only 80! From now on, privacy, independence, sovereignty, and "isolation" are going to be hard indeed to come by.

As one who is convinced that the only way to defeat Communism is to outperform it, I would urge that every effort be made to combine the best features of all of the several Free World patent systems, and that the emphasis should be on the effectiveness of the system rather than on the convenience of control. No doubt the President's Commission did make some study of these matters, especially taking into account European experience. But in recommending a change to the "first-to-file" concept the two main justifications given seem to be (1) convenience for the Patent Office and (2) the tacit assumption that "the first to file is more apt to be the inventor who first appreciated the worth of the invention and promptly acted to make the invention available to the public."

---

[5]Gilfillan, note 1, *supra*, p. 98.

In my opinion the first of these should not be controlling and the second argument is certainly not convincing.

In my reading in this area I stumble again, as I stated in the beginning of my talk, on a lack of definition of words. First to file, O.K.—but first to file what? This is the critical point. How is the potential flood of half-baked ideas to be controlled?

To those of us working in the field it has finally become obvious that an invention must be more than a bright idea—it must be a feasible and useful device or process. To the general public it is still merely a bright idea. In my company we have a large activity called the New Devices Section in our Engineering Staff, whose sole duty it is to handle the bright ideas that we all get by mail. They arrive at the rate of 700 per month and all must be processed and answered as a matter of business courtesy, as well as screened for the rare useful nuggets for which we might wish to negotiate licensing agreements.

Over my desk recently have come letters noting that the limitation on the electric car lies in the constantly depleting battery, and suggesting a very simple solution—namely, to use a generator (which never wears out!)—instead of the battery!

On the face of it this suggestion is so preposterous as to be amusing. However, in all seriousness there is the germ of an idea here. A hybrid car with a small prime mover running continuously, and through a generator charging a battery, which in turn provides power for the wheels, is indeed a possibility for future low-smog cars. Actually many companies including GM are seriously exploring this possibility. The problem is not to conceive of a combination which can work. Many combinations are entirely feasible. The problem is to devise one which is really practicable and economical. For this, much experimental work is required.

Now suppose our enthusiastic inventor continues to follow developments in the literature and elsewhere, and files for a series of paper patents approaching closer and closer to technical feasibility. At some point long before the experimental work necessary to prove commercial practicality is finished, a first-to-file patent may be granted to our paper inventor. Is he to receive royalties from other inventors or companies who took the time and trouble for actual reduction to practice? Would it be just that the actual inventor should be denied the right to use the results of his own extensive work by someone who had done much less much later? On the other hand should it really be necessary for every inventor who can think up a feasible combination of prime mover, generator, and battery to file promptly for a patent? Twenty years ago we used to say that every time three engineers got together with four bottles of beer a new guided missile was born. Unless more safeguards for the first-to-file procedure are revealed than have so far been explained, I would predict that the number of claims for inventions for low-smog cars alone might quickly approach infinity.

Certainly the purpose of our patent system should be to encourage and reward the true inventor, and not the purveyor of unproven paper proposals. "First to file" seems to substitute appearance for substance. It is not surprising that the patent community is resisting the proposed change—although it is both interesting and significant that in this case the large companies (traditionally accused of being most reactionary) are less inclined to raise objections than small business and independent patent lawyers. While the difference of opinion is real, to me it is reassuring for the long run that any conflict between the U.S. and European patent systems is not like the difference between the English and the metric systems, completely irreconcilable.

Compromises should be possible, and with further discussion and debate, opposition may well be reduced to a point where some accommodation to a system for world-wide use may become possible. Complete conformity is unnecessary to genuine and effective international cooperation. To illustrate, there may be compulsory licensing in one country and not in another without preventing effective interaction. Scholarly studies to this end might well be a project for the Research Institute to undertake, for considerable give and take will be involved and arguments more persuasive than that of convenience will be required.

On the question of the overload of the Patent Office, as a layman I do not feel competent to make suggestions. It seems clear that some procedural change might be possible to reduce the amount of work spent on unimportant claims. Since vested interests are involved, this is as much a political as a technical matter. Again, a scholarly study by an objective group would seem to be indicated. In matters of this kind it is often useful to take steps to separate carefully the question of what *ought* to be done from the questions of what *can* be done.

In conclusion and in summary, I wish to be on record that I feel that our present patent system and procedure has served us well and promises to continue to do so. Evolutionary changes certainly may prove to be desirable but even such changes should be made with due caution. The overall objective must be to handle fewer and more significant claims more justly—rather than a high

378   N<small>URTURING</small> N<small>EW</small> I<small>DEAS</small>

volume of weak claims more conveniently. Compared to other activities on which much government money is now being spent, the cost-effectiveness of our patent system, measured in returns to the economy and therefore to the tax-paying citizen, is very high indeed.

Author's Postcript—

After the preparation of this paper, a number of bills were introduced in the Senate and the House of Representatives as alternates to the 1967 Patent Reform Act. These include S. 1691 (Dodd), S. 2164 (Yarborough/Tower), S. 2597 (Dirksen), H.R. 7454 (Giamo), H.R. 10006 (Bush), and H.R. 11447 (Broyhill). I leave patent law details of these bills for discussion by the patent experts. The fact that there are these various alternatives to the 1967 Patent Reform Act, and particularly that many of them appear to retain the first-to-invent concept and other traditional features of the American patent system, suggests that there are ways to achieve patent law revision without the herioc surgery involved in the 1967 Patent Reform Act.

Also, after the preparation of this paper, some testimony was given in the Congress to the effect that the 1967 Patent Reform Act was especially desired by large industrial concerns. In my opinion, large concerns having extensive international operations can be expected to support steps toward a more uniform international system. However, the great majority of large concerns, as well as smaller concerns, while recognizing the advantages of uniformity, I am sure, really prefer the traditional American patent system, which has served us so well.

Proposed Legislation Deriving From Presidential Commission's Report

JOSEPH GRAY JACKSON

Patent Reform Bills S. 1042 and H.R. 5924 flow from suggestions made by the President's Commission on the Patent System. The following radical changes are at the heart of this proposed legislation:

(1) The grace period, by which it is possible to file a U.S. patent application after the subject matter of the invention has been in public use or on sale within the United States, or has been published anywhere, will be repealed so that a patent application will have to be filed before public use, sale, or publication.

(2) Priority will be entirely on the basis of first-to-file, rather than first-to-invent, so that a race to the Patent Office will be instituted.

(3) Interferences by which priority contests are now determined will be discontinued.

These proposals are not calculated to achieve the objectives of the President's Commission, but actually oppose these objectives as follows:

(1) Instead of raising the quality of a patent application, they will lower the quality because of the urge to file immediately rather than prepare a careful patent application.

(2) The pendency of a patent application will be lengthened by the requirement in the bill that one year be available after filing a preliminary application within which to file more preliminary applications and then a complete application.

(3) While the President's Commission wants to encourage immediate disclosure, this will delay disclosure because:

(a) It will delay sale, since sale cannot be accomplished before filing. At the present time, judging by a sampling obtained by Barkev S. Sanders, of The PTC Research Institute, about 40 percent of the inventions are put on sale before filing in the United States, often for the purpose of market testing.

(b) This will delay publication and will undoubtedly embar-

EDITOR'S NOTE: This paper and the following three were presented at a conference conducted by The PTC Research Institute on June 22-23, 1967. (*IDEA*, Vol. 11, Conference No. 1967.) Postscripts by Mr. Mossinghoff and by Mr. Parry appear with their respective papers.

rass the scientific community, since many scientists prefer to publish papers in scientific journals before filing in the United States.

(c) This will also delay public use. Now many inventors prefer to put their inventions in public use before filing, in order to discover and correct difficulties in operation before filing.

(4) The proposed law will increase the expense. The filing of preliminary applications alone will be expensive, since, as pointed out by Howard K. Nason of the President's Commission, it will be necessary to prepare preliminary applications with all the attention to formalities necessary in a complete application (except for the claims), as the preliminary application must be relied on to antedate publications, public uses and sales. They will be a booby trap for uninformed inventors who file preliminary applications which they have themselves prepared, in this respect resembling caveats which were abolished in 1910.

(5) One of the major purposes of the President's Commission was to make United States law compatible with foreign law. This fails in that respect also. The laws of major foreign countries differ widely between countries which examine patent applications and countries which merely register them. The proposed law bears some relation to the law in countries like France, Italy and Western Germany, but it fails to include protections which are present even in these laws, such as the right of prior user and the personal grace period in force in West Germany.

(6) Another objective of the President's Commission is to keep up with exploding technology. The proposed law hinders this objective because one must take time to compare a complete application with possibly three or four preliminary applications to know what its effective date is.

Thus the proposed law will impose on the inventor an intolerable burden of activity. Within one year after he files his first preliminary application, he will have to do each of the following things:

(1) File preliminaries on all further developments and improvements since he cannot rely on priority except from preliminary applications.

(2) Complete tests necessary for the complete application.

(3) Make market tests required to determine whether it is worthwhile to file the complete application.

(4) Conduct exhibits (except for special international exhibits which give him an exception from the first-to-file rule).

(5) Aid his attorney in drafting, and finance the filing of a complete application.

(6) Get special licenses for foreign filing, since licenses will no longer issue automatically as at present.

(7) File all foreign convention cases.

All these things must be done in this one-year period, even though the American Chemical Society says that you cannot complete a sophisticated chemical application within one year.

Radical changes in plant operation will result from these provisions of the proposed law. Notwithstanding that many companies now believe that it is good public relations to permit visitors to go through their plants, every plant will have to operate like an armed camp, with exclusion of visitors.

One of the national disgraces, commercial espionage, will become more widespread, and spoiling publications by competitors to bar the inventor from patenting will become general. Even an honest person's making an improvement and filing first on that improvement will prevent patenting of the basic invention.

Is it any wonder, therefore, that the overwhelming majority of the relevant informed public is against these provisions?

Another feature of the proposed law which will disastrously increase the cost of obtaining and litigating patents is world-wide prior art in respect to commercial use. Contrary to what one would think from casual inspection of the Commission's Report, world-wide commercial use is in vogue in only a minority of countries as follows:

France	Portugal
Italy	Spain
Mexico (after one year)	Sweden

On the other hand the following countries apply national boundaries in respect to commercial use:

Australia	Finland	New Zealand
Austria	West Germany	Republic of South Africa
Belgium	Great Britain	United States
Canada	Ireland	Norway
Denmark	Japan	Switzerland

Three important areas with which the Commission did not deal, but which urgently require attention, are:

(1) Claims

(2) Disclosure

(3) Petty patents

There is one aspect of the proposed legislation which is widely applauded. This permits filing by the assignee. This will lower the cost because it will not be necessary to file separate applications for employees' inventions because of difference in inventorship, and it will avoid great resentment in determining who are the inventors. Many needless questions of double patenting will be avoided.

Another provision which I strongly favor is early publication of patent applications. This permits the filing of oppositions and goes hand in hand with a cancellation procedure. To the extent that these procedures are used, they will raise the quality of patents. Regrettably, however, these features plus preliminary applications will greatly increase the cost. While in Dallas recently I talked to two corporate patent executives about cost estimates for operation under the proposed law. One told me that costs would be 150 percent of the present level, and another thought they would be 200 percent. Several corporate patent executives have since agreed with these views. There is one area in the proposed law which I personally favor, though I am in a minority of less than 5 percent. I would like to see a limited experiment on deferred examination. And I mean limited! One chemical, one electrical, and one mechanical class should be selected, and the experiment should be conducted only on the subject matter in these classes for a period of at least 25 years, so that we can draw conclusions after the first group of patents has expired. This would permit an examiner to concentrate on urgent cases.

The Commission has made a whole series of unwise proposals dealing with minor irritants in the Patent Office. One is that a terminal disclaimer should no longer help in cutting the Gordian knot on double patenting. Another is that no longer can mistakes be corrected by broadened reissue. In this respect the Commission has ignored the saving effect of intervening rights. A third unwise proposal is that a cutoff date be provided for continuation-in-part applications. This assures, as the American Chemical Society has pointed out, that the patent will include less-advanced technology.

The nadir of this group of proposals (the one that rings the bell) is the suggestion of appealing from the five-judge Court of Customs and Patent Appeals to the three-judge Court of Appeals for the District of Columbia. I have a suggestion in this respect. Both courts can sit together and hear one appellate argument, the Court of Customs and Patent Appeals can then render its decision, and the Court of Appeals for the District of Columbia can then reverse it. In a single word, this is superjudgegation. You say that my proposal is nonsense, and I agree, but I point out that the proposal of the Commission is equally arrant nonsense. This would add to the already heavy expense of obtaining a patent.

Another proposal by the Commission that seems to follow its pattern of favoring the large corporation and hurting the small inventor is that computer programs should not be patentable. A computer program of course is something which can be produced by a lone inventor. The provision in the proposed law, Section 106, is so broad as to render unpatentable all cams, gearing, jacquards, and other control mechanism. This proposal by the President's Commission is coupled with the irresponsible suggestion to repeal the patent law on designs and plants.

Thus in summary the proposed legislation will have a disastrous impact on the U.S. patent system by concentrating patents in large corporations, and impeding the individual inventor who makes most of the startling new contributions. If enacted, it will set the patent system back many years. I say this without hesitation, notwithstanding that there are many trivial good features in the proposed law.

Fortunately, indications are that among sophisticated people, only an insignificant minority favors the new law.

You may ask how it is possible that the fine, capable men on the Commission came up with such unfortunate proposals. The answer is, I believe, that they are mainly by experience knowledgeable in problems of government and large corporations, with inadequate representation of small inventors and small companies. And let's face it, most of them do not know much about the subject.

Proposed Patent Reform Act*

GERALD J. MOSSINGHOFF

In the title of this session the question is asked—I assume not rhetorically—"Will [the] Proposed Legislation Deriving from the Report of the President's Commission Meet the Challenge?"

Appropriately, this leaves it to the individual speakers not only to provide their answers to the question but, perhaps more significantly, to define the scope and boundaries of the challenge which must be met. In this context, I can answer the question positively and unequivocally: The Patent Reform Bill will meet the challenge; and no one can intelligently disagree with me—at least until I define what I view the challenge to be.

A major premise of the Presidential Commission in shaping its recommendations, and a major premise of the Johnson Administration in translating these recommendations into a legislative proposal, is the conclusion that the protection of intellectual property is fundamental to our free enterprise economic and political system. A corollary of this is that if systems protecting intellectual property can be strengthened internationally, the type of economic and political system in which we believe will be correspondingly strengthened.

Another premise underlying the Commission's recommendations is that the effective protection of intellectual property across national boundaries will have an increasingly significant and beneficial impact on the pattern of this country's international trade.

Technological change affects international trade in many ways. It permits us to replace decreasing exports in low-technology products with increasing exports in high-technology products. A recent study of the Secretary of Commerce's Advisory Panel on Invention and Innovation demonstrated this in relation to this country's exports of yarns and fabrics. In 1956, we exported $187 million of cotton and wool, low-technology products, as compared with only $125 million of these products exported in 1965, a decrease of $62 million. During this same period, however, the exports of high-technology synthetic fibers increased from $158 million to $241 million, resulting in a net *gain* in exports of yarns

*See covering Editor's Note, p. 379.

384

and fabrics by the United States of over $20 million during the ten-year period.

An element of this country's international balance of payments is what is sometimes called the "technological" balance of payments. This international account reflects payments for technical know-how, data and patent royalties. In general, this "technological" balance of payments is favorable to the United States. For example, a study of the Organization for Economic Cooperation and Development (OECD) determined that in 1961 there was a balance favorable to the United States of $514 million; during this year we received $577 million in payment for technical know-how, patent licenses, data, etc., while paying out only $63 million to other countries. There was no attempt to determine the amount either paid or received for patent licenses alone; but patent license agreements are generally regarded as an effective, and sometimes indispensable, vehicle for the interchange of technical data and know-how across national borders. Accordingly, if the "technological" balance of payments is to remain in our favor, it is important that U.S. businessmen and inventors obtain patent protection on their inventions in other countries.

The United States, of course, does not have a monopoly on the creation of new technology or its exploitation commercially. For example, while transistor technology originated in the United States, and although this country sold over $10 million worth of transistor radios in world markets in 1966, during this same year we imported $94 million worth of transistor radios from Japan alone. In this same context, no one would doubt the benefits to the U.S. economy resulting from the discovery and use of superconductivity by Kamerling Onnes, the Dutch Nobel Laureate; or in the earlier era, of antennas of the type invented by Professor Yagi of Japan. If patents serve as an important incentive to the development, exploitation and marketing of an invention—and I am convinced they do—making the U.S. patent system more accessible to foreign applicants would necessarily stimulate the use and development of valuable foreign technology in this country.

This whole area of the popularized "technology gap," the "technological" balance of payments and the efforts toward export expansion is highly complex, involving economic, social and political considerations as yet not precisely defined. There is general agreement, however, that to serve as a stimulus to international trade and lead to an improved standard of living in all countries of the world, the legal systems protecting new technology should facilitate the transfer of this new technology across national borders, while at the same time provide adequate protection and incentives for the creators of the new technology.

The first aspect of the "challenge" which must be met, therefore, is to provide the legal framework to facilitate this interchange of technology under an effective system of legal protection.

The second and overriding aspect of the "challenge" which must be met by the U.S. patent system is the role ordained for it by the Constitution. It must "promote the progress of science and the useful arts" to the greatest extent possible; and it must do this in the framework of a social and legal tradition in which monopolies are well defined and carefully circumscribed exceptions to the general rule of free and open competition. To be justified in this environment, the patent system must continue to serve effectively its constitutional purpose of promoting early public disclosure and use of technological advances.

Much of the opposition to the Presidential Commission's recommendations is based on the belief that the patent system was intended under the Constitution to secure an inventor's natural or moral rights to his invention. Those who take this position either overlook or choose to ignore the fact that the Supreme Court has emphasized that the Constitution makes no provision for the moral or inherent rights of the inventor. In tracing the history of the U.S. patent system, Justice Clark, speaking for a unanimous Supreme Court in *Graham* v. *John Deere Corporation*, 383 U.S. 1 (1966), was clear in the conclusion that "the patent monopoly was not designed to secure the inventor his natural rights in his discoveries. Rather, it was a reward, an inducement, to bring forth new knowledge."

The patent system, therefore, was indeed intended to serve the interests of scientists and inventors; but overriding this, the system was designed to serve the interest of the public.

The fact that a patent grant has this dual aspect—creating rights for the inventor while serving the public interest—led to a number of the Commission's recommendations, including the most far-reaching and controversial: that the United States adopt a first-to-file or filing-date system of priority.

Under the patent system there is, in effect, an exchange between the inventor and society. In return for disclosure to the public, the state will grant a legal monopoly when a person has made an invention. This monopoly is granted—and quite properly and beneficially in my view—notwithstanding, as I have said, the aversion to monopolies which characterizes our free enterprise system. Based upon this concept of the patent system, however, it is an anomaly for the state to give a monopoly to anyone but the inventor who first took steps under the patent system to make the invention available to the public.

This factor, among others, led the President's Commission to conclude that where there are competing claims to the same invention it would be as equitable—and certainly more in keeping with the disclosure-promoting concept underlying the patent system—to award the limited monopoly which a patent confers to the inventor, in the Commission's words, "who first appreciated the worth of the invention and promptly acted to make the invention available to the public." Since the first step in making the invention available to the public under the patent system is the filing of a patent application, the Commission recommended, and the Patent Reform Bill would establish, a system which gives a patent to the first to file.

The proposed first-to-file system would increase the quality and reliability of United States patents:

(1) By removing the uncertainties which necessarily arise when events and dates prior to filing an application are proved by oral testimony or affidavits;

(2) By eliminating the defense of prior inventorship under 35 U.S.C. 102(g) which can now be urged by someone who took no active steps to make his invention known to the public.

Complemented by the preliminary application technique, the filing date system of priority will reduce the time and expense of obtaining a patent by eliminating the burdensome interference practice and the necessity of keeping witnessed or corroborated records to establish early dates of conception. Preliminary applications, if properly used, will be of obvious advantage to small businesses and individual inventors who may wish to establish an early legal filing date, but who are not ready to pay the substantial fees for the preparation and filing of a formal application.

The proposed system of priority will necessitate the prompt filing of patent applications by inventors and their attorneys. This, together with the publication of patent applications by the Patent Office after 24 months, will hasten the public disclosure of new technology and inform the public of the inventor's rights.

The international implications of the first-to-file recommendation are apparent. Seventy-four of the 77 countries which belong to the Paris Union base priority on a first-to-file basis. The United States, Canada, and the Philippines are the only countries which base priority on a "first-to-invent" basis. And a Royal Commission in Canada, empaneled to study their patent system, strongly urged in 1960 that Canada amend its laws to award priority on a first-to-file basis. As an aside, we understand that Canadian officials are now actively considering this recommendation, particularly in light of steps towards international cooperation in the patent field.

The draft of a proposed Patent Cooperation Treaty was released in Geneva on May 31, 1967, by BIRPI, the Secretariat for the Paris Convention. A copy of this treaty was published in the June 13 issue of the Official Gazette.

As Commissioner Brenner noted in a press conference releasing the treaty on June 1, full participation in Phase II of the treaty, which would involve the issuance of international Certificates of Patentability, would, as the treaty is now drafted, require a first-to-file system of priority.

Under Article 27 of the treaty, a Certificate of Patentability transmitted to this country from abroad could be rejected within a year on various grounds, including the existence of prior art or the fact that the invention was not patentable under national laws. This latter category would include, for example, atomic weapons in the United States or drug compounds in Italy. The draft treaty, however, makes no provision for the rejection of a Certificate of Patentability on the ground that an applicant of a later filed application could prove acts in this country establishing a conception of the invention prior to the international filing date. Adoption of a filing date system of priority, in one form or another, therefore, would be essential for the participation by the United States in Phase II of the proposed treaty. (See Author's Postscript.)

In releasing the proposed treaty, Dr. Hollomon, Acting Under Secretary of Commerce, characterized it as "a major step toward the long-range goal of a universal patent system." Commissioner Brenner observed that a major advantage of the treaty is that "it will form the basis for the buildup of mutual respect and confidence among the patent offices of the world as an indispensable step toward the ultimate goal of a universal patent system."

Mr. Eugene Braderman, Deputy Assistant Secretary of State, stressed the importance of the treaty to the developing countries many of which are today unable to support adequate patent examining procedures. He stated:

> The proposed system offers a clear and simple solution to this dilemma by enabling such countries to utilize a search and examination system developed through an international bureau. Thus, we believe that the developing countries would also benefit from the proposed system in being able to offer meaningful protection for inventors and businessmen, as well as for foreign investors who con-

sider the effective protection of inventions as an important factor in the total climate for investment in these countries.

Although the proposed treaty is still in the formative stages, there is no doubt that its release is a milestone in the development of an intellectual property system, in the words of the theme of this meeting, for greater social progress.

In summary, then, the challenge to be met, in my view, has two aspects:

(1) To design a patent system which inherently achieves the constitutional purpose of prompt public disclosure and use of new technology; and

(2) To insure that such a system will facilitate the interchange of new technology across national borders under an effective incentive system of legal protection.

The recommendations of the President's Commission, including the controversial first-to-file feature, complemented by the historic efforts toward closer international cooperation in the patent field will, I am firmly convinced, serve to meet this challenge.

Author's Postscript—

At a Committee of Experts meeting held in Geneva, October 2-10, 1967, to consider the first draft of the proposed Patent Cooperation Treaty, there was general agreement that this draft would be revised to require a minimum of changes in the substantive patent laws of the prospective Member States. One of the changes agreed upon was that Article 27 would be amended so as not to require adoption of a filing-date system of priority. See the Report of October Meeting released by the United International Bureaux for the Protection of Industrial Property (BIRPI), 846 O.G. 5 (January 2, 1968).

Foreign Experience with Patent Law Provisions Similar to Proposals of Presidential Commission*

MALCOLM W. PARRY

My task is that of attempting to project, in terms of probable effect in the United States, the foreign experience with patent law provisions which have counterparts, either identical or basically similar, in the proposals of the President's Commission on the Patent System.

An examination of the Commission's proposals from this point of view is certainly warranted, since it is abundantly clear from the Report of the Commission, from subsequent statements of members of the Commission, and from statements emanating from the Patent Office and Commerce Department that an important, if not the principal, motivation behind the Commission's proposals is the desire to obtain a harmonization between U.S. and foreign patent law.

How many times in presentations by members of the Johnson Administration have we heard it said, in effect, "I am not sure that I can explain the virtue of this suggestion, but please bear in mind that it is in harmony with foreign law"?

For one who has for some years been concerned with foreign patent laws and who has been able in the past to obtain from U.S. practitioners only grudging condescension in respect of the possible virtues of some procedural aspects of foreign law, it is a rather startling turnabout to find the vast amount of respect which is now being given to foreign patent law and the eagerness, at least in some circles, to embrace quickly and with very little regard to the consequences provisions of foreign patent law which run counter to long established basic principles of U.S. patent law.

It is my view that the patent law of any country should reflect the legal, social, political, and economic philosophy of that particular country and that the best patent law for the United States is that which best serves to advance the interests of the United States. It is naive and unrealistic, I believe, to assume that there is such a harmony between countries in the legal, political, social, and economic areas that there is necessarily one model, harmonized patent law, that is best for all of them.

*See covering Editor's Note, p. 379.

390

In the absence of better evidence, the state of our economic development and well-being as compared with that of other countries having patent laws proposed to be emulated should be given its proper weight as a measure of the efficacy of the U.S. patent system. Therefore, I urge that my comments to follow be taken with due regard to the recent admonition of the Section of Patent, Trademark and Copyright Law of the American Bar Association as expressed in its Resolution No. 28 that changes in the U.S. patent law intended to achieve harmony with foreign patent systems should be resisted "unless it be shown that such changes will favorably affect the domestic operation and effectiveness of the U.S. patent system."

An initial general problem should, I think, be indicated in considering the question as to how the proposals of the Presidential Commission have worked abroad in their foreign-law equivalents. This is the necessity of considering these proposals one at a time. In other words, it is not altogether valid to consider what has been the foreign experience with a certain Commission proposal unless we know that the foreign country in question, having a counterpart to the Commission proposal, also has a provision corresponding to this proposal; and even so, this may not give the true picture if the foreign country has a relevant third provision which is not among the Commission's suggestions.

Only as an example, the Commission has proposed a first-to-file system with an absolute novelty standard. Therefore, as to these proposals, the German experience may not provide a basis for judging these proposals, since under the German law public use outside Germany does not destroy novelty. Furthermore, under German law there is a grace period of six months prior to filing during which any publication or public use emanating from the inventor does not destroy novelty.

This is only to say in short that a proposed law can only be finally assessed in the totality of its provisions, and unfortunately, from the point of view of true comparison, there is no patent law existing that embodies all of the proposals of the President's Commission.

With these general remarks aside, I shall turn to a particular consideration of those proposals of the President's Commission which bring innovation into the U.S. patent law and which may be said to have a counterpart in some foreign patent law.

Certainly, the one proposal of the Commission which is considered to bring the most drastic change into U. S. patent law and which has caused most controversy and discussion is that a patent be given to the first to file rather than to the first to invent as heretofore. There is no lack of foreign experience in this approach since of all the countries of the world only the United States, Canada, and the Philippines have patent laws which go into the question of priority of inventorship. Strangely enough no country except the United States, Canada, and the Philippines ever seems to have even considered a patent law which, like the United States, would award a patent to the first inventor.

There has always been this basic difference in law. No country having a first-to-file system has changed over to a first-to-invent system. Similarly, the United States and Canada have remained true to the first inventor approach although the Canadian Royal Commission of 1960 made a rather tentative suggestion which has never been implemented in the Canadian law to go over to a first-to-file system.

Parenthetically, the English patent law still speaks of the "true and first inventor." However, from the inception of the British patent system, this has meant something quite different from our understanding of "true and first inventor" since it originally meant, and still includes, that person first bringing the inventive concept into England, whether or not he conceived it. If English law could and still does recognize as an inventor a person who had no part in conceiving the invention, then it is not surprising that it can consider the first inventor to be the first to file an application.

It is difficult to ascertain exactly how much the English approach influenced the law of other countries, but certainly the inquiry into priority of inventorship has always been alien to the great majority of patent systems of the world.

What has been the foreign experience with the first-to-file system? I have found practically no one abroad who feels that awarding a patent to the first to file has resulted in unfairness from the point of view of a patent being awarded to a person who is not the first inventor. However, this failure of foreign practitioners to see any problem in this regard, I think, may arise at least in part, from a long term and complete acceptance of the concept that the first-to-file is the first inventor, so that in fact those living under the first-to-file system are never concerned with who is the first inventor in the U.S. sense.

In connection with the proposals here to have a first-to-file system, there is probably most often heard the criticism that this will result in a race to the Patent Office. Is there a race in those countries where the first-to-file system exists? In this regard, it is only of value I believe to consider technologically advanced countries where economic competition is as intense as in the United States. In those countries there is no question but that there is a race to the Patent Office. Has this race to the Patent Office resulted in rewarding the speculator as opposed to the inventor? There is no answer to this question since in most of the countries where the first-to-file system exists the speculator is the inventor. Under the systems of those countries, a patent can be and is awarded to a person who has arrived at an inventive concept and it is not necessary to describe an invention in detail.

All must be aware of the fact that the usual German, Dutch, or Japanese patent is only about a page or so in length. It may include drawings or it may not. If drawings are included they may be completely schematic. In chemical cases it is not required to give large numbers of examples. If further exemplification is called for, it can be added during prosecution.

Similarly, the specification can be amplified after filing in respect of utility. A German patent attorney in writing to me has stated it well:

> Your present system of "conception priority" has enabled the requirement and its fulfillment for disclosure "up to the last screw or most detailed manipulation," because the inventor need not be afraid of a "quicker" working competitor.
>
> Contrarily thereto, our system of rewarding the first to file cogently requests lower standards as to sufficient disclosure and allows a "more generalized broad disclosure."

A French patent attorney writes:

> There is no doubt that this provision causes the applicant to rush to file his application, and evidently compels the inventor to place the application on file before the invention has been thoroughly developed or tested.
>
> This governing principle has for result that the characteristic which the inventor wishes to protect is described in general terms which do not entirely find support in the specification. The invention is, consequently, not sufficiently exemplified.

I believe the same could be said in respect of applications in Holland and the Scandinavian countries.

The race to the patent office in Great Britain must be run somewhat differently. This is because British requirements with respect to application disclosure are more like our own. In Great Britain, the practice is in very many instances to file a provisional application to obtain the earliest possible filing date. This type of application, which must be completed within a year, can be short, generally worded, and without drawings or claims. The

President's Commission has recommended a similar procedure in its preliminary application.

The Commission conceives of this as a paper which "could be prepared by someone having little knowledge of patent law and procedure." To the contrary, one who has had experience with British provisional practice knows that this type of application must be most carefully drafted since it must later face the test of affording the basis of priority for claims.

The provisional application under British practice will generate a date only for what it discloses, and a person who discloses too little or too poorly may later find his provisional filing was practically worthless. Furthermore, it should be pointed out that the question of deciding whether a claim in a complete application is entitled to the priority date of the provisional application can be most difficult and would introduce a new complication in U. S. patent prosecution.

Summing up, it is my view that the foreign experience indicates that the first-to-file system undoubtedly does result in a race to the Patent Office. Therefore, unless the United States radically changes its present practice as to what constitutes an adequate patent application disclosure, in many instances the race will be won by the organization having the resources and personnel to insure that such adequate disclosure is developed without delay.

In speaking of the first-to-file system, a German attorney has stated this as follows: "Our system is based and can only be successful on two suppositions: (a) thinking in function; and (b) lower standards of detailed disclosure of the invention."

The second most significant proposal of the Commission is the new definition of prior art and the abolition of a grace period. As to the first, the general understanding of the Commission's recommendation and Section 102 of Senate Bill S.1042 embodying these recommendations, is that oral disclosure of an invention would not destroy novelty.

I find it difficult to reach this conclusion. Section 102 states that a person shall not be entitled to a patent if "prior to the effective filing date of the application, the subject matter sought to be patented was known to the public, or made available to the public by means of a disclosure in tangible form." This construction would seem to me to clearly mean that the requirement as to being in tangible form only limits the making available and does not apply to the "known to the public." This arises grammatically from the presence of a comma after "known to the public" and from the use of the word "or." It also arises logically from the fact that if only tangible disclosure made available to the public is a bar, why is it necessary to also state that public knowledge is a bar. How else would public knowledge be obtained other than by disclosure in tangible form, obviously by oral disclosure. The Commission's comments seem to me to strengthen this interpretation.

On page 7 of the Commission Report, it is stated that prior art is "that either publicly known or made available in a preservable form." The Commission's use of the word "either" would appear to make it clear that the following "or" is used in the disjunctive sense.

In any event, the Commission's proposal is for some sort of a strict novelty rule with no grace period. This provision can be equated therefore with the present law of France, Holland, and Italy. In these countries it is essential that testing of an invention prior to filing be carried out under the greatest security and that all publications concerning the invention be suppressed until an application is filed.

On this problem a Swedish associate has written to me:

A number of scientists whose cases I am handling have pointed out that a similar principle as in U.S.A., Canada and Germany regarding the possibility to file patent applications within a certain period after the first specific publication would be appreciated by them.

On the same question a French associate has written:

The obligation to avoid any divulgation before the filing of an application certainly hinders the tests numerous firms would wish to conduct before filing a patent application.

However, it is possible and permitted by the French law, to conduct tests at third parties' plants provided they are treated confidentially and that agreements for the secrecy of such tests have been concluded between the parties.

In cases where drugs have to be tested, the clinical tests are most of the time conducted with drugs not yet patented. These drugs are forwarded to clinical doctors in hospitals under a code number, and clinical doctors, having no knowledge of chemistry, are unable to analyze the products they are receiving for testing.

The French firms have not even to make sure that their researchers, whether working in the firm premises or outside the firm, do not publish any information, for any research personnel has, for common practice over here, to inquire on the patent situation before publishing any information.

Before leaving this particular point, I should like to indicate that the German patent law provides a six-month period as to the inventor's own publication and use. The same is true in Japan.

The British act and acts modeled thereon provide a year excusal for public use of the invention for purposes of reasonable trial. Furthermore, it should also be pointed out that in Great Britain and countries following the British law, such as New Zealand, Australia, and Israel, publication of an invention must take place in the country itself in order to constitute a bar.

In other countries such as Switzerland, Sweden, Norway, Denmark, Austria, and others, a publication must be in printed form to constitute a bar. In Belgium and Spain any disclosure of an invention resulting from an official publication such as issuance of a corresponding patent is not a bar to a so-called importation patent. Similarly, in most South American countries and in a number of other countries, valid patents can be obtained, notwithstanding the fact that a corresponding patent has issued elsewhere.

I would like to revert for a moment to the language of Section 102 of Senate Bill S.1042 that provides that patentability is defeated if the invention was known to the public prior to the effective filing date of the application. An almost exact counterpart appears in the South African act where it is provided that an invention is not novel if it was known in South Africa prior to the application effective date.

There has recently come across my desk the decision of the Court of the Commissioner of Patents for the Republic of South Africa in the case of an opposition against the application of W. A. Scholtens Chemische Fabriken. This may be found in the *Patent Journal,* Vol. 7, No. 293, January 11, 1967. Here it was alleged by the opponents that an employee of their German subsidiary came to South Africa and orally disclosed the subject matter of the opposed application to officers of the opposing company. This was established by oral testimony. The opposition was successful and the application was refused, the court saying, "Knowledge even by a single person, if openly acquired, is sufficient to invalidate a patent." Presumably, a similar decision could be arrived at under the Commission's proposals concerning prior art.

Particular attention has been directed to the proposal of the Commission that novelty should be destroyed by public use of an invention anywhere before the application filing date. The dangers of such a rule have been much discussed emphasizing particularly the possibility of witnesses from far off parts of the world attesting to use.

What has been the foreign experience in this regard? In this connection, there seems to be a misconception that the law in

Italy, France, and Holland speaks of an invention lacking novelty if there was public use of the same prior to the filing date. In point of fact, the laws of none of these countries even mention the word "use." Although the statutory language in these three countries differs somewhat, in general it can be said that novelty is destroyed if the invention has been made known to the public sufficiently in any way to enable it to be carried out.

As a practical matter, if in these countries a patent is sought to be invalidated by a foreign use which is alleged to have made the invention known to the public, the courts have generally held that such making known to the public cannot be completely established by testimony, but must be documented by concrete physical evidence. In any event, it would be almost impossible under the present state of foreign patent law to invalidate a patent on the basis of public use outside the country established by testimony, and I believe that prudence and good sense dictate that the same should be true in the United States. This could be most easily accomplished by excluding from any future legislation foreign public use as a ground for invalidity.

Another facet of the Commission's recommendation with respect to prior art is that a U.S. patent or published application shall constitute prior art as of its effective filing date. The Commission in its explanatory test states that this provision is a necessary adjunct of a first-to-file system. This reasoning is difficult to follow since in practically all countries having a first-to-file system, there is no such rule, and a patent of earlier date is only citable as to what it claims and is not citable as a prior publication unless it was in fact published before the effective filing date of the application it is to be cited against. The requirement of avoiding conflict of claims with a patent of earlier date is quite sufficient to the issuance of two patents on the same invention.

I believe that probably the next most significant of the Commission's proposals is for publication of pending patent applications. The foreign experience as regards this provision is practically nil since of major countries only Australia and the Netherlands—the latter quite recently—have had such provisions in their law. Great Britain some years ago had such a provision for applications filed with Convention priority, but this was abandoned with the present 1949 Act.

The experience has been to move away from this. I have found with this early publication, there are two major drawbacks. First, once the publication takes place, this operates as a bar to the filing of further patent applications. Also, I think it will be found that in any country where an application is laid open, the ambit of claims, as laid open, sets the final ambit for protection. I would think that same concept would come into U. S. law.

In summing up, I think it must be apparent from what has been said that evaluation of the Commission's proposals in the light of foreign experience is not clearly fruitful, first because, setting aside the first-to-file proposal, the other proposals of the Commission do not in fact have significant counterparts in existing foreign patent laws.

As to the first-to-file system, I have tried to show that its practical operation would require a drastic change in U. S. patent practice. Finally, I would suggest again that the fact that a particular type of patent system is considered successful in some foreign country having different institutions, economic structure, and political philosophy from those in the United States should not be given great weight in deciding what is best for the United States.

Author's Postscript—

In contrast to the past rather gradual and evolutionary development of national patent laws, there have been in the short time since this paper was written substantially changed new patent laws enacted in no fewer than seven countries, i.e., West Germany, Sweden, Norway, Denmark, Finland, France, and Israel. I think that it is not unfair to say that the primary impetus behind most of this new legislation has been a desire to simplify administrative operations of the patent offices concerned, and it would be unwise to assume that the new provisions embodied in the legislation will lead to a strengthening of the respective patent systems.

There is one provision that appears for the first time in all the new laws except that of Israel, and this is the provision that pending applications be made available to public inspection 18 months following the filing date or the Convention priority date if claimed. Although the public interest in having inventions made known in a reasonable time is apparent, the author still believes that it is equally important to the patent system that the inventor have the option of keeping his invention secret until his application has been allowed. This may not be feasible where, as in the new West German law, there is provision for deferred examination and the date of allowance is therefore controlled by the applicant. However, in those countries where there will not be deferred examination and prosecution will be controlled by the patent offices, the provisions for a laying open to the public before allowance suggest only that these patent offices would prefer not to face up to the problems of making the necessary administrative improvements in examination of applications whereby applications could be allowed and published within a short enough time reasonably to satisfy the public interest.

International Aspects of Presidential Commission's Report*

JOHN R. SHIPMAN

In connection with the international aspects of the President's Commission, I have at times heard some disturbing questions and comments such as: Why should we be concerned about this international stuff? Our U. S. inventors aren't interested in foreign filing. Why should we make changes for the benefit of foreigners? If the foreign people want more compatibility between our patent systems, let them change over to our system.

I think two things should be noted right away. First, the Commission gave as one of six objectives "to make U. S. patent practice more compatible with that of other major countries, wherever consistent with the objectives of the U. S. patent system." Thus, the idea is to harmonize "wherever consistent" with U. S. objectives.

Second, the changes proposed are to be for the benefit of U. S. people, not for the benefit of foreigners.

Why should we be concerned? It is true that less than half the U. S. originated cases are filed outside the United States. However, in 1965, when U. S. residents filed about 72,000 applications in the U. S. Patent Office, they also filed approximately 118,000 applications outside the United States. That is a lot of applications for people who aren't interested in foreign applications.

In 1966, U. S. people filed approximately the same number of complete specifications in the United Kingdom alone as did the British people. That is a lot of applications for people who aren't interested.

The United International Bureaux for the Protection of Intellectual Property (BIRPI) has reported filing statistics for the year 1965 for 56 other countries besides the United States and the United Kingdom, not including the Communist countries. Of these 56, 38 countries reported more applications of U. S. origin than of local origin, and a 39th country said they were about equal. With the United Kingdom this would seem to make 40 out of 57 countries, or 70 percent in which the United States filed more than the local people. That is a lot of applications for people who aren't interested.

---

*See covering Editor's Note, p. 379.

One might think that these 40 countries were mostly the little ones of the group with little patent activity. But, if we consider only the 20 with the greatest patent activity, we find the U. S. originated applications exceeded the local ones in nine of the 20 countries, and in a tenth, the United Kingdom, they were about equal in 1966. That is a lot of applications for people who aren't interested.

Further, in this connection, the rate of increase in U. S. filing abroad is far greater than the rate of increase in U. S. filing at home. Here are some of the percentage increases in U. S. originated applications filed in 1965 over 1960: Japan, 93 percent; Germany, 52 percent; France, 46 percent; United Kingdom, 51 percent; Canada, 20 percent; Italy, 59 percent; Switzerland, 62 percent; Netherlands, 74 percent; Sweden, 59 percent; Belgium, 95 percent.

In all, the top 20 countries had an increase in U. S. originated cases filed in 1965 over 1960 of about 55 percent, while in the same period the increase in U. S. originated cases filed in the United States was only 11 percent. It is therefore evident that there is a very substantial amount of filing by U. S. people outside the United States, and this is increasing at a very rapid rate.

If you or your company or your clients are not interested, maybe you should be. Almost any invention of value in the United States has considerable value in the rest of the world, if properly protected by patents. Are you missing the boat?

In view of these facts, I think the Commission's Report, from an international aspect, indicates an understanding of the real world as it is today, rejecting U. S. isolation in the patent area. It recognizes that the world's patent systems promote the beneficial exchange of products, services and technological information across national boundaries, thereby stimulating inventive activity.

It recognizes that making the world's patent systems more compatible and moving toward the goal of a universal patent system would provide benefits for all inventors and all business, and help to raise the standards of living everywhere, thereby serving our own national interests.

It recognizes that the large filing activity by U. S. people in other countries includes much duplication of effort and, therefore, extra expense in time and money to U. S. patent applicants.

Accordingly, in the broad sense, we find the Commission proposing the goal of a universal patent and recommending pursuit thereof through: (1) international harmonization; (2) the formation of regional patent system groups; and (3) a universal network of mechanized information storage and retrieval systems. While these are not the type of recommendations calling for legislation now, they are most important and seem to meet with general approval of interested parties.

I must admit, however, I occasionally feel that they are approved by my colleagues in the patent profession simply because they sound like unassailable virtues in the category of God, Flag, and Mother, although even God and the Flag seem to be collecting a few brickbats these days. Maybe the approval is qualified by "if they do it our way." Then I talk with them, recognize their sincerity, and my faith is restored.

There are, however, several other recommendations of the Commission incorporated in the Patent Reform Act which have some international aspects and are considerably more controversial.

For example, the first-to-file concept, with elimination of the grace period and the possibility of a preliminary application; the extension of prior art to include foreign knowledge, use and sale; filing by either the assignee or the inventor; early publication and the opportunity for the public to cite art.

Also, provisions for standby authority for optional deferred examination; the opportunity for limited cancellation proceedings; term of patent based on filing date; infringement through importation into the United States of a product made abroad by a process patented in the United States.

Of these, I would like to discuss the most controversial; that is the first-to-file concept with elimination of the grace period and the provision of a preliminary application.

Let me emphasize again the international aspect was only one of several factors considered by the Commission in making these recommendations. We have heard much against this proposal. However, let me raise some points on the other side and describe some of my own experiences, which I hope will be helpful in arriving at the answers. There are valid arguments on both sides of the questions. I think it is essential that we consider carefully both sides from an unemotional, cold, realistic point of view.

The United States now follows a so-called first-to-invent philosophy for granting patents with a one-year grace period. It is not exactly a first-to-invent system.

Actually, it is a first-to-file system with exceptions, the exceptions being that the later-filed application can receive the patent, if, but only if, the inventor can prove he conceived the invention first and then reduced it to practice first and the other party cannot establish a first conception coupled with diligence.

There is, unfortunately, a substantial gap here between theory and practice. It might even be called a "credibility gap" because our practice does not lend much credibility to what an inventor says or writes. It requires "proof" of a nature which necessitates a departure from the way most inventors work. Most inventors have a number of ideas from time to time, only a few of which are really good. At the time of conception the good ones often are not readily distinguishable by him from the poor ones. He does not normally have a tendency to describe all of these in writing and explain them to someone else capable of understanding, who in turn will make a record of it. And when he reduces an idea to practice, and shows it to someone else, there is a substantial likelihood that person would either not understand or not be able to see all the essential parts or not make a record or otherwise fail to do things important to establishing the required "proof."

How many inventors would normally keep a sufficient record of their activities to establish diligence, or are actually diligent in the degree required, or, for that matter, understand what constitutes diligence? Unfortunately, the patent legal meanings of conception, diligence and reduction to practice do not always coincide with the inventor's understanding. I often wonder how many poor, misguided inventors delay filing in reliance on the theory of first-to-invent, where their actual practices and records are completely insufficient to establish their conception of a reduction to practice or diligence.

It is reported that only 1 percent or less of the U. S. applications get into interference and, therefore, the complicated and long-drawn-out practices for handling interferences affect only a few. But this overlooks the fact that because of this system, the inventors of the country must keep records with witnesses, and worry about diligence, for all the other 99 percent as well, and in addition for all the possible inventive ideas which did not ultimately form the basis of an application. No inventor I ever heard of has applications filed on every one of his ideas.

In my company, the inventors have many more ideas than they themselves ultimately submit for consideration for filing, and they submit seven for every one that is filed. If this is typical, you can see that if they did what they should, the U. S. inventors who filed 72,000 applications in 1965 would have kept records for more than seven times 72,000 or more than 500,000 ideas. That is a lot of paper; for what purpose? As possible support for the 700 or so of these applications which will probably get into interference? And with what result?

The large majority of the interferences are won by the applicant who was first to file. I wonder how many interferences are won simply because the other inventor was caught with insufficient evidence to support his own statements. I venture to guess there were quite a high percentage in this class, and as to these, our first-to-invent system was merely a beautiful theory creating a lot of sound and fury and amounting to nothing.

How fair is all this? How much additional stimulation does this so-called first-to-invent system give our inventors when it requires them to go through such a mass of additional paper work?

I have heard it said that if the first-to-invent system produces "justice" for only one inventor, it is worth it. But how about producing injustice; injustice to the small inventor who cannot be expected to know all the niceties of interference proofs?

There are thousands of Americans working outside the United States. What about injustice to them? If they make an invention in the United States and happen to know about interferences, they can go back to provable conception dates for first inventorship purposes. But, if the same man happens to make that invention in England, he is limited to his filing date. Justice? We used to rationalize this on the basis of difficulty of taking testimony and establishing proofs, besides which, many years ago many of us just didn't trust foreigners.

I have a daughter who lives in Austin, Tex., at the University of Texas. I can get to England just as quickly and more conveniently than I can get to see my daughter. I can pick up the telephone and converse just as quickly with my co-workers in England as with her.

I can get mail delivered from England just as quickly and often more quickly than from her. Goodness knows what it would be if she lived in the State of Alaska. Yet here is Great Britain, with an outstanding legal history far longer than ours, and we won't let a resident of that country even attempt to establish proof of any acts prior to filing an application. Is that justice? The United States has no monopoly on brains, ingenuity, honesty, and integrity, but we often act as if we do.

Not long ago I attended a conference in Frankfurt which was attended by representatives of the major companies in Europe and by leading people in the patent profession. By far the greatest applause in two full days of meetings came in response to statements by Gordon Grant, head of the British Patent Office, when he said, in effect, that there is no part of American practice that is more passionately disliked by Europeans than our first-to-invent and interference system; that because it is so thoroughly hated, it has become a symbol—rightly or wrongly—but, nevertheless, a symbol, and if the United States truly wants to promote wholehearted cooperation in the international patent field it must remove that symbol.

You may ask, a symbol of what? Mr. Grant did not say in his talk, but the audience knew and I knew; a symbol of the United States saying, loudly and clearly, "We don't trust you."

Comments are made about the proposed first-to-file system favoring the large corporations. But who do you think in the present system would most likely have the best records to establish the required proof—the large corporation—which because of their volume can afford to educate their inventors and establish rules and controls over inventors' records and test procedures and provide witnesses; to the small company or so-called small inventor, who makes an invention only once in quite a while and sees his patent attorney at widely spaced intervals and usually after he has already done, or rather failed to do, things which might be important in proving first inventorship?

The proposed first-to-file system is supposed to favor the big corporations because the system will produce a "race to the Patent Office," and the big corporations allegedly will be better able to run that race. With respect to this aspect, I have one or two comments.

Large corporations are notoriously slow-moving and less able to act quickly than a small company or individual. My company has six good-sized laboratories in six different countries of Europe, all of whom have a first-to-file system, and yet we have not found it necessary, or even desirable to handle our inventions and filing because of this any differently than we do in the United States.

In the six and one-half years in which my responsibilities have included protecting the inventions from these European labs, I have never once run into a situation where anyone—inventor, patent attorney, or anyone else—became concerned about a "race to the Patent Office." In my many, many discussions with patent agents and patent management of all kinds outside the United States, I have heard many complaints, but I have never heard them complain about or raise any criticism about operations under a first-to-file system.

It has been suggested that the "race to the Patent Office"

will result in poorly prepared applications and the European prepared applications are pointed out as illustrating this position. Now certainly it is true that the less work that is done, the shorter the time it takes and, usually, the poorer the case. But that is not always so. I have seen some cases which were prepared after quite some months of work, and they were pretty poor. In any event it depends upon the amount of time and effort actually given to preparing the case and not on the date when done.

Nevertheless, I think we also have to consider whether or not the difference in the European and U. S. prepared applications are the result of differences in the ideas and standards of what constitute a well prepared application rather than with the first-to-file system. Here you might wish to know, most Europeans think U. S. applications are very poorly prepared. I wonder if that is because of our first-to-invent system.

I have heard statements to the effect that the first-to-invent philosophy is a basic part of our patent system, and to go to a first-to-file system is to depart from that which made our industrialization so successful. While our patent system has been of great assistance in our country's development, I think attributing it to the first-to-invent system is somewhat of an exaggeration. Japan in recent years has had a phenomenal growth at a rate far exceeding ours. Is this because of their first-to-file system? Is our industrial development due to, or in spite of, our first-to-invent system?

Now a part of our present system, which goes right along with our first-to-invent philosophy, is the grace period. With a first-to-file system, the grace period cannot be used. Our grace period does not give the inventor any priority rights, but it does give him a one-year period following publishing of his invention to file his U.S. application without the publication being a bar. There is no question this gives a degree of leeway insofar as U. S. practice is concerned, which is welcomed by both inventors and patent attorneys. But we must also realize this grace period can be, and often is, a treacherous snare and delusion.

The average inventor or businessman naturally tends to believe that if he can get a U.S. patent he will be able to get a patent in any other country. But this isn't so. If his invention is published or if someone else filed before he files his first application, he is barred from getting a patent in many countries of the world.

Keeping in mind the large and rapidly increasing number of U. S. applications already being filed outside the United States, one can readily see how an inventor can be led right down the primrose path in reliance on the U.S. grace period to find he has lost out on foreign protection which might double the value of his invention.

I think a patent attorney today has an unusually strong obligation to advise his clients of the possibilities of foreign protection and the necessity to avoid such things as publication before filing to leave himself the option of foreign filing if he desires. As a result, all who are even considering foreign filing must operate in effect without the grace period.

Many scientists and people in the academic world in the United States have a strong desire to publish their ideas. Presently, they do so in the grace period and lose their foreign rights to patent protection. The Commission attempted to provide a convenient means for them to do so without losing either their U. S. rights under a first-to-file system or their foreign rights to patent protection. To this end a preliminary application was recommended.

I personally don't care for this idea, and we have had no trouble outside the United States on this score. The United Kingdom has a similar provisional application, but we have used it only twice in ten years, and even then, wondered why we bothered.

However, I must say I do not understand many of the arguments advanced against this recommendation. Those who argue for the first-to-invent system, requiring extensive record-keeping on the part of the inventors with the accompanying difficulties of proofs and the necessity of complete descriptions, not only in written records but with witnesses, also argue against the preliminary application on the ground it will require too much writing and will have to be prepared by skilled attorneys to carry the date back and will add litigation-type difficulties.

It seems to me that no more care needs to be exercised in writing a preliminary application than in recording a description for use in a future interference. Or if for purposes of scientific meetings, the difference is in a preliminary application, you don't have to worry about proving a date or of having competent witnesses or of exercising diligence and being able to prove it. It also seems to me the preliminary application will require study no more often than an interference would occur.

Now we have a first-to-invent system with grace period which has faults. It requires excessive record-keeping, witnesses, worry about diligence, proofs, etc. It can give unknowing inventors a false sense of security. It produces some injustices. It has little effect on the ownership of patents. It is expensive and time-consuming. It can lead an unsuspecting inventor down the primrose path in reliance on the grace period.

On the other hand, we have the proposed first-to-file system with preliminary application, which is not ideal. But it eliminates the record-keeping, witnesses and diligence questions. It is relatively simple for an inventor to understand, so he will not be misled.

There is less chance of an unsuspecting inventor losing his option to obtain foreign patents without even considering the question. It provides, in effect, a grace period through the filing of a preliminary application of the same nature as the desired publication.

So I, too, ask you: Look at this coldly, realistically, practically. Is there really much difference, or are we letting ourselves become involved in theoretical abstractions. Let us remember too the flaws, as well as the advantages, in our present system.

Although we must look to the true merits of the situation, I think too we must face up to the real world; to the fact that the world is smaller; that all the world is our market; that international cooperation is essential for the future of patents; and that the rest of the world passionately hates our first-to-invent system and views it like another version of the ugly American.

In this light let us take another look, make another effort, and come up with constructive suggestions.

PART V

INTERNATIONAL CONTEXT

The strong commitment of countries to rapid industrialization that has given increased international significance to industrial property as a technological and economic resource, and the vigorous sentiment in certain quarters, both here and abroad, in favor of harmonization of national patent laws and of proposed international arrangements and treaties relating to industrial property, make it most important to assess the implications of such arrangements for U.S. interests. In previous chapters we considered the performance of the industrial property systems primarily in the United States. This chapter is directed to the international role of the industrial property systems and its relevance to our domestic systems and to the systems of other countries.

Our contribution to, and our stake in, the international interchange of industrial property are investigated in Dr. Behrman's paper on the licensing abroad of patents, trademarks, and know-how owned by U.S. companies. After appropriate protective measures are taken, industrial property is licensed in other countries in return for royalties or other business considerations. Although many companies would rather export products than license patents, under certain conditions it may be more advantageous to collect royalties than the proceeds of sale. Moreover, licensing can be a substitute for investment in foreign countries. There is much current interest in the subject of foreign licensing by reason of the need to limit the transfer of funds overseas. The report by Dr. Behrman, a former Assistant Secretary of Commerce, is a pioneer study and includes considerable information not hitherto available.

The importance of know-how in international agreements prompts the inclusion of Dr. Ladas' paper on the "Legal Protection of Know-How." His discussion of the civil and common law literature, the implications of the International Chamber of Commerce 1961 Resolution, and "the inclusion [by the Commission of the EEC] of know-how, together with the other rights of industrial property, in the special dispensation from notification of agreements relating to industrial property" is invaluable reading for the patent attorney in foreign practice or the businessman engaged in foreign trade.

Mr. Lightman's report on "Domestic and International Trade

Aspects of the USSR Trademark System" concerns the increasing commercial relations with the East and the role that trademarks can play for U.S. interests. This paper contains much new and useful information on the Soviet trademark system. In view of the desire of the USSR to augment its transactions with the West—as manifested in the "Westernization" of its trademark law—this article will profit careful scrutiny by persons engaged in, or planning to enter into, commercial arrangements with the Soviets.

The profit potential for American business in Canada, the United Kingdom, and Australia makes these markets attractive to U.S. enterprise, and license agreements "provide a convenient and common method of exploiting them." The three taxation studies deal with the taxation of foreign licensor in these non-U.S. jurisdictions; particular attention is directed to the taxation of the U.S. licensor. To make the information useful to the nonspecialist, technicalities have been kept to a minimum. The authors are regarded as tax experts in their respective countries.

European industrial property "climate" with respect to harmonization and international industrial property arrangements is explored in the seventh paper, the initial report on a study of the experience and attitudes of foreign experts under provisions of their laws that embody recommendations of the Report of the President's Commission on the U.S. Patent System. Because it probes deeper levels of sentiment relating to industrial property, this paper contains an important message for U.S. interests. The author counsels that "We should not reject opportunities to harmonize our laws with those of other nations and to enter into agreements that are in the *national* as well as the international interest"; however, he cautions, "While accepting patent ideas of common advantage, we need not concede initiative or the upper hand to other states."

A recent international development of great importance is a proposed Patent Cooperation Treaty. In May of 1967, BIRPI released the first draft of this treaty "as a result of a proposal made by the United States to the Executive Committee of the Paris Union." Numerous private and governmental conferences and meetings have discussed the proposed treaty and suggested revisions and alternatives, and a second draft was issued by BIRPI in July 1968. Former Assistant Patent Commissioner O'Brien, responsible for the operations of the Office of International Patent and Trademark Affairs in the Patent Office, outlines the principal features of the Treaty; he emphasizes the contributions that the Treaty should make toward solving international patent problems of American companies. Dr. Ladas' paper which follows, analyzes and evaluates the 1968

Draft and offers alternatives calculated to carry out the objectives sought by the American proposal.

A major spur to international action was the address of General David Sarnoff in 1966 on "A World Patent System," upon the occasion of his receipt of the 1965 Charles F. Kettering Award. The gist of his provocative paper is that "a global patent system could now be accommodated technically in a world-wide communications system just as readily as global television, global weather reporting, and global computer services." In view of our objectives in this volume "to inform more people about the potential of the patent and related systems for technological progress, for world cooperation and trade, and for world peace," we conclude this last chapter with the eloquent coincident observations of General Sarnoff: "With this remarkable record of achievement, and with his continuing acquisition of new knowledge, is it too much to expect that man can also find the ways and means to fulfill the elemental needs of life for everyone on this planet? Surely, there could be no greater contribution to human welfare and world peace."

Licensing Abroad Under Patents, Trademarks, and Know-How by U.S. Companies

J. N. BEHRMAN*

INTRODUCTION: 1969

During the past 10 years there has not been a reassessment of the quantitative aspects of foreign licensing. From the returns of royalties and the data on payments by other countries, we know that the practice is continuing to grow. The data, therefore, may appear to be dated; though we do not know what the distribution of licensed assets might be among patents, trademarks, and know-how, we can be fairly certain that the flow of licensing is still stronger to the advanced countries but probably growing more rapidly to the less developed countries.

The problems of licensing remain much as before, and the analyses relating to the areas of taxation, antitrust, contract terms, etc., remain applicable in general. Some new aspects have come on the scene, however. Thus, some of the advanced countries are concerned about the "balance of payments" for technological advances as represented in payments for licenses, and some have become concerned about the dominance of foreign technology which is represented by the uneven flow of proprietary rights among countries. They are, therefore, examining ways of altering the terms of the arrangements, and of stimulating domestic research and its licensing abroad.

On the other side of the argument, some countries are concerned that direct investment is too often tied to licensing, which should be divorced from equity ownership and thus reduce the threat of dominance. Efforts are being directed, therefore, to means of stimulating licensing without the accompanying direct investment. Conversely, many licensors have now tested the

EDITOR'S NOTE: This paper is a condensed version (with a new Introduction) of a report on a pioneer study on foreign licensing of patents, trademarks, and "know-how." The complete report appeared in *IDEA,* Vol. 2, No. 2.

*Acknowledgment is made of the contribution to this study by Jerome Jacobson, who served as consultant; by John Lindeman, who initiated it; by W. E. Schmidt, Lawrence Eckstrom, Joe S. Cardinale, and Wilbur Fugate, who commented on part or all of the manuscript; and by members of the executive and research staff of the Institute, who offered technical advice and criticism.

market sufficiently and are interested in establishing either joint-ventures with their licensees or in buying them out, or simply terminating the license at some convenient time.

We may introduce this analysis, therefore, with the assertion that the problems it adumbrates and examines are not only alive today but will be with us in intensified forms in the next decade.

SIGNIFICANCE AND SCOPE OF STUDY

Purpose and Scope

The Institute's pilot study on foreign licensing was conceived as an examination of the relation of U. S. patents and trademarks and U. S.-owned foreign patents and trademarks to their use abroad. We were interested initially in the ways in which the results of the U. S. patent and trademark systems are extended abroad. Obviously, U. S. patents and trademarks confer no rights as to manufacture abroad. But they are usually the basis for filing and registration in foreign countries. It is only after the foreign rights are obtained that the U. S. company can license the use of these rights to foreign firms. To this extent foreign licensing of patents and trademarks is an outgrowth of the U. S. systems for protection of marks and inventions.

The subject of licensing cannot be restricted to patents and trademarks. It must encompass the transfer of technical know-how. "Know-how" includes whatever *unpatented* or unpatentable information the licensor has developed and which the licensee cannot readily obtain on his own and is willing to pay for under the agreement; such as techniques and processes, the trade secrets necessary to make and sell a patented (or other) item in the most efficient manner, designs, blueprints, plant layouts, engineering specifications, product mixes, secret formulae, etc. Transfers of know-how most frequently accompany a patent license and sometimes are important in making a trademark license valuable to the licensee. This investigation has, therefore, encompassed all three types of transfer of intangible industrial property rights from the United States to foreign companies under license agreements.

Basically there are four types of licensing agreements, though they are usually found in combination. The agreement may transfer rights to *patents* (either for products, processes, or machines) which have been obtained abroad by the U. S. firm. It may be a means of granting rights under U. S.-owned *trademarks* registered abroad. It may be an arrangement to make available or sell *know-how* relating to either technical or managerial skills or both.

A fourth type adds to any of these types a reciprocal arrangement under which certain rights are extended from the foreign company to the U. S. company; this sets up a *cross-license* seldom involving payment of royalties or fees. Any of these types may extend the right to merely manufacture, or to use, or to sell, or any combination of these.

The initial study has been restricted to the U. S. side of the picture in order to limit the scope of investigation to one which could be covered within a reasonable period of time. A full-scale study would require examination also of *foreign* patent and trademark systems, legal protection, commercial and financial regulations, antimonopoly policies, taxation, and governmental attitudes toward licensing. A larger study would also encompass the problems foreigners face in licensing U. S. companies to produce in the United States and the extent to which such activities affect U. S. licensing abroad.

Extent of Foreign Patenting and Licensing

In order to determine the economic significance of the subject studied, we requested data from our respondents upon the extent to which they patented inventions abroad, registered their trademarks abroad, and licensed either to foreign companies.

Few, if any, U. S. companies patent all their patentable developments in the United States; relatively few of those patented in the United States are patented abroad. Less than 2 percent of the companies we interviewed or questioned asserted that all of their U. S. patented inventions were patented abroad; and such was the case *only* when the company had relatively few patents. About 20 percent patented none of their inventions abroad (or had no U. S. patents). Within the extremes, the experience shows the following distribution: about one fourth of the companies applied abroad for between 1 and 25 percent of their U. S. patented inventions (about half of these applied for 10 percent of them abroad); another fifth applied for between 26 and 50 percent abroad (most of these being at the 50 percent level); surprisingly, about a fifth applied for between 65 and 95 percent.

A higher proportion of U. S. trademarks was registered abroad than was the case with respect to patent applications abroad on U. S. patented inventions. Nearly one fourth of those responding indicated that they registered all their marks in one or more foreign countries. Another fourth registered abroad between 76 and 95 percent of their U. S. marks; and a third quarter registered between 25 and 75 percent, with most of these being at the

50 percent level. Less than a fifth registered under 25 percent, and only about 10 percent indicated that they did not register any of their U. S. marks abroad. The heavy registration of marks abroad is probably a reflection of a general rule that they should be registered even before exporting.

The significant number of patents obtained and of marks registered abroad would indicate that these companies had considerable foreign assets which could produce income through licensing. But this was not the main objective of foreign patenting or registering for most respondents. The primary objective in four fifths of the cases was to obtain protection. The protection was for the company's own exports, for sales of its subsidiaries, or against the nuisance of having to deal with poachers abroad. Though protection was the primary consideration, about 75 percent of the respondents replied that future licensing was at least a secondary (though minor) factor.

Several companies, however, indicated that their patenting and registering abroad was done wholly in the light of future licensing. Others said they paid no attention to the possibility of future licensing. Other reasons for patenting or registering abroad were to improve its opportunities for cross-licensing, to keep open the door for foreign expansion itself in the future, and to gain benefit in the form of advertising and prestige.

Use of the patents obtained abroad and trademarks registered in other countries is shown by the following data on the proportion licensed by the responding companies:

Percent of Foreign Trademarks Licensed	Percent of Responding Companies	Percent of Foreign Patents Licensed	Percent of Responding Companies
0	13	0	17
1– 5	22	1– 5	15
10	10	10	7
11–49	20	11–49	15
50–95	15	50–95	20
100	20	100	16*

*Licensees were usually subsidiaries *or* the licensors held only a few foreign patents.

The growing attention paid to licensing has made many companies more cautious about their policy on foreign patenting and registering. While the cost of maintaining many and widespread foreign patents and trademarks is extremely high, it has happened that one item has returned the costs of all foreign protection and more. Some companies have missed protecting that item. Because of the cost of maintaining patents, many firms review their foreign positions periodically. They seek to discover why licensing under a patent has *not* occurred and whether it is to be expected. If not, it may be dropped or assigned to a foreign company contingent upon the payment of royalties if the item involved is ever produced.

There is no way of calculating the proportion of know-how licensed abroad. Thus, we had to be satisfied with a subjective evaluation by the respondent of its relative importance. By far the majority of U. S. companies questioned replied that know-how was much more important to them as an asset which could be successfully licensed than were patents or trademarks; it was much more sought after by potential licensees. When asked to rank these according to importance, know-how licenses were placed first two times out of three; the other first place listings went more to patents than to trademarks. A mild predominance fell to patent licenses in the second-place slot, and a strong predominance of third-place listings fell to trademarks.[1] In a few cases, however, the respondent indicated that only one of the three was important to his company. Others showed that trademarks were of no value in their licensing, but that patents and know-how went together hand in hand; still others coupled trademarks and know-how.

---

[1]The reasons given for these attitudes may be enlightening:

Trademarks were given first rank when the commodities involved were those close to the ultimate consumer; they were considered important in increasing sales, raising prestige, and getting the eye of the consumer.

Patents were considered most important in the experience of some for these reasons: higher royalties were gained from patent licenses than from other types; cross-licensing could be more effective under patents than under know-how exchanges; only patents provide the government protection desired by many licensees; foreign licensees respect patents more than simple know-how agreements; the existence of patents eases the licensing negotiations and provides some tax advantages; and, patents are a positive asset while trademarks are usually defensive.

Know-how attained much of its importance by making each of the other types of agreements more effective; in licensing subsidiaries, the licensee generally receives rights to patents automatically and thus is more eager for the know-how to use with it. In many instances, the know-how of the licensor was considered unique; in others, the large amount of engineering involved made technical knowledge indispensable. Where the art of the industry had been developed over a long time and manufacturing could not be carried on without it, know-how was of first importance. Also, patents do not disclose all development; the additional know-how makes the license worthwhile, but the existence of the patent provides the means of ensuring that the licensee will have to make payments during the period of use of the know-how; that is, without a patent, the licensee may take know-how and then cancel the agreement. Some companies considered know-how licensing a less expensive substitute for licensing of patents. They felt foreign companies seek know-how licenses because of the complexity and expense of obtaining know-how on their own.

Postwar Expansion of Foreign Licensing

The increase in licensing since World War II has been reflected in greater activity by companies already licensing and a rise in the number of companies entering into licensing programs. Among the companies interviewed and questioned, some have been licensing abroad as long as 50 and 60 years, but these are relatively few. Nearly 20 percent of the companies have been licensing more than 30 years. The largest proportion (about 40 percent) have been licensing abroad between 15 and 30 years. About 15 percent began foreign licensing during World War II, and nearly one-third began after the war—most during 1947 and 1948.

Nearly 95 percent of the companies responding indicated an increase in their licensing activities since World War II. The predominant rise was in licensing of know-how—nearly twice as great as increases in licensing of patents and nearly three times as significant as the rise in licensing of trademarks. Again, this experience is not the same for all, but increases in licensing of know-how were given a first-place ranking by nearly three to one over either patent or trademark licensing. Patents and trademarks received an equal number of second-place votes, but trademarks nosed out patents for third-place honors.

Main factors affecting the postwar increase in foreign licensing were three: a policy decision of the licensor to become more aggressive, expansion of commercial activity abroad, and increased interest shown by potential licensees. Respondents were asked to rank these factors and add (and rank) any other significant ones affecting their own postwar expansion. The results indicate that expansion of licensing in the postwar period was only partly a result of an aggressive policy by U. S. business; the initiative was in the hands of the potential licensee about half the time.[2] However, many licensors took positive decisions to expand their licensing operations once commercial conditions improved abroad. It is difficult to draw a precise line between these various factors

---

[2]"Expansion of commercial activity abroad" usually ranked first, followed by a "policy decision of the company," and then "increased interest of the licensee." "Commercial expansion abroad" was indicated as first three times to two for a "policy decision of the company" and two to one for "increased interest of the licensee"; "commercial expansion abroad" was also given the highest number of second-place votes, being five to four over each of the others; whereas "interest of the licensee" was in third place—two to one over "policy decision of the company" and three to one over "increased interest of the licensee."

since they have tended to meld together in a large number of instances. Other factors affecting the increase in licensing were of first importance to less than 10 percent of the respondents.[3]

Countries of Licensees

There is little information as to the countries in which licensing occurs by American companies, but the information obtained through the questionnaire shows a pattern not too dissimilar from the educated guesses of some of the persons interviewed. Only 20 percent of the companies responding to the questionnaire refused to answer the question on the number or area of licensees. Most respondents supplied precise information. Several had over 100 licensees in a group of more than 20 countries and the physical work of listing them was too great.

The countries having the most licensees of U. S. companies were found to be the most highly industrialized: England, France, Germany, Canada, Australia, and Japan. Canada might well be in first place but for the fact that subsidiary operations predominate there, and these may not be formally licensed. Some of the more rapidly developing countries came close behind: Mexico, Brazil, Italy, Argentina, and South Africa. Further down the list of the number of licensees came the countries in Europe which are smaller and more specialized in their industrial production: Belgium, Netherlands, Sweden, and Switzerland. Although the above rankings were the order of the countries according to numbers of licensees (see the following table), nothing can be said by the investigators at this time about the *value* of the returns from these licensees.[4]

Many of those interviewed orally did not have the time to provide a country breakdown of their licensees; and some of the respondents merely wrote that they had "more than 75" or "about 175" licenses, but we have estimated that the companies reporting had agreements aggregating well over 1,500 in number.[5]

---

[3]*See IDEA*, Vol. 2, No. 1 (1958), pp. 137-158.

[4]One group of company officials guessed that France was the most important licensee country in terms of royalties, but it is far below Britain both in number of licensees and in number of U.S. companies extending licenses.

[5]The larger number of licenses represented may account for the discrepancy in the order of countries in the table with that found by the NICB in its report relating to only 483 licensees. (NICB, *Foreign Licensing Agreements*, 1958, p. 14).

Country	Number of U.S. Companies Reporting Licenses*	Number of Licensees Reported*	Rank by Number of Licensees
Europe			
United Kingdom	70	190	1
France	42	95	2
West Germany	37	87	3
Italy	25	38	9
Belgium	16	23	11
Netherlands	12	18	13
Sweden	13	16	14
Switzerland	10	16	15
Spain	11	12	17
Denmark	7	8	--
Norway	4	5	--
Austria	4	5	--
Portugal	4	4	--
Finland	3	3	--
Greece	2	2	--
Turkey	1	1	--
Iceland	1	1	--
Liechtenstein	1	1	--
Canada	45	77	4
South America			
Mexico	34	47	7
Brazil	30	39	8
Argentina	21	24	10
Colombia	8	10	19
Venezuela	5	9	20
Uruguay	5	6	--
Chile	5	5	--
Peru	4	5	--
Cuba	3	4	--
Ecuador	2	2	--
Salvador	2	2	--
Middle East and Africa			
South Africa	15	22	12
Israel	3	3	--
Egypt	1	1	--
Southern Rhodesia	1	1	--
Asia and the Pacific			
Australia	46	69	5
Japan	30	48	6
India	7	13	16
New Zealand	10	10	18
Philippines	4	5	--
Pakistan	1	2	--
World-wide licenses	4	4	
	100*	823	

*As reported by the 100 companies replying with a specific number of licenses; some few gave overall totals or "more than" figures.

The percentage distribution of the companies reporting *both* the number of their licensees and the countries was as follows:

Number of Countries	Number of Licensees				
	1-5	6-10	11-15	16-20	>20
1- 5	37	8	—	—	—
6-10	—	16	4	6	—
11-15	—	—	—	3	4
16-20	—	—	—	—	—
>20	—	—	—	—	4

The distribution cannot be considered more than indicative that most companies have fewer than 10 licensees in as many countries; and, of these, the majority have fewer than 10 licensees in five or fewer countries.

Statistical reporting on the volume of licensing abroad is made difficult not only by the differences in "value" of licenses but also because one licensee may be given the right to manufacture, use, or sell in more than one foreign country. Thus, a British company may have rights in the entire British Commonwealth; and a French company throughout the French Union. In addition, several companies license only *through* their subsidiaries; others license their subsidiaries themselves and permit some sublicensing. A more accurate picture would require an examination of the subsidiary relationship as well as the *value* of the licenses in the various countries.

U. S. Companies as Licensees

Although it was not an integral part of the project to study the extent of licensing of U. S. companies by foreign enterprises, we included a question to determine whether one flow or the other was relatively the more important. Slightly more than one third of our respondents indicated that they were licensees of foreign companies. In some instances the licensor was a subsidiary. In some cases the field of the license was not related to the area of the U. S. company's own licensing program. We did not attempt to determine the nature or extent of cross-licensing, for a host of problems arise in that area which would have extended the study too greatly.

Among those indicating that they were licensees, one tenth were unable or unwilling to state whether or not their payments under the licenses were greater or less than their receipts from those they extended abroad. One firm stated that its payments were 10 times its receipts; another reported payments twice receipts. And two stated that both receipts and payments were zero; this occurred when the relationship was with a subsidiary and where the payments were replaced by an agreement to purchase materials or component parts.

For 80 percent of those who were also licensees, payments under these agreements were anywhere from one-for-one, compared to receipts under the licenses it extended abroad, to "infinitely" smaller than receipts. Two stated that receipts equaled payments; one firm indicated a five-to-four ratio of receipts over payments; several reported receipts twice the size of payments; several four and five to one, and several nine and ten to one. Three reported receipts 15 to 20 times payments, three showed them at a ratio of 100 to one, while the final three reported large-scale receipts but no payments.

On the whole, payments by U. S. companies to foreign licensors probably aggregate no more than 15 percent of their receipts as licensors. The relative insignificance of such payments has not made us feel the study was improperly restricted by our having excluded the reverse licensing situation. However, a full-scale study would have to take these contracts into account, for they are important not only in the overall picture but also in that some of them arise as part of the payment for licensing by U. S. companies through the return of improvements. And some of them are part of significant patterns of cross-licensing, which have historically been the basis for extensive international business cooperation.

EXCLUSIVITY, ANTITRUST, AND INTERNATIONAL RESTRICTIVE BUSINESS PRACTICES

There are many types of restraints upon the competitive freedom of either party that may subject the licensing agreement to scrutiny and the parties to penalties under the antitrust laws of the United States. We have not attempted a full analysis of the impact on foreign licensing of antitrust legislation. In order to delineate the antitrust problems which U. S. businessmen face in licensing abroad, we have examined the reasons advanced by businessmen for the various restraints which each party might wish to impose in the agreement. Preliminary to a larger study of what the law on antitrust violations *is*, and the counsel given by legal departments relating to licensing operations, we have sought also to determine the problems concerning which legal opinion is required in view of the antitrust laws. The importance of legal counsel in decisions on licensing is exemplified by the following colloquy before a subcommittee of the U. S. Senate Committee on the Judiciary:

> MR. LADAS: I have here three or four letters of various companies telling me that they are not entering into [licensing] agreements because of the Timken decision.

> MR. BURNS: Is it your conclusion with respect to Timken that while students of the law and practicing lawyers might construe the decision in such a way as to not invalidate these practices, that nevertheless, because of the language of certain of the Justices, business is, in fact, concerned, and that the decision is resulting in retarding agreements which might otherwise be entered into?

> MR. LADAS: That is right.[6]

In view of the divergence of antimonopoly policies in foreign countries as compared with those of the United States and the necessity of U. S. business competing abroad, we present in this section some of the views concerning an international agreement on restrictive business practices. Many U. S. businessmen consider it too difficult (and even inequitable) to have to operate abroad in competition with others not under antitrust restraints. Yet if the United States does not impose restraints on the foreign operations of its companies, not only may its imports and exports be adversely affected but indirectly also its domestic production and sales. The background for the various attitudes toward an international coordination of national antitrust policies is given to stimulate discussion of the problem.

Business Motives for Imposition of Restraints

The restraints which either the licensee or the licensor sometimes wishes to place in the agreement relate to the actions of each other in the market. They are restrictive of competition in some way, such as dividing the market, setting prices, sharing production quotas, or limiting entry of third parties. While it is legally dangerous to use the license as a front for a "naked" restraint of competition, the reduction of potential competition through licensing may be a strong motive for the agreement in the first place. Both the licensor and the licensee may have an interest in reduced competition, but it will not always be to the interest of each to permit the other the particular restraint he wishes. The following presentation of motives is a summation of views of officials we interviewed and stresses their interest in a more "reasonable" interpretation of antitrust law. It should be emphasized that not all the officials inter-

---

[6]"A Study of the Antitrust Laws," Hearings before the Subcommittee on Antitrust and Monopoly, Part 4, 84th Cong., 1st Session, p. 1725.

viewed expressed a desire to impose the types of restraints discussed below. Nearly half the companies we questioned held the view that both they and the licensor benefited from competition with others, and a few considered that competition from them kept the licensee on his toes. Most of these officials found that they could bargain away restrictive clauses with changes in royalty rates. Thus, the agreements below reflect the views of only those companies using such provisions and willing to discuss their motives with us.

Motives of the Licensee

There are three broad circumstances which may give rise to a desire on the part of the foreign licensee to restrict his competition: either he is unsure of his position in the market and would like to have a period of "infant-industry" protection to warrant the initial investment; *or* his market under competition would be too small to serve efficiently; *or* he is accustomed to operating and selling in a monopolistic (or cartelized) market and wishes to have the same situation with reference to the product covered by the license. Each reflects a desire on the part of the licensee to increase the value of what he has obtained through the license by eliminating competition of the licensor or others in the market.

The competitive weakness of the licensee may be in comparison to the dominance of the licensor or in comparison to companies in third countries. He may be protected against each by tariffs, currency restrictions, shipping costs, or quantitative import restrictions. If so, the desire for exclusivity under the license will be less. Without these protections, however, he may feel that the only way in which he can obtain a period of grace is under an exclusive provision in the licensing agreement.

The desire for "infant-industry" protection may stem, however, from the fact that the manufacture of the licensed product requires a large amount of capital investment. In order to induce the licensee to make such heavy outlays, it may be necessary to provide him a respite from immediate competition in a given market. The economic justification for such protection stands on all fours with that for commercial tariff protection under similar circumstances; it is subject to the same criticisms, however, as far as general economic policy is concerned.

A third justification for exclusivity, at least for an initial period of development, is that the internal market may be so small as to accommodate only one manufacturer at efficient levels of operation. If the licensee has to share the market with others, his portion may be such as to keep his costs high and prevent him from enjoying the benefits of larger scale production and prevent the consumer from having a lower priced commodity. On the presumption that his costs would fall with a larger market, the licensee is justified in asking for exclusivity at least for the time necessary to prove his ability to supply the market at reasonable cost.

If it is considered that even the domestic market is too small for the more efficient scale of operation, the licensee may also request a share in third markets, or even an exclusive portion of them.[7] This request has sometimes been supported by the government if the economy is in need of foreign exchange and if the right to a larger market would expand exports into a desirable area.

The above reasons for exclusivity stem from conditions which may be short-run and may, thereby, justify only a temporary privilege of exclusion of competitors. However, as with tariff protection,

---

[7]The following report in a statement by the American Chamber of Commerce in Paris is illustrative: "In many industries the French market is comparatively small, and it is essential to have an exclusive license for a period of at least a few years in order to build up the business and supply the market without danger of having it cut into by others. In some instances, with mass production techniques, even the entire French market is not large enough to support economical production. In such instances, a French company would require an exclusive license in one or two other European countries in order to assemble a large enough market to make production economical. It was pointed out that the size of some European countries is smaller than some American states and that an American company would hesitate to have its sales limited to any one state. Until such time as there is a United States of Europe, the entire European continent must be considered in determining the extent to which patent licenses should be limited to particular areas.

"They claim the hesitancy of American attorneys in allowing their clients to grant exclusive rights to manufacture in France has caused losses to the American companies. One instance which was cited was where a French company would not risk manufacturing under the American invention without an exclusive license, so that particular product was not made for several years. Finally a German company came along with a process similar to the American company and granted the exclusive license to the French company. The result of this hesitancy on the part of the American lawyers was to deprive their client of the benefit of royalties for several years, while depriving the French consumer of the benefit of the product. These products were absent from the French market because of the uncertainty of the American antitrust laws. The product was one which could not have been imported into France at the time." ("Foreign Trade Conferences," *Committee Print*, Committee on the Judiciary, U.S. Senate, 84th Cong., 1st Sess., pp. 15-16.)

Although not all the relevant facts are given, it may be questioned whether the American attorney's advice was sound in this case. Depending on the circumstances (such as whether there would be a substantial *effect* upon U.S. commerce resulting from exclusivity), exclusivity can be well within antitrust interpretations. Thus, if a patent was held in both the United States and France, the licensor could have given an exclusive license under the French patent and have been protected from exports by the French company through its American patent. Obversely, the French licensee would have been protected from imports into France by virtue of its French (licensed) patents which it could have asserted against the imports.

the history of exclusive clauses during the prewar period seems to be dominated by those which were either intended to be permanent or which were continued long after the initial justification was past. The second major justification—that of continuation of a desirable privilege of market control—became the dominant one.

The monopolization of a market is permitted in foreign economies, though it is not legal (save in a few instances) in the United States. When a potential licensee has been operating under cartelized conditions both at home and in his own foreign markets, it is difficult for him to understand the reluctance of some American licensors to extend exclusive privileges. And, from his own view, there is no justification for such recalcitrant behavior. The laws of his land and the administration of his government permit and sometimes encourage restriction of competition; so do his business mores. When such a licensee feels strongly that he must continue to operate in the same milieu as before, he may insist on exclusive provisions. The mere fact of his insistence—to the extent that without exclusivity the contract will not be written—may become adequate justification in the eyes of the U.S. licensor for the inclusion of the privilege. In this case, the license, even with exclusive provisions, creates more production and commerce (though not necessarily U. S. trade) than would have occurred without the license.[8]

Motives of Licensor

Two of the same motives are behind the licensor's desire for restraint of competition: to protect himself against creation of a strong competitor from abroad or to gain the benefits of monopoly in the market. But the U. S. licensor's justification for these is quite different. In the case of the former he cannot claim "infant-industry" status, and in the case of the latter he cannot claim to have acquired the habit of monopoly operation.

Economic justification for restraining competition arising from the licensee is nevertheless asserted by some U. S. businessmen. It is that the licensor did not, in the first place, have to give birth to the licensed production and was therefore, *ex ante* license, not subject to the competition which might ensue *ex post* license. However, in several antitrust cases and in the *Combustion Engineering* consent

---

[8]Analysis of bilateral trade agreements in the postwar period shows that *restricted* trade may be larger than *free* trade when conditions of stress exist, as occurs where foreign exchange is scarce. R.F. Mikesell and M.N. Trued, "Postwar Bilateral Trade Agreements" (International Finance Section, Princeton University, 1955), pp. 80-89. See also J. E. Meade, *The Theory of Customs Unions* (Amsterdam: North Holland Publishing Co., 1955) on the trade-creating and trade-diverting effects of restrictions.

decree, the Supreme Court frowned on a license provision which prohibited, in positive language, the licensee from exporting to the United States.

Once again, the strength of the licensor's desire for restraints rests on his own competitive position. If he is operating behind commercial protection by the government or under conditions which provide him a competitive advantage in production, shipment, or selling so that he need not fear sales from abroad, then his desire is likely to be weak. However, if the licensor is a small firm, producing (e.g.) only one item in a large product line, and sharing the market at home with foreign firms, *and* if the potential licensee is a large, strong firm and is already in the domestic market of the licensor though in other products of the line the licensor may feel justified in requesting that the licensee restrict his operation in the product concerned to other markets. One must be careful, however, not to generalize too quickly that low labor (or other single factor) costs in the country of the licensee automatically provide him with such competitive strength. It is widely held that low labor costs abroad are a prima facie justification for restraining the licensee for he thereby has a competitive advantage. Such contentions do not withstand close scrutiny; the foreign firm may be more efficient and thereby a stronger competitor than the licensor; but, if so, that strength rests on the *entire* agglomeration of cost factors, including managerial techniques and inventiveness, *in comparison with* the same aggregate cost factors in the United States—not just on a comparison of labor costs, which themselves may be low in money terms abroad but high in terms of labor's productivity.

The U. S. licensor may, however, be strong enough to withstand the competition of his foreign licensee (or even be operating behind protection) in the home market and still wish to restrain the activity of the licensee(s); the motive then is higher profits from restriction of competition abroad. Such action may not come under antitrust laws, since the antitrust legislation covers only U. S. commerce. However, the courts have implicitly defined "U. S. commerce" quite broadly.

It is quite true that in certain types of markets, the profits (sales price, and therefore the royalties) may be greater if the volume or production is limited. If the licensor extended the privilege of production abroad to any and all companies applying, he might well cut the profit margin so low, without increasing the total value of sales, that his royalties would be less than if he restricted the number and activities of his licensees. He may, for example, extend the privilege of production and sale to *one* licensee, urging him to

take advantage of his monopoly position. Or he might divide territories among several licensees so as to provide the same advantages over a larger market.

Whether or not the licensor attempts this type of restraint is
largely a reflection of the company philosophy rather than of any
economic or market analysis which shows the existence of demand
relatively unresponsive to price. Market conditions may be such
that an expansion of production should be encouraged to reach the
point of maximum returns, but if the licensee has been given an
exclusive privilege on the basis that he can maximize profits
through restriction of sales, it is unlikely that he will attempt to
expand production. Yet, it is not at all certain that the licensor and
licensee can discern the precise conditions which would make restriction of sales profitable to them both and thereby justify exclusive
licensing.

The special conditions of international commerce today do
give rise to another set of conditions which might make it profitable
to extend exclusive licensing. These arise from the currency and
trade restrictions imposed by numerous governments. Many governments favor trade with certain other countries, providing greater
premiums in prices (or favorable exchange rates) and permitting
larger volumes of imports and usually discriminating against dollar
goods. *If* the division of third markets is involved in the licensing
program of the American company, and *if* the licensor can determine what the currency and trade picture will be for the duration
of his license agreements, it is possible that he would want to assign
certain territories to licensees in a country which is treated most
favorably in those territories, thus making their sales larger and
increasing his royalties. His action must be qualified, however, by
the fact that, in turn, the currency of the licensee must be converted
into dollars; the "gain" which the licensee made in terms of third-
currency prices and sales may turn into a "loss" when translated
into dollars at the rate provided the licensor. Once again, then, the
special condition which would seem to justify an effort at discriminating monopoly may be quite difficult to discover or to turn into
profits.

Finally, in both of the last two situations it may be necessary
to control not only the territories but also the sales volume and
prices (as well as the quality) of the products sold by the licensee.
Unless this is done—with the licensor coordinating the actions of all
licensees—the advantages of discriminatory pricing may be lost.
Such provisions in licensing agreements are, however, violations of
antitrust legislation if there is the requisite effect on U. S. foreign
commerce.

It must be admitted, however, that exclusivity which is aimed at maximizing the benefits of specialization and large-scale production may be economically appropriate. Thus, if the entire European market is required in order to increase the size of the market to a level where production of an item becomes efficient, the licensor may wish to extend the privilege of production of one item in his line to a manufacturer in Germany, and of another item to a company in England, and still a third product to a company in France. In each case, exclusive rights to the whole European area would be provided. Also, the licensor's reasons for exclusivity when a large number of licensees exist is to prevent destructive competition, especially in the early stages, from co-licensees in the home market of each licensee.

Finally, as indicated in the section concerning the licensee's motives, the licensor may be "blackmailed" into extending exclusive rights through the insistence of either the licensee or the government of the licensee that there will be no agreement without such a provision. It is not suggested, however, that even a large number of licensees are so recalcitrant as to reject a good opportunity merely because they cannot obtain exclusive privileges. Many U. S. licensors have found that this provision is subject to bargaining against others—especially against the royalty rate.

Methods to Restrain Competition

The methods (legal or not) of restraining business competition through licensing arrangements vary from tacit acceptance of restraints to specific restrictive provisions. The fact that each party recognizes the benefit to each from a restriction of operations to "home territory" may be sufficient to cause them to act in that fashion, in the absence of an express provision embodied in the agreement. In addition, however, when licensing involves patent rights (or trademarks), the extension of a privilege to use the rights under a given patent (or mark), filed in a given country, itself limits the licensee; the licensee must stay out of countries in which the licensor has patents (or marks) under which he has not received rights. In this fashion, the patent (or trademark) itself divides the market.

Where the licensor does not wish rigidly to restrict the operations of the licensee but at the same time does not wish to encourage an expansion of the latter's area of operations, the license may provide that a higher royalty be paid on sales outside of the country of the licensee. Such action, however, has brought one firm under a recent consent decree on the ground that a "penalty" was imposed on the foreign commerce of the licensee. Finally, some earlier agreements spelled out the precise areas in which the licensees could and could not operate; some leniency was extended through separating the rights to manufacture, use, and sell in different territories.

PROFITABILITY AND INCENTIVES

A major motive, if not *the* motive, for foreign licensing is profit. Without a fair estimation of profitability, the entrance of a company into licensing is a complete "shot in the dark." To determine whether it would be more profitable for a firm to enter licensing arrangements than to sell abroad directly, or to invest abroad, there must be adequate or accurate accounting of costs and returns. Once profitability is determined, there are other incentives which may make the licensor more venturesome, and there are some obstacles which may deter him. We record below the reactions of our respondents to the profitability of licensing and its relation to investment abroad.

Profitability and Cost of Licensing

About 90 percent of our respondent companies counted licensing as directly profitable; that is, returns were larger than estimated costs. This view was held despite the fact that most of these firms do not calculate costs. The lack of cost calculations was a result of the fact that royalty returns are usually a small *percentage* of total net income—though for many companies aggregate royalties run to six digits and for a few, to seven. Recent information indicates that the value of royalties returned to the United States annually is on the order of $150 million—*exclusive* of royalties left abroad (received in local currency and spent or invested), royalties coupled with dividends, and returns under cross-licenses.

Nearly 80 percent of the firms responding to a question on gross income—about half of those filling in the questionnaire did answer this question—stated that their gross income from licensing was less than 2 percent of their total income, and many of these counted the percentage as less than one. This was the case for both years 1946 and 1955. About 10 percent of those answering indicated a percentage of licensing income to total gross income in the range of 3 to 5 percent during 1946, *rising* to between 5 and 8 percent in 1955. Another tenth of the respondents showed a *rise* in the percentage from the 0 to 2 percent range in 1946 to the 3 to 5 percent range during 1955. Only one company reported a decline from the 3 to 5 percent range to the 0 to 2 percent range. Thus, licensing is showing greater activity, and as licensees gain standing in their foreign markets, their sales are picking up. Licensing, like investment, is a long-run operation.

Eighty percent of the companies replying reported royalty returns greater than costs (however calculated). In addition to the direct returns of royalties, one out of every three companies counted an increase in export sales of complementary items or component parts as an indirect return to licensing. This nonroyalty return was the entire basis for the statement of 10 percent of the respondents that their licensing was profitable; they received no royalties at all, having licensed their subsidiaries under contracts but *without* royalty payments. Of course, an increase in dividends also resulted, but no allocation to licensing was made. A final 10 percent of the companies answering asserted that licensing was not profitable directly to them. One gave no reason for the statement; others asserted that they were still too new in the operation and had not received royalties, though profitable returns were anticipated. One indicated that no royalties were obtained at all from its licenses, since it had only cross-licenses and the benefit came in the form of an exchange of information. A final company pointed out that it was under a consent decree which took all of the profitability out of its licensing programs.

By far the majority of firms interviewed or questioned treat gross licensing returns as *net* income. They agree that the costs of research and development, of patenting abroad, of registering trademarks abroad, and of the engineering and legal departments should be allocated to licensing; but they actually do not do so. A partial justification for this procedure is that these costs would be incurred in any event to support the domestic and foreign sales of the company. Another is that it would be too time-consuming and somewhat arbitrary to make the required allocations. This being so, they count licensing as essentially "costless."

The second largest group of companies charge only the "out-of-pocket" costs of direct administrative and technical services connected with negotiating and fulfilling the agreement. The remainder of the royalty returns are considered a net addition to total profits.

A third group, far in the minority, attempt to allocate the proportionate costs of the engineering and legal departments, of patent costs (including translation, attorney's fees, government expenses, renewal taxes, etc.), and of research and development. To these charges are added the direct costs of technical services, laboratory expenses, blueprints, etc., and the administrative costs of negotiation and fullfillment of the agreement. Where a department of foreign operations (or an international division) exists, a proportionate share of its costs are allocated to licensing.

The precise formulae for allocation of such expenses were not divulged, but it is generally agreed that the procedures are almost wholly arbitrary. One company, after taking pains to allocate expenses carefully among its various overseas operations, decided that the cost of making such calculations was much greater than the benefit from the supposed knowledge obtained, especially when they themselves recognized the arbitrariness of the allocation. They ceased to make the effort because the "netted" figure did not really reflect the profitability of the foreign licensing program.

Almost all the respondents were satisfied with the procedure they used for accounting profitability—whether it was to consider all licensing income as net, or not. Only 12 respondents stated that they *should* change their procedures. Of these, two stated unqualifiedly that all costs involved should be charged against royalties. The remainder asserted that they would attempt to do so only if foreign royalties became more important in the income picture. And a few of the latter questioned whether the results obtained would be useful in view of the time consumed and the arbitrariness of the results.

In sum, we may conclude that the majority of companies find licensing directly profitable as indicated by returns greater than "costs" (calculated or not calculated). A few consider the operation unprofitable, despite the fact that they have returns greater than "costs," presumably on the grounds that the *net* returns would be zero or negative if all appropriate costs were charged against royalties. Others, though they estimate costs greater than returns, still consider licensing profitable as a result of an increase in direct exports; this is particularly true of an operation which licenses subsidiaries under contract. And, finally, many companies do not know whether their operation is profitable but would not change their accounting procedures because it would be too time-consuming to do so.

Motives and Incentives to License Abroad

To determine why U. S. companies had moved into licensing, we asked them to rank a list of alternative reasons and add others they had found significant. The questionnaire list included: royalty returns, increased profits from subsidiaries, cross-licensing, expectation of future licensing from abroad, attempt to meet currency and trade restrictions by foreign governments, and attempt to aid economic development abroad.

As would be expected, more than 80 percent of the firms listed as important in *some* rank the possibility of *royalty returns*. Over 50 percent placed this motive first, and many considered this their only incentive. But for about one fourth of the firms responding, direct royalty returns were a second-rank motive; it was a third- or fourth-rank motive for less than 10 percent. Those companies not indicating royalties as a motive at all were either licensing only subsidiaries, and thus counted *an increase in subsidiaries' profits* as a prime motive, or they licensed only under *cross-licensing* arrangements and listed this first. Thus, more than 20 percent of the respondents gave *subsidiary profits* as the primary incentive, and just over 10 percent listed *cross-licensing* first. Nearly one third of the companies ranked *subsidiary profits* first, second, or third, and about one fifth gave *cross-licensing* either first, second, or third place.

Apart from the possibility of direct returns to the company through royalties, profits of subsidiaries, or rights granted under cross-licenses, the major incentive to license abroad since World War II has been a negative one. *Currency and trade restrictions* of foreign governments have made other means of doing business abroad relatively less attractive. Nearly 60 percent of the respondents said this situation was an incentive in their licensing program, and more than 40 percent indicated it was of first importance. (The number of first-rank votes for the various incentives will add to greater than 100 percent since a few respondents merely checked the factors leaving us to count them of equal rank, while others indicated that two factors were of first-place and equal rank.)

The fifth-ranking motive was *assisting in the economic development of foreign countries*. Despite the derisive laughs of one or two respondents who seemed to think that such motives were "un-American," more than 20 percent of the respondents indicated that a sincere desire to "help others help themselves" was an incentive of some degree in their licensing programs. One tenth of the respondents to the mailed questionnaire indicated that this motive was first for their company, and another tenth placed it in second or third position, with a few companies placing it fifth or sixth. The extent to which this motive is important in the overall foreign economic policy of the United States has been suggested in a previous report.[9]

The last-ranked motive among those listed in the questionnaire was using licensing to *open up opportunities* for obtaining licenses from abroad. Only 15 percent indicated this was a factor in their decision, and less than 10 percent ranked it first. In the experience of most firms, there is little that foreign companies have to provide American companies in the way of patents, trademarks, or

---

[9]*IDEA*, Vol. 2, No. 1 (March 1958), pp. 137-158.

even know-how—at least through a separate licensing agreement. The most valuable returns apparently came through cross-licenses, though there are a significant number of separate agreements under which the U. S. company is a licensee.

The questionnaire did not exhaust the motives of business firms in embarking on licensing programs abroad. Respondents added nearly a dozen of their own, which were sometimes placed first, second, or third.

Of special interest is the relation of licensing to direct investment. Some respondents have preferred licensing to investment and the reverse has been true of others. Even some foreign governments, such as Brazil and Japan, have at times preferred licensing to investment and/or have strictly controlled both. A group of Brazilian manufacturers recently asserted that they would prefer to see an expansion of licensing over U. S. direct investment because the shipment of U. S. machinery would (1) alter the competitive position if others in the industry could not obtain the same equipment, and (2) lead to overproduction in the industry.

A large number of companies are, reportedly, coupling investment with licensing—or licensing with investment. Nearly two thirds of the respondents reported a financial interest in their licensees. The actual percentage may be greater since some respondents replied that they had no financial interest in licensees but answered in the same question that they licensed subsidiaries. Thus, they made a distinction between licensing a subsidiary (probably wholly owned or at least controlled) and investing in an "independent" licensee.

To check on the extent to which subsidiaries were licensed, we asked each of those having subsidiaries to state whether they were licensed and why. Eighty percent of the respondents to the mailed questionnaire reported that they had foreign subsidiaries. Of these, exactly two thirds *did* license the subsidiary, while the remaining third did not. The reasons for *not* licensing the subsidiary were that the foreign company was wholly owned, and it was thus not necessary, or that licensing was not required in order to assure a return of profits. One of the major reasons for licensing the subsidiary stemmed from the desirability of recording a basis for royalty payments so as to increase returns from the subsidiary; this was a reason in about 15 percent of the cases where subsidiaries were licensed. The reason given most frequently (in 30 percent of the cases) was that licensing made for legal preciseness; it gave control over the name, patents, trademarks, and techniques in the event of nationalization, sale of an interest, or even local infringement. This reason was stated to be even more important when the subsidiary was not wholly owned, but it was important for many even when it was a trademark that was licensed. Additional reasons given were that licensing permitted the subsidiary to sublicense abroad, that licensing reduced the tax burden for the subsidiary, and that sometimes exchange control regulations required or induced licensing of a subsidiary; in the last instance, the authorities have sometimes become convinced that the royalties are a necessary *expense* which warrants more ready remission. In addition, where profits of the subsidiary are high, it may be desirable to "reduce" them by royalty payments to the parent. This action increases the "expenses" of the subsidiary and cuts taxable income; it also reduces profits as seen by potential competitors, thus tending to cut unwanted competition.

In order to determine the pattern of financial relationships, we requested respondents to indicate the number of licensees which were wholly owned subsidiaries, partially owned subsidiaries, subsidiaries in which they held a controlling interest, and licensees in which they held no financial interest. Rather than give the numbers involved, several respondents merely indicated that the ratio of wholly owned to non-wholly-owned was 15:1, 2:1, or 1:10. The statistical picture of those replying quantitatively is as follows:

Number of Licensees	Wholly Owned	Partially Owned	Controlling Interest	No Financial Interest
0	25	32	28	7
1-5	31	25	26	45
6-10	4	2	7	13
11-15	2	—	1	7
16-20	1	1	1	5
21-50	—	—	—	4
100/Over	—	—	—	2

As indicated above, a major reason why many subsidiaries were not licensed was the fact that they were wholly owned; the above table indicates that 25 companies reported that they had wholly owned subsidiaries which they did not license; in comparison, 38 companies reported licensees (totaling over 100) which were wholly owned subsidiaries. Thirty-two (not necessarily different) companies reported that they had partially owned subsidiaries which they did not license; 28 reported that they had a controlling interest in subsidiaries which were not licensed. And only seven stated that they had no licensees in which they had *no* financial interest at all.

The three "investment with licensing" relationships were

overwhelmed by that of "pure" licensing. Forty-five companies reported one to five licensees in which no financial interest was involved; 13 reported six to ten, etc., up to a total of 76 companies reporting well over 600 licensees in which they had no financial interest. This compares with just over 200 licensees in which these (and other) licensors had some financial interest.

In order to find the reasons behind the decisions to invest or not to invest in licensees, we asked whether the relationship was a result of an overall policy position or accidental and *ad hoc.* Those companies which had both types of arrangements (investment and independent licensees) usually did not reply to the question. About 20 firms stated that they had made a definite decision to license only where they had an investment, but five which licensed only when they held an equity interest indicated that no overt decision had been made. The major reasons given by those who had made such a decision was that they desired (1) the added control (especially where know-how was licensed) and (2) the commercial interest (returns) available through investment. Only a few indicated that they had adopted a policy of gradual investment from licensing an independent firm to finally purchasing controlling interest in the licensee. Some stated that they generally licensed only subsidiaries but had no *policy* against investing in independent licensees; it was just that capital was already so scarce that all available funds were needed for expansion of the company's own production. Others reported, however, that they had a strong bias toward investing in licensees and that where they held no financial interest it was because it was impossible to buy into the licensee.

While it might seem odd that companies would license subsidiaries or invest in licensees without taking an overt policy decision, this was the situation with two thirds of those who stated that they had no financial interest in their licensees. Only one third of those having no financial interest in licensees stated that it was the result of a definite policy decision by their executives. The others had apparently not given the matter sufficient thought, or had just drifted into the easiest practice at the behest of licensees.

Among the reasons given by those who had given the matter consideration sufficient to have taken a policy decision, the main factors were that the licensees were all established manufacturers who did not require and would look askance at contributions of capital from the licensor *or* that the desired returns could be gained without investing. Variations of these two positions were reflected in the assertions that "it would be like the tail wagging the dog since all have ample capital"; that "we have not had to invest, so why do so"; that "there has been no occasion to invest"; or that "we have tried to avoid investing because greater returns can be gained at home." One respondent merely asserted that the company had adopted a policy of not expanding abroad, without giving a reason; (this company had 20 independent licensees). Another reason, given without explanation, was that the company believed the licensee does a better job if he has control of the foreign firm himself. Finally, one licensor, having only *one* financially related licensee out of 12, asserted that it makes licensing agreements with independent firms only when the financial interest might be endangered by local conditions; in other words, the company had apparently taken a decision to invest yet had found only one in 12 to be a "safe" situation.

Without knowing the periods in which the financial interests developed and whether those with financial interests grew out of prior licensing arrangements, we cannot conclude from the above that licensing is a precursor to investment or that licensing with investment is growing. We must wait on more extensive and intensive investigation. But the close tie between the two is demonstrated by the fact (see above tabular data) that 50-odd companies had more than 100 financially related (*non*-wholly-owned) licensees.

Obstacles to Licensing of Patent Rights and Know-How

So far we have examined the various *advantages* of licensing abroad—those which are independent of any other technique for operating abroad and those which arise in comparison with exports and direct investment. There are also some *obstacles* to licensing which arise apart from any comparison with other methods of doing foreign business. In order to obtain the experience of U. S. companies, we asked whether they had refused any requests for licenses and why. Nearly half the respondents indicated that they had never refused an applicant. Such an experience resulted either from a policy of "open" licensing or from a small number of requests from desirable licensees.

There is not a clear dominance of one reason over others of why licenses were refused. "Inadequacy of the foreign market," "general economic conditions abroad," "political instability abroad," and "reputability of applicant company" were each considered of the same importance. However, "inadequate market" was the factor placed first by nearly 20 percent of the respondents; "political instability," "reputability of the applicant," and "incompetency of foreign executives" were each placed first by about 10 percent of the respondents. The preponderance of second-place ranking went to the factors of "an inadequate market" and "general economic conditions." Only about 15 percent of the companies replying listed disagreement over terms of the license as being important in a negative decision; most seemed able to iron out negotiating differences. However, a few could not convince foreign governmental agencies of the desirability of provisions the parties had agreed upon, so lack of approval became the deciding obstacle. Less than 3 percent of the respondents listed as obstacles at all the taxation of royalties by the United States or a foreign government, the risk of antitrust violation, or the fact that costs appeared greater than anticipated returns.

The following reasons for denying applicants were added by a few firms:

a) a lack of technicians abroad,

b) prior commitments not to set up competing licensees,

c) extreme care by licensor to control quality and maintain reputation of the product,

d) existence of a conflicting trademark situation,

e) U. S. military classification preventing disclosure,

f) choice of the best prepared licensee, thereby denying the less able or the poorly equipped,

g) affiliation of the applicant with a U. S. competitor, and

h) unwillingness to set up competition in a market already served or to be exploited later.

THE LICENSE CONTRACT

The profitability of any licensing arrangement depends significantly on the terms of the agreement. The licensee requires some guarantees, and the licensor wants some assurances and protection. The promises of each form the license contract. Some U. S. licensors have stated that no contract is worth more than the mutual respect and confidence underlying it and that, given good faith, there is little need for a written contract. Such a statement is admittedly an oversimplification. The reasoning behind it is that the licensee will respect the license so long as the rights or information is useful to him—whether or not the contract is written. Mutual benefit and good faith are the *sine qua non* of successful licensing. Although some few licenses *have* been verbal and some have been arranged more or less informally in letters, almost all those contracted today are written. The death of officials who negotiated longstanding agreements, the transfer of officials to other companies, or mere misunderstandings as to what *was* agreed upon—each is a reason for having a written contract.

The growing importance of licensing operations has caused several firms with longstanding contracts to renegotiate them along the pattern of more recent agreements. About half of the companies queried in our investigations had succeeded in establishing a more or less standardized form for their license contracts, which is altered as little as possible for each licensee. A few companies are able, because of very large licensing programs and a policy of extending licenses readily to all applicants, to print contract forms into which are written appropriate names, rights transferred, and applicable payment terms with each individual licensee.

The advantage of a standardized form does not rest wholly in the simplification of negotiations. The potential licensee is assured that he is being treated in the same fashion as all other licensees; nondiscrimination may be important in the eyes of the licensee. This equality of treatment may be important also in helping the licensor to bargain more effectively when the applicant-licensee desires certain provisions that the licensor does not wish to grant—e.g., exclusivity—he may then argue that he cannot break his *pattern* of non-exclusivity and treat one licensee more favorably than all others. Contrarily, of course, a printed form reduces the flexibility of negotiations. "Tailoring" of the contract by making concessions to a particular situation is more difficult, though it can still be done to some extent by varying the royalty rates. Some licensors, however, have standard rates also. In some companies' experience, "tailoring" is more important than the advantages of standardization. This can be decided only on a case-by-case basis.

Purpose and Use of Major Provisions

The observations in this section are drawn from our interviews and questionnaires. So as not to impose on the hospitality of our respondents, we did not attempt to obtain a complete and detailed picture of their contracts. Rather we questioned them on some of the more critical provisions. We therefore did not try to obtain the most detailed information concerning *each* company's experience.

The questionnaire did not provide for ways to distinguish between provisions of licenses with a subsidiary or an independent company abroad. Many of the respondents volunteered information broken down according to the type of license or business relationship. Thus, the question concerning exclusivity provisions was answered differently by the same firm when referring to trademark licenses and to patent licenses. And, the provisions of quality control were strongly affected by whether the license was of a trademark or patent. Although it is difficult to separate the answers, it may be that protective provisions also are closely related to the type of license; the evidence gathered so far cannot be used to support either contention, however. On the other hand, the *form* of royalty provisions does not seem to be greatly affected by whether the license covers patents, trademarks, or know-how—though the rates employed vary greatly.

Another qualification concerning the replies is that they, perforce, related to the *general* experience of the company. It would be impossible to categorize all the provisions of every contract, and it would be meaningless to do so. Different provisions are meaningful only when they are related to the specific problems in each case. Thus, a case study would have to be made of the circumstances surrounding each contract. What we hoped to obtain was a picture of the more usual practices; this can be a guide to companies newly entering the field and will provide older hands some knowledge of what others are doing. With these objectives in mind, our question was limited to provisions which seem to involve the more important policy problems.

Exclusivity[10]

Exclusive rights are generally extended under trademark licenses, and there is apparently a willingness on the part of a large number of U. S. licensors to extend them under other types. Over two thirds of the respondents indicated that they commonly extend exclusive rights to manufacture abroad; one fourth stated that they did not usually do so; a few respondents failed to answer this question. These replies do not, of course, mean that all licenses extended by a company provide exclusivity; the replies reflect only its general practice.

One fourth of the respondents stated that they did not give the licensee exclusive rights to use patented inventions abroad, but about half of them stated that they usually did so; 28 percent failed to answer. Over a third indicated that they normally extended the licensee exclusive rights to sell in his territory; about 20 percent failed to answer.

These answers show that there is a general willingness on the part of most of the respondents to extend exclusive rights *or* that they considered it necessary to do so in order to get the contract signed by the potential licensee. Some interviewed officials stated that the latter was the case, but others asserted that exclusive rights <u>could be</u> bargained away with a lower royalty rate. Exclusivity is

[10]The reasons for, advantages and disadvantages of and problems resulting from exclusivity are raised and partially examined in the previous section on antitrust problems.

generally a cause for higher royalty rates, and inadequate performance by the licensee is usually cause for removal of exclusive rights.

In about one fifth of the cases, the grant of exclusivity was
coupled with prohibitions against the licensee operating or selling
in any other territory than his own. That is, he would not be permitted to sell in third areas not covered by the trademark or patent;
his competition with the licensor was thus restricted. Over 70 percent of the respondents, however, indicated that they did permit
the licensee to sell in third countries in competition with themselves or other licensees; (we sought no information as to whether
the licensees actually did make such sales). Where coupled with
exclusivity provisions, this action does provide for some area of competition; and when exclusivity is not extended to all, it is a generali-
zation of the competitive spirit.

Another provision which affects the degree of exclusivity is
that extending rights to the licensee under patents and trademarks
held by the licensor in third countries. For example, a French company might be given rights under patents and trademarks which the
licensor holds in Belgium or Holland. If the rights extended are
exclusive, this expansion makes the market even more exclusive.
But if nonexclusivity exists, the extension of rights under patents
and trademarks in third countries in not necessarily a reduction of
competition. In fact, it may increase the competition among licensees and possibly with the licensor. Respondents split almost 50:50
in their writing of such provisions. Nearly half of them indicated
that they did give rights to a single licensee under patents or marks
in more than one country; over 40 percent stated that they did not,
with the remainder not answering. Coupled with the fact that a
large percentage of licensors extend exclusive rights to manufacture,
to use, and to sell, it might appear that this provision and the extension of rights in third countries increase exclusivity. But such a
conclusion would be unwarranted without more detailed information concerning how many firms coupled these provisions in a *single*
contract of a type which would in fact lead to greater exclusivity.

Supervision and Quality Control

Although it is a widely accepted proposition that control of
quality is essential to trademark licensing, there is a significant
amount of supervision and control under patent licensing also
However, many patent licenses do not include supervision or
quality control; the rationale is that poor quality will hurt only
the licensee and it will be to his interest to maintain a high quality
Know-how licenses or technical assistance agreements seldom in-

volve quality control. In all, 25 percent of the respondents indicated that they imposed no supervisory restrictions on the licensee's production.

Among the two thirds of the respondents who asserted that they did include supervisory provisions, there was no distinct pattern of implementation. The largest number imposed quality controls through inspection of samples returned to the home office *and* by sending representatives or technicians abroad. But there were nearly as many which employed only one of these two methods. Inspection of samples was used only slightly more frequently than inspection in the field. Presumably, for those whose foreign operations are important enough to require inspection, representatives or technicians traveling abroad are available to perform the job.

Inspection of products is not the only method of quality control. There are a few firms that require the licensee to send plant designs and product specifications before production is approved by the licensor.

Nor is quality control the only purpose of supervision of the licensee. Some few of the licensors control labeling of the product, especially where the license covers a trademark and component parts are supplied. Others also control advertising and sales procedures. Although this aspect was not covered in our questionnaire, some licensors also control the pricing of the final product.

Access to Improvements and Future Developments

One of the reasons why definitions of the subject matter to be transferred and the product market to be served are so important is that improvements by the licensor are frequently made available to the licensee. In order not to be giving away what was not originally intended, the precise area of improvements must be carefully delineated.

Well over 80 percent of our respondents stated that they extend the licensee access to *all* relevant information concerning the products licensed. About 10 percent did not reply to the question, but of the remaining 10 percent some indicated that they provided any and all "necessary" information. This provision usually includes improvements made in the product or process during the life of the agreement. The licensor is, obviously, arbiter as to what is and what is not relevant to the licensed rights. As one licensor has stated: "I will tell the licensee all of what I am doing, but nothing of what I am thinking." Thus, actual improvements made in the licensed product or process which are applied by the licensor will often be given to the licensee without additional payment. If blueprints, design drawings, or engineering layouts are involved, sometimes a fee is charged for these services.

But access to improvements in a licensed product or process does not give the licensee rights to new developments. Once again, careful definition is required to distinguish a mere improvement from a new development. However, for three fourths of the licensors questioned, the distinction is not so important since they apparently readily extended future developments also to the licensee. Just over one fifth of the licensors queried did not usually accept a contractual obligation to supply the licensee with future developments; however, some of these respondents did so in practice.

The argument against providing future developments under one contract is that very profitable developments may be discovered which warrant different treatment. A hedge against such a possibility would be a clause permitting renegotiation of royalty provisions, but this seems seldom to be used. Licensors would apparently rather keep the contract simple—either excluding or clearly including future developments within the initially negotiated contract.

Compensation

The basic principles underlying provisions covering compensation are, of course, the simple ones of cost to the supplier and value to the purchaser. To state the principles does not explain them nor show how they should be applied. There are, apparently, two rules of thumb applied by licensors: one is to cover allowable costs—i.e., some portion of research and development and out-of-pocket costs; the other is to charge whatever more than this amount the traffic will bear. The rules reduce, then, to charging what the licensee will pay and not signing the contract when this amount is less than calculated "costs."

Where definite costs of providing specific information can be isolated, the agreement will frequently require the payment of fees for this information. And where costs of developing the information and maintaining the patent can be ascertained, a down payment is frequently charged to cover them. Such a payment is coupled with additional types of remuneration aimed at getting something of the value of the rights to the licensee. Nearly 40 percent of the respondents employ a down payment as part of their compensation requirements. The major reason for a down payment is to enable the licensor to justify making available the people necessary to set up and supervise the program and to meet the needs of the licensee. Licensing makes the licensor a sort of management engineering firm; top executive talent will be required, and it is expensive to divert it to foreign operations. It is usually not profitable to provide the licensee merely with blueprints, specifications, and know-how; he must also be given some "show-how." He may even have to be shown what to ask of the licensor. The down payment is a means of paying for the initially heavy use of such executive and technical talent.

The different compensation arrangements, which may or may not be coupled with a downpayment, include: fixed annual payments, royalties according to volume of sales by licensee, minimum royalty payments, royalty rates decreasing over the life of the agreement or as volumes increase, a royalty-free period or royalties set low in early years to help licensee get started, maximum payments, stock payments, payments per unit volume of production, and profits from sales of components.

Royalty rates are usually fixed but may be of the sliding scale variety—starting low to ease the burden on the licensee as he gets the business into operation, or going down with increased volume. Percentage rates provide some protection against inflation as compared to fixed payments per unit. A minimum royalty return provides an incentive to the licensee to produce at least a certain volume and not "sit on" the rights. Progressive minimums are sometimes stipulated; they are especially valuable as an escape clause. Down payments, when prohibited by governmental authorities, are sometimes prorated over the royalty rate.

Where subsidiaries are involved, the returns from licensing may be undistinguished from dividends on investments. A significant number of licensor-investors do have contracts with subsidiaries, however, in order to keep the records straight and to make it easier to transfer earnings to the parent company. And, it is sometimes easier to persuade the foreign government that payments for licensed rights are an expense of operation necessary to the continuation of the business.

The amount of compensation will vary according to the bargaining power of the parties, the custom in the industry, and the provisions of the contract which make it more or less valuable to the licensee. We can say little about relative bargaining power except that the licensor has an asset which he must guard carefully to maintain its value and that most of the respondents entered into license agreements at the behest of foreign licensees. Thus, the greater bargaining power would seem temporarily to rest with the U. S. licensor. This position is receiving some strong competition from European licensors.

We do not yet have enough evidence to set forth the patterns of rate-making within each industry. But, apparently throughout all of them, the following situations give rise to a higher return to the licensors:

a) an especially valuable process or product in the country of the licensor,
b) a high degree of "completeness" of the process or product; that is, little additional research necessary to make the development commercial abroad,
c) extension of exclusive rights under the contract,
d) extension of rights to sublicense or assign,
e) a large-size territory,
f) a longer duration of the contract,
g) a relatively strong patent position,
h) extension of the right to use future improvements and/or developments,
i) agreement by licensor not to export to country of licensee —but this may lead to antitrust indictment.

The methods of obtaining the returns may be classed according to whether the royalties are based on sales or on another means of calculation.

Royalties based on sales. Over two thirds of the respondents employ as the only or major method of compensation a royalty rate based on volume of *net* sales by the licensee. This rate has a distinct advantage over other bases of calculation in that it hedges against inflation in the country of the licensee. In addition, a rate *per unit* becomes more burdensome to the licensee when prices drop and may make him antagonistic toward the agreement. The value calculation is usually based on total sales less cost of advertising, packaging, delivery, taxes, etc., and may be net of the value of any component parts supplied by the licensor. The rate itself varies widely from one fourth of 1 percent to as high as 30 percent.[11] Different ways of calculating net sales may account for some of the spread, but the differences are accounted for mostly in terms of volume of sales expected and the number of rights for which each rate is applicable. For example, when rates are less than 1 percent, several different patents are involved in the agree-

---

[11]What the parties may agree upon as an appropriate rate may not actually govern. Several governments insist on approving the financial terms and they may allow remittance only of smaller amounts than the agreement would provide. Some licensees have apparently been "willing" to agree on higher royalties, under the knowledge that either the authorities would reduce them *or* they could persuade the authorities to clamp a lower ceiling on royalty payments.

ment, each with a separate rate; the total royalty on a finished product may then rise to 5 percent or more.

It is safe to say that 5 percent is close to the mode of the rates based on net sales. The reason for this is that a rule of thumb has apparently been adopted among many negotiators that 20 percent of net profits is a fair portion for the licensor, and expected net profits were apparently habitually estimated to be 25 percent of net sales. However, in the case of some food processing licenses, the royalty was calculated at 34 percent of net profit of the licensee; and in the licensing of Sulphanilyl—Aminopyridine 50 percent of net profits was charged.[12]

Examples of rates based on *net* sales are provided by the licensing of a petroleum cracking catalyst, of sulfadiazine, and of polysulfide synthetic—each licensed at 5 percent of net sales. Crude rubber and polysulfide synthetic, when licensed to the government, have been compensated at the rate of 2.5 percent of net sales.

Gross sales have been the base for calculating royalties on methods of drilling, mud control, and treatment of petroleum emulsions, carriers, and styrene—all either 2.5 percent or 5 percent of *gross* sales. Modifications have been used in the cases of sponge rubber products, under which the rate was 5 percent of net sales plus a minimum annual payment of $4,000. Cheese wrapping materials have been licensed at 10 percent of net sales to a given date and 5 percent thereafter.

A modification of royalties based on sales is the use of a minimum annual royalty payment. This may be set as a fixed amount or as a requirement that the licensee sell a minimum volume. Either works out as a guarantee of an annual return of a given amount to the licensor. Over 40 percent of our respondents indicated that they impose minima. Minima help to keep the licensee on his toes and provide a justification for the licensor requiring a renegotiation of some of the provisions of the license (e.g., exclusivity) or for cancelling the license.

In order to ease the burden of payments on the licensee either as his performance improves or as the period of the license lengthens, some licensors have provided for a decreasing royalty rate. The rate may be permitted to decrease in any given period as volume of sales rises from one plateau to another, or the rate may begin to decrease after the fifth year or so. Only about 10 percent

---

[12]Rate examples in this section are taken from a study by Robert S. Aries, "Licensing Your Process," *Petroleum Refiner*, February 1956, pp. 147-148.

of our respondents stated that they employed this procedure. An alternative way of achieving much the same purpose is the provision of a maximum royalty payment—or, as one interviewee put it, "a knock-out" payment. When an annual payment would rise above this maximum, the licensee has to pay only the stipulated maximum. This guards against the licensor "over-charging" the licensee. However, only about 5 percent of the respondents use this method. The others apparently accept the philosophy of one official who replied that when he had a good thing he wanted to get all that he could out of it; in part, such profitable situations balanced out those which did not return so much.

Other payment methods. In order to cover annual costs and to make certain that some income is returned, some agreements are drawn with fixed payments per period. Some 15 percent of the respondents indicated that they write such provisions into their agreements. Most of them are coupled, however, with royalties based on sales.

Another method of payment which is coupled with royalties on sales is that of payment in equities. In order to obtain a larger participation in the profits of the licensee and to reduce the burden of remittances during the early periods of growth, payment in equities has been accepted by about 5 percent of our respondents. While we did not include this method as one of the possibilities on the questionnaire, several volunteered that they were employing it. There is growing interest in this method to obtain an equity interest especially when the licensor would like to invest abroad but does not have the capital at hand.

A method which substitutes for royalties based on sales is that requiring a payment per unit of production or per unit of feed-in. Several of the firms stated that they employ this technique. For example, payments under a license covering polysulfide synthetic rubber and another for styrene require payment of $0.00125 per pound produced. A coal carbonization process requires payment of one cent per ton of coal delivered to the retort. Modifications of the per unit rate are exemplified by a license for polysulfide synthetic rubber which carries a rate of $0.0236 per pound, but such rate never to be less than 3 percent of the net selling price. A license covering lubricating oils carries a rate of $0.035 per pound adjusted to the index of wholesale commodity prices and the chlorine content.

A specific payment (10 U.S. cents) per unit should be made subject to adjustment; if inflation is rampant in the licensee country, the specific payment in dollars may increase the burden on the licensee; contrarily, the licensor will be burdened if the payment is in local currency.

Rates combining per unit output, inputs, and/or sales volumes are exemplified by some licenses in the field of catalytic petroleum refining. A license covering a fluid catalytic cracking process requires payment of five cents per barrel of fresh feed stock, plus five cents per barrel of aviation products, and 3 percent of the price of other special liquid products.

One covering hydro catalytic reforming requires 5.5 cents per barrel of fresh feed stock and the same additions as above. A license covering insecticidal compositions requires 5 percent of net sales with a maximum rate, plus $0.0004 for each percent DDT content up to and including 10 percent and $0.000333 for each percent DDT over 10 percent.

A final means of payment under licensing agreements is used when the sale of component parts is extremely important in the arrangement. Though such a case is exceptional, one licensor has eschewed all other methods of payments and takes his entire returns through the pricing of component parts. This has the advantage of greater certainty and would probably bring more ready approval by the foreign government of imports since the license arrangement demonstrates the necessity of meeting this expense in order to produce at all. Even where such sales occur, most licensors do not rely on them heavily for income. They apparently agree on a "cost plus 15 percent" or similar formula; they seem to feel that a low price will enable greater sales by the licensee and return more in royalties than in profits on components.

Return of improvements. A possible compensation for licensing arises when and if the licensee makes an improvement in the product or process licensed. Over 60 percent of those responding stated that they required the return to them of improvements developed by the licensee; nine out of every ten of these required them to be returned royalty free. Some 30 percent of the respondents did not anticipate any value from such a clause.

The rationale for including a grant back of improvements is that the licensor might find himself in a position of not being able to make the best product despite the fact that he had developed most of it. He would also be in a position of not being able to license his other licensees unless he obtains permission to sublicense the improvement. One licensor multilateralizes improvements by extending them freely to all licensees who have signed a grant back clause on improvements.

The experience of our respondents and interviewees, however, is that grant backs of improvements have resulted in few benefits. Of course, a subsidiary relationship makes the problem largely irrelevant.

Protection

A stong patent or trademark position enhances the value of the license and is a basis for a higher return to the licensor. To maintain such a position requires yearly payments. About 60 percent of our respondents prefer to keep the reins in their own hands and maintain the patent or trademark (and pay the costs) themselves. Only about 15 percent require the licensee to undertake the maintenance of the patent or trademark (and pay the costs); and most of these are apparently subsidiaries. However, in some countries (e.g., Italy) local companies pay at lower rates than do foreign companies. The licensee is more frequently required to maintain the asset and pay costs if the license is exclusive. In this way, a patent which the licensor would otherwise drop may be kept alive by the licensee. About 10 percent of the respondents share the costs with the licensee on some agreed formula.

Protection of the patent or trademark position involves the responsibility of preventing infringement by others. Once again, the U.S. licensors responding usually take this responsibility upon themselves; half of them stated that they defend against any infringement. About 30 percent share the responsibility with the licensee. The licensee may sometimes initiate action, but it is usually permitted only after consultation with the licensor. Costs of litigation are to be shared as well as awards. In about 10 percent of the programs, the licensee is usually given the responsibility or privilege of bringing action; this procedure is probably followed most frequently when a subsidiary is the licensee. The responsibility is sometimes placed upon a licensee if he is given exclusive rights.

Infringement cases may also arise from the suit of third parties against the licensee based on his use of the patent or trademark. Most respondents do not guarantee the validity of a patent or the trademark registration. Over 40 percent of the respondents, therefore, place liability for infringements of others' rights upon the licensee. Less than 30 percent take the responsibility wholly upon themselves, and about 15 percent share it with the licensee. Some licensors make themselves liable to damages up to the amount of royalties already received but no more. A subsidiary-licensee relation makes the procedure largely formal.

In order to protect against changes in the laws or policies of either government, it has been suggested that agreements include an "escape" clause permitting either party to call for renegotiation or even to cancel if governmental attitudes change or the agreement is found to be in violation of any laws. Use of such a provision is not accepted by the majority of our respondents. Its use and nonuse is evenly balanced. About 40 percent of the respondents indicated that they usually include it, while an equal percentage stated that they usually did not. Many do not consider that it is necessary, especially if it is stated in the agreement what laws the agreement is to come under.

Another type of protection is sought from unlicensed action by the licensee. Under patents, the licensee has no rights to continued use if the contract is terminated before the patent life is ended; he has use of information in the public domain if the patent has run out. If a trademark license is terminated and the licensor has been careful to maintain ownership, the licensee must stop using the mark. But, the case of a know-how license is blurred by the absence of legal redress. Nearly two thirds of our respondents insert a clause prohibiting the licensee from using the know-how after the license is terminated; about 30 percent do not usually include such a provision. Even those who do write it have had little experience in attempting to enforce it, and no one seems to know how to enforce the prohibition in the case of know-how. The clause seems, therefore, to be mainly a warning or a statement of rights.

Termination

Provisions for the duration and termination of agreements are usually different depending on whether they cover patents or trademarks. Only about half of the respondents indicated that they licensed their trademarks at all. Of these, over 60 percent licensed the marks for a definite and renewable period. The periods were usually in multiples of five: that is 5, 10, 15, or 20 years. This provision has the advantage of permitting renegotiation or cancellation at definite and known periods without stated reasons. In an exceptional case, a trademark was licensed on a year-to-year basis. Over a third of those licensing their marks did so for indefinite terms but with provision for termination. Under 10 percent extended licenses for the life of the registration; however, these also were presumably terminable under specified conditions.

It might appear to the layman that the fact that a patent has a definite number of years to run would cause any license agreement concerning it to be made for the same length of time. But only about 40 percent of those licensing under patents made the duration of the license coterminous with the life of the patent. An equal percentage usually wrote agreements having a duration shorter than the life of the patent. The advantage to such an arrangement would seem to lie in the ability to cancel the agreement if desired without prior cause or to force renegotiation if the licensee's performance was not adequate. Agreements are also written to terminate one year before the end of the life of the patent apparently in order to protect the licensor's title and to avoid having the license declared as a sale or assignment.

About 15 percent of the respondents licensing under patents indicated that they usually wrote agreements for a duration longer than the life of patents covered. Such an arrangement would come about when know-how was also important and future developments of the licensor were considered important to the licensee. Three percent of those responding indicated that they wrote patent license agreements for indefinite periods.

IMPLICATIONS OF THE STUDY

Profitability and Accounting Procedures

We found in our investigations of profitability and cost practices that most of our respondents do not accurately account for the costs of their licensing program. The implications of this lack of accounting may be serious in the long run, especially as licensing increases in importance, since decisions may be made on the wrong bases.

Effect of Accounting Inadequacy

Without an accurate account of the costs and returns of licensing, most officials are continually in doubt as to whether the apparent rewards of foreign licensing are actual or merely "book" profits, arbitrarily allocated to that department of the company. Obviously such doubts affect their business decisions—especially those of the Board of Directors who may be highly skeptical of any operation purportedly returning income which is 100 percent "net profit."

The first thing that can be said of the procedure of not "costing" the licensing program is that it makes the activity look much more profitable than it really is and thereby makes domestic business or foreign sales look relatively less attractive. This result obviously occurs if *no* costs are attributed to licensing. There is little disagreement that costs which are incurred directly as a result of the licensing program should be set against licensing returns; the disagreement arises over whether the effort required to keep time sheets on the services of technicians, draftsmen, legal counsel, and executives is worth the more accurate accounting which would be obtained.

A few firms do keep time sheets on personnel who are related to both domestic operations and foreign licensing. This decision was based on the view that a procedure which lumped all costs in one department together to be set against domestic sales would raise the costs of the domestic sales or even of foreign sales. This rise in cost might result in a drop in sales, depending on the pricing technique followed.

If pricing of the end product is on the basis of cost plus a percentage mark-up, then the procedure of not "costing" licensing increases the price of direct sales. This higher price may well reduce profits of the firm if there is any inclination for total revenue to fall off when prices rise. With a slightly lower price, the company may be able to attract enough additional customers to increase its total net income. Depending on the procedure of offsetting costs and on the size of the licensing program, the company may be harming itself by not keeping a more accurate account of its activities.

However, if the company is operating in a non-competitive market or one in which sales volume is not greatly price-responsive, the cost procedure will not affect price so directly. That is, the price will be determined more on the basis of "what the market will bear." The impact of the cost procedure falls on the level of operations of the firm; it decides how much of the commodity to offer to the public and then asks as much as it feels the public will pay for that amount. If cost procedures are not accurate, the level of operations may be greater or smaller than the optimum, thereby reducing the profits of the firm.

In no instance, therefore, is the cost procedure irrelevant; it may be unimportant if the level of licensing operations is insignificant. However, the level of operations is important in shaping a company's attitude toward licensing; thus, if only one or two licenses are anticipated, the cost of making new decisions, carrying out negotiations, and fulfilling the contract may seem excessive. But, if more licenses are anticipated, the overhead costs of familiarizing the officials with procedures and setting up the required organization can be spread over larger revenues. Whereas a few licenses may seem unprofitable, a larger program can become quite profitable. Company officials may decide that greater accuracy in cost procedures will pay off in more efficient, and therefore profitable, decision-making as to the firm's activities. Unless a better picture of costs is obtained than is now usually done, licensing will appear to return a higher rate than other operations open to the company.

"Maximization" Procedure

Ideally, in order to maximize profits of the company, domestic sales, direct exports, investment at home or abroad, and licensing at home or abroad should each return the same rate of profit *at the margin*. That is, each should be carried to the point where an additional transaction or activity under it will return the same net income as an equal expenditure would in any of the company's other operations. Under this approach, no one operation could be said to be "more profitable" than another save through comparing the *aggregate* profit which each returned. If a company has not equalized the marginal profit returns from each of its different operations, it should be readily discernible which one of them should be expanded next; and, total net income will not be at a maximum (assuming an efficient operation) until marginal returns *are* equal.

The argument as to whether direct export (as a whole) is more profitable than foreign licensing (as an entire program)[13] is a reflection of a confusion over cost and pricing procedures. It is unlikely that direct sales abroad will be "more profitable" throughout *all* levels than some volume of foreign licensing. The problem is to discover the proper balance between licensing and exports and also between exports and foreign investment. This can be done only after a more careful examination of the procedure which will maximize total net profits of the company and of how closely this procedure may be approximated in practice.

Allocation of Research and Development (or Other "Fixed") Costs

Some firms allocate *all* research and development (as well as legal, administrative, and foreign patent) costs to domestic operations and foreign sales; others follow this procedure but employ a per-unit-of-production base for determining a "down payment" (initial payment) by the licensee. Although all such costs are already allocated to sales, the same unit basis is extended to licensing. For example, suppose that the company had an expenditure of $200,000 for research and development and produced 20,000 units, the per unit cost of research and development would be $10.

---

[13]See *IDEA*, Vol. 2, No. 1 (March 1958), pp. 137-158.

If the licensee were expected to produce 5,000 units yearly of the licensed product, a down payment might be asked of $50,000. This procedure is usually followed for *each* licensee.

The company practicing this procedure for determining licensing returns should, more precisely, divide the entire cost of $200,000 by total output at home and under license, obtaining a per-unit cost of $8; a down payment of $40,000 would then be required. The difference between the $40,000 and $50,000 would be recouped on domestic operations, which cost $2 less per unit; the drop in price (if demand were at all elastic) would increase sales at home. The lower down payment by the licensee would permit him to cut prices and increase sales. If accounting procedure is to remain precise, this same reduction of the burden of research and development should be redivided each time a licensee is added. Although the licensor may consider that this will not obtain him "all that the traffic will bear," if both he and the licensee are imbued with the idea of small profit rate to increase sales and thereby raise total profits, he may well find that increased royalty returns more than offset any cut in the down payment requested. Alternatively, such "fixed" costs may not be allocated to *any* type of revenue-earning operation of the business but merely absorbed under "total" revenue. Then a comparison of "variable" costs at the margin provides the decision-making criterion.

What the above argument reduces to is that when research and development costs are already fixed—or are already determined by considerations unrelated to licensing abroad—total revenue should be maximized from the areas of licensing and of sales combined. Where research and development costs are not allocated to both but are allocated to sales, the result will be a diversion of activity from sales to licensing since the additional return from an expansion of licensing will be greater than from sales. Either such costs must be allocated over the entire production of licensor and licensees, or they must be considered a sort of "fixed" costs of doing business and not be permitted to enter into the decisions of whether to expand operations in any one area.

To illustrate this conclusion, let us suppose that research and development costs are $10 per unit of domestic production; suppose also that domestic sales are returning $2 net income per unit and royalties from abroad are $11 per unit of sales by the licensee. Obviously, it would maximize profits if greater attention were paid to licensing operations so as to increase sales of licenses. But, if research and development were allocated, as in the above example, to sales by both the licensor and the licensee, the net profit on the licensor's sales rises from $2 per unit to $4 per unit, and that from the licensee's sales would drop from $11 per unit to $3 per unit (unless the cost could be passed on to the customers of the licensee without too greatly dampening his sales); the apparent profitability of the expansion of licensing over sales would disappear.

The same, more accurate, decision could be obtained by not allocating research and development costs to either activity (sales or licensing) when a decision is made to expand. Thus, the net profit on domestic sales (*ex* costs of research and development) would, in our example, rise to $12 per unit compared to $11 per unit from the licensee's production; the same differential of $1 in favor of the licensor's sales would be found. The decision of whether or not to sell directly or to license could then be made with a much firmer recognition of the costs and returns. This procedure of excluding research and development costs from any comparison of sales and licensing is an extension of the principle that maximization of profits will occur when the additional costs of expanding operations by one unit in each market are equalized; research and development costs are thus considered as "past," or as "fixed," costs.

A different problem arises if the company finds that research and development costs are related to the opportunity of obtaining royalties from licensing abroad. In some instances, research and development expenditures are not independent of the demand for know-how by the licensee. That is, either a demand by the licensee for techniques or products adaptable to his market might raise the costs of research and development, or a large expenditure by the licensor for research and development might increase the demand of potential licensees for his particular know-how and thus raise the royalty rate which he may ask; alternatively, the provision of techniques adapted to the foreign conditions or the breaking of a bottleneck for the licensee might increase his sales and significantly raise royalty returns.

When there is such an interdependence between expenditures for research and development and licensing returns, it is even more important that the costs be allocated accurately. It is then desirable to know whether a proposed increase in research and development expenditures may be expected to be covered more or less by sales and licensing returns. And it is useful to know whether requests from licensees are requiring research expenditures in excess of their royalty payments.

Desirability of More Accurate Accounting

As a result of a more accurate accounting procedure, many firms may find licensing slightly less profitable than they now count it. However, some few may discover that, with a bit more attention to their programs of research and development and to their licensing programs over-all, they can increase royalty returns by considerably more than the cost—especially if they can increase the number of licensees.

Some officials in interviewed companies objected to any analysis which downgrades the returns from licensing, for they are convinced that licensing is an important and valuable aspect of the company's operations and are afraid that it will not be pushed if net income from licensing is shown to be less than currently calculated. It may well be true that licensing *should* be expanded (for reasons other than immediate direct income returns), and such operations will not be pushed in many firms unless reluctant boards of directors can be shown exceedingly high rates of return compared to other activities. Thus, a rationale for the view that "licensing returns are all gravy" is established.

The impartial observer cannot countenance such specious arguments, even if results can be shown to coincide with reasoned conclusions. Rather, it is to be hoped that repeated searching out of the facts in a given situation will bring even reluctant directors into the view that profit differentials between domestic and foreign operations need not be 100 percent to justify expansion of foreign activity. Better information and keener analysis should lead to more profitable business operations.

Legal Protection of Know-How

STEPHEN P. LADAS

Know-how is a subject of increasing importance in international agreements and international investment. The subject matter designated by it has come to be the handmaid of progress and the core of industrial competition. Efficiency of production, effective pricing, superior quality standards, are based on know-how. The success of an industry in the competitive market depends on its being able to develop know-how by research of its own or its ability to obtain the benefits of know-how developed by others. New inventions permit an industry to make a leap but these have to be set in a broader technological framework and supplemented by the practical procedures which will make them workable particularly by resolving the cost problem. Know-how has also assumed an aura of fascination for newly developing countries which see in it a mystical factor which may resolve or bridge over the difficult initial steps of technical and economic development.

In international trade, know-how may be involved in various forms. It may be part of an agreement relating to patents, designs, or trademarks, and may be secondary to those rights or, on the contrary, these may be mere appendages to the principal grant of know-how. Or know-how may be the sole subject matter of a license agreement. Finally, know-how may be in a package deal of a construction or engineering contract under which a firm undertakes to erect a plant and supply the know-how for the construction and operation of the plant.

Newly developing countries, because of their general lack of traditional techniques and skills and inability to invest in local research, depend even more heavily on foreign know-how. Indeed, in such countries, it is not the local industrialists or inventors who are the prime movers but rather the government that sees the political future of its country in industrialization and is pushing its citizens along the road of progress. In such cases, know-how agreements replace even patent agreements, since foreign patentees do not generally take out patents in underdeveloped countries in view of the lack of local industry that may use the inventions covered by the patents.

In connection with all these types of agreements involving

EDITOR'S NOTE: This paper appeared in *IDEA*, Vol. 7, No. 4.

know-how, several legal problems arise, such as: the propriety and adequacy of clauses seeking to protect the licensor's know-how; their legal enforceability and the kind of remedies available not only against licensees but also against third parties; tax problems on the royalties or other compensation payable by the licensee in the country of the payee and in the receiving country; and finally, antitrust law problems with respect to restrictive clauses included in the agreement. These problems depend largely on the question of the legal nature of the right in know-how.

Some of the difficulties in dealing with this basic question stem from the absence of precise definition of the expression "know-how." While this is a convenient term to denote a variety of different matters, it does not define protectable subject matter. Indeed, in ordinary use know-how may include tangible materials: recipes, formulae, designs, drawings. patterns, blueprints, technical records, specifications, lists of materials, technical product and process manuals, written instructions for operating the process, and analytical means for checking and controlling the product and the process and the like; and intangible information consisting in practical procedures, details of workshop practice, technical training, personal visitation and inspection, etc. It also may include singly or in combination:

information relating to a patented invention not included in a patent specification;
inventions capable of being patented but not patented;
inventions incapable of being patented in a particular country because the subject matter is excluded in the patent law;
inventions incapable of being patented by reason of lack of inventive height;
industrial designs capable of being registered but not registered;
industrial designs having functional characteristics;
skill, experience, and craftsmanship of technicians.

The element of secrecy may not be indispensable as to all of the subject matter involved, yet the possessor of the know-how, the subject of a grant, must want to preserve it against unauthorized publication. Nor is the element of "exclusiveness" indispensable since more than one person may develop the same know-how, and if each of them preserves it from publication, each of them may have a right to his creation.

Because of these differences and the indefiniteness of the term "know-how," agreements often avoid the use of such terms or use it subsidiarily and instead employ terms describing and defining the subject matter of the grant more specifically, such as secret or tech-

nical information, manufacturing processes, or knowledge relative
to the use and application of the industrial technique required for
the establishment and operation of a particular plant or the production of the subject matter of the agreement.

II

The question of the legal nature of the right in know-how
usually proceeds with the query whether in the particular country
this is recognized as a property right or not. The answer to this requires a definition of the word "property" which raises difficult
problems under the law of various countries. In countries with a
codified civil law, there is a definite classification of "property"
rights and the only class available for know-how would be that of
"intangible rights."[1] But there has been no thoroughgoing legal analysis of this right in know-how so as to distinguish the various types
of relationships involved and give it an orderly pattern. There is a
recognition that know-how can be sold, licensed, assigned, taxed,
subjected to levy, exchanged for stock in a corporation, etc., but no
conscious attempt on the part of writers or the courts to resolve all
problems created by dealings with know-how.[2]

There has been a tendency to dodge the issue by pointing out
that there is always the contract which is law between the parties
and that any violation of undertakings under the contract with respect to know-how may be reached by an action under the contract.
This, however, leaves out the whole aspect of protection against
third parties—employees and competitors who may obtain unauthorized disclosure of know-how and use it without the owner's
consent—and does not dispose of the necessity to supplement the
absence of a contract by reference to other law.

In common law countries, the concept of property is more flexible and the courts have granted protection by reference to rules of
law or equity in all cases of inequitable or unfair conduct. As Justice
Holmes was able to say in *DuPont Powder Co.* v. *Masland* (1917)
244 U.S. 100:

> The word "property" as applied to trade secrets is an unanalyzed ex-
> pression of certain secondary consequences of the primary fact that the
> law makes some rudimentary requirements of good faith.

The British courts also have avoided the question of definition.
The Master of the Rolls, Lord Greene, in *Saltman Engineering Co.*

---

[1] Bouvier, *Le Droit de la Propriété Industrielle*, p. 372.
[2] Nash, "The Concept of Property in Know-How," *IDEA*, Vol. 6, No. 2
(Summer 1962), pp. 289, 294, 295.

v. *Campbell Engineering Company,* 65 R.P.C. 203, 213 (1948), held that:

> Even if Mr. Ransom did not make a contract with the defendants, it does not alter the fact that the confidential drawings handed to the defendants for the purpose of executing the order placed with them were the property of Saltman Engineering Co., and the defendants knew that.

and stated the general principle as follows:

> If a defendant is proven to have used confidential information directly or indirectly obtained from the plaintiff, without the consent, expressed or implied, of the plaintiff, he will be guilty of an infringement of the plaintiff's rights.

Most interesting in connection with the nature of know-how are the statements of Lord Radcliffe in *Rolls-Royce Ltd.* v. *Jeffrey.*[3] He said that the case involved first "the nature of this asset of the appellants which is conveniently comprehended in the word 'know-how,' " and continued:

> I see no objection to describing this as an asset. It is intangible, but then so is goodwill. . . .It is a reality when associated with production and development as that of Rolls-Royce, and a large part, though not the whole of it, finds its material record in all those lists, drawings, and manufacturing and engineering data that are specified in the various license agreements. . . . An asset of this kind is, I am afraid, that I must use the phrase, sui generis. It is not easily compared with factory or office buildings, warehouses, plant and machinery, or such independent legal rights as patents, copyrights or trademarks, or even with goodwill. "Know-how" is an ambiance that pervades a highly specialized production organization and, although I think it correct to describe it as fixed capital so long as the manufacturer retains it for his own productive purposes and expresses its value in his products, one must realize that in so describing it, one is proceeding by an analogy which can easily break down owing to the inherent differences that separate "know-how" from the more straightforward elements of fixed capital. . . . Know-how has the peculiar quality that it can be communicated to or shared with others outside the manufacturer's own business, without in any sense destroying its value to him.

It is submitted that it may be advisable to look closely into the genesis of know-how and its development in the most common cases. We have really two situations:

(a) An invention is made, and application is filed for a patent. This necessarily must be filed as quickly as it is completed so that it may not be anticipated by another inventor working in the same field. So far as the requirements of the patent law are concerned, the disclosure may be complete. The public is advised as to what the invention is, and the process or method of manufacture is fully disclosed. But

[3] 1 All E.R. 801, 805 (1962).

after the application is filed the inventor must still work out practical details of workshop technique so that the invented process or product may be manufactured at the least possible cost. Indeed, the cost of manufacture is an important consideration of any new invention. If the making of the product is too expensive, or if the new process cannot be fitted into existing machinery or tooling, the invention may be impracticable. The manufacturer or inventor works these details out, and it may take years before these are fully developed. These details are not patentable, because they are not inventions; they are merely improvements of workshop technique. Competing manufacturers working in the same field of research are able to absorb the invention immediately, and all they may need is a license under the patent. But other competing manufacturers cannot by themselves work out these details except by research, which takes time and expense, and they are therefore anxious to acquire the knowledge of these details, i.e., the know-how. There may not be holding back of information which should have been disclosed in the patent application because these details are not patentable and they are not even known to the inventor at the time of filing the application.

(b) On the other hand, research is a continuous process of improvement of technology step by step. There may be nothing in these improvements that is patentable because there is nothing that can be deemed a real invention, i.e., an advance in the art which is not obvious to a person having ordinary skill in such art. The improvement may consist in adjusting machinery or tooling, using a certain type of metal rather than another, the laying out of a plant, the siting of the various types of equipment, the layout of the valve system, and the use of one known chemical rather than another. Each of these steps may be in the public domain, but their combined effect is what does the trick. It may take research of many years and considerable investment to work out all these improvements step by step, but no patent can be obtained on them because they are not patentable inventions. If they were patentable, the manufacturer would rather take a patent and be protected by the patent law than rely on the uncertainties of know-how protection, or take the risk that the same know-how may be developed by others or may be published. A competing manufacturer making similar research and spending time and money can work out the same technological improvements but it is economically advantageous to acquire such know-how from one who developed it rather than remain behind in the technological progress.

III

Thus, know-how appears to be essentially a supplement to patented or patentable inventions or a variety of technical achievements in the process by which industry seeks to gain a competitive position in the marketplace. It follows that the legal relationship between the person coming into the original possession of know-how and other persons in privity or without privity to the former is of the same nature as the relationship that governs the owner of a patent or design or trademark and other persons. Law has grown out of relationships, and there is a relationship of competitors in the marketplace, whether the subject matter is patents, designs, trademarks, or know-how.

In this relationship we are seeking to recognize, reconcile, and satisfy competing interests, claims, and demands. An attempt has been made elsewhere to recognize and identify these in the legal ordering involved in patent law, design law, and trademark law.[4] With regard to know-how, we recognize the following competing interests, claims, and demands:

(a) The interests, demands, and claims of an enterprise which by costly research and experiment has developed information, inventions, skills, and knowledge, i.e., know-how, that gives to such enterprise an advantageous competitive position in the marketplace. This is a valuable business asset for the acquisition of which other enterprises are willing to pay a price, and the unauthorized disclosure or misues by others would inflict a serious damage to the originating enterprise.

(b) The interests, demands, and claims of competing enterprises which desire to obtain the benefit of know-how developed by others as an effective instrument for the promotion of their interests. They are looking out for the publication of any information on such know-how and desire to enter into agreements to obtain communication of know-how maintained in secrecy.

(c) The interests and claims of the community in the widest possible intercommunication of know-how by enterprises and the resulting high quality standards and low cost of goods, and in the avoidance of undue or excessive restraints between those competing in the marketplace.

(d) The interests of the social and legal order of the country concerned which would be fatally injured if the spirit of invention and

---

[4]See Ladas, "Industrial Property and Economic Development," *The Trademark Reporter* (1955) Vol. 45, p. 615.

creation and the investment in research and development of know-how were to be discouraged, and if it should be permitted to enter-prises to engage in unlawful competition and unauthorized use of secret know-how of others, or in the disinclination to share techni-cal knowledge and skills.

The competitive relationships involving these interests, claims, and demands are the same whether we are dealing with national or international markets.

There is need for a legal control by which we recognize, recon-cile, and satisfy all these interests, claims, and demands, just as we need similar legal control in the relationship involved in patents, designs, and trademarks. In connection with patents, such legal control is exercised by the statutory law on patents which defines patentable inventions, the requirements of patentability and nov-elty, the conditions for applying for a patent wherein particularly a full disclosure of the subject matter is required, the rights and obli-gations of the patentee, the term of the patent, etc. Analogous is the situation with respect to the design law and trademark law.

With respect to the know-how, there is generally no specific all-embracing statute which attempts to define and regulate the competitive relationship, analogous to the patent, design or trade-mark legislation, but one may be permitted to inquire whether such detailed statute is really necessary if other general legislation appli-cable to know-how does in fact recognize, reconcile, or satisfy the competitor relationship involved, and if the courts have in fact de-fined and circumscribed the right by the remedies granted. We have in most countries a law of unfair competition which generally is not a full statutory law. Most often this law has been fashioned as a full-bodied law by the courts on the basis of a single provision in the civil code or of a general principle formulated by a succession of court decisions. Yet we have a quite clearly established legal order-ing of the conflicting interests, claims, and demands of competitors in the marketplace through this type of unfair competition law.

It is precisely the same thing that appears to be the case in re-spect to the right in know-how. A review of the law of a number of countries is revealing.[5]

First, we have the German law of 1909 against unfair compe-tition which outlaws generally, in its first section, competitive con-duct contrary to honest practices, and specifies and prohibits in sub-sequent sections various acts of unfair competition, such as acts

---

[5]The writer's attention was called, after this paper was completed, to the article by Mr. Van Notten, "Know-How Licensing in the Common Market," 38 *N.Y.U. Law Review* (1963), pp. 525, 541 ff.

causing confusion of the public, deceptive and unfair advertising, discrediting of competitors, interference with contracts, etc. Then in Sections 17-19 it prohibits unauthorized disclosure and misuse of business or manufacturing secrets. These sections read as follows:

Section 17

(1) An employee, worker or apprentice of a firm who unlawfully imparts a business or manufacturing secret entrusted or made accessible to him by reason of his employment relationship to anyone during the term of service for the purpose of competition or for personal gain or with the intention of damaging the owner of the firm, will be liable to imprisonment of up to three years and to a fine, or to either.

(2) Anyone making use for purposes of competition or personal gain of a trade or manufacturing secret or imparting the same to third parties, knowledge of which he obtained through the means described in paragraph (1) or through conduct of his own contrary to the law or contra bonos mores, will be punished in the same manner.

(3) If, when imparting the said information, the perpetrator knows that use is to be made of the secret in foreign countries, or if he himself makes use of it in foreign countries, he may render himself liable to imprisonment up to five years.

(4) The provisions of paragraphs (1) to (3) also apply in cases where the person receiving the information is already familiar with the secret or is entitled to know it, without the perpetrator being aware of this fact.

Section 18

Anyone unlawfully making use of or imparting to third parties for the purpose of competition or personal gain any designs or instructions of a technical nature confided to him in the course of his business dealings, particularly drawings, models, stencils, cuttings and formulae, is punishable with imprisonment up to two years and with a fine, or one of these two measures.

Section 17, par. 4, applies equally.

Section 19

Acts contrary to the provisions contained in Sections 17 and 18 entail liability for the resulting damages. Where several persons are involved in such an infringement, there is a joint liability.

Thus, the German act deals with the following relationships in respect to know-how:

(a) the relationship between the owner of know-how and his employees;

(b) the relationship between the owner of know-how and a competitor to whom the employee makes an unauthorized disclosure of the know-how;

(c) the relationship between the owner of know-how and a competitor who, through any conduct contrary to law or to good morals, obtains knowledge of the know-how;

(d) the relationship of the owner of know-how and a person who obtains confidential communication of such know-how and proceeds to use it without the authorization of the owner;

(e) any other relationship or situation involving unauthorized use or misuse of know-how would also come under the general principle of the first section of the act of 1909, which condemns and prohibits any act contrary to honest practices.

In all these cases, the owner has a right to sue for damages under Section 19 and may also file criminal complaint under Sections 17 and 18. He may also obtain an injunction against such unauthorized use or threatened misuse of his know-how under the general provisions of the German law. It is highly significant that Germany had dealt with the relationships involved in know-how under the general provisions of the Unfair Competition Act. Indeed, the German Supreme Court (Bundesgericht) in a decision in 1951 (17 B.G.H. 2, p. 42) placed the whole subject of know-how squarely under the general principles of unfair competition. It stated:

> With respect to so-called secret processes and other commercial or manufacturing secrets, the protection involved is in accordance with the general provisions of the Civil Code and the law against unfair competition. Secrecy is protected by the right to unrestricted exercise of commercial activity (Section 823, par. 1, and Section 826 of the Civil Code, and Arts. 1, 17 and 18 of the Act against Unfair Competition). Under these articles a petition, by application of Section 1004 BGB for injunction of unauthorized use is available against the person to whom the licensor has entrusted a commercial secret in business relationship. If, under manufacturing arrangements, the licensor communicates to the licensee process instructions based on commercial secrets, this constitutes entrusting of technical instructions in the meaning of Art. 18 of the Act against Unfair Competition.

Next, it should be noted that similar legislative handling of the competitive relationships in know-how is made in other countries. Indeed, provisions analogous to those of the German Unfair Competition Act exist in the Austrian Act against Unfair Competition of 1923, Sections 11 and 12; the Norwegian law of July 7, 1922, Section 11; the Danish law of March 29, 1924, Section 11; and the Swedish law of May 29, 1931, Sections 3-5.

Belgium has a special Arrêté Royal of December 23, 1934 which provides in Article 2 for a summary remedy by the president of the tribunal, akin to an injunction, in certain cases of unfair competition, and these cases specifically include "the unauthorized use of models, specimens, technical combinations and formulae of a competitor and generally of all information or documents entrusted to another." Here, again, misuse or unauthorized use of know-how is dealt with by analogy to other acts of unfair competition. This is in addition to the action for damages available under the broad provision of Article 1382 of the civil code, which is the foundation of all law of unfair competition.

In other civil-law countries, such as France, Italy, and the Netherlands, the basis of protection of know-how is also unfair-competition law,[6] as the foundation of all law of industrial property to which know-how is generally assimilated. Know-how is deemed a combination of things organized toward an industrial purpose which constitutes a new value that the law protects against interference, and such protection is the proper function of the law of unfair competition.[7]

Articles 1382-1383 of the French and Belgian civil codes, which are the basis of the unfair competition law in these two countries, find their counterpart in Article 2598 of the Italian codes and Articles 1401—1402 of the Dutch. In Italy, there is also a special provision in Article 2105 which affords protection against the divulging of "information relating to the organization or methods of production of an enterprise, or the making use thereof in a manner that may prejudice it." Thus, for the purpose of this action, it is quite immaterial whether the secret information which is abused is directly misappropriated by someone concerned with it or has been acquired through third parties. In the Netherlands, injunction may be issued by the courts against the unauthorized use of know-how.

All four countries also contain specific provisions in their penal codes. Article 309 of the Belgian and Article 418 of the French codes provide for criminal punishment of anyone who fraudulently, or with intention to cause harm, communicates manufacturing secrets to third parties. In Italy, Article 623 of the penal code subjects to criminal punishment anyone who, having had access by reason of his status or profession to information intended to remain secret, communicates such information to others or exploits the same for his own benefit. In the Netherlands, Articles 272 and 273 of the penal code contain penal provisions against intentional divulgation of secret information which should be kept confidential because of the actual or previous professional position of the person who divulges, or because a commercial or industrial enterprise had ordered that such information be kept secret.

Cases of dealing with know-how which are not reached by these penal provisions are covered by the law of unfair competition.

---

[6]See Bouvier, *Le Droit de la Propriété Industrielle*, Vol. II, pp. 368 *et seq.*
[7]Mario Rotondi, "Unfair Competition in Europe," *American Journal of Comparative Law*, Vol. 7, No. 3 (1958), pp. 327, 333.

In common-law countries, the position is somewhat different. Wrongful appropriation, misuse, or unauthorized divulgation of know-how is essentially an equitable wrong against which the courts will grant a remedy. The courts will do so under the rules of law and equity of the common law, rather than in application of any statutory law. Thus, the law for the protection of know-how has developed entirely through case law, by the courts administering relief in cases where they considered that inequitable conduct was involved. Heretofore, there has been no effort to classify and distinguish the various cases, examine the relationships involved, and suggest a possible general theory of the nature of the right in know-how.[8] The laws in the United States and Great Britain are now remarkably similar in essence, although the reasoning, emphasis, and legal theory may not be alike.

In Great Britain, and generally in British-law countries throughout the world, the notion of a law of unfair competition as such has not found acceptance as yet. In the absence of explicit contractual provisions relating to know-how, in which case the position is defined by the contract, the English courts look to the relationship and give relief on the basis of a theory of implied contract or breach of confidence or trust.[9]

In the United States, on the other hand, in addition to these theories, a doctrine of unjust enrichment also is applied concurrently, complementarily, or in the alternative.[10]

But while the legal jargon used may be different from that in civil law countries, what the courts really do is to find a relationship between the parties which makes it unfair for the defendant to appropriate, misuse, or make an unauthorized disclosure of know-how communicated by the owner thereof, and in essence they apply the basic principles of the unfair-competition law. Indeed, the conduct prohibited involves not so much the revelation, wrongful appropriation, or misuse of know-how as such, but the economic implication of interference with an advantageous competitive position represented by the value of the know-how to the owner thereof.

This appears in a particularly clear light in the cases involving an unrelated third person who obtains disclosure of the know-how innocently, and the question is whether such person may be restrained. In *Stevenson, Jordan & Harrison Ltd.* v. *MacDonald & Evans,*[11] Lloyd-Jacob J. remarked:

---

[8]The first such attempt is made in the excellent book by Amédée Turner, *The Law of Trade Secrets,* London, 1962.

[9] *Id.,* p. 235.

[10]*Id.,* p. 265.

[11]68 R.P.C. 190 and on appeal 69 R.P.C. 10. On appeal, the judgment was

Counsel for the plaintiff expressly disclaimed any suggestion that . . . the defendants were aware that . . . Mr. Hemming was acting in breach of his duty to the plaintiff. Does this circumstance frank their avowed intention to consummate Mr. Hemming's wrongdoing? The original and independent jurisdiction of this Court to prevent, by the grant of an injunction, any person availing himself of a title which arises out of a violation of a right or a breach of confidence, is so well established as a cardinal principle that only a binding authority to the contrary should prevent its application by this Court.

In the United States[12] the decisions of the courts have established the position which the Restatement of Torts (Section 758(b), comment (e)) summarizes to the effect that the answer depends upon weighing the loss to the innocent party against the benefit to the plaintiff. It would be wrong to charge the defendant with damages or profits for the period after he knew the facts of the disclosure in the case when he has changed substantially his position by exploiting the disclosures beforehand. Otherwise, an innocent recipient of a disclosure becomes liable for any use he makes after he learns the facts of the disclosure. This is an obvious case of application of unfair-competition-law principles.

From the point of view of taxation of this asset, it is of interest to consider two decisions of the House of Lords. In the first case, *Moriarty (Inspector of Taxes)* v. *Evans Medical Supplies Ltd.,*[13] a British company, carrying on business as a manufacturer of pharmaceutical products and wholesale druggist, made an agreement with the Government of Burma to supply information as to certain secret processes relating to the manufacture of pharmaceutical products and technical data, drawings, designs, and plans for the erection of a factory and the installation of machinery therein. The consideration to be received in return was £100,000. The question arose as to whether this sum was ordinary income or a capital gain. The Court of Appeal held that, insofar as the consideration was in respect of the imparting of information as to secret processes, the receipt was a capital receipt, such secret processes and formulae being in this respect akin to patents. On the other hand, insofar as the consideration related to the drawings, designs, and plans and information relating to the supply of prototype machinery, laying out and installation of such machinery, etc., it was a payment for services and therefore an income.

The House of Lords held that there was no case for apportioning the sum in the manner directed by the Court of Appeal and

---

reversed on the ground that the confidential nature of the subject matter was not substantial enough to warrant protection.

[12]Turner, note 8, *supra*, pp. 414, 417.
[13]3 All E. R. 718 (1957).

concluded that the whole sum was a capital profit and therefore not taxable. Viscount Simonds and Lord Tucker pointed out that the ownership by this company of these secret processes and know-how had enabled the company to acquire a substantial share of the market for pharmaceutical products in Burma. Even though the whole value of these secret processes and know-how might not be lost at once to the company as the result of the agreement, their value would be greatly diminished and it was doubtful whether, within a measurable period of time, any value at all to the company would remain.

In the more recent decision in *Rolls-Royce Ltd.* v. *Inland Revenue Commissioners,*[14] the House of Lords upheld the decision of the Court of Appeal that lump-sum payments made by certain foreign governments and companies to Rolls-Royce in return for technical knowledge, plans, and a license for an interchange of staffs to enable them to manufacture specified types of aircraft engines did not represent the value of a capital asset and was assessable for income tax. The taxpayer's position was that its know-how was part of its fixed capital. The House of Lords, particularly Lord Radcliffe, looked into the nature of know-how[15] and admitted that this was a capital asset so long as the manufacturer retained it for his own productive purposes. It is the kind of intangible entity that can very easily change its category according to the use to which its owner himself decides to put it. Rolls-Royce turned the know-how to account by undertaking for reward to impart it to the others in order to bring about an alternative way of deriving profit in lieu of manufacture and sale of their own engines to the governments or companies with whom they entered into license agreements. The case was distinguished from *Moriarty* v. *Evans* in that in the latter the company had sold to the Burmese Government a secret process on which the success of its business in Burma had to depend, and it had, in effect, disposed altogether of its Burmese trade.

Indeed, the reconciliation of the two decisions is possible on the facts of each case: a more or less total loss of the asset in the first case, and a more or less limited dilution of the asset in the second case, particularly since the information disclosed was only that bearing on the production of a single type of engine.

IV

The general conclusion resulting from an analysis of legislation

---

[14] 1 All E. R. 801 (1962).
Similar holding by the Court of Appeal in *Musker (Inspector of Taxes)* v. *English Electric Co., Inc.*
[15] See text accompanying note 3, *supra.*

and court decisions being that the competitive relationships involved in know-how are governed by the broad principles of the law on unfair competition, it should then follow that in the international field the stipulations of Article 10bis of the International Convention are applicable. This article reads as follows:

(1) The countries of the Union are bound to assure to persons entitled to the benefits of the Union effective protection against unfair competition.

(2) Any act of competition contrary to honest practices in industrial or commercial matters constitutes an act of unfair competition.

(3) The following in particular shall be prohibited:

1. all acts of such a nature as to create confusion by any means whatever with the establishment, the goods, or the industrial or commercial activities of a competitor;

2. false allegations in the course of trade which are of such a nature as to discredit the establishment, the goods, or the industrial or commercial activities of a competitor;

3. indications or allegations the use of which in the course of trade is liable to mislead the public as to the nature, the manufacturing process, the characteristics, the suitability for their purpose or the quantity of the goods.

The general principle announced by this article is that any act of competition contrary to honest practices in industrial and commercial matters is prohibited, and this should apply to unauthorized disclosure or misuse of know-how.

The International Chamber of Commerce in 1955 undertook to study the problem of protection of know-how on an international basis. After long investigation of the law and practice of the various countries, it adopted a resolution in 1961[16] setting forth rules for the protection of know-how. This resolution reads as follows:

Technological improvements developed by business enterprises whether patentable or not, commonly referred to as know-how, have become in recent times tremendously valuable subjects of industrial property supplementing patents and other rights, have assumed a great economic importance, and are the subject matter of an increasing number of very important agreements between business enterprises.

The protection of know-how on an international basis is therefore a keenly felt need if the communication of know-how between enterprises to promote economic and technical progress is to be encouraged.

Hardly any country so far has dealt in an adequate and comprehensive way with the protection of industrial know-how, although existing national laws on contract, breach of trust and unfair competition are sometimes applicable to the subject.

Accordingly, the International Chamber of Commerce has set out hereunder in a summary form provisions which are highly recommended for incorporation in national legislation:

[16]International Chamber of Commerce, Statements and Resolutions 1959-1961, pp. 98, 99.

1. Industrial know-how means applied technical knowledge, methods and data necessary for realizing or carrying out in practice techniques which serve industrial purposes.

2. Where such know-how is of a secret character it constitutes a valuable business asset and should be protected in law.

3. Know-how should be regarded as secret in character if it has not been published in a form available to the public and the undertaking which has developed it or lawfully acquired it takes all reasonable steps to prevent its unauthorized disclosure. Such know-how is hereinafter referred to as "secret know-how."

4. It should be unlawful for an undertaking to use industrial know-how which it knows or ought to have known to be the secret know-how of another undertaking, without the consent of that undertaking.

5. It should also be unlawful to divulge the secret know-how of an undertaking, or to transfer it to others, without the consent of that undertaking.

6. Nothing in these provisions should affect the right of an undertaking to use, divulge or transfer any industrial know-how which it has itself originated and developed by its own independent means or to use any such know-how which has been published in a form available to the public.

7. An injunction or an order to pay damages or both should be available in respect of the unlawful use, divulgence, or transfer of secret know-how.

8. In addition to the above provisions, it should be possible, even in the case of a bona fide use of the secret know-how of another, to order the user to compensate that other, if the circumstances make it equitable to do so.

The following comment is suggested on this resolution.[17] It will be noted that it is limited to industrial know-how. Thus, it does not deal with commercial, financial, or other know-how. The reason for this is one of practical expediency. It was felt that the need for protecting other types of know-how may not be as great as that for protecting industrial know-how, and attention should primarily be directed to the latter. Then the resolution is limited to know-how of a secret character used for industrial purposes. "Secret know-how" is that which has not been published in a form available to the public and which the owner thereof has taken all reasonable steps to prevent from being published. This means:

(a) that the owner thereof ensures that nonlicensed third parties do not use, publish, or transfer it to others;

(b) that know-how which has been divulged or transferred to others without the authorization of the owner may still be considered "secret" if the owner has taken all adequate measures to prevent its disclosure;

[17]See Document No. 450/198, dated December 27, 1960, of the International Chamber of Commerce.

(c) if the know-how has been published in such a way that not only an unauthorized third party has obtained knowledge of it but it has become available to the public generally, the know-how is no longer revocable and the only remedy may be damages by the person who published the know-how.

Ex contrario, paragraph 6 of this resolution clarifies that secrecy does not imply exclusivity. Therefore, if another party should develop or possess similar know-how or acquire such from another owner or come to know of it from a publication available to the public, it is free to use it, divulge it, or transfer it without regard to the fact that another enterprise has a secret know-how of its own.

The resolution then proceeds to suggest a system of protection of know-how. Paragraph 4 deals with unlawful use of know-how, and this is deemed to exist in all cases of bad faith. If the user knows or ought to know that the know-how is the secret know-how of another, and uses it without the consent of the owner, the use is unlawful.

Paragraph 5 deals with unauthorized divulgation or transfer of secret know-how. Both are deemed unlawful when there is no consent by the owner of the know-how. No requirement of bad faith is included in this provision. The transferee may have received the know-how in good faith, for instance, as a licensee or sublicensee or employee thereof, or may be an independent third party who paid value for the same. The act of transfer by such person and particularly the act of publication constitutes a serious damage to the owner. If the latter asserts his rights before such transfer or divulgation, the act by the transferor is unlawful.

Paragraph 7 of the resolution recommends that the remedies against unlawful use, transfer, or divulgation should be an injunction or an order for payment of damages, or both. The International Chamber of Commerce would have recommended the remedy of injunction generally but it had to take note of the fact that this is not known in the legal system of a number of civil-law countries.[18]

Finally, paragraph 8 provides that even in the case of a bona fide use of secret know-how by an independent third party distinguished in paragraph 4, the law should provide for equitable com-

---

[18]Because of the basic need of preserving the secrecy of know-how, the courts may adopt procedures to prevent publication as a result of litigation. Thus, in *Amber Size & Chemical Co. Ltd.* v. *Menzel*, 2 Ch. 239; 30 R.P.C. 433 (1913), where it was obvious that the question of the aspects of plaintiff's processes that were claimed to be secret had to be disclosed to someone on behalf of the court, the court's solution was for the parties to agree on an expert or experts to whom disclosures could be made on behalf of the court, or to a small list of experts from whom the court could make a selection.

pensation of the owner of the know-how. In other words, no unjust
enrichment should be allowed in the case where one in good faith
obtains knowledge of secret know-how and uses it for his purpose.

V

It is as a result of this resolution that the International Chamber of Commerce insisted on the Commission of the European Economic Community for the inclusion of know-how, together with the
other rights of industrial property, in the special dispensation from
notification of agreements relating to industrial property.

It will be recalled that the first draft of the regulations submitted by the Commission to the Council of Ministers of the
European Economic Community provided for compulsory registration of all agreements containing restrictions prohibited under
Article 85(1) of the Treaty of Rome. As an exception to this rule,
no registration was required in respect of agreements imposing on
the transferee or licensee of patents, designs, and trademarks
limitations in the exercise of these rights. Thus, the exception was
limited to patent, design, and trademark agreements. As a result of
strong representations on the part of the International Chamber of
Commerce, the final text of Regulation No. 17 extended this particular exception to know-how agreements as well.

Indeed, this regulation, which now requires notification of
agreements for the purpose of obtaining the benefits of Article 85(3)
of the Treaty, dispenses from such notification, under Article 4(2)
(ii)(b) of Regulation No. 17:

> agreements to which two enterprises only participate and which have
> the sole effect
>> to impose upon the purchaser or the user of rights of industrial
>> property—namely, patents, utility models, designs or trademarks
>> —or upon the beneficiary of contracts involving the transfer or
>> licensing of manufacturing processes or knowledge relative to the
>> use and application of industrial techniques, limitations in the
>> exercise of these rights.

This is a recognition, by what constitutes a legislative act of the
European Economic Community, of know-how as a right equivalent to industrial property. The regulation recognizes the *right* in
know-how, since it speaks of limitations which may be imposed in
the exercise of the right in know-how as they may be imposed in the
exercise of the patent right, the design right, or the trademark right.

The terms used in this provision are:

> manufacturing processes or knowledge relative to the use or applica-
> tion of industrial techniques.

It is interesting in this connection to compare these terms with those used in the German Act of 1957 Against Restrictions of Competition. This act in Section 20 deals with permissible restrictions in agreements relating to patents, utility models, and rights relating to varieties of plants. Section 21 applies, so far as applicable, the provisions of Section 20 to agreements involving the transfer or exploitation of:

> legally unprotected inventions, manufacturing processes, technical designs and other technological achievements . . . if such achievements constitute business secrets.

The terms describing know-how in Regulation No. 17 are broader than those in the German Act of 1957 and do not even include the requirement of secrecy contained in the latter. Thus, the German law not only recognizes and protects, under the law of unfair competition, business and manufacturing secrets but it also permits, so far as applicable, the same restrictions in agreements relating to such secrets as in the case of agreements relating to patents.

Since, then, both Section 21 of the German Act of 1957 Against Restriction of Competition and Article 4(2)(ii)(b) of Regulation No. 17 of the Common Market deal with limitations in agreements relating to know-how, it is of interest to consider the effect of the German antitrust law before proceeding to consider the provisions of the Common Market antitrust law.

To understand the scope of the exemption of restrictions in know-how license agreements under Section 21 of the German law, we must relate them to the restrictions permitted in patent license agreements under Section 20 of the German law.

First is the restriction relating to the character, the extent, the quantity, the area, or the time of the use of a patent. Certainly this is applicable to know-how. The owner of the know-how may dispose of his right by transfer or license for a limited purpose or application only, for a limited area, or for a limited time.

Second are the restrictions imposed on the acquirer or licensee of a patent justified by the interest of the owner or licensor in the technically unobjectionable exploitation of the object protected by the patent. It is difficult to conceive how this restriction may be generally applicable to the grant of know-how, except in two cases. The first is where the licensee of the know-how uses a marking on his goods referring to the name of the licensor. In such case the interest of the licensor in the reputation of his name justifies his right to insist on technically unobjectionable exploitation of the know-how. Another case is where the licensor of the know-how also licenses the use of his trademark. In such case the validity of his trademark as well as the interest in its reputation and goodwill may justify the same restriction.

Third is the obligation assumed by the acquirer or licensee regarding the pricing of the patented article. The object of the restriction is to prevent the licensee from underselling the patentee and competing unfairly with him. It does not seem possible to permit such a restriction in the case of the licensing of know-how.

Fourth is the obligation imposed on the acquirer or licensee for the granting back of information or of a license for the use of inventions relating to improvements on condition of a reciprocal obligation by the seller or licensor. It is not seen why this obligation would be objectionable with respect to grant of know-how. Subject to the condition of reciprocity and to the condition that the license back to the licensor should not be exclusive to the latter, this tends to encourage the sharing of knowledge and promotes rather than restricts competition.

Fifth is the obligation of the acquirer or licensee not to challenge the licensed patent. It is not seen why this obligation on the communicatee of know-how would be objectionable when it is not on the patent licensee. Contesting the right of the licensor in his know-how is violation of the basic foundation of the contract. However, it must be understood that the licensee should have the right to show that the know-how furnished by the licensor has become public property without the fault of the licensee.

Finally, there is the obligation imposed on the acquirer or licensee relating to regulation of competition outside the area of applicability of the law. This provision in the German law meant that the licensee might be restricted with respect to competition outside Germany. The same restriction could apply in Germany with respect to the grant of know-how. However, this provision is no longer applicable insofar as interstate trade in the Common Market countries is concerned, and the same would be true with respect to know-how.

VI

Coming now to the Common Market antitrust law, we have before us Article 4(2)(ii)(b) of Regulation No. 17, which dispenses from notification agreements relating to know-how and containing "limitations in the exercise of the right" in know-how. What are these limitations, which are presumably outside the prohibition of Article 85(1) of the Treaty.[19]

The Commission of the EEC in its "Communication" on patent license agreements published December 24, 1962, has specified certain restrictions which it deems as not included within the scope of the prohibitions of Article 85(1) of the Rome Treaty. In this "Communication" the Commission explains why it has not attempted to specify restrictions in agreements relating to know-how, which may also be deemed outside the scope of prohibitions of Article 85(1), and states:

> The question of application of Art. 85(1) of the Treaty . . . to agreements relating to the exploitation . . . of creations not protected by law which represent technical improvements . . . must be the subject of a further decision.

The words in this statement "not protected by law" are unfortunate since it is obvious from the above exposition that know-how is protected by law. Obviously the Commission refers only to the fact that there is no full statutory law governing the relationships involved in know-how, and indicates its uncertainty as to how far it may consider applicable to know-how agreements restrictions analogous to those in patent license agreements deemed outside the scope of prohibitions of Article 85(1). But whether or not the Commission determines to issue a statement of interpretation with respect to restrictions in know-how license agreements, it is undeniable that restrictions "within the exercise of the right" in know-how are permissible. This is true not only because of the inclusion of know-how in Article 4(2)(ii)(b) of Regulation No. 17, but also because of the saving clause of Article 222 of the Rome Treaty, which provides that "the Treaty shall in no way prejudice existing systems and incidents of property." Certainly the right in know-how is an existing system and incident of property.

Indeed, precisely because the right in know-how is not fully defined by statutory law and is broadly governed by the protection of the law of unfair competition, it becomes essential for the parties concerned to at least define their respective rights and duties in the license agreement. This fixes the limits for which the use and application of the furnished know-how are granted or authorized.

It follows that a know-how license agreement may contain the following restrictions as outside the scope of prohibitions of Article 85(1) of the Treaty:

(a) Restrictions calculated to protect the know-how against unauthorized disclosure or transfer to third parties. This is necessary to preserve the secrecy of the know-how and the right of the owner in the know-how.

(b) Restrictions against the use of the licensed know-how beyond the use or application for which it is being licensed. This is a limitation within the scope of the right in the know-how.

(c) Limitations on the use of the know-how with respect to time. This means that the license to use the know-how may be limited for a certain term only, and therefore the licensee may be required not to use such know-how after termination or cancellation of the agreement. This is, of course, subject to the qualification that the know-how has not become available to the public.

(d) Limitations with regard to area. This refers to the *use* of the know-how and not the marketing of merchandise made by the use of such know-how. It is not possible, with respect to know-how, to conceive of separate rights in know-how granted by separate states as independent rights. The right in know-how is a single right, and it may be enforced under the law of any country. But once this right has been licensed and products have been made by the use of such know-how, it is not possible to limit the sale of such products to a particular country.

(e) Limitations with respect to person. The owner of the know-how may provide that the licensee shall not assign the license or grant a sublicense to another. This is both a limitation inherent in the right in the know-how and a means of protecting the secrecy of the know-how.

(f) An obligation on the licensee to affix on the product a legend referring to the owner of the know-how. This is a means of promoting the reputation of the licensor of the know-how and involves no restriction on competition.

(g) The license of the know-how may be granted on an exclusive or nonexclusive basis. The former means that the owner of the know-how undertakes not to furnish such know-how to any other party. This involves no more of a restriction than an exclusive license under a patent does. Indeed, it is of lesser importance since the exclusivity under a patent may endure for 15 to 20 years whereas ordinarily the value of the know-how has a commercial value of a much more limited time.

Finally, the restrictions discussed above in Section V as permissible under the German antitrust law in know-how license agreements should be deemed proper "limitations in the exercise of the right" under Article 4(2)(ii)(b) of Regulation No. 17.

Domestic and International Trade Aspects of the USSR Trademark System

Joseph M. Lightman

INTRODUCTION

Trademarks as competitive marketing tools are obviously less significant in a state-enterprise economy, such as the USSR, than in the competitive economies of industrialized countries outside of Eastern Europe. As in other Eastern European countries, trademarks[1] in the USSR have served primarily as "grade marks" to facilitate government surveillance over the quality of factory output rather than as marketing tools. Registrations under its trademark law have been relatively low when compared with those in industrialized non-Eastern European countries (see Table 1 at end of paper).

It is to be noted nevertheless that sweeping economic reform measures instituted by the USSR since 1965, and its apparent desire to improve trade relations with the West, have had important ramifications in the country's industrial property rights sector,[2] including the trademark system. The government's emphasis on strengthening and improving its industrial property laws in recent years has been reflected among other ways in a continuing series of measures designed to update its trademark system.

An earlier article published in IDEA in 1966 on the USSR trademark system spotlighted its relationship to Western concepts of trademark protection and East-West trade.[3] Developments since then, which appear to have an important bearing on the USSR trademark picture, have prompted a new assessment by The PTC Research Institute of that picture, with particular reference to the trade situation.

Since 1966, new insights into the role of trademarks in the USSR's domestic and foreign trade picture have emerged from

EDITOR'S NOTE: This paper appeared in *IDEA*, Vol. 12, Nos. 2-3.

[1] I.e., marks registered as industrial property rights under the USSR Trademark Law, as distinct from "production" or other markings assigned to each factory for government identification purposes.

[2] E.g., in the updating and complete codification of its legislation pertaining to patents and inventions (see texts in *Industrial Property*, published by United International Bureaux for the Protection of Intellectual Property, No. 4 [Geneva: April 1967]) and in the promulgation of a new Industrial Design Law, July 9, 1965 (*id.*, No. 12 [December 1965]).

[3] "The USSR Trademark System and East-West Trade," *IDEA*, Vol. 10, No. 1 (Spring 1966), pp. 11-31.

information now brought to light on the "sales, profit, and rate of return on capital" criteria which many enterprise managers are now required to use. Also, detailed data on industrial property rights activities are now being published by the USSR through the United International Bureaux for the Protection of Intellectual Property (BIRPI) and through its own channels since adhering to the Paris Union Convention in July 1965.

The main thrust of the comprehensive Soviet economic reform measures enacted in September and October of 1965 is to help improve economic performance by vesting in enterprise managers more independence from their superior agencies. They are also made more responsible for maintaining a profitable production operation and are guided in this respect by criteria aimed at producing high-quality marketable products rather than meeting production quota targets as such.[4] The new "success indicators" instituted under the reform movement have resulted in a growing awareness among participating enterprise managers of the need for distinctive markings on their products, not only for identification and quality control purposes but as marketing tools. An apparent manifestation of this awareness was the unusual number of domestically originated trademark applications filed and registered in the USSR in 1965, the year the reform movement began (see Table 2).[5]

The basic significance to U.S. businessmen, and those of the 83 other member countries, of the USSR's adherence to the Paris Union Convention is, of course, the fact that such businessmen are now accorded national treatment and other special benefits for protection of their trademark, as well as patent, industrial design, and trade name rights in that country.[6] Another important facet

---

[4]During 1966, 704 enterprises accounting for 10 percent of the industrial work force, and 12 percent of industrial production had been transferred to this new system. By 1967, total enterprises in the new system had grown to 7,000 accounting for about 40 percent of total industrial production; by the end of March 1968, this figure reached 10,000 enterprises accounting for about 50 percent of production of about 45,000 enterprises. (Source: *Soviet Economic Performance, 1966-67*, Committee Print of U.S. Congress Joint Economic Committee's Subcommittee on Foreign Economic Policy, 90th Cong., 2nd Sess. (Washington, D. C.: G.P.O., May 1968), p. 129). In a July 1968 issue of *Ekonomicheskaya Gazeta*, it was reported that 20,000 enterprises producing 60 percent of total industrial output had been transferred to the new system.

[5]Another contributing factor to this unusual activity in the trademark field in 1965 may also have been the USSR's adherence to the Paris Union Convention that year. Foreign trade organizations wishing to exercise various rights under the Convention, such as the six months' "right of priority," and also seeking domestic approval of the marks they intended to use in the member countries, presumably filed an unusually large number of applications in 1965.

[6]The USSR Council of Ministers Decree of March 8, 1965 (No. 848), announced Soviet accession as of July 1, 1965.

The Paris Union Convention is the major intergovernmental agreement in the

of this adherence, however, is that the USSR is now affording the Western world (through BIRPI) details on such matters as filings, registrations, legal procedures, and other information relative to Soviet industrial property laws never before available. Such material has appeared not only in recent issues of BIRPI's monthly publication, *Industrial Property,*[7] but also in certain other BIRPI publications, such as that on an East-West Industrial Property Symposium it conducted in Budapest in 1966,[8] at which several Soviet patent and trademark officials spoke on the state of their country's laws. In the past several years two comprehensive English language publications by the USSR have also appeared in the United States on Soviet industrial property systems and have been given fairly wide distribution.[9] Additionally, other material translated into English has appeared in growing quantity in the past two years relative to speeches and analyses by Soviet officials on that country's patent and trademark system.

Much has been written on the subject of patent protection in the USSR in English language technical, trade, and legal journals. This element of industrial property rights is, of course, most important to U. S. firms interested in the Soviet market. The PTC Re-

industrial property rights field and is now adhered to by about 85 countries including the United States and Canada, eight countries in Latin America, all of the industrialized countries in Europe, most of the African countries, and many in the Middle East and Asia. Industrial property rights are defined in the Convention as patents, utility models, industrial designs, trademarks, service marks, trade names, and indications of source or appellations of origin (Art. 1, Revision of 1958). The Convention's basic principle is a guarantee by each member country to provide foreigners the same protection for their industrial property rights that it provides its own nationals (i.e., national treatment). The Convention goes beyond national treatment, however, and also provides certain special benefits and advantages for nationals of member countries, such as a one-year period after the first filing of a patent application in a member country (or a six-month period in the case of trademarks) in which to file a corresponding application in another member country and receive in the latter the benefit of the first application filing date. Other advantages include protection in each member country of a member national's patent against arbitrary forfeiture for nonworking and a right of a member national to file a trademark without first having to register the mark at home. (The 1958 Revision, which is the latest in effect, to which most of the countries including the USSR adhere, incorporates this latter feature. Earlier revisions (1911, 1925, and 1934), to which some countries still adhere as their latest revision in force, still enable them to retain the "prior home registration requirement" if they so desire.) By adhering to the Convention, the USSR has now joined most other nations in agreeing to abide by those internationally accepted protection principles that have been in effect for industrial property rights since the Convention was adopted in 1883.

[7]Pertinent material from this publication will be cited further in this article.

[8]"BIRPI East-West Industrial Property Symposium, Budapest, 1966" (Geneva: March 1967).

[9]*Protection of Invention in the U.S.S.R.: Basic Principles,* Committee for Inventions and Discoveries Attached to the Council of Ministers of the U.S.S.R. (Moscow: 1966); M. Boguslavsky and I. Cherviakov, *Protection of Industrial Property in the U.S.S.R.* (Novosti Press Agency Publishing House).

search Institute feels, nevertheless, that the trademark aspect is now deserving of more emphasis than it has been given in the English language press in the context of U. S.-USSR trade relations. As U. S. firms consider marketing prospects in the USSR, they will want to be fully aware of the protection available to them in that country for their valuable trademark rights. Also, the USSR has shown considerable interest in technical interchanges and licensing agreements with the West. In this connection, it has taken important steps to develop favorable conditions for licensing activities— including changes in the trademark as well as patent laws to make them more compatible with Western systems, creation of an agency specifically designed to handle licensing and other industrial property transactions with foreigners,[10] and the retailoring of patent, technical know-how, and trademark provisions in its commercial agreements to conform more to Western standards of accepted protection.

Foreign trademark filings and prosecutions are generally handled by the USSR Chamber of Commerce's Patent Bureau. The Chamber, which, among other activities, represents various organizations interested in foreign trade promotion, is one of the principal Soviet entities delegated the responsibility for making contact with foreign business organizations.

Administration of all industrial property laws, including trademarks, is coordinated within the framework of one agency—the State Committee for Inventions and Discoveries (hereinafter called the "Committee").[11] Here it is to be noted that trademark administration has not been relegated to any lesser agency than that responsible for administering the important laws pertaining to protection and utilization of inventions and technology.

Based on the new information which has been brought to light on the USSR trademark system, this article will examine these latest developments in detail with particular reference to their trade implications.

TRADEMARKS AND SOVIET TRADE

The USSR's trade turnover (exports and imports) in 1967, which amounted to $18.2 billion, represented an increase of about 8 percent over its $16.8 billion trade figure in 1966. On the basis of

---

[10]The All-Union Export-Import Association, "Litsensintorg." Among other things, this agency endeavors to interest foreigners in selling or licensing their industrial property in the USSR.

[11]An "independent agency" reporting directly to the Council of Ministers.

its total trade turnover, the USSR ranked among the eight major world trading nations; the others in descending order of magnitude were the United States, West Germany, United Kingdom, France, Japan, Canada, and Italy.[12] U.S. exports in 1967 to the USSR rose to $60.2 million from $41.7 million in 1966.[13] The USSR continued to manifest a strong interest in purchasing from the U.S. and other western countries machinery, chemicals, and other manufactured products of the type generally advertised and marketed under trademarks.

Procedural Considerations

Most American companies seriously interested in foreign trade generally register abroad anywhere from one fourth to two thirds of their U.S.-owned trademarks, for defensive as well as marketing purposes.[14] In the USSR, as in many countries, the first person to apply for a mark is entitled to its registration and to legal recognition of its exclusive use. Unlike the situation in the United States, the right to a trademark in the USSR does not arise out of a system of common-law appropriation and use; it is based on registration.

The owner of a foreign mark who finds that someone else has already applied for or registered it in the USSR is faced with a problem of contesting the "pirated" application or registration. Should he decide not to contest it, or should he be unsuccessful in such action, he is then faced with possible foreclosure of his trademark in the Soviet market. More important, the possible Soviet registration of a "pirated mark" may create problems for the rightful owner of the mark in third-country markets, particularly in less-developed areas.

Companies having an internationally used trademark (a "house mark," product, or service mark) which they publicize abroad find it highly desirable to register such a mark in every country where a possible sales interest or piracy problem may exist. Under the Paris Union Convention, member countries are required to protect "well known" marks against registration by persons other than their rightful owners.[15] Past experience, however, has indicated that

---

[12]*Soviet Economic Performance, 1966-67*, note 4, *supra*, p. 97, for USSR statistics; International Monetary Fund, *International Financial Statistics*, Vol. XXII, No. 4 (April 1968), pp. 34-35, for other countries' statistics.

[13]*Export Control*, 83rd Quarterly ·Report, 1st Quarter (U.S. Department of Commerce, May 15, 1968), pp. 8-9.

[14]For further information on foreign registration practices of U.S. firms, see *IDEA*, Vol. 11, No. 4 (Winter 1967-68), "Economic Aspects of Trademark Utilization," pp. 472-499; and *IDEA*, Vol. 10, No. 3 (Fall 1966), "The Economic Role of Trademarks and Their Utilization as Business Assets," pp. 323-336.

[15]Under this Convention, a member country must provide the rightful

the term "well known" is subject to a wide variety of interpretations among many member countries. A U.S. mark widely used and registered abroad may not necessarily qualify as well known in a particular country. Most companies engaging in foreign trade therefore find it desirable to register their more important marks for protection in the first instance, rather than to rely on the Paris Union Convention premise that well known trademarks shall be protected even in the absence of a registration.

It is likely in many instances that trademarks will be coupled closely with patents or know-how in the licensing of U.S. products to Soviet enterprises. In this connection, licensing consultants in the United States may strongly advise their clients, in the interest of their future safety as potential licensors as well as trademark owners, to register their marks in their own name abroad and to protect them as such.

Marketing Techniques

Foreign firms interested in the Soviet market, bearing in mind that imports are controlled by state trading organizations and that distribution is still geared to state planning directives, may nevertheless look into various marketing techniques focusing on trademarks that might possibly be utilized in the USSR.

Advertising seems to be growing in the USSR. Trade journals are the media primarily used by production enterprises to advertise their goods to other industries and the consumer trade, but radio and television advertising is expanding. An increasing number of foreign firms, including American, are using Soviet media to advertise their products and impress their brand names upon appropriate Soviet purchasing authorities and the consumer public.[16] It is interesting to note that in the USSR the Soviet lawmakers themselves now recognize the role of trademarks in advertising. The first paragraph of the present trademark law emphasizes that the purpose of a trademark is not only to distinguish an enterprise's goods and services but also "to advertise them."

The Soviet enterprise Vneshtorgreklama handles advertising of Soviet goods abroad and of foreign goods in the USSR. Advertising

owner of a "well-known" mark registered to someone else, a period of at least five years from the date of such registration in which to seek its cancellation. After that time, however, the country can prohibit a party from seeking such cancellation on grounds of being the rightful owner of the well-known mark.

[16]The advertising and brand promotion activities of several American firms in the USSR are described in the December 1967 issue of *Marketing/Communications,* in an article by Sol Fox, entitled "The Odd Couple: Marx and Marketing." pp. 51-52.

of Soviet-made products domestically is directed by the state enterprise Soyustorgreklama, which also supervises such advertising
organizations in each of the 15 Soviet Republics. On January 16,
1967, Vneshtorgreklama ran a large ad in *The New York Times*
(pages 56-57) inviting American firms to utilize its services in advertising their products in the USSR newspaper, magazine, radio,
and television media. For the U.S. foreign trading community's
edification, the ad also provided information on about 30 Soviet
foreign trade organizations that serve as the country's import and/
or export monopolies for particular commodities. Also described
were activities of Litsenintorg (see note 10) and the patent and trademark activities of the USSR Chamber of Commerce. The ad also
showed for these and the other Soviet trading organizations the
trademark each used exclusively to identify itself abroad.

As in other Eastern European countries, trade fairs in the
USSR also appear to provide good showcases for the trademarked
goods of foreign firms. Two such fairs were held in 1966, three in
1967, and four in 1968, according to the available schedules. Four
have been firmed up so far for 1969 and two for 1970.[17] These
exhibitions cover a variety of industrial and consumer-type goods,
each year attracting exhibitors from Western as well as Eastern
Europe. Soviet trademark law provides recognized protection for
an unregistered trademark on goods displayed at such exhibitions
should the applicant wish to file for its registration within six
months after he puts the goods on display. In such instances his
application filing date is the date on which he first displayed his
goods.[18]

Recent U.S. Action Pertinent to Trademark Interests in Soviet Trade

President Johnson, in his State of the Union message delivered
January 17, 1968, noted the progress that had been made in U.S.-
USSR relations despite the fact that "Serious differences still remain between us. . . ." He cited, as examples, the recently concluded Consular Convention and Commercial Air Agreement
between the two countries.

Also to be noted is a Joint Resolution (S.J. Res. 169) intro-

---

[17]*International Commerce* (June 27 and December 26, 1966; June 26 and
December 25, 1967; and July 8, 1968), published by U.S. Department of Commerce. The interest of U.S. manufacturers of trademarked goods in these fairs
is exemplified by the participation of 18 U.S. firms in the automatic food-handling
equipment (Inprodmash), 15 U.S. firms in the clothing exhibition (Odezha), and
about 10 U.S. firms in the mining equipment (Intergormash) fairs in 1968.

[18]Soviet Trade Mark Law of 1962, Art. 11, para. 5 (see Appendix B).

duced in the U.S. Senate, May 9, 1968 (90th Cong., 2nd Sess.), calling for a reexamination of the export control regulations and Export-Import Bank financing restrictions to permit an increase in peaceful goods trade between the U.S. and Eastern Europe. It was referred to the Senate's Banking and Currency Committee and was still pending as of the writing of this article.

Recent U.S.-USSR Agreements

The above agreements are among the specific actions taken since 1966 to implement the President's appeal that year in his State of the Union message, and a later major policy speech, that we build bridges of peaceful trade with Eastern Europe.[19] Trademark owners interested in the Soviet market may find the treaties particularly interesting.

The Consular Treaty, which entered into force July 13, 1968, establishes the conditions under which Consulates may be opened by each country in the other's territory, and also provides for certain basic safeguards for individual rights of each country's nationals in the other's territory.[20] Additionally, it establishes the framework for enhancing commercial contacts between the two countries by enabling the creation of centralized sources for each country in the other's territory to render commercial advice, services, and assistance. The U.S.-USSR Civil Air Transport Agreement, signed November 4, 1966, and amended May 6, 1968, provides for direct flight services between New York and Moscow to be implemented by Pan American World Airways and the Soviet airline Aeroflot. The flights began July 15, 1968. A number of U.S. businessmen were among the first to book passage aboard the initial flights.[21]

Export Control Actions

In 1966, the Department of Commerce removed requirements of export licenses on about 400 nonstrategic items for shipment to the USSR and other Eastern European countries with which we have diplomatic relations.[22] Most of these items are of the con-

---

[19]State of the Union Message, January 12, 1966; Speech of October 7, 1966, to The National Conference of Editorial Writers, New York City.

[20]President's Transmittal Message of June 12, 1964, and Text of Treaty signed June 1, 1964, appear in U.S. Senate Document, *Consular Convention with Russia*, Executive D, (88th Cong., 2nd Sess.).

[21]State Department, *Treaties and Other International Acts, Series 6135;* amendment appears in State Department Press Release No. 94, May 6, 1968. *Business Abroad,* Vol. 93, No. 15 (August 1968), p. 9. Published by Dunn & Bradstreet, Inc.

[22]As a direct follow-up to the President's major policy speech of October 7, 1966. See note 19 and *Current Export Bulletin, No. 941* (U.S. Dept. of Commerce, October 12, 1966).

sumer and industrial type generally identified by trademarks, such as clothing, prepared foods, hardware and tools, electrical, measuring, and air conditioning equipment. There are now around 900 products which are exportable to the USSR and Eastern Europe under general (open) license.

Also of interest to exporters of trademarked goods is the Department of Commerce announcement in May 1968 of a new procedure to expedite export licensing of sample shipments of certain commodities to the USSR and to other Eastern European countries.[23] Under this procedure it will approve "without extended review" applications to export samples valued at no more than $200 to these countries. This should save considerable time to prospective exporters of trademarked goods who do not specifically seek advance indication of approval for subsequent commercial shipments. Issuance of a license for a sample does not constitute a commitment by the Department to approve shipments in commercial quantities at a future date. The new procedure is limited to five product categories: chemicals, drugs, and pharmaceuticals; synthetic rubber; petroleum and petroleum products; lubricants, additives, and operational fluids; and metals and minerals. Coupled with this action was the removal of certain power-operated tools from requirements of export licensing to Eastern European countries.

U.S. Trade Mission

In addition to liberalizing the export control regulations affecting shipments to the USSR and other Eastern European countries, the Department of Commerce sponsored a trade mission organized by the Minneapolis Chamber of Commerce which visited the USSR as well as Poland, Romania, Bulgaria and Yugoslavia. The mission members were impressed by the keen interest of Eastern European commercial officials in U.S.-branded products and a desire for appropriate catalogs and literature.[24]

SALIENT FEATURES OF THE TRADEMARK SYSTEM

Trademarks in the USSR, as previously noted, have served primarily as factory identification and quality control symbols. Until enactment of the present trademark law in 1962 (superseding the earlier law of 1936), little attention was paid to their potential

---

[23]Since then, additional items have been added to the list as a result of continuing review. See *Current Export Bulletin, No. 965* (U.S. Dept. of Commerce, May 10, 1968).

[24]*International Commerce*, note 17, *supra* (November 27, 1967), pp. 14-16.

function as competitive sales and advertising devices, and as distinctive identifications to enable prospective buyers to choose among similar goods made by different enterprises. There appears to have been little attempt by the Soviets before that date to make any significant changes in their trademark system to bring it more into conformity with international standards of practice and procedure.

Long before the Soviets joined the Paris Union Convention, the six other Eastern European countries (Czechoslovakia, Bulgaria, Romania, Hungary, Poland, and Yugoslavia) were members and adherents to its international standards of trademark as well as patent protection. In the USSR, where articles have been produced mostly for industrial usage and for domestic consumption, the trademark system in effect before 1962 did little more than force state enterprises to use certain markings on their goods so that liability could be established in cases of quality defects or faulty handling of goods. The earlier Soviet Trademark Law of 1936 is summarized in Appendix A.

The present law came into force June 23, 1962 (see Appendix B for text). It does not deal specifically with "Production or Factory Marks" included in the 1936 law. Such marks are apparently not abolished although it seems that they will become obsolete for identification and liability purposes in view of Council of Ministers' Decrees of February 16 and May 15, 1962, requiring enterprises to register and use trademarks on consumer and capital goods.[25]

Scope of Present Trademark Protection

The law provides that "Every trademark, before it is used in the USSR, shall be subject to compulsory State registration with the Committee for Inventions and Discoveries. . . ."[26] The owner of a registered mark is entitled to its exclusive use in the USSR.[27] It is not clear whether a nonregistered mark may be used in the USSR with no recognized exclusive rights therein or whether no trademark whatsoever may be used unless it is first registered in that country. No legal decisions or other clarifying official rulings from the government are available.

Trademarks are registered for the term indicated by the applicant up to 10 years from the application filing date; renewals also

---

[25]M. Boguslavsky and I. Cherviakov, note 9, *supra*, p. 48. These Decrees also contained other provisions governing the registration and use of trademarks which were incorporated in the present Law of June 23, 1962.

[26]See Appendix B, "Union of Soviet Socialist Republics Law Concerning Trademarks," Art. 2.

[27]*Id.*, Art. 4.

cannot be made for more than 10 years at a time.[28] The rights to a trademark lapse upon expiration of the validity term, waiver of such rights by the owner, or liquidation of the enterprise.[29] The applicant is not obliged to show prior use of his mark in order to apply for and receive a registration.[30] However, where there is a dispute over several applications on file for similar or identical marks, registration may be granted to the first applicant as determined by the date his application was received by the Committee.[31]

Soviet law includes protection for service marks.[32] Thus, in line with Paris Union Convention principles embodied in the Lisbon Revision of 1958, the law provides for protection of marks used to identify services as well as to distinguish goods. "A trademark or service mark" is defined as "an artistic representation, original in its form," and can consist of "original names and words, separate combinations of letters and figures, vignettes, different forms of packaging, artistic compositions and drawings whether combined or not with letters, figures, words etc. . . ."[33] Not registerable as trademarks are "marks commonly used to denote goods of a well-known kind (free marks)," marks which constitute national emblems and insignia; marks of international organizations, including the Red Cross and Red Crescent; business-type summary information about the product and the applicant; marks containing false or misleading information about the manufacturer or geographic origin of the product; marks "contrary to the public interest or the requirements of Socialist morality," and marks which conflict with international conventions to which the USSR adheres.[34]

Filing and Registration Particulars

The USSR Chamber of Commerce's Patent Bureau generally handles all filing and prosecution actions for foreigners' applications.[35] It requires an appropriate power of attorney and also

---

[28]*Id.*, Art. 19 and 20. (Time period is calculated from date of receipt of application by the Committee.)

[29]*Id.*, Art. 25.

[30]*Id.*, Art. 9. (This article details the required documentation but mentions no need of evidence of prior use.)

[31]*Id.*, Art 11, para. 1.

[32]Service industries in the USSR have reportedly received far less attention, so far, than industrial and consumer goods production industries in governmental planning operations. The government has, however, announced plans to increase capital investment in the services sectors.

[33]Note 26, *supra*, Art. 1, para. 1.

[34]*Id.*, para. 2.

[35]Details on filing procedures and fees can be secured by writing to the Bureau at 6 Kuibyshev Ul., Moscow.

collects the various fees charged by the government in addition to
its own agent fees.

Since the USSR has ratified the Paris Union Convention, a
trademark owner in the United States or any other Convention
country is entitled to claim a six-month "right of priority" therein
after a first filing of his trademark application in another Convention country.[36] Soviet citizens of course have the same "priority
rights" in the United States and other Convention countries on
the basis of USSR Convention membership. The filing date of a
foreigner's application in the USSR is determined by the date it
was received by the Committee.[37]

Applications are subject to examination, and, if refused, the
applicant is entitled to an administrative appeal.[38] There are no
provisions for opposition. An application will be refused if the mark
applied for is similar to one already registered in the same class of
goods or to one which is the subject of a previous application in
the USSR on which a decision has not yet been made.[39] If the
application is acceptable to the Committee, the trademark is recorded in the State Register of Trademarks and a certificate is
granted entitling the registrant to the exclusive right to use of the
mark.[40] Soviet law provides a preliminary examination system
to persons desiring to know if their trademarks are registerable
before they decide to file formal applications. Upon request by
such person the Committee may examine his mark and then certify
whether it is suitable for registration. If the applicant is informed
that he is entitled to the registration, the searched mark may be
reserved for him for three months. If he fails to apply for it within
that period, the mark (or one similar to it) may be registerable to
another applicant.[41]

Classification Procedures

The Soviets have established a classification system for trademark registrations.[42] It consists of product classes, one through
34; and service classes, 35 through 42. The classes are comparable
to those in the present "International Classification for the Registration of Trademarks" adopted by an Arrangement at Nice which
came into force April 8, 1961. The USSR is not a party to this

---

[36]Note 26, *supra*, Art. 11, paras. 2, 3, and 4.

[37]*Id.*, Art. 11, para. 1.

[38]*Id.*, Art. 16.

[39]*Id.*, Art. 15.

[40]*Id.*, Art. 17.

[41]*Id.*, Art. 18.

[42]*Id.*, Art. 8.

Arrangement, although it applies the same system. A separate application must be filed in the USSR for each class of goods.[43]

Infringement Actions

The law prohibits the use of a trademark without the registrant's consent and enables him to seek injunctive action against its unauthorized use and damages for infringement.[44] Infringement action can presumably be taken against unauthorized use of a mark on imports. Civil lawsuits, including those on trademark infringements, are apparently within the jurisdiction of District (City) People's Courts unless a higher court (i.e., Moscow City Court or the Supreme Court of a Republic) decides to have a case referred to it as the Court of First Instance. So far as can be determined, U.S. nationals reportedly have the same benefits as Soviet nationals in exercising rights under USSR judicial procedures. The USSR Civil Code, which provides for indemnification of property damages, is also applicable in the case of trademark infringement.[45] Few trademark infringement suits appear to have been filed in the USSR in recent years.[46] Infringement of trademark rights may also be subject to penal action under the USSR Criminal Codes.[47]

Transfers, Assignments, and Licenses

Exclusive rights to a trademark may be transferred from one enterprise to another upon reorganization, or by assignment from one party to another, in which case the existing registration is voided and a new one issued in the new proprietor's name. Transfer agreements must be registered with the Committee to be legal.[48]

A trademark registrant is permitted to license his mark. Li-

---

[43]*Id.*, Art. 9, para. 2.

[44]*Id.*, Arts. 4 and 21.

[45]M. Boguslavsky and I. Cherviakov, note 9, *supra*, p. 62-65.

[46]In a prominent case two years ago involving a foreign mark, the Belgian-West German firm Gevaert-AGFA N.V. of Antwerp was subject to an infringement suit as a result of its use of AGFA in a Soviet trade fair. The suit was brought by an East German firm, Volkseigener Betrieb (VEB) Filmfabrik Wolfen, which had acquired an AGFA registration in the USSR in 1955. The Moscow City Court ruled in the case in January 1966 that Gevaert-AGFA could not use its name in the USSR because AGFA had already been registered there by the East German firm. The Soviet Supreme Court upheld this verdict in a decision of April 28, 1966. (Reported in *The Journal of Commerce*, April 29, 1966.)

[47]For example, the Criminal Code of the Russian Soviet Federative Socialist Republic (§ 155) provides that "illegal use of a trademark belonging to another person is punishable by reformatory labor for a period of not more than six months or by a fine of not more than 300 rubles." ("BIRPI East-West Industrial Property Symposium," note 8, *supra*, p. 187; also, M. Boguslavsky and I. Cherviakov, note 9, *supra*, p. 68).

[48]Note 26, *supra*, Arts. 22 and 23 (para. 3).

censing agreements, which also must be registered with the Committee to be legal, must contain commitments by the parties that quality standards not inferior to those of the licensor will be maintained on the goods bearing the licensed mark.[49]

Any amendments to the registration certificate, including designation of the registrant, changes in classes to be covered, and basic changes in the trademark itself, must also be registered with the Committee.[50]

Other Major Characteristics

There is no requirement in the law for a registered mark to be used, but it would seem that most marks are registered in the USSR with the expectation of their eventual, if not immediate, use. Trademark registrations, renewals, transfers, licensing, amendment, and annulment actions are required to be entered in the State Register of Trademarks and are published by the Committee in its *Official Bulletin of Inventions, Trademarks and Designs*.[51]

The law contains a reciprocity provision for foreign nationals, i.e., it applies only to those foreigners whose countries extend national treatment to Soviet citizens under their trademark laws.[52] This reciprocity provision, however, is no bar to U.S. filings, since our trademark law, as mentioned earlier, makes no distinction as to nationality so far as rights of applicants to file for and secure registrations are concerned. Also, the principle of national treatment is established in the Paris Union Convention.

In the USSR, a state production or service enterprise can own one mark for use on all its goods or services or a separate one for use on each type of product it sells or type of service it renders. Also, a Soviet commercial enterprise may use its own trademark on all its documentation and may use the mark in place of or together with the trademark of the manufacturer on goods handled by it or made to its special order.[53] Goods manufactured by state enterprises must bear a trademark before they can be sold (see note 25).

The present Trademark Law was approved by the Committee on June 23, 1962. It was amended on May 4 and 19, 1965, to reflect changes needed to implement the Paris Union Convention and on March 31, 1967, to clarify further its provisions on transfers of trademarks.

---

[49]*Id.*, Art. 23.
[50]*Id.*, Art. 24.
[51]*Id.*, Art. 26.
[52]*Id.*, Art. 27.
[53]*Id.*, Arts. 5, 6, and 7.

CONCLUSION

In the USSR, where the distribution of goods and services is subject to a system of state directives, trademarks have served primarily as symbols of identification for guarantee and quality control purposes. They have played a lesser role as tools for marketing, business promotion, and "good will" development. Nevertheless, American businessmen interested in Soviet trade might consider applying for trademark registrations in the USSR for a number of reasons. The trademark registered in accordance with the law will thereby become a legally recognized form of protection subject to enforcement against unauthorized imitations, including those on imported goods. Also, such marks will be useful focal points around which to develop any market promotion that can be accomplished within the limitations of the Soviet system. Furthermore, such registered marks, entitled to exclusive use under Soviet law, will provide important identification for a firm's products imported into the USSR. Trademark registrations will also facilitate conclusion of licensing agreements in those product areas where "package deals," including licensing of patents and technical know-how, as well as trademarks, may be the only type of arrangements that can be negotiated.

The USSR has Westernized its Trademark Law and is participating in the world "Union" of countries that abide by internationally accepted principles of patent and trademark protection. So far, there is little experience by which to determine how successful American firms will be in protecting their rights in that country. The American businessman will have to consult carefully with his attorney and licensing advisor for guidance on the procedures to be followed in acquiring and maintaining the fullest possible protection available under Soviet law.

It is possible that disputes concerning trademark matters that might be involved in an overall foreign trade transaction could be decided through arbitration procedures rather than the courts. The Foreign Trade Arbitration Commission of the USSR Chamber of Commerce in Moscow is the arbitral body in that country. Western firms, however, have been known successfully to resist Soviet enterprises' requests for arbitration in Moscow and have been able to agree, in a number of instances, upon arbitration in the country desired by the Western party.

About 17,000 trademarks are reportedly now registered in the USSR (Table 1). While this overall figure is small compared with the numbers of trademarks registered in the United States and many other industrialized non-Eastern European countries, the number of applications filed and registrations granted in the USSR from foreign sources have increased in recent years. U.S. nationals reportedly had about 500 trademark registrations in that country as of October 1, 1965.[54] Any increase in U.S. filings is undoubtedly attributable to anticipation of better trade opportunities, the greater flexibility in licensing provided by the new law, and adherence by the USSR to the Paris Union Convention. In the past, many U.S. marks were filed through, and in the name of, Western European subsidiaries of U.S. firms to take greater advantage of trading opportunities. In recent years however, more U.S. firms have become interested in filing directly in the USSR.

Table 3 shows U.S. filings in 1965 and 1966 in the USSR and other Eastern European countries as compared to filings in leading Western countries on a regional basis, where figures are available. Although U.S. filings in the USSR may be far below those for other leading trading countries, the Soviet Government's increasing emphasis on consumer goods production, the growing market potential in that country for imports, and its adherence to the Paris Union Convention may change this picture considerably in the next few years.

---

[54]United Kingdom nationals reportedly had 417, Italy 209, France 189, West Germany 143, Switzerland 110, East Germany 927 and Czechoslovakia 248, as of this date. (M. Boguslavsky and I. Cherviakov, note 9, *supra*, p. 53).

TABLE 1

TRADEMARK REGISTRATIONS IN FORCE IN SELECTED
COUNTRIES IN 1965 and 1966
(Listed by Declining Order of Magnitude in 1966)

	Total in Force End of 1965	Total in Force End of 1966
Japan	377,463	407,789
U. S.	339,360	344,550
Fed. Rep. Germany	251,431	257,459
United Kingdom	220,982	222,854
Canada	98,623	102,449
Netherlands	79,799	81,317
India	80,251	81,290
Sweden	54,543	56,865
Chile	48,828	54,081
Colombia	42,475	44,218
Czechoslovakia	29,653	30,832
Rhodesia	19,426	19,575
Syria	17,510	17,705
USSR	16,391	16,597
Lebanon	13,902	14,561
Israel	12,339	13,007
Philippines	9,419	9,961
Uganda	7,171	7,650
Hungary	5,664	5,856
Yugoslavia	4,329	4,613
Bulgaria	3,947	4,366

Source: *Industrial Property*, note 2, *supra* (Statistical Annex, No. 12, December issues for 1966 and 1967).

TABLE 2

TRADEMARK APPLICATIONS FILED IN AND REGISTRATIONS GRANTED BY USSR (1965 & 1966)

	1965		1966	
	Number Applications Filed	Number Registrations Rec'd.	Number Applications Filed	Number Registrations Rec'd.
By Foreign Nationals from:				
Austria	n.a.	n.a.	6	0
Belgium	n.a.	n.a.	14	4
Canada	0	3	2	0
Cuba	1	1	2	0
Czechoslovakia	16	13	26	19
Denmark	2	1	17	2
Finland	3	0	2	0
France	24	34	19	20
Fed. Rep. Germany	137	0	280	199
East Germany	56	68	41	46
Hungary	1	5	1	1
India	n.a.	n.a.	1	0
Ireland	n.a.	n.a.	1	1
Italy	11	7	14	6
Jamaica	1	0	0	1
Japan	40	27	36	33
Netherlands	19	4	40	21
Norway	5	0	2	5
Panama	n.a.	n.a.	1	0
Poland	n.a.	n.a.	2	0
South Africa	2	2	1	2
Spain	n.a.	n.a.	2	0
Sweden	6	4	10	6
Switzerland	95	20	61	92
United Kingdom	165	46	77	146
United States	83	56	79	60
Others	0	1	3	1
Total Filings by Foreign Nationals	668		740	
Total Registrations Received by Foreign Nationals		292		665
Total Filings by USSR Domestic Nationals	4,356		1,862	
Total Registrations Received by USSR Domestic Nationals		2,219		765
Total Filings and Registrations in USSR (Foreign and Domestic Nationals)	5,024	2,511	2,602	1,430

Source: *Industrial Property*, note 2, *supra* (Statistical Annex, No. 12, December issues for 1966 and 1967).

TABLE 3

UNITED STATES TRADEMARK APPLICATIONS FILED
IN SELECTED COUNTRIES
(By Number of Filings in 1965 and 1966)

Country of Filing	1965	1966
Eastern Europe		
USSR	83	79
Poland	65	104
Rumania	n.a.	
Hungary	84	146
Czechoslovakia	43[1]	48[1]
Bulgaria	57	72
Yugoslavia	109	106
Western Europe		
United Kingdom	1,962	2,032
France	1,771	632
Germany	1,626	1,510
Netherlands	957	1,001
Belgium	842	846
Sweden	871	909
Switzerland	715[1]	649
Norway	579	657
Austria	522	525
Canada	2,340	2,521
Latin America		
Chile	1,022	1,191
Venezuela	945	1,275
Colombia	389	496
Far East		
Japan	2,607	2,378
New Zealand	610	764
India	443	468
Thailand	332	481
Malaysia	226	276
Ceylon	97	148
Pakistan	247	237
Philippines	285	591
North Africa and Middle East		
Israel	355	389
Lebanon	302	267
Iran	194	237
Morocco	151	169
United Arab Republic	161	198
Africa (Other)		
South Africa	988	1,002
Rhodesia	198	214
Sudan	98	179
Ghana	115	133
Uganda	114	153

[1]Registrations

Source: *Industrial Property*, note 2, *supra* (Statistical Annex, No. 12, December issues for 1966 and 1967).

APPENDIX A

THE EARLIER USSR TRADEMARK LAW
OF 1936 (SUMMARY)

The earlier Soviet Trademark Law of 1936 established two classes of marks—production marks and trademarks. A production mark was obligatory on all manufactured goods, their containers or wrappers, and had to show the factory's name, location, state agency in charge of the factory, quality of its goods, and its standard number. Certain factories producing military-type goods were exempted from this requirement to avoid disclosures for security reasons. The other class of mark—the trademark—was an industrial property right similar to that afforded by the U.S. and other Western industrial property laws. Adoption of a trademark by a factory or other producing enterprise to distinguish an article was voluntary. Marks not registrable were those confusingly similar to marks already registered, those containing false or misleading connotations in relation to their goods, those simulating the Red Cross or Red Crescent, and those too generally descriptive of the goods for which they were intended. Trademarks could be "graphic images, original names, combinations of letters, etc.," and different marks could be used for different goods or the same mark for all goods produced by a factory. An enterprise, such as an exporting entity, dealing with goods produced by others, was also permitted to have, and to use in connection with its sales, its own mark.

The trademark registration system was originally decentralized into three categories. The People's Commissariat for Heavy Industry registered all marks used on machines, tools, building supplies, and chemicals; the Commissariat for Public Health registered all marks used on medical supplies and instruments; and the Commissariat for Internal Trade registered marks used on other classes of goods. In 1959 the registration system was centralized in the State Committee for Inventions and Discoveries, which today administers the patent and industrial design laws, as well as that on trademarks. The earlier trademark law contained no use requirement, but conditions were such that once a mark was registered it was put to use. The law permitted the owner of a registration to sue for infringement against unauthorized use of his mark on imported as well as on domestically manufactured products and to seek injunctions and recover damages in infringement cases. Action could also be sought to invalidate a registration.

Under the 1936 law foreigners could register their marks in the USSR only if their home countries extended the benefits of their trademark laws to Soviet nationals. This was no bar so far as U.S. nationals were concerned since our trademark law makes no distinction as to nationality and enables a Soviet or any other national to apply for and receive trademark protection. The Soviet law also required a foreign applicant to have a prior home registration for his mark before it could be registered in the USSR. Registration was issued only for a term not exceeding the home registration.

Appendix B
USSR STATUTE ON TRADEMARKS[55]
Approved by the Committee for Inventions and Discoveries
Attached to the Council of Ministers of the USSR
on June 23, 1962, as amended up to March 31, 1967

1. — A trademark or service mark is an artistic representation, original in its form (original names and words, separate combinations of letters and figures, vignettes, different forms of packing, artistic compositions and drawings whether combined or not with letters, figures, words, etc.) used to distinguish goods or services of one enterprise from similar goods or services of other enterprises, and to advertise them.

The following shall not be used as trademarks and cannot be accepted for registration:

(a) marks commonly used to denote goods of a well-known kind (free marks);

(b) State insignia, facsimiles, seals, stamps; control, guarantee or other marks; emblems of international organizations without the consent of the appropriate bodies; or marks containing a representation of the Red Cross or Red Crescent;

(c) representations consisting exclusively of a text containing information concerning the time of manufacture of the goods, the address of the enterprise, price, quantity, size, etc. Where such information is additional to the basic representation of a mark, only the basic representation may be registered as a trademark, without the text. The text may be used together with the trademark but not as part of the representation of the mark itself;

(d) representations containing false information, or information capable of misleading a purchaser, concerning the manufacturer or the place of production (origin) of the goods;

(e) representations contrary to the public interest or the requirements of Socialist morality;

(f) representations conflicting with international conventions to which the USSR is a party.

2. — Every trademark, before it is used in the USSR, shall be subject to compulsory State registration with the Committee for Inventions and Discoveries attached to the Council of Ministers of the USSR, in accordance with Decree No. 442 of the Council of Ministers of the USSR, of May 15, 1962, "Concerning Trademarks."

3. — Trademarks cannot be used for liquid, gaseous, or loose and unconsolidated substances supplied or sold without packing, or for other goods exempt from all kinds of marking in accordance with State All-Union Standards (GOST) and Technical Specifications.

4. — An enterprise shall be entitled, in the territory of the USSR, to the exclusive use of a trademark or service mark registered in its name. The use of a trademark or service mark without the consent of the enterprise in the name of which it is registered is prohibited.

5. — An enterprise (organization, or production associations thereof) shall be entitled to possess a single trademark (service mark) for all the

[55]BIRPI translation. Revised version of texts published in 1965 and 1966, incorporating changes partly in the legislation and partly in the translation.
Source: *Industrial Property*, note 2, *supra*, No. 6 (June 1967), pp. 133-136.

goods it markets or all the services it renders, or to use different marks for various kinds of goods or services.

6. — An enterprise may also place trademarks or service marks registered in its name on technical drawings, prospectuses, invoices, forms, labels, and other documentation accompanying goods or connected with their distribution operations.

7. — A commercial enterprise (organization) shall have the right to place its own trademark instead of or beside the trademark of the manufacturing enterprise on goods marketed by it and manufactured to its special order (according to models, special formulae and prescriptions, etc.). The same right shall be granted to foreign-trade organizations in respect of goods marketed by them.

8. — Trademarks and service marks shall be registered for a definite class of goods (services). The same mark may be registered for different classes of goods (services) in the name of one enterprise (organization).

9. — State registration of trademarks and service marks shall be carried out by the Committee for Inventions and Discoveries attached to the Council of Ministers of the USSR on the basis of applications filed by enterprises (production associations of enterprises) and by organizations either directly or through agents duly authorized for the purpose. An application for registration of a trademark filed through an agent must be accompanied by a signed power of attorney in the prescribed form. Powers of attorney executed abroad must be duly legalized in consular offices of the USSR unless such legalization is not required by virtue of international treaties.

A separate application must be filed for each class of goods for which a trademark (service mark) is to be registered.

The application shall comprise the following materials:

(a) two copies of a declaration stating the full designation and postal address of the enterprise (organization) in the name of which the trademark is to be registered, and also the duration of the trademark registration;

(b) two copies of a complete list of the goods for which the trademark is to be registered, together with an indication of the classes of the goods and the manner in which the mark is to be applied to these goods;

(c) twenty copies of a specimen and two copies of a description of the trademark;

(d) a receipt from the State Bank for payment of the prescribed application fee (2.50 roubles for each class of goods);

(e) one copy of a document certifying the subordination (or affiliation) of the enterprise.

If the trademark or service mark contains information concerning the origin of the goods, the applicant must append to the application one copy of an official document certifying the correctness of the information concerning the origin of the goods contained in the representation of the trademark.

10. — A trademark (service mark) submitted for registration in color shall be registered and protected only in that color. A trademark (service mark) submitted for registration without indication of color shall be registered in black and white and may be used in any color unless it repeats a similar mark registered in a specified color.

A trademark (service mark) of similar representation may not be registered in other color combinations for other goods of the same class in the name of other proprietors.

11. — The date of priority of an application for a trademark (service mark) shall be the date on which the application is received by the Committee for Inventions and Discoveries attached to the Council of Ministers of the USSR. Applications may be sent by registered post. In case of dispute, the date of application shall be deemed to be the date of dispatch as fixed by the postmark, and for foreign applicants the date of dispatch to the Committee by a patent agent domiciled in the USSR.

In the case of nationals of foreign countries and foreign legal entities, the priority of an application for a trademark, in conformity with the International Convention to which the USSR is a party, shall be established as the date of priority of the first lawfully valid application filed in a country which is also a party to the said Convention, provided that the application is filed in the USSR within a period of six months after that date.

Any person who wishes to avail himself of the priority established in accordance with the International Convention shall immediately, upon filing the application, make a statement to that effect, and shall indicate the date of priority and the country where the trademark was first filed.

The requisite certified copy of the foreign application and all other materials necessary for establishing the date of priority may be furnished subsequently, but not later than three months from the date of filing of the application in the USSR.

The priority of an application for a trademark used on exhibits displayed in international exhibitions organized in the USSR shall be determined by the date on which the exhibit is put on display in the exhibition, provided that the application is filed not later than six months after that date.

12. — The Committee for Inventions and Discoveries attached to the Council of Ministers of the USSR shall examine all applications received in order to ascertain that the documents comprised in the application and the representation of the trademark (service mark) submitted for registration satisfy the requirements of this Statute.

13. — The Committee for Inventions and Discoveries attached to the Council of Ministers of the USSR shall be entitled to require an applicant to submit the additional materials necessary for its decision concerning the registration of the trademark (service mark).

If the applicant does not submit the required additional materials within three months from the date on which he receives the request of the Committee for Inventions and Discoveries attached to the Council of Ministers of the USSR, the application shall not be considered.

14. — The Committee for Inventions and Discoveries attached to the Council of Ministers of the USSR shall notify the applicant of the decision concerning registration of the trademark (service mark) within one month from the expiration of a six-month period after the date of filing of the application or of receipt of the required additional materials.

In the event of refusal to register the trademark, the decision, together with the grounds therefor, must be communicated to the applicant within three months from the date of filing of the application or the date of receipt of the required additional materials, and, if the refusal is based upon the application of a national of a foreign country or a foreign legal entity, benefiting from an earlier priority in accordance with the International Convention, within one month from the date on which the application is filed with the Committee for Inventions and Discoveries attached tò the Council of Ministers of the USSR.

15. — The Committee for Inventions and Discoveries attached to the Council of Ministers of the USSR shall refuse to register a trademark (service mark) if the mark for which application is made for a specified class of goods is similar to:

(a) a trademark (service mark) registered in the same class of goods in the USSR;

(b) a trademark (service mark) for which an application has already been filed in the USSR on which no decision has yet been made.

16. — An applicant who disagrees with a refusal to register a trademark (service mark) may, within two months from the date on which he receives the decision, lodge with the Committee for Inventions and Discoveries attached to the Council of Ministers of the USSR an objection with grounds therefor. The objection shall be accompanied by a receipt for payment of the prescribed fee (2.50 roubles for each class of goods).

The Committee for Inventions and Discoveries attached to the Council of Ministers of the USSR shall consider the objection within two months. The decision of the Chairman of the Committee or his Deputy shall be final.

17. — After reaching a decision to register a trademark (service mark), the Committee for Inventions and Discoveries attached to the Council of Ministers of the USSR shall enter the same in the State Register of Trademarks of the USSR and issue to the applicant a certificate granting him the right to exclusive use of the mark.

Copies of the certificate granting the right to the exclusive use of the trademark may be issued only upon presentation of an official announcement of the loss of the said certificate published in the local press, and, in the case of an irrecoverable loss, upon presentation of documents confirming the loss of the certificate.

18. — An applicant may request the Committee for Inventions and Discoveries attached to the Council of Ministers of the USSR to conduct a preliminary examination of a trademark in order to determine whether its registration is possible. Such preliminary examination shall be conducted on submission of one copy each of the application, a specimen of the trademark, and a list of the goods in connection with which it is proposed to use the trademark, together with the receipt of the State Bank for payment of the prescribed fee (2.50 roubles for each class of goods).

If, within three months from the date of dispatch to the applicant of the positive conclusion of the preliminary examination of the trademark, an application for registration of the said trademark (service mark) has not been filed with the Committee for Inventions and Discoveries attached to the Council of Ministers of the USSR by the applicant, the mark (or marks similar to it) may be registered in the name of another applicant.

19. — Trademarks (service marks) shall be registered for the term specified by the applicant, but not longer than ten years calculated from the date of receipt of the application by the Committee for Inventions and Discoveries attached to the Council of Ministers of the USSR.

20. — The term of validity of the certificate granting the right to the

exclusive use of a trademark (service mark) may be extended for not more than ten years each time. The term of validity of a certificate shall be extended on application filed by the proprietor during the last year of validity of the certificate, but not later than six months after the expiry of such term.

An application for extension of the term of validity of a certificate shall be accompanied by:

(a) the original certificate granting the right to the exclusive use of the trademark;

(b) a receipt from the State Bank for payment of the application fee (2.50 roubles for each class of goods);

(c) a receipt for payment of the publication fee.

21. — During the term of validity of the certificate granting the right to the exclusive use of a trademark, the proprietor of the certificate may demand, in the manner prescribed by law, the cessation of unlawful use of an identical or analogous trademark or service mark in connection with goods or services of the same class, and damages for any loss caused to him.

22. — The right to the exclusive use of a trademark (service mark) may be transferred from one enterprise (organization) to another upon reorganization, and/or on assignment of the trademark (service mark).

In such cases, the certificate granting the right to the exclusive use of the trademark shall be cancelled and a new certificate shall be issued in its stead in the name of the new proprietor, who shall submit to the Committee within three months:

(a) a notarized copy of the deed or other document concerning the transfer of the right;

(b) the original certificate granting the right to the exclusive use of the trademark;

(c) a receipt for payment of the prescribed fee (2.50 roubles for each class of goods);

(d) a receipt for payment of the publication fee.

23. — An enterprise (organization) in the name of which a trademark (service mark) is registered shall be entitled to grant a license for full or partial use of its trademark to another enterprise (organization).

A license may be granted only on condition that the license agreement provides that the quality of the goods of the licensee shall not be inferior to the quality of the goods of the proprietor of the trademark for which the mark was registered, and that the proprietor who has transferred the mark shall control the fulfillment of this condition.

The agreement to transfer the right to a trademark (service mark) or to grant a license must be registered with the Committee for Inventions and Discoveries attached to the Council of Ministers of the USSR.

Unless so registered, the agreement shall be invalid.

24.—Amendments to the designation of the proprietor of the certificate granting the right to exclusive use of a trademark (service mark), to the list of classes and goods protected by the certificate, and to the registered trademark (if amendments relate to certain elements of the mark and do not change its substance) are subject to compulsory registration with the Committee for Inventions and Discoveries attached to the Council of Ministers of the USSR.

To amend the certificate granting the right to exclusive use of a trademark the following documents shall be submitted:

(a) the request indicating the nature of the amendment;
(b) the original certificate granting the right to exclusive use of the trademark;
(c) a receipt for payment of the prescribed fee (2.50 roubles for each class of goods);
(d) a receipt for payment of the publication fee (3 roubles);
(e) twenty photocopies of the trademark (if the mark is amended).

The request for amendment of the certificate shall be examined within three months from the date of its receipt by the Committee.

25. — The right to the exclusive use of a trademark shall lapse:

(a) on expiry of the term of its validity;
(b) in virtue of a declaration by the proprietor of the certificate waiving his right to use the mark;
(c) on liquidation of the enterprise.

26. — A note of every registration of a trademark (service mark), extension of a term of validity, transfer of the right to a trademark, grant of a license, amendment referred to above in Article 24, and annulment of a certificate, shall be entered in the State Register of Trademarks of the USSR and published in the *Official Bulletin* issued by the Committee for Inventions and Discoveries attached to the Council of Ministers of the USSR.

The applicant shall pay 3 roubles for the publication of each of such notices, except for the notice of annulment.

27. — Foreign legal entities and nationals of foreign countries shall, subject to reciprocity, enjoy the rights provided under this Statute on equal terms with enterprises and organizations of the USSR.

Author's Postscript—

Since the original publication of this article, attention, within its context, is called to the U.S. Government's review, instituted following the USSR-led invasion of Czechoslovakia on August 20, 1968, of relations with the USSR and the other invading countries. A summary of actions and conclusions following this review is quoted from the State Department's Annual Report on the Battle Act.

". . . .Steps were taken to express concretely the disapproval of the American people and the U.S. Government to the unprovoked invasion and occupation. For example, some cultural programs with the invading countries were canceled and unnecessary contacts and travel to that area were discouraged. The U.S. Government exhibit at the Plovdiv Trade Fair (Bulgaria) was canceled as were other governmental trade promotional efforts with respect to the invading countries.

"With respect to the longer term question of U.S. commercial and economic relations with these countries, it was concluded that the national interest of the United States would not be served by severing trade relations with them, and that the policy of permitting nonstrategic trade and related business contacts should be maintained. However, U.S. businessmen inquiring about transactions with these countries have been informed that the concern and uncertainty introduced by the invasion and occupation of Czechoslovakia should not be ignored in making plans to do business with these countries.

"The Department of Commerce has continued to process export license applications for these Eastern European destinations with care, to screen out commodities and technical data the use of which might adversely affect the national security of the United States. To this end, proposed transactions for which export licenses were sought for these countries have been considered on their individual merits, and licensed or denied according to their implications for U.S. national security welfare. In assessing these implications, the Department of Commerce, in consultation with the Departments of State and Defense, as well as other U.S. Government agencies, has continued to take into account prevailing security and foreign policy considerations, as well as the government's long-range trade policy." (*The Battle Act Report,* 1968, Department of State Publication 8426, released January, 1969, p. 16).

Taxation of the Foreign
Licensor in Australia

JOHN K. CONNOR

The U.S. Department of Commerce estimated that in January 1963 there were approximately 800 license or similar arrangements then in force between U.S. licensors of industrial property and like rights and Australian licensees.[1] The tax implications of such arrangements are therefore of considerable significance to the U.S. business community. The purpose of this paper is to outline briefly the impact of Australian taxes on these and related agreements and transactions.

For the most part, the only significant Australian tax imposed on the receipts from licenses of, and other transactions in, industrial property and allied rights is the income tax imposed by the Commonwealth of Australia. (Australia, like the United States, is a federation of states with distinct governments in addition to a commonwealth (i.e., federal) government.) Discussion in this article will therefore be confined to the incidence of the commonwealth income tax.

BASIC CONCEPTS

Australian income tax law hinges around three basic concepts— taxable income, residence, and income source. Some explanation of each of these is essential to any proper understanding of the Australian income tax system and is a necessary preamble to the discussion which follows.

Taxable Income

The concept of income for tax purposes is, for the most part, as ill-defined in Australian tax law as it is in the United States.[2] Ba-

EDITOR's NOTE: This paper was published in *IDEA*, Vol. 8, No. 1. Recent changes in the relevant tax laws of Australia appear in the author's postscript. This and the following two papers are reports by tax experts on a series of studies in a project conducted by John F. Creed, dealing with the taxation of the foreign licensor in certain non-U.S. jurisdictions.

[1]U.S. Department of Commerce Trade List of American Firms, Subsidiaries and Affiliates in Australia issued January 1963.

[2]The basic test was propounded by Chief Justice Jordan of the New South Wales Supreme Court in *Scott* v. *C. of T. (N.S.W.)*, 3 S.R. (N.S.W.) 215, 219 (1935) as being whether a receipt is income by the "ordinary concepts and usages of mankind."

sically, taxable income for Australian tax purposes is ascertained by deducting from the taxpayer's "assessable income" the appropriate "allowable deductions."[3] "Assessable income" approximates gross income for U.S. tax purposes with the exception of capital gains, there being no Australian income or similar tax on capital gains. "Allowable deductions" may be classified into general and concessional deductions, the former comprising principally business expenditures while the latter arise as a consequence of a taxpayer's personal status or needs, location in Australia, or domestic responsibilities.[4]

One significant difference from U.S. tax law is that all royalties are specifically deemed to be income receipts, even though on a conceptual analysis they might be considered as being capital items.[5] However, the converse is not necessarily true; a royalty payment may well be a nondeductible capital expenditure on the part of the payor.[6]

Residence

Residence is a concept of considerable significance, since it may determine not only basic liability to Australian income tax[7] but also the rate of tax payable,[8] the appropriate method of tax collection,[9] entitlement to concessional deductions,[10] and the scope of protection afforded by the Double Taxation Conventions to which Australia is a signatory.[11]

An individual will be taxed as an Australian resident if he is in fact resident there by ordinary legal standards.[12] In Australia, the general legal concept of residence is to be distinguished from that of domicile, which may be governed by place of birth or operation of law or secured by choice but is not necessarily dependent on having an actual residence in the place of domicile. Residence, on the

---

[3]Income Tax and Social Services Contribution Assessment Act 1936-1963 (hereinafter referred to as "the Act"). §§ 6 and 48.

[4]The Act, § 48 *et seq.*

[5]The Act, § 26 (f). and see *McCauley* v. *F.C. of T.*, 69 C.L.R. 235 (1944). cf. *Minister of National Revenue* v. *Spooner*, A.C. 684.

[6]See *Colonial Mutual Life Assurance Society Ltd.* v. *F.C. of T.*, 89 C.L.R. 428 (1953).

[7]The Act, §§ 25 (1) and 23 (r).

[8]See p. 510, *infra*. It affects only the rate of tax imposed on certain corporate dividend income.

[9]The Act, §§ 219, 255, and 226.

[10]§ 82A of the Act limits concessional deductions to residents of Australia, including residents of certain external territories.

[11]See p. 510, *infra*.

[12]The Act, Section 6 (1) and see *Gregory* v. *D.F.C. of T.*, 57 C.L.R. 774 (1937).

other hand, turns solely on the existence of an actual home or place of abode in the relevant jurisdiction.[13]

In addition, an Australian domiciliary will be treated as an Australian resident for tax purposes, even if he has currently no actual residence in Australia, unless he can satisfy the Commissioner of Taxation that he has his permanent place of abode outside Australia.[14] A taxpayer will also be taxed as an Australian resident if he is actually in Australia for more than one half the tax year unless he can satisfy the Commissioner that his usual place of abode is outside Australia and that he does not intend to take up residence there.[15]

A company will be resident in Australia for tax purposes if it is incorporated in Australia, if its central management and control are located within the country, or if it carries on business in Australia and has its voting power controlled by shareholders who are Australian residents.[16] The prime but not the only criterion for determining the central management or control of a company is the situs of its directors' meetings.[17] However, if real management and control are not exercised by the directors at their meetings, or if these are in fact shared with other individuals or corporate organs, then the situs of the directors' meetings will not in itself be decisive. The test to be applied is, in essence, one that looks to the locus of the "voice" which controls the company's business.[18]

Income Source

An Australian resident (as defined above) is subject to Australian income tax on his world-wide income, with certain exceptions, while a nonresident is subject to tax only on Australian source income.[19] For this reason the concept of income source is of particular significance to nonresidents.

In a watershed case, Isaacs J. of the High Court said of the word "source," when used in a statutory context very similar to that of the present commonwealth income tax legislation, that it "meant, not a legal concept, but something which a practical man would

---

[13]See *Davies and Jones* v. *Western Australia*, 2 C.L.R. 29 (1904); *Udny* v. *Udny*, L.R. 1 H.L. Sc. 441, 9 C.T.B.R. Case 64 (1869).

[14]The Act, § 6 (1).

[15]*Ibid.*

[16]*Ibid.* and see *Malayan Shipping Company Ltd.* v. *Federal Commissioner of Taxation*, 71 C.L.R. 156 (1946).

[17]See *De Beers Consolidated Mines Co. Ltd.* v. *Howe*, A.C. 455 (1906); *John Hood & Co.* v. *Magee*, 7 T.C. 327 (1918); *North Australian Pastoral Co. Ltd.* v. *F.C. of T.*, 71 C.L.R. 623 (1946).

[18]*Unit Construction Co. Ltd.* v. *Bullock*, A.C. 351 (1960); *Koitaki Para Rubber Estates Ltd.* v. *F.C. of T.*, 64 C.L.R. 241 (1940), and *North Australian Pastoral Co. Ltd.* v. *F.C. of T.*, note 17, *supra*.

[19]The Act, § 25 (1) and 23 (r).

regard as a real source of income . . . the ascertainment of the actual source of a given income is a practical, hard matter of fact."[20] Despite frequent reiteration of this statement, the Australian courts have perhaps proved to be more influenced by conceptual legal criteria than have their U.S. counterparts when determining income source.

In general, it may be said that earnings derived from the rendering of services will be allocated to Australian source if the services are actually rendered in Australia, while income derived from the systematic exploitation, renting, or licensing of property located in Australia will normally be said to have an Australian source as a matter of course.[21] In some other cases the place of making of a particular contract may influence the source of the income to which it gives rise, and the place of receipt of the income may also be a relevant factor. (Obviously, other rules may apply in areas, e.g., that of mercantile profits, dividends, and interest, outside the scope of this article.) These are, of course, broad generalizations, and as such are subject to many exceptions and modifications in particular cases. Their particular application in the present area of inquiry will be further developed in this article.

TAX CLASSIFICATION OF COMPANIES

Since the great majority of foreign licensors and owners of Australian industrial property and like rights are undoubtedly corporations, it may be convenient at this stage to refer briefly to a distinction adopted in Australian income tax law between so-called "private" and "public" companies.[22] This distinction is only incidentally related to that adopted for Australian Company Law purposes between public and proprietary companies, and a company's status for corporate law purposes does not necessarily give any accurate indication of its tax status .

The distinction between the two classes of companies is important, since not only are differing rates of tax imposed on the two types of companies but, in addition, an undistributed-profits tax is imposed on certain private companies if they fail to make a sufficient distribution of their after-tax income.[23] No undistributed-profits or similar tax is imposed on public companies.

---

[20]*Nathan* v. *F.C. of T.*, 25 C.L.R. 183, 189-190 (1918). See also *Rhodesia Metals Ltd. (in liq.)* v. *Taxes Commissioner (Southern Rhodesia)*, A.C. 774 (1940), and *C. of T. (N.S.W.)* v. *Cam & Sons Ltd.*, 36 S.R. (N.S.W.) 544 (1936).

[21]See *F.C. of T.* v. *United Aircraft Corporation*, 68 C.L.R. 525 (1943); *Curtis Brown Ltd.* v. *Jarvis*, 14 T.C. 744 (1929); *F.C. of T.* v. *French*, 98 C.L.R. 398, 13 T.B.R.D. Case No. N36 (1957).

[22]The Act, Part III, Division 7.

[23]*Id.*, § 104 (1).

In brief, a private company, whether resident or not, is a company in which, on the last day of the tax year, all of the shares are held by 20 or fewer persons and which is capable of being controlled by seven or fewer persons (the concept of control being spelled out by explicit statutory criteria),[24] unless:

    a) it is a company in which the public is substantially interested, or

    b) it is a subsidiary of a public company, or

    c) it is unreasonable that it be so treated.

Dealing with each of these exceptions in turn:

    a) A company is a company in which the public is substantially interested if, generally, shares of the company have, in the current fiscal year, been quoted on the official list of a stock exchange, unless shares carrying not less than three quarters of the voting power in the company are, at the end of each fiscal year, beneficially held by or for 20 or fewer persons.

    b) A company is a subsidiary of a public company if, by reason of beneficial ownership of the shares, the control of the company is in the hands of one or more companies, none of which is a private company.[25]

    c) If it can be established, to the satisfaction of the Commissioner, that, because of special circumstances existing as of the last day of the year of income, it is unreasonable to treat a company as a private company, then it will not be so treated. The operation of this exemption is, of course, de-

---

[24]A company will be one capable of control by seven or fewer persons, the word "person" including a company, if they:

    1. are capable of exercising more than half the voting power, or

    2. hold more than half of its paid-up capital, other than capital comprised of shares having a fixed dividend rate only, or

    3. are capable of exercising three-quarters or more of the voting power, or

    4. hold shares comprising three-quarters or more of its paid-up capital, other than capital represented by shares bearing a fixed dividend rate only, or

    5. are capable of controlling the company by any means whatsoever, the word "control" here referring to shareholding control in the sense of being able to secure the passage of a resolution at a general meeting of the company.

(See *F.C. of T.* v. *Sidney Williams (Holdings) Ltd.,* 100 C.L.R. 95 (1957). For the purposes of tests (1) and (2) above, a person and his nominees are deemed to be one person (the Act, Section 105 (2)), while for the purposes of tests (3) and (4) a person as well as his nominees and certain relatives is deemed to be one person (the Act, Section 105 (3)).

[25]If one or more public companies are capable, as a matter of shareholding power, of controlling a particular company, then that company will be public despite the fact that such control is not actually exercised. See *Adelaide Stevedoring Co. Limited* v. *Federal Commissioner of Taxation,* 8 A.I.T.R. 440 (1961).

pendent on a favorable exercise of his discretion by the Commissioner, and such exemptions are not lightly given.

Any company which is not a private company is a public company.

THE UNDISTRIBUTED-PROFITS TAX AND THE NONRESIDENT COMPANY

As previously mentioned, an undistributed-profits tax is imposed on certain private companies if they fail to make a sufficient distribution of their after-tax income.[26] This tax, which is imposed at a flat rate (currently 50 percent) on so much of a company's undistributed after-tax income as exceeds fixed maximum percentages, is levied in addition to the normal income tax otherwise payable by the company.[27] The undistributed-profits tax is imposed on a nonresident private company only if it has a branch or head office in Australia, in which event all of its Australian source income is brought into account in determining whether a sufficient dividend distribution has been made to avoid the tax.[28] Since the computation of the undistributed amount on which the tax is imposed is based on a company's taxable income, and since, in the case of a nonresident company, its taxable income will include only Australian source income, such a company's foreign-source income is not taken into account in determining its distributable income and hence whether it has made a sufficient distribution.[29]

---

[26]The Act, § 104(1).

[27]The Act, §§103, 104(1), 105(A), and 105(B), and Income Tax and Social Services Contribution Act 1961-1963, Sixth Schedule § (3) (c).

[28]The Act, § 104(1).

[29]As explained earlier, a nonresident's assessable income and hence his taxable income includes only Australian source income. The procedure for arriving at the amount subject to the undistributed-profits tax is as follows, bearing in mind that the tax is imposed on the "undistributed amount" of the company's income:

1. "Distributable Income" = Taxable Income—(Commonwealth and any State and Foreign Income Taxes + Net Foreign Trading Losses).
2. "Reduced Distributable Income" = Distributable Income—Income from Property.
3. "Retention Allowance" = A sliding percentage (see table below) of the Reduced Distributable Income + 10 percent of the Taxable Income from Property (except dividends from other private companies for which no retention allowance is granted).
4. "Undistributed Amount" = Distributable Income—(Retention Allowance + Dividends Paid).

It should be noted that although the taxable income of a nonresident company will include only its Australian source income, it may pay dividends out of other income and still bring such dividends into account when ascertaining whether it has made a sufficient distribution.

RATES OF TAX

Although special tax rates are imposed in some circumstances upon dividends and interest received by nonresidents, no special rates of tax are imposed on taxable income of the type with which we are concerned which is derived by a nonresident.

The Double Taxation Conventions with the United States, the United Kingdom, Canada, and New Zealand do not in any way affect the rate of Australian tax payable by residents of these countries on taxable income, other than dividends, but do operate to exempt certain income from tax.[30] The rates of tax currently payable by individual taxpayers range from zero on an income of less than £100 ($225) per annum up to a maximum of 66.66 percent on taxable income in excess of £16,000 per annum.[31] The present rates of tax imposed on corporate income of the type with which we are concerned are as follows:[32]

Type of Company and Quantum of Income	Rate
Resident public companies on first £5,000 ($11,250) of taxable income	35%
Resident public companies on the balance of the taxable income over £5,000	40%
Nonresident public companies on the balance of first £5,000 of taxable income after subtracting taxable dividend income therefrom	35%
Nonresident public companies on all taxable income over £5,000	40%
Resident and nonresident private companies on first £5,000 of taxable income	25%
Resident and nonresident private companies on balance of taxable income over £5,000	35%

SPECIAL PROBLEMS OF NONRESIDENT LICENSORS AND OWNERS

Australian or Foreign Source Income?

To reiterate, a nonresident is liable to Australian income tax only on Australian source income, and the problem of source allocation is, therefore, a major one.

RETENTION ALLOWANCE TABLE
FOR INCOME OTHER THAN THAT DERIVED FROM PROPERTY

Reduced Distributable Income	Retention Allowance
First £5,000 ($11,250)	50%
Second £5,000	45%
Amount exceeding £10,000 ($22,500)	40%

[30]See p. 510, *infra.*

[31]Income Tax and Social Services Contribution Act 1961-1963, First Schedule.

[32]*Id.,* Sixth Schedule.

In this area it is possible to make several dogmatic assertions. Thus, we may confidently assert that receipts directly derived by a nonresident proprietor or licensor from the licensing, sublicensing, or sale for a royalty, of patents, designs, trademarks, and copyrights registered in Australia will definitely have an Australian source.[33]

An interesting example of the application of this principle was recently provided by a Commonwealth Taxation Board of Review decision.[34] A nonresident owner of certain inventions patented in Australia granted an exclusive license not registered under the Patents Act 1952 to a nonresident company which in turn granted an unregistered sublicense to an Australian resident. The Board held that royalties paid to the nonresident company were derived from an Australian source despite the fact that neither the head license nor the sublicense was registered in Australia and that the agreement was executed, and the royalty payments made, outside Australia. The decision seems an eminently sensible one, but is contrary to a view formerly held by many in Australia and is currently being appealed.[35]

One may also assert dogmatically that an agreement by a nonresident to render technical services completely outside Australia will not give rise to Australian source receipts, especially if the agreement is concluded abroad and payments are received outside the country.[36] Until recent years it was possible to be equally dogmatic as to a license of unpatented or unregistered inventions, processes, formulae, and the like, and confidently to classify such licenses for Australian tax purposes as in fact no more than agreements to provide technical services which, if the above rules were observed, would not give rise to Australian source income. Now, however, as a consequence of some of the judgments given in the English Courts in *Evans Medical Supplies Ltd.* v. *Moriarty,*[37] it is no longer possible to be quite so cavalier.

In the 20-year-old case of *United Aircraft Corporation* v. *F. C. of T.,*[38] the High Court of Australia held, by a two-to-one majority, that a license to use unpatented technical data granted by a U.S. licensor to an Australian company did not give rise to Australian source income where the agreement was concluded and

---

[33]See *Curtis Brown Ltd.* v. *Jarvis,* 14 T.C. 744 (1929); 9 T.B.R.D. Case J22 (1958).

[34]13 T.B.R.D. Case No. N36.

[35]But see *George Kent Ltd.* v. *C. of T. (N.S.W.),* 2 A.I.T.R. (1943).

[36]See *United Aircraft Corporation* v. *F.C. of T.,* 68 C.L.R. 525 (1943), discussed *infra.*

[37]1 All E.R. 336 (C.A.) (1957), 3 All E.R. 718 (H.L.) (1957).

[38]68 C.L.R. 525 (1943).

royalty payments made in the United States and the technical data
was communicated principally by depositing written materials in
the mail in New York City, even though the quantum of royalties
payable was determined by reference to production in Australia.
The reasoning of Latham C. J., in particular, rested largely on the
premises that there could be no legal property in unpatented inventions, whether secret or otherwise, and that income could be derived
only from acts done or from the ownership of property.[39] Basing
his reasoning on these two premises, he concluded that since the
data licensed did not constitute property in a legal sense, the agreement in fact amounted to a contract to communicate information
which, being communicated outside Australia, could not give rise
to Australian source income, especially when the relevant agreement
was executed and payments made in the United States. The decision
of Rich J. in the other majority opinion rested on somewhat different grounds and utilized a balance-of-contacts approach, looking
less to purely legal concept and reasoning and more to the practical
hard matter-of-fact, case-by-case approach enunciated in other
cases.[40]

Some of the views of Latham C. J. would appear to be in conflict with those enunciated by Viscount Simonds of the English
House of Lords in *Evans Medical Supplies* v. *Moriarty* insofar as
secret matter is concerned. Viscount Simonds, in a speech concurred
in by one other member of the House of Lords,[41] adopted the
view that secret processes and formulae can in fact constitute property in a legal sense, his opinion in this regard actually bearing a
striking similarity to the dissenting judgment of Williams J. in the
United Aircraft case. Thus, for instance, Viscount Simonds remarked that "it is manifest that a secret process . . . is something
which can be disposed of for value and that, by imparting the secret
to another, its owner does something which could not fairly be
described as 'rendering a service.' " He also held that the particular
taxpayer in the case had "parted with its property for a purchase
price, and when I say its property, I mean . . . a capital asset. In
this respect I see no difference between a patent and a secret process."

Williams J. in his dissenting judgment[42] in the *United Aircraft* case adopted a view as to the nature of secret processes and
inventions quite compatible with the views expressed by Viscount
Simonds and others in *Evans Medical Supplies Ltd.* v. *Moriarty*.
In his view, a secret process or invention in fact constitutes prop-

---

[39]*Id.* at p. 536.
[40]*Id.* at p. 539.
[41]Lord Tucker.
[42]68 C.L.R. 525 at 540 (1943).

erty, and a license to use it amounts to something more than a mere agreement to make disclosure. Having arrived at the view that such a license was indeed a license to use property, he then examined the question as to whether incorporeal property of this type could be said to have a situs and concluded, on the basis of an earlier English House of Lords decision relating to goodwill,[43] that it could, especially if assigned such a situs by the parties themselves in their contractual arrangements. His Honour pointed out that in the particular agreement in issue, the parties had acted upon the assumption that a license was necessary to use the relevant inventions in Australia and had expressly limited the right of use to Australia and New Zealand. He therefore concluded that the agreement was in fact a license to use industrial property in Australia, which gave rise to Australian source income in the same way as would a lease of personal property to be used in Australia.

The recent English case of *Rolls-Royce Ltd.* v. *Jeffrey*,[44] and more particularly the judgments rendered in the Court of Appeal, would seem to indicate that a distinction is to be drawn between secret processes and formulae property so-called, and mere "transient by-products of advanced engineering science," which is "ever growing, ever changing."[45] It would appear that the less-secret types of technical data and know-how are not property and that a purported license to use them is in fact simply an agreement to communicate or impart knowledge.

In sum, the theoretical position as to the source of royalties paid to a nonresident in respect of a license to use secret processes, formulae, and inventions in Australia remains obscure. The Australian Taxation Commissioner may well continue to apply the *United Aircraft* decision even in respect of such licenses, especially since the decision in *Evans Medical Supplies Ltd.* v. *Moriarty* is a confused one from which it is difficult to extract a *ratio decidendi* of broad application, a fact which has been given judicial recognition in England.[46] Moreover, the precise issue raised in the English cases related not to income source but instead to the question of whether particular receipts constituted capital or income items.[47]

If a U.S. licensor desires to avoid Australian income tax on such royalties, he would be well advised to stress the service aspect in the relevant agreement (assuming such services are supplied from out-

---

[43]*Commissioner of Inland Revenue* v. *Muller & Co's Margarine Ltd.*, A.C. 217 (1901).

[44]1 All E.R. 801 (H.L.) (1962); 2 All E.R. 469 (C.A.) (1961).

[45]*Per* Holyroyd Pearce L.J., 2 All E.R. 469, p. 474 (1961).

[46]*Id.* at p. 471.

[47]See p. 516, *infra*.

side Australia) and to minimize or otherwise express the secrecy aspects. Even slight differences in contractual terminology may be of considerable practical assistance in this regard.

A source allocation problem will frequently be encountered by U.S. residents when registered Australian industrial or artistic property is licensed and the licensor also agrees, either in the same or different agreements, to license unregistered technical data and know-how or to provide technical services to the licensee from outside Australia. In these circumstances, considerable difficulty may be experienced in allocating territorially the resultant income and expenses for both U.S. and Australian tax purposes. A U.S. foreign tax credit may well be granted for only a portion of the Australian taxes assessed because the U.S. tax authorities may allocate a smaller proportion of the income to Australian sources than the Australian Tax Commissioner.[48] Similar problems may arise in the allocation of expenses.

If the one agreement encompasses both a license to use registered Australian industrial or artistic property and a contract to provide information or services which, on a *United Aircraft* analysis, would be free of Australian tax (because supplied from outside Australia), the Australian Tax Commissioner may seek to allocate all or most of the income to Australian sources.

If the information and services provided are clearly subservient to the registered Australian industrial or artistic property (e.g., explanations as to the method of use of a patented invention), then the Taxation Commissioner is probably justified in allocating all of the resulting income to an Australian source and taxing it accordingly. If, however, the Commissioner seeks to allocate part only of the income to Australian sources when the parties themselves have contracted for a single indivisible royalty or fee payment, the position is not so clear.[49]

---

[48]See §904(a) of Internal Revenue Code of 1954 (as amended).

[49]The provisions of §§ 25(1) and 23(r) of the Act provide respectively that a nonresident is to be taxed on Australian source income and he is not to be taxed on income derived from sources wholly outside Australia. These two sections have not been specifically judicially interpreted in the context of allocating otherwise indivisible items of income between Australian and ex-Australian sources. However, the present Chief Justice of the High Court, Dixon C.J., would seem to have regarded source allocation in such a case as improper, in the absence of express statutory authorization (see *Hillsdon Watts Ltd.* v. *C. of T. (N.S.W.),* 57 C.L.R. 36, 51-52 (1937). The same judge in a case concerning §23(q) of the Act, which exempts from tax income derived from sources outside Australia where that income is not exempt from tax in its country of derivation, expressly reserved the question as to whether apportionment was ever possible in the particular statutory context there being considered (*F.C. of T.* v. *French,* 98 C.L.R. 398 (1957)). On the other hand, in the same case, Williams and Taylor JJ. specifically affirmed the principle

In other cases the parties themselves may allocate payments so as to distinguish between income sources, either by entering into two distinct agreements or by a specific allocation within a single agreement, or by executing one agreement confining itself to technical services and unregistered information and data (supplied from outside Australia) while the nonresident *de facto* allows the other party to use a particular Australian patent, design, copyright, or trademark without formal agreement. In such cases the Commissioner may seek to reallocate a portion or all of the royalties or fees paid for the use by the licensee of the registered industrial or artistic property and to tax the nonresident accordingly. If the parties are related and one is an Australian resident while the other is a resident of one of the countries with which Australia has a Double Taxation Convention, then the Commissioner could conceivably seek to apply a provision which, with some variations, appears in each of the Conventions to which Australia is a party and which is designed to impose an arm's-length standard on transactions between related parties.[50] In addition, in an extremely gross case, the Commissioner may try to apply a general tax-avoidance provision of the principal Australian Income Tax Act which is essentially an annihilating section (see *infra*).

Similar problems may also arise when a license to use industrial property registered in Australia is granted by one nonresident legal entity and another agreement with the same licensee is entered into by an entity related to the first licensor providing for the rendering of technical services or the licensing of technical data in a fashion which does not give rise to Australian source income. In such a case, the Commissioner's power to reallocate income from the tax-free arrangement to the taxable license would seem even more conjectural than when the two agreements run between the same

of apportionment (see also *C. of T.* v. *Cam & Sons Ltd.*, 36 S.R. (N.S.W.) 554 (1936)).

Section 42 of the Act provides that the Commissioner may make regulations as to the allocation of the whole or any part (and, if a part, what part) of any profit derived by a person from sources in Australia. However, no such regulations have ever been made, and it is in any event an open question as to whether this section should not be confined to the case of a sale of goods since it occurs in and is by its terms directly related to the other sections of a special division of the act dealing with this topic.

[50]See Article IV of the Double Taxation Convention with the United Kingdom, the United States, Canada, and New Zealand. However, Article IV of the Convention with the United States differs from the others in that there is no specific authorization for deeming profits of a U.S. enterprise attributed to it pursuant to the article to be income derived from Australian sources and hence taxable by Australia—cf. Article IV(2) of the other treaties. These conventions form part of domestic Australian income tax law by virtue of their forming schedules to the Income Tax (International Agreements) Act 1953-1960.

parties, unless the arrangement is so transparent as to attract the annihilating provision.

In cases where it is obvious that the parties have adopted particular arrangements solely or primarily to avoid taxation of the nonresident party, or to minimize to an exaggerated extent his Australian tax liability, then the Commissioner may seek to apply Section 260 of the Act. This is an annihilating section which allows the Commissioner to void, as against himself, all contracts, agreements, or arrangements that have or purport to have the purpose or effect of directly or indirectly altering in any way the incidence of any income tax or, *inter alia,* defeating, evading, or avoiding any duty or liability imposed on any person by the principal Income Tax Act, or preventing the operation of that Act in any respect. This section for the most part can be applied only in the grossest cases.[51] Its applicability to the type of license situation with which we are presently concerned has not been tested in the courts, and it would seem most unlikely that it could be applied except in the most flagrant circumstances.

If a nonresident owner of Australian patents, trademarks, copyrights, or designs does not license them or sell them on a royalty basis, but instead sells them outright for a fixed sum, then he will probably not derive Australian source income if the relevant agreements and payments are made outside Australia. An exception will perhaps be made if the industrial or artistic property disposed of was developed in Australia (e.g., by composing a particular literary or other copyrighted work in Australia or developing a particular patented invention there),[52] or if the particular sale in question forms part of a pattern of trafficking in Australian industrial and artistic property or like rights.[53]

Capital Gain or Assessable Income?

Having determined that a particular receipt derived by a nonresident has an Australian source, it is then necessary to determine

---

[51]Needless to say, a section of such extraordinary breadth as this one, which, if read literally, would allow the Commissioner to disregard almost any business transaction, since very few transactions do not have some effect on the incidence of income tax, has been the subject of a flurry of litigation in recent years as the ingenuity of Australian professional tax advisors has developed. The section has not yet been applied in any reported case to the type of transaction with which we are concerned. For the leading case on the Section, and an example of the confusion to which it gives rise, see *Newton* v. *F.C. of T.,* 98 C.L.R. 1 (1958).

[52]See the South African case of *Millin* v. *I. R. Commr.,* 3 S.A.T.C. 170 (1928) and the Commissioner's decision referred to in *Gunn's Commonwealth Income Tax Law and Practice* (7th ed.), para. 931.

[53]*Rhodesia Metals Ltd. (in liq.)* v. *Taxes Commr. (Southern Rhodesia),* A.C. 774 (1940).

whether or not it is a capital or an income receipt and hence excluded from or included in the recipient's assessable income.

The general conceptual approach adopted by the Australian courts is expressed in the statement by Dixon J. in *Sun Newspaper Ltd.* v. *F. C. of T.* that "the distinction between expenditure and outgoing on revenue account and on capital account corresponds with the distinction between the business entity structure or organization set up or established for the earning of profit and the process by which such an organization operates to obtain regular returns by means of regular outlay, the difference between the outlay and the returns representing profit or loss."[54] The type of analysis here suggested has been adopted in the Australian cases both in seeking to ascertain the character of the receipt on the one hand or an outgoing on the other, but its application to actual cases is often difficult. The application of similar tests in the United Kingdom has evoked an exasperated judicial comparison to a "spin of a coin."[55]

As has already been noted, amounts received as or by way of royalty are specifically deemed to be assessable income (i.e., revenue items) for Australian income tax purposes, regardless of whether they arise from the disposal of a capital asset.[56] It has been said that it is inherent in the conception of "royalty" as used in the Australian Income Tax Act that "the payments should be made in respect of the particular exercise of the right . . . and, therefore, should be calculated either in respect of the quantity or value taken on the occasions upon which the right is exercised."[57] In other words, a receipt will be said to be a royalty if its quantum varies with the use or exploitation of the right granted.

If particular industrial property or like rights are licensed or disposed of for a lump sum or a fixed sum payable in installations rather than for royalties, it is necessary to determine in each case whether the amounts so received constitute income or capital receipts. In this regard the Australian case law is sparse, and reference must be made to the English case law.[58] For the most part, the applicable tests are:

---

[54]61 C.L.R. 337, 359-360 (1938).

[55]*Per* Sir Wilfred Green in *I.A. Commrs.* v. *British Salsmon Aero Engines Ltd.*, 2 K.B. 482, 498 (1938).

[56]The Act, §26(f).

[57]*Per* Dixon C. J., Williams, Webb, Fullagar and Kitto JJ. in *Stanton* v. *F.C. of T.*, 92 C.L.R. 630 (1955); see also *A. G. for Ontario* v. *Mercer*, 8 App. Cas. 767 (1883); *Re Graydon*, 1 Q.B. 417 (1896); *Nethersole* v. *Withers*, 28 T.C. 501 (1948); and *Pacific Coal Co. Pty. Ltd.* v. *Perpetual Trustee Co. Ltd.* 91 C.L.R. 486 (1954).

[58]For an analysis of English taxation of the foreign licensor, see p. 545, *infra*.

1. Whether the particular property right being disposed of was acquired for the purposes of its disposal at a profit or whether its disposal forms part of a profit-making scheme, undertaking, business, or vocation.[59]

2. Whether the transaction in fact amounts to disposal of a property or similar right, or whether it is in fact an agreement to render services or communicate information not involving secret processes, formulae, or inventions.[60]

3. Whether, in the case of a disposition of the right to use know-how, all or part of the consideration granted by the vendor can be viewed negatively as a restrictive covenant. Many so-called sales of know-how can be viewed as being wholly or in part a covenant not to compete. It is clear law that a covenant not to compete, if given for a lump sum or fixed or definable amount payable in installments, may constitute a capital receipt.[61] Thus such a sale may in fact consist of two elements, a covenant to provide "know-how," which in an Australian tax analysis will probably be treated as a contract to perform services or to communicate information,[62] coupled with a covenant not to compete, the granting of which may give rise to a capital receipt.[63]

The Problem of Deductibility

For Australian income tax purposes, losses and outgoings are deductible to the extent to which they are incurred in gaining or producing assessable income or are necessarily incurred in carrying on a business for the purpose of gaining or producing such income, unless they are of a capital, private, or domestic nature.[64] These provisions apply in the case of a foreign licensor or recipient of Australian source income derived from the sale or exploitation of industrial property rights in the same way as with any other taxpayer. But it will be noted that since assessable income in the case of a nonresident includes only income derived from an Australian source,[65] the losses and outgoings will be deductible only to the

---

[59]The Act, § 26(a); see also *Rolls-Royce Ltd.* v. *Jeffrey*, 2 All E.R. 469 (C.A.) (1961) and 1 All E.R. 801 (H.L.) (1962).

[60]See p. 512 *et seq., supra,* and in particular the cases of *Evans Medical Supplies Ltd.* v. *Moriarty* and *Rolls-Royce Ltd.* v. *Jeffrey* there discussed.

[61]*Margerison* v. *Tyresoles Ltd.*, 25 T.C. 29 (1942); *Higgs* v. *Sir Laurence Olivier*, Ch. 899 (1951); *Dickenson* v. *F.C. of T.*, 98 C.L.R. 460 (1958); 7 T.B.R.D. case G82 (1957).

[62]See p. 512, *supra.*

[63]See also *Musker* v. *General Electric Co.*, T.R. 199 (1962).

[64]The Act, § 51(1).

[65]*Id.*, § 23(r) and 25(1).

extent to which they are incurred in producing Australian source income or in carrying on a business for the purpose of producing such Australian source income. Obviously, difficult allocation problems can arise, especially in the case of know-how and similar licenses, and for this reason if for no other it is generally desirable to avoid the incidence of Australian income tax on such receipts insofar as is possible. In the case of know-how licenses and technical-service agreements, this is not usually a very difficult matter under present Australian tax law.[66]

The question of whether a particular outgoing is a capital or revenue item is one which frequently troubles both Australian residents and nonresidents in the type of situation with which we are involved. The nonresident may be immediately concerned with the deductibility of some item which is clearly referable to his Australian source income. He may also be concerned with the extent to which an amount paid to him will be deductible on the part of the Australian resident payor, since this may affect the type of arrangement to which the resident party will agree or, if the two parties are related, may affect the overall tax position of the nonresident.

Since the resident will be liable to Australian tax on his worldwide income, with the exception of certain exempt income, the expense if it is a revenue item will in most cases be deductible unless it happens to relate to the production of income that is exempt from Australian tax in his hands.[67] A determination of whether an outgoing is a capital or a revenue item will therefore conclude the issue of deductibility in most cases for a resident taxpayer. The rules for distinguishing capital from revenue outgoings are intimately connected with, and no clearer than, those applied to distinguish between capital gains and assessable income. The same type of approach may be adapted to both questions in many cases. However, it is self-evident that the character of a particular receipt in the hands of its recipient will not necessarily be decisive of its character as an outgoing on the part of the payor. Thus, for instance, it is obvious that a manufacturer of a commercial refrigerator will take the purchase price received into his assessable income while the corner grocery store which purchases it will have to treat it as a capital expense, and hence not deductible.

In the area with which we are concerned, the situation may arise in which a royalty paid by an Australian resident will be assessable income in the hands of its nonresident recipient, and yet will

---

[66]See p. 512 *et seq., supra.*

[67]E.g., by being not exempt from tax in some foreign country where it has its source. (See the Act, § 23(q).)

not be deductible by the resident party because it represents a capital outgoing. While there is an express statutory provision that specifically deems all royalties to be income receipts,[68] there exists no comparable specific provision rendering a royalty automatically a deductible revenue item.

The legal or equitable proprietor or licensee of registered Australian patents, copyrights, or designs is, however, permitted to amortize capital expenditures made in acquiring such rights or, in the case of an original owner, directly incurred in relation to inventing or producing the protected invention, work, or design.[69] In addition, a taxpayer who acquires such industrial or artistic property by virtue of a disposal by the previous owner otherwise than for valuable consideration will be allowed an amortization deduction if the assignor was, or would have been, entitled to a similar deduction.[70]

No provision is made for the amortization of expenditures made in acquiring or developing trademarks or foreign patents, copyrights, or designs, or made in acquiring or developing unregistered industrial rights such as unpatented secret processes, formulae, inventions, technical data, and know-how. Moreover, the statutory method prescribed for calculating an amortization deduction would seem to preclude the possibility of amortizing royalties paid to acquire such rights, even though such royalties might be considered capital expenditures and therefore not deductible by the payor.

The method of amortization is simple, being determined each year by dividing the residual value of the industrial property right concerned (e.g., its cost less the sum of past amortization deductions taken) by the number of years in its remaining effective life.[71] In the case of a taxpayer who has acquired a right other than for valuable consideration, the residual value is determined by reference to the residual value at the time of acquisition in the hands of the person from whom the right was acquired, unless part only of the rights held by the previous owner was so acquired, in which case the Commissioner of Taxation is given power to determine the residual value.[72]

Provisions complementary to those outlined above provide for an accrual to a taxpayer of taxable income if he disposes of an amor-

[68]See *Colonial Mutual Life Assurance Society Ltd.* v. *F.C. of T.*, 73 C.L.R. 604 (1946).

[69]The Act, § 124K *et seq.*

[70]*Id.*, § 124L(1)(c).

[71]*Id.*, § 124S and 124M.

[72]*Id.*, § 124R.

tized industrial property right at a price in excess of its residual value, the taxable income so derived being limited to the sum of the previous deductions taken by the taxpayer in respect of the right.[73] As a necessary corollary, a deduction is granted in the event of its disposal at a price less than its residual value.[74]

Other provisions allow the Taxation Commissioner to allocate part of a particular purchase price to amortizable industrial rights if these are purchased together with other assets and no separate price is allocated by the parties to the industrial property so purchased, and to disregard such part of any purchase price paid for such property as he may deem excessive.[75]

Of particular interest to nonresidents is a provision which allows the Commissioner to reduce amortization deductions which would otherwise accrue to the benefit of the owner of an industrial right if he has obtained benefits from a related right exercised outside Australia, the reduction being made by reference to the overseas benefit so derived.[76]

The above summary of the amortization provisions is by no means exhaustive. Of secondary importance are a number of other provisions contained in the Act dealing with special situations and providing for coordination with other sections. These provisions endeavor to close off techniques which taxpayers have devised in the past to secure advantages from the amortization sections not intended by the legislation.

Finally, it should be mentioned in passing that the Commissioner has on occasions attempted to use Section 51 of the Act (the section governing deduction of business expenses) as a means of attacking tax avoidance arrangements.[77] He has not been particularly successful in this regard except where a payment was quite obviously not made for a business purpose, but was instead of a private or domestic nature. In particular, his efforts to use the section to disallow otherwise justifiable business expenditures on the ground that they are excessive have met with little success.[78]

Assessment and Collection of Tax From Nonresidents

No special withholding or other tax is imposed upon income of the type with which we are concerned. However, the Act makes

---

[73]*Id.*, § 124P.
[74]*Id.*, § 124N.
[75]*Id.*, § 124R.
[76]*Id.*, § 124Z.
[77]For an example, see *Cecil Bros.* v. *F.C. of T.*, 8 A.I.T.R. 523 (1962).
[78]*Ibid.*

general provision for the collection of tax due from nonresidents and special provision for collection of the tax due in respect of royalties.

In the case of royalties, the payor, who need not necessarily be a resident,[79] is required to furnish a statement to the Commissioner of the royalty due before making payment. He is then required to retain the tax assessed by the Commissioner from the royalty payment, and if he fails to do so is personally liable.[80]

With other types of payment, the payor who again need not necessarily be a resident,[81] is required to pay the tax due by the nonresident only when required to do so by the Commissioner, e.g., after the Commissioner has made an assessment. However, the payor is again personally liable for the tax payable by him on behalf of the nonresident, being given statutory authority to retain sufficient amounts for this purpose and being indemnified for payments made to the Commissioner.[82]

The only difference between the provision applicable to royalties and the more general provision is, therefore, that in the case of royalty preliminary assessment must be made by the Commissioner before payment is made, while in the case of other receipts assessment may be made after payment, and the payor, if he is willing to take the risk of being subsequently liable after assessment, may make the payment in full if he believes that the nonresident will not be liable to Australian tax thereon.

In practice, if an agreement involving payment of royalties is concluded, it will generally be submitted to the Commissioner of Taxation for an informal ruling as to whether or not the nonresident will be liable for Australian tax thereon. For instance, in the case of a technical service agreement fulfilling the criteria laid down by the *United Aircraft* case,[83] the Commissioner should rule that the royalty will not be subject to Australian tax, and payments may then be made without deduction of tax. In the case of periodic payments other than royalties, the Commissioner will generally assess the nonresident directly and if payment is not made will then apply to the payor the general provisions of the Act allowing for what is, in effect, garnishment of any future sums due to the nonresident.[84]

---

[79]The Act, §256 refers simply to a "person" making payment—not necessarily a resident "person."

[80]The Act, §§256 and 255.

[81]*Id.*, § 255.

[82]*Ibid.*

[83]See p. 512 *et seq., supra.*

[84]The Act, § 218.

IMPACT OF DOUBLE TAXATION TREATIES

The Double Taxation Convention between Australia and the United States, like those with Canada and New Zealand, but unlike that with the United Kingdom, does not make any special provision for the tax treatment of royalties, other than certain copyright and mining royalties, except to exclude them from the class of "industrial and commercial profits" protected by the more general provisions of the Treaties.[85] The Convention with the United Kingdom on the other hand exempts from Australian income tax all royalties (with the exception of certain motion picture royalties) derived by residents of that country from Australian sources if paid as a consideration for the use of, or for the right of using, copyrights, patents, designs, secret processes or formulae, trademarks, or other like property, unless the recipient has a permanent establishment in Australia or is not subject to tax in the United Kingdom.[86] The Conventions with the United States, Canada, and New Zealand do protect from Australian tax copyright royalties (other than motion picture royalties and, in the case of New Zealand, television royalties) derived from Australian sources by residents of these countries, provided the taxpayer in question does not have a permanent establishment in Australia.[87] It should be noted that, unlike the exemption granted by the United Kingdom Convention, the protection given to United States, Canadian, and New Zealand residents does not depend on their being subject to tax in their country of residence.[88]

There would seem to be no *a priori* reason why receipts, other than royalties, derived from the exploitation of industrial or artistic property or like rights by residents of any of the countries with which Australia has a Double Taxation Convention should not fall within the general class of "industrial and commercial profits" protected by the general provisions of the treaties, if the overall conditions prescribed by the particular Convention are otherwise fulfilled and if they are not classifiable as management charges or remuneration for personal services.[89]

---

[85]The term of "industrial and commercial profits" is defined in Article II(1)(n) and Article II(1)(k), respectively, of the Conventions with the United States and Canada so as to exclude royalties.

[86]See Article VII.

[87]See Article X of the Convention with the United States and Article IX of those with Canada and New Zealand.

[88]*Ibid.*

[89]See Article II(1)(i), Article II(1)(n), Article II(1)(k) and Article II(1)(h) of, respectively, the U.K., U.S., Canadian, and New Zealand treaties.

CONCLUSION

The picture which Australia presents in this field is one of a country to which nonresident licensing of industrial property and similar arrangements are and have been for some time of great importance. It is a nation with a high standard of living and rapidly growing industrialization which itself does not have sufficient experience and resources to develop more than a fraction of the technology which its economy and social life demand. Its tax system as a whole, being of relatively recent origin, is reasonably straight-forward and its application in the area with which we have been concerned is fairly well defined vis-a-vis the more traditional types of industrial and artistic property, such as patents, copyrights, and trademarks. But, as with many other countries, the law is less well defined in relation to unregistered industrial and commercial technology of one type or another. The tax system probably also reflects, in its lack of discrimination against nonresidents in this area, a recognition of Australia's need for the fruits of foreign experience and talents.

Author's Postscript—

There have been some changes in Australian law since the original publication of this article. The relevant changes are as follows:

Income Source: The High Court of Australia has again emphasized that the question of income source is a matter of fact to be determined on a case by case basis. (*F.C. of T.* v. *Mitchum,* 9 A.I.T.R. 559 (1965).) As a consequence it is now a little more difficult to lay down hard and fast rules as to income source, but as a practical matter the Taxation Department continues to apply the precepts enunciated in earlier cases where they are relevant.

Tax Classification of Companies: New tests have been defined for determining whether a company is public or private. (The Act, Section 103A). Now all companies that are not public companies are deemed to be private companies, and a public company is defined as a company that is listed on a stock exchange in Australia or elsewhere, a cooperative company, a nonprofit company, a mutual life assurance company, a government-owned corporation, or a subsidiary of a public company. Additionally, a company may be treated as a public company if the Commissioner of Taxation is of the opinion that it is reasonable that it should be so treated having regard to the spread of its share ownership and certain other items. A number of U.S. corporations have been classified as public by the Commissioner even though not listed on a stock exchange because their stock is extensively traded over the counter and is widely held.

Companies which are listed on a stock exchange and cooperative companies are not considered public if 20 or fewer persons hold three fourths or more of their paid-up capital, are entitled at any time during the year of income to exercise three fourths or more of the voting power in them, or have received three fourths or more of any dividends paid by them during the tax year or would have received three fourths or more of such dividends had they been paid.

A company is a subsidiary of a public company if one or more public companies beneficially own more than half of its paid-up capital, are capable of controlling or obtaining control of more than half of the voting power in it, would be beneficially entitled to receive more than half of any dividends paid by it, and would be beneficially entitled to receive more than half of any distribution of capital made by the company in the event of a winding up or reduction of capital.

It will be appreciated that this summary of the provisions defining a public company is oversimplified and that there are a number of qualifications that should be considered in any particular case.

Impact of Double Taxation Treaties: A new double taxation convention has been negotiated with the United Kingdom which substitutes a 10 percent withholding tax for the previous tax-exempt status of royalties derived by residents of the United Kingdom from Australian payors.

Taxation of the Foreign Licensor in Canada

SCHUYLER M. SIGEL AND SAMUEL R. BAKER

Development of the profit potential in the Canadian market has in the past proved to be a natural step for many successful U.S. enterprises. Licensing arrangements have provided a convenient and common method of market. This article explores the basic Canadian tax concepts applicable to foreign licensors, and by way of background outlines the taxation of domestic licensors in that country.

GENERAL SCHEME OF CANADIAN TAXATION

The Canadian Income Tax Act[1] imposes a tax at graduated rates on the world-wide taxable income of residents[2] and on the taxable income of nonresidents if such income emanates from employment in Canada or from a business carried on there.[3] Under Part III of The Income Tax Act, certain payments credited by residents to nonresidents in respect of income from property are subjected to a designated flat rate of tax, commonly referred to as a "withholding tax."

Capital gains are not subject to tax under existing Canadian tax legislation. However, it is anticipated that some form of tax on capital gains may shortly be introduced in Canada. In the recent Report on the Royal Commission on Taxation,[4] the proposition was advanced that certain capital gains ought to be assimilated to gains on income account and taxed at full rates.[5] While the report may not receive full acceptance, it is expected to have considerable influence upon proposals for new tax legislation to be introduced by the Government of Canada in the form of a White Paper later in 1968.

At present, in cases where the proceeds from the disposition of

---

EDITOR'S NOTE: This article is a substantially revised version of a paper written by Hubert J. Stitt and John A. Gamble for *IDEA,* Vol. 8, No. 2.

[1]Unless otherwise indicated, statutory references throughout this article are to the Income Tax Act, R.S.C. 1952 c. 148, as amended.

[2]§ § 2(1) and 3.

[3]§ § 2(2) and 3.

[4]On September 28, 1962, The Government of Canada constituted a Royal Commission under the Chairmanship of Kenneth LeM. Carter to "enquire into and report upon the incidence and effects of taxation imposed by Parliament." The resulting "Carter Commission Report," dated December 22, 1966, was released on February 24, 1967.

[5]See Vol. 4, p. 222 *et seq.*

industrial property rights may be classified as capital gains, such proceeds will not be subject to Canadian taxation.

Residence

Since Canadian taxation is imposed upon the world-wide taxable income of a Canadian resident, the foreign licensor will normally attempt to limit his activities in Canada to avoid resident classification. An individual is deemed to be a resident of Canada if he sojourns there for a period of 183 days or more in a taxation year.[6] It is a question of fact whether a sojourn of less than 183 days will in any particular case constitute residence,[7] and "the graduation of degrees of time, object, intention, continuity, and other relevant circumstances"[8] will be considered. It is possible that a resident of a foreign country may also be considered a Canadian resident.

Although the word "resident" applies to corporations as well as to natural persons,[9] the underlying tests are dissimilar. A corporation is considered to be resident in the country where its central control and management are actually exercised.[10] Control is ordinarily considered to be exercised at the place where a company's board of directors meet,[11] although on occasion the courts will disregard this criterion if the board does not in fact control the company, and will deem the company's residence to be located where the actual as distinct from ostensible control exists.[12] Any corporation incorporated in Canada after April 26, 1965, is deemed to be resident in Canada.[13] A corporation incorporated in Canada prior to April 27, 1965, is deemed to be resident in Canada if it was resident in Canada or carried on business in Canada at any time during a taxation year ending after April 26, 1965.[14]

For Canadian tax purposes, prior to the passing of Section 139(4a) in 1965, dual residence was as possible for Canadian incorporated entities as it is today for individuals.[15]

A corporation might be found to be resident in Canada as well

[6]§ 139(3)(a).
[7]*Beament* v. *M.N.R.*, 6 D.T.C. 1183.
[8]*Thomson* v. *M.N.R.*, 2 D.T.C. 812, 815 (Supreme Court of Canada).
[9]*Egyptian Delta Land and Investment Company Limited* v. *Todd*, A.C. 1 (1929).
[10]*De Beers Consolidated Mines Ltd.* v. *Howe*, A.C. 455 (1906).
[11]*American Thread Company* v. *Joyce*, 6 T.C. 163.
[12]*Bulloch* v. *Unit Construction Company Limited*, 38 T.C. 712.
[13]§ 139 (4a) (a).
[14]§ 139 (4a) (b).
[15]*Swedish Central Railroad Company* v. *Thompson*, 9 T.C. 342.

as elsewhere if, for example, its control and management were exercised more or less equally from each jurisdiction.

Carrying on Business

Although the foreign licensor may limit his time spent or corporate control exercised in Canada so as to avoid classification as a Canadian resident, the income reasonably attributable to such activities will nevertheless be taxed at full Canadian personal or corporate rates, in the absence of treaty protection, if his activities in Canada are sufficient to constitute carrying on business.[16] The relevant statutory provisions have been modified in some instances by conventions for the prevention of double taxation entered into between Canada and certain other countries. A U.S. enterprise, for example, is taxed only on Canadian business income attributable to a permanent establishment located in Canada. The effect of double taxation is more fully discussed below.

Although the term "business" is not extensively defined in The Income Tax Act, it is stated to include "a profession, calling, trade, manufacture or undertaking of any kind whatsoever and includes an adventure or concern in the nature of trade but does not include an office or employment."[17] Section 139 (7) extends the meaning of "carrying on business" as it applies to nonresidents by providing that a person will be deemed to carry on business in Canada if such person

> produced, grew, mined, created, manufactured, fabricated, improved, packed, preserved or constructed, in whole or in part, anything in Canada whether or not he exported that thing without selling it prior to exportation, or soliciting orders or offered anything for sale in Canada through an agent or servant whether the contract or transaction was to be completed inside or outside Canada or partly in and partly outside Canada.[18]

The case law delineating what constitutes carrying on business in Canada is extensive, but the courts have deliberately refused to formulate an exhaustive definition. Where contracts of sale are involved, one test that has consistently been relied upon is that the business is conducted at the place where the offer is accepted.[19] In the final analysis, the foreign licensor with extensive activities in Canada must attempt to ascertain whether a business is being carried on there by analyzing the particular facts in relation to the pertinent statutory provisions and case law.

---

[16] §§ 2(2) and 31(1) (a).
[17] § 139(1) (e).
[18] § 139(7).
[19] *Crookston Bros.* v. *Furlado*, 5 T.C. 602, 615.

Income of Nonresidents Taxable Under Part III

Part III[20] of the Act imposes a tax on specified classes of income paid or credited to nonresidents "from Canada." (In this context income "from" Canada is to be distinguished from income earned "in" Canada.) The tax imposed is a flat percentage of gross payments without the deductions and exemptions ordinarily permitted in calculating taxable income.[21] Thus, if substantial expenses are attributable to a particular licensing agreement, the tax incidence under Part III may in some cases be greater than that under the other parts of the Act although the applicable tax rate is less.

Capital Gains

A fundamental principle of Canadian taxation has been that capital gains are not subject to tax. Thus, a potential foreign licensor may be motivated to consider the possibilities of an outright sale of a particular right if such a sale would result in a nontaxable gain.

The test as to whether the profit on a sale or like disposition of property can be regarded as a trading (taxable) receipt has been expressed as follows:

> Now the principle I think is very clear and has been established by many cases. The appreciation of an article, the subject of property, whether it is the property of an individual or whether it is the property of a company, is not taxed as such; but it is taxed if the realization of that appreciation forms part of a trade, because then the trade is taxed, and this is an item in the trade.[22]

It is a question of fact in each case, whether a given receipt constitutes income or a capital gain. Factors relevant to this determination include the recipient's whole course of conduct in relation to the property disposed of and any similar property which he has dealt with, the intention of the taxpayer in holding the property, the number of similar sales made by the taxpayer, and the relationship between the particular transaction and the taxpayer's normal business.[23] It should be noted that even a single transaction may constitute carrying on business if it is an "adventure or concern in the nature of a trade."[24]

Although the Report of the Royal Commission on Taxation recommends the imposition of a capital-gains tax, it restricts the impact of the tax to those nonresidents who carry on business in

---

[20]§§ 106-110.
[21]§ 108(1).
[22]*Collins* v. *Firth-Breanley Stainless Steel Syndicate*, 9 T.C. 520, 564.
[23]*M.N.R.* v. *Taylor*, 56 D.T.C. 1125.
[24]§ 139(1) (e).

Canada. The Commission takes the position that "Canada should not seek to tax nonresidents on their Canadian property gains except those realized in connection with a business carried on in Canada (defined to include transactions in real property or an interest in real property which is located in Canada)."[25]

TAXATION OF CANADIAN RESIDENTS
ON ROYALTY OR SIMILAR PAYMENTS

Imposition of Tax

Amounts received by a Canadian resident in the form of royalties or similar amounts under agreements granting the right to use patents, copyrights, trademarks, and similar industrial property rights will ordinarily be taxable as income from property.[26] If, however, the taxpayer's pursuit of such revenue constitutes carrying on business or an adventure or concern in the nature of trade, the profits so derived could be classified as business income. Once the taxable income is calculated, the distinction between income from property and business income is normally of little significance, as income from both sources is taxed at equivalent rates. If, however, the receipt is classified as income from property the capital nature of the income producing property is more likely to be preserved, and this may prove important if the property is ultimately sold or disposed of at a gain. This difference will be eroded if the Carter Report proposals with respect to taxation of capital gains are adopted.

Income or Capital Receipt

For payments made in connection with the transfer of industrial property rights to qualify as nontaxable receipts, these conditions must be met:

1. The transaction must effect an absolute transfer to the purchaser of all rights to use the industrial property or to sell products incorporating it in the territory to which the contract of sale extends;

2. The transaction must *not* have occurred in the ordinary course of a business carried on by the transferor; preferably the seller has not previously sold any tangible property rights;

3. The price must not be dependent upon the use of or production from the property rights.

With respect to the first condition, an absolute assignment of

---

[25]Vol. 4, p. 571, Conclusion 9.
[26]§ 3(b).

industrial property rights for valuable consideration clearly effects their sale.[27] Generally, the exclusive and perpetual licensing of such rights will be similarly construed.[28] In the case of a patent, it is sufficient that the exclusive license extend for the remaining term of the patent.[29] However, the grant of nonexclusive rights,[30] or of exclusive rights for a limited period of time,[31] is a mere license and not a sale.

The standard applied in determining whether or not the second requirement is met is discussed above under the heading "Capital Gains."

The third condition for a nontaxable capital gain is specifically imposed by Section 6(1)(j) of The Income Tax Act, which provides that there shall be included in taxable income "amounts . . . that were dependent upon use of or production from property," property being broadly defined to include intangible property, such as patents.[32] Thus, a receipt that would otherwise be a capital item is converted to income under that section. A case in point would be an arrangement calling for the payment of royalties based on the sales of products manufactured by the licensee under the licensed patent.

The mere fact that the sales price is payable by installments of fixed amounts will not render the profit taxable income.[33] On the other hand, if the sales price is basically dependent upon the use of property, the fact that there is an agreed maximum price will not prevent the profit from being deemed taxable income.[34]

Status of Know-How

a. *Disposal of Know-How*—There are no Canadian cases dealing with the classification of receipts from the disposition of know-how as income or capital gains. In an English decision, *Evans Medical Supplies* v. *Moriarty*,[35] the House of Lords held that the transfer by an English pharmaceutical company to the Burmese Government of certain secret processes resulted in a capital gain. In

[27]It should be noted that the courts frequently do not discuss specifically whether a "sale" has occurred, but rather whether all substantial rights to the property were transferred.

[28]See *M.N.R.* v. *Paris Canada Films Ltd.*, 16 D.T.C. 1338, dealing with motion picture film rights.

[29]*442* v. *M.N.R.*, 11 D.T.C. 435.

[30]*Rustproof Metal Window Company Limited* v. *C.I.R.* T.R. 337 (1947); *Peat Business Systems Limited.* v. *M.N.R.*, 51 D.T.C. 341.

[31]See *M.N.R.* v. *Paris Canada Films Ltd.*, n. 28, *supra* (second issue).

[32]§ 139(1) (ag).

[33]*Benard* v. *M.N.R.*, 50 D.T.C. 428.

[34]*Ross* v. *M.N.R.*, 50 D.T.C. 775.

[35]T.C. 540. Canadian courts treat decisions of the House of Lords as being of the highest persuasive value.

more recent English cases, such as *Rolls-Royce* v. *Jeffrey*[36] and *Musher* v. *English Electric Ltd.*,[37] the House of Lords has shown a strong tendency to limit the circumstances in which capital gains treatment may be allowed and to classify the communication of technical knowledge and procedures as the performance of teaching services wherever possible. Nevertheless, it would appear that a capital gain may be realized on the disposition of know-how which is the exclusive and secret property of the seller if the three requirements set out above under the heading "Income or Capital Receipt" are present and certain additional safeguards are observed. For example, any arrangement between the seller and buyer relating to technical services should be completely divorced from the sale of know-how; otherwise the transaction may be classified as the performance of services rather than a conveyance of a capital asset. In such cases it is preferable for technical expertise to be provided by a transfer of personnel from seller to buyer rather than by a continuing relationship involving performance of technical services. Further, it should be made clear in the sale agreement that the purchase price is paid for definable know-how existing at a specified date and does not relate to future discoveries. Provision for future transfers is suggestive of a business of trading in know-how.

b. *Licensing of Know-How*—The essential question with respect to the tax status of licensed know-how would seem to be whether and in what circumstance, if any, know-how qualifies as property that may be used in Canada (thereby giving rise to Canadian source income taxable under the ordinary rules or under Section 106(1)(d) of The Income Tax Act in the case of nonresidents not carrying on business in Canada). This question was considered in 1964 by the Tax Appeal Board, the Canadian tax forum of first instance, in *Technical Tape Corporation* v. *M.N.R.*[38] In *Technical Tape Corporation*, the question was whether contingent payments made by a Canadian company to a U.S. licensor were subject to the 15-percent withholding tax under Part III of The Income Tax Act as royalty-type payments for the use of property. The subject matter of the license was broadly designated as technical assistance, research and secret information and "know-how." No patents were involved.

Relying upon the *Rolls-Royce* case referred to above, the Board ruled that the licensed rights, collectively termed "know-how," were undoubtedly "property" for Canadian tax purposes. Accordingly, the contingent payments were held subject to the withholding tax.

---

[36]T.C. 443.

[37]T.C. 556.

[38]64 D.T.C. 428.

The same question was brought to the forum of the Canadian Exchequer Court recently in the case of *Quality Checkd Dairy Products Association (Co-operative)* v. *M.N.R.*[39] In this case, the nonresident appellant allowed a dairy in Canada to use its certification mark, "Quality Checkd," and its mark, including the symbol "Q" with a check mark. In addition, the appellant provided services to the dairy, such as "production advice on an ad hoc basis to individual members according to their needs; the holding of production seminars on an annual basis in each district at which sometimes experts outside the staff of the appellant were included in such things as panel discussions; laboratory analysis of products; preparation of advertising programmes and materials; marketing and sales advice, also on an ad hoc basis; and the holding of sales workshops at which sales people from various member companies attended to exchange ideas and also to share other ideas and suggestions from the staff of the appellant and sometimes outside consultants." In return, the appellant received a certain fee. The Tax Department alleged that the amounts paid by the dairy were either in satisfaction of rents, royalties, or similar payments for the use in Canada of the certification mark, or in satisfaction of rents, royalties, or similar payments for the use in Canada of "know-how," and that "know-how" is "property or . . . other thing" within the meaning of Section 106(1)(d) of The Income Tax Act. The court held the payments to be both in respect of the certification mark and in respect of the "know-how" of the appellant.

After reviewing the cases dealing with "know-how" (including the *Technical Tape* case), the court concluded that there is but an illusory difference between "know-how" as a capital asset and "know-how" on income account, being in relation to services performed. Furthermore the court found that the portion of the payment representing compensation for "know-how" was not "property" or "other thing" within the meaning of Section 106(1)(d) and thus was not subject to the Canadian withholding tax. On the basis of this case, the careful drafting of an agreement compensating a nonresident for availing a resident of its know-how would appear to offer the nonresident a payment free of Canadian tax.

PROBLEMS OF FOREIGN LICENSORS

Nonresident Licensors Carrying on Business in Canada

As stated earlier, a nonresident is liable to income tax upon all income derived from any business carried on in Canada.[40] Al-

[39] 67 D.T.C. 5303.
[40] §§ 2(2) (b) and 31(1).

though royalties received by a nonresident under a license, or payments to a nonresident on the sale of a patent or similar property, may very well, under the principles discussed above, constitute the profits from a business activity, it does not necessarily follow that, because the patents or other property licensed or sold are situated in Canada, the business is being carried on in Canada. For example, royalties received outside Canada by a foreign company under a patent license registered and executed outside Canada would not appear to constitute income from a business carried on in Canada if no further activity takes place there. Thus, a licensor may, under the principles of Canadian tax law, be carrying on business by retaining the rights to and by further exploitation of its patents or trademarks, but the profits from this business activity may nevertheless be profits from a business with Canada as opposed to a business in Canada. In such circumstances the licensor will be liable to tax in respect of payments received from such business under Part III of the Act, as discussed later.

Different considerations will apply if the licensor performs duties or services in Canada under an obligation contained in the license. Where, as is frequently the case, a manufacturer receives technical services in Canada under its patent license from the licensor, the performance of those services in Canada may constitute the carrying on of business by the licensor in Canada, with the result that at least a portion of the royalty profits may be subject to full Canadian tax.[41] Unless protection can be claimed under a double-taxation convention, a licensor would be well advised to separate and apportion his profits attributable respectively to the performance of technical services and to the rights granted under the license. Alternatively, an effort could be made to ensure that all technical services are performed outside Canada.

TAXATION OF NONRESIDENTS ON INCOME FROM PROPERTY

Rents, Royalties, or Similar Payments

Under the provisions of Part III of the Canadian Act, a resident of Canada must deduct tax at the rate of 15 percent on rents, royalties, or similar payments paid or credited to a nonresident for the use of property in Canada.[42]

The Carter Report recommends that this rate of tax be increased to 30 percent except when "specific circumstances warrant

---

[41]§§ 2(2) (b) and 31(1).
[42]§§ 106(1) (d).

a lower rate for certain countries and certain kinds of payments[43] and save and except where same are reduced by double taxation duties."

The withholding tax levied under Part III applies to royalties payable under a patent or trademark license. Payments in respect of know-how categorized as services rendered were held to be free of the confines of this tax in *Quality Checkd Dairy Products Association (Co-operative)* v. *M.N.R.*, discussed above. Royalties paid in respect of copyrights are, however, expressly excluded from the provisions of Part III[44] and are not taxed to a nonresident not carrying on business in Canada.

Amounts paid as rentals or royalties for the use of motion pictures or films or video tapes that are reproduced or used in Canada are given separate treatment, being subject to a withholding tax of 10 percent.[45]

Where the rents or royalties paid can reasonably be attributed to a business carried on by the nonresident licensor in Canada, then the nonresident will not be subject to a withholding tax thereon but to ordinary income tax.[46]

If the expenses incurred by the licensor in earning his royalties are substantial, a comparison of the withholding tax based on 15 percent of gross income and the ordinary corporate tax imposed on the net taxable income of the resident taxpayer is called for. The federal corporate tax rate is 21 percent on the first $35,000 of taxable income and 50 percent on taxable income in excess of $35,000.[47] There is, in addition, imposed on every nonresident corporation carrying on business in Canada a tax of 15 percent on the amount by which net income (after regular corporate taxes) exceeds the increase in capital investments for the year.[48] While the tax on the profits from carrying on a business in Canada is imposed at rates that are higher than the rate of the withholding tax, the higher rates may in a given case be preferable because expenses reasonably attributable to earning the royalties will be deductible in computing the taxable income of the nonresident. Such deductions are not

---

[43]Vol. 4, p. 547.
[44]§ 106(1) (d) (A).
[45]§ 106(2).
[46]§ 805 of Income Tax Regulations.
[47]§ 39; these rates include Old Age Security Tax of 3 percent.
[48]§ 110B. Capital investment is generally defined as the aggregate of:
    (1) the undepreciated capital cost of depreciable property, and
    (2) the cost of land (other than land held for sale), less
    (3) certain amounts owing on the purchase price of these two categories of property.

allowed for the purpose of calculating the 15-percent withholding tax.[49]

Any person paying or crediting to a nonresident a royalty liable to the withholding tax must make the appropriate deduction and forthwith remit the amount deducted to the Canadian revenue authorities.[50] The payor who does not so withhold is personally liable for the tax, although he may recover it from the recipient of the royalty by deductions from later payments.[51] Tax must be withheld from all royalties paid to nonresidents unless the payor satisfies the Minister of National Revenue that tax need not be withheld on the ground that the royalties constitute income which may reasonably be attributable to a business carried on by the nonresident in Canada. Where the Canadian revenue authorities are satisfied that the royalties can be so attributed, they will permit payment without any deduction.[52]

Royalties Distinguished From Technical Service Fees

The withholding tax must be deducted from any "rent, royalty or similar payment." Such a payment will include a payment for the use in Canada of property or an invention, or for the sale or use in Canada of any "property, trade name, design or other thing."[53] The provisions include payments on account of a purchase price for the sale of property rights if the price is dependent upon the quantity of production under the rights.[54]

Interesting problems arise when payments for technical services are involved. The words "rent or royalty" would not seem appropriate to payments for services rendered. Furthermore, the history of the relevant legislation seems to indicate that technical services were not intended to be covered by Part III.[55] Exclusion of technical service fees from the withholding tax would be consistent with the fact that where technical services are rendered by a nonresident in Canada the profit from the fees normally and in the absence of treaty relief will be taxable as a profit from carrying on a business in Canada.

---

[49] § 108(1)
[50] § 109 and Regulations, § 202.
[51] § 109(5).
[52] Income Tax Regulations, § 805(2).
[53] § 106(1)(d)(i)-(iii).
[54] *Ross* v. *M.N.R.*, 50 D.T.C. 775.
[55] In § 96 of the Income Act, 1948, there was express reference in subsection (1)(f) to "management, technical, professional or other services." The repeal of this subsection in 1949 would, therefore, seem to justify the conclusion that fees for technical services are not included under Part III. See also *Warsh & Co. Ltd.* v. *M.N.R.*, 62 D.T.C. 247, p. 250.

Difficult problems of construction arise when periodic payments are made under an agreement which grants the right to use property and provides that the grantor shall provide technical services. The problem came before the courts in the case of *Warsh & Co. Ltd.* v. *M.N.R.*,[56] where a Canadian manufacturer of dresses paid monthly sums to a U.S. company in consideration for the right to use all the styles and patterns of the U.S. company. The Canadian company claimed that the payments were at least in part for services rendered by the U.S. company, and to this extent it was not required to withhold. The services consisted of advice as to styles, fabrics, market conditions, and similar matters. The court found it impossible to distinguish between the right to use dress designs and information and advice in relation thereto. It regarded the services as complementary and incidental to the license and, accordingly, as not meriting separate payment. The entire payments were, therefore, held to be royalties liable to deduction of a 15-percent withholding tax.

Thus, in order to ensure that technical service fees are not liable to deduction on payment, and that accordingly they shall be free from Canadian income tax if they are not derived from a business carried on in Canada, it would be advisable to provide a separate agreement and thus a separate consideration for the performance of such services.

Management Fees

The deduction of a withholding tax under Part III of the Act was extended to management or administration fees by Bill C-95, which was given Royal assent on December 5, 1963.[57] The duty to withhold applies to a "management or administrative fee or charge" paid or credited to nonresidents after June 13, 1963. This amendment was introduced as a result of the Canadian Government's concern as to the use of management and similar fees to reduce Canadian taxes on profits of foreign-owned Canadian subsidiaries. Prior to the enactment, a foreign company could charge management fees to its Canadian subsidiary and thereby avoid with respect to such fees the 50-percent corporate tax (on earnings above $35,000) and the 15-percent withholding tax imposed on dividends. It should be noted in general that the amendment does not impose the 15-percent tax on management fees paid to an unrelated party who performs the service as part of the ordinary business activity of such party or on like fees paid to a related party in reimbursement of

---

[56] 62 D.T.C. 247.
[57] § 106(1)(a) and (1c).

specific expenses incurred by it in performing services for the benefit of the Canadian payor.[58]

The Department of National Revenue has issued an *Information Bulletin* regarding payment of management or administration fees, and once again no mention is made of technical service fees as such.[59]

It would seem that if the Minister of National Revenue had intended that the term "management or administrative fees" should cover payments for technical services, he would have expressly included them in the amendment. An aid to the interpretation may be had from past legislation. The 1948 Income Tax Act expressly provided for the imposition of a 15-percent withholding tax on payments for, *inter alia,* "management, technical, professional and other services, information or advice and know-how."[60] This provision, which was subsequently repealed and until now has had no successor, clearly shows that the legislature drew a distinction between management fees and technical service fees.

In the absence of any judicial interpretation, the correct view would seem to be that technical service fees, properly so-called, are not covered by the new provision because they have no connection with the administration or management of the Canadian payor, even where payor and recipient are related parties. Nevertheless, licensors will be well-advised to ensure that technical service fees are not in any way connected with the performance of management or administration functions.

The Carter Report deals with the taxation of management services and like services under the heading "Personal Service Income."[61] The Commission recommends that where the benefit of all like services are enjoyed in Canada and where the payment was deductible in computing business or property income for Canadian tax purposes, a 10-percent withholding tax should be applied.[62] The tax, being one levied on payments for services, would not apply to amounts paid in reimbursement of expenses; this is consistent with the provisions of the present Section 106(1c) of the Act.[63] The

---

[58] § 106(c) and Bulletin cited n. 59, *infra.* Strangely enough, the Ontario tax department will *not* permit the deduction of management fees paid from the taxable income of the payor for Ontario corporation tax purposes if the payment attracted the 15-percent tax under § 106(1)(a) of the Act. See § 23(1)(i) of The Corporations Tax Act, Ontario.

[59] Department of National Revenue *Information Bulletin* No. 23, dated January 27, 1964.

[60] § 96(1)(f) of the Income Tax Act, 1948.

[61] Vol. 4, p. 551.

[62] *Id.,* p. 553.

[63] *Id.,* p. 553.

Commission restricts the tax as above so that same would not be imposed on payments for services of a personal nature.

THE EFFECT OF DOUBLE-TAXATION CONVENTIONS

A nonresident licensor may be able to claim exemption from Canadian tax if there is a double-taxation convention in force between Canada and the country in which the licensor is primarily liable to tax. Canada has at the present time entered into conventions with 16 countries, although not all have been ratified.[64] The 16 countries are the United States, Ireland, Trinidad, Tobago, Norway, Denmark, Finland, Japan, Sweden, South Africa, the United Kingdom, France, Germany, The Netherlands, Australia, and New Zealand.

The Carter Commission has recommended that Canada enter into additional treaties, especially with those countries with which Canada has "close or growing trade and financial relations, such as Italy, Switzerland, Mexico, Venezuela, India and Brazil."[65]

The conventions contain three provisions that may give relief to a nonresident licensor. The first, and most general, is that which exempts the industrial and commercial profits of the nonresident from tax if he does not carry on business in Canada through a permanent establishment situated there; the second gives exemption from tax on capital gains; and the third relates to royalties payable to nonresidents. Not all of these exemptions are found in every convention. Furthermore, the relief provided may vary from convention to convention. In the discussion that follows, particular reference will be made to the convention with the United States.

Industrial and Commercial Profits

Article I of the convention with the United States provides that a U.S. enterprise is subject to Canadian income tax on its industrial and commercial profits except insofar as those profits are allocable to a permanent establishment in Canada. Industrial and commercial profits are expressly defined to exclude royalties, management charges, or gains from the sale of capital assets. Such items of income are taxed under the ordinary principles of Canadian law. It should be noted that, where those principles would treat royalties as profits from a business, no relief will be available under the convention and tax will be assessed at the full rate, notwithstanding the fact that

---

[64]The Canada-U.K. convention has been extended to some 29 English colonies and former colonies.
[65]See Vol. 4, p. 569.

under Canadian law the profits of the nonresident will be treated as commercial profits.[66]

Technical service fees for services rendered by a corporate licensor would normally constitute commercial or industrial profits. It has been held in a U.S. case that remuneration for personal services can constitute commercial or industrial profits for purposes of the convention with Canada.[67] Therefore, a U.S. licensor receiving fees for technical services should be exempt from Canadian tax on such fees if he has no permanent establishment in Canada; and this should be so whether or not the services are performed in Canada. Once again, to ensure treaty protection, technical service fees should be segregated from royalty payments in the drafting of license agreements.[68]

Permanent Establishment

The convention with the United States contains an extensive definition of the term "permanent establishment." It is defined to include:

> . . . branches, mines and oil wells, farms, timber lands, plantations, factories, workshops, warehouses, offices, agencies and other fixed places of business of an enterprise, but does not include a subsidiary corporation. The use of substantial equipment or machinery within (Canada) at any time shall constitute a permanent establishment of such enterprise in (Canada) for such taxable year.[69]

The reference to use of substantial equipment or machinery contemplates use by contractors or builders who move such equipment from place to place as part of their normal operations. The Tax Appeal Board has held that subway and seaway construction equipment worth $600,000 qualifies as substantial equipment.[70] In another case, the Supreme Court of Canada ruled that "substantial" refers to substantial size.[71] In that case the equipment consisted of samples of appliances ranging in value from $4,000 to $11,000. The court considered that the reference to substantial equipment or machinery was intended to apply only to machinery and equipment such as is used by contractors or builders. In the same case it was held that the machinery, to constitute a permanent establishment, must be used for the purpose for which it was created. The mere

---

[66]Possibly such payment might qualify for exception under Article XI, which sets a maximum rate of 15 percent on "non-earned income."

[67]*Consolidated Premium Iron Ores Ltd.*, 28 T.C. 127 (1957), aff'd., 265 F.2d 320 (6th Cir., 1959).

[68]*Warsh & Co. v. M.N.R.*, 62 D.T.C. 247.

[69]§ 3(f) of the Protocol.

[70]*No. 630 v. M.N.R.*, 50 D.T.C. 300.

[71]*Sunbeam Corporation (Canada) Ltd. v. M.N.R.*, 62 D.T.C. 1390.

display of the appliances or samples did not involve their "use" in Canada.[72]

The mere storing of goods in a warehouse in Canada does not create a permanent establishment unless some control is exercised over the warehousing facilities by the nonresident, or unless the nonresident has an agent who regularly fills orders from the stock of goods in the warehouse.[73] If a nonresident has a partner who has a permanent establishment in Canada, the nonresident will be considered to have the same permanent establishment.[74]

If the U.S. cases that have interpreted the meaning of the term "permanent establishment" are followed, an isolated transaction does not give rise to a permanent establishment. One such case emphasized the importance of permanence and held that "establishment" implies the existence of an office or other place of business capable of carrying on the day-to-day business of the nonresident.[75]

If a foreign company receiving fees for technical services performed in Canada desires to avoid having a permanent establishment there, it will be well-advised not to maintain personnel permanently in Canada. At the very least such personnel should not operate from their own permanent premises in that country or from premises of the licensee that are permanently allocated to them.

All the conventions entered into by Canada contain a provision exempting a nonresident from Canadian tax on commercial or industrial profits unless they are attributable to a permanent establishment. The extent of the relief generally follows the U.S. convention.

Gains From Sales of Capital Assets

The U.S. convention exempts from Canadian taxation gains derived in Canada from the sale of capital assets by a U.S. resident or a U.S. corporation, provided the seller has no permanent establishment in Canada.[76] Although at present Canada does not tax capital gains, this relief as applied to U.S. persons will become of great importance if the Carter recommendations with respect to taxing capital gains are implemented.

It will be recalled that Canadian tax is imposed on payments for the sale of a capital asset, such as a patent, even if on strict economic and accounting theory the sale is a capital sale, if payments in respect of the purchase price are dependent upon the use of or pro-

---

[72]See also the lower court (Exchequer Court) opinion, 61 D.T.C. 1053.
[73]*No. 630* v. *M.N.R.*, 59 D.T.C. 300.
[74]*Ibid.*
[75]*Consolidated Premium Iron Ores Ltd.* v. *C.I.R.*, n. 67, *supra.*
[76]Art. VIII.

duction from the property that is sold.[77] In such case, although Canadian tax law would tax the gains from the sale of the capital asset, the vendor should be able to claim relief under the convention.

Capital-gain exemptions are not contained in the majority of the conventions entered into by Canada. There is, however, similar relief in the conventions with Sweden, Germany, and Finland.

Royalties

The conventions to which Canada is a party generally provide relief from Canadian tax on royalties paid to a nonresident licensor.[78]

Under the U.S. convention an exemption is provided for royalties paid for the right to use copyrights or the right to produce or reproduce any literary, dramatic, musical, or artistic work, so long as the nonresident has no permanent establishment in Canada.[79] The withholding tax of 15 percent on royalties for industrial property rights, such as patents, trademarks, and know-how, paid to a U.S. resident remains unaffected by the convention. Royalties for rights in connection with motion picture films are also expressly excluded from treaty protection.

The reason the convention does not give relief to royalties paid with respect to patents and trademarks is presumably that Canada would suffer from a reciprocal arrangement with the United States. The licensing of such rights in Canada by U.S. residents has a much higher incidence than the corresponding licensing in the U.S. by Canadian residents.

Most of the other Canadian conventions give relief only in respect of copyright royalties. Many of the conventions do, however, expressly limit the Canadian tax on royalties for industrial property to 15 percent, which is, of course, the rate of the present withholding tax.[80]

Non-Arm's-Length Transactions

Because royalty and like fees provide a method whereby foreign interest can extract funds from controlled subsidiaries free of the double impact of Canadian corporate tax and withholding tax on dividends, the Department of National Revenue has adopted a policy of strict enforcement of the reasonableness test with respect to such

---

[77] § 6(i)(j).

[78] The only convention which gives no relief for royalties of any kind is the South African convention.

[79] Art. XIII C.

[80] See, e.g., Art. VI of the U.K. convention and Art. VIII of the German convention.

payments. Both the Canadian Income Tax Act and the Canadian conventions contain provisions which permit the Department to reallocate unreasonable payments. Section 12(2) of the Act provides that no deduction shall be made in respect of an outlay or expense except to the extent that it is reasonable under the circumstances. Thus, by so limiting the expense deduction to the Canadian taxpayer, a deterrent to such payments is created.

All Canadian conventions contain a provision whereby non-arm's-length payments can be adjusted appropriately for the purpose of calculating the payor's Canadian tax liability. Under the U.S. convention, the Canadian authorities are given the right to disallow unreasonable deductions to the payor where a U.S. resident through its participation in the management or capital of a Canadian enterprise permits unreasonable amounts to be charged as royalties or technical service fees.[81]

PROVINCIAL TAX

The discussion in this article has centered on liability under the federal Income Tax Act. It should therefore finally be noted that the Canadian provinces have enacted their own corporate income tax acts. These acts are either modelled on the federal Income Tax Act or give rise to the payment of tax as a percentage of the federal tax payable. Liability is dependent upon the existence of a permanent establishment within the province, and the tax is imposed upon that portion of a corporation's total income earned or deemed to be earned in the province. The federal act provides for a tax credit for provincial taxes and, except for Quebec, Ontario, Manitoba, and Saskatchewan, the credit is equal to the provincial tax.[82]

CONCLUSION

As may be seen from the foregoing analysis, the impact of Canadian tax will vary with the method of operation adopted by the nonresident in licensing in Canada and by the country from which the nonresident licenses in Canada. Practical business decisions will, of course, ultimately dictate the form of operation that will prove most effective. Nevertheless, within the confines of those decisions

---

[81]Art. IV.

[82]Corporate rates in those provinces are: Quebec, 12 percent; Ontario, 11 percent; Manitoba and Saskatchewan, 10 percent. By reason of the credit against federal tax bestowed by § 40(1), these rates are effectively reduced to 2 percent, 2 percent, 1 percent, and 1 percent, respectively.

it may frequently be possible by the careful drafting and execution of licenses and by the careful selection of a base from which to effect the licensing to minimize Canadian taxation or to avoid unnecessary exposure to it.

Taxation of the Foreign Licensor in the United Kingdom

MALCOLM J. F. PALMER

INTRODUCTION

This article will discuss taxation in the United Kingdom[1] of profits derived from patents and other industrial property rights owned by those persons or corporations who are not resident within that jurisdiction. This is a topic which has been, and will continue to be, of major importance to manufacturers in the United States. Statistics show that in 1963 U.S. manufacturers had more new licensees located in the United Kingdom than in any country other than Japan.[2]

There are four taxes imposed in the United Kingdom which may affect the foreign licensor. The first, and the most important for the foreign licensor, is the income tax imposed at present at the rate of 41.25 percent. Normally the rate is fixed for each year in the annual finance act, which is introduced each April. The three other taxes, namely, the profits tax, the corporation tax, and the capital gains tax, normally will not affect the corporate foreign licensor unless it is carrying on a business in the United Kingdom through a branch or an agency.

INCOME TAX

Basic Charge

A person resident in the United Kingdom is charged with income tax on all his annual profits from any property and any trade, whether in the United Kingdom or elsewhere. A person not resident in the United Kingdom is charged on his annual profits from any property in the United Kingdom or from any trade exercised there.[3]

EDITOR'S NOTE: This paper appeared in *IDEA*, Vol. 9, No. 3. Recent changes in the relevant tax laws of the United Kingdom appear in the author's postscript.

[1]The title to this article refers to taxation in "the United Kingdom." The United Kingdom, which in its full description is the United Kingdom of Great Britain and Northern Ireland, covers England, Wales, Scotland, and Northern Ireland. It does not include the Channel Islands or the Isle of Man.
[2]The report of Booz-Allen & Hamilton, Inc., entitled "New Foreign Business Activity of U.S. Firms" states that in 1963, 745 U.S. companies investigated entered into a total of 42 licenses in the United Kingdom. Only Japan with 66 exceeded this figure. Canada with 32 licenses was next after the United Kingdom.
[3]Income Tax Act, 1952, §122 (1)(a)(iii).

The standard rate of income tax is now 41.25 percent. An individual may be liable at a higher rate if he has assessable income in excess of £2,000. Income in excess of that amount may be liable to additional income tax (generally known as surtax) at progressively higher rates on different slices of the excess. The top slice of an individual's income may be taxed at a rate as high as 91.25 percent. On the other hand, certain individuals may be entitled to personal reliefs which will result in an effective rate of less than 41.25 percent, but a nonresident normally will be entitled to these personal reliefs only if he is a British subject.[4]

A nonresident corporation which is carrying on business in the United Kingdom through a branch or agency will be liable to the corporation tax and not to the income tax on the income arising directly or indirectly from that branch or agency.[5]

Residence

The residence of an individual or corporation has to be determined for each tax year. Four main factors are relevant to the determination of the residence of an individual.

(a) *The period of presence within the United Kingdom*

If the individual is present in the United Kingdom for a period or periods totalling six months or more in any tax year (which runs from April 6th to April 5th), he is a resident.[6]

(b) *Dwelling place*

An individual is a resident if there is a dwelling place in the United Kingdom at his disposal and available for his occupation;[7] but if he works full time in a trade carried on wholly outside the United Kingdom, or if he has an employment the duties of which are performed outside the United Kingdom, the question of his residence is determined without reference to any dwelling place maintained for his use in the United Kingdom.[8]

(c) *Regularity of visits*

An individual who regularly makes visits of substantial length to the United Kingdom may become a resident even if he is not present for more than six months in a year and has no dwelling place available for him.[9] The Inland

---

[4]*Id.*, §227.
[5]Finance Act, 1965, §§46(2) and 50.
[6]Income Tax Act, 1952, § 375.
[7]*Loewenstein* v. *de Salis*, 10 T.C. 424 (1926).
[8]Finance Act, 1956, § 11.
[9]*Lysaght* v. *I.R.C.*, 13 T.C. 511.

Revenue normally regards visits of three or more months each in four consecutive years as resulting in residence.[10]

(d) *Citizenship*

It is harder for a British subject who has been a resident to lose that status than it would be for an alien in similar circumstances.[11] As a general rule, a British subject does not cease to be a resident until he has been out of the country continuously for a whole tax year.

The test to determine where a company is resident can be clearly stated. A company resides where its real business is carried on, and its real business is deemed to be carried on where the central management and control is exercised.[12] What matters is where control is in fact exercised and not where it ought to be exercised under the constitution of the company.[13] Thus, a company normally will be resident at the place where the directors meet and make their decisions. If, however, persons other than the directors exercise *de facto* control of the company, the place where those persons meet will be the deciding factor. A company, like an individual, can be resident in more than one country. It will be resident in any country where a substantial part of the central management is located and the control of its affairs is carried out.[14]

Incorporation in the United Kingdom, at least in the case of a company carrying on an active trade, will not in itself make a company resident there.[15] Furthermore, if a company, irrespective of its place of incorporation, carries on business within the United Kingdom through a branch, that will not in itself make the company resident. Admittedly, there are no reported cases holding that a company carrying on substantial business activities in the United Kingdom is not resident in the United Kingdom, but the cases which lay down the principle of central management and control are clear authority for the view that the existence of a substantial branch business does not in itself render a company resident. This conclusion is supported by legislation which recognizes that a nonresident company may have a branch or management in the United Kingdom.[16] In principle it follows that a company will not be resident

[10]See leaflet issued by the Board of Inland Revenue, September 1960.
[11]See Income Tax Act, 1952, § 368.
[12]*De Beers Consolidated Mines Ltd.* v. *Howe*, 5 T.C. 198.
[13]*Unit Construction Co. Ltd.* v. *Bullock*, 38 T.C. 712.
[14]*Swedish Central Rail Co. Ltd.* v. *Thompson*, 9 T.C. 342; *Union Corporation Ltd.* v. *I.R.C.*, 34 T.C. 207, 259 (1953). See also *Koitaki Para Rubber Estates Ltd.* v. *Federal Commission of Taxation*, 64 C.L.R. 15 (1940), and *Gasque* v. *I.R.C.*, 23 T.C. 210.
[15]Compare *Swedish Central Rail Co. Ltd.* v. *Thompson*, 9 T.C. 342, and *Todd* v. *Egyptian Delta Land and Investment Co. Ltd.*, 14 T.C. 119.
[16]See for example Finance Act, 1965, §§50(1) and 89(2)(b).

in the United Kingdom even if it is incorporated in that jurisdiction and it carries on all of its business there, provided that the central management and control is exercised outside the United Kingdom. But, again, there is as yet no direct case authority for this proposition.[17]

Throughout the remainder of this article, it will be assumed that the foreign licensor is not resident within the United Kingdom.

Withholding of Tax at Source From "Annual Payments" and Assessment of Nonresidents

The U.K. tax system has adopted, whenever practicable, the principle that tax will be deducted at source. The pertinent statute provides for deduction of income tax at source by the payor from "any yearly interest of money, annuity or other annual payment."[18] The procedure for this deduction has several distinctive features.

1. If the payment is made by an individual who has sufficient taxed income in the year of payment to cover the payment, he is entitled to deduct income tax at the standard rate from the payment. He need not account to the Revenue for the tax deducted. No assessment is made on the recipient, who must accept the payment subject to the deduction of tax.[19]

2. If the payment is made by an individual who does not have sufficient taxed income to cover the payment, he must deduct income tax at the standard rate from the payment and account to the Revenue for the tax deducted, or so much as exceeds the income tax otherwise payable by him.[20] If he fails to do so, the Revenue can assess the recipient.[21]

3. If the payment is made by a corporation resident in the United Kingdom, it must deduct income tax at the standard rate from the payment and account to the Revenue for the tax deducted.[22] If it fails to do this, the Revenue can assess the recipient.[23] Normally the gross payment will be deductible in computing the liability of the payor to the corporation tax.[24]

4. In the exceptional case where the payment is made by a

---

[17]It seems likely that this point will be litigated in the future in view of the desirability under the Finance Act, 1965, for subsidiaries of foreign companies operating in the United Kingdom to establish themselves in this manner.

[18]Income Tax Act, 1952, §§ 169 and 170 (§ 170 refers to "any interest").

[19]Id., § 169.

[20]Id., § 170.

[21]Grosvenor Place Estates Ltd. v. Roberts, 39 T.C. 433.

[22]Finance Act, 1965, § 48(5).

[23]Grosvenor Place Estates Ltd. v. Roberts, 39 T.C. 433.

[24]Finance Act, 1965, § 52(5).

corporation which is not resident in the United Kingdom, the treatment will be the same as if it were made by an individual. Normally, the payor will not have sufficient income liable to income tax to cover the payment, and, therefore, it will have to account to the Revenue for the tax deducted. No deduction will be permitted in computing the liability of the nonresident corporation to the corporation tax.[25]

In each of these cases the withholding of tax at source applies only to income tax payable at the standard rate. If the recipient is an individual, who in addition has a liability to surtax, he must be separately assessed for the surtax payable by him.

The foregoing treatment applies whether the recipient is a resident or a nonresident. A nonresident may, however, be able to claim exemption under a double-taxation treaty. In addition, a nonresident who is not liable to income tax will be entitled to claim the annual payment in full (i.e., without deduction of tax at source) if the proper law of the contract or other obligation under which the payment is made is other than that of the laws of the United Kingdom.[26] But in practical terms it would be unreasonable for the foreign licensor to demand that the contract be governed by, say, the law of Illinois rather than that of England, because although this would ensure that the licensee would have to pay in full, he would not be entitled to any deduction for the payment.[27]

Not every payment which is made annually is subject to tax deduction at source as an "annual payment." The payment must be similar to interest or to a payment under an annuity. This is usually expressed by saying that it must be "pure income profit" in the hands of the recipient.[28] This means that it must not be a receipt, such as a trading receipt, which is merely taken into account in the calculation of the profits of the recipient that are liable to income tax[29] or corporation tax. It must be the type of payment which will almost inevitably increase the total taxable income of the recipient. The procedure for deduction of tax at source is highly

---

[25]*Ibid.*

[26]*Keiner* v. *Keiner*, 34 T.C. 346, *Bingham* v. *I.R.C.*, 36 T.C. 254.

[27]Income Tax Act, § 137, and Finance Act, 1965, §§ 52(5)(a), 53(5)(b). Furthermore, the licensee, if corporate or if an individual whose taxed income is insufficient to support the payment, would probably have to account to the Revenue for the tax which he would otherwise have deducted. See *Keiner* v. *Keiner*, 34 T.C. 346, Donovan J. at p. 348.

[28]*Re Hanbury*, 38 T.C. 588; *C.I.R.* v. *Whitworth Park Coal Co. Ltd.*, 38 T.C. 531.

[29]See *British Commonwealth International Newsfilm Agency Ltd.* v. *Mahany*, 40 T.C. 550.

relevant for the foreign licensor because it has been specifically extended to cover patent and copyright royalties.[30]

A nonresident who is liable to income tax which is not withheld at source may be directly assessed if he is himself present in the United Kingdom. In addition, he may be charged in the name of any factor, agent, receiver, branch, or manager, whether or not that person receives any of the profits or gains.[31]

Capital or Income Receipt

Traditionally, income tax is a tax on income, and sums which are capital receipts in the hands of the recipient normally will not give rise to liability to income tax. The importance of determining whether a sum is a capital or an income receipt is considerably less now than it was in the past. Any capital sum received on the sale of patent rights is taxable as income, and there is now a capital-gains tax on any capital gain realized on the disposal of other industrial property rights.[32] But the distinction between capital and income receipts is still often relevant, and it is particularly so for the non-resident, who will not be liable to the capital-gains tax unless he is carrying on a business in the United Kingdom[33] through a branch or agency.

Whether any particular payment is a capital or income receipt is a question of fact to be determined in the light of all of the circumstances. In the final analysis the courts regard it as a question to be answered in accordance with sound accounting principles.[34] Nevertheless, the cases lay down several guiding principles. A lump sum paid on the sale of a patent or similar right is a capital sum (although the gain element is taxed as income),[35] unless the recipient is carrying on the trade of dealing in industrial property rights. In the same way, a lump sum paid on the grant of an exclusive license, whether for the full term of the patent or merely for a fixed term, will be regarded as a capital receipt.[36] On the other hand, if the lump sum is paid on the grant of a nonexclusive license, it will be treated as an income receipt.[37] If the sum paid is based on actual use, as in the case of a royalty hinged to production or sales, it will clearly be in-

---

[30]Income Tax Act, §§ 169(3), 470.
[31]Income Tax Act, 1952, § 369.
[32]Finance Act, 1965, § 22.
[33]*Id.*, § 20(2).
[34]*British Salmson Aero Engines Ltd.* v. *C.I.R.*, 22 T.C. 29, Sir Wilfrid Greene at p. 43.
[35]*Handley Page* v. *Butterworth*, 19 T.C. 328, Romer L.J. at p. 359.
[36]*British Salmson Aero Engines Ltd.* v. *C.I.R.*, 22 T.C. 29, and see *Nethersole* v. *Withers*, 28 T.C. 501.
[37]*Rustproof Metal Window Co. Ltd.* v. *C.I.R.*, 29 T.C. 243.

come, and this will be the case whether there is a mere license or an outright sale of the right.[38] A lump sum paid on account of or as an advance against royalties will be an income receipt.[39]

Patents

The U.K. law of patents closely resembles the U.S. law. The term of a patent is 16 years from the date of filing of the complete specification, and it is subject to the payment of annual renewal fees from the end of the fourth year.[40]

Patent royalties are treated as annual payments, and, therefore, income tax must be deducted from them by the payor. This applies not only to royalties but also to any other payment of an income nature that is made in respect of the use of a patent. In many cases, patent royalties and other payments of an income nature in respect of the use of a patent will not be "pure income profit" in the hands of the recipient,[41] but the withholding procedure has been specifically extended to them.[42]

The recipient has an option to spread the royalties paid for patent use that has extended for more than two years.[43] If, for example, a royalty is paid in respect of use that has extended for four years, the recipient may be treated as receiving one quarter of the royalty in the year of payment and one quarter in each of the three preceding years. The maximum period over which the spread can be made is six years. This particular option is not available if the sum received is of a capital nature, and it will not affect the payor, who will deduct tax at the stadard rate at date of payment. Where necessary, relief will be given by a refund of tax. Normally, spreading will be of benefit to the nonresident recipient if the standard rate of income tax has been increased during the relevant period of use or if he is an individual liable to surtax.

A nonresident who receives a capital sum on the sale or exclusive license of a U.K. patent will be liable to income tax on the gain realized. The payor of the capital sum must deduct income tax at the standard rate from the payment and account to the Revenue for the amount deducted.[44] The recipient may elect within two

---

[38]*Jones* v. *C.I.R.*, 7 T.C. 310, and see *Rustproof Metal Window Co. Ltd.* v. *C.I.R.*, 29 T.C. 243, Lord Greene M.R. at p. 268.

[39]*C.I.R.* v. *Longmans Green & Co. Ltd.*, 17 T.C. 272; *Rye and Eyre* v. *C.I.R.*, 19 T.C. 164.

[40]Patents are covered by the Patents Acts, 1949-1961.

[41]See *Wild* v. *Ionides*, 9 T.C. 392.

[42]Income Tax Act, 1952, § 169(3).

[43]*Id.*, § 472.

[44]*Id.*, § 318.

years from the end of the tax year in which the payment is made to be taxed as if he had received in the year of payment and each of the five succeeding years one sixth of the total payment. Exercise of this election will not affect the payor, as he must still deduct tax from the whole payment and account to the Revenue. However, it will entitle the recipient to refund of tax if it turns out that excessive tax has been deducted in any of the six years. He will be treated as though he had received one sixth of the payment subject to a deduction of one sixth of the original deduction in each of the six years. Exercise of the election therefore will be an advantage if the standard rate of income tax is reduced during the six-year period or if the recipient would be liable to surtax on the capital sum. The amount of the capital sum on which tax is assessed will be reduced by the amount of any capital expenses incurred on purchase of the patent rights. This relief will permit the recipient to claim a refund of tax, but again it will not affect the liability of the payor to deduct tax from the whole payment.[45] In addition to the opportunities for spreading, the liability of a nonresident may be totally or partially relieved in the following ways:

1. If the taxpayer incurred capital expenditure on the acquisition of patent rights, he will be entitled to an annual allowance which can be set off against his income from the patent rights and carried forward as may be necessary. The amount of the annual allowance will be the amount of the expenditure divided by the number of complete or partial years remaining for the patent at the time of the acquisition of the patent rights, or where appropriate, the specific period of the exclusive rights acquired by the licensor.[46] Relief will be given by way of a refund of tax. If the patent rights are subsequently sold for an amount that is greater or less than the balance of the capital expenditure remaining unallowed, there will be a balancing charge or allowance of the appropriate amount.[47]

---

[45]*Id.*, § 318(3).
[46]*Id.*, § 316.
[47]*Id.*, § 317.

Example 1: Assume a taxpayer acquires for £5,000 patent rights which have five years to run. The taxpayer, therefore, is entitled to an annual allowance of £1,000 in each of the five years. If in the second year he sells the patent rights for £2,000, he will not be entitled to any further annual allowances, but will be entitled to a balancing allowance calculated as follows:

Cost of patent rights	£5,000
Less allowances for tax years	2,000
Unallowed expenditure	£3,000
Less proceeds of sale	2,000
Balancing allowance	£1,000

2. Fees and expenses, such as the patent agent's charges, incurred in connection with the grant or renewal of a patent will be deductible and may be offset against income from the patent rights. Relief will again be given by way of a refund of tax.[48]

3. Tax treaty relief. If the nonresident licensor is a resident in the United States, he may be entitled to relief from U.K. tax under the terms of the tax treaty between the United States and the United Kingdom. That treaty provides that royalties paid to a resident of the United States for the use of U.K. patents will be exempt from U.K. tax if the licensor is subject to U.S. tax on the royalties and is not engaged in trade or business in the United Kingdom through a permanent establishment or, if he is, if the royalties are not associated with that permanent establishment.[49] Thus, in the normal case the licensor who is a resident in the United States will be able to obtain an exemption from the U.K. tax. Claims for exemption must be made by the licensor to the Inspector of Foreign Dividends in England. If the claim is accepted, the licensee will be directed to make payment in full without deduction of tax. As a result, the payment will be deductible for income-tax and profits-tax purposes by the licensee.[50] The deductibility of royalties paid by a corporate licensee will be discussed later in the section on the new corporation tax.

The treaty with the United States and certain other treaties entered into by the United Kingdom prior to 1949 provide exemption only if the royalties or other amounts are paid "for the use of" patents.[51] It is, therefore, generally considered that relief will not be available under these treaties if the payments which are subject to tax in the United Kingdom are capital payments on the outright sale of a patent. The reason for this is historic. At the time the treaties with the United States and other relevant countries were negotiated, these payments were not taxable in the United Kingdom. As a concession, the U.K. Revenue will usually grant relief under

---

Example 2: Assume similar facts, but a sales price of £4,000, in which event there will be a balancing charge of £1,000, which is the sales price of £4,000 less the unallowed expenditure of £3,000.

[48] Income Tax Act, 1952, § 320.

[49] Article VIII of the Double Taxation Convention between the United States and the United Kingdom.

[50] S.R.&O., 1946, No. 466, Regulation 3(4).

[51] Treaties which give similar relief include those with Australia, New Zealand, Sweden, Denmark, The Netherlands, France, Norway, Burma, Finland, Greece, Belgium, Switzerland, Federal Republic of Germany, Pakistan, Austria, Italy, Israel, and numerous colonies and former colonies. The exact terms of relief differ in certain of the treaties. Only partial relief is given under the treaties with South Africa and Japan. It should be noted that the former treaty with Canada, which is now being renegotiated, gave no relief in respect of patent royalties.

these treaties in respect of capital payments. Nevertheless, where the U.S. licensor is seeking to obtain capital-gains treatment, it is advisable to express the transaction as an exclusive license for the full term of the patents, and not as a sale. If this is done, any royalties will be treated for U.K. tax purposes as paid "for the use of" the patents and relief will not be merely concessionary. Treaties negotiated after 1949 also give relief in respect of capital payments.

Where the foreign licensor himself is liable to make royalty payments in respect of the patent rights, in theory he normally will be entitled under U.K. tax law to the equivalent of a deduction equal to the amount of the royalties payable by him.[52]

Copyright[53]

Copyright in the United Kingdom subsists in literary, dramatic, musical, and artistic works for a period of 50 years beyond the end of the year in which the author died. Copyright also subsists in sound recordings, films, television, and sound broadcasts normally for a period of 50 years from the end of the year in which the item was first published or broadcast.

Royalties payable to a nonresident for copyright are expressly brought within the withholding procedure applicable to annual payments. Where the recipient of a royalty or other periodic payment for U.K. copyright has his "usual place of abode" outside the United Kingdom, the payor must deduct income tax at the standard rate and account to the Revenue for the tax deducted.[54] This procedure will apply whether the owner of the copyright is an individual or a corporation; corporations are treated as "abiding" where they are managed and controlled.[55]

The withholding procedure does not apply to royalties payable in respect of film rights or copies of works which have been exported from the United Kingdom for distribution outside the United Kingdom.[56] Nor does the withholding procedure apply where a capital

---

[52]Under the withholding procedure relating to annual payments, a foreign licensor will be entitled to deduct income tax at the standard rate from the royalties. If he is not entitled to deduct tax, because, for example, the royalties are payable outside the United Kingdom under an obligation which is not governed by English law, the position is complex. There is no authority on the point, but it would seem that a foreign licensor in such a position may be entitled to claim a deduction for the royalties as expenses necessarily incurred in earning his royalty income. However, there would appear to be no machinery for permitting a refund of tax deducted from the royalties paid to the nonresident licensor unless he elects to spread the royalties or other payments in one of the two ways discussed.

[53]Copyright is covered by the Copyright Act, 1956.

[54]Income Tax Act, 1952, § 470.

[55]See, e.g., *De Beers Consolidated Mines Ltd.* v. *Howe*, 5 T.C. 198, 212.

[56]Income Tax Act, 1952, § 470(1).

sum is paid for the copyright. However, it will apply to a lump sum which is of an income nature. For example, it would apply to a lump sum paid as an advance against royalties.[57] If the taxpayer is an author who has spent more than 12 months creating the work in which the copyright exists, he may spread any royalties or taxable lump sum over the period of work, with a maximum spread of three years.[58] No allowance will be made on account of any capital expenditure incurred on the acquisition of the copyright.

As in the case of patent royalties, relief for copyright royalties may be available under a treaty. Relief given under the treaty with the United States is the same as the relief in respect of royalties and other payments made for the use of patents. Motion picture rentals are expressly included within the definition of royalties.[59]

Registered Designs[60]

Certain designs which are applied to articles by any industrial process or means are registrable. Registration gives copyright for five years from the date of registration. The period may be extended by two further periods of five years each.

The property rights acquired by the proprietor of a registered design are described under English law as copyright.[61] Accordingly, for U.K. tax purposes the treatment of a payment in respect of a registered design is the same as for a payment in respect of copyright. A deduction may be permitted for expenditure incurred in registering or renewing a registered design. However, this deduction often will not be of relevance to the nonresident licensor, since normally it will be available only if he has a permanent establishment in the United Kingdom and is taxed on the profits of a trade or business in respect of which the registered design has been acquired.[62] Again, relief may be given under treaty.

It might be mentioned here that although the rights in a registered design are regarded as copyright for English law purposes, it is considered that they will be regarded as patent rights and not as copyright for the purposes of the U.S. Internal Revenue Code. This distinction may be relevant if capital gains treatment is to be given

---

[57]*I.R.C.* v. *Longmans Green & Co. Ltd.*, 17 T.C. 272.

[58]Income Tax Act, 1952, § 471 and Finance Act, 1953, § 22.

[59]The treaties with several countries expressly exclude royalties for television or film rights from the relief given. Examples are the treaties with Sweden, Pakistan, and Israel.

[60]Registered designs are covered by the Registered Designs Acts, 1949-1961.

[61]See § 7, Registered Designs Act, 1949: "The registration of a design under this Act shall give to the registered proprietor the copyright in the registered design."

[62]Income Tax Act, 1952, § 139.

for sums received on a sale of the rights. The essential difference between the rights of the proprietor of copyright under U.S. law and the rights of the proprietor of a U.S. design patent is that the former has the right to restrain copying only, while the latter has a monopoly in his design. The difference is clear. Two individuals may independently of each other prepare identical maps of the same area; each will have the exclusive right to prevent any other person from copying his own map. The proprietor of a design patent, on the other hand, has a monopoly; he can restrain another from using a similar design, even if that other devised the same design independently and without knowledge of the registration.

In the light of this distinction, it seems clear that the proprietor of a registered design in the United Kingdom has rights which are equated more closely under U.S. law to the rights of a proprietor of a design patent than to the rights of a proprietor of copyright. The owner of a registered design in the United Kingdom has the exclusive right to use that design in relation to particular articles; he can restrain another from using the same, or a substantially similar design, even if that other devised the design himself and without knowledge of the registration.[63]

Trademarks

The basic concepts of U.K. trademark law are comparable with those of the U.S. law. It should be noted, however, that when a trademark is licensed, it is advisable to do so by means of a user agreement registered with the Registrar of Trademarks. Otherwise there is a danger that the validity of a trademark may be lost.[64] This is true even if the licensee is the subsidiary of the registered proprietor.[65] The initial period of registration for a trademark is seven years, but it may be renewed from time to time after that period without limit for additional periods of 14 years each.

In theory, the income of a nonresident licensor of U.K. trademarks is liable to income tax as income from property in the United Kingdom. There is no authority directly on this point, but by analogy with cases on other statutory industrial property rights, it seems indisputable that trademarks are "property" for this purpose.[66]

---

[63]The Registered Designs Act, 1949, § 7.

[64]Failure to register, however, will not necessarily invalidate the trademark if use by the licensee has not resulted in the loss of distinctiveness in the trademark. See *Bostitch Inc.* v. *McGarry & Cole Ltd.*, R.P.C. 183 (1963).

[65]There is no provision in the U.K. trademark law similar to § 5 of the U.S. Trademark Law, 1946.

[66]See *Curtis Brown Ltd.* v. *Jarvis*, 14 T.C. 744 (Copyright); *Internal Combustion Ltd.* v. *C.I.R.*, 16 T.C. 532 (Patent); and *I.R.C.* v. *Rolls Royce Limited* (No. 1), 29 T.C. 14 (Patent).

In practice, the Revenue does not attempt to assess trademark royalties that are paid to a nonresident licensor. Presumably this is because there is no convenient machinery for collection of the tax. The Revenue takes the view that trademark royalties are not normally annual payments for the purpose of the withholding procedure that has been described above. This view is probably correct, since trademark royalties are not normally "pure income profit" in the hands of the recipient, but are revenue receipts of his trade.

If there is an agent in the United Kingdom who collects the royalties on behalf of the licensor, the licensor could be assessed in the agent's name.[67] But this normally does not help the Revenue because the licensee paying the royalties will clearly not be the "agent, receiver, branch or manager" of the licensor in whose name an assessment might otherwise be made.

Where there is no relief available under a double taxation convention, two steps can be taken to strengthen the argument that trademark royalties are not taxable. The first is to provide that the royalties shall be payable by the licensee at some bank outside the United Kingdom. This will prevent any argument that they are collected by an agent in the United Kingdom. Secondly, it is advisable to base the royalties on some quantum of use, such as net sales, rather than to make them annual payments of a fixed amount. This will strengthen the argument that the royalties are not annual payments for the purposes of the withholding procedure.

The expenses of registration or renewal of a trademark are deductible, but as in the case of these expenses for a registered design, this deduction normally will not be relevant to the nonresident licensor.

Most of the tax treaties which have been concluded by the United Kingdom specifically state that royalties or other sums paid to a nonresident for the use of the U.K. trademarks will be exempt from U.K. tax. Under the treaty with the United States, the conditions necessary to obtain this relief are the same as for payments for patents. But this relief will not often be relevant. The U.K. licensee should pay trademark royalties in full, even if no application for relief has been made, because the withholding procedure does not apply to trademark royalties. The treaty relief will, therefore, be relevant only in exceptional circumstances where, for example, a direct assessment could otherwise be made on the nonresident licensor.

---

[67]See text accompanying note 31, *supra*.

Know-How

Know-how is not a term of art in English law. For the purpose of this article it is used to mean confidential and secret data relating to machines, processes, designs, and inventions and any other secret information pertaining to the means of manufacture or trading, which amounts to something more than the mere skill or experience of technical employees. Information will be secret in this sense, even if some competitors or others know it, provided that it is not generally available to those who might want to acquire it. It is firmly settled that a person who reveals know-how to another in such circumstances that an obligation of confidence is imposed will be substantially protected if the other uses the know-how without his consent.[68] This will be the case even if there is no contractual relationship. The protection is given as a result of the breach of confidence. An obligation of confidence will be found where, for example, know-how is given by a manufacturer to a subcontractor or an intended licensee.[69]

There is a fundamental difference between the license of industrial property rights that consist of know-how and the license of other types of industrial property. The latter is the voluntary waiver of preexisting statutory rights which give a monopoly that is good against all others (except in the case of copyright, against an innocent, independent creator). The owner of know-how has no preexisting rights against third parties; he merely has information which is not known to them. He cannot prevent third parties using that information if they can acquire it legally, for example, by their own research or by inspection of an item manufactured and sold by him. The licensor of know-how, therefore, reduces the secrecy surrounding his know-how and as a result he acquires rights against the recipient of the secret information.

There is no clear authority as to what is the correct treatment for tax purposes of sums paid to a nonresident for the right to use his know-how. In the past such sums usually have created no problem. In practice, the U.K. Revenue normally does not assess royalties for the use of know-how payable to nonresidents. The reasons for this practice are the same as in the case of trademark royalties. Sums payable for the right to use know-how usually are not regarded as pure income profit in the hands of the recipient, but as his trading

---

[68]*Saltman Engineering Co. Ltd.* v. *Campbell Engineering Co.*, 65 R.P.C. 203 (1948).

[69]For recent examples of the application of this principle see *Ackroyds (London) Limited* v. *Islington Plastics*, R.P.C. 97 (1962), and *Peter Pan Manufacturing Corporation* v. *Corsets Silhouette Limited*, 1 W.L.R. 96 (1964).

income; and therefore, the withholding procedure described above will not apply. Secondly, there is usually no agent of the nonresident in the United Kingdom in whose name he can be assessed. As a result, it is not often of concern to the nonresident licensor whether the correct analysis of these payments is that they are royalties for the use of property or for technical service fees. Nor has it been material for the payor who usually can claim a deduction in either event.[70] But this may not always be so in the future. As will be discussed later, "close companies" will not be able to deduct for the purpose of the corporation tax royalties that are paid to members for the use of intangible property.

There seem to be two alternative grounds on which payments for the use of know-how can be assessed. Such payments are either income from property within the United Kingdom or, alternatively, income from services which will be taxable if performed within the United Kingdom. Which is the correct analysis depends upon whether know-how is "property" for the purposes of the Income Tax Acts and, if so, how that property is utilized when licensed.

In cases where improper use of know-how has been claimed, the courts have generally avoided any discussion as to whether know-how creates proprietary rights. Decisions in these cases have normally been based on whether the know-how was acquired in such circumstances that a confidential relationship was created and, if so, whether there was a breach of the confidence imposed by that relationship.

The judgments of the House of Lords[71] in four tax cases have discussed the treatment of sums paid on the disposal or license of know-how. Each case considered whether lump-sum payments made to a person resident in the United Kingdom constituted revenue receipts or receipts in the nature of capital.

The first case is *Handley Page* v. *Butterworth*.[72] The point at issue was whether the aircraft designer, Mr. Handley Page, was taxable in respect of compensation paid by the U.K. Government for wartime use of his designs. The compensation had been paid to Handley Page Limited, a company of which Mr. Handley Page was managing director and the major shareholder. The designs were not registerable and were not covered (except as to minor details) by patent protection. As a result of the wartime use, the designs had become common knowledge. Two questions were at issue. Were the payments in the nature of capital receipts? And secondly, were

---

[70]See *Paterson Engineering Co. Ltd.* v. *Duff*, 25 T.C. 43.
[71]The House of Lords is the highest court of appeal in the United Kingdom.
[72]19 T.C. 328

they received by the company as agent for Mr. Handley Page? Lord Tomlin in the unanimous opinion of the House of Lords stated:

> In such a design there is no legal monopoly or property. There is property no doubt in the drawings and plans in which it is embodied, and if the design is kept secret, it may be protected by those remedies which are available against breaches of confidence.

These remarks cannot be regarded as definitive. Notwithstanding his denial of any property, Lord Tomlin concluded that the payments were in the nature of capital receipts, and hence presumably (although he did not actually say so) were payments made in respect of the disposal of a capital asset. Furthermore, the alternative reason for his decision was that the company did not receive the payments as agent for Mr. Handley Page.

The second case is *Evans Medical Supplies Limited* v. *Moriarty*.[73] The company was a pharmaceutical manufacturer with world-wide sales and in particular with sales in Burma handled through an agency. After the Second World War it became apparent that the Burmese Government intended to set up its own manufacturing plant. The company successfully bid for the contract to supply the Burmese Government with the necessary know-how to erect a plant and commence manufacture of certain pharmaceutical products. The company received a lump-sum payment of £100,000 in consideration for the disclosure of secret processes relating to the storing and packing of certain of the products as well as for the disclosure of other information that, although known to some competitors, was not common knowledge. By a majority of three to two, the House of Lords held that no part of the lump sum was taxable. Two of the judges giving the majority decision based their decision on the grounds that the know-how was a capital asset, and that by entering into the transaction the company had realized a considerable part of the capital value of that asset. Lord Denning, who was the third member of the majority, based his decision on totally different grounds. He considered that, although the know-how was a revenue producing asset, no part of it was disposed of since the company retained full right to use the know-how as before. He likened the transaction to the instruction of a pupil by a professional man and thus as an agreement to provide services. Nevertheless, he held that the lump sum was not taxable on the narrow ground that it arose from a new trade and not the existing trade assessed by the Revenue. A fourth judge held that the receipt was taxable to the extent that it was allocable to the acquisition of information other than the secret processes. The fifth judge found the receipt was wholly taxable as a profit arising from the exploitation of the know-how in the

---

[73] 37 T.C. 540.

course of the existing trade, but he did not attempt to analyze whether the exploitation took the form of sale of parts of the asset or for the provision of services.

The *Evans* case is difficult to apply because it is difficult to ascertain a common *ratio decidendi* of the judges. Nevertheless, it is clear that all five members of the House of Lords regarded the know-how as property; the only difference of opinion was as to whether it was exploited in the course of trade or whether it was in part sold in a capital transaction.

The next case is *Jeffrey* v. *Rolls-Royce Limited.*[74] The company was a manufacturer of aero engines and had acquired a considerable fund of know-how in relation to their manufacture. After the Second World War the engines were used in the military aircraft of many countries throughout the world. Frequently, the company considered that the only method of getting its engines adopted in a certain market was by arranging for local manufacture by a licensee. For example, it entered into license agreements with governments or manufacturers in the Republic of China, France, the United States, Australia, Belgium, Argentina, and Sweden. The agreements commonly provided that in consideration of a lump-sum payment, the company undertook to supply the licensee with drawings and information necessary for the manufacture of certain of its engines.

All five judges in the House of Lords regarded the know-how involved as a capital asset of the business. But they held that all the lump sums were trading receipts arising from the exploitation of that asset in the course of the company's trade. They did not consider that the company had parted with any capital asset, but that it was trading with its know-how in the most advantageous, and in some countries the only, way open to it. What is interesting is that two of the judges specifically likened the sums to awards for teaching, that is to say to fees for services rendered. This approach is best exemplified by the judgment of Lord Radcliffe.[75]

> First, as to "know-how." I see no objection to describing this as an asset. It is intangible: but then, so is goodwill. . . . "Know-how" is an ambience that pervades a highly specialized production organization, and, although I think it correct to describe it as fixed capital so long as a manufacturer retains it for his own productive purposes and expresses its value in its products, one must realize that in so describing it one is proceeding by an analogy which can easily break down owing to the inherent differences that separate "know-how" from the more straightforward elements of fixed capital. For instance, it will be wrong to confuse the physical records with the "know-how" itself, which is the valuable asset, for, if you put them on a duplicator and

---

[74] 40 T.C. 443.
[75] 40 T.C. 443, 493.

produce one hundred copies, you have certainly not multiplied your asset in proportion. . . . Whatever else the lump sum or capital sums payable under the agreement are paid for, it is not for a license in the ordinary sense: it is for the making available, the imparting, of the "know-how," both as recorded in the drawings and other data and as conveyed by direct instruction, advice and information. . . . No doubt the things to be supplied are tangible objects; but then, so are textbooks, formulae or recipes. The company is teaching at long range.

The fourth and most recent case is *Musker* v. *English Electric Co. Limited.*[76] The company, at the request of the British Government, had entered into licensing agreements with the government of Australia and the Glenn L. Martin Company in the United States for the manufacture of the Canberra bomber. These agreements provided for the payment of lump sums of £200,000 and $1,500,000, respectively, in consideration for the supply by the company of the manufacturing techniques, engineering data and other information necessary for the manufacture of the aircraft. The lump sums were again treated as taxable receipts. All the judges except one (who merely stated that the case was covered by *Jeffrey* v. *Rolls-Royce Limited*) agreed that the transaction was in reality the teaching of the licensee by the company. In the words of Lord Donovan[77] the company

has taught for reward, as Rolls-Royce taught for reward; and just as that reward was held to be trading income in the hands of Rolls-Royce, so also must the reward accruing to the company.

To summarize these cases, it would seem that know-how is an intangible asset which can be turned to a profit by the manufacturer in two ways. He can use it himself in the manufacture of goods for sale at a profit, or he can teach it to others when his fees and rewards will be revenue in his hands. A lump sum received on the disposal of know-how by a manufacturer or other owner will normally be a capital receipt only if the manufacturer no longer retains the right to use the know-how. A lump sum may also be a capital receipt if in an isolated case the know-how is disposed of with a business carried on in a particular territory, and the seller of the business is precluded from using the know-how in that territory.

Where a nonresident licensor grants a manufacturer in the United Kingdom the right, whether exclusive or nonexclusive, to use his know-how in the United Kingdom, but otherwise retains the know-how for his own benefit, any sums received by him will be rewards for services rendered, and not income from property used in the United Kingdom. Consequently, the liability of the nonresi-

[76]41 T.C. 556.
[77]41 T.C. 556, 587.

dent to assessment of income tax will depend upon whether any of those services are rendered in the United Kingdom. If all drawings and other written data are made available to the licensee outside the United Kingdom and all instruction of the licensee's employees takes place at the licensor's premises in the United States or elsewhere outside the United Kingdom, there would seem to be no grounds on which an assessment can be made on the licensor.

Although a lump-sum payment in the hands of a licensor will usually be regarded as a payment for teaching services rendered, it will not necessarily be a deductible revenue expense of the U.K. licensee. As a result of the instruction the licensee receives, he will obtain know-how which may become a capital asset of his business. This would certainly seem to be the case where the licensee is entitled to retain and use the know-how at the end of the license period. Therefore, a lump-sum payment for know-how will be treated normally as a nondeductible capital payment. There will be no means whereby the licensee can depreciate that payment. Thus, if the licensor insists upon a lump-sum payment, it may be in the interests of the licensee to allocate the lump sum specifically to any patent rights that may be involved. As has been described, a capital sum paid for the acquisition of patent rights can be depreciated.

The tax treaty with the United States and with most of the other countries specifically gives relief in respect of royalties and other sums paid for the use of "designs, secret processes and formulae." The conditions for relief under the treaty with the United States are the same as for relief in respect of patent royalties. This relief, like the relief in respect of trademark royalties, will not often be relevant to the U.S. licensor. In any event, royalties for the use of know-how are payable in full without deduction of tax.

PROFITS TAX

Until recently, nonresident companies carrying on business in the United Kingdom were liable to profits tax at the rate of 15 percent. Thus, in the exceptional case where the income of a nonresident licensor was attributable to a branch in the United Kingdom, that income would have been liable to profits tax. However, as a result of the new corporation tax (described later), profits tax will not apply to any profits earned after April 6, 1966,[78] and, therefore, this tax will not be discussed in further detail.

---

[78]Finance Act, 1965, § 46(3).

CAPITAL GAINS TAX

The United Kingdom has recently introduced a capital gains tax on any gains arising on the disposal of an asset after April 5, 1965.[79] Only so much of the gain as is attributable to the period after that date will be taxable. A nonresident will be liable to this tax only on gains arising from the disposal of assets located in the United Kingdom and used in a trade carried on there through a branch or agency. This tax, therefore, will be of concern to the nonresident licensor only in exceptional cases.

Where the taxpayer is a corporation, the gain will be charged to the corporation tax discussed below. An individual will be liable to the capital-gains tax at the rate of 30 percent unless his total capital gain for the year is less than £5,000, in which event he may elect to be taxed at half his marginal rate.

CORPORATION TAX

A nonresident company will be liable to the new corporation tax if it is carrying on trade in the United Kingdom through a branch or agency.[80] The rate of this tax has not yet been announced, but will probably fall between 35 and 40 percent. It will be chargeable on the trading profits arising from the branch or agency of the nonresident company and on any income from any property or rights used or held by the branch or agency.[81] Thus, where a corporate nonresident licensor has a branch establishment in the United Kingdom which itself uses the industrial property rights licensed to the U.K. licensee, its license income will be subject to the corporation tax. Where a nonresident licensor is chargeable in this manner and receives income, such as patent royalties, subject to deduction of income tax, that income tax can be set off against its liability to the corporation tax.

It will probably be the unusual case in which the nonresident licensor is chargeable to the corporation tax as described above. An aspect of the corporation tax which will be of more frequent relevance for the nonresident licensor will be the deductibility of royalties by the licensee. There are three circumstances in which a corporate licensee may find that royalty payments are not deductible. The first is merely a transitional problem; the second will probably be removed by amending legislation; and the third will arise only if the licensee is a close company.

---

[79]*Id.*, §§19-45.
[80]This tax is introduced by the Finance Act, 1965, §§ 46-89.
[81]Finance Act, 1965, § 50.

The transitional problem arises from the fact that payments, such as patent royalties, that must be made after deduction of tax under the withholding procedure will not be deductible for the corporation tax if paid before April 6, 1966.[82] The problem is that many, if not most, companies carrying on business in the United Kingdom will be subject to the corporation tax on accounting periods commencing before that date.[83] Admittedly, the licensee will sometimes get an effective deduction because it will be withholding tax for which it will not have to account to the Revenue.[84] However, where the licensee does not have sufficient income to cover the payments or where a tax treaty applies and the payments must be made in full, they will be nondeductible if paid prior to April 6, 1966, but in an accounting year in which the licensee is subject to the corporation tax.

Insofar as the licensee is concerned (and subject to what is said in the next paragraph), an effective method of overcoming this transitional problem may be to delay payment of patent royalties until April 6, 1966, or later. The deductibility of patent royalties will not be on the accrual basis, but will be strictly on the basis of actual payments made in the accounting year. It must be emphasized that this problem only arises in respect of royalties which are paid subject to the deduction of tax under the withholding procedure, or would be so paid if it were not for a tax treaty. The problem, therefore, does not arise in respect of trademark or know-how royalties.

Payments such as patent royalties that are made after April 6, 1966, and that must be made subject to the withholding procedure will not be deductible for the corporation tax unless the payor deducts tax and accounts to the Revenue for the tax deducted. No provision has been made to cover the situation where the licensee is required by a tax treaty to make the payments in full.[85] Thus, it would seem that as the law now stands many licensees will lose the right to deduct patent royalties for the purposes of the corporation tax if the licensor has obtained exemption from U.K. tax under a tax treaty. It is understood, however, that the U.K. Revenue intends to introduce amending legislation or regulations permitting deductions in these circumstances.

If a corporate licensee is a close company, any royalties or other consideration paid for the use of intangible property paid to a

---

[82]*Id.*, § 52(1).

[83]In the normal case a company will be liable to the corporation tax on its earnings in its first complete accounting period after April 5, 1964.

[84]On or after April 6, 1966, the licensee withholding tax at source will be required to account to the Revenue.

[85]See Finance Act, § § 52(5), 53(5).

member of the close company will be treated as a dividend distribution.[86] As a result the royalties will not be deductible and, subject to any relevant tax treaty provision, will be subject to a withholding tax at the rate of 41.25 percent. It is beyond the scope ·of this article to consider in detail the definition of a close company. Briefly, a close company is a company which is under the control of five or fewer members.[87] Family groups are treated as one, as are partners and certain trustees and beneficiaries. Persons who can control the company or who have an option to acquire shares will be treated as members. Where a company is under the contol of one or more companies, it will be a close company only if those companies are themselves under the necessary degree of close control. Any licensor who receives patent or trademark royalties from a U.K. company of which it is a member, therefore, should investigate whether its licensee is a close company. If it is, one solution may be to transfer the license agreement to a sister subsidiary which does not directly control the U.K. licensee.[88]

Royalty payments made by a close company to a member will not be deductible if they are "for the use of property." Copyright in a literary, dramatic, musical, or artistic work is specifically excluded from "property" for this purpose. Royalties paid for the use of patents, trademarks or registered designs are clearly covered. But if the analysis of payments for the right to use know-how made earlier in this article is correct, royalties for the right to use know-how should be deductible. They are not royalties for the use of property, but payments for teaching services rendered. They should, therefore, be deductible as ordinary revenue expenditure. It must be emphasized, however, that although this proposition appears to follow from the previously discussed decisions of the House of Lords, there is no direct authority for it at this time.

CONCLUSION

The U.K. tax law relating to patent royalties and other sums paid for the use of or on the sale of patents is well developed. Nevertheless, in view of the extensive range of tax treaties concluded by the United Kingdom, the licensor resident in the United States, or in one of most other developed countries, will not be affected often

---

[86]*Id.*, Schedule 11, Paragraph 9(1)(c).

[87]*Id.*, Schedule 18. In fact, the statute reads in terms of control by five or fewer "participators," a term defined to include not only shareholders, but loan creditors, persons entitled to become shareholders and certain other persons.

[88]In most circumstances, such transfer would give rise to U.S. tax implications that would have to be evaluated before a decision was made to effectuate the transfer.

by any U.K. tax liability. The law relating to the taxation of royalties and other sums paid in respect of trademarks and know-how is less well developed. But this is usually to the advantage of the nonresident licensor, since the lack of development chiefly consists in the failure to apply an effective method of collecting tax from nonresidents in respect of income from these types of intangible property. The major practical problem which is likely to concern the nonresident licensor is the deductibility by the licensee of patent and trademark royalties for the purposes of the new corporation tax.

Author's Postscript—

There have been several changes in the relevant law since the publication of this article in 1965.

The tax treaty between the United States and the United Kingdom was amended in 1966 to take into account the changes in the U.K. tax law as a result of the introduction of corporation tax and capital gains tax. Royalties beneficially owned by a resident of the United States are exempt from tax in the United Kingdom provided that they are not effectively connected with a permanent establishment of the licensor in the United Kingdom. It is no longer a condition for exemption that the royalties be subject to U.S. tax. The treaty relief now expressly extends to payments made not only from the use of patents and other industrial property but also from the sale or exchange of any such rights. Thus, a U.S. proprietor of U.K. industrial property rights who wishes to obtain capital-gains treatment may safely express the transaction as a sale. Furthermore royalties paid by a close company to a resident of the United States cannot be treated as a dividend distribution and, therefore, will be deductible unless persons who are residents of the United Kingdom control both the licensor and the licensee. New and revised treaties on similar lines have also been negotiated with several countries including New Zealand (10 percent), Switzerland, Canada (10 percent except on copyright royalties), Singapore, Trinidad & Tobago (15 percent except on copyright royalties), Belgium, the Netherlands, and Luxembourg (5 percent). In certain of the treaties U.K. income tax is chargeable at the reduced rate indicated.

As anticipated on page 565 of the original article, legislation was introduced (The Double Taxation Relief (Taxes on Income) (General) Regulations 1966) permitting a licensee to deduct royalties that are payable in full or subject only to a reduced rate of withholding tax as a result of treaty relief.

It has been announced that the Government intends to introduce legislation in the next Finance Bill to increase the corporation tax rate to 42.5 percent.

In *Murray* v. *Imperial Chemical Industries Limited,* 3 W.L.R. 301 (1967), it was held that lump-sum payments expressly made for "keep out" covenants which were ancillary to the grant of exclusive patent licenses were to be treated as capital receipts. The "keep out" covenants were given by I.C.I. to exclusive licensees of its Terylene products in several different countries. It was held that the lump-sum payments were not taxable as receipts from the exploitation of the company's assets in the course of its trade. The case, however, is unsatisfactory because it would seem that, if the lump sums were to be treated as arising on the sale of the patent rights, the receipts should nevertheless have been taxable under Section 318 of the Income Tax Act, 1952. It is not clear from the report why it was not contended by the Revenue that this should have been the case.

Notes on Informed European Opinion
Regarding Industrial Property

L. JAMES HARRIS

In the summer of 1967 I personally collected material on the experience of European experts under provisions of laws that already largely embody the Recommendations of the Report of the President's Commission on the United States Patent System.[1] My purpose in this article is to present a brief account of my impressions concerning the European industrial property "climate," particularly with respect to harmonization and regional and international industrial property arrangements. A later, more formal, report will deal in detail with the implications of Recommendation 35[2] and of other Recommendations covered in my conversations abroad.[3]

In a sense, this note constitutes a byproduct of one of the studies[4] that The PTC Research Institute has undertaken on the Report of the President's Commission on the United States Patent System. The purpose of the Institute studies is to reveal, insofar as possible, the potential effects of the changes proposed by the Commission on innovation and economic progress. The Institute studies are being conducted by means of depth interview,

---

EDITOR'S NOTE: This paper appeared in *IDEA*, Vol. 11, No. 3.

[1] *Report of the President's Commission on the Patent System* (Washington, D.C.: G.P.O., 1966).

[2] Recommendation 35 states that: "The Commission believes that the ultimate goal in the protection of inventions should be the establishment of a universal patent, respected throughout the world, issued in the light of, and inventive over, all of the prior art of the world, and obtained quickly and inexpensively on a single application, but only in return for a genuine contribution to the progress of the useful arts.

"To this end the Commission specifically recommends the pursuit of: (1) international harmonization of patent practice, (2) the formation of regional patent system groups, and (3) a universal network of mechanized information storage and retrieval systems." See note 1, *supra*, at p. 55.

[3] I discussed the following topics with foreign experts: first to file; grace period; opposition and cancellation; interpretation of claims and effectiveness of examination system; novelty and obviousness; deferred examination; preliminary applications; protection against importation; early publication of patent application; foreign public knowledge, use and sale included as prior art; advisory council; burden of persuasion; damages for infringement before patent issues; and patent office finance.

[4] See "Institute Research Bearing on Report of President's Commission on the Patent System," *PTC News Notes*, Ref. 709 (March 1967). Also see *IDEA*, Vol. 11, Conference No. (1967).

questionnaire, and literature search. My own assignment was to
interview foreign participants in the Workshop on Industrial and
Intellectual Property that I had been asked to organize and moderate at the World Peace Through Law Conference in Geneva in
July 1967. I took further advantage of my trip abroad to interview
in depth many government officials, private practitioners, and
business executives in Switzerland, Germany, Denmark, France,
and the Netherlands.[5]

HARMONIZATION: COMPETING AND CORRELATIVE OBJECTIVES

My encounters with experts in industrial property and with
other European industrial and professional leaders suggest that
Europe is prepared to accept a greater degree of legal, technological, and economic harmonization and integration than at any other
time since World War II. But there is also evidence of ambiva-
lence. There is an underlying reluctance, distrust, or drag, particularly where a closer rapport may logically require political integration. While Europeans strive for more concord, they remain animated
by keen economic and political competition. Their history cannot
be shed, and they literally cling to the sovereignty of the present
and past as they look to the future.

When I raised the question of international patent cooperation, the responses were generally favorable. However, further
discussion disclosed doubts, particularly as the exploration extended
to other questions. At deeper levels, it became certain that the kind
of cooperation that the experts deemed acceptable was also strictly
circumscribed.

Frequently, I asked: "For the purposes of international cooperation, do you think it is essential that there be substantially
identical patent laws? If so, why?" In every case I stressed the word
"essential" and the phrase " substantially identical." I also made it
a point to explain that their responses would be evaluated in accordance with this emphasis.

Most of the respondents thought that harmonization of patent laws would be helpful, if not essential, to international cooperation. But, in almost every case, the reply was carefully hedged; that
is, harmonization was usually considered essential for certain types
of provisions only. Thus, the impression was conveyed that harmonization was deemed feasible precisely because it required a limited

[5]On several occasions I interviewed two and three experts representing
different disciplines at one time. Happily, in all these multiparty interviews the
effect on the discussions was synergistic.

amount of legal and political change. Several of the interviewees seemed to have some kind of international arrangement in view as the goal. This impression was most strongly conveyed in Germany; it also emerged from discussions in France, Denmark, and the Netherlands.

Let me cite a few examples: A highly placed official of the German Government stated that "substantially identical patent laws are needed," but went on to explain that he was referring to laws relating to the patentability of invention. Indeed, he felt that it was "not necessary that the procedural requirements be the same in different countries." A representative from German industry repeated this position in almost the same language. He stated that "patentability, including utility, novelty, and inventive height, should be substantially identical although procedural laws may differ." Another response from a German government employee was focused on "search results from the various industrial countries." He thought that, to assure similar results, "certain procedures should be instituted on a step-by-step basis." The first step he advocated involved patent documentation: "The prior art should be classified in the same way in the various countries." The second step "should bring the patent application form, including the claims, into conformity in those countries."

In France, a well-informed government official responded in terms that recalled my experience with German interviewees. He favored "substantially identical patent laws relating to patentability, such as novelty, inventive step and subject matter." He, too, thought it "not essential that patent laws be identical for that part of the law relating to procedures after the patent is granted."

In Denmark, an industry executive expressed the limitation another way. He said that: "With respect to certain patent provisions, substantial identity would be essential. For example, registration versus examination, first-to-invent versus first-to-file."

In the Netherlands, a quasi-government official also hedged while seeming to assert a broader basis of commonality. For the purposes of novelty-searching, he felt that it was "not essential that there be substantially identical patent laws to achieve international cooperation." He added, however, that "a common definition of novelty would be extremely important." Referring to "inventive height," he stated that "substantially identical patent laws are not essential because its presence or absence is a subjective determination." But it was also his belief that achievement of real uniformity with respect to patentability would require "a supranational court that would have jurisdiction over all the national courts dealing with patents in the participating countries, and to which their respective decisions can be appealed."

Several of the experts responded to my query by referring to regional arrangements. For example, several Danes directed their remarks to the proposed Nordic Patent Convention,[6] while some French experts cited the proposed draft Common Market Patent Convention.[7] Since a BIRPI[8] meeting in Stockholm on administrative reorganization and U.S. government conferences on the proposed PCT Treaty[9] had occurred at about the time of my European trip, the treaty too was cited. In general, each such respondent considered his country not yet ready to enter into a regional patent arrangement, although it might well be or become a member of a group for other purposes. Thus, the position on group patent integration seemed far less advanced than the position on patent harmonization or on some form of international negotiation. Further implications of the responses bearing on regional arrangements will be considered in the next section of this paper.

Another question on international cooperation that I asked the

[6]". . . there has been a somewhat surprising development in the Scandinavian countries. For many years a Nordic Patent Convention has been proposed and discussed. In the last few months it has suddenly come to active life under Swedish leadership.

"Essentially this involves the enactment of substantially identical patent laws in Sweden, Norway and Denmark and probably Finland, and a treaty between these countries whereby an application filed and granted in any one of them could also be automatically issued in some or all of the others, at the request of the patentee.

"This would be an open Convention available to nationals of any country. It is believed that there are no important political objections, and the Nordic Convention may possibly be in effect before the end of the present decade. In view of the existing similarities in practice and language among the Scandinavian countries, this is actually in the nature of harmonization rather than a supranational system." Leonard J. Robbins, *IDEA*, Vol. 8, Conference No. (1964), pp. 107-108.

[7]For a comprehensive paper on the Convention, see Franz Froschmaier, "Progress Toward the Proposed Convention for a European Patent and for a European Trademark," *IDEA*, Vol. 6, No. 4 (Winter 1962-1963), p. 479.

[8]Bureaux Internationaux Reunis pour la Protection de la Propriété Intellectuelle, the Secretariat of the Paris and Berne Unions, is located in Geneva, Switzerland.

[9]See "BIRPI Plan for Facilitating the Filing and Examination of Applications for the Protection of the Same Invention in a Number of Countries," *Industrial Property* (March 1967).

On May 31, 1967, BIRPI released a draft of a proposed Patent Cooperation Treaty "as a result of a proposal made by the United States to the Executive Committee of the Paris Union." Thereafter, during the spring and summer of this year, a number of briefing conferences were held in different cities in the United States under the auspices of the Patent Office, U.S. Department of Commerce.

For an expert appraisal of the proposed treaty, see Gerald D. O'Brien, "A Realistic Appraisal of the Draft Patent Cooperation Treaty," p. 585, *infra;* for a constructive counterproposal, see Stephen P. Ladas "The BIRPI Plan for a Patent Cooperation Treaty," *IDEA,* Vol. 11, No. 2 (Summer 1967); see also "The 1968 BIRPI Draft Treaty for Patent Cooperation," p. 606, *infra.*

foreign experts was this: "Is it necessary to have a first-to-file procedure if a country is to participate in BIRPI's proposed PCT Treaty?" The answers to this question (which was intended to elicit information concerning harmonization, international arrangements, and the European attitude toward an important element of American patent practice) were generally negative. In almost every case, the two parts of the Treaty were treated discretely—as well as discreetly. There was much support for the first part of the Treaty relating to the novelty report, but little, if any, for the certificate of patentability. The replies to this question reinforced my impression that great store is placed by cooperation, particularly harmonization and international instruments; and that, at the same time, domestic interests were deemed paramount.

A French expert from industry stressed that, for the purposes of BIRPI's certificate of patentability, it was essential that the patent laws (which are in reality an expression of national sovereignty) first be made substantially identical. In his view, "such a certificate of patentability is not feasible until the laws of the participating countries are harmonized."

A German university professor counseled that the first phase of the BIRPI Treaty was "essential to avoid double work." On the other hand, he believed that the second phase was "not realistic."

I should cite some of the thought-provoking comments made on the first part of the Treaty. According to a well-known French patent agent, all participants would have to accept a first-to-file procedure if they were to participate in the proposed BIRPI Treaty. Although he was favorably disposed toward the Treaty proposal relating to a novelty report, he voiced four objections from a "practical standpoint." Specifically, "(1) in order to determine whether patents had defense implications, it would be necessary to compel applicants to file first in their national patent offices; (2) the intervention of an agency like BIRPI would further complicate patent application proceedings; (3) the organization of the examination proposed by BIRPI would be impossible because of the current lack of uniformity; and (4) there might also be problems with the application of the International Convention."[10]

A government official in the Netherlands thought that the proposed BIRPI Treaty would represent an improvement in international cooperation precisely *because* it would lead to increased collaboration between parties operating under a first-to-file system

---

[10]Paris Convention for the Protection of Industrial Property of 1883, revised at Brussels 1900, at Washington 1911, at The Hague 1925, at London 1934, at Lisbon 1958, and at Stockholm 1967.

and parties operating under a first-to-invent system. This view struck me as thoughtfully different. He noted, however, that "the BIRPI Treaty would be much easier to realize if all the countries had a first-to-file procedure."

In short, the viewpoints expressed by the respondents indicate a uniformly favorable opinion on harmonization and on international cooperation, but not on group arrangements involving integration. Even when the need for harmonization was expressed as a necessary prelude to group or international patent arrangements, no conviction was communicated for a full and vigorous group integration, nor was there any optimism that integration would be realized within the near future. Lack of uniformity of patent laws was considered by some respondents to be responsible for the lack of progress in group patent arrangements. On closer examination, however, the responses revealed a surprising lack of enthusiasm for such arrangements anyway. Support for group arrangements was even more limited among the French experts than among the experts interviewed from other countries.

HALTING PROGRESS TOWARD
REGIONAL ARRANGEMENTS

I made a special effort to obtain information on attitudes of experts toward patent arrangements within regional groupings of nations. The responses were "unofficial"; but, again, deeper considerations seemed to influence the disposition to reply and the quality of the information given. The opinions on integration, as I mentioned in the previous section, were generally consistent with their points of view concerning harmonization and other varieties of international cooperation.

The respondents recognized industrial property as an important avenue by which regional groups may pursue economic and technological integration. Nevertheless, the expressed objections to integration were often unequivocal. Clear overtones of doubt were heard even in otherwise favorable observations on the state of integration. The attitude toward integration is very different from that toward harmonization or international treaties; and, moreover, the intercountry variation in this attitude toward group patent arrangements was much less than I had anticipated.

An eminent Danish patent agent informed me that the political parties in Denmark and Norway raised national sovereignty and other objections to Nordic patent legislation after the government representatives of various Scandinavian countries had agreed and after the patent agents in these countries had been consulted. He said that "there is a very strong likelihood that the new Danish law will be passed with Chapter III eliminated—or made effective at some future date."[11] Chapter III of the new Danish law is the chapter that provides for Nordic cooperation. It is apparently feared that applicants will tend to apply to the patent office of the country considered most liberal, and that a lack of uniformity is implicit in the failure to provide for a common appeals board or court.

Contrary Danish sentiment was also encountered. A government official expressed belief that a Nordic patent was getting closer than ever, and he even hoped "that Danes will be able to put the Nordic patent into effect."

In France, the Strasbourg Convention[12] was favorably mentioned by a high government official and a leading patent agent. However, the agent stated that it would be impossible to obtain identical patent laws. But harmonization had to take place and provision for examination of patents made in the national patent laws of the six countries involved for a common EEC patent to become possible.[13] In his opinion, such a patent will not be instituted for a long time to come. Moreover, he felt that the EEC common patent proposal implies an overcomplicated system. He amplified as follows: "An infringement action must first be brought in the national court. If invalidation of a patent is determined, the proceedings in the national court must come to a halt and an action must be brought in the European court to determine the validity of the patent. Only after the action of the European court has been concluded and a determination made can the national court proceed with the action that was originally instituted therein."

Another well-known French patent agent did not think substantially identical patent laws essential for international coopera-

---

[11]As this paper went to press I received a letter from a Swedish patent attorney informing me that the new Swedish patent law was enacted by the Swedish Parliament on November 1, 1967, to take effect January 1, 1968. He writes that ". . . the special Rules regarding 'Nordic' patent applications which will mature into patents in all the four Nordic countries—Sweden, Denmark, Norway and Finland—will only come into force later on."

[12]"Harmonization has also just won a quiet victory in the countries belonging to the Council of Europe—which include the six Common Market countries. There are already two existing minor Conventions relating to classification and formalities. A new Convention has been signed dealing with harmonization of several important substantive aspects of patent law, particularly relating to novelty and patentability. While no one could say this makes the German and French systems similar, at any rate it does bring them closer together." See note 6, *supra*, at p. 108.

[13]. . . it should be remembered that many proponents of the European Patent Convention, while approving in principle, have stated that harmonization of national patent laws must come first." See note 6, *supra*, at p. 108.

tion. He gave the very revealing reason that "national judges are unimpressed by what happens in other countries."

In only one of my interviews abroad was a clear and spontaneous sentiment expressed in favor of regional patent arrangements. In response to my inquiry on the necessity for a first-to-file procedure for participating in the proposed BIRPI Treaty, a German university professor expressed doubts as to the practicability of the second phase of the Treaty. In this connection, he stated a preference for "regional arrangements such as those proposed for the Scandinavian countries and for the Common Market countries."

In general, I experienced more support for regional integration in Germany than in France. Although a Common Market patent was not often mentioned even in Germany, I nevertheless got the impression that the Germans would encourage agreements leading to greater group cohesion. Apparently, the integration sought by the Germans is based primarily on nationalism, or self-interest: it involves the political unification of Germany, a goal that has wide support.

Discussions of the different modes of economic and legal integration available made it clear to me that the Germans are anxious for the Common Market to be made attractive. The industrial property potential is recognized. If the Eastern European nations could be included, particularly East Germany, eventual political unification of the two Germanies would be easier. On becoming aware of the deeper implications of the West German attitude, I also acquired an insight into the changing policies of De Gaulle—toward the Common Market, the independence for the Poles, and the separation of the French Canadians. The admission of countries like England to the EEC, and any further steps to advance integration in the Market, would encourage extension to other European countries and thus facilitate the eventual unification of Germany. De Gaulle anticipates that Germany would assume the leading role in the EEC, perhaps in all of Europe.

IMPLICATIONS FOR U.S. INDUSTRIAL PROPERTY POLICY

The theme of the Workshop on Industrial and Intellectual Property at the World Peace Through Law Conference in Geneva which I moderated was "the improvement of the international role of industrial property with a view to transferring technology to developing countries as a means of accelerating their economic growth." If patent protection could induce investment in, and transfer of, technology to less industrialized nations, these nations could presumably achieve a higher material standard of living and a greater degree of economic development. Greater tangible wealth might make nations less inclined to take military risks, and the cause of world peace would accordingly be promoted.

The transfer of technological information was, indeed, uppermost in the minds of the representatives from the less developed nations to the Geneva Conference. The representatives of the industrialized nations to the Conference were sympathetic, of course, but their interest seemed to center on the development of international trade, the problems of world peace, and the ethical obligations of the "have" nations to provide for the "have-not" nations. The last consideration was, as might be expected, most evident in the talk of American representatives.

In the interviews I conducted after leaving Geneva, I did not find as much interest as I had anticipated in the transfer of technological information from the highly developed to the lesser-developed nations. I had somehow expected that a U.N. resolution[14] and subsequent report[15] on the subject would have a greater impact than they did. Perhaps, the dominant economic position of the United States is encouraging other nations to feel less concerned with the technological welfare of the less-developed nations. Another possible explanation is the belief in an R&D "gap."[16] Since

[14]"In 1961, in the General Assembly of the United Nations, a draft resolution originating with the Brazilian delegation was presented demanding an investigation of the role of patents in the transfer of technology to underdeveloped countries.

"The original wording almost implied condemnation, but was toned down, as a result of well reasoned criticism by a number of interested organizations. The final resolution, dated December 19, 1961 directed the Secretary General to make a broad study of patents, and in particular the effect of patents granted to foreigners on the economy of underdeveloped nations." See note 6, *supra*, p. 109.

[15]*The Role of Patents in the Transfer of Technology to Developing Countries*, (Annes E): U.N. Publication 65 II BI (1964).

"The resulting U.S. Report has now been issued, dated February 14, 1964. It is fair, objective, and is based not only on theoretical research, but on an extensive questionnaire sent to over fifty countries and many interested organizations. It is well worth reading for itself, and as a sample of U.N. activity. It establishes factually and conclusively that there is an unbalanced distribution of capital, technological skills and managerial skills between the developed and underdeveloped countries.

"The conclusion is that the grant of patents to foreigners in the underdeveloped countries is actually a factor for the correction rather than the creation of this unbalance." See note 6, *supra*, at p. 109.

[16]Smith Hempstone, a European correspondent of *The Washington Star*, reported that British Prime Minister Harold Wilson, in a speech delivered at the Lord Mayor's banquet in London's Guild Hall on November 13, 1967, stated that

we allegedly are so far ahead of the Europeans in our research and development, it may be believed that we can afford better than anyone to dispense technological largess.

Despite the lack of emphasis on transfer, the subject was never minimized, and was sometimes mentioned by interviewees. For example, when I asked a Dutch executive in a quasi-government position for his opinion of the proposed BIRPI Treaty, he added, after responding comprehensively, that, "for the underdeveloped nations, it might be wise to institute a cheap, practical system attuned to their simple needs for the next 25 years."

We should not overlook the fact that the industrial property laws of various European countries already have striking similarities.[17] Furthermore, an organized effort is being directed toward the reworking of such laws within the context of trading blocs.[18] Indeed, the countries of Europe seem to be engaged in harmonization on a European basis.[19] The commonalities which already exist in the industrial property laws of these countries portend a successful outcome of the harmonization process. References by interviewees to new laws enacted and to other laws being enacted or still contemplated evidenced satisfaction with action toward harmonization. The reworking of the laws of the cooperative economic groups, on the other hand, did not seem to signify for the respondents any early successful achievement of a common multinational framework for industrial property. The current interest in patent cooperation seems pan-European,[20] or even more broadly international.

The Netherlands law granting patents under a deferred exam-

(in Mr. Hempstone's words) "the technology gap between Europe and the United States . . . is 'ominously widening' year by year and if allowed to continue would leave Europeans as 'hewers of wood and drawers of water,' " *The Evening Star*, November 14, 1967.

[17]Although two basically unlike systems are operating in Western Europe today, certain provisions appear more or less similar, (e.g., provisions relating to first-to-file procedure, grace period [derived from inventor or invention], applicants entitled to apply, cancellation proceedings, renewal fees, and licensing or compulsory working).

[18]E.g., proposed European Patent Convention, Nordic Patent Convention, European Free Trade Association Patent Convention.

[19]Witness the Conventions of the Council of Europe relating to: (1) formalities required for patent application, (2) international classification of patents for invention, and (3) unification of certain points of substantive law on patents for invention.

[20]" . . . Wilson called on the continental nations to create with Britain 'a collective European technology.' "

"He emphasized that his proposals were separate from but not a substitute for, British membership in the Common Market. . . ." Smith Hempstone, note 16, *supra*.

ination procedure went into effect on January 1, 1964,[21] and a new law including a deferred procedure will shortly go into effect in Germany.[22] There, a major revision—which may take a number of years to complete—is under consideration in connection with the contemplated "great German patent law reform." The French contemplate extending their unique examination system to all technical fields;[23] and Denmark will very probably amend its patent laws to conform with those of the draft Nordic Patent Convention, except for Chapter III as previously mentioned. The inevitable accommodation between the industrial property laws of Europe, as they emerge from their current state of flux, was pointed up by a representative of Danish industry, who explained that the "grace period in the Nordic patent stems from the grace period in the EEC proposed patent law."[24] He added that, although there is no grace period in the present Danish law,[25] the new Danish patent bill includes a six-month grace period if the invention is derived from the applicant in bad faith (a similar period is provided under German law).[26] In referring to the proposal for absolute novelty under the new Danish law, he also pointed out that a provision for absolute novelty is at present part of the French patent law.

A French government official went even further with respect to novelty. He stated that "the Strasbourg Convention incorporates absolute novelty; and, if the countries are to cooperate, they must all have provision for absolute novelty in their laws."[27]

----

[21]A report on deferred examination in operation is made by the head of the Dutch Patent Office in "Industrial Property Relations with Industrialized Nations: The Deferred Examination System," C. J. de Haan, *IDEA*, Vol. 9, Conference Number (1965), p. 227.

[22]For background information on the new German law, see Dr. Gerd Hiete and Dipl. Ing. Anton Huber, "Vorschläge der Prüfer des Deutschen Patentamts und der Richter des Bundespatentgerichts zur Neuregelung des Patenterteilungsverfahrens," *Mitteilungen der deutschen Patentanwälte*, Vol. 57, No. 6 (June 1966), p. 105.

[23]Bill No. 244, on the reform of the French Patent Law, was introduced in the French National Assembly in the Spring of 1967.

[24]"The interesting thing is that the final proposals [for the Nordic Patent Convention] were made after very careful study of the draft European Patent Convention and consultation with the officials of the Common Market Commission in Brussels. Certain of the proposals in the European Patent Convention have been incorporated." See note 6, *supra*, at p. 108.

[25]The Danish Patent Act of 1st September, 1936, with Amendments, Latest by Act No. 508 of 20th December, 1950, English translation published by The Comptroller of Patents, Copenhagen (1951).

[26]This is a narrower and shorter type of grace period than the period provided under U.S. law, which extends for a year and also covers third party disclosures.

[27]In discussing the recommendation for absolute novelty in the Report of

An appreciation of the strength of the tide running in favor of harmonization can be obtained from the enactment of deferred examination laws in certain countries and from the imminence of such laws elsewhere despite formidable opposition. Thus, the deferred examination system took root in the Netherlands notwithstanding opposition from many highly regarded individuals.[28] Likewise, it will become the law in Germany over the opposition of a majority of German patent examiners and patent attorneys and many industrialists. In the words of a German government official, "some support for the new law came from industry and the Patent Office, but the major sponsor was the Ministry of Justice." There also appears to be opposition to the deferred examination in France.

A French patent attorney confided to me that "a deferred examination system would not be introduced in France." He was convinced that, for France, "one likely alternative would entail the immediate examination of the patent application; and another would allow the patent application to be issued without any examination at all."

A representative of French industry thought differently. He considered a deferred examination system likely, although he was unhappy about the prospect: "Deferred examination is not a good system. It keeps all parties uncertain of their rights for too long."

In Denmark, I learned from an industry representative that the deferred examination system "was discussed in the Danish Parliament as a substitute for a Nordic patent system (to which the Danes are opposed). Danish industry particularly prefers deferred examination to the Nordic patent." A Danish patent agent sup-

the President's Commission on the U.S. Patent System, a highly regarded American expert on foreign patent law points out that "the extension of prior art to include public use anywhere in the world does not harmonize with the laws of Great Britain or any of the British Commonwealth countries, West Germany, Japan and Canada but does correspond to the definition of prior art in the unratified 'Substantive Patent Law Convention' of the Council of Europe, the proposed Nordic Patent Convention, and the ill-fated draft Common Market Patent Convention." S. Delvalle Goldsmith, "The United States Patent System: Has It Come to the End of the Line?," *IDEA*, Vol. 11, No. 3 (Fall 1967), p. 333.

[28]"Mr. Chairman, I know I am not unbiased, because before the new Dutch law was introduced I wrote an article in which I argued that the system would be a complete failure on account of the fact that Dutch inventors would request the novelty search immediately in order to determine whether it would be appropriate to file the same patent application abroad, whereas foreign applicants would have already made up their mind to this effect and would only file patent applications in Holland to obtain a patent, but would not be interested in having their patent applications pending. I must admit I was wrong and that the new system gives more than the expected savings. Like any new convert I am perhaps fanatical, but this has the advantage that you did find a convinced defender of the system for giving this talk to you." Unpublished talk given by C. M. R. Davidson on November 3, 1967, before the Institute of Patent Agents in Canada.

ported deferred examination on economic grounds. He stated that: "Deferred examination would relieve the Patent Office from wasting time and effort on inventions that may prove to be without practical purpose. Eighty percent of the applications in the Danish Patent Office are of foreign origin, and probably already have had the benefit of a novelty search in the patent offices of countries from which they came."

What message emerges for American industrial property policy from the foregoing brief discussion? Greater European harmonization and an increase in international arrangements[29] are inevitable, and we have much to gain from such cooperation. Although there is general awareness of American law and even admiration for parts of it in certain European quarters, the changes in European patent provisions are not likely to use our model. One of the obvious major reasons for this involution of patent law is that European countries face similar problems. A striking manifestation of this similarity is to be found in domestic-foreign distribution of patent applications processed by European patent offices—practically the reverse of the ratios which prevail in the United States.[30] Furthermore, European languages, attitudes, customs, traditions, institutions, and legal and social systems differ despite many "Western" commonalities; and Europeans must compete with each other in a relatively small geographic area.

This European quest for further harmonization extends even to the point of radical alteration of examination systems. Deferred examination is being commonly embraced by patent offices abroad as the solution to the influx of applications—which, in large part, are of foreign origin. Although this solution is not universally admired, it has caught the fancy of some[31] and is reluctantly acknowledged by others as the lesser of two evils. The Dutch, not yet entirely certain, are nevertheless advertising the effectiveness of the deferred-examination solution.[32] Curiously, a strong interest in

[29]For a recently published paper on current international patent problems and proposed international solutions, see Gerald O'Brien, note 9, *supra*.

[30]In this connection the reader may find of interest a paper comparing the inventiveness of nations by means of the relative proportion of domestic patented inventions also patented in other countries. See Barkev S. Sanders. "American Inventiveness," *IDEA*, Vol. 5, No. 2 (Summer 1961), p. 114.

[31]See proposal on deferred examination in Leonard J. Robbins' paper "Reform of the U.S. Patent Law and the Proposed Patent Cooperation Treaty," prepared for the FICPI meeting in Cannes in February, 1967.

Also see John Robert Duncan, "The European Patent Convention as a Guide to Modernizing Our Patent Examining System," *IDEA*, Vol. 8, No. 3 (Fall 1964), p. 405.

[32]"Results of the Netherlands Procedure for Granting Patents with Deferred Examination," unpublished paper by J. B. van Benthem, October 3, 1967; C. J.

harmonization was reflected in the reference by several experts to the "Substantive Patent Law Convention" of the Council of Europe, which has not yet been ratified by all the member countries. This interest also seems intimately associated with attitudes toward the proposed BIRPI PCT Treaty, supported only in part, however, by the interviewees. Indeed, some felt harmonization had to precede the Treaty; others felt that the Treaty would make for more harmonization; still others felt that harmonization should somehow replace the Treaty.[33]

Whatever the future of group arrangements, such as the proposed Common Market Patent Convention or the proposed Nordic Patent Convention, their emergence has had a definite impact on the European countries. Lack of vigorous support for these proposed group compacts (even though certain changes in domestic legislation originating from group patent proposals is favored) has, perhaps, resulted in more favorable action toward other modes of cooperation, such as harmonization.[34] Harmonization, like other international accords, appears to have a special fascination for the Europeans, but group arrangements cannot yet be counted out.

CONCLUSIONS

I am impressed that the industrial property policies of European nations are being pursued with a clear understanding of national purpose. We, too, should promote an understanding of our national objectives and pursue them consistently in international industrial property transactions. An ill-defined feeling has taken hold in certain quarters that our system somehow is out of step with other systems almost everywhere, that this lack of rapport is having an inhibiting effect on our international dealings. Is this notion exaggerated by the vigor of our energetic debates? Are the seeming advantages of European patent provisions due at least in

---

de Haan, "Industrial Property Relations with Industrialized Nations: Deferred Examination System," *IDEA*, Vol. 9, Conference No. (1965), p. 227; "Experiences with the New Dutch Patent Law," unpublished talk given by C. M. R. Davidson, note 28, *supra*.

[33]For alternate plans to the BIRPI PCT Treaty, see Stephen P. Ladas, note 9, *supra;* Leonard J. Robbins, note 31, *supra,* and the Patent Cooperation Treaty (Alternative Draft) dated September 20, 1967, prepared for the National Association of Manufacturers and presented by William R. Woodward at the Conference on International Patent Cooperation Treaty sponsored by The Federal Bar Association and The Bureau of National Affairs, September 20, 21, 1967.

[34]In discussing this point a colleague remarked: "In spite of all the talk about harmonization, the actual substantive changes in European patent laws that have gone into effect in the last decade or so, have really been of a very minor character. That is, most of the long established national 'flavor' still exists."

part to the paternalistic nature of European governments? How would such provisions actually stand up in our more open, pluralistic society? More important, can our own objectives be consistently pursued, given the peculiarities of our own democratic institutions?

Despite limited public appreciation of the fact, the United States already constitutes a highly advanced "common market."[35] Maybe, attention has not been directed toward the United States as such a market because it has always been one; because, being so much a part of our life, it is accepted as a matter of course. In contrast, the accomplishment of the EEC represented such a decisive break with a past of intense nationalistic and military rivalry that it shocked the world into a new attitude of respect.

My examination leads me to believe that we may not be appreciating our actual performance. We may be trying now to discard our experience and our historical advantage in vain pursuit of other systems developed under another sky and rooted in another soil. Thus, if we once again bring our situation into focus, we may find that we have the only group industrial property system that is operating, and that we should remain different from other nations to meet our continuing peculiar needs. Indeed, our group patent system began[36] and developed during a long period of ascent to, and maintenance of, technological dominance. Other countries that excel in particular branches of technology, nevertheless envy the scope and depth of U.S. superiority.[37]

In an earlier paper, I wrote: ". . . when the time comes for direct confrontation by the United States with the EEC, we might consider reciprocity of the U.S. Common Market with that of EEC, supported by a common political sympathy and cultural background. It behooves the free world to develop arrangements among the large trading blocs it comprises which maintain them in their full vigor and which are compatible with their long range interests and common objectives."[38] The potential of our group patent sys-

---

[35]See L. James Harris, "The First Modern Common Market: A Reinterpretation of the (British) Commonwealth," *IDEA*, Vol. 6, No. 2 (Summer 1962), p. 199.

[36]For a recently published scholarly treatise on early American patent history see Bruce W. Bugbee, *The Genesis of American Patent and Copyright Law* (Washington, D.C.: Public Affairs Press, 1967).

[37]". . . the widening technology gap between the United States and Europe are sore points in all continental countries.

"European dependence on American scientific advances is illustrated by the fact that Europe pays five times as much for the use of U.S. patents as America pays for European patents." Smith Hempstone, see *supra* note 15.

[38]L. James Harris, note 36, *supra*, at p. 223.

tem has amply been demonstrated; and much is to be gained by all from the reciprocal exchange of ideas and goods.

We should not reject opportunities to harmonize our laws with those of other nations and to enter into agreements that are in the *national* as well as in the international interest. Specifically, we should deal on more even terms, and even enhance our competitiveness, with other countries. Guilt over our achievement of technological and industrial supremacy, over our continuing benefit from a so-called "brain drain,"[39] is needless. In our relations with our own states, we have developed national systems of law, including our patent system, and we have developed skills of diplomacy. This experience and the instruments we have shaped should facilitate international harmonization and the fashioning of international arrangements relating to industrial property. While accepting foreign patent ideas of common advantage, we need not concede initiative or the upper hand to other states.

[39]"Scientific Brain Drain to U.S. Alarms Bonn," *The Evening Star*, November 16, 1967, p. A21.

A Realistic Appraisal of the Draft Patent Cooperation Treaty

GERALD D. O'BRIEN

On May 31, 1967, the United International Bureaux for the Protection of Intellectual Property (BIRPI) released to the public a draft Patent Cooperation Treaty. The Treaty was subsequently published in the June 13, 1967, issue of the *Official Gazette* of the U.S. Patent Office.

The purpose of this paper is to review the background underlying the proposed Treaty and to explain some of its important features.

THE PROBLEM

As has been stated so many times in recent years by prominent American businessmen, patent practitioners, and officials of patent offices through the world,[1] the international patent system is inadequately equipped to serve today's needs. Added to an unprecedented explosion of patent applications of increased complexity being filed world-wide is the all but impossible burden of effectively managing these applications within the structure of more than 80 separate and widely divergent patent laws and procedures. The increasing number of duplicate and multiple patent applications for the same invention is a natural and proper consequence of the rapid acceleration of world trade, especially during the past decade.

Solutions must be found to minimize those difficulties for applicants and patent offices which are the consequence of the multiplicity of complex and divergent national patent procedures. Most commentators are frank to admit that there is no other escape and that the clear alternative is an utter collapse of the patent system or such seri-

EDITOR'S NOTE: This paper was published in *IDEA,* Vol. 11, No. 2. The author has written a postscript for this volume.

[1]Kurt Haertel, President of the German Patent Office: "Crises of National Patent Systems and Necessity of International Solutions." Conference on "World Patent Systems," conducted by the National Association of Manufacturers at New York City in June 1965.

Martin Kalikow, Patent Counsel, IGE Export Division: Speech at The 175th Anniversary of the U.S. Patent System, October 20, 1965.

John R. Shipman, Director of International Patent Operations, IBM Corporation: "International Patent Planning," *Harvard Business Review* (March-April 1967).

ous alteration of its fundamental principles as to render it virtually impotent to serve its proper function as an impetus to innovation and as a stimulant to world trade.[2]

Typical of comments addressed to this problem is the recent statement of David Sarnoff, Chairman of the Board of RCA, at an Inter-Industry Conference on International Patents held in Frankfurt, Germany, on June 7, 1967. General Sarnoff said:

> Nearly 350 years after the introduction of the first patent law, we are still burdened with a fragmented territorial concept of patent coverage. An inventor is still compelled to go through separate and often widely different procedures in nearly every nation where he seeks to establish title to his work.
>
> A sharp rise in the volume of patent applications strains the facilities and manpower of individual patent offices. In member countries of the Paris Union, the number of applications grew by nearly 50 percent during the last ten years.

One year earlier, General Sarnoff, speaking at the Tenth Annual Public Conference of The PTC Research Institute, challenged his audience with the following statement:

> One of today's principal challenges is to design an international patent structure that can accommodate the revolutionary changes in technology and spread its benefits more evenly around the world. Through the tremendous advances that have been made in one aspect of this technology—in communications—the physical means are available to accomplish this purpose. It is now technically feasible to establish a universal patent system, utilizing the latest communications devices and concepts, to bring swiftness, order, and reasonable uniformity to the entire patent structure.[3]

Surprisingly, the occasion for such statements of the problem and calls for remedial action have not been limited to the past few years. In fact, the same points have been made time and time again, each time with the same sense of urgency, at least for the past half-century. Indeed, as early as 1909, a French patent attorney named Reymond, in proposing an international patent convention to the very first meeting of AIPPI, the International Association for the Protection of Industrial Property, was frank to express a degree of frustration about the dilemma which has persisted down to this day. On that occasion, Reymond said:

> While complaints are heard on all sides about the continually overburdening of the patent offices, serious men sit in the various offices and torment themselves in carrying out the same work.[4]

---

[2]*EFTA Reporter* (European Free Trade Association), No. 165 (June 26, 1967): Excerpts from an interview given by E. Armitage, Assistant Comptroller in the British Patent Office and Chairman of the EFTA Working Party on Patents.

[3]See p. 622, *infra.*

[4]C. P. Tootal, "Prospects of Further International Cooperation in the Field of Patents," *Transactions of the Chartered Institute of Patent Agents,* Vol. LXXIX (Session 1960-61), p. C92.

Little did he dream that almost 60 years later a world which is capable of sending a manned space vehicle to the moon would tolerate more than a quarter million duplicate or multiple patent filings. The point is rested here because much has been said and written about the problems—so much that more than one prominent patent attorney has been frankly critical of the many meetings, surveys, and studies which have been devoted to the preparation of groundwork for action in this field. These people have been urging, "We already know what the problems are in international patents. What we want to hear about are solutions!"

OFFICE OF INTERNATIONAL PATENT AND TRADEMARK AFFAIRS

The Office of International Patent and Trademark Affairs (OIPTA) was established in September 1964, largely as a result of initiative from Commissioner Edward J. Brenner and Assistant Secretary J. Herbert Hollomon, for the express purpose of developing positive programs for solving the problems which were apparent to everyone in both the private and public sectors of the patent system.[5] At the time of the formation of this new office, a significant aspect of the situation was that most of the post-World War II initiative towards multilateral cooperation had been developed and sponsored by European patent people under the sponsorship of European institutions. Accordingly, a corollary purpose of OIPTA was to seek a leadership position for the United States in its search for practical solutions.

International Patent Program and Objectives

Initially, OIPTA launched a series of statistical studies, surveys, and analyses of the situation in order to provide a basis for formulating a program and a strategy for achieving the desired objectives. The program which emerged consisted of several parts, the central direction of which was toward the ultimate goal of an international patent system.[6]

---

[5]Address by the Commissioner of Patents, Edward J. Brenner, before the Indiana State Bar Association, Fort Wayne, Indiana, September 19, 1964.

[6]"U.S. to Launch World Patent System Drive," *Journal of Commerce* (September 25, 1964).

Vincent Travaglini, "Exporters Have Important Stake in Protecting Their Industrial Property Rights Outside the U.S.," *Daily Commercial News and Shipping Guide* (Los Angeles, California).

"International Patent Situation Examined During 3-Day Conference," *International Commerce* (October 25, 1965).

The central core of the program consisted of a series of bilateral studies and exchanges with other patent offices which had also expressed considerable concern about the international patent problems and indicated their desire to enter into cooperative programs with the United States that hopefully would point the way toward solutions. As a consequence of this initiative, bilateral programs are now under way with the patent offices of a large number of countries, including West Germany, Switzerland, Sweden, France, Japan, Philippines, Czechoslovakia, and Austria.

The principle purpose of these programs was to develop a data base for further cooperation.

United States—West Germany Search Exchange

For example, the first program launched was an experimental exchange of search results on 2,000 patent applications on each of which a later corresponding case had been filed either in the United States (1,000 cases) or in West Germany (1,000 cases).[7]

Although the results of this experimental exchange are not conclusive, the exchange was both beneficial and encouraging from several standpoints.[8]

First, in a substantial number of cases, examiners in both countries received material assistance from the search results of the other office both from the standpoint of improving the quality of their examinations and as a means of saving time.

Second, the exchange served to isolate those differences between the U.S. and German practice which would affect the usefulness of search results in the receiving office. Several follow-up studies on the cases involved in the exchange promise to produce still further insight into these differences.

Third, and perhaps most important of all, the exchange provided a unique opportunity for examiners in the patent offices of each country to share, in the context of active cases, the experience of qualified examiners in the other country while examining the same disclosures.

Although the above-listed benefits were limited to the small

---

[7]Harvey Winter, Business Practices Division, U.S. State Department, in his address entitled "USG International Patent Policy," before the International Patent and Trademark Association in Washington, D. C. January 25, 1966, stated:

> The long range goal of the United States in the international patent field is the development of an international system under which a single patent would be effective in many countries. And we do not believe this is a utopian goal.

[8]Joint Report on U.S.-German Search Exchange, 838 O.G. 1225 (May 23, 1967).

number of cases involved, the patent offices of the United States and West Germany have concluded that the exchange produced sufficient benefits to warrant proceeding with a continuing search exchange, on all cases filed in both countries.[9] This continuing exchange, which eliminates the elaborate record keeping of the experiment, is now in effect for some cases and will be fully implemented within the next few months.

Other Bilateral Programs

Other bilateral exchange and study programs are intended to provide the Patent Office with further insight into the differences in patent examination practices, while at the same time, hopefully will provide savings of time and increased quality of examination. The Swiss exchange, for example, is providing a unique opportunity to evaluate the quality of searches performed by the International Patent Institute at The Hague (IIB). This international searching organization does all of the searching for the Swiss in the fields of horology and textile treatment, the only fields in which the Swiss patent office performs an examination. The IIB also supplies search reports on a contract basis for other member countries.[10]

The United States—Philippine program, details of which are soon to be announced to the public, involves the exchange of examination results rather than merely search reports and includes a procedure, optional to applicants, under which we will be able to test whether savings in the burden of duplicate prosecution will be possible for U.S. applicants as well as for the Philippine patent office.

A bilateral program with the French patent office, including an exchange of search results quite similar to the Swiss program, is soon to be initiated. This exchange concerns only one field of technology, pharmaceuticals, which is the only field in which the French presently conduct an examination. However, its importance may be much greater in the future, since France has recently intro-

---

[9]Address by Commissioner of Patents, Edward J. Brenner, before the Patent, Trademark, and Copyright Section of the American Bar Association, August 5, 1967.

[10]The International Patent Institute is a nonprofit organization established as a result of a diplomatic agreement signed at The Hague in 1947 on behalf of the governments of Belgium, France, Luxembourg and the Netherlands, to which agreement the governments of Monaco, Morocco, Switzerland, Turkey and the United Kingdom have also subscribed. The official name of the Institute is "Institut International des Brevets." The Institute's function is to carry out documentary research novelty reports and others of a technical nature for the benefit of the governments of the member countries and also on behalf of industrial undertakings, inventors and others who require technical information for the protection of industrial property interests.

duced legislation which would eventually expand examination to all fields, using the IIB as its searching facility.[11]

Parallel to the bilateral exchange and study programs has been involvement of the U.S. Patent Office in international efforts toward harmonization of patent laws and procedures and improved documentation and information retrieval techniques.

Harmonization and Documentation

The Paris Convention has over the years been strengthened from the standpoint of bringing the nations of the world closer together in regard to some fundamental aspects of patent law. There have also been harmonization efforts on a regional basis, the best known of which are the three conventions of the Council of Europe on patent application formalities, points of substantive law, and patent classification.[12] The Nordic countries have virtually accomplished a complete conformity of patent laws after a concerted effort of an intergovernmental committee which has been working toward this goal over the past 15 years.[13]

In documentation, the United States was a leader in establishing ICIREPAT, an informal intergovernmental organization of examining patent offices which has been engaged for a number of years in coordinating the development by member countries of mechanized search systems for shared use by other members.[14] Similarly, the last few years have seen a considerable increase in the amount of collaboration in the field of patent classification. Cooperation is now contemplated in the equally important development of microform reproduction systems for patent documents.[15]

[11] The French National Assembly in the session ending July 1, 1967 adopted the proposed Bill, No. 244, introduced May 23, 1967 on the reform of the French Patent Law. Action by the Senate is expected in the course of the next fall session.

[12] Council of Europe—Convention on the Unification of Certain Points of Substantive Law on Patents for Invention (1963); European Convention on the International Classification of Patents for Invention (1954); European Convention Relating to the Formalities Required for Patent Application (1953). The background of these conventions is summarized in the Report of the Secretary General of the United Nations entitled "The Role of Patents in the Transfer of Technology to Developing Countries," Document E/3861/Revil, (1964).

[13] S. Lewin, Chief of Division, Swedish Patent Office: "The Proposal for Unification of the Patent System in Scandinavia," *JPOS* (June 1965).

[14] Proceedings of International Patent Office Workshop for Information Retrieval, Part II of Proceedings of The 175th Anniversary of the U.S. Patent System.

Proceedings of the 2nd, 3rd, 4th, and 5th Annual Meetings of ICIREPAT (Committee for International Cooperation in Information Retrieval Among Examining Patent Offices).

Proceedings of the Executive Sessions of the 2nd, 3rd, 4th, 5th, and 6th Annual Meetings of ICIREPAT. ICIREPAT *Bulletins* Nos. 1-17.

[15] Address by the Commissioner of Patents, Edward J. Brenner, delivered at the Annual Meeting of the Industrial Research Institute, Inc., May 31, 1967.

Background of Multilateral Approach

Until the spring of 1966, this three-phase program of the International Office constituted the principal thrust toward achieving some relief to the pressing international patent problems. However, at about that time, considerable evidence began to emerge that the program and strategy were inadequate to produce practical benefits soon enough to relieve the near impossible burden on applicants or to provide significant assistance to examining patent offices.

First was a realization based on experience that bilateral programs could only be developed beneficially to a certain point. The difficulty with bilateral programs, it was found, was not only the slowness of their progress but the fact that increasing the scope of cooperation in these programs and the corresponding benefits to be derived from them required changes in practices and law on a bilateral basis. While such changes might improve the results as between the two involved countries, these changes might not be at all consistent with the situation called for with a third country, and so forth. Accordingly, it was recognized that the program should be expanded to include a multilateral phase.

Confirming this conclusion were the results of an international survey conducted by the Office of International Patent and Trademark Affairs during the fall of 1965, the returns of which were received and tabulated in the spring of the following year. The forum for this survey consisted of approximately 235 companies which had been assigned more than 200 U.S. patent applications between the years 1942 and 1962. Replies to the survey questionnaire were received from 140, or approximately 60 percent, of the companies in this category. These replies, by and large, reflected the viewpoints of patent counsel for these companies which represented a meaningful sampling of the view of patent professionals on the international problems which existed in the patent field and the solutions which seemed to them to be called for. In addition, the survey provided valuable statistical information on the extent of foreign filings, particularly as to the magnitude of duplication involved in these filings. Two of the questions in this survey were open-end requests for the opinions of respondents on the problems encountered in international patent practice and solutions which they deemed most practical to consider.

The survey also indicated an interest in more advanced steps, especially in the areas of simplification of filing procedures for international patent protection, the harmonization of formal requirements and the elimination of duplicate searching, examination, and prosecution of patent applications filed in more than one country.

These points will be covered in more detail later in this paper, but the survey is mentioned here as part of the evidence which stimulated the Patent Office toward expanding the outlines of our program to include a broader, multilateral approach.

The Patent Office participated in a number of meetings, seminars and individual discussions with patent practitioners in the United States which served to reinforce the notion that more dramatic and far-reaching action would be required. Indeed, the whole tenor of attitudes expressed at meetings sponsored by the National Association of Manufacturers, The PTC Research Institute, and the Commemorative Committee for The 175th Anniversary of the U.S. Patent System was that the Patent Office should do more toward expanding the scope and extent of its international programs.

Another indicator came from other countries, principally in Europe. Reports from these countries revealed a sense of urgency about the need for international cooperation as constituting the last hope to preserve sound and effective patent systems. Efforts by the European Common Market countries to develop a European patent were bogged down because of various political considerations.[16] Implementation of the Nordic patent system was delayed. European officials expressed to Commissioner Brenner and other officials of the Patent Office a strong desire to support cooperation on a broader basis with the United States and other non-European countries included as working partners.

All of these indications culminated in a proposal by the Departments of Commerce and State to initiate action on a multilateral basis under the sponsorship of BIRPI[17] which had long been the focal point for worldwide collaboration in the patent field.

---

[16]See Statement by Jean Monnet "Scope of Patent Protection Within the Common Market" in "Creative Ferment in World Patent Systems." National Association of Manufacturers, June 1965.

[17]BIRPI is the joint international Secretariat of the Paris and Berne Unions. It is one of the oldest international secretariats in the world. It started functioning more than 80 year ago and continued functioning without interruption through two world wars.

BIRPI stands for Bureaux Internationaux Réunis pour la Protection de la Propriété Intellectuelle. The expression "Intellectual Property" covers both industrial property and copyright. "Bureaux" means in this context Office or Secretariat. "Réunis" refers to the fact that it is a joint or united Secretariat for both the Paris and the Berne Unions.

Since 1960, BIRPI's headquarters have been in Geneva, Switzerland. Before that date they were in Berne, Switzerland.

Among other things, BIRPI carries out a program of legal technical assistance for developing countries, helping them to deal with their patent, trademark, and copyright problems. BIRPI's revenues (approximately $1,000,000 per year) come from the contributions of member States, from the fees paid by applicants for the international registration of trademarks and from the sale of publications.

Before taking this step, a plan to present a resolution to the Executive Committee of the Paris Convention was explained to a representative group of interested patent practitioners in the United States. The group included inhouse patent counsels for companies having extensive international patent filings, representatives of leading international patent firms engaged in the filing of patent applications for large and small American companies, and members of prominent domestic patent law firms.

With this background, the United States presented a resolution to the Executive Committee of the Paris Union in Geneva, Switzerland, on September 29, 1966.[18] This resolution took note of the substantial and growing volume of patent applications of increasing complexity, of the considerable duplication involved in these filings, and of the need to simplify the procedures for obtaining protection of inventions throughout the world. The resolution recommended that studies be undertaken on an urgent basis and that such studies include the consideration of concluding special agreements within the framework of the Paris Union.

The resolution was adopted by a unanimous vote. This was particularly significant because the membership of the Executive Committee which acted upon it was broadly representative of the world patent community, including in addition to important European countries, the United States, Japan, and many other countries widely scattered geographically and diverse in their approach to industrial property protection. It seemed clear that the unanimous vote evidenced widespread interest in early and serious efforts to find solutions.

The decision to opt for a broader multilateral approach was announced publicly by Commissioner Brenner at a meeting sponsored by the National Association of Manufacturers in Washington on October 11, 1966. At this time, Commissioner Brenner said:

> You will appreciate, from what I have already said, that we believe that a total systems approach is needed to solve the problems we face. One might easily argue that the foundations of harmonization ought to precede a multilateral exchange and acceptance agreement. However, it seems to us that such a limited approach is neither essential nor feasible at this stage of our dilemma. This does not mean we are going to blithely ignore the necessary foundation work. However, we believe it is necessary to begin prefabricating the structure of the system itself while the foundation is being laid.

Two monthly periodicals in two languages—one dealing with industrial property, the other with copyright—report on the changes in the Unions and in the national legislations; they contain information on BIRPI's activities and articles on intellectual property questions.

[18]*Industrial Property*, No. 10 (October 1966), p. 229.

Initially, the extent to which the results will be able to eliminate duplication and to expedite the obtaining of protection may be limited. In some cases the principal benefit will be to improve the quality of issued patents. However, as the foundation stones of harmonization are set into place, the prefabricated structure of the system will more quickly take shape and we will then be in striking distance of the eventual goal.

There is really nothing very unique about this kind of approach to development of a patent system. Indeed, our own system in its infancy 175 years ago was composed of a very simple, uncomplicated framework consisting merely of the formalities of filing and issue. The solid substance which has made it into one of the most effective patent systems in the world was added later and only then as a result of many years of dedicated work and gradual evolution of its fundamental principles and its administrative refinements. However, I don't believe any of us would suggest that it was not an historically significant achievement that it was boldly launched in spite of the fact that its founders must have appreciated its apparent deficiencies at the outset.

In response to this resolution, the officials of BIRPI moved promptly by organizing a series of consultations with experts from six states which had the largest number of patent applications, including a representative from the International Patent Institute at The Hague. The energy displayed by BIRPI in these steps was all the more impressive since BIRPI at the same time was heavily involved in preparations for the Stockholm Conference of 1967, which involved significant proposals in the field of international copyright protection as well as a move to strengthen the administrative structure for the various conventions for which it had secretariat responsibility. In spite of this full schedule of other activities, BIRPI prepared a first draft which was distributed to selected consultants on January 1, 1967.[19] Several drafts followed before the draft released on May 31, 1967, was published for broad scale consideration. During this period of time, the U.S. Patent Office followed the progress of BIRPI in this effort. The Office of International Patent and Trademark Affairs and the Department of State engaged in numerous informal discussions of the provisions of the preliminary drafts with various patent professionals.

A meeting of a six-country expert team was held in Geneva in February 1967, as a result of which the first draft was extensively revised. Prior to this meeting, the Departments of State and Commerce met with selected representatives of the same interests previously consulted and their views were taken into account in preparing

[19]"BIRPI Plan for Facilitating the Filing and Examination of Applications for the Protection of the Same Invention in a Number of Countries," Copy of BIRPI document PCT/INF/1, dated February 28, 1967. *Industrial Property*, No. 3 (March 1967).

for the February deliberations in Geneva. On March 30, 1967, the Deputy Director of BIRPI released a Progress Report on the Treaty at a Federal Bar Association Briefing Conference in Boston attended by more than 200 patent attorneys. The Departments of State and Commerce held a briefing session on the Treaty in April 1967, to which representatives of 50 U.S. companies were invited.

The preparation of the draft of the Treaty released on May 31 followed these meetings. BIRPI then scheduled a meeting of a Committee of Experts, October 2-10, 1967.

Attendance at this October meeting includes representatives of 23 Paris Union countries, seven intergovernmental organizations, and numerous private associations, including the International Association for the Protection of Industrial Property, the International Chamber of Commerce, and the National Association of Manufacturers.

OUTLINE OF DRAFT PCT TREATY

The proposed Treaty is a highly integrated proposal which, nevertheless, for purposes of analysis, may be divided into two phases.

Phase I is called "Central Filing Plus Search Report." This phase would be obligatory for all Contracting States and for all applicants wishing to file internationally.

Phase II is a more advanced stage which involves the establishment of what is called a "Certificate of Patentability." Cooperation in this second phase would be optional for the Contracting States, and each applicant would decide for himself whether he wanted to take advantage of this advanced phase.

It is important to note that the drafters did not contemplate in either phase a universal patent which would have extraterritorial effect in the member countries. Although the President's Commission on the Patent System recommended this as an eventual goal,[20] the present proposal does not go that far. National patenting remains the function of each country.

Under Phase I, the applicant files a single international application with the International Bureau. This filing may be made directly to that Bureau or, more likely, through the intermediary of the applicant's national office. For U.S. applicants it would likely be filed in the U.S. Patent Office. The applicant designates the coun-

---

[20]*Report of the President's Commission on the Patent System* (Washington: G.P.O., 1966).

tries in which he desires protection. This initial designation is tentative, required to be made final with payment of a small designation fee only after the search results have been seen and an opportunity to amend the claims given. The application is filed in English (one of several selected official languages—French, English, German, and perhaps others). In addition, the international application is drafted according to a standard format which would be acceptable to all member countries.

If found acceptable as to form by the International Bureau, the international application is searched by a qualified searching authority, which then sends out a search report to the applicant as well as to the International Bureau. It is anticipated that the technical operations of the International Bureau will be handled by such searching authorities functioning under contract with the central Secretariat. These searching authorities would probably include three or four of the principal national patent offices which are willing and able to undertake these responsibilities, as well as the International Patent Institute at The Hague.

Upon transmittal of the search report to the applicant, he is then allowed to amend his claims. Thereafter, the application together with the search report is sent to the Contracting States designated by the applicant.

During this first phase of the Treaty, the application and search reports are to be published in an *International Gazette* within 18 to 24 months from the effective filing date of the application. In most cases, this publication will not take place until the applicant has had an opportunity to review and consider the search report and to amend the claims or withdraw his application.

If the country receiving the application and search report is a registration country, such as France, the application is likely to be published in that country as a French patent. France could refuse this effect, if for example, the application covered subject matter not considered to be patentable subject matter in France. Perhaps a better example is Italy, another registration country which does not today consider pharmaceutical patents to be proper subject matter.[21] However, if the country receiving the application plus the search report is an examining country, such as Germany, the

---

[21]Another example can be found in the United States in the Atomic Energy Act of 1964, 42 US 2181, which states "No patent shall hereafter be granted for any invention or discovery which is useful solely in the utilization of special nuclear material or atomic energy in an atomic weapon."

application may be subjected to examination by that country, which would be the sole judge to decide whether the international application complied with its national law. The German system includes a provision for opposition by third parties based on the knowledge of prior art which has not been found in the course of the examination. Such procedures would continue to be applicable to the international case.

In other words, the effect of an international application in each Contracting State is that of a regular national application.

To summarize the first phase:

(1) A *single* application is filed in one of several selected languages;

(2) After a formal check this application is then submitted to a single worldwide *search*;

(3) Upon modification of the claims by the applicant, the application and the search are then *communicated to the* designated Contracting States;

(4) And, shortly thereafter, worldwide publication of this document occurs within 18 to 24 months from the effective filing date.

Under Phase II, the applicant may, at any time before the expiration of the time limit allowed for amending claims, request a full examination and obtain an international Certificate of Patentability. This certificate is issued, or denied, after an examination carried out by a qualified examining office. Here again the operations of the International Bureau would be carried out by three or four principal patent offices and the International Patent Institute at The Hague. The conditions which each invention has to meet in order to be entitled to an international certificate include worldwide novelty, nonobviousness, and utility or industrial applicability. In the case of a denial, the applicant can be heard by an international review board comprising highly qualified examiners. If issued, the international certificate is communicated to the states designated by the applicant and would provide the basis for issuance of national patents provided requirements of national law are satisfied.

The international certificate is then communicated to the designated countries and published in the *International Gazette*. In the receiving countries, the certificate would furnish a basis for issuing national patents. The Treaty does not, even in this second phase, preempt the authority of national offices. Thus, in some countries today, there are provisions for the citation of prior art by third parties which might take over at this stage.

INTERNATIONAL PATENT SURVEY

The key features of the Treaty are directly responsive to a number of the international patent problems as they were expressed in the survey referred to above. These features of the treaty will be outlined in the context of the survey responses.

Diversity of Formal Requirements

There is today virtually no consistency or agreement among the various countries on the formal requirements of a patent application. The diversity extends to such routine matters as the size of paper which must be used or the size and type of drawings which must be included.

A recurring complaint of the respondents to this survey was that this unnecessary diversity all but precluded the possibility of using a single format for international filing. Not only does this increase costs of preparation, it leads, in many instances, to bickering with foreign patent officials on purely formal matters having little or no relationship to the value or substance of the invention.

The Treaty seeks to respond to this concern by providing as an alternative to the many national filings that are now required a single international application format. So long as the international application conforms to the standard format it must be accepted by the member countries. Of course, if it fails to comply with the standard format, the application may be rejected, this rejection being subject to review either by an international bureau or, in certain cases, by recourse to the national patent office involved. In any event, the remedy is broader than it exists today under national filing requirements.

Time for Committing Resources

To obtain the benefits of the Paris Convention with respect to priority, an applicant today must file all of his foreign patent applications within one year of his national filing. Because of the time involved in obtaining translations and in preparing the foreign applications, decisions as to filing abroad must usually be made before the commercial or scientific worth of the invention is determined.

The largest number of comments addressed to a single problem area were concerned with this difficulty. Companies stated that because of the timing they were either required to file on applications which later turned out to be of little value or, alternatively, neglected on those applications which proved important.

Several aspects of the Treaty are pertinent to this problem. By providing a single international filing under which the applicant may tentatively elect the countries in which he is interested, applicant may defer committing his resources until he has obtained an indication of the patentability of the invention which will occur, in most cases, outside the 12-month Convention period. Thus, it may be anticipated that applicants filing internationally under the Treaty will elect all or substantially all of the participating countries since there is no additional cost for such an election.

The Treaty offers two alternatives to enter the international filing system: by first filing an international application, either directly with the International Bureau or through the intermediary of his own national patent office; or by first filing a national patent application in a country which is a member of the Paris Union followed by the international application which will benefit by the priority of the first filed national case, provided it is filed within the priority year.

In the context of the Paris Convention, a distinction must be made between the date of filing and the date of receipt of the international application by the International Bureau. In every case, where the international application is a second application claiming priority benefits it must be filed, just as at present, within the priority year else the applicant will lose his priority. Thus, in such a case, if the international filing is made directly at the International Bureau it must be filed there prior to the expiration of one year from the date of the first filing.

If, on the other hand, it is made throught the intermediary of a national office then the application must be filed in such national office prior to the end of the one-year priority term. The mere fact that, in this latter case, the national office is given a reasonable time for forwarding the second application to the International Bureau does not mean that the Paris Convention deadline has been extended.

While not altering the Convention priority term, the draft Treaty does offer a substantial advantage, equivalent to one of the principal purposes of the priority term, in deferring the time when the heaviest cost obligations of foreign filing must be committed. Chief among these is the expense of translations into the national language of each country in which protection is desired. Under present practice, this cost must be obligated by about the ninth month in order to assure that national filings are made prior to expiration of the twelfth month. Under the Treaty, applicants filing in one of the official languages can defer this expense until after the international application is communicated. This could be up to 24 months under Phase I and even longer if a Certificate of Patentability is requested under Phase II.

The Language Barrier

A recurring and underlying problem frequently mentioned in the survey by many respondents rests in the basic realm of communication of ideas. The most important aspect is the language barrier which increases expense and lowers effectiveness both in dealing with foreign patent offices and with attorneys and agents located in foreign countries. This frequently leads to a misunderstanding of the invention by the foreign patent office. Moreover, this misunderstanding frequently cannot be conveyed through the intermediary of double translations required when U.S. concerns attempt to respond to the foreign patent office objections and rejections. By providing for the basic filing, search, examination, and prosecution of the application in English, the language problems now encountered are minimized.

Moreover, in the prosecution of an application, a U.S. applicant may deal with his U.S. attorney, who is most familiar with his case. In most cases for U.S. applicants, this will result in completion of the examination in foreign countries sooner than is now possible.

Multiple Searches

A problem frequently mentioned in the survey resulted from the fact that each searching office now conducts its own search of the invention as though a search on the same application was not being carried out in another office. This results in evaluating the invention against different prior art and involves a substantial amount of duplication both for the applicant and for the search offices. In turn, this latter duplication creates backlogs which delay the issuance of patents.

The Treaty in part alleviates this problem by providing for a single international search to be conducted by qualified searching facilities. While the search files of these facilities will—at least in the initial steps of the Treaty—not be identical and while additional national searching may still be required, the Treaty moves in a direction of the goal of a single highly qualified search using an international search file. Moreover, the Treaty draws upon the existing facilities both of national patent offices and the International Patent Institute, which is more realistic at this point in history than to attempt to create a single international organization capable of handling the expected workload.

CONCLUSION

Certainly one of the benefits of the Treaty is to simplify international filing of patent applications and these simplified procedures will naturally lead to an increased interest in broader protection.

The U.S. patent system has been designed to encourage the patenting of new inventions. Indeed, substantially the entire patent profession strongly urged this point in connection with the patent fee legislation which resulted in increased fees in the United States a few years ago. The point was made at that time that an effective patent system should encourage the filing of patent applications. No one has ever suggested that we should make it more difficult for foreign inventors to file and obtain patent protection in the United States.

Looking at this question from an overall viewpoint, it is clear that the Treaty is not designed to reduce the number of inventions for which patent protection is requested. The aim of the Treaty is to eliminate the duplication of effort found in the multiple processing and examination of these inventions. The number of inventions for which applications are filed in a single country (usually the home country of the inventor) is not increasing to any marked extent. Rather it is the multiple filing of the same invention that has created the international problem. It is the view of most people that the patent system of the world should and must be capable of dealing with increased inventive activity.

Clearly, the draft Patent Cooperation Treaty does not purport to be a cure-all for all problems. Nor is it considered to be a perfect draft in many respects. Indeed, it may be expected there will be numerous drafts and considerable discussion before the time is reached to decide whether to participate in formal treaty negotiations.

The BIRPI Treaty effort has recently been characterized by one European patent official as the last chance for effective worldwide cooperation. At the Conference on International Patents, sponsored by the National Association of Manufacturers in Frankfurt, Germany, on June 8, 1967, Gordon Grant, Comptroller of the Patent Office of the United Kingdom, said: ". . . This is the eleventh hour of the examining patent system."

As far as the proposed Patent Cooperation Treaty is concerned, Mr. Grant went on to say that he believed this Treaty is "at any rate, for the time being, the last chance we have for a real international project."

Author's Postscript—

CURRENT STATUS OF PATENT
COOPERATION TREATY

Subsequent to the preparation of the above article (and as referred to in the second full paragraph on page 000 thereof), a meeting of a Committee of Experts was held in Geneva to examine further the proposed draft of the Patent Cooperation Treaty. As a result of this meeting a report of "Committee of Experts on the BIRPI Plan for Facilitating the Filing and Examination of Applications for the Protection of the Same Invention in a Number of Countries," BIRPI Document PCT/I/11, was released by BIRPI on October 20, 1967. This report is in the nature of a general summary of the majority views of the participants at the October meeting. The stated purpose of the report is to assist BIRPI, its working groups, and committees of experts in their work in preparing new drafts of the PCT plan.

The report contained numerous objections to many provisions in the first draft and it was considered that the draft would require extensive revisions to accommodate the interests of applicants. In general, the consensus of the report was two-pronged:

1. It favored reducing to the extent possible all unnecessary transmittal of documents between national offices and the International Bureau.

2. It favored modification of the treaty so as to require a very minimum of changes in national law.

The Committee unanimously adopted the report on October 11, 1967, and the Director of BIRPI indicated that he would report to the competent organs of the Paris Union and, subject to their approval, he would convene working parties and a second Committee of Experts in 1968 to which interested intergovernmental and nongovernmental organizations would again be invited as observers.

As a result, a meeting of a working group was held from March 25-29, 1968, in Geneva to consider in detail the subject of searching under the PCT. A report of this meeting was released by BIRPI as PCT/II/7, dated April 3, 1968. A copy of this report was reproduced in the *Official Gazette* of April 30, 1968. Thereafter, meetings were held in April and May to consider the questions of international application and international preliminary examination. Finally, meetings were held in Geneva June 25-29 and July 1 to consider in detail the proposed treaty. On the basis of the advice received in these meetings, BIRPI released on July 15, 1968, a new draft treaty with full draft regulations. Copies of this new draft, the

Regulations, a brief summary, and an evolution of the plan were reproduced in the August 13,1968, issue of the *Official Gazette*.

In considering the highlights of the 1968 Draft, it is interesting to compare the main differences between it and the 1967 Draft:

1. *Where to File:* It is no longer proposed that the international application be filed with the International Bureau. According to the 1968 Draft, the international application would be filed with the national patent office of the state of which the applicant was a resident.

2. *Checking:* It is no longer proposed that checking of the minimum requirements of the international application be entrusted to the International Bureau. Under the 1968 Draft, this task would be entrusted to the receiving office.

3. *Languages:* It is no longer proposed that the Treaty specify the language in which the international application must be written. Under the 1968 Draft, any language might be used which the competent searching authority was able to handle.

4. *National Fees:* The 1967 Draft provided that national filing fees would be replaced by "designation fees" which would be the same for each designated state. The 1968 Draft does not provide for any designation fees. National filing fees would not be replaced.

5. *Time of Publication:* It is no longer proposed that the international application be automatically published between the 18th month and the 24th month from the priority date. Under the 1968 Draft, the international application would be published promptly after the expiration of the 18th month only if, among the designated states, there was at least one which provides for publication after 18 months. Otherwise, the international application would be published at the time when, according to the law of the designated state whose law provided for the earliest publication, publication became due.

6. *No Publication When Application Is Withdrawn:* Unlike the 1967 Draft, the 1968 Draft expressly provides that an international application that was withdrawn before the technical preparations for the publication were completed would not be published.

7. *Delaying of Translations and National Fees:* Under the 1968 Draft, the applicant would have the guarantee that no state might require him to furnish a copy of his application and a translation of the same, or to pay the national fees, prior to 20 months after the priority date if the state was a designated state, or 25 months after the priority date if the state was an elected state.

8. *Delaying of National Processing:* Under the 1968 Draft, the applicant would have the guarantee that the examination and

other processing of his application would not be started in the national office of the designated or elected state prior to the expiration of the 20-month or 25-month period.

9. *Amendment of Claims:* Under the 1968 Draft, the applicant would be guaranteed the right to amend the claims not only in the international phase, but also before the national office of each designated state, even if that state had a "registration system."

10. *No Automatic Effects:* It is no longer proposed that inaction by the national office of a designated state could lead to the maturing of the international application into a national patent in that state.

11. *Limited Scope of Examination:* It is no longer proposed that international examination go into almost all questions of patentability. Under the 1968 Draft, the examination would mainly go into the questions of novelty, nonobviousness, and industrial applicability.

12. *No International Review:* It is no longer proposed that the opinion of the preliminary examining authority be subject to an appeal to an international review board.

13. *Establishment of Search Report:* It is no longer proposed that the international search report be established by the International Bureau after preparation by the searching authority. Under the 1968 Draft, the search report would be established directly by the searching authority.

14. *Immediate Effect of Filing:* It is no longer proposed that the international application have the effect, albeit retroactive, of a national application in each designated state only after it has been communicated with the search report. Under the 1968 Draft, the said effect would start immediately upon the filing of the international application. Such effect might later be lost only for specific reasons.

15. *National Route:* Under the 1968 Draft, if an international application ceased to be processed internationally because of some defect in it or omission by the applicant, it would on request, be submitted to the national offices of the designated states, which would be obliged to form an independent judgment on the question whether the application had failed to comply with the requirements of the PCT. No such guarantee of review in each designated state was provided for in the 1967 Draft.

16. *No "Certificates of Patentability":* The concept of an "international certificate of patentability" has been abandoned. The document issuing after the international examination—which is called "preliminary" to emphasize that it is not the final one (the final being the national examination)—is called in the 1968 Draft "the international preliminary examination report."

17. *No Limits for Substantive Law:* It is no longer proposed that the Treaty contain an enumeration of the grounds on which a state might deny the grant of a national patent. Under the 1968 Draft, any state could deny the grant of a national patent on any ground. Consequently, any substantive rules of the patent law of any. country are and will be compatible with the Treaty.

18. *No Limits for Procedural Law:* The 1968 Draft does not contain any provisions on national procedures except that the applicant would be guaranteed an opportunity to amend before the national office of any elected state. Otherwise, any procedural rules of the patent law of any country are and will be compatible with the Treaty.

The 1968 Draft was widely publicized and was the subject of numerous discussion and briefing conferences in some 14 major cities throughout the United States in the fall of 1968.

All member states of the Paris Union, together with more than 20 international intergovernmental and nongovernmental organizations, were invited by the Director of BIRPI to attend a Committee of Experts meeting in Geneva from December 2-10, 1968, in order to consider in detail the 1968 Draft. Given encouraging results, plans for the conclusion of a diplomatic conference in 1969 for the establishment of the Treaty were to be made.

The 1968 BIRPI Draft Treaty
for Patent Cooperation

STEPHEN P. LADAS

I

The BIRPI plan was considered, as scheduled, at a Conference of Experts in Geneva on October 2-10, 1967. This was a meeting of government experts of 23 countries. Intergovernmental organizations and nongovernmental organizations were invited as observers and were able to submit comments. A great many problems and difficulties were revealed by the discussion, and it was agreed that several basic questions had to be reexamined by working groups to be convened by BIRPI and by further consultations. In the first six months of 1968, numerous consultations took place and meetings of working groups were held in January and March.

As a result, BIRPI prepared a second draft of the PCT and also draft regulations. These together with a memorandum on the evolution of the plan and a summary were published by BIRPI in July 1968 as Documents PCT III.

A committee of government experts and observers was convened by BIRPI for December 2-10, 1968 to discuss the new draft. The substance of this is essentially the following: The applicant files an international application with his national office. This, if filed within the 12 months' priority term of the Paris Convention, is deemed by legal fiction to be a national filing in each of the designated countries. The national office checks the application to see whether it is in order as to form, in accordance with the formal requirements provided by the draft. It will then send one copy of the application to the International Bureau and one copy to the searching authority. The searching authority will examine the application with respect to relevant prior art and establish a report consisting of bare citations of documents believed to be relevant. This search report will first be communicated to the applicant, who may then maintain the application as it is, withdraw it, or amend the claims by communicating these to the International Bureau. The Bureau will then send copies of the application and search report to the designated countries at the latest within the 20th month from the

---

EDITOR'S NOTE: The original paper, published in *IDEA,* Vol. 11, No. 2, has been completely rewritten for this volume by the author.

priority date. Thereafter, the applicant will proceed with individual applications in the designated countries in compliance with their requirements.

Thus, certain improvements limiting the old draft's dominance of the International Bureau have been made, but the essential plan remains, insofar as it involves a single international application of standardized format, international search, and the use of BIRPI as a forwarding agency, certifying agency, accrediting agency, and publication agency. There is also retained the optional international patentability examination.

At first sight, the plan seems marvelous. It appears to save work and money both for patent applicants and for patent offices in cases where one seeks patent protection in a number of countries. However, legal men must look under the surface and analyze carefully the position. It is surely one of the most difficult problems of international agreements to determine beforehand how far a particular country would benefit from it and how far it might be hurt. The dynamics of the new internationalism in world economic and political relations is the source of many unresolved problems. The impetus towards it must be matched by a careful search for certainty about the goal towards which we are moving. Thus, we must put a pragmatic footnote to the internationalist impetus. It is this effort at a pragmatic look that leads to the following observations.

1. The plan seeks to embrace too much—too many authorities to deal with, too much formalism, too much bureaucracy, too many steps, too many fees.

Applicants will have to deal with the national office; receiving office; the International Bureau; the searching authority; the designated offices; the preliminary examining authority; and the elected offices.

Study of the Draft Treaty and the Rules indicates over 50 steps that must be taken before handling of the international application begins. Moreover, six new fees would have to be paid in addition to the national fees, i.e., transmittal fee, international fee, search fee, additional search fees, BIRPI's handling fee, and international examination fee.

2. The plan would superimpose an international bureaucracy over the existing patent offices, which still would have to operate to the full extent. It has been estimated that at this stage 600,000 foreign applications are generated by national applications. Assuming an average of six foreign applications so generated for each national application, the BIRPI plan seeks to deal with 100,000 international applications. To handle this number of applications,

BIRPI would need a very substantial work force, not all of it clerical. Experience has shown that one highly trained clerical employee is required to handle the filing documents for 1,000 patent applications per year. Therefore, BIRPI would require some 300 to 400 clerical employees if only a few of the major countries joined PCT. This does not include the record keeping generated by filing. BIRPI has to perform 22 acts in connection with each patent application. The possibility of errors and inadvertent mistakes and omissions are numerous. The dangers of loss of rights of applicants created by the sheer fact of the intervention of BIRPI are many.

The significant point is that while we are creating this international bureaucracy, we are not alleviating the condition of the national patent offices except in some respect with regard to the novelty search. Indeed, the national patent offices will have to retain and increase their facilities and personnel, if only to deal with national applications, both those that are purely local and those that give rise to foreign applications, and to handle international applications received from BIRPI.

With respect to examination-system countries, the plan may lessen the work of the patent offices with regard to search of novelty, assuming that the international search report will not be followed in each country by a local national search—a most unlikely supposition. Moreover, the plan would create new problems for examination offices in respect of examining international applications as to form, correspondence with applicant with respect to defects, watching for time limits, transmitting record copy to BIRPI and search copy where required, transmitting certified copy for Convention priority purposes, and the like. On the other hand, the designated offices also would have new duties and functions in correspondence with BIRPI: asking for advance copy of international applications, comparing translation filed later with copy of international application, considering amendments filed after search report, and the like.

All of these are new problems to be faced by national offices which are not present in today's system. There is some question as to whether these new tasks are counterbalanced by the availability of the international search report.

With regard to nonexamination-system countries, the PCT plan definitely would add new tasks and functions to local patent offices. Under the present system, such countries merely receive the foreign application in the required local translation, perhaps examine certain formal aspects and particularly with respect to the payment of national fees, and proceed with the grant of the patent. Under the BIRPI plan, they would have to wait for the international search report and eventually for the preliminary examination report. They would have correspondence with BIRPI, and they would face new problems with respect to what to register and publish as the subject matter of the grant, since they would have to look at the original international application, the search report, the amendments, if any, etc. If anything, these offices would have to increase their facilities and personnel to suit themselves to the requirements of the proposed Treaty. Moreover, with regard to any international applications filed by their own citizens, they would have to assume new duties of correspondence with BIRPI and the searching authority, examination of the application as to form, etc.

3. Dr. Krieger of the German Patent Office, in a recent article in *Industrial Property*, has described the severity of the problem of examining patent offices as due to three reasons:

(a) a constantly increasing number of new applications for patents filed—a consequence of increasing industrialism and technological expansion covering ever more widespread fields of activity;

(b) the extraordinarily rapid development of "the state of art" and technical literature, which inevitably means longer time for examination of every application; and

(c) a growing differentiation of technology, making patent applications more complex so that it is more difficult for the examiners to understand and evaluate them.

If this statement is correct, does the PCT plan really improve this situation? It would appear doubtful so long as there is no single international search center and so long as the substantive law on patentability of inventions has not been harmonized. Indeed:

1. In nonexamination countries, the plan would create complications rather than alleviate difficulties. It would delay the grant of patents, since the patent office must wait for the copy of the international application for 20 or 25 months, for translations, appointment of agent, new conditions for the payment of fees, etc.

2. In countries where local limited examination is made, usually by farming out to local government experts—for instance, in Latin America—the international search report itself is not of much interest. These countries from a spirit of national independence are most unlikely to give up local search and examination. The same is also true of countries which examine novelty essentially with respect to local patents, such as Canada and Australia. These will continue to make such novelty search since their patents are not within the minimum documentation of the searching authorities required by Rule 32.

3. In strict examination countries, the novelty search report

would be useful, but since under Rule 39 it would give merely the citations of documents considered to be relevant, it would save an insignificant part of the examination process. Even at that, it would have to be supplemented in each such country because no patent office today has all the documentation prescribed or has personnel with complete foreign language knowledge, and also because of pending conflicting applications. Moreover, according to the nationality of the applicant, the application will be submitted to more or less strict regime. The minimum required documentation exceeds the present documentation in some searching offices but falls short of that in others. Under Article 15(a) the latter group would have to extend their search to these other documents. Consequently, with five searching offices, and excluding countries which will perform additional searches in their own extensive material, the possibility is that five different classes of patents will eventually emerge, each of which will be characterized by a different scope and quality of search. (See ICC Doc. 450/303, par. 7).

II

Looking at the plan from the point of view of U.S. interests primarily, it is obvious that any plan which seeks to change the workings of the patent system on an international level has effects on American inventors and owners of inventions in two directions: in the domestic operation of the Patent Office and in the filing and obtaining of patents in foreign countries.

Filing and Obtaining Patents in Foreign Countries

The PCT plan at first sight seems most favorable to American applicants. They would file the international application in the U.S. Patent Office. It would be examined by such Office with regard to formal requirements. The international search would be made by such Office. The search report would be communicated by the U.S. Patent Office to the U.S. applicant, who might then amend his claims. If Chapter II is also considered, the U.S. Patent Office would issue the international preliminary examination report, after communication and discussion with the applicant, and the report would be filed with all the elected states. With unbridled optimism, it is felt that foreign states would largely accept the American search report and the American preliminary examination report and would proceed with the issue of the foreign patents—thus accomplishing, as a patent counsel of a large company put it, "the extension of the American patent system to the whole world." It is further believed that this would make the obtaining of foreign patents much less expensive because the plan substitutes BIRPI for foreign patent agents.

To deal with the question of expense first, Commissioner Brenner was more realistic in stating the purpose of the Treaty as destined "to enable applicants to *defer* the substantial expenditures involved in multiple translation, prosecution and other aspects of foreign filing practice." Indeed, once BIRPI communicated a copy of the international application to each designated office (Article 20 of the Treaty), the national procedure would begin and the applicant would have to comply with the national requirements. In the meantime, the applicant would have paid the six new fees of the BIRPI procedure, as indicated above.

Nonexamination countries would call for a translation as required and for the payment of national fees. These would have to be submitted by the American applicant through a local agent, who would have to make the payment in the form required by national law, and who would be recorded as an Address for Service, as is generally required by such law. Thus, the expense of translation, the expense of the national fees, and the expense of fees to a local patent agent would have to be incurred at that time. The idea of deferment of this expense for 20 months is that the applicant after the search report might decide not to file in the nonexamination countries which have been preliminarily designated. Whether doubts as to novelty of an invention would persuade an American applicant not to file in nonexamination countries in which he originally desired to file is quite questionable.

Examination countries would examine the application after the 20th or 25th month, quite probably with regard to novelty in respect of their own documentation, particularly if the applicant had amended the claims, and certainly with regard to patentability. The American applicant would have to appoint local patent agents to deal with these examining patent offices. Translation as required would have to be filed. National fees would have to be paid. Official actions of the Office would have to be dealt with in respect to questions of novelty, inventive height, usefulness or industrial application, sufficiency of documents filed—indeed, the whole gamut of national requirements. Therefore, fees of patent agents would have to be paid, and these probably would not be less than on direct national filing.

Thus, the plan would mean practically only a deferring of expense for eight to 13 months as compared with the defraying of expenditure at the present time. If some saving would result in the sense that local patent agents' charges might be somewhat less, this would be compensated for by the new fees payable under the proposed Treaty.

Leaving aside the question of expense, the most important question is whether the procedure of dealing with a single international application is really advantageous to the American applicant. In this connection:

1. In the absence of an international search center making all searches and a binding obligation of all contracting countries to accept the search report of such center as conclusive, it is most unlikely that examination countries would be prepared to dispense with their own novelty search. It is hardly conceivable that the Netherlands, Japan, the Scandinavian countries, Soviet Russia, or Germany would accept the U.S. Patent Office's search report and not make any novelty search of their own. Were it even possible for the patent offices of these countries to determine not to make their own search, we would have to reciprocate by accepting their searches, and, as stated before, we would then have in effect five different types of patents in the world—an American search patent, a Russian search patent, a German search patent, a Japanese search patent, and an IIB search patent, each of which would have a different value, depending on the thoroughness or adequacy of the search. This would create considerable confusion and uncertainty in the international patent system and in the economic value of patents.

2. In nonexamination countries, American applicants would find themselves unable to obtain a patent before the end of 20 months or more in view of Article 23. This would prevent quick grants in respect of inventions which allow for immediate commercialization; prevent action against an infringer during this period; and also delay the licensing of patents locally. There is no substance to the argument made by BIRPI that in this way nonexamining countries would issue better patents and would not be imposed upon by developed countries to grant unjustified monopolies. These countries will still have no capacity to consider the validity of the patent and will rely merely on the fact that the foreign patentee has obtained a corresponding patent in one of the important examination countries, such as the United States, Germany, or the Netherlands.

3. The most important limitation of an international application would be its frozen character and the hidden dangers which this would involve. This relates to the description and claims of the application. Article 5 of the draft Treaty provides that "the description shall disclose the invention in a manner sufficiently clear and complete for the invention to be carried out by persons skilled

in the art", and then Rule 6 sets out the manner in which the description must be drawn up. These are typical legal provisions, present in many countries, and yet the patent offices and the courts do not apply a uniform standard to questions of sufficiency of description. Article 5 of the Treaty and Rule 6 in effect leave the question of sufficiency of description to the courts of each country on the basis of the background of national jurisprudence. It is not conceivable that the courts will construe the description of an international application differently from the description of a national application, or that the courts will apply the standards, if any, of the Treaty to national applications. Yet, under Article 28 of the Treaty, the applicant could not change the description before each designated office. He could only amend the claims. This fixed text of the description in the international application would involve hidden dangers for the American applicant. Under the present system, in consideration of the form of claims called for by various countries, there is a corresponding adaptation of the description in foreign applications. A peripheral or central approach to the formulation of claims calls for the framing of the description to support it. In countries where products are not patentable, a full description of the process or a full description of the product or a detailed description of both may be necessary. More or less information about utility of the invention may be required to be included in particular countries, etc. It is true that the first national application could be filed as an international application, in which case (under Article 11(3) of the Treaty) it would be treated as a regular national filing within the meaning of Article 4 of the Paris Convention. In such case, if the search report were sought and obtained quickly, the applicant could rewrite his specification as well as his claims within the Convention priority. But in such case, the applicant would lose the benefit of the extension of time under the BIRPI plan.

4. The problem of combination or division of an application also would be seriously handicapped by the frozen character of the international application. Under the present system, combination is of major importance for effective foreign filing, particularly for U.S. applicants, who can protect a series of developments by combination-in-part applications. Combination permits a comprehensive case to be filed with broad claims and maximum disclosure. This of course must be done within 12 months from the first basic Convention date. The PCT plan would not change this with respect to the filing of an international application, but when the international search report was obtained, the original combination might

need drastic revision in several possible ways. Division might be advisable along quite different lines. Alternatively, new combinations with other cases without priority might be advisable, or it might be advisable to include entirely new matter to complete the original disclosure. Under the BIRPI plan, the applicant after the search report could only amend the claims of the international application. He could not change the description, or combine several international applications.

Domestic Effects of PCT Treaty in the United States

Any treaty has two sides, and we are prone sometimes to look at what we are "getting" by the treaty and to forget what we are "giving." One must also guard against the argument that if the treaty should prove not always to be helpful to us, we could go the old way and make use of the treaty only when it suited us. The point is that foreigners would use the treaty if it served their interests, regardless of how much we used it ourselves. What then would be the effects of foreigners using the PCT route?

1. Statistics show that we receive at the present time 25,000 foreign patent applications. Presumably we should receive through BIRPI a far larger number because of the advantages promised by the PCT plan. Indeed, BIRPI specifically claims (Summary, par. 69) that the proposed system would "induce inventors to seek protection in more countries for more inventions than at the present time." In any case, under the draft Treaty, in the absence of a designation, all contracting countries would be deemed to be designated, and the international application filed in the Receiving Office would be deemed to be filed in each of the contracting countries. Thus, the U.S. Patent Office would have to presume that all international applications extended to the United States and wait for 20 or 25 months from the priority date before it could touch such applications.

2. It is impossible, of course, to forecast how many foreign international applications would ultimately designate the United States as a country to which such applications extended, but one must reasonably expect a large increase. Soviet Russia, where the state in fact owns all the inventions filed by an application for a certificate of inventorship, might as a matter of state policy determine to designate the United States as a country to which all their international applications extended. It might be induced to do so because under the PCT plan Soviet Russia would not have to file translations until more than 20 or 25 months from the priority date, and send their own search report and their own preliminary exami-

nation report. It is not inconceivable that Soviet Russia might designate the United States in respect of a large proportion of the 100,000 applications filed in Russia at this time, while in the past only 250 Soviet applications were filed in the United States. The Soviet Union is mentioned not because of anticommunist sentiment but because it is a prime example of a government-controlled economy where important inventions are developed.

3. It is not likely that the U.S. Patent Office would accept the search report or the preliminary examination report sent in by BIRPI as issued by another country, such as by the Soviet Patent Office or the Japanese Patent Office, or indeed any other office. If these were to be accepted at face value, the quality of U.S. patents would be reduced. Otherwise, these reports coming into the U.S. Patent Office with copy of the international application would be only of some help in reducing the work of our Patent Office. Insofar as a larger number of international applications should come to us, the work of our Patent Office would greatly increase.

4. Foreigners' international applications would be communicated to the U.S. Patent Office at the end of 20 months from the priority date or at the end of 25 months under Chapter II. Moreover, translations of such applications would not be submitted until some time later. Since examination of copending applications is part of the examination system, completion of novelty examination of national U.S. patent applications by American citizens or corporations would have to be delayed until 20 or 25 months to wait for these foreign international applications. Even if we were to take advantage of Article 13 of the Treaty and demand from BIRPI that it communicate to us copy of the international application promptly after the expiration of the one-year priority, this would not be of much use to the U.S. Patent Office if the text was in Russian, Japanese, or indeed in many other foreign languages. The delay in handling the U.S. applications of our nationals would be prejudicial both to the applicants themselves and to American industry.

5. New duties would develop for our Patent Office in respect of communications, notifications, and other correspondence with BIRPI, thus increasing the cost of operation of the Patent Office. The draft Treaty sets up a new administration with an assembly, executive committee, and advisory committee. The assembly would determine the contribution of each contracting country, and the amount of such contribution would be determined with due regard to the number of applications emanating from each state each year. Since the largest number of foreign-owned applications are American, we would necessarily pay the largest part of the establishment of the international bureaucracy under this Treaty.

6. If we should be so ill-advised as to accept Chapter II of the draft Treaty, this would mean:

a. That the U.S. Patent Office would have to be a preliminary examining authority. Any foreign applicant might choose to have the international preliminary examination report issued by our Patent Office, which would add further to the work of our Office.

b. Foreign applicants would file with our Patent Office a preliminary examination report issued by another country. If we expect other countries to respect such a report issued by our Patent Office for American national applications, we should similarly have to respect preliminary examination reports issued by other countries. This raises serious questions with regard to our industry and the position of our courts.

The net conclusion of these general observations is that it would have been far better to limit the PCT plan in the beginning to certain essentials on which harmonization is easily practicable and then gradually move toward greater harmonization in the future. The essentials on which there is general agreement and general desire to accomplish them are:

(i) a single International Search for novelty of inventions.
(ii) availability of a period after the expiration of the one-year priority period (provided that an extension of the right of priority itself could not be agreed upon) within which the foreign application could be filed with the search report.
(iii) uniformity of the basic application as to format for the purpose of the international search.

It has been stated that the government representatives participating in the preparation of the PCT plan are anxious to have BIRPI as a certifying, accrediting, and publication agency by reason of international confidence in it. For 80 years now, the right of priority of Article 4 of the Convention has played its most useful role on the basis of mere certification by the national patent offices of the copy of the original application and of its date of filing. It is not understood why suddenly we are no longer willing to trust the patent offices of these contracting countries. In any case, there could be no objection to sending to BIRPI for record keeping a copy of the international application.

Possible Alternatives

It is to secure this simpler harmonization on the aforesaid points (i), (ii) and (iii) that certain alternatives have been suggested.

The simplest alternative would be an extension of the Convention priority under Article 4 of the Paris Convention to 18 months. This would give an applicant time to obtain his search report or even a preliminary examination report and to determine whether to file in foreign countries and if so, in which ones. This would accomplish the object of deferral of expense as in the PCT plan. It would enable the applicant to amend his description and claims, to combine or divide cases, and to file his foreign applications in accordance with his best interests.

It might conceivably be objected to that it is not desired to extend the Convention priority because this would be prejudicial to competitors, and several countries are adverse to such extension. However, there is no reason why the effects of the Convention priority may not be varied with respect to the extension by a proper amendment of Article 4 of the Paris Convention. We may preserve the 12-month priority with respect to its present effects, i.e., the priority claimant prevails over an intervening applicant, and publication or use during the 12-month priority term does not destroy novelty. The applicant then would have an extended period of six additional months only for the purpose of filing his foreign applications with an international search report.

A second alternative is the FICPI-II plan, which is similar to the above except that it calls for the filing within 18 months of a provisional foreign application to be converted into a regular national application within a time prescribed by each country, and also it provides that the applicant shall file within 24 months from the priority date with BIRPI a declaration of particulars to enable BIRPI to coordinate and publish all relevant information on the multiple filings.

A third alternative accepts the idea of a single international application filed in the national patent office with a request for international search. The search report would be sent to the applicant (and not also to BIRPI), who might amend the specification and claims and send the certified copy of the international application with all desired amendments listed separately to the countries where protection was desired, with translations, if required, appointment of local agent, and payment of national fees. This would eliminate the extensive activities to be performed by BIRPI as a forwarding agency and certifying agency, but retain it as an accrediting agency for searching authorities. A variant of this would be to have the home patent office forward copies of the international application to each of the foreign countries within the one-year priority, but to require the applicant to file the regular foreign application within a prescribed period, with translation fees and the search report.

III

The principal difficulty may reside in the fact that the initiative for the BIRPI plan has come from government officials without previous consultation with private interests. These officials are now unwilling to give up the general outline of the BIRPI draft. Conscious particularly of the administrative features of the draft Treaty, they are anxious to retain them. Moreover, they have persuaded certain American corporations filing a large number of applications in foreign countries that the advantages of the draft in multiple foreign filings far outweigh any disadvantages.

Considering this situation realistically, it is suggested that we retain in effect the general draft of the Treaty (subject to any improvements in form or substance that could be made to particular articles), and adopt only certain changes in three articles which, while hardly disturbing the general scheme as a whole, would introduce an optional alternative procedure designed to protect vital aspects of an applicant's rights in foreign countries along the lines indicated in the preceding exposition.

Indeed, Article 12(2) of the draft Treaty contains an alternative, which, however, is not carried out fully. This article provides that if the applicant so requests, the receiving office shall give to the applicant the record copy, which then shall be forwarded by him to the International Bureau, instead of the receiving office transmitting it directly to the International Bureau. However, Article 12(2) does not also provide that the applicant himself may send the search copy of the application to the competent searching authority. If the applicant is given this option also, then he will be given a certain freedom. If he wishes to withdraw the international application and substitute a new one, or a combined application, or add new information in the disclosure, he should be able to do so and thus initiate the search under his direct control, rather than being closed out through the receiving office communicating directly with the searching authority. In fact, this is possible under the draft Treaty in the case where one has filed no national application in his country but files instead only an international application, which is treated under Article 11(3) as a regular national application within the meaning of Article 4(A)(2) of the Paris Convention.

Much more important, of course, is the applicant's freedom at the time of actual filing abroad. After the applicant has received the search report and, if he wishes, has amended the claims of the international application, the actual filing in the foreign countries, under the BIRPI draft, is taken out of his hands and consummated by the International Bureau by direct contact with the designated patent offices. But it is just at this moment that the applicant may decide to drop the whole project, file on the basis of different international applications, file in certain contemplated countries, add others, or proceed in different names.

Moreover, the BIRPI draft does not provide for the combining of original applications for foreign filing and the claiming of multiple priority or for incorporating subject matter not having a priority (partial priority). Under the present procedure and under the BIRPI draft, all of this has to be done within the Convention year.

If a real extra benefit is to be obtained by extending the Convention year through postponing the actual foreign filing up to 20 months, then the applicant should be permitted to combine applications and add subject matter after receiving the search report, while preserving unity of invention and without requiring further search. These several results can be obtained by amending Articles 19 and 20 in the following manner:

Article 19

The applicant may, after having received the international search report, amend the specification and/or claims of the International Application, or submit a new combined specification and claims based on a plurality of related International Applications, and in either event may include suitable additional subject matter without priority and not requiring further search, by filing such amended or new documents with the International Bureau within the prescribed time limit.

Article 20

The International Bureau, or the applicant or his agents if the applicant so requests, shall communicate the original International Application including any amendments of the specification and/or claims, or shall communicate the plurality of related original International Applications and the new combined specification and claims, together with the International Search Report or Reports and their translations (as required) to each Designated Office.

If the applicant exercises this option, the applicant shall simultaneously advise the International Bureau what documents are filed in each Designated Office, and shall furnish copies of any new documents in addition to the original International Application or Applications.

Corresponding revision of the regulations should be simple. The proposed optional direct filing by applicants with the foreign countries after the search report has been received under the procedure provided for in the draft Treaty would not alter the scheme of the Treaty, and the certifying function of BIRPI would remain because any national patent office or court could always, if and when required, check the documents filed by an applicant against those on record in the International Bureau.

A World Patent System

DAVID SARNOFF

The rights of inventors were established in Article One of the Constitution, and the Congress, in 1790, gave legal substance to those rights.

Since then, more than three million American patents have resulted from the government's encouragement to "science and the useful arts." Taken as a group, they have contributed profoundly to America's technological, economic, military, and political leadership, and have reshaped the course of history.

The patent procedures which made possible this early flow of inventiveness were attuned to the requirements of individual artisans and inventors who worked independently on their own inventions. With their limited resources, they sought to create for a market that extended no farther than the boundaries of their region or nation, and the device or product they created could nearly always be clearly defined as their own.

Today, the character and scope of the inventive process has changed profoundly. The application of new ideas to practical uses has created new industries and stimulated the growth of old ones, giving new impetus to a growing economy.

The search for new ideas commands the resources of government, education, and private enterprise. Under the stimulus of new concepts, vast and complex facilities have been constructed and industries have grown up almost overnight. The development of new products, processes, and systems has engaged hundreds of thousands of our finest minds, and the fruits of their interlocking efforts are evident wherever civilization extends.

Against this background of extraordinary technological growth, it is ironic that the very instrument designed to advance this progress has not kept pace with the progress it has stimulated. In this age of mass invention which has produced deep space probes, supersonic flight, and satellite communications, the patent structure of most

EDITOR'S NOTE: This paper was presented by the author at the award dinner of the Tenth Annual Public Conference of The PTC Research Institute held in Washington, D.C. on June 16, 1966, when General Sarnoff received the Institute's 1965 Charles F. Kettering Award. (*IDEA*, Volume 10, Conference Number (1966))

nations is no longer capable of meeting the requirements imposed by technological change and economic growth.

The United States, for example, is the world leader in quantity and variety of invention, but an average of three years is still required for passage from patent application to patent issue. In some instances, both here and abroad, the time period is even longer. These delays have in some cases retarded the progress of an idea from the mind to the marketplace.

When we can transmit an idea around the world in less than one seventh of a second, why must years elapse before that idea can be validated within or outside the country of origin? Why must an inventor still make separate application in every country where he wishes to protect his idea? Why should some countries make no provision at all for patent filings, or impose severely restrictive conditions upon the inventor?

The answers lie in the fragmented array of national patent systems, most of them working in isolation from the others. This condition inhibits the swift and equitable worldwide distribution of patent benefits—through new technology, new industry, and expanded markets. The consequences are unfortunate enough in the industrialized nations, but they are even more damaging to the underdeveloped members of the world community.

As technology becomes more complex, the problem of sharing it with others becomes more difficult to solve. Today, material wealth is largely concentrated in a group of nations with only one third of the world's population. The remaining two thirds account for less than one tenth of the world's industrial production, generate less than one quarter of the world's energy, and produce little more than one third of the world's food.

In the face of growing abundance induced by technology, the supreme paradox of our times is the fact that the gap between the have and have-not nations continues to widen. This imbalance obviously carries the seeds of new disorders and further violence in an uneasy world. In 87 percent of the nations classified by the World Bank as very poor—those with per-capita income of less than $100 a year—there has been an average of two major outbreaks of violence per country during the last decade.

To help overcome this disturbing situation, I believe there must be a more equitable distribution of technical know-how and stronger encouragement of inventiveness in the nations that have been left behind in the wake of modern technology. True, the problem cannot be solved overnight, and it certainly will not be solved without the full cooperation of the underdeveloped nations them-selves. But through an appropriate international patent structure, we can make an intellectual as well as a capital investment in these countries.

The input of know-how and ideas can be as great a stimulant to their progress as money and machinery. As Oliver Wendell Holmes said, "A man's mind stretched by a new idea can never go back to its original dimensions."

One of today's principal challenges is to design an international patent structure that can accommodate the revolutionary changes in technology and spread its benefits more evenly around the world. Through the tremendous advances that have been made in one aspect of this technology—in communications—the physical means are available to accomplish this purpose. It is now technically feasi-ble to establish a universal patent system, utilizing the latest com-munications devices and concepts, to bring swiftness, order, and reasonable uniformity to the entire patent structure.

The concept of a global patent system has been proposed both here and abroad, but a combination of political and technical prob-lems has until now prevented its achievement. Today, however, the mounting pressure of economic necessities may overcome the polit-ical obstacles. And a global patent system could now be accommo-dated technically in a world-wide communications service just as readily as global television, global weather reporting, and global computer services.

Hovering in synchronous orbit above the equator is the first stage of a world-wide system of high-capacity communications sat-ellites. Soon a complete system of such satellites and their ground terminals will link all points on earth with thousands of channels for simultaneous voice, data and message transmission.

A new generation of electronic data-processing systems is emer-ging, capable of storing up to 100 million bits of information and retrieving them in fractional millionths of a second. These systems are beginning to provide central computing and reference services for subscribers scattered over large areas.

Other new electronic devices are being joined to computers to transmit, store and retrieve information by sight or sound, and by the display of words, diagrams, or pictures. It will become common-place, for example, to speak directly over any distance to a computer and to receive the answer within seconds in either sound or sight, on a display screen or in electronically printed form.

These various systems can be combined to perform all of the technical functions for a world patent center that could receive and process applications from inventors everywhere. This center would be the focus of the world patent system, linked to all countries by high-capacity satellite communications and built around a large data-processing and information-storage system.

Incoming data on inventions, appropriately coded in the country of origin, would be compared with key data on prior patents in the same field, retrieved from the computer memory. The novelty and patentability of the idea could be determined within an infinitely shorter time than is now the case—and it could be determined on a world-wide rather than simply on a national basis. In addition, the means of instant access to all data could speed immensely the comparison and adjudication of conflicting claims.

Since vast amounts of data accumulate over a short time in this era of growing invention, it has become increasingly difficult to keep track of the progress being made and the patents being issued. Therefore, the patent center also could serve as an international reference source of invention and technology. It could, upon request, provide copies of patents and distribute technical data to interested parties.

In a project of such magnitude, with its many potentialities for service, we cannot expect universal operation to begin overnight. Practical experience suggests that nations will move slowly toward the concept of a single world patent system. But it should be possible to begin applying such a concept on a limited scale among a few major patent countries, sophisticated in the use of technology and conscious of the need. Later, as its advantages became evident, other nations could join the project and its services would correspondingly expand.

Assuming that such an international agreement can be achieved, it is possible within the next several years to foresee an inventor, patent attorney or other interested party sitting in his office and submitting a patent application and the accompanying designs through a desk instrument linked by satellite to the central or regional computer of the world patent office. Should there be no problems, the inventor would be informed within a matter of days that his patent has been approved and registered in as many countries as requested.

With this transformation in the world patent process, we could expect many advantages to emerge. Among them would be:

A basic simplification of the total process. By providing quick and complete access to all the relevant information in a patent search, the resolution of conflicting claims could be expedited. The result should be less costly and less time-consuming, and should produce a greater respect for the patent system;

The ready availability of know-how to people in all countries, through a swift and orderly system protecting the interests of inventor and user alike;

A spur to improved education in the underdeveloped nations, in order to take maximum advantage of newly available technology;

A greater incentive to intellectual investment by the governments and enterprises of the industrialized nations, leading to a climate more conducive to invention and innovation everywhere;

And, finally, a narrowing of the gap created by today's imbalance in technology between the have and have-not nations.

Certainly, there are numerous precedents for international cooperation in the distribution of ideas and knowledge. It exists, for example, in the orderly use of radio spectrum for message traffic, and in the written communication of ideas through the mails. Moreover, progress already is being made in the merging of national patent laws for common use by groups of nations, and in developing patent procedures for the nonindustrialized countries.

These developments are moving forward on several continents, and through the United Nations. And, of course, two multinational organizations, the International Patent Bureau and the International Patent Institute, have long been active in the field.

Strong and imaginative steps have already been taken by the U.S. Patent Office to cut in half the time now required to handle patent applications. A further major advance toward modernizing our patent structure was made in 1965 with the Executive Order establishing the President's Commission on the Patent System. These activities deserve the full support of all who are concerned with the problem—government and the legal profession, science and invention, trade and industry.

The great challenge of our time is to match the capabilities of technology to the needs of humanity. A world patent system, functioning as I have suggested here, could play an important role in meeting that challenge.

In his mastery of the electron and the atom, modern man already has given us a glimpse of where technology can lead.

He has invented satellites to carry him through space and circle the globe at 24 times the speed of sound.

He has learned to walk in space around the world in approximately 90 minutes.

He has guided a satellite by remote control to a selected spot on the surface of the moon and televised its features back to earth.

With this remarkable record of achievement, and with his continuing acquisition of new knowledge, is it too much to expect that man can also find the ways and means to fulfill the elemental needs of life for everyone on this planet? Surely, there could be no greater contribution to human welfare and world peace.

TOPICAL INDEX

A